Title:~ Practical Handbook of

INDUSTRIAL TRAFFIC MANAGEMENT

RICHARD C. COLTON
EDMUND S. WARD

Fifth Edition Revised by
CHARLES H. WAGER

Published by **THE TRAFFIC SERVICE CORPORATION**
Washington • New York • Chicago • Philadelphia
Boston • Atlanta • Palo Alto

First Printing, 1973
Second Printing, 1977

© *The Traffic Service Corporation, 1973*
815 Washington Building, Washington, D.C. 20005

Fifth Edition, Completely Revised and Reset

Library of Congress Catalog Card Number 72–95464

Printed in the United States of America

Production by Stephen R. Hunter

To All Of My Transportation Colleagues
For their support in our effort to encourage true
and worthwhile accomplishments at all levels
of our industry.

C. H. W.

PREFACE

A far-reaching galaxy of all-star innovations in transportation has come to be very much with us since the last edition of this book was published. Most spectacular, of course, has been the movement to and from the moon of the astronauts. In more down-to-earth fields a new Department of Transportation has been established with its Secretary having Cabinet status. Important increases in the nation's freight bill have occurred with annual figures being in amounts of real magnitude. Substantial advances in operations capabilities have been attained by the rails, trucks, water carriers, airlines, and other modes. If such is possible, transportation's importance to industry today is more so than ever before.

Along with its advancements and importance transportation's needs continue for knowledgeable, result-getting individuals who are both specialists and generalists. Students of economics and established businessmen frequently have little, if any, practical information on what constitutes good shipping practices. They have yet to be exposed to the details of the over-all distribution/transportation complex involving thousands of transportation carriers, freight rates, bills of lading, proper packaging, warehousing, and so on. College graduates may have majored in transportation and still, despite this discipline, have little knowledge of how to manage and buy transportation economically. The prime purpose of this text is to be helpful in these regards and to assist anyone involved in combining facts, logic, and broad sensitivities and coming up with wise decisions.

Every effort has been made to present the subject of freight and distribution and transportation in a direct, easily understood manner from a practical, everyday viewpoint. This

Handbook is for the practicing traffic man; it is for the young man desirous of making transportation his career; it is for the student of economics anxious to complete his understanding of the major functions of modern business; and it is for the businessman who seeks pertinent facts on the transportation of his inbound raw material and the over-all distribution of his outbound finished products. The problems of economical and adequate distribution and transportation apply with equal force to the small business and the large corporation.

This treatise cannot cover all subjects in complete detail, but the authors have made every effort to cover all of the principal responsibilities and functions of industrial traffic management and it is hoped that our readers will find a few new ideas herein along with the basic information. Because rates, services, etc., are subject to more or less frequent change, the information in this *Handbook* is usually either basic or general, not dealing with specific rates or services. Neither is it claimed that all statements herein are technically correct to the hundredth degree. That would be quite impossible in a handbook such as this, which covers so much subject matter in a broad over-all approach. It is suggested, however, that the subject matter does provide a good, sound working basis from a strictly practical viewpoint.

One word of advice. Do not look for perfection in the handling of your distribution and transportation responsibilities. There is no such thing as perfection in either over-all physical distribution or just the transportation factor. While all concerned may strive toward millennial perfectionism, none actually achieves it due to the many uncontrollable factors and the carriers' complicated rate structure. One must be prepared to compromise on many situations, to take the hurdles as best one can as they develop. A professional traffic manager can procure the best results under any set of circumstances.

This handbook has been published for something like the last twenty-five years and has been a respected reference work during that period. Its updating has been done with this in mind and changes have been limited to those which seem validly indicated by new conditions. As examples, data processing in transportation has progressed to the point where more specifics can be discussed properly and this has been done. There are indications that a trend may be developing for industrial companies (particularly small ones) to tighten and administer more carefully their freight payments and related activities. The outline of the steps that might be taken in this regard has been accentuated.

As regards designations of transportation work (i.e. whether physical distribution, transportation, or traffic "titles" are assigned) the text has been carefully prepared to be applicable whatever may be the designation. Excellent jobs are done for many industrial companies by departments designated in each of the categories. Various transportation developments in the federal government have made it more important that transportation men know how activities of interest to them "fit" into others there. As will appear from Chapter 2 on "Regulation" organization charts and other information have been augmented to help those involved in "knowing their way around Washington." Other features receiving particular attention have included the addition of a chapter on hazardous materials transportation. Coverage is principally of its high-lights; undoubtedly considerably more will be heard on this subject in the years ahead.

ACKNOWLEDGMENT

The cooperation from those members of the transportation and related industries which made possible the up-dating of this text is gratefully and sincerely acknowledged. Assistance came in many ways and this is to thank all who participated for their generous contributions. They were fine and are genuinely appreciated.

Along with the assistance generally which was so kindly given, particular help on certain features came also from a rather wide range of individuals. Among them are A. G. Anderson and W. W. Bixby of the Transportation Association of America, Vic Angerame of Trans World Airlines, W. J. Augello of the New York Bar, A. E. Baylis of the National Committee on International Trade Documentation, George Berry of C.B.W. Transport, F. L. Betz of Lykes Bros. Steamship Lines, C. E. Blanck of United States Freight Company, John Blair of the Southern Railway System, Harold Brown of Associated Transport.

Michael Camhi of The Valley Line Company, J. R. Canavan of the Eastern Weighing & Inspection Bureau, R. J. Delmontagne of The Material Handling Institute, W. H. Ducey of Midwestern Shipping Agencies, L. J. Dorr of the National Industrial Traffic League, L. J. Fitch of Mobil Oil, G. A. Gecowets of the National Council of Physical Distribution Management, A. P. Grellet of Penn Central Transportation, E. A. Guilbert and Tom Desnoyers of the Transportation Data Coordinating Committee, Stanley Hoffman of Union Carbide, J. P. Ingrassia, Transportation Consultant, R. J. Janer of Denenholtz & Janer, Inc., Ray Johnson of Shell Canada, Limited.

Thomas Lynch of the Fibre Box Association, W. H. Magrath of Ingersoll-Rand, C. D. Marshall of the Associated Latin

American Freight Conferences, G. L. McGrath of Mitsui & Co. (U.S.A.), W. H. Morley, Jr., of the New York Bar, Allan D. Musgrove of I.M.L. Freight, C. B. O'Hara of The Port of New York Authority, John Peterson, Transportation Consultant, R. J. Sullivan and H. S. Nelson of Shell Oil, W. H. Sardo, Jr. of the National Wooden Pallet & Container Association, and J. S. Wager of the Washington, D.C. Bar. Richard C. Colton, author and co-author of earlier editions, was particularly helpful also.

Additionally, assistance came from the office of the publisher with E. F. Hamm, Jr., Richard Coleman, and Stephen Hunter providing also kindly and important guidance and encouragement. Various dealings accorded "production" features mirror publisher oriented and generated activities and attention. Locally, Bertha Bullwinkel and Katherine Mertz were most helpful with necessary secretarial work and correspondence.

A last, but far from least, word of appreciation is much in order for my family for their thoughtful consideration and patience at all times as they lived with the "book" from its inception.

Charles H. Wager

CONTENTS

1. MANAGING TRANSPORTATION 1
2. REGULATION AND OTHER GOVERNMENT FUNCTIONS . . 11
3. FREIGHT CLASSIFICATION 31
4. THE DOMESTIC BILL OF LADING AND SHIPPING RULES 65
5. FREIGHT RATES 81
6. FREIGHT ROUTING 121
7. PACKAGING, LOADING AND MATERIALS HANDLING . . . 163
8. FREIGHT CLAIMS 215
9. DISTRIBUTION AND WAREHOUSING 251
10. CONTRACT MOTOR CARRIAGE 291
11. PRIVATE MOTOR CARRIAGE 317
12. EXPEDITING AND TRACING 339
13. DETENTION CHARGES, DEMURRAGE, SIDING AND
     WEIGHT AGREEMENTS 359
14. ORGANIZING, OPERATING AND EQUIPPING A TRAFFIC
     DEPARTMENT 383
15. DATA PROCESSING IN TRANSPORTATION 433
16. UNITED STATES GOVERNMENT TRAFFIC 449
17. INTERNATIONAL SHIPMENTS 461
18. THE TRANSPORTATION OF HAZARDOUS MATERIALS . . 571
     APPENDIX 1—STANDARD RAIL, MOTOR CARRIER, AND
     FREIGHT FORWARDER BILL OF LADING CONTRACT
     TERMS AND CONDITIONS 585
     APPENDIX 2—OCEAN BILL OF LADING CONTRACT
     TERMS AND CONDITIONS 593
     GLOSSARY 603
     INDEX 632

LIST OF ILLUSTRATIONS

Transport Responsibilities In the Executive Branch . . . 12

Department of Transportation—Organization Chart . . . 14

Standing Congressional Committees Having Jurisdiction
    Over Transportation 16

Federal Transportation Regulatory Agencies 18

Organization Diagrams
    Interstate Commerce Commission 21
    Federal Maritime Commission 25
    Civil Aeronautics Board 28

Excerpt National Motor Freight Classification Released
    Value Ratings 40

Index Page—Uniform Freight Classification 43

Example—Bill of Lading Commodity Description, etc.—
    U.F.C. 45

Airbill Form—Air Freight Shipments 70

Uniform Straight Bill of Lading 78

History—New York Chicago Rail Freight Rates 82

Excerpt—Typical Class Tariff Showing Application of
    Rate Bases 85

Excerpt—National Rate Base Tariff 85

Typical Class Tariff Arrangement 86

New England Motor Rate Bureau—Class Rates 88

Modern Auto Rack Rail Freight Cars 127

New "Big Boy" Rail Box Cars 129

Typical Piggy Back Rail Loading 134

Tandem Trailers—Motor Carriers 137
Water-Truck Freight Operations 150
Jet Aircraft Cargo Loading System 154
Loss and Damage Claim Payments 166
The Packaging Equation and Application 177
Excerpt—Rule 41—Fibre Box Minimum Specifications . 183
Certificate Forms—Fibre Box Makers 184
Special Box Certificate Forms 185
Package Groups—Fibreboard Containers 187
National Safe Transit Label 192
Stringer and Block Pallets 200
Notched Stringer Pallet Design 201
Four Basic Pallet Loading Patterns 202
Sizes and Types of Containers 210
Standard Form For Overcharge Claims 221
Indemnity Agreement 223
Standard Form—Loss and Damage Claims 227
Some Modern Railroad Equipment and Handling Tech-
    niques .248, 249
Section of Automated Warehouse 259
An Automated Warehouse 260
Utilization of Storage Space 268
Combination Clamp-Fork Lift Truck 273
Trucking Contract Form 295
Chart Form for Relating Truck Costs to Rates 301
Trucking Agreement Form 308
Private Carrier Cost Analysis
    Work Sheet 321
    Special Form 322
Truck Lease and Service Form for Shippers 330

Expediting and Tracing Record 353
Chart—Railroad Storage Rates and Charges 365
Motor Carrier Detention Charge Chart 366
Rail Demurrage Charge Chart 370
Weight Agreement Form—Rail 376
Shipper Weight Agreement Certification 378
Chart—Traffic Department Organization 392
Traffic Office Layout 409
Monthly Traffic Bulletin Form 422
Commodity Code Numbers—Data Processing—U.F.C. . 437
U.S. Government Bill of Lading 458
LASH-España, of Prudential Grace Lines 473
International Shipments—Modern SEABEE Vessel . .474, 475
Ocean Bill of Lading Form 480, 481
Letter of Indemnity 484
Federal Maritime Commission—Conference List . . .494, 495
Typical Ocean Freight Tariff
    Title Page 497
        Commodity and Rate Page 498
Steamship Conference Tariff Analysis Form 502
Shippers Export Declaration 513
Consular Invoice 515
Foreign Collection Letter 530
Sight Draft 531
Ninety Day Draft 532
Irrevocable, Confirmed Letter of Credit 533
Example—Packing Case Marking 554
Hazardous Materials Code—DOT—Excerpt 573
Specimen—"Chem-Card" On a Particular Chemical . . . 581

1

MANAGING TRANSPORTATION

VERY LITTLE OF WHAT IS PRODUCED IN THIS COUNTRY IS CONSUMED where it is grown, mined or manufactured. From its earliest raw material state until its ultimate consumption, the commerce of the nation requires a series of decisions involving transportation, whether it be across town or halfway around the world. For the most part, these decisions are the responsibility of industrial traffic managers whose over-all basic objective is to obtain transportation services tailored to fit the commodity in question and best suited to the needs of their employers as far as cost, speed, and plans for manufacturing, marketing and supplies are concerned.

The purchase of transportation demands a high degree of skill and care. Intelligently and imaginatively administered, this function can make a material contribution to a company's profit and prestige. If its importance is not fully understood at top levels of management or if it is in the hands of incompetent personnel, however, the transportation responsibility can degenerate into chaos and financial loss.

Substantial monetary expenditures are involved in choosing between rail, highway, water, air and pipeline; and, in more detail, between common, contract, exempt or private carriage; and, in still more detail, in planning the best type of packaging, proper shipping quantities, warehousing en route, and so on.

The complexity of the transportation industry and of the

1

many rules and regulations surrounding the purchase and use of transportation is such that getting the most for a company's transportation dollar involves much more than "getting the best rate." Indeed, the many radical changes in the transportation industry in recent years, such as new price levels, new concepts of setting them, increased world-wide trade, the application of electronic data processing techniques, the push toward lower inventories and exciting new transportation services and shipping practices, have made it almost essential for companies of any size to retain competent traffic management, if only to keep abreast of these changes and to measure and control their effect on buying and marketing practices. *An industrial traffic department, given sufficient authority and latitude with which to carry out its ideas, can guarantee the ultimate in value for every dollar paid out for transportation.*

An important specific objective of every purchaser of transportation is to satisfy *service* requirements at the lowest possible cost. That is to say, he would not arrange to ship a vital and needed electronic part by a comparatively slow water service, merely because of low rates; nor would he get "caught short" and order several hundreds of tons of industrial sand shipped by a premium transportation service. The added cost of crating and packing shipments for low-cost transportation might be greater than the added cost of shipping the same products with little or no crating via premium transportation. Similarly, there would be cases where part of a shipment might be sent via premium transportation in order to keep a production line going, while the rest might be sent by slower and cheaper methods and still arrive in time. Then there is the potential of high-speed, premium transportation for reducing over-all costs by lessening warehouse and inventory requirements and thus freeing capital that might otherwise have been tied up in both warehouse space and large inventories.

While there can be no hard and fast rules about managing transportation that will apply for every company, there is no doubt that the function requires an individual who is both trained and skilled and is granted the authority to formulate a transportation policy that is suited to his company's requirements and *is binding upon the company's other departments.*

For example, it should not be the production man's decision as to what *form* of transportation will overcome a supplier's failure to ship on the date specified; the factory expediter should not dictate the form of expenditure of extra transportation dollars to make up for delays in production schedules; nor should the sales department necessarily have the last word as to the *routing* to be used to preserve its customer relations. The tendency of departments not in day-to-day touch with domestic and world-wide transportation services and facilities is frequently to demand the most expensive service without regard for the possibility that less costly alternatives would achieve the desired ends. The responsibility for those decisions should devolve on an organization that is equipped to consider all factors and make its choice accordingly. It is an essential function of a traffic department.

Other than in those instances where the over-all cost is lower because of less packaging, situations involving perishables, and so on, the higher-cost premium services should be used only for the occasional emergency order. Premium transportation cost is defined as the expense of service that is costlier than other cheaper and normally available service. Premium transportation costs can be held to a minimum (1) by scheduling shipments to be released in most economical quantities and with sufficient time in transit to permit routing via lowest-rating services, and (2) by contacting Traffic personnel *for best emergency routing if normal routing is not satisfactory.*

The top managements of many concerns are given reports on the dollar savings effected by their traffic or shipping organizations. *Similar reports covering the excess of premium transportation used for alleged service reasons might well put the finger on practices that succeed only in dissipating company profits without producing commensurate benefits.* A survey of the cost of providing superlative transportation service might well be the basis for producing considerable additional savings through effective control.

Charts of a general nature illustrating costs and transit-time relationships between the various modes of intercity transportation have been provided in the past to show graphically the extra charges that are incurred for premium transportation, rail versus truck versus air, and so on. Transportation complexities have increased to the point, however, that chart-use of this type has come to be of a less general nature. Much of the time it is refined and adapted to particular situations.

The charts take different forms, and an important aim regarding them is that they be simple for quick reading and understanding. A typical individualized chart could well be one with origins and destinations on the left and appropriate columns on the right for the types of service, their respective transit times, and their costs. In some cases they are personalized to a particular plant or area, in others to a particular product, and so on.

These charts can be quite illuminative of what is involved when the transportation dollar could be better spent. To illustrate, a practice on the common side is to simply and without analysis place orders for shipment "fastest way." This often incurs avoidable extra costs. The data on charts of this nature can be of help in correcting uneconomic ordering patterns.

As a general rule, but dependent upon the type of business involved, *premium transportation costs* should not exceed a small percentage of the total transportation expense. If they exceed such a percentage (as determined by a particular company) there is, of course, a definite indication that action should be taken to reduce them.

Questioned as to why his company did not have a traffic department, an executive explained that all of its inbound materials were purchased F.O.B. destination and all of its finished products were sold F.O.B. factory; hence the company had no transportation problems. "So you see," said the spokesman, "we do not need a traffic department and therefore save ourselves a great deal of expense."

Plausible as it sounds, a trained traffic man would have little difficulty in exploding this naive theory. In the first place, a

vendor selling on an F.O.B. destination basis must include in
his price a factor to include the cost of transportation. He also
must include an added factor as reimbursement for advancing
capital funds to prepay freight, for assuming the risks of transportation, for filing loss and damage claims, for expediting urgent shipments and for the delays in receiving payment for
goods due to the fact that invoices are not usually payable until
goods have been received. Without traffic assistance, those factors cannot be measured against the desirability of purchasing
F.O.B. origin. Nor may the purchaser route the freight via the
service best suited to his operations, conduct negotiations for
reductions in freight rates considered too high, and arrange for
consolidation into pool carloads or truckloads.

When it comes to selling finished products on an F.O.B.
factory basis, this may be all very well in connection with that
rare article that has no competition, but *it may be tantamount
to suicide in a competitive market*. It will tend to localize sales
to the area within which freight rates are lowest from that particular factory, whereas a system of freight equalizations or absorptions worked out in collaboration with the traffic department might open up additional highly profitable areas for sales
operations. Additionally, a traffic department can help in developing distribution arrangements that will permit competing in
markets which otherwise could not be touched. And, too, small
inventories mean money saved by reducing investment, by
eliminating the possibility of warehouse stock suddenly becoming obsolete and by more direct deliveries to customers, with
fewer handlings during the factory-to-customer cycle. To accomplish this requires precise timing and precise transportation
planning. Inventory control requires a traffic department constantly functioning at its best.

On neither outbound nor inbound shipments does this no-
traffic-department concern have the control of tonnage that
would enable it to establish effective public relations with carriers. This can be a serious handicap in matters of mutual interest and in dealing with emergencies. Well operated traffic departments can not only effect substantial savings by efficient

handling of incoming and outgoing shipments but can also be instrumental in widening company markets, opening up new sources of supply, and building customer good-will, thus lowering costs and increasing sales. Too many industrial executives lack a clear understanding of what can be expected of a traffic department. As a result, they deprive themselves of experienced counsel on a subject that can have a profound effect upon company profits.

Today's traffic manager is a far cry from the glorified shipping clerk who so often misused the title in years past. The complexity of the field of *physical distribution* is demanding men of many talents.

The transportation complex is changing constantly, and it is essential to be well informed on a current basis. For example, consider private motor carriage. It is doing a great deal; it is making it necessary for the railroads and common motor carriers to depart from the age-old rate making basis of *what the traffic will bear* or *ability to pay!* Common carriers must compete, so they quote all-commodity rates and make specific commodity rates to meet the competition of private carriage. Developing or pioneering rural areas really are aided by private carriage, since there often is not sufficient cargo volume to support regularly scheduled common carrier service.

Contentions are heard that private carriage takes the cream of the cargo, and this is not to be denied completely. Too often, however, losses of important tonnage by common carriers occur for reasons known by the carriers to be resting at their own door steps. Such reasons are similar in many ways to the reasons for loss by an industrial company of particular pieces of its business. Over and above these facets, the common carriers' "secret weapon" of being able to haul freight both ways and to charge for doing so is used quite effectively at times by them in these matters. In most instances private trucks return empty, with no tonnage carried and no revenue. Under the law this is all they can do. The common carriers do not have a similar handicap.

The traffic administrator should operate on a level high

enough to allow him a voice among those who set his company's over-all policies and to permit his decisions to be effective. He must be well versed in transportation law and the requirements of the various governmental regulatory bodies, not only to keep his company from violation of regulations, but to fully protect its rights under the law. More and more he is expected to handle overseas shipments entailing complicated routing, documentation, etc. And because the details of his job may not be too well known to his management, he must be a *self-starter*, with resourcefulness, a creative imagination, a nose for research, and the ability to *sell* his ideas and services. He must have the type of personality that will enable him to deal effectively with both subordinates and superiors and at the same time be a credit to his company from a public relations standpoint. As will be developed in subsequent chapters, he must be equipped to supervise and perform the following clerical and managerial traffic functions:

Clerical functions

Audit of freight bills
Claims
Classification
Demurrage
Diversion and reconsignment
Expediting and tracing

Household goods moving
Passenger reservations
Rate and routing guides
Rate quotations
Routing
Stop-off cars and pooling

Managerial functions

Classification adjustments
Collaboration with packing
   and materials handling
   engineers
Consolidations
Contracts
Credit arrangements
Demurrage, siding and weight
   agreements

Distribution and warehouse
   studies
Economical distribution
Insurance
Intraplant and interplant company truck operations
Inventory control
Location of new plants

Packaging and materials handling studies

Private motor carriage operations

Public relations with carriers

Rate adjustments

Relations with other company departments such as accounting, legal, manufacturing, purchasing, receiving, sales, shipping, warehousing

Tonnage distribution policy

Transit privileges

Chapter 14 reviews in detail the various functions in which the traffic department and other company departments share mutual interest and responsibility for the over-all good of the company.

Not every company can support a traffic department of the size and scope generally indicated in this book. But even if a company is too small to justify even one trained traffic man there is no need for it to be deprived of professional traffic services. From one end of the country to the other there are traffic consultant firms or individual traffic consultants. They will assume any or all of these functions on a fee basis. Chambers of commerce and manufacturers' associations usually provide certain transportation services and counsel. *The point is that skilled counsel in the many aspects of traffic management is a good investment!*

The Traffic Manager's First Consideration

No student of transportation, nor any individual in the industrial traffic department, should approach the procurement of transportation without a sound knowledge of the basic principles of the common carrier transportation system.

The first of these is that carriers may not discriminate; they are obligated to offer the same services to small shippers as to large shippers, and the same rates, although the equivalents of volume discounts are permissible in much the same way they are in any business. Another important aspect of this is that carriers may not establish and discontinue services at will; in other words, a carrier may not discontinue unprofitable operations in order to concentrate on profitable ones. It has, for the most part, been held that in the granting of rights to a carrier the volume of business in its profitable operations will be balanced to compensate for possible losses in its unprofitable services, and that therefore the same scales of rates must apply for shippers in remote and out-of-the-way places as for those in the large urban centers. In other words, the right of a carrier to engage in interstate transportation carries with it certain obligations which have as their net result that large and small shippers, no matter where they may be located, shall receive equal treatment and equal rates.

A second concept which is of importance is that of *inherent advantages*. This is no more than saying that each form of common carrier transportation has its distinct advantages for shippers in terms of speed, capacity, flexibility or cost. At the two extremes of the scale would be the air carriers, with tremendous speed but limited load-carrying capacity and relatively high rates on the one hand and the water carriers, with their tremendous capacity, much lower rates and longer transit intervals, on the other. The increasing use of pipelines for transportation of liquids and semi-solids adds another dimension to the competitive picture, just as current research into nuclear energy and guided missiles may bring about changes in the future.

A threat to profitable operations of the nation's common carrier system exists, and has existed for some time, in the transportation of freight by motor carriers operating in ways that are questionable or are not authorized under the law. It has been estimated by the Interstate Commerce Commission that millions of dollars annually in freight revenue are being diverted from the common carrier system by such operators. Their activities persist and appear to have their origins in: (1) The complexity of the governing laws and attendant confusion as to what is or is not permissible and (2) pressures to reduce transportation costs, which bring on unauthorized steps in the attempts to accomplish the reductions. Dangers of fines and other penalties are, of course, ever present in these matters.

Basically, however, if the common carrier system is to realize its full potential as a dynamic force in the economy, it must have the full cooperation of every shipper and receiver of freight. They must differentiate between the legal and the unauthorized and steadfastly refuse to be drawn into situations that are not proper or are not recognized under the law.

Various leaders in transportation have expressed concern about the future of the common carrier transportation system. It has stood us in good stead. As to many features our transportation policy which involves them was formulated before trucks and airplanes were considered carriers. Modernization of the legal structure and of its anachronisms is needed but will take time. The melding process of doing this is not an easy one the way transportation legislation goes these days. In the years ahead we shall undoubtedly see more attempts to help the common carrier system in the interests of our national economy and defense, and, in a continuing effort, to avoid government ownership of transportation facilities.

It is strongly and sincerely felt by the great majority of those involved that continued patronage by shippers of common carriers whenever practicable, like utilization of United States flag liners in export and import, is simply good business. The transportation and transportation-supply industries employ millions of persons in the United States and pay billions each year for wages, equipment, and supplies as well as for local, state and federal taxes! The additional billions of private dollars invested in transportation plant and equipment, plus the genius, know how, and superlative capabilities of those participating have given the United States a transportation system that is unequalled anywhere in the world. While the common carrier system is by no means perfect, it is extremely useful and helpful in most situations, and it is generally in the best interest of shippers to take advantage of its many potentialities for maintaining the high standards of living and business that are possible under free enterprise!

2

REGULATION AND OTHER GOVERNMENT FUNCTIONS —WHAT ARE THEY?

THE TRANSPORTATION INDUSTRY OF THE UNITED STATES, AS private enterprise, has performed a remarkable feat in achieving its present high degree of excellence within the framework of control imposed by law and administered by government regulatory agencies. Recognizing that a transportation system made up of strong carriers in each of the various modes is indispensable to the nation's economy and defense, Congress, aided by recommendations of various parties in interest, from time to time amends the laws and enacts new ones designed to maintain that strength in the face of changing conditions.

These laws passed by Congress involve important functions in addition to those of a regulatory nature. While regulatory matters are of concern to transportation men on substantially a day-to-day basis, involvements in other functions often occur. This chapter is written with the broad picture of these aspects in mind.

The Department of Transportation (DOT), headed by a Secretary having Cabinet status, came into existence in 1967. The regulatory agencies in existence now and before the creation of DOT are the Interstate Commerce Commission (ICC), Federal Maritime Commission (FMC), and the Civil Aeronautics Board (CAB). Some of their functions, such as those of the ICC on safety, were transferred to DOT as it was created.

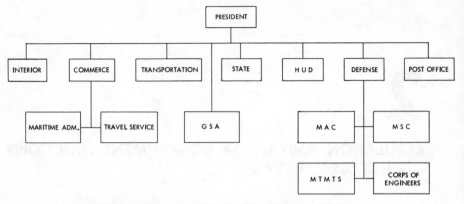

TRANSPORT RESPONSIBILITIES IN THE EXECUTIVE BRANCH

OFFICE OR AGENCY	RESPONSIBILITY
President	Rules on matters relating to international air transport by U.S. air carriers and foreign air carrier operations to the U.S. Appoints members of Federal agencies and appoints chairman of I.C.C., CAB and FMC.
Department of State	Develops policy recommendations and approves policy programs concerning international aviation and maritime transportation.
Department of Housing and Urban Development	Administers a variety of federally aided housing and community development programs, consulting with and advising the Department of Transportation in order that the urban transport programs of DOT are compatible with the development programs of HUD.
Department of Interior	Develops and coordinates policy for oil and gas (including pipelines), and provides for a standby Emergency Petroleum and Gas Administration.
U. S. Travel Service	Develops, plans and carries out a comprehensive program designed to stimulate and encourage travel to the United States by residents of foreign countries.
Maritime Administration	Promotes merchant marine; grants ship mortgage insurance; determines ship requirements, ocean services, routes and lines essential for development and maintenance of the foreign commerce of the United States; maintains the National Defense Reserve Fleet; develops ship designs, marine transportation systems, advanced propulsion concepts, and ship mechanization and management techniques. Its Maritime Subsidy Board awards subsidies, determines the degree of services and specific routes of subsidized operators.

DOT is an arm of the executive branch of government. The others are arms of the legislative branch.

DOT's sphere of responsibilities involves considerably more than regulation. The responsibilities of the ICC, FMC, and CAB, in a very broad way and except as to safety, continue generally as they were during recent years and remain generally in the fields of regulation.

The charts that appear here illustrate the line-up as to regulatory functions of the various federal agencies, the areas of federal assistance, and the departments and others working in particular areas. They provide thumbnail sketches of the present status of those responsible for a wide variety of dealings. For

OFFICE OR AGENCY	RESPONSIBILITY
Post Office Department	Establishes and administers policies, programs, regulations, and procedures governing the procurement and utilization and transportation of mail and mail equipment, including policies governing the distribution, routing and dispatch of mail both foreign and domestic.
General Services Administration	Develops and operates transportation programs within the Federal Government; provides and procures transportation services; develops and implements procedures for improving motor equipment management, operation and rehabilitation programs of the Federal Government including assigning, regulating or performing the operation of interagency motor pools and motor transport systems.
Military Sealift Command	Provides ocean transportation for personnel and cargo of the Department of Defense and, as directed, for other agencies and departments of the United States. Also operates ships in support of scientific projects and other programs of the Federal Government.
Military Airlift Command	Provides air transportation for personnel and cargo for all the military services on a worldwide basis; in addition furnishes weather, rescue and photographic and charting services for the Air Force.
Military Traffic Management and Terminal Service	Directs military traffic management, land transportation, and common-user ocean terminal service within the United States, and for worldwide traffic management of the DOD household goods moving and storage program. Provides for the procurement and use of freight and passenger transportation service from commercial for-hire transportation companies operating between points in the continental U.S., except for long-term contract air-lift service.
Corps of Engineers	Constructs and maintains river and harbor improvements. Administers laws for protecting navigable waterways.

From 8th edition of Transport Facts & Trends, published by Transportation Association of America.

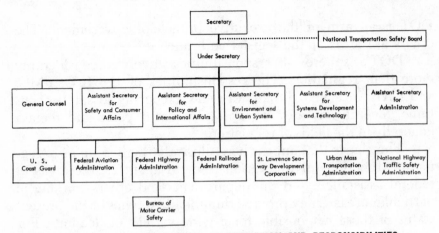

DEPARTMENT OF TRANSPORTATION—ORGANIZATION AND RESPONSIBILITIES

OFFICE OR AGENCY	RESPONSIBILITY
Secretary of Transportation	Under direction of the President, exercises and provides leadership in transportation matters, develops national transportation policies and programs, including compliance with safety laws pertaining to all modes of transport.
National Transportation Safety Board	Determines and reports causes, facts and circumstances relating to transportation accidents, reviews on appeal the revocation, suspension or denial of any certificate or license issued by the Department, and exercises all functions relating to aircraft accident investigations.
General Counsel	Legal services, including the legal aspects and drafting of legislation.
Asst. Secy. for Safety and Consumer Affairs	Safety coordination; regulation of movement of hazardous materials; pipeline safety regulations; and representation of the public viewpoint, in the Department, with regard to transportation matters.
Asst. Secy. for Policy and International Affairs	Economic and systems analysis; policy review; transport data; international transport facilitation; and, technical assistance.
Asst. Secy. for Environment and Urban Systems	Coordinate policies, programs, and resources of DOT transport program with public and private efforts to solve environmental problems having an impact on transportation.
Asst. Secy. for Systems Development and Technology	Scientific and technologic research and development relating to the speed, safety and economy of transportation; noise abatement; and, transportation information planning.
Asst. Secy. for Administration	Organization, budgeting, staffing, personnel management, logistics and procurement policy, management systems and other administrative support for the Department.
U. S. Coast Guard	Provides navigational aids to inland and offshore water and trans-oceanic air commerce; enforces federal maritime safety, including approval of plans for vessel construction and repair. Administers Great Lakes Pilotage Act of 1960. Has responsibility for water vessel anchorages, drawbridge operation, and locations and clearances of bridges over navigable water (Previously under the Corps of Engineers).

convenience they are broken out to the executive and to the legislative branches.

The charts on pages 12 and 13 depict the transport responsibilities in the executive branch. The Post Office, Military Service Management, Corps of Engineers, U.S. Travel Service and others with their functions are included here, and those functions are quite substantial.

The charts here show the organization and responsibilities of the Department of Transportation. Of particular note are the responsibilities for safety, systems development and technology, and urban mass transportation. The latter carries with it substantial burdens. Further discussions of the Depart-

OFFICE OR AGENCY	RESPONSIBILITY
Federal Aviation Administration	Promotes civil aviation generally, including research and promulgation and enforcement of safety regulations. Develops and operates the airways, including facilities. Administers the federal airport program.
Federal Highway Administration	Responsible for implementation of the Federal-Aid Highway Program; National Traffic and Motor Vehicle Safety Act of 1966; and the Highway Safety Act of 1966. Responsibility for reasonableness of tolls on bridges over navigable waters (previously under the Corps of Engineers). Administers federal highway construction, research planning, safety programs, and Federal-Aid highway funds (formerly under Bureau of Public Roads).
Federal Railroad Administration	Responsible for the operation of the Alaska Railroad; administration of the High-Speed Ground Transportation Program; implementation of railroad laws; and advises the Secretary on matters pertaining to national railroad policy developments.
St. Lawrence Seaway Dev. Corp.	Administers operation and maintenance of the U.S. portion of the St. Lawrence Seaway, including toll rates.
Urban Mass Transportation Administration	Responsible for developing comprehensive coordinated mass transport systems for metropolitan and urban areas, including R & D and demonstration projects; aid for technical studies, planning, engineering, and designing; financial aid and grants to public bodies for modernization, equipment, and training of personnel.
National Highway Traffic Safety Administration	Formulation and promulgation of programs for use by the States in driver performance; development of uniform standards for keeping accident records and investigation of accident causes; vehicle registration and inspection and the safety aspects of highway design and maintenance. Planning, development and enforcement of federal motor vehicle safety standards relating to the manufacturing of motor vehicles.
Bureau of Motor Carrier Safety	Administers and enforces motor carrier safety regulations (formerly under ICC) and the regulations governing the transportation of hazardous materials.

From 8th edition of Transport Facts & Trends, published by Transportation Association of America.

STANDING CONGRESSIONAL COMMITTEES HAVING JURISDICTION OVER TRANSPORTATION

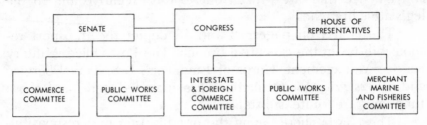

The present standing committee structure of Congress includes several committees which have both direct and indirect jurisdiction over policies affecting the transportation industry. The organizational chart above indicates the positions of these committees within the structure of the Congress. The table of functions points up the major areas of the transportation industry covered by the various committees, as well as the similarity of their respective jurisdiction.

SENATE COMMITTEE	HOUSE COMMITTEE
Commerce Regulation of interstate railroads, buses, trucks, pipe lines, freight forwarders, domestic water carriers and domestic and international air carriers. Inland waterways. Promotion of civil aviation, including subsidies and airport construction.	**Interstate & Foreign Commerce** Same basic jurisdiction, plus railroad labor and retirement and unemployment. Handles ICC regulated water transportation and domestic inland water transportation in general.
International water carriers generally, including registering and licensing of vessels and small boats; navigation and the laws relating thereto; measures relating to subsidies; and the inspection and safety of vessels. Approve Maritime Administrative programs.	**Merchant Marine & Fisheries** Same basic jurisdiction, plus unregulated domestic ocean-going water transportation. Approve Maritime Administration programs.
Public Works Projects for the benefit of water navigation and rivers and harbors. Measures relating to the construction or maintenance of highways.	Same basic jurisdiction.

Legislation affecting transportation also comes within the jurisdiction of several other Congressional committees, such as:

Appropriations	Actual appropriation of funds.
Government Operations	Transportation operations of Federal agencies.
Judiciary	Rules and procedures for regulatory agencies.
Post Office & Civil Service	Parcel post service.
House Ways & Means Senate Finance	Financial matters, with House Committee originating all tax bills.
House Education & Labor Senate Labor & Public Welfare	Transport labor generally, including mediation or arbitration of disputes. (Note House I & FC Committee's jurisdiction over rail labor.)

From 8th edition of Transport Facts & Trends, published by Transportation Association of America.

ment appear in later pages with particular emphasis on its regulatory activities in the safety field and its systems development and related work.

Moving from the executive branch to the legislative, the chart at left shows the standing congressional committees having jurisdiction over transportation. Of those closely tied to the field, the Senate has two and the House three. The Commerce Committee of the Senate along with the Interstate and Foreign Commerce and the Merchant Marine and Fisheries Committees of the House have been particularly important. The Post Office, Government Operations, House Ways and Means, Senate Finance, and others which are shown in the lower section have also been involved in substantial ways in industrial transportation.

The federal transportation regulatory agencies that are arms of the legislative branch are shown on the following page. These are the ICC, CAB, and FMC. Individual organization charts are shown for them later and additional information on their regulatory functions and activities are reviewed. The ICC has been the body with which most industrial traffic men have been involved through the years and it continues to be probably the most important arbiter of freight rates and practices for the substantial majority of them.

As a part of moving to review in more detail governmental regulative activities it should be borne in mind that the Shipping Act of 1916, the Reed-Bulwinkle Act and other laws give carriers the right to set prices, rules and regulations collectively under anti-trust exemption. The regulatory philosophy considers this warranted in that it helps preserve their economic well-being and enables them to avoid price cutting and other practices which might weaken the system.

At the same time, there are laws that protect the users of transportation from abuses which might arise from carriers' actions, collective or otherwise. References to the various provisions of these laws appear throughout this book. High on the list of every traffic manager's responsibilities is a thorough understanding of his company's rights and limitations under the

FEDERAL TRANSPORTATION REGULATORY AGENCIES

The Federal transportation regulatory agencies are arms of the legislative branch of the Government. They are not courts, but they do have recourse to the courts in order to enforce their orders. They exercise quasi-judicial powers as well as quasi-legislative powers. Their members are appointed by the President with Senate approval at salaries of $38,000 with chairmen receiving an additional $2,000. Not more than a majority of one can be from any one political party.

INTERSTATE COMMERCE COMMISSION

The ICC was created in 1887 by the Act to Regulate Commerce. It currently consists of eleven members who serve terms of seven years. Its Chairman is appointed by the President, and its Vice Chairman is elected annually by the members. The following table indicates the types of domestic interstate carriers over which the Commission has economic jurisdiction, as well as its other major functions.

Modes Regulated	Major Functions

Railroads (1887), Express Companies, Sleeping Car Companies (1906)
 Oil Pipe Lines (1906)*—Common carriers only
 Motor Carriers (1935)
    Private carriers and carriers of agricultural commodities exclusively are exempt, as are motor vehicles used by farm co-ops.
 Water Carriers (1940), Water carriers operating coastwise, intercoastal, and on inland waters of the U.S.
    Private carriers and carriers of liquid bulk or three or less dry bulk commodities in a single vessel are exempt.
 Freight Forwarders (1942)
    Non-profit shippers' associations exempt.
 *Gas Pipelines regulated by Federal Power Commission.
	Regulates, in varying degrees by mode of transport, surface carrier operations, including rates, routes, operating rights, abandonment and mergers; conducts investigations and awards damages where applicable and administers railroad bankruptcy. Prescribes uniform system of accounts and records, evaluates property owned or used by carriers subject to the act; authorizes issuance of securities or assumption of obligations by carriers by railroad and certain common or contract carriers by motor vehicle.
	
	 Develops preparedness programs covering rail, motor, and inland waterways utilization.

CIVIL AERONAUTICS BOARD

The CAB, as it exists today, is an outgrowth of the Civil Aeronautics Act of 1938, Presidential Reorganization Plans of 1940, and the Federal Aviation Act of 1958. There are five Board members, each serving terms of six years. The Chairman and Vice Chairman are appointed annually by the President.

Regulates	Major Functions
U.S. domestic and international air carriers. Foreign air carrier operations to, from, and within the U.S.	Regulates carrier operations, including rates, routes, operating rights, and mergers; determines and grants subsidies. Assists in the development of international air transport, and grants, subject to Presidential approval, foreign operating certificates to U.S. carriers and U.S. operating permits to foreign carriers.

FEDERAL MARITIME COMMISSION*

The present FMC was established by Presidential Reorganization Plan 7 of 1961, although most of its regulatory powers are similar to those granted its predecessor agencies by the Shipping Act of 1916 and subsequent statutes. The Commission consists of five members appointed to four-year terms by the President with Senate approval. The President designates the Chairman. The Vice Chairman is elected annually by the members.

Regulates	Major Functions
American-flag vessels operating in the foreign commerce of the U.S. and common carriers by water operating in domestic trade to points beyond the continental U.S.	Regulates services, practices, and agreements of water common carriers in international trade. Regulates rates and practices of water common carriers operating in domestic trade to points beyond continental U.S.

*Note entry and route-designation functions of Maritime Subsidy Board on chart of executive branch.

From 8th edition of Transport Facts & Trends, published by Transportation Association of America.

laws affecting transportation. A current copy of the Interstate Commerce Act should be available for his ready reference.

For the rest of this chapter we shall explore the regulatory roles of the government bodies in the administration of the law, as well as clarify the part played by the Interstate Commerce Commission, Federal Maritime Commission and the Civil Aeronautics Board in the establishment of charges for transportation. Their roles may be important but ordinarily their involvements are minimal. Shipper-carrier negotiations can effect most adjustments.

The Interstate Commerce Commission

The establishment of the ICC in 1887 dates it as the oldest of the administrative agencies. Its board of eleven commissioners is more than twice the size of comparable groups for the CAB and FMC. Their seven year terms also are longer.

The "Act to Regulate Commerce," under which the ICC was established, has been amended many times since its original passage and is now known as the "Interstate Commerce Act." The parts of particular interest to industry parallel each other closely as to most of the provisions affecting freight rates and are:

Part I, covering railroads and pipe lines

Part II, added 1935, covering motor carriers

Part III, added 1940, covering water carriers

Part IV, added 1942, covering freight forwarders

The act enunciates the national transportation policy of Congress as being ". . . . *to provide for fair and impartial regulation of all modes of transportation subject to the provisions of this act . . . . to the end of developing, coordinating, and preserving a national transportation system by water, highway, and rail, as well as other means, adequate to meet the needs of the commerce of the United States, of the Postal Service, and of the national defense.*"

It requires of common carriers that they furnish transportation upon reasonable request therefor; that they establish reasonable through routes with other such carriers; and that they establish just and reasonable rates, charges and classifications. Certificates of public convenience and necessity, issued by the ICC, must be obtained in advance of the construction of new railroad lines or the abandonment or consolidation of existing ones and are necessary before motor carriers, water carriers and freight forwarders may extend their routes.

Unjust discrimination among persons whereby one might be called upon to pay a greater or lesser charge than another person for the same service is declared unlawful. The granting of any undue preference or advantage to one shipper, locality or kind of traffic over another is unlawful, too.

Among those provisions of the Act having important influence on the day-to-day determination of freight rates are the requirements of Section 4, Part 1 (sometimes known as the "long haul-short haul" section). Briefly, these make it unlawful for the rail and water common carriers to charge more for a short haul than for a longer haul over the same route without specific authorization of the ICC, or to make a greater charge based on a through rate than would result from the aggregate of separately established intermediate rates. No comparable provisions exist regarding the motor carriers or freight forwarders.

The ICC is empowered, under the Act, to prescribe rail and freight forwarder rates and charges to remove unjust discrimination against interstate commerce. Known as "thirteenth section proceedings," this power is invoked when state commissions require the maintenance of rates so low as to be noncompensatory and thus create a burden on interstate commerce by requiring that intrastate losses be made up out of interstate revenues. The Act does not give the ICC this power over motor and water carrier rates.

Persons claiming to have been damaged by acts of commission or omission on the part of carriers subject to Parts I and III of the Act may make complaint to the ICC or bring suit in a federal district court, but may not use both remedies. ICC decisions are administrative, and the test of their validity ultimately resides with the courts. Only a minute percentage of the thousands of formal cases decided each year are placed under judicial scrutiny and fewer still are overturned.

The ICC is permitted by the Act to investigate rates and charges on its own motion and to determine, after full public hearing, what rates and charges will be lawful for the future. However, the overwhelming majority of the changes in rates that take place daily are set by the carriers themselves, usually after negotiation with affected shippers. In such cases, the only part the Commission plays in the establishment of the rates is to receive the tariffs for filing (thirty days before the effective date unless ICC order permits "Sixth Section less-than-statutory notice") and to make sure that the tariffs conform to its tariff publication rules.

The divisions are each composed of three commissioners

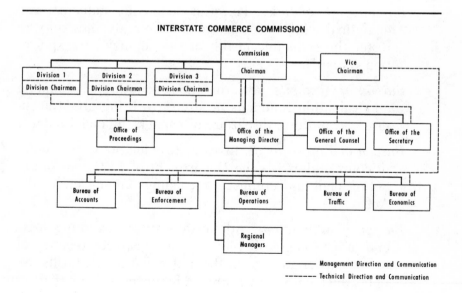

INTERSTATE COMMERCE COMMISSION

——— Management Direction and Communication
------- Technical Direction and Communication

and are each assigned a definite share of the Commission's work load. Their areas of responsibility are:

Division One—Operating Rights.

Division Two—Rates, Tariffs and Valuation.

Division Three—Finance and Service.

Each division is assisted by one or more of five bureaus, which handle most of the preparation and detail work and dispose of matters that do not require the personal attention of the commissioners. The names of these bureaus and a brief summary of their functions follow:

Bureau of Traffic. Supervises the filing of tariffs, suspension of their provisions pending investigation of lawfulness and renders informal opinions concerning the application of tariff provisions.

Bureau of Economics. Performs economic, statistical and analytical work necessary to the Commission's duty to foster the economic health of the country's transportation system.

Bureau of Accounts. Performs the accounting, cost finding and valuation functions necessary to bring about accurate and uniform disclosure of carriers' financial data.

Bureau of Enforcement. Investigates violations, prosecutes in court and assists the Department of Justice in prosecuting civil and criminal proceedings arising under the Act.

Bureau of Operations. Administers rules governing lease and interchange of vehicles and inspects records of motor carriers to inform them of violations in tariffs, rebates, accounts, etc.; also administers regulation of water carriers and freight forwarders under the provisions of Parts III and IV of the Act.

In addition, there is a field organization, comprising nearly one-third of the Commission's total staff, which is set up in six regions, each with a manager, and with offices in 76 principal cities throughout the country. This group takes care of inspection of carrier accounts and other records for compliance with regulations, inspection of equipment and facilities, and investigation of complaints from shippers, carriers and the general public.

State Commissions

Many state regulatory statutes covering movements within their borders are patterned after the interstate commerce act, follow in many ways ICC procedures, and often recognize ICC decisions as precedents. As to these, the industrial traffic man can operate on the basis that ICC guidelines will control, as a general rule, and he can govern his actions accordingly.

The ICC pattern by no means prevails in all states, however. Some states have no rate regulation at all. Others have laws vesting in their commissions powers considerably more extensive than those of the ICC. In the latter category are some that require approval by their commissions of each change in a rate or tariff provision prior to its publication.

Other variations occur in the territorial zones or areas which are established as being exempt from motor carrier rate regulation and operating rights requirements. These, figuratively, can vary "all over the map." The lists of products (agricultural versus others, etc.) which may be hauled by truck on an exempt basis also vary substantially. In some states motor carriers can haul without operating rights on a much broader basis than others. One state statute which comes to mind, and there are undoubtedly others, calls for freight rate regulation in a commercial zone designated as exempt by the ICC.

Questions regarding the applicability of intra- versus inter-state regulations at times arise. Ordinarily the decision rests on whether the movement is within a state or whether it crosses a state line. Interstate applicability is clear where state lines are crossed, but the problem arises when there is no such crossing. An example would be, say, a combination box car and truck move where material comes from out of state by rail and moves on within the state by truck (immediately on arrival, in its original form, and in accordance with a continuing and original intent of the shipper to so deal with it from the out-of-state origin to the destination). Under applicable standards the truck part of this transportation would be considered interstate.

The intent of the shipper is accorded considerable importance in these matters and is to be given substantial weight in deciding what to do about them and the variances in them which occur. In many instances, of course, the same freight rates apply, there are no incompatible regulations, and so on. These have an end result of making the inter- versus intrastate problem a moot one. This is not always the case, however, and this feature of the traffic of many industries bears constant watching.

Where intrastate tonnage volumes are substantial or other related conditions exist it can be as important for a traffic man to know the state rules and regulations as it is for him to know those applicable to interstate transportation. References to the state statutes or to pamphlets outlining them, which generally can be obtained at the state capitols, can be helpful in this regard. Familiarity with them can be valuable and worthwhile.

As has been indicated before there is a tendency in some states to keep rail rate levels so low that intrastate traffic becomes a burden on interstate traffic and it is necessary for the ICC to correct them through proceedings under Section 13 of the Interstate Commerce Act.

The Federal Maritime Commission

The FMC should not be confused with the Maritime Administration of the Department of Commerce. The latter is responsible for the promotion of the merchant marine. The former deals with water carriers, but its functions are primarily regulatory in nature.

A more explicit outline of the FMC's functions would be that it regulates common carriers by water in foreign trade. In addition, the Commission has regulatory powers in the domes-

FEDERAL MARITIME COMMISSION*

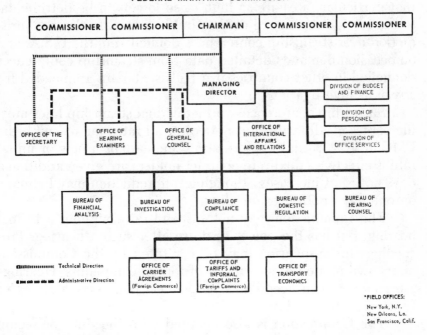

tic offshore trades, i.e., trades between the United States and its non-contiguous states, territories and possessions, over terminal operators and foreign freight forwarders. All this is as provided in the Shipping Act of 1916, as amended, or other related statutes. One of the basic provisions of the 1916 Act is that no carrier or other person subject to the Act may give any undue or unreasonable preference or advantage to any particular person, locality or classification in traffic. In other words, the Act endeavors to assure, within the law, that all cargo interests similarly situated, are similarly treated.

The Commission has control over the reasonableness of freight rates via common ocean carriers in the domestic offshore trades. In the oceanborne foreign commerce common carrier services the FMC has more limited authority, due to the freedom-of-the-seas principle. The Commission can, however, take action on its own motion if it concludes, after a hearing, that particular rates are so high or so low as to be detrimental to the foreign commerce of the United States. It also has jurisdiction over steamship conferences domiciled in the U.S.A. and on occasion demands detailed data from steamship conferences domiciled in other countries if it feels such data are needed for any of its investigations.

Steamship conferences and individual steamship lines must file copies of all tariffs and notices of all rates quoted with the FMC at least 30 days before a rate increase or a new or initial rate is effective (dual-rate contract holders are given additional days notice of increases) though a rate reduction may be made on one day's notice, or on filing.

The Commission may not suspend rates without a formal hearing, but has the power to do so after such a hearing. Proceedings for suspension may be instituted by the Commission on its own motion or as a result of formal complaints. Hearings are conducted in accordance with the Commission's Rules of Practice and Procedure.

The Commission is also charged with the duty of seeing that water carriers do not engage in practices which are forbidden by the Act. These include the use of rebates, fighting ships, retaliation against shippers by refusing space because a shipper has patronized another carrier or has filed a complaint with the FMC. Also involved are the making of unfair or unjustly discriminatory contracts with shippers, or unjust discriminations in the allocation of cargo space and accommodations and the settlement of claims.

Because the foreign trade of our country is also the foreign trade of other countries, and neither the United States nor the foreign country of origin or destination has complete control, the Federal Maritime Commission encourages self-regulation with government supervision to prevent violations of the Act. To a large extent such self-regulation is accomplished through the organization of steamship conferences, which today exist on virtually every important trade route in the world.

Under amendments to the Shipping Act of 1916 in the 1960s, steamship conferences domiciled in the U.S.A. must regulate themselves by maintaining a *neutral body* for each conference. A neutral body is a disinterested or outside individual or company (frequently an auditing firm) that investigates all alleged and suspected violations of conference agreements or operational rules. Each member line must post a cash bond to guarantee adherence to the conference rates, practices, etc.

The Federal Maritime Commission has indicated that it believes that conferences, when properly functioning, promote stability of rates and uniformity of treatment of all cargo interests and obviously also tend to improve the calibre of steamship service.

The Civil Aeronautics Board

The regulatory activities of the CAB are of particular interest to industrial traffic departments because of their effect on air freight and air passenger charges and service. Traffic men also may be called upon from time to time to provide user support to requests by the individual air carriers to the CAB for expanded operating rights, more frequent landings, and so on. In actual practice considerable responsibility for Board activities rests with the chairman.

The CAB is vested with economic regulatory powers over civil aviation within the United States and between the United States and foreign countries. It has jurisdiction over tariffs and over the rates and fares charged the public for air transportation. Carriers initiate tariffs and fares and the Board approves or disapproves them. The principal objective of this regulatory function is to insure reasonable and adequate service to the public without unjust discrimination, undue preference or advantage, or unfair competitive practices. The Board may act on its own initiative or in response to complaints in connection with any of these matters.

The Federal Aviation Act is by no means as complicated as the Interstate Commerce Act and grants considerably more latitude to carriers in the publication of rates, rules and charges. *For example, the establishment of through services*

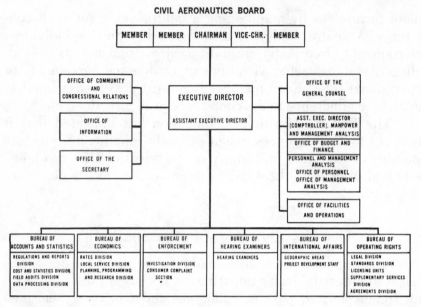

CIVIL AERONAUTICS BOARD

and joint rates with other airlines is permissive, not mandatory as is the case in Part I of the Interstate Commerce Act. This, of course, is in keeping with the comparative youth of the industry and an apparent desire on the part of Congress to avoid provisions which might restrict the industry's development. The anti-trust situation applicable to the airlines is such that they go to the CAB for approval before undertaking in concert many joint fare publications and other industry-wide activities.

Department of Transportation

Earlier it was mentioned that DOT's regulation of safety matters and some of its systems work would be discussed in greater detail. Its safety work is discussed in later chapters where pertinent as are special features of the activities of other regulatory agencies.

A non-regulatory activity of DOT of particular interest to industry has been the work it has been doing on the simplification of international trade documents. The situation regarding these has been receiving concentrated attention in recent years, and DOT has provided worthwhile help in the important progress that has been made in easing unneeded burdens there. Help also has been provided by DOT in the coordination of data processing in transportation, which has outstanding shipper-carrier possibilities.

A number of states have established departments of transportation in recent years. There are currently about 15 of them. Jurisdictions and powers vary, with mass transportation being high on the list of their responsibilities. As with state commissions functioning along lines related to the ICC, the state DOTs can be important to industrial traffic men and may be more so in the future.

General

Along with groups previously mentioned, there are numerous other aspects of the transportation regulatory picture. Illustrations could well include hours and wages of employees, weights and lengths of highway vehicles, carrier fuel taxes, and so on. Several are discussed and referred to later in the text, the chapter on hazardous materials being particularly pertinent.

Top dealings with these aspects generally require more than reading the regulations and statutes. Problem areas are to be reconciled, updated data applied, and other features covered with transportation being administered accordingly.

Illustrative of a problem area is that under the federal Motor Carrier Act a 60 hour driver work week is recognized whereas under the Fair Labor Standards Act it is 40 hours. The latter requires payment of wages at time and a half when 40 hours are exceeded. Numerous problems have arisen in this connection. Generally speaking, where interstate commerce is involved and I. C. C. regulations apply, the 60 hour specification is recognized. Galbraith v. Gulf Oil (C.A. 1969) 413 Fed.2 941.

To be mentioned also is that price controls applicable to carrier charges were with us in the early 1970's but have lapsed although they exist internationally in other countries. Additionally, somewhat special regulatory situations follow.

Recent activity concerning industrial safety stem particularly from the Occupational Safety and Health Act of 1970 (84 Stat. 1590) which is administered by the Department of Labor. Its provisions, and the standards and rules promulgated thereunder, are quite broad. These are framed, generally speaking, to pertain to entire plants, manufacturing works, refineries, and so on. They may also include, however, loading and unloading facilities together with other operations which involve traffic. The Act requires attention because of this.

Environment regulations of particularly recent origin stem from the National Environment Policy Act of 1969 (42 U.S.C. 4321) and related statutes. This, again, is legislation which is quite broad in scope; its administration falls to the Council of Environmental Quality, the Environmental Protection Agency, and others. Among various things, it calls upon other federal agencies to cooperate on and to consider (and make findings on) environmental aspects in matters before them. The I. C. C. does this in line with an implementation ruling it has promulgated (Implementation — Natl. Environmental Policy Act 1969, 340 I. C. C. 431). Where indicated, the Commission specifically rules whether or not "the quality of the human environment will be significantly affected" as a part of its decisions. Developments in this field of regulation are emerging as to the extent they bear on transportation.

Rights and liabilities of industrial companies under antidumping laws applicable to foreign trade are receiving more attention because the activity in this field has increased substantially. The general situation is such that probably this activity will be further increased. While only a limited number of transportation departments are now involved in these matters, more may be later and possibilities in this regard should be kept in mind. Laws on dumping have been in effect for a number of years and are discussed in more detail in the Customs section of the International Trade chapter. Substantial sums of money closely allied to transportation functions can be involved in these cases.

3

FREIGHT CLASSIFICATION

IT IS A FUNDAMENTAL REQUIREMENT OF EVERY INDUSTRIAL TRAFFIC
manager that he give adequate recognition to the importance
of correctly classifying his freight. The National Motor Freight
Classification has summed up the reason for this as follows:

"To insure the assessment of correct freight charges and avoid
infractions of Federal and State laws, shippers should acquaint themselves with the descriptions of articles in the tariffs under which they ship. Commodity word descriptions
must be used in shipping orders and bills of lading and must
conform to those in the applicable tariff, including packing
specifications where different rates are provided on the same
article according to the manner in which it is prepared for
shipment."

Failure to use correct classification nomenclature in describing shipments on bills of lading not only will result in carriers assessing incorrect rates, but may subject the shipper to
suspicion of false billing. False billing is a punishable offense
by the terms of the Interstate Commerce Act (see Chapter 4).
But even if no violation occurs and carriers charge high rates to
protect themselves, this is wasteful if freight charges are absorbed by the shipper. If the customer bears the freight
charges, poor descriptions may well exert a strain on customer
relations. Subsequent adjustment with the carriers often is extremely difficult.

31

Purpose and Background

The need for a system of classification dates back to the time when the railroads first held themselves out to the general public as transporters of goods, for it soon became evident that to make charges *per box, per barrel, per bushel, etc.,* was inadequate and that it was necessary to base freight charges on units of weight. In doing so they had to distinguish between that commodity of which 5,000 pounds filled a freight car and that of which 20,000 pounds or more could be loaded in a car. Similarly, they felt that they were entitled to greater compensation for the transportation, for example, of a shipment of expensive and easily damaged furniture than for a shipment of the same weight of the much lower priced and virtually indestructible rough lumber from which furniture might be made.

To publish specific rates on each of the thousands of different articles found in transportation and to do it in such a way as to make them applicable between all of the different railroad stations in the United States would have been impractical, if not impossible. Consequently, a system of *class rates* was developed, with a limited number of graduations, or classes. By means of the classification the various articles were placed into related categories and assigned class ratings which were determined by the transportation characteristics of each article, such as *weight per cubic foot, value per pound, susceptibility to damage and pilferage, competitive relationship to other articles of similar nature and use, regularity and volume of movement,* etc. Each of these categories was given two class ratings, one for use on carload shipments coupled with a minimum carload weight and a higher one for use on shipments of less-than-carload quantities.

Originally, each railroad published its own classifications, one for traffic moving locally on its own line and another for traffic handled jointly with other connecting lines. There were classifications that differed according to the direction of movement, and some railroads had separate classifications for their different divisions. One railroad had nine different classifications in effect at the same time, each with its own rules, packing requirements, minimum weights and ratings.

Under these circumstances, it is not difficult to visualize the chaotic conditions which existed in 1887, when the Interstate Commerce Commission came into being, charged with the responsibility of putting the nation's transportation house in order within the framework of the Interstate Commerce Act. As early as 1888, the ICC had before it a resolution calling for it to order the railroads to publish a single classification for nationwide application, but the difficulties of reconciling the widely divergent views on the subject then held in various sections of the country caused the resolution to be tabled and carried on the Commission's agenda from year to year without action. Some progress did take place, however, for the railroads dropped their individual classifications and participated jointly in four publications which were issued on territorial lines, as follows:

> *Official Classification* applied in that portion of the country situated north of the Ohio and Potomac rivers and east of the Indiana-Illinois state line and on shipments between that territory on the one hand and Illinois and the eastern part of Western Classification Territory on the other.

> *Southern Classification* applied in the territory east of the Mississippi and south of the Ohio and Potomac rivers.

> *Western Classification* applied in the territory comprising the states west of the Mississippi River, also the Upper Peninsula of Michigan, the State of Wisconsin and the northwestern portion of Illinois.

> *Illinois Classification* applied between points in Illinois.

While this was a step in the right direction, it did not completely solve the problem, for in addition to the different ratings that applied in each territory, there were different rules, packing requirements, commodity descriptions and carload minimum weights. There were very few interterritorial class rates, and most shipments moved on combinations of rates constructed over border points of the respective territories. Thus, a shipment from New York to New Orleans might carry a *de-scription* which would assure it the correct rate for that part of the haul to the border of Southern Classification Territory, but which might not appear at all in the Southern Classification. Or a shipment from Atlanta to Dallas might be in packages which conformed fully to the requirements of the Southern Classification but which would incur a penalty under the Western Classification.

The great expansion of interterritorial commerce which had been taking place in the opening years of the twentieth century made this a most unsatisfactory arrangement, working hardships on shippers and carriers alike. Finally, during the regime of the United States Railroad Administration, which controlled the railroads in the years of World War I and immediately thereafter, the Commission decided that if ratings could not be made entirely uniform, at least commodity descriptions, rules and regulations, packing requirements and carload minimum weights could be. An investigation was ordered, as a result of which the railroads were instructed to create committees representing Official, Southern and Western Classification territories for the purpose of planning the publication of a *consolidated* freight classification.

Out of these proceedings came the publication of Consolidated Freight Classification No. 1, which became effective December 30, 1919. Although it preserved the individual differences of rating peculiar to each territory, it was a significant advance toward uniformity. The Illinois Classification, which had continued as a separate publication, was incorporated into the Consolidated Freight Classification effective November 15, 1933.

Until the 1920s, the various class rate scales were graduated according to numbered or lettered classes, none of which bore a fixed relationship to the first class rate. Thus a third class rate might be anywhere from 60% to 80% of the first class rate for the same distance, while the fifth class rate might range from 32½% to 45% of the same first class rate. In a series of decisions which caused the revision by December 3, 1931 of all class rate scales east of the Rocky Mountains, the Commission prescribed fixed percentage relationships to the first class rate for each of the numbered or lettered classes. Thus, in Official Classification Territory, second class always was 85% of first, third class 70%, fourth class 50%, fifth class 35% and sixth class 27½%. In Western Classification Territory, second and third classes carried the same percentages as in Official, but fourth class was 55%, fifth class 37½% and there was no sixth class. The lettered classes started with A at 45% and scaled down to 17½% for class E. Southern Classification Territory classes were numbered from 1 to 12 and corresponded to Western as far as fourth class, fifth class being 45%, sixth class 40% and so down to twelfth class at 17½%.

The Commission still was not satisfied with the rail classification situation, for in addition to the wide differences in ratings in the various territories, a vast number of *exceptions to these ratings* had found their way into the railroads' tariffs to meet a variety of competitive situations. Although the Commission on several occasions had declared that the interests of the shipping public pointed up the desirability of uniform classification ratings and urged the railroads to remedy the situation, no voluntary action was forthcoming. Consequently, as it is permitted to do under section 13(2) of the Interstate Commerce Act, the Commission initiated an investigation on its own motion and placed it on the docket under No. 28310, Uniform Freight Classification. In a decision handed down May 15, 1945, the Official, Illinois, Southern and Western Classifications were found to be unjust and unreasonable for the future, in violation of section 1(4) and (6), and the railroads were ordered to prepare within a reasonable time a classification embodying the principle of *basic uniformity of classification ratings* for application in all territories. The order directed them to weave into the new classification as many of the exception ratings as possible and to refrain from using the order as a means of increasing their revenues.

Complying with the order, the railroads appointed a committee, which held public hearings in major cities during 1948 and 1949 and considered in four separate dockets the reclassification of all articles then listed in the Consolidated Freight Classification. Finally, after seven years of preparation and study, Uniform Freight Classification No. 1 was published to become effective May 30, 1952. In it, the old system of numbered and lettered classes was dropped and all ratings were expressed as percentages. Thus Class 70 is 70% of Class 100, while Class 250 is 2½ times Class 100. It resulted in many increases and decreases in ratings and brought about several hundred requests for suspension by shippers who claimed to be affected adversely by the increases. However, so determined was the Commission to realize a goal of more than sixty years standing that it denied them all and suggested that adjustment of the items under attack be sought through the regular docket procedure of the Uniform Classification Committee.

Originally, these uniform ratings applied only in connection with the *uniform class rates* which went into effect on the same date as the result of the Commission's order in a companion case, Docket 28300. These rates applied in the territory east of the Rocky Mountains and with their establishment practically all of the LCL and many of the carload *exception* ratings in the same territory were cancelled. Then in 1956, the Commission extended the Docket 28300 principle to the entire country by its decision in Dockets 30416 and 30660, and the Uniform Classification governed all interstate class rates effective August 15, 1956. The Consolidated Classification remains in effect, but applies only in connection with a few very old tariffs which, for one reason or another, it has not been possible to cancel completely.

The Uniform Classification has as its current edition number 10. Numerous supplements have been issued and are to be consulted as a part of making sure any referrals are up-to-date. Examples from number 7 were part of the last edition of this text.

The Motor Carrier Classification

In 1935, when Part II of the Interstate Commerce Act brought motor carriers under regulation, the American Trucking Associations, as agent for most of the regulated motor carriers, published and filed with the Commission, National Motor Freight Classification No. 1. The ratings conformed closely to those published in the rail classification except for articles rated lower than 30% of first class and certain bulky articles on which the motor carriers elected to publish higher ratings. The "volume" minimum weights were generally the same as the rail carload minimum weights, but in almost all territories exceptions to these minimum weights were published separately because the size of the motor carrier equipment then in use and state laws as to maximum loading prevented shippers from loading that much. The rules of the National Motor Freight Classification differ from those of the rail classification and both will be summarized at the end of this chapter.

With the introduction of the rail Docket 28300 class rates and the Uniform Classification, the motor carriers brought out National Motor Freight Classification No. A-1, patterned along the same lines as the rail Uniform Classification. At first, it had very limited application, but gradually motor carriers adopted class rate scales designed to be competitive with the rail Docket Nos. 28300, 30416 and 30660 scales and it now governs all motor carrier class rates. The National Motor Freight Classifications are published by the National Motor Freight Traffic Association, Inc., as agent for participating carriers.

The current publication of this Classification is NMFC A-12. Subsequent to the time of the last edition of this text "Items," rather than "Rules," have come to be used in designating individual provisions. The changed terminology is reflected in the comparisons of the Classifications that are later tabulated herein.

The motor carriers in New England have had their own distinctive classifications since the early days of motor carrier regulation. Originally two separate publications, issued by the Eastern Motor Rate Bureau and the New England Motor Rate Bureau, they were combined under the name Coordinated Motor Freight Classification when the two bureaus merged in 1954 as the New England Motor Rate Bureau. This classification regards density as its principal standard and confines itself to eight ratings: 2½, 2 and 1½ times first class, first, second, third, fourth and fifth classes. Illustrative of the importance and effect of density to this Classification is Rule 210 which states criteria that must be met to warrant "compressed" ratings. Under it material weighing less than 5 pounds per cubic foot is rated Class 1; 5 to 10 pounds, Class 2; 10 to 15 pounds, Class 3; 15 to 20 pounds, Class 4; over 20 pounds, Class 5. Each article is assigned but one class rating, the class rate scales being constructed on a series of *weight breaks* which provide progressively lower rates in each class for each increase in minimum weight.

For one reason or another, more than 200 motor carriers participate in the rail classification. Some of these are trucking subsidiaries of rail lines; others are independent carriers that join with the railroads to provide through services on rates published by the railroads. Conversely, a number of railroads participate in the National Motor Freight Classification for various purposes, including that of joining with motor carriers in through rates published by the motor carriers.

Water Carrier Classifications

Class rates via domestic water carriers which are published jointly are subject to either the rail or motor classifications according to the nature of the joint service. Local class rates, also, may be subject to either classification. For the most part, these have been subject to the rail classification in the past.

Freight Forwarder Classifications

The rail or the truck classification governs the class rates of domestic freight forwarders. Some forwarders are shown as participants in both publications.

General Comments

A freight classification publication in many ways is simply another part of the carrier-shipper contract-agreement for the hauling of goods and articles through out the continent. The principal "rail" classification ("Uniform Freight Classification") is some 1,000 pages in size and the principal "motor carrier" classification ("National Motor Freight Classification") is quite similar. You might say their aim is to include all articles moved for all shippers by all carriers and they are therefore rather large and bulky. The broad coverage of the subject matter and the all-inclusiveness of its treatment leads to this somewhat "telephone book" result. They fill a real need in arriving at proper freight rates.

The name, "Classifications", comes from the principal purposes of such classifications which are to "classify" individual goods and articles for freight rate purposes so that proper charges can be made and paid for transporting them. Other important purposes are served also and are discussed elsewhere in this chapter. Their publication of general shipping rules is one of those purposes. The "classifying" function, however, is a paramount one. This "classifying" feature is used by some, particularly newcomers, to help in identifying "Classifications" in rate terminology as they come on for discussion.

Each tariff that is governed by the ratings or rules of a classification will contain a definite statement to that effect and name the classification to which it is subject. By such reference, it is possible to obviate the reproduction of voluminous rules in each of the many thousands of individual tariffs in effect, as well as assuring the uniformity of such rules in all tariffs. There are occasions when exceptions to the classification ratings and rules are published and, if they do not appear in the tariff itself, reference to the tariff in which they are published must receive prominence equal to the reference to the governing classification.

In all the rail and motor classifications there are ratings which differ according to the *released valuation* of the goods shipped and others which vary according to the *actual valua-*

tion. The distinction between these two types of ratings is important and should be understood fully by shippers of articles so rated (see illustrations below).

Ratings for *released valuation* limit the carriers' liability for loss or damage to the amount stated and, because of this change in the bill of lading contract, may be published only with the express permission of the Interstate Commerce Commission. In such cases, the shipper is not obligated to declare the full value of the goods, but may elect to release the shipment to the valuation that will entitle him to the lowest rating and then cover the balance of the value either by self-insuring or taking out a commercial transportation insurance policy.

Item	ARTICLES	CLASSES (Ratings)		Min. Wt. Factor
		LTL	TL	(See Rule 115)
99400	**HIDES GROUP,** subject to item 98800: **Hides, Pelts or Skins,** dressed or tanned or not dressed nor tanned, NOI, dry, see Note, item 99402:			
Sub 1	Released to value not exceeding $1.50 per pound, in packages	100	85	12.2
Sub 2	Released to value exceeding $1.50 per pound but not exceeding $5.00 per pound, in packages	250	150	12.2
Sub 3	Released to value exceeding $5.00 per pound but not exceeding $7.50 per pound, in packages	300	200	12.2
99402	**Note**—The released value **must** be entered on the shipping order and bill of lading in the following form: The agreed or declared value of the property is hereby specifically stated by the shipper to be not exceeding .... per pound. If the shipper fails or declines to execute the above statement or designates a value exceeding $7.50 per pound, **shipment will not be accepted,** but if shipment is inadvertently accepted, charges initially will be assessed on the basis of the rating for the highest value provided. Upon proof of lower actual value, the freight charges will be adjusted to those that would apply if the shipment had been released to the amount of its actual value. Ratings herein based on released value have been authorized by the Interstate Commerce Commission in Released Rates Order No. MC-519 of October 12, 1962, as amended November 19, 1962, subject to complaint or suspension. (See page 2 for state authorities.)			

Item	ARTICLES			
88150	**GLASSWARE GROUP,** subject to item 87500: **Glassware,** NOI, in barrels or boxes, see Notes, items 88152, 88154, 88156 and 88166, or in Packages 563, 845, 1004 or 1024:			
Sub 1	Actual value not exceeding 35¢ per lb.	70	37½	24.2
Sub 2	Actual value exceeding 35¢ per lb., but not exceeding $1.50 per lb.	85	55	24.2
Sub 3	Actual value exceeding $1.50 per lb., but not exceeding $2.00 per lb.	100	70	20.2
Sub 4	Actual value exceeding $2.00 per lb., but not exceeding $3.75 per lb.	150	85	20.2
Sub 5	Actual value exceeding $3.75 per lb., but not exceeding $5.00 per lb.	200	100	20.2
Sub 6	Except as otherwise provided, see Note, item 88172, if actual value exceeds $5.00 per lb., or if shipper declines to declare value		NOT TAKEN	
88152	**Note**—Shipper must certify on shipping order and bill of lading the actual value of the property as follows: "The actual value of the articles herein described as Glassware NOI is embrasive of any authorized accompanying articles in the same package, and is specifically stated by the shipper to be 'not in excess of 35¢ per lb.', or 'in excess of 35¢ per lb., but not in excess of $1.50 per lb.', or 'in excess of $1.50 per lb., but not in excess of $2.00 per lb.', or 'in excess of $2.00 per lb., but not in excess of $3.75 per lb.', or 'in excess of $3.75 per lb., but not in excess of $5.00 per lb.' as the case may be."			

Excerpts from National Motor Freight Classification illustrating manner of publishing *released value* ratings and *actual value* ratings. The figures in the extreme right-hand column are minimum weight factors which, when used in connection with the table provided in Item 997, produce the truckload minimum weight.

Those ratings which call for the declaration of *actual valuation* are quite another matter, for the carriers' liability is not limited. The shipper must declare that the valuation of the goods falls within the stated ranges published in connection with the rating. Failure to do so will subject him to the penalties provided in the Interstate Commerce Act for false billing and make him liable to a fine of as much as $5,000.

The Interstate Commerce Act, Part I, section 1(4) and corresponding sections in Parts II, III and IV require of common carriers that they establish just and reasonable classifications. The monumental task of performing this duty for the railroads is in the hands of the Uniform Classification Committee, while motor carrier classification is handled by the National Classification Board. Both groups are composed of men who have made a specialty of classification matters for many years and it is a tribute to this skill that relatively few formal complaints involve the results of their work.

While the recent increase in the number of carload and trailerload "Freight-All-Kinds" rates, the cost-related scales for shipments weighing less than a certain number of pounds, and other developments are taken by some people to herald the breakdown of traditional classification principles, it is doubted that the classifications as we now know them will be discarded in the foreseeable future. The ratings presently in use appear to offer the best means of arriving at price levels for the transportation of an important part of the country's commerce; they have been upheld on many occasions by the Interstate Commerce Commission; and they seem to continue to have important endorsement by the transportation industry and shippers alike.

Using the Classifications

At best, classification is far from being an exact science; rather it is a matter of judgment born of long experience. Because of the many factors which are considered in the development of a classification rating, no precise formula is available to provide the shipping public with a key to the basis for the Committees' judgment. Some things can be stated with a degree of certainty, however. For example, the *use* to which an article is put does not control its rating; instead, the Committee will be guided by its *transportation characteristics* and *what it is represented to be.* Thus a manufacturer who sells an article of hardware made of brass may not expect as low a rating as the same article made of steel, even though his article is sold in competition with the steel product. Nor may something represented as "Miracle Cleaning Compound" but which consists of nothing but trisodium phosphate take advantage of any lower ratings which may apply on trisodium phosphate.

In selecting a classification description for a given article, it is not necessary to secure a ruling from the classification committee unless it proves difficult to locate its description among the 10,000 or more listed in the Classification. These various articles usually are grouped with others of similar nature under generic headings, such as Automobile Parts or Accessories, Chemicals, Hardware, Machinery, Seeds, or Tools (See illustrations, page 43, 45). If the article shipped plainly belongs under one of these generic headings but is not listed by name, a "noibn" (Not Otherwise Indexed By Name) description may be used if provided. The Uniform Classification furnishes an aid in assigning such descriptions by listing certain articles in the index only, referenced by an asterisk (*) and the item number for the "noibn" description which it has determined as being suitable for the article. Thus, the entry

       * Scoops, ice cream 91810

appears in the index and reference to Item 91810 shows that the general description to be used is "Tools, noibn."

In the absence of any definite indication as to what the description should be, the matter may be resolved by submitting to the Committee as much information about the article as possible, including *trade name, use, material from which made, weight per cubic foot, value per pound* and *how it is packed*

UNIFORM FREIGHT CLASSIFICATION 10

INDEX TO ARTICLES

STCC No.	Article	Item	STCC No.	Article	Item
37 299 35	Nacelles or nacelle sections. aircraft. 4705		32 959 59	Natural stone,ground or pulverized, noibn. 47715	
28 169 46	Nacreous pigment (pearl essence). 24745		19 411 50	Naval gunfire control systems, armored. 73020	
25 421 60	Nail bins,revolving. metal . . . . 44070,↑44220,↑44230		38 111 40	Navigating logs,vessel. . . . ./. . 11740	
25 411 50	Nail bins,revolving. wooden. . . . . 44070,↑44220,↑44230		38 111 35	Navigation sounding machines, vessel,ot radar. 65930	
31 999 60	Nail head protectors.leather 80085		20 861 20	•Near beer. 56850	
34 298 37	Nails and picture hangers combined. . . . .↑49771,50210		20 143 30	Neatsfoot oil,noibn. 72470	
	Nails:		29 919 15	Neatsfoot oil,petroleum 77240	
33 992 10	Aluminum 5670		20 144 40	Neatsfoot stock 70095	
33 992 15	Brass,bronze or copper,not plated. . . . .↑49771,50220		38 421 10	Nebulizers. 8095	
	Cement-coated. . . . .↑21070		34 998 28	Neck rings,gas cylinder, iors . . . . .49670,↑49781	
33 992 25	Copper-clad. . . . . ↑49771,↑49781,50230		26 471 35	Neck strips paper 76405	
33 152 40	Crate fastener,iors. 54410		34 449 66	Necks,can,sheet steel . . . .85710,↑86010	
33 152 83	•Egg case 54430		20 119 10	•Necks,hog,fresh or chilled. 67910	
33 152 45	Horse shoe,iors. 54420		34 298 49	Necktie racks 52710	
33 992 50	Hungarian,noibn,brass,bronze or . copper. . . . .↑49771,50810		31 999 63	Neckyoke centers,leather or leather and metal combined 94180	
33 152 25	Hungarian,noibn,steel,with ot steel or zinc heads 50820		37 994 11	Neckyokes,steel,or wooden in the white,ironed . . . . ↑4050,32830	
33 152 30	Hungarian,noibn,steel,with steel heads . . . .↑49781,50830		37 994 12	Neckyokes,wood,in the white,not ironed . . . . ↑4050,32830	
34 994 70	Hungarian,noibn,steel,with zinc heads. 50840		37 994 10	Neckyokes,wooden,finished . . . ↑4050,32830	
33 152 50	Iors,noibn,plain,galvanized, japanned or tinned,or coated with brass,bronze,cadmium,cement or copper,or with lead-covered or lead-rimmed heads 54430		37 994 13	Neckyokes,wooden,in the rough . . . 57810	
			20 334 40	•Nectar,guava,unfermented,ot frozen 40210	
			20 334 40	•Nectar,juice,unfermented,ot frozen 40210	
			20 334 40	•Nectar,papaya,unfermented,ot frozen 40210	
33 992 55	Nickel,nickel-copper,or nickel- iron-chromium alloy 70220		20 371 30	•Nectarines,fresh,cold-pack (frozen) 40050	
33 992 25	Nickel-plated. . . . ↑49771,↑49781,50230		01 225 10	Nectarines,fresh,ot cold-pack . . . 41830	
33 152 20	Picture. . . . .↑49771,50210		10 929 20	Needle antimony (antimony sulphide), concentrated ore,lump. 27080	
33 992 50	Shoe,noibn,brass,bronze or copper. . . . .↑49771,50810		10 929 25	Needle antimony (antimony sulphide), concentrated ore,pulverized or powdered 27090	
33 152 25	Shoe,noibn,steel,with ot steel or zinc heads 50820			Needles:	
33 152 30	Shoe,noibn,steel,with steel heads . . . .↑49781,50830		35 321 61	Miners',copper. 91030	
34 994 70	Shoe,noibn,steel,with zinc heads 50840		35 321 64	Miners',iors. 91040	
			39 642 65	Noibn 70100	
33 152 10	String,boot or shoe,steel. coiled. 13630		36 511 55	Phonograph. 88530	
33 992 60	Zinc 98400		08 619 46	Pine (pine straw) 77480	
34 619 36	Name diagram plates,rwy,iors . . . 82130		36 511 55	Talking machine 70100	
34 998 31	Name plates,metal. . . ↑49771,↑49781,50350		35 321 61	Well diggers',copper. 91030	
29 119 82	Naphtha distillate 77240		35 321 64	Well diggers',iors. 91040	
29 919 18	Naphtha solvent,coal tar . . . 23415,33800		41 114 74	Negatives,photograph,glass.old. . . 46160	
29 919 31	Naphtha,coal tar,crude 72370		28 134 75	•Neon gas. 45580	
29 119 82	Naphtha,petroleum. 77240		28 999 29	Neon sign leads or lead wires . . . 34890	
28 141 49	Naphthalene,crude. 24640,33800		28 212 20	Neoprene rubber,crude 84270	
28 151 39	Naphthalene,ot crude 24650,33800		28 186 86	Neo-decanoic acid 2345, 33800	
28 141 46	Naphthenic acid. 77330		28 186 88	Neo-heptanoic acid. 2345, 33800	
28 151 13	Naphthol,alpha 22110,33800		28 186 84	Neo-pentanoic acid. 2345, 33800	
28 151 17	Naphthol,beta. 22880,33800		28 186 87	Neo-tridecanoic acid. . . . 2345, 33800	
28 799 80	Naphthyl methyl carbamate. . . . . δ		28 185 52	Neopentyl glycol. 23980	
26 471 40	Napkin holders and paper napkins in combined packages. 76635		35 228 23	Nest eggs,poultry equipment 36290	
			35 228 45	Nest traps,hens', steel. . . . . ↑35980,↑36000,36800	
26 218 20	Napkin paper 75700		35 228 28	Nests,hens' . . . . ↑35980,↑36000,36460	
26 471 35	Napkins,paper. 76405		33 612 35	Net floats,aluminum 38783	
26 471 40	Napkins,paper and napkin holders in combined packages. 76635		24 941 62	" floats,cork. 38784	
			30 716 22	" floats,plastic.cellular or expanded. 38785	
26 472 10	Napkins,sanitary . . . .↑74540,↑74550				
23 .924 10	•Napkins,table,cotton,or cotton and rayon or flax 28160		30 713 37	" floats,plastic.ot cellular or expanded. 38786	
32 411 15	Natural cement . . . . 21680,↑77130		34 449 36	" floats,sheet steel 38787	
13 211 10	" gasoline,suitable only for mixing,blending,or refining purposes 77240		24 999 21	" floats,wooden. 38788	
			41 111 17	" outfits,camouflage,military. . 73530	
08 422 90	" gums,noibn 48040,33800			Nets:	
08 423 25	" rubber,crude. 84270		39 496 58	Basketball. 7690	
14 219 90	" stone chips,noibn 47715		22 981 78	Camouflage,noibn. 70110	
32 959 59	" stone dust,noibn 47715		34 819 80	Camouflage,woven wire,interwoven cloth,glass fibre,or steel wool. 70120	
40 271 45	" stone waste,noibn 47715		22 981 81	Fish. 70125	
14 219 90	" stone,crushed,noibn 47715		31 999 33	Fly,horse 51250	

For explanation of reference marks,see top of page 17;for abbreviations,see last page of this Classification.

Alphabetical Index to Articles, Uniform Freight Classification. Included
are Standard Transportation Commodity Code numbers.

for shipment. Upon consideration of these facts, the Committee may

    (1) Select a description already in the Classification.

    (2) Rule that it is to be described *by analogy* to another article of comparable characteristics.

    (3) Proceed as in (1) or (2) above as a temporary expedient and place the matter of their formal docket for the determination of description and ratings to be used.

Item numbers from the index (page 43) are "matched" with those for bill of lading descriptions to determine such descriptions and other information (see page 45). In using a bill of lading description, care should be exercised to avoid ignoring an obviously applicable description in favor of another one which is not as specific, merely because the latter carries a lower rating. To illustrate, hand blown Lamp Chimneys, although they are articles of Glassware that could be valued at less than 35 cents per pound, may not be described as Glassware to obtain the Class 70 LCL rating applicable thereon because they are *listed specifically* and take a rating of Class 125. Also, it is important to bear in mind that classification by analogy, as provided in Rule 17 of the Uniform Classification is not the shipper's prerogative, but is reserved exclusively to the carriers and their classification committees.

Shippers desiring changes in descriptions, ratings, minimum weights or packing requirements may file an application with the appropriate classification committee, either by letter or by using the regular forms provided for the purpose. The application should include the following information:

    1. Name and complete description of article, material from which made and use to which put.

    2. Photograph, line drawing or blueprint in triplicate.

    3. Length, width and height of package, in inches.

    4. Weight, in pounds, per package or piece, as ready for shipment.

    5. Weight, in pounds, per cubic foot (length times width

UNIFORM FREIGHT CLASSIFICATION 10   40150-40360

ITEM	ARTICLES	Less Carload Ratings	Carload Minimum (Pounds)	Carload Ratings
	FOODSTUFFS,BEVERAGES OR BEVERAGE PREPARATIONS,NOT NAMED IN OTHER MORE SPECIFIC GROUPS,NOT COLD-PACK NOR FROZEN,NOT FREEZE-DEHYDRATED NOR FREEZE-DRIED,UNLESS OTHERWISE SPECIFIED (see also Item 33800) (Subject to Item 39410)-Continued:			
40150	Jams,jellies or preserves,edible,noibn,in kits,pails,tubs or metal cans in crates,in barrels,boxes,kits,pails or tubs,or in Package 1264	60	36,000	35
40160	Jelly,corn syrup,in kits,pails,tubs or metal cans in crates; or in barrels,boxes,kits,pails or tubs	60	36,000	35
40170	Juice,citrus fruit,frozen,in containers in barrels or boxes,in bulk in barrels,in metal cans in crates or in Packages 575,1164 or 1415; also CL,in Package 1188.	100	36,000	37½
40180	Juice,citrus fruit,other than frozen,noibn,see Note 36,Item 40182: In barrels,boxes or Packages 575 or 1415; also CL,in Packages 835 or 1164.	60	36,000	35
40182	In insulated tank cars,Rule 35,except as to minimum weight. . . .	. . . .	40,000	35
	NOTE 36.-Ratings also apply on fruit juice coloring,the gross weight of which does not exceed 5% of gross weight of shipment when shipped with fruit juices in the same outer container.			
40190	Juice,citrus fruit,with sugar,citric acid,vegetable gum and oils, certified food color and water added,other than frozen,in glass in boxes,in metal cans in boxes or crates,in bulk in barrels or in Package 575.	60	36,000	35
40200	Juice,fruit,artificial or natural,frozen,noibn,in barrels or boxes, in pails or metal cans in crates or in Package 575	100	36,000	37½
40210	Juice,fruit,artificial or natural,other than frozen,noibn,in barrels or boxes,in pails or metal cans in crates or in Packages 575,592, 1264 or 1331	60	36,000	35
40220	Juice,grape,other than frozen,noibn,in barrels,boxes or Package 575; also CL,in glass in crates with solid tops,in Package 454,or in tank cars,Rule 35.	60	36,000	35
40230	Juice,grape,with sugar or other sweetening and water added,other than frozen,in metal cans in boxes or crates,in bulk in barrels or in Package 575.	60	36,000	35
40240	Juice,pineapple,other than frozen,in barrels or boxes; also CL,in Packages 838 or 873.	60	36,000	35
40250	Juice,prune,other than frozen,in barrels,boxes or Package 1304. . .	60	36,000	35
40260	Juice,vegetable,frozen,noibn,in barrels or boxes,or in pails or metal cans in crates; also CL,in metal cans,loose.	100	36,000	37½
40270	Macaroni,noodles,spaghetti or vermicelli,in barrels,boxes or double bags,or in Packages 58,852 or 1119	60	36,000	35
40280	Macaroni,noodles,spaghetti or vermicelli,prepared,with or without cheese,hominy,meat or vegetables,in containers in barrels or boxes or in metal cans in crates	60	36,000	35
40290	Macaroni,noodles,spaghetti or vermicelli,dry,not cooked,with cheese, meat,vegetables or other ingredients,in combined packages in boxes.	60	36,000	35
40300	Malt and milk compound (not malted milk),in barrels,boxes,paper lined cloth bags or in metal cans in crates,see Note 38,Item 40312 .	65	36,000	40
40310	Malt or milk and chocolate or cocoa compounds,beverage preparation, in double bags,barrels or boxes,or in metal cans in crates,or in Package 1100,see Note 38,Item 40312.	65	36,000	40
40312	NOTE 38.-With LCL shipments there may be included paper cups and paper lids for such cups,wooden ice cream sticks and printed advertising matter,subject to packing requirements provided therefor,in an amount not exceeding 20% of the weight of the entire shipment,the entire mixed shipment to be subject to the Class 65 rating.			
40320	Malt extract,liquid:			
	In glass in barrels or boxes.	70	30,000	40
	In metal cans in barrels or boxes,or in bulk in barrels	65	36,000	35
40330	Malt extract,other than liquid,malt powder (dehydrated malt syrup), or maltose (malt sugar):			
	In glass in barrels or boxes.	70	30,000	40
	In bulk in barrels,boxes or 4-ply paper bags,in containers other than glass or earthenware in barrels or boxes.	65	36,000	35
40340	Meat substitutes,processed from vegetables,soybean products,peanuts or grain products,with or without seasoning,in glass or metal cans in barrels or boxes,or in metal cans in crates; also CL,in Package 1437	60	36,000	35
40350	Meats,cooked,cured or preserved,with or without vegetable,milk,egg, fruit or cereal ingredients,noibn,in glass (Rule 5,Sec.2 (b) not applicable) or metal cans in barrels or boxes,in metal cans in crates,or in Packages 223,1307 or 1400; also CL,in Package 1345. . .	60	36,000	35
40360	Milk,cream,buttermilk,or dry milk solids,powdered or flaked,with or without vegetable fats not exceeding 1% by weight,in containers in crates or cloth bags,or in double bags,multiple-wall paper bags, barrels or boxes,or in Packages 3,197,864,1227 or 1307; also CL,in bulk in covered hopper cars,Rule 37,see Note 56,Item 41046,or in bulk in metal shipping containers.	60	36,000	35

For explanation of abbreviations,numbers and reference marks,see last page of this Classification; for packages,see pages following rating section.

Bill of lading descriptions, ratings and carload minimum weights — Uniform Freight Classification.

times height in inches, divided by 1728, and the result divided into the weight per package).

6. Value per pound, as ready for shipment.

7. Details if packaged differently for carload and less-than-carload shipment or truckload and less-than-truckload shipment, as the case may be.

8. Details, if article can be or is nested (see Rule 21, end of this chapter).

9. Details, if article is knocked down (see Rule 19, end of this chapter).

10. Present classification description, ratings, minimum weight and packing requirements.

11. Details of change desired.

12. Data as to weight shipped annually, broken down by origin point and destination territory, CL and LCL or TL and LTL, as the case may be.

13. Complete justification for change.

The application will appear on the next public docket of the classification committee. Hearings are conducted by the rail committee six times a year at Chicago and elsewhere when required. Motor carrier classification docket hearings are held five times a year at Washington, D.C., New York, Chicago and Atlanta and elsewhere upon occasion. It is not absolutely necessary, but often it is desirable, that a representative of the shipper requesting the change make a personal appearance at the hearing to answer questions the committee may have in connection with the proposal. Rather searching questions are likely to be asked and the representative should be thoroughly familiar with the article and all aspects of the proposal.

Decisions on proposals are not made at the hearings, but only after the committee members have had an opportunity to study and discuss the matter among themselves. Proponents then are notified whether or not the application received a favorable disposition, or if a modification was recommended. If the disposition was unfavorable or the modification unacceptable, a new application with additional justification may be submitted for docketing. If the committee then reaffirms its previous action and the matter is thought to be of sufficient importance, it may be made the subject of a formal complaint before the Interstate Commerce Commission.

The dockets of the Uniform Classification Committee appear weekly in THE TRAFFIC BULLETIN; the dockets of the National Classification Board are furnished by the Board to the public for a nominal charge and are published also as a special section of THE TRAFFIC BULLETIN, while the monthly docket of the New England Motor Rate Bureau Classification Committee is distributed free of charge to all tariff subscribers. Each one should be reviewed promptly upon receipt for the detection of proposed changes which might affect a given firm's commodities. Those thought to be favorable can be supported, and those considered objectionable can be protested, either by letter or by personal appearance at the hearings. In the latter case, the Committee should be asked for an assignment of time at the most conveniently located hearing. Shipper proposals appearing on the rail classification dockets will be heard by the full committee only in Chicago, but arrangements may be made for a hearing by one committee member in New York or Atlanta when necessary.

The skill with which the classification job is done in any company can have a far-reaching effect on that company's sales and over-all costs as well as its compliance with the law; therefore it should be entrusted only to trained personnel, with the best possible background, who are thoroughly familiar with the transportation characteristics of their companies' products, as well as those of their competitors. It will assist them in the performance of their duties if they have a knowledge of Classification Committee procedure and the history of previous Interstate Commerce decisions and Classification Committee rulings affecting their own and other kindred commodities. See Chapter 14 for the Traffic Department's functions in this regard.

Even though a company may have no direct *cost* interest in the freight charges on its shipments, it pays to make certain that correct descriptions are used on the commodities it ships and that packaging is such as to command the most favorable rating. For example, one shipper may describe his product as "Hardware, iron" rated Class 70, LTL, while his competitor may correctly use the description "Iron, Hangers, pipe" rated Class 50, LTL. (NMFC A-12 Items 95190 and 105500, respectively, are involved in this connection). FOB origin prices being equal, the difference in freight charges soon would force the former out of a given market or compel him to reduce his prices. On the other hand, the price of raw materials or supplies purchased FOB destination may include a transportation factor which would be inflated if an incorrect description or improper package were used.

Personnel responsible for shipping a company's products, as well as those charged with auditing its freight bills, should be kept posted currently as to the correct descriptions to be used. Those companies having but a limited number of products may do this by preparing and using a bill of lading on which both trade names and correct bill of lading descriptions are printed in the "Description of Articles" column, somewhat as follows:

Boxes Muffo (Muffin Preparations with Canned Fruit)

Boxes Gellina (Dessert Preparations, N.O.I.B.N.)

Boxes Bonzo (Malt and Milk Compound)

If the list of articles is too long to make a printed listing on a bill of lading practicable, they may be similarly listed on a sheet or card which can be displayed prominently in the shipping room and elsewhere for easy reference.

An extension of this idea may be found in a *company classification*, which may be prepared along the general lines and arrangements of the rail and truck classifications. It should contain a section devoted to an explanation of its use, shipping rules pertinent to the company's needs and a digest of such rules of the carriers' classifications as may be applicable to the company's shipments. Another section should consist of an index arranged alphabetically by trade names or numerically by product, piece part or specification numbers. By means of a system of *keys* or codes, these individual entries in the index are linked to a third section containing bill of lading descriptions and, if desired, packaging requirements, ratings and carload or truckload minimum weights. A simple publication of this kind might be set up along the following lines:

Section 1 — Rules

Explanation of use. To find the correct bill of lading description, locate the name or number of the product in the index in Section 2, note the key (or code) number shown in connection with it and use the description provided in Section 3 for this key (or code). *Example:* Armatures are shown in the index as taking key (or code) 151. Reference to No. 151 in Section 3 indicates that the description "Electrical Equipment, Armatures" should be used on bills of lading and that they carry a rating of 77½.

Mixed Packages. When different articles are shipped in the same container, the rate for the article taking the highest rating will apply to the total weight of the package. Do not pack a small weight of high rated material in the same container with a greater weight of low rated articles. When it is necessary to ship different articles in the same container, the description for the highest rated article should be shown on the bill of lading followed by "and other articles rated the same or lower."

Grouping Shipments. All freight shipped on one day to one consignee at the same address should move on one bill of lading to assure lowest freight charges.

(Other rules regarding Packaging, Marking, Loading, Damage, Preparation of Bills of Lading, etc., as are needed may follow.)

Section 2 — Index

Article	Key No.
Ammeters	13
Amplifiers	1
Anodes, Copper	215
Armatures	151

Section 3 — Bill of Lading Descriptions and Ratings

Key No.	Bill of Lading Description	Rating
1	Electrical Equipment, Sets, Amplifiers	125
13	Meters, Electric, noibn	100
151	Electrical Equipment, Armatures	77½
215	Annodes, copper (may be shipped loose if each weighs 25 lbs. or more)	55

In a simple publication such as this, only LCL ratings are shown. *Since it would be designed primarily for use in shipping departments, any rules shown should be confined to those actually affecting shipping functions and should be stated in terms that can be understood easily by shipping personnel.*

Larger firms may find it desirable to expand on this format by adding packing requirements, ratings for both LCL and carload and those applicable via truck when different; also carload minimum weights. It is difficult to show truckload minimum weights because they tend to vary from territory to territory and even from carrier to carrier.

Publications of this sort must be under *constant* review for changes and additions, and for this reason it is best that they be issued in loose-leaf form. Each reissued page should bear a correction number or other identification by which it may be determined whether or not the publication is in current condition.

The bare bones of these three ways to help in assuring the use of correct commodity descriptions and in obtaining proper freight charges are preprinted bills of lading, card lists, and company classifications. Combinations of them and the personalizing of them to individual situations where warranted are also important. To illustrate, partially preprinted bills of lading may be used in which the preprinting is of the most moved commodities and blank lines left to be used for the occasional movers. Also, partially preprinted bills of lading may be used along with card lists and company classifications where indicated.

The index of the Uniform Freight Classification carries the

Standard Transportation Commodity Code (STTC) designation for all articles listed (see page 43). This Code was originally developed to facilitate the reporting via computer of transportation statistics more quickly and simply and with greater accuracy than previously possible. Subsequently its uses have been broadened to include freight rate matters and other purposes. A number of industries are using the Code in their classification work and in other ways. Its use is explored more thoroughly in Chapter 15.

Classification Rules

The carriers' classifications also set forth those rules governing the transportation of freight as are general in application. This eliminates the necessity of repeating those rules in each of the thousands of currently effective carrier tariffs.

The rules of the various classifications govern class and commodity rates (for discussion of commodity rates, see Chapter 5) to the extent provided in the tariffs naming those rates. *Thorough* familiarity with these rules is an absolute necessity for all traffic men because of the prominent part they occupy in the transportation job. The following summary is not intended as a substitute for a careful reading of the rules themselves, but is designed to point out and explain the salient features of each. The listing shows the rules of the rail classification, with reference to the corresponding provisions, if any, in the truck classifications.

Rule 1. Gives shippers the privilege, rarely used, of tendering shipments with carriers' liability limited by common law instead of by the bill of lading contract, and provides an increase of 10% in freight charges for doing so.

Also provides for bill of lading forms to be used generally, except when shipments are tendered as above.

(*Items 360 and 365 of National Motor Freight Classification do not carry the alternative privilege, but merely prescribe bill of lading forms to be used; Rule 20 of Coordinated Classification.*)

Rule 2. States that bill of lading descriptions should conform to those in the classification and provides for inspection of shipments by carriers if they deem necessary. See Chapter 7 for additional details.

(Item 360 of National Motor Freight Classification; Rule 20 of Coordinated Classification.)

Rule 3. Prohibits acceptance, either by themselves or as premiums accompanying other articles, of property of extraordinary value and other named articles.

(Item 780 of National Motor Freight Classification; Rule 150 of Coordinated Classification.)

Rule 4. Relieves carriers of obligation to accept freight liable to impregnate or otherwise damage equipment or other freight. See Chapter 7 for additional details.

(Item 780 of National Motor Freight Classification; Rule 150 of Coordinated Classification.)

Rule 5. Requires that articles be tendered for shipment in such condition and so prepared as to render transportation of them reasonably safe and practicable, defines various packages and provides basis for assessment of freight charges on articles found in transportation packed otherwise than required in the classification, *but prohibits use of these provisions as a basis for quoting rates.* See Chapter 7 for additional details.

(Items 680, 685, and 687 of National Motor Freight Classification contain provisions along generally similar lines as well as alternate forms of packing and packaging.)

Rule 6. Gives instructions for the marking or tagging of individual pieces of freight. See Chapter 7 for additional details.

(Item 580 of National Motor Freight Classification; Rule 40 of Coordinated Classification.)

Rule 7. Prescribes information to be shown on bills of lading and describes conditions under which delivery of shipments will be made under both Order and Straight Bills of Lading, as well as import shipments.

(Various items, e.g., 360 sec. 4, of National Motor Freight Classification and Rule 20 of Coordinated Classification are similar but make no reference to import shipments.)

Rule 8. Prohibits advancing charges to shippers, owners, consignees, their draymen or warehousemen unless specifically provided for in carriers' tariffs. This means that, for example, a warehouseman may not collect storage charges on a shipment from a carrier and ask the carrier to collect them, in turn, from the consignee.

(Item 300 of National Motor Freight Classification; Rule 130 of Coordinated Classification.)

Rule 9. Requires prepayment or guarantee of freight charges on shipments which, in the event of non-delivery, might not yield enough at forced sale to cover the amount of freight charges.

(Item 770 of National Motor Freight Classification; Rule 120 of Coordinated Classification.)

Rule 10. Prescribes the basis for freight charges on carloads consisting of a mixture of differently rated articles or articles carrying different carload minimum weights.

(Items 640 and 645 of National Motor Freight Classification and Rule 70 of Coordinated Classification prescribe bases for charges on LTL shipments as well as truckload.)

Rule 11. Provides that freight charges shall be computed on gross weights or on estimated weights when specifically authorized.

(Item 995 of National Motor Freight Classification; Rule 60 of Coordinated Classification.)

Rule 12. States basis for assessment of freight charges on LCL shipments of one or more classes and for packages containing differently rated articles, less carload or carload.

(Items 640 and 645 of National Motor Freight Classification; Rules 70 and 80 of Coordinated Classification.)

Rule 13. Provides minimum charges per LCL shipment

and per carload. This means that, if the weight multiplied by the rate results in lower charges, these minimum charges are applied.

(No corresponding provisions in National Motor Freight nor Coordinated Classifications. Carried in individual tariffs.)

Rule 14. Defines carload freight and states conditions under which carload rates will apply on shipments accorded services ordinarily not included in carload rates.

(Item 110 of National Motor Freight Classification and Rule 10 of Coordinated Classification define all shipments; otherwise no corresponding provisions.)

Rule 15. States conditions under which LCL shipments may be subject to carload charges and carload shipments may be subject to LCL charges. It specifically excludes from the application of carload rates shipments that have been accorded railroad pickup or delivery service, or an allowance in lieu thereof, unless carriers' tariffs provide otherwise.

(No corresponding provisions in National Motor Freight nor Coordinated Classifications.)

Rule 16. Defines less carload freight.

(Item 110 of National Motor Freight Classification; Rule 10 of Coordinated Classification; LTL.)

Rule 17. Provides for classification by analogy when articles are not specifically provided for nor embraced by an "noibn" description.

NOTE: This may be done only by carriers or their agents, which also would include Classification Committees.

(Item 421 of National Motor Freight Classification; Rule 220 of Coordinated Classification.)

Rule 18. Provides that, when the combination is not specifically listed, articles which are combined or attached to one another will be charged for at the rating applicable to the highest rated article in the combination and, on carload shipments, at the highest carload minimum weight.

(Item 422 of National Motor Freight Classification; Rule 100 of Coordinated Classification.)

Rule 19. Defines "knocked down" articles by stating that KD ratings will apply only on articles taken apart in such manner as to reduce bulk by at least 33⅓ percent. See Chapter 7 for additional details.

(Item 110 of National Motor Freight Classification; Rule 10 of Coordinated Classification.)

Rule 20. States that parts or pieces constituting a complete article, when received on one bill of lading, will be charged for at the rating applicable to the complete article. Thus, for example, it is not permissible to ship a sidewalk sign consisting of a metal sign weighing 7 pounds, a pipe upright weighing 12 pounds and a cast iron base weighing 30 pounds on the same bill of lading and describe them separately in order to obtain the lower ratings provided for the pipe and base.

(Item 424 of National Motor Freight Classification; Rule 110 of Coordinated Classification.)

Rule 21. Defines the term "nested". See Chapter 7 for additional details.

(Item 110 of National Motor Freight Classification; Rule 10 of Coordinated Classification.)

Rule 22. Defines "in the rough," "in the white" and "finished" as used in connection with classification descriptions of wooden articles. See Chapter 7 for additional details.

(Item 110 of National Motor Freight Classification; Rule 10 of Coordinated Classification.)

Rule 23. Prohibits loading of freight in the bunkers (ice compartments) of refrigerator cars.

(No corresponding rule in National Motor Freight nor Coordinated Classifications.)

Rule 24. Provides for manner of handling and basis for charges on quantities of freight in excess of that which can be loaded in or on a single car.

NOTE: This rule is recommended for careful study by shippers of carload freight because proper use of its provisions can operate to save considerably in transportation charges. Many exceptions to this rule appear in individual tariffs and in connection with individual rates.

(No corresponding rule in National Motor Freight nor Coordinated Classifications. Carried in individual rate tariffs.)

Rule 25. Provides for the interchangeability of the word "iron" with the word "steel" and states that where reference to the gauge of metal, it means U.S. Standard Gauge.

(Item 110 of National Motor Freight Classification; Rule 10 of Coordinated Classification.)

Rule 26. Does not appear in the Uniform Classification.

Rule 27. Requires shippers to load, and consignees to unload, carload freight and heavy or bulky LCL freight; also requires safe loading of cars and protection of detachable parts of articles shipped on open cars.

(Item 568 of National Motor Freight Classification, confined to heavy or bulky freight, which is defined. No similar provisions in Coordinated Classification.)

Rule 28. Provides that the word "rubber" shall indicate the natural or synthetic varieties; defines "synthetic plastics" and provides that references to aluminum, magnesium, zinc and metal, noibn, shall include alloys thereof.

(Item 110 of National Motor Freight Classification; Rule 10 of Coordinated Classification; rubber and plastics only.)

Rule 29. Provides basis for charges on carload and less carload shipments which, because of length or dimensions, require two or more cars or series of cars and specifies four cars as the maximum number in a series. Provision also is made for loadings which cannot be accomplished through a box car's side door measuring 6 feet wide by 9 feet, 4 inches high.

(No comparable rule in National Motor Freight nor Coordinated Classifications.)

Rule 30. Defines dunnage as "temporary blocking, flooring or lining, standards, strips, stakes or similar bracing or supports not constituting a part of the car" when required to protect and make carload freight secure for shipment. It specifically excludes from the term "dunnage" packing material such as excelsior, hay, sawdust, shavings, shredded paper, straw or packing cushions. Dunnage must be furnished and installed by the shipper at his expense. If the actual weight of the dunnage is specified on the bill of lading, carriers will allow up to 2,000 pounds of it to move in each carload free of transportation charges provided the carload minimum weight is met.

(Item 995 of National Motor Freight Classification and Rule 170 of Coordinated Classification. The latter is silent as to a provision for free transportation.)

Rule 31. Provides that ratings do not include the expense of refrigeration nor obligate carriers to maintain heat in cars, except to the extent that their tariffs provide otherwise.

(Item 810 of National Motor Freight Classification, Rule 160 of Coordinated Classification.)

Rule 32. Provides that transportation charges will not be assessed on the weight of ice in the bunkers of refrigerator cars unless removed and appropriated by the consignee, in which case it will be charged for at the carload rate applicable to the freight it accompanies.

(No corresponding provisions in National Motor Freight nor Coordinated Classifications.)

Rule 33. Provides for the alternative application of varying carload ratings and minimum weights.

(Item 595 of National Motor Freight Classification; see Rule 290 in Coordinated Classification as to Connecticut traffic.)

Rule 34. Deals with the matter of carload minimum weights which are made subject to the rule by specific reference or listed in the classification suffixed by the letter "R". In such cases, when a closed car longer than 40 feet 7 inches but not over 52 feet 8 inches is ordered for loading, the carload minimum weight is increased 40%, and if a car over 52 feet 8 inches is ordered, the carload minimum weight is increased 100%. Open cars are subject to a graduated scale whereby the carload minimum weight is applicable on cars up to 41 feet 6 inches and when longer cars are ordered the carload minimum weight is increased as follows:

Over 41 ft. 6 in. and not over 42 ft. 6 in.   22%
Over 42 ft. 6 in. and not over 46 ft. 6 in.   42%
Over 46 ft. 6 in. and not over 50 ft. 6 in.   62%
Over 50 ft. 6 in. and not over 52 ft. 6 in.   72%
Over 52 ft. 6 in.   100%

The rule also makes provision for the furnishing of two cars when a single car of the length ordered is not available.

> NOTE: This rule is of utmost importance to shippers of light and bulky freight and should be studied carefully for its effect on a given firm's shipping practices.

(No comparable rule in National Motor Freight nor Coordinated Classifications.)

Rule 35. Contains a number of basic provisions for the computation of carload minimum weights and freight charges on shipments in tank cars. It relieves the carriers of the obligation to furnish tank cars.

(Item 370 of National Motor Freight and Rule 160 of Coordinated Classification deal with tank truck shipments.)

Rule 36. Provides that, when applying a percentage factor to a given rate, fractions of less than ½ or .50 of a cent in the result will be dropped and those ½ or .50 of a cent or greater will increase the result to the next whole cent.

(Item 565 of National Motor Freight Classification; Rule 230 of Coordinated Classification.)

Rule 37. Specifies that publication of rates on shipments in covered hopper cars does not obligate carriers to furnish such cars. This rule is not applicable on Texas intrastate traffic.

(No comparable rule in National Motor Freight nor Coordinated Classifications.)

Rule 38. States that an exception rating must be used instead of the corresponding classification rating and that the establishment of a commodity rate on a given article supersedes both unless the tariff publishing the exception rating or the commodity rate specifically provides otherwise. It also permits alternation of class and commodity rates on Illinois intrastate traffic. Rule 38 does not apply on Florida intrastate traffic.

(Item 765 of National Motor Freight Classification, and Rule 180 of Coordinated Classification, except that they do not contain the provisions for Illinois and Florida intrastate traffic.)

Rule 39. Requires that explosives and other dangerous articles transportation comply with the rules and regulations prescribed by the ICC and published in the tariff of the Bureau of Explosives or in the *Federal Register* or, if by water carrier, those prescribed by the Commandant, United States Coast Guard. It also requires that if the description in the Bureau of Explosives tariff differs from the classification, exception or commodity rate description, the former must appear first on the bill of lading with the latter following in parentheses. See Chapter 7 for additional details. (ICC means DOT here).

(Item 540 of National Motor Freight Classification is comparable but refers to Department of Transportation; Rule 40 of Coordinated Classification provides for marking and packing per the New England Motor Rate Bureau Explosives tariff.)

Rule 40. Carries detailed specifications for numerous forms of shipping containers made of materials other than fibreboard. See Chapter 7 for additional details.

(Items 200-297, inclusive, of National Motor Freight Classification; Rule 30 of Coordinated Classification.)

Rule 41. Carries detailed specifications for shipping containers made of solid or corrugated fibreboard, including the form of certificate required to be imprinted thereon by the manufacturer of the container. See Chapter 7 for additional details.

(Items 200-297, inclusive, of National Motor Freight Classification; Rule 30 of Coordinated Classification.)

Rule 42. Provides that reshipping documents, invoices, assembly or operating instructions or X-ray photographs may be forwarded in packages with other articles at the rate or rating applicable on the articles they accompany.

(Item 428 of National Motor Freight Classification; Rule 200 of Coordinated Classification is along related lines but provides for forwarding without charge with truck loads.)

Rule 43. Prescribes the form of separate contract to be used when men accompany shipments of property, other than live stock, live wild animals or ostriches.

(No corresponding provisions in National Motor Freight nor Coordinated Classifications.)

Rule 44. Describes the method by which changes in individual items will be designated in supplements to the classification by use of lettered suffixes. *Example:* Item 1500-B cancels Item 1500-A of a prior supplement, which in turn had cancelled Item 1500.

(Item 381 of National Motor Freight Classification; Rule 50 of Coordinated Classification.)

Rule 45. Contains provisions for the acceptance of and assessment of charges on advertising matter, advertising signs, store display racks, stands and premiums when they accompany the articles they advertise or are given with. Ordinarily, the advertising materials may not exceed 10% of the gross weight of those articles they accompany, and no more than one premium may be enclosed with each inner package. Freight charges then will be computed at the rate applicable to the article they accompany; any excess will be charged for at the rate applicable to the advertising matter or premiums.

(Item 310 of National Motor Freight Classification; Rule 90 of Coordinated Classification.)

Rule 46. Explains that the word "and" is used to couple

the terms between which it appears and that "or" provides for alternation or use of either or both of the terms between which it appears, sometimes a very important distinction. It also states that a name appearing in parentheses is to be read as another description of the article preceding the parentheses. There is an explanation of the indentations used in the text of the classification to the effect that an entry so set away from the left margin must be read in relation to the heading to which it is subordinate. *Example:* Item 53630 reads "Angles, noibn" but because it is indented from the heading "IRON OR STEEL" in Item 53610, it must be read as "Iron or Steel Angles, noibn". This rule defines "rate" as the specific figure published in tariffs to be used in computing freight charges, and "rating" or "column" as signifying the numerals used in the classification or exceptions to identify the "rate" published in class or commodity column tariffs.

(Item 110 of National Motor Freight Classification; Rule 10 of Coordinated Classification.)

Rule 47. Contains rules under which carriers will make collection of COD charges (not their freight charges) on LCL or any quantity shipments and provides a scale of charges based on the amount to be collected for performing this service.

(Item 430 of National Motor Freight Classification; Rule 190 of Coordinated Classification. These are not limited to LCL or AQ shipments.)

Rule 48. Provides that where reference is made to tariffs, items, notes, rules, etc., such reference includes supplements to and reissues of those tariffs and reissues of those items, notes, rules, etc.

(Item 845 of National Motor Freight Classification; Rule 240 of Coordinated Classification.)

Rule 49. States conditions under which the Classification Committee will issue permits for the experimental use of otherwise unauthorized containers for the purpose of determining the merits of such containers. See Chapter 7 for additional details.

(Item 689 of National Motor Freight Classification; Rule 300 of Coordinated Classification.)

Rule 50. Provides that up to 25 pounds of empty shipping containers may be included in carloads for the purpose of reconditioning the car's contents at destination. See Chapter 7 for additional details.

(Item 426 of National Motor Freight Classification as to bags; no corresponding provisions in Coordinated Classification.)

Rule 51. Provides that when packing requirements call for wooden barrels, drums, pails or tubs, such containers may be constructed of fibreboard. Also provides penalties when specifications are not met. See Chapter 7 for additional details.

(Items 200-297, inclusive, of National Motor Freight Classification; Rule 30 of Coordinated Classification.)

Rules 52 and 53. Provide basis for computation of carload weights on shipments of Liquefied Petroleum Gas, Butadiene, and Isoprene.

(No comparable provisions in National Motor Freight nor Coordinated Classifications.)

Rule 54. Provides that, as to multi-level flat cars, rates and weights published in U.F.C. shall not be applicable. This provision is currently under suspension by the I.C.C.

(No comparable provisions in National Motor Freight nor Coordinated Classifications.)

Rule 55. Describes method of denoting matter brought forward from one supplement to another without change.

(No comparable provisions in National Motor Freight nor Coordinated Classifications.)

Rules 56-59, inclusive. Do not appear in Uniform Classification.

Rule 60. Provides minimum charge for the use of certain types of flat cars.

(No comparable provisions in National Motor Freight nor Coordinated Classifications.)

Rule 61. Specifies calculations to be made in determining weight per cubic foot.

(Item 110 Sec. 8 of National Motor Freight Classification; Rule 10 Sec. s of Coordinated Classification.)

National Motor Freight Classification Rules

The National Motor Freight Classification has several items not referred to above. They include:

Item 360. Certain sections establish charges for extra copies of shipping documents, other papers, and related matters. Exceptions include documents incident to Bank and Sight Draft plans.

Item 370. Application of minimum weights in connection with freight shipped in tank trucks. This is somewhat related to tank car UFC 35.

Item 420. Explanation of classes.

Item 535. Table of expiration dates in connection with certain temporary provisions.

Items 997. The purpose of this rule is similar to that of Rule 34 of the Uniform Classification in that it attempts to adapt truckload minimum weights to the size of equipment available. Articles in the classification are given individual "minimum weight factors" (see last column, illustration, page 40) instead of minimum weights stated in pounds. Application of the minimum weight factor to the proper table will indicate the truckload minimum weight in pounds.

Coordinated Classification Rules

The Coordinated Classification likewise has several rules

not previously referred to which include:

Rule 210. Defining the word "compressed" as used in individual descriptions of articles such as rags, waste paper, etc.

Rule 250. Containing individual carriers' restrictions against the handling of shipments on order bills of lading.

Rule 260. Relating to bill of lading descriptions for articles classified as to density, actual value or released value.

Rule 270. Providing that a shipment consisting of two or more articles taking different minimum charges shall be subject to the highest minimum charge provided for any article in the shipment.

Rule 280. Requires that overcharge claims against carriers and undercharge claims against shippers be presented within two years on intrastate traffic.

Rule 290. Provides for a maximum charge based on the truckload rate and minimum weight on Connecticut intrastate traffic.

Rule 310. Provisions for the collection of consolidation and forwarding charges.

Rule 320. Restrictions against the application of ratings to articles made of Plastic, Polyurethane or Urethane unless these materials are specifically mentioned in the item.

Rule 330. Provides for classification of gold and silver plated articles not specifically covered.

Rule 340. Prohibits partial prepayment or collection of freight charges.

Rule 360. Establishes charges for extra copies of certain shipping documents and related matters. Exceptions are provided as to Bank and Sight Draft plans.

In addition to these rules, the several classifications illustrate the various forms of bills of lading which are discussed fully in Chapter 4.

4

THE DOMESTIC BILL OF LADING AND SHIPPING RULES

OF ALL THE DOCUMENTS REQUIRED IN THE TRANSPORTATION OF goods, none is more important than the bill of lading, the origins of which extend far back into the annals of commerce when ships were the only carriers. The form and terms of the bill of lading have evolved over the years and varied according to the country in which used, but its basic purpose has remained unchanged. In the United States, standardization of its form and contract provisions took place on January 1, 1917, under the Federal Bills of Lading Act.

This act, in addition to standardizing, clothed the bill of lading with much of its high standing as a document by making provision for heavy penalties for altering, forging, counterfeiting or falsely making a bill of lading for criminal purposes. *Conviction on such charges subjects the guilty parties to imprisonment for as long as five years, $5,000 fine, or both, for each offense.* The Interstate Commerce Act imposes upon common carriers the duty of issuing bills of lading and prescribes the general terms of the contract of carriage. The actual form of the bill of lading is set forth in the carriers' classifications (see Chapter 3).

The importance of the bill of lading lies in its several functions in connection with the shipment it covers. It must be prepared in no less than three copies.

No. 1 Copy—Original. This copy, bearing signatures of shipper's and carrier's agents, serves as a description of the shipment and its contents and as a receipt by the carrier for the goods; thus it is acceptable as proof that shipment has been made and as evidence of beneficial ownership. At the same time, *it is a contract and clearly fixes the carrier's liability* (see Appendix 1). Under ordinary circumstances, it should be in the possession of the party having title to the goods while in transit, for it is required in support of loss and damage claims.

No. 2 Copy—Shipping Order. This copy is retained by the carrier and serves as forwarding instructions and as a base for billing.

No. 3 Copy—Memorandum. This copy is an acknowledgment that a bill of lading has been issued and, while it does not have the standing of the original as a receipt and contract, is valuable as a record, especially in cases where the original must be surrendered.

Additional Copies. As many additional copies as are desired may be prepared for record purposes but they will not be receipted by the carrier nor will they have any standing as documents in connection with the transaction.

Although the Interstate Commerce Act requires carriers to issue bills of lading, their actual preparation almost always is attended to by the shippers. Sometimes they are on blank forms supplied by the carriers, but more and more frequently they are on forms designed to suit an individual shipper's needs, carrying printed lists of his principal commodities and printed at the shipper's expense. The carrier then signs it as a firm contract. Often, the three bill of lading copies are part of a manifold of six or more which also may include an order acknowledgment, warehouse release, shipping notice, invoice, ledger copy or other forms incident to the transaction. There are no restrictions as to what may be manifolded with the bill of lading as long as the bill of lading itself conforms to the illustrations published in carriers' classification (See page 78). Slight shifts in the arrangement of the printed bill of lading text are permissible, and extraneous matter may be printed on the form to accommodate the shipper's needs, provided such matter is referenced by a dagger symbol (†) and the symbol explained elsewhere on the form to indicate that it means: "Shipper's imprint. Not a part of the bill of lading prescribed in carriers' classifications."

■ *Uniform straight bill of lading and short form.*—Formerly the model forms shown in the classifications required that all bill of lading forms reproduce the complete contract terms and conditions, as well as refer specifically to the name of the classifications whose rules governed the acceptance of the shipment. As a result, it was necessary to provide separate forms for rail and truck shipments or, if the rail form were used for all shipments, that it be overstamped on truck shipments. This created considerable dissatisfaction and misunderstanding, as well as providing a document of questionable legal standing, and led to the introduction of what is known as the *Straight Bill of Lading—Short Form*, which contains uniform provisions applicable to either rails or trucks. Also, this form provides for receiving the shipment subject to the contract terms and conditions in the classification which governs and thus obviates the reproduction of the entire text. Short form bills of lading are not furnished by carriers, but are recommended for use by those shippers having their own specially imprinted forms. In addition to the Uniform Straight Bill of Lading and its short form, there is an optional form, called a *unit bill of lading,* which is prepared in four copies, the extra copy serving as the railroad's waybill. Use of this form is beneficial in eliminating transcription errors from bill of lading to waybill and helps expedite shipments by assuring that the bill will travel with them instead of following them. This can be especially important in the case of a small station at which a large volume of LCL shipments originates. All Straight Bills of Lading forms must be printed on white paper.

■ Uniform *order* bill of lading.—This bill of lading, often called "Order-Notify" or "Sight Draft" bill of lading, is printed on yellow paper and is also offered in the optional "unit" form. It embodies the same contract terms and conditions as the Straight Bill of Lading, but unlike the straight variety, it is a negotiable instrument and must be surrendered to the carrier's agent at destination before delivery of the goods it covers may be obtained. Its principal use is to prevent delivery until payment is made for the goods, although it sometimes serves as a safeguard against unauthorized delivery when terms of sale or credit investigations have not been completed at the time shipment is made. To obtain payment against an Order Bill of Lading, the shipper attaches the original, receipted by the carrier's agent and endorsed in the space provided on the reverse, to a sight draft for the amount to be collected and gives them to his bank for collection. Upon payment of the draft at destination the collecting bank detaches the bill of lading and hands it to the person making the payment, who may obtain his goods by surrendering it to the carrier's agent. The use of an Order Bill of Lading limits the usual privileges accorded a shipment, for such a consignment may not be stopped in transit for completion of loading or for partial unloading, nor may it be diverted or reconsigned without surrender of the original bill of lading. Inspection of contents may be made only under specific conditions, such as written authorization by the person to whose order the shipment is consigned, deposit of the invoice value of the goods in cash or presentation of a bond of indemnity. Delivery of goods may be obtained without surrender of the Order Bill of Lading, but only upon presentation to the carrier of security in the form of cash in an amount equal to 125% of the invoice value of the property or a bond of indemnity with surety in an amount equal to double the invoice value. To obtain delivery by other means is a punishable offense for anyone connected with the transaction and is particularly hard on the carrier's agent involved, for he usually is held for the full amount of his company's liability.

■ Uniform *live stock* contract.—Because of the special conditions attending the shipment of live stock and wild animals, the rail classification prescribes a Uniform Live Stock Contract to be used instead of a bill of lading, under which the carrier's liability is somewhat limited. In preparing this contract, shippers must declare whether the live stock is "ordinary" (animals shipped for grazing, fattening or slaughter) or "other than ordinary" (animals valuable for breeding, racing or show purposes). Freight rates on the latter vary according to the value which must be declared by the shipper on the contract, and the carrier's liability is limited to this value. The Uniform Live Stock Contract has no counterpart in the truck classifications, for when shipped by truck, live stock is exempt from regulation.

■ Uniform *through export* bill of lading.—Still another bill of lading prescribed in carriers' classifications is the Uniform Through Export bill of lading which is discussed in Chapter 17.

■ Ocean bill of lading.—*Domestic, between U.S.A. ports only.* The contract terms and conditions of the railroad bill of lading (Appendix 1) differ materially from those of the ocean bill of lading (Appendix 2) in that the carrier's liability under the latter is considerably more limited than under the former. Steamship companies operating between United States ports will accept shipments subject only to the ocean bill of lading. Unlike rail and truck bills of lading, the ocean bill of lading for coastwise and intercoastal shipments always is prepared by the carrier and submitted to the shipper for signature, frequently several days after the vessel has sailed. Interim protection is afforded by what is known as a Dock Receipt or other similar form of receipt signed by the carrier subject to the contract terms and conditions of its regular long-form bill of lading.

■ Ocean bill of lading.—*Export.* Explanation of the use of the ocean bill of lading on export shipments will be found in Chapter 17.

■ Air.—An airbill specimen (the air bill of lading) follows. It is computer oriented, and provides governing tariffs control. It is non-negotiable, there being no negotiable form. A carrier liability limit (50¢ per pound or $50 per shipment) is imposed unless a higher value is declared. Many shippers show the full amount in the "Declared Value" blank and make the extra pay-

UNIFORM AIRBILL — NONNEGOTIABLE
Subject to Conditions of Contract on Back of Shipper's Copy of the Airbill

TO

FROM

CARRIER	ORIGIN			AIRBILL NUMBER		DATE DA MO YR	DECLARED VALUE

Carrier's liability is limited per Item 3 on reverse side unless shipper requests additional declared value (subject to additional charge).

: AIRLINE ROUTING APPLIES UNLESS SHIPPER INSERTS SPECIFIC ROUTING HERE   AIRPORT OF DESTINATION

1 | TO | VIA | TO | VIA | TO | VIA |

☐ PREPAID ☐ COLLECT

2 CONSIGNEE'S ACCOUNT NO.

▼ **CONSIGNEE** ▼

	CARRIER	RATE	CHARGES
			A. WEIGHT CHARGES

NAME

CODE NUMBER

STREET ADDRESS   PICKUP TRUCKER | PICKUP ZONE | B. PICKUP CHG. |

CITY, STATE, ZIP CODE   DELIVERY TRUCKER | DEL. ZONE | D. DELIVERY CHGS |

3 SHIPPER'S ACCOUNT NO.

▼ **SHIPPER** ▼

E. EXCESS VALUE

TO EXPEDITE MOVEMENT, SHIPMENT MAY BE DIVERTED TO MOTOR OR OTHER CARRIER AS PER TARIFF RULE UNLESS SHIPPER GIVES OTHER INSTRUCTIONS HEREON.

G. SHIPPER'S C.O.D.

NAME

STREET ADDRESS   RECEIVED BY CARRIER AT   H. C.O.D. FEE
☐ SHIPPER'S DOOR ☐ CITY TERMINAL ☐ AIRPORT TERMINAL

CITY, STATE, ZIP CODE   DESCRIPTION OF ORIGIN ADVANCE CHGS. | K. ORIG. ADV. CHGS. |

7 INSTRUCTIONS TO CARRIER: INCLUDE CUSTOMER REF. NO. & BILLING INSTRUCTIONS

8 DESCRIPTION OF DESTINATION ADVANCE CHARGES | L. DEST. ADV. CHGS. |

DESCRIPTION OF OTHER CHARGES | F. OTHER CHARGES |

PCS/PKGS LENGTH WIDTH DEPTH CUBIC INCHES | J. SHIPPER'S RFC.
X   X   =

C.O.D. SHIPMENT
IF AMOUNT ENTERED HERE BY SHIPPER

DIMENSIONAL WEIGHT – LBS. | I. TAX |

5 **R.F.C. SHIPMENT**
IF AMOUNT ENTERED HERE BY SHIPPER

TARIFF AUTHORITY | ITEMS PREPAID | R. TOTAL SHIPPER PAYS
$

SHIPPER'S SIGNATURE   GBL. GTR. NO. | ITEMS COLLECT | S. TOTAL CONSIGNEE PAYS.
$

X

NO. PCS.	GROSS WEIGHT	CHARGEABLE WEIGHT	DESCRIPTION OF PACKING, PIECES AND CONTENTS	CARRIER COMMODITY GROUP NO.	MULTIPLE CONTAINER/COMMODITY		
					CODE	RATE	CHARGE
6							
			CARRIER REMARKS				

8
A WEIGHT CHARGES	B PICKUP ZONE	PICKUP CHARGES	D DEL. ZONE	DELIVERY CHARGES	K ORIG. ADV. CHGS.	DESCRIPTION OF ORIGIN ADVANCE CHARGES	
E EXCESS VALUE	L DEST. ADV. CHGS.	DESCRIPTION OF DEST. ADVANCE CHARGES			F OTHER CHARGES	DESCRIPTION OF OTHER CHARGES	
I TAX	G SHIPPER'S C.O.D.	H C.O.D. FEE	J SHIPPER'S R.F.C.		X 1ST RATE	2ND RATE	3RD RATE
R SHIPPER PAYS $	ITEMS PREPAID	S $ CONSIGNEE PAYS		ITEMS COLLECT			

SHADED AREA FOR CARRIER USE ONLY

THIS IS NOT AN INVOICE

EXECUTED BY	DATE	TIME	CARRIER	ORIGIN	SERIAL NUMBER

FORM AC-17-A (1-77)   1 - SHIPPER'S RECEIPT

Airbill form used on air freight shipments. The designation "Uniform" relates principally to information called for in the blanks and to provisions applicable. Forms vary as to size, placement or omission of data, and so on. Amendments are to be published shortly.

ment. Further, aircraft space can be particularly dear and critical and size versus weight of shipments as related to airbill provisions, rates, and so on often receive special shipper attention because of density provisions.

■ Government bills of lading.—Not prescribed by carriers' classifications, but requiring explanation in this book because of its radically different nature, the Government Bill of Lading is discussed in Chapter 16.

The Bill of Lading of the Future

Recent years have seen the introduction of several new types of bills of lading; some of them have developed to be of real value; others have limited uses; still others appear to be destined to have considerably more influence on shippers' and carriers' billing practices. An important factor in their design is the elimination in some measure of the duplicative clerical operations involved in the preparation by the shipper and the transcription to a different form by the carrier for a freight bill and other bills and record purposes.

Some of these bills of lading consist of a form composed in such a manner that it can be reproduced by photo-copying in the billing office of the carrier after rates are determined and extensions computed. The shipping order copy thus becomes, without transcription, a freight bill, auditor's copy, waybill, delivery receipt and consignee's copy, as well as any other record the carrier requires. Others reach somewhat similar results by having carbon papers so arranged that only certain features are reproduced on forms that are engineered for other uses. These methods not only cut down clerical effort, but minimize the possibility of error due to transcription.

Electronic data processing techniques make possible far more sophisticated systems of bill of lading production. Some computer arrangements are set-up so that a shipping room in one city reports by coded teletype message the loading of a given shipment. Within minutes of the receipt of this message at the computer center in a distant town, another teletype in the shipping room starts writing a nine-part combination bill of lading—freight bill form, complete with route, commodity description (including the classification item number), rate, extension, total charges and even the division of total revenue among interline carriers. The original bill of lading, memorandum copy and prepaid freight bill are retained by the shipper, while the remaining six copies are handed to the driver before he has had time to start his motor and pull away from the loading platform.

The use of bills of lading as a practical matter has been by-passed at a paper mill in the South as to a substantial amount of its inbound shipments. The computers of the plant owner and of the rail carrier serving the plant working severally and in unison have permitted this to˙be done. In essence the records, calculations, and so on made by the computers of the parties are all that are needed by them. More results along these lines will be attained in the future. Chapter 15 discusses this further.

The expense of installing systems of this sort is great for shippers and, for that matter, all concerned. It represents something that in many cases simply has to be done to operate efficiently and economically and merits attention importantly in that light along with other factors. The Interstate Commerce Commission has permitted nominal allowances for some of the unit billing when forms are supplied by shippers, but these allowances are related to the cost of the forms themselves.

The Bill of Lading Contract

In stressing the importance of a bill of lading as a contract, it naturally follows that the contract terms and conditions be fully understood. The fine print on the reverse of a bill of lading form sometimes makes their reading difficult; hence the Uniform Straight Bill of Lading contract has been reproduced verbatim in Appendix 1, and an example of an Ocean Bill of Lading Contract appears in Appendix 2. Their thorough reading and periodic reexamination is strongly recommended.

Section 1 (a) of the contract establishes carrier liability for loss of or physical damage to the shipment *as at common law*. This means that any legal action surrounding such loss or damage is pursued through the courts and not before the Interstate Commerce Commission as in matters involving violations of the Interstate Commerce Act.

The operation of section 7 is also worthy of special mention. Ordinarily, the consignee is liable for the payment of charges on a collect shipment and is required to make such payment before receiving the shipment. However, he may establish credit arrangements with the carrier and thus obtain his shipment without such payment. If, by hook or crook, the consignee were to evade payment of the charges, the shipper would be held liable for them. On the other hand, even though it was thought that full charges had been collected at the time of delivery, an audit of the carrier's books might establish an undercharge at a considerably later date. Meanwhile, if the consignee had moved or gone out of business, the carrier would have to look to the shipper for satisfaction of his undercharge bill. *This liability may be avoided if the shipper signs the section 7 clause provided in a box on the face of the bill of lading.* Even on a prepaid shipment, section 7 may be used to prevent a balance due bill being presented or to permit partial prepayment of charges. This is particularly useful in cases where the price of the goods is calculated to include a precise amount of transportation charges and where the liability for additional charges would work hardship and financial loss upon the shipper. The "no recourse" provision may not be used in connection with shipments consigned to stations at which railroads maintain no agents, shipments of perishable commodities or those billed to stop in transit for completion of loading or for partial unloading.

It should be stressed that the carrier *does not have to sign any bill of lading* to make a firm contract unless he is satisfied as to the dependability of all facts indicated and this of course would include bills of lading on which the shipper had signed the section 7 clause. A signing of the section 7 clause by the shipper has a distinct advantage for him. Such action operates to close the door on various possible liabilities that might be asserted against him. It is not unusual for an industrial traffic department to have matters set up so that these are signed routinely as a part of its shipping activities on outbound movements from its plants unless valid reasons to the contrary exist.

As in the case of any other contract, all of the provisions of the bill of lading must be clear and in such terms as to be understood by both parties. This means that it must be prepared legibly and that it contain no conflicting provisions or requirements impossible of execution. An example of a conflict is where a rate shown on a bill of lading is not applicable via the route specified thereon. In such cases, the carrier's agent is required to resolve the conflict or unworkable provision or, in the alternative, refuse to handle the shipment. Failure on his part to do so will result in the matter being resolved against the carrier for, although it may not have prepared the bill of lading, it is nevertheless charged with the issuance of it and thus is held to be the framer of the contract.

Particular attention is also directed to section 10 of the Terms and Conditions which requires that any alteration, addition or erasure on the bill of lading bear the special notation (or initialing) of the agent of the carrier before it is valid. In the absence of such acknowledgment by the agent, the original provisions of the bill of lading will hold. Any alteration of any written instrument without the full consent of all concerned, of course, involves considerable risk of the document being declared void by the courts if litigation results.

It is also important that a clear, legible and complete signature be affixed to the document by the carrier's agent. The courts have held that a bill of lading becomes an enforceable contract without the signature of the shipper or his agent, but they have refused to recognize the validity of bills of lading which did not bear the complete name of the carrier and the personal signature (not initials) of its agent. This does not present as much of a problem when freight is tendered directly to the line-haul carrier as it does when a local cartage company is employed by that carrier to pick up its shipments. In such cases, care should be exercised that the local cartage company indicate that it is acting as agent for the line-haul carrier and that its driver sign his full name in the following manner:

> CROSS COUNTRY CARRIERS
> Local Delivery Co., Inc., Agent
> per John Smith
> September 25, 1971

Many progressive motor carriers, alert to their responsibility to provide a clear receipt and aware of its advantages from a record standpoint, supply their pickup drivers with a pocket-size combination rubber stamp and ink pad. The wording thereon may vary considerably but will usually be made up somewhat as follows:

```
┌─────────────────────────────────────┐
│              RECEIVED               │
│         X-Y-Z TRUCKING CO.          │
│    By  ...........................  │
│             Driver No. 24           │
│    Date  ............... Pieces.... │
└─────────────────────────────────────┘
```

If the carrier's agent signs the bill of lading without showing a date, the date entered by the shipper in the place provided on the bill of lading will stand as the date on which the carrier received the shipment. A date entered by the carrier's agent with his signature, if different from that shown by the shipper, will be considered the date received. This can be very important when shipments are made close to the date of a change in rates.

Preparation of Bills of Lading

A bill of lading must be prepared for each shipment. Definitions of the word "shipment" vary and are reproduced from the carriers' classifications, as follows:

Carloads—Uniform Freight Classification No. 10, Rule 14.

Carload ratings or rates apply only when a carload of freight is shipped from one station, in or on one car, except as otherwise provided in Rules 24, 29 or 34, in one calendar day from midnight to midnight, by one shipper for delivery to one consignee at one destination and is loaded by shipper and unloaded by consignee.

Less carloads—Uniform Freight Classification No. 10, Rule 16.

A single shipment of less carload freight is a lot received from one shipper, on one shipping order or bill of lading, at one station, at one time, for one consignee and one destination.

Truckload and LTL—National Motor Freight Classification No. A-12, Item 110, Section 5.

A shipment consists of a lot of freight tendered to the carrier by one consignor at one place at one time for delivery to one consignee at one place on one bill of lading.

The steps in a bill of lading's preparation described later are numbered to correspond with the numbers encircled in the form on page 78.

(1) Shipper's Number. In this space may be inserted the order number, invoice number or any other number that will enable the shipper to identify the shipment. (2) The name of the originating carrier (*not* the full route) appears here. (3) On this line is written the name of the town or station of shipment, followed by the date. Street addresses or postal zones must not be shown in this space. (4) This line is for the name of the shipper. (5) On Straight Bills of Lading, the name of the consignee, followed by the mail or street address at which he is to be notified, appears on this line. (6) This line is for the name of the city and state in which delivery is to be made and, if there is more than one point by that name in the state, the county should be shown. (7) If it differs from that appearing on the line above, the delivery address should be written in this space. On Order Bills of Lading after "Consigned to ORDER of" is shown the name of the person or firm controlling the shipment, usually the shipper. On the next line is entered the destination city, state and county. After "Notify", the name of the person or firm expected to present the original bill of lading is shown, with the address on the following line. (8) This line

contains space for the route or such part of it as may be designated by the shipper (see Chapter 6). (9) If the services of a particular carrier are required to make delivery at destination, its name should be inserted here. (10) This space is for the car or vehicle identifying initials and number.

The bill of lading now is ready for a description of the shipment. An accurate count of the number of packages or pieces is necessary (except in the case of bulk commodities) whether or not the shipment moves under "Shipper's load and count" notation and the correct number should be entered in the appropriate column. (11) A separate entry should be made for the number of each *kind* of package (box, crate, bundle, barrel, etc.) under each commodity description. (12) Chapter 3 stressed the importance of developing the proper description for each shipment, and the entry of that description on the bill of lading is the key to the assessment of correct freight charges. The use of abbreviations should be avoided wherever possible and, in cases where they must be used, they should be confined to standard and easily understood terms. (13) Any weights used in the column provided should either be set forth in carrier weight agreements (see Chapter 13) or be the result of careful test weighing. If weights are shown, they should appear separately for each kind of package under each commodity description. Even though all weights are subject to correction by the carrier, haphazard guesses at weights are likely to be costly and can be extremely troublesome to a motor carrier, who may unintentionally overload a vehicle on the basis of misstated weights and thus expose himself to penalties at law. (14) In the column headed "Class or Rate" may be inserted the classification rating or the rate applicable, but it is important to note that doing so can in no way affect the assessment of legal published charges. Regardless of whether the shipper understates or overstates the rate or rating, the carrier is obligated to charge the legal rate. (15) As noted in Chapter 3, some rates are dependent upon value and in such cases the declaration on the bill of lading must be filled in and signed. (16) The shipment will move with *charges to be collected from the consignee* unless *prepayment* is requested in the box provided. If the shipment is prepaid and charges are paid in a cash transaction, the agent may receipt for charges in the space allotted; otherwise it is customary to collect freight charges upon presentation of a regular freight bill. (17) After the shipper's name and signature of his agent should be shown the address at which shipper desires prepaid freight bills or other notification to be sent. (18) The bill of lading then is ready for receipting by the carrier's agent.

When freight is loaded by the shipper and tendered to the carrier with seals applied to the car or motor vehicle, the car-

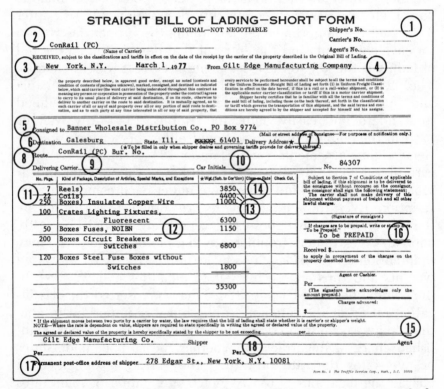

Uniform straight bill of lading—short form, illustrating manner in which it is prepared for receipting by carrier's agent. Encircled numbers correspond with numbers in text on adjoining pages. See Appendix 1 for bill of lading contract terms and conditions.

rier's agent naturally cannot check the number, kind or condition of the packages therein. In such cases, the bill of lading is signed subject to a *Shippers Load and Count* notation, which means that the carrier will not entertain claims for shortage except under certain well defined circumstances (see Chapter 8).

One bill of lading may be used to cover unlimited quantities of freight as long as the freight meets the definition of "shipment." Thus, several carloads or trailer loads may be listed on a single bill of lading even though they actually move away from the shipper's place of business at different times during the day. Preparation of bills of lading in this manner is particularly important to take advantage of "follow-lot" or "overflow" provisions of carriers' tariffs. These rules usually provide that when a quantity of freight offered for shipment is greater than can be accommodated in a single car or vehicle, each car or vehicle used for the shipment must be loaded to full visible capacity or weight limit *except that unit carrying the overflow.* Each load will be charged for at the carload or truckload rate and the actual weight or carload or truckload minimum weight, whichever is greater, but the overflow will not be subject to a minimum weight. Obviously, these provisions can be met only with a single bill of lading for the entire shipment; the savings to be realized will be lost if a separate bill of lading is prepared for the overflow.

Additionally, before the bill of lading is presented to the carrier to sign under (18), certain aspects of at least three other features should have further attention than it was practical to indicate, in the previous summarization, they should be given. One is whether in showing the route under (8) a junction should be specified. Another is whether a reasonably firm stand should be taken that in all cases practical rates are to be inserted by the shipper in the appropriate column under (14). The third is whether the Section 7 block (unless known reasons for not doing so exist) should be signed by the shipper simply as a matter of course. The first two of those questions are discussed further in Chapter 6; the third was discussed earlier in this chapter. Please refer to those discussions. While there are respectable negative views an important group of knowledgeable industry transportation executives has affirmative answers to those questions on the basis that they are so treated by their own companies.

It is to be noted that as ConRail is specified in a rail bill of lading the initials of the former (predecessor) carrier involved should be added. ConRail is new (April 1, 1976), extensive (17,000 miles), and has much to do to meld into one its operations. It comprises the former Penn Central, Erie Lackawanna, Reading, Central of New Jersey, Lehigh Valley, Lehigh-Hudson River, and Ann Arbor properties. Particular situations exist in many cases as to these. To illustrate, under (2) and (8) "ConRail (PC)" is used; Penn Central was the originating carrier. If, say, Penn Central was a part of the movement in some other way (such as a line haul, connecting carrier), the ConRail participation should be similarly treated or, if, say, the Central of New Jersey were involved, the designation should be "ConRail (CNJ)".

A well prepared bill of lading is excellent insurance that a shipment will travel to its destination as desired by the shipper, that freight charges will be correct and billed to the proper party and that all concerned will have a clear understanding of the transportation phase of the transaction. These benefits are well worth the effort.

5

FREIGHT RATES

WHEN A TRAFFIC MAN TALKS ABOUT FREIGHT RATES, HE IS discussing the very heart of his job, for whatever else he is expected to do, he must be extremely well-informed in obtaining transportation. This, of course, requires that he have full knowledge of current developments in transportation technology, the services available to him and, most importantly, the prices charged by each of these services. For *freight rates are transportation prices* and unless he is skilled in determining these prices, the traffic man cannot make an informed choice of the service best suited to a given situation. Anything but the best selection can have a serious effect on his company's profits and place his employer at a competitive disadvantage.

The transportation pricing structure of this country probably is the most comprehensive system of user costs ever devised. It has been developed to embrace every known article of commerce, grouped into about 30,000 categories, moving from any given point to any of upwards of 50,000 other points in the country. *According to estimates, some 40 trillion prices are involved!*

Necessarily, then, carriers' price lists are complicated; much more so than, for example, those of the manufacturer of a line of hardware. Whereas a manufacturer's price list will quote the price on a named article in a given size or quantity at a given place, the price of transportation contains an additional dimension, that of *distance*. Small wonder, therefore, that all

HISTORY OF FIRST CLASS OR CLASS 100
ALL-RAIL RATE
NEW YORK—CHICAGO
1900—1971

Rate in Cents	Date Effective	Case
75	1900	
78.8	2-23-15	Five percent case, 32 ICC 325
90	6-27-17	Ex Parte 57
113	6-25-18	General Order No. 28
158	8-26-20	Ex Parte 74
142	7- 1-22	Reduced Rates, 1922
152	12- 3-31	Docket 15879
154	1- 4-32	Ex Parte 103
152	10- 1-33	Expiration of Ex Parte 103
163	4-18-35	Ex Parte 115
152	1- 1-37	Expiration of Ex Parte 115
167	3-28-38	Ex Parte 123
177	3-18-42	Ex Parte 148
167	5-15-43	Voluntary Suspension of Ex Parte 148
186	7- 1-46	Reinstatement of Ex Parte 148
209	1- 1-47	Ex Parte 162
225	8-22-47	Docket 28300 Interim Basis
247.5*	10-13-47	Ex Parte 166, Interim Decision
270*	1- 5-48	Ex Parte 166, 2nd Interim Decision
292.5*	5- 6-48	Ex Parte 166, 3rd Interim Decision
293	8-21-48	Ex Parte 166, Final Decision
311	1-11-49	Ex Parte 168, Interim Decision
322	9- 1-49	Ex Parte 168, Final Decision
334.9*	4- 4-51	Ex Parte 175, Interim Decision
351*	8-28-51	Ex Parte 175, 2nd Interim Decision
370.3*	5- 2-52	Ex Parte 175, Final Decision
373.8*	5-30-52	Docket 28300 Final Basis
374	12- 1-55	Ex Parte 175, Rate Conversion
396	3- 7-56	Ex Parte 196
424	12-28-56	Ex Parte 206, Interim Decision
444	8-26-57	Ex Parte 206, Final Decision
453	2-15-58	Ex Parte 212
454	10-24-60	Ex Parte 223
477	8-19-67	Ex Parte 256
501	11-28-68	Ex Parte 259B
531	11-18-69	Ex Parte 262
563	11-20-70	Ex Parte 265B
642	4-12-71	Ex Parte 267B

* Approximation—increases were granted as percentage surcharges on total freight charges and rates themselves were not converted.

Note: Interim adjustments from 1960 are not separately specified; this is to help in streamlining.

History: New York Chicago Class 100 Rail Freight Rates

this, when coupled with rather rigid rules and regulations growing out of government regulation, becomes an intensely specialized subject in which proficiency is achieved with experience and study.

In common parlance, a carrier's freight charge schedule is its tariff. Tariffs are publications containing the rates and charges required to be paid by the shipper or receiver of freight and to be collected by a transportation company. These publications must be filed with the Interstate Commerce Commission or other appropriate authority, and by law the transportation company is prohibited from charging either more or less than the published rates and charges. Tariffs also describe the various supplemental or accessorial services that may be performed by the carrier. A charge is usually provided for each service.

Although volumes could be written on the subject of freight rates, a book of this size can do no more than approach it from a somewhat general viewpoint.

The Various Kinds of Rates

As has been noted in Chapter 2 and as just mentioned, the Interstate Commerce Act and the corresponding laws of those states which regulate transportation within their borders require that common carriers publish schedules naming their charges for all services they hold themselves out to the public to perform. Even though a railroad's rails may extend from point A to point B or a motor carrier's certificate entitle him to transport commodities between these points, such transportation may not be performed unless tariffs (compiled in the form and manner required by such publications as the ICC's various tariff circulars) have been filed with the appropriate regulatory body and publicly posted in accordance with that body's rules. These charges fall into four principal categories: Class Rates, Exception Rates, Commodity Rates and Accessorial Charges.

■ *Class Rates.* In Chapter 3 the development of class rates was traced in connection with their close relationship to the classifications which govern them. As a result of the system of class rates established under ICC Dockets 28300, 30416 and 30660 and similar scales adopted by motor carriers, virtually every community in the nation enjoying common carrier transportation service is linked with every other such community by an underlying freight rate structure. Thus, there exists a basis for the calculation of freight charges on just about anything that is likely to be shipped from one place to another.

A tabulation showing the history of the first class (Class 100) rail rate New York to Chicago is shown on Page 82. Of particular interest are the increases and the times at which they have occurred during the period which represents about three quarters of the century.

Class rates applicable via all-rail routes are published in most of the tariffs listed later in this chapter. Because it would greatly increase the bulk of each tariff if it were to list every individual point between which it applied, the class rate tariffs are arranged to apply between groups of points. These groups, or *rate bases*, are roughly 40 miles in diameter and usually are named for either the most prominent or most central point therein. The class rate tariffs refers the user to the National Rate Basis Tariff issued by Tariff Publishing Agent Robert H. Lindsay (formerly Fred Ofcky) in behalf of the agencies listed on Page 92, to ascertain the names of the rate bases in which origin and destination are located. Certain of the transcontinental class rates in the Transcontinental Freight Bureau tariffs are published to apply between groups of much larger size and the National Rate Base Tariff is not applicable to those larger groups.

An excerpt of a page from the National Rate Base Tariff applicable to Illinois appears at the top of Page 85. The first column specifies the railroad station; the second, the railroad and its station number; the third, the SPLC (Standard Point Location Code—more about this later in the discussions on computers); and the fourth, the city that controls as the rate base point.

| 6170000 | NATIONAL RATE BASIS TARIFF 1-B | 6170000 |

ALPHABETICAL INDEX OF STATIONS BY STATE
LOCATION, STANDARD POINT LOCATION CODE, RATE BASIS
RATE BASIS APPLICABLE

STATION	RR	NO	SPLC	RATE BASIS	STATION	RR	NO	SPLC	RATE BASIS
ITEM 6170000			CONT'D		ITEM 6170000			CONT'D	
		ILLINOIS					ILLINOIS		
Abingdon	CNW	11105	385995	Galesburg IL	Arthur	PCP	25875	391642	Mattoon IL
Adair	BN	1695	389364	Vermont IL	Ashburn	GTW	25	380210	No Rate Basis
Addieville	LN	11145	396543	Centralia IL	Ashburn 12	NW	15700	380210	Chicago IL
Addison	IC	3120	382219	Chicago IL	Ashkum	IC	180	387128	Sheldon IL
Adeline	MILW	585	382844	Freeport IL	Ashland	BO	13375	388952	Jacksonville .IL
Adrian	BN	1555	389844	Carthage IL	Ashland	GMO	885	388952	Jacksonville .IL
Aetna	IC	320	391498	Mattoon IL	Ashley	IC	750	396562	Mt Vernon . . .IL
Agnew	CNW	175	383435	Dixon IL	Ashley	LN	11125	396562	Mt Vernon . . .IL
Ahern	MILW	9365	384437	Kankakee IL	Ashmore	PCC	34905	391418	Paris IL
Aiken	CNW	11505	383479	Galena IL	Ashton	CNW	140	382923	Dixon IL
Akron	CNW	565	388225	Peoria IL	Assumption	IC	2065	392735	Pana IL
Albany	MILW	650	383583	Morrison IL	Astoria	BN	1710	389198	Vermont IL
Albers	SOU	11535	396492	Centralia IL	Athens	CIM	120	388884	Lincoln IL
Albion	SOU	11425	394960	Carmi IL	Athol	GMO	325	388634	Lincoln IL
Aldridge	IC	1525	399531	Murphysboro . . .IL	Atkinson	RI	385	385333	Galva IL
Aledo	BN	1120	386440	Gladstone . . .IL	Atlanta	GMO	310	388618	Bloomington . .IL
Alexander	NW	15335	393132	Jacksonville . .IL	Atlanta	PCP	25965	388618	Bloomington . .IL
Alexis	BN	1180	386612	Galesburg . . .IL	Atterbury	CIM	100	388845	Lincoln IL
Algonquin	CNW	360	382387	Harvard IL	Atwater	BN	1885	392936	Litchfield . .IL
Alhambra	IC	1740	396233	Litchfield . .IL	Atwood	BO	15630	387882	Champaign . . .IL
Alhambra	NW	12215	396233	Litchfield . .IL	Augusta	GMO	460	392496	Springfield .IL
Allen	CNW	584	388732	Lincoln IL	Augusta	BN	1465	389483	Carthage . . .IL
Allenby	IC	716.05	398715	Marion IL	Aurora	BN	140	382480	Aurora IL
Allendale	PCC	36190	394713	Olney IL	Aurora	CNW	330	382480	Aurora IL
Allentown	PCP	26000	388456	Peoria IL	Aurora	EJE	260	382480	Aurora IL
Allenville	IC	2425	391673	Mattoon IL	Ava	GMO	1225	398932	Murphysboro . .IL
Allerton	CEI	875	387698	Paris IL	Aviston	BO	13145	396465	Centralia . . .IL
Alma	IC	370	395631	Edgewood . . .IL	Avon	BN	1420	389128	Galesburg . . .IL
Alonzo	CEI	675	387188	Sheldon . . .IL	Avondale 12	CNW	605	380453	Chicago IL
Alpha	BN	965	385395	Galva IL	Ayers Siding	BN	870	383696	Morrison . . .IL
Alpine	NW	15745	381458	Chicago . . .IL	Baileyville	IC	3150	382842	Freeport . . .IL

Excerpt from page of National Rate Base Tariff.

Freight Tariff No. I-1002

APPLICATION OF RATE BASES

BETWEEN (See Item 100) AND (See Item 100)	Alexandria...Mo.	Aurora...Ill.	Barry...Ill.	Barstow...Ill.	Bloomington...Ill.	Brooklyn...Wis.	Burlington...Iowa	Cairo...Ill.	Carmi...Ill.	Carthage...Ill.	Centralia...Ill.	Champaign...Ill.	Chicago...Ill.	Clinton...Iowa	Danville...Ill.	Davenport...Iowa	Decatur...Ill.	DeKalb...Ill.	Dixon...Ill.	Dodgeville...Wis.
						RATE BASES APPLICABLE (For rates, see pages 16 and 17)														
Alexandria...............Mo.	40																			
Aurora...................Ill.	205	40																		
Barry....................Ill.	54	244	40																	
Barstow..................Ill.	117	127	163	40																
Bloomington.............Ill.	144	107	157	128	40															
Brooklyn.................Wis.	260	121	304	144	196	40														
Burlington..............Iowa	42	169	91	79	130	221	40													
Cairo....................Ill.	315	356	264	366	249	445	333	40												
Carmi....................Ill.	274	287	245	312	193	388	292	103	40											
Carthage.................Ill.	40	205	51	117	144	260	42	315	274	40										
Centralia...............Ill.	203	243	178	253	136	332	222	113	71	203	40									
Champaign...............Ill.	192	136	186	175	48	244	177	239	155	192	126	40								
Chicago..................Ill.	243	40	282	161	127	130	206	365	279	243	252	127	40							
Clinton.................Iowa	149	104	195	40	131	110	116	380	324	149	267	179	138	40						
Danville................Ill.	224	131	213	208	80	251	210	258	157	224	145	40	123	210	40					
Davenport...............Iowa	117	127	163	40	128	144	79	366	312	117	253	175	161	40	208	40				
Decatur.................Ill.	165	151	168	168	44	210	170	205	149	165	93	47	167	174	74	168	40			
DeKalb..................Ill.	200	40	240	103	113	97	164	362	305	200	249	160	59	81	155	103	157	40		

Excerpt from typical class tariff showing application of rate bases.

The class rate tariffs spell out the applications of the rate base points through the use of tables having headline and side line cities. The numbers shown at the junction of each vertical and horizontal column are known as the *rate basis number* and are used to determine the scale of rates, applicable in either direction between those two rate bases.

These rate scales appear as tables of rates elsewhere in the tariffs. Examples of tariff sheets showing the application of rate bases are shown at the lower part of page 85 and of the tables of rate scales on this page. These are partial only and the tariffs themselves are much more extensive.

To illustrate the use of these on a representative move, say, from Addieville, Illinois, to Chicago the first reference is to the rate base tariff (third line) which shows Centralia as the rate basis city for Addieville. Thereafter, by matching Centralia and Chicago on the table for applying rate bases (also on page 85), we find the rate base number is 252. The next step is to relate the number to the appropriate rate scale on this page. If we assume the material moving takes Class 100, the rate would be $2.36 per 100 pounds; Class 70 would be $1.65 and so on.

TARIFF I-1002-C

SECTION 2

TABLE OF RATES

CLASS RATES IN CENTS PER 100 POUNDS

RATE BASIS NUMBERS (Numbers, inclusive)	CLASSES																							
	400	300	250	200	175	150	125	110	100	97½	95	92½	90	87½	85	82½	80	77½	75	73½	72½	70	67½	66
40 . . .	484	363	303	242	212	182	151	133	121	118	115	112	109	106	103	100	97	94	91	89	88	85	82	80
41 to 45	496	372	310	248	217	186	155	136	124	121	118	115	112	109	105	102	99	96	93	91	90	87	84	82
46 to 50	508	381	318	254	222	191	159	140	127	124	121	117	114	111	108	105	102	98	95	93	92	89	86	84
51 to 55	528	396	330	264	231	198	165	145	132	129	125	122	119	116	112	109	106	102	99	97	96	92	89	87
56 to 60	540	405	338	270	236	203	169	145	135	132	128	125	122	118	115	111	108	105	101	99	98	95	91	89
181 to 190	816	612	510	408	357	305	255	224	204	199	194	189	184	179	173	168	163	158	153	153	148	143	138	135
191 to 200	832	624	520	416	364	312	260	229	208	203	198	192	187	182	177	172	166	161	156	153	151	146	140	137
201 to 210	856	642	535	428	375	321	268	235	214	209	203	198	193	187	182	177	171	166	161	157	155	150	144	141
211 to 220	872	654	545	436	382	327	273	240	218	213	207	202	196	191	185	180	174	169	164	160	158	153	147	144
221 to 230	888	666	555	444	389	333	278	244	222	216	211	205	200	194	189	183	178	172	167	163	161	155	150	147
231 to 240	904	678	565	452	396	339	283	249	226	220	215	209	203	198	192	186	181	175	170	166	164	158	153	149
241 to 260	944	708	590	472	413	354	295	260	236	230	224	218	212	207	201	195	189	183	177	173	171	165	159	156
261 to 280	968	726	605	484	424	363	303	266	242	236	230	224	218	212	206	200	194	188	182	178	175	169	163	160
281 to 290	1000	750	625	500	438	375	313	275	250	244	238	231	225	219	213	206	200	194	188	184	181	175	169	165

Excerpt from typical class tariff showing rate basis numbers and application of class rates to them.

In Tariffs 1000 or 1011 and 1016, the rate basis number is the approximate short line mileage between the two groups. These were established some 25 years ago and there have been some abandonments and other changes since that time.

In Tariffs 1014 and 1015 it is the Class 100 rate which applied on August 15, 1956, when the original tariffs became effective. The rate tables contain columns headed by the class rating percentages appearing in the classification and in the exceptions tariffs. Rates are expressed in cents per 100 pounds.

Motor carrier class rates are published in much the same manner as the rail class rates; but in some tariffs, group numbers are substituted for named rate bases. It is in the tables of rates that the motor carrier rates depart radically from the pattern set in the rail tariffs. In most if not practically all cases the rate scales are divided into varying weight breaks in addition to those specified for truck loads.

For example, the LTL rates will have separate scales for various weights, such as: Under 2,000 pounds, 2,000 to 5,999 pounds, and 6,000 pounds or over. Furthermore, the rates do not always reflect the actual percentage of Class 100 indicated by the rating, particularly the lower ratings for long hauls.

Additionally, as mentioned in Chapter 3, the scales of the New England Motor Rate Bureau are entirely different from all others, not only because of the numbered classes and their lack of fixed percentage relationship one to another, but because each class is divided into weight breaks, with the truckload minimum weight theoretically representing the quantity that can be loaded conveniently in the equipment generally available. On page 88 is a tariff excerpt illustrating these features. Class 5 has a 32,000 truckload minimum; Class 4 has 24,000; and so on. The less-truckload break patterns have but few common features.

The Interstate Commerce Commission has held on numerous occasions that class rates constitute the *maximum reasonable* basis for freight charges. Therefore, any other rates which exceed that basis may be attacked as unreasonable unless they have been established with clear justification. When the ICC Docket 28300 rates went into effect on May 30, 1952, many commodity rates and exceptions to the old class rates which were higher than the new class rates on the same articles remained in effect and Tariffs 1000 to 1011 each contained an item stating that the new class rates would not apply under such conditions. In the order that created the new class rates, the Commission recognized the fact that it would be some time before tariffs could be cleared of the higher commodity and exception rates and gave the railroads five years in which to do so. Meanwhile, it denied all requests for reparation (discussed later in this chapter) on shipments which moved prior to May 30, 1957. Since that date, the existence of a higher commodity or exception rate has been accepted as *prima facie* evidence of unreasonableness and usually produces an award of reparation. Tariffs 1014, 1015 and 1016, published as a result of the decision in ICC Dockets 30416 and 30660, alternate with exceptions and commodity rates and the lower charges resulting from either apply.

■ *Exception Rates.* It might be said that, if the classifica-

RATE SCALE NOS. (AS SHOWN IN SECTION 2)	CLASS 5 L.T.L. LBS., INC.					CLASS 4 L.T.L. LBS., INC.					CLASS 3 L.T.L. LBS., INC.					CLASS 2 L.T.L. LBS., INC.					CLASS 1 L.T.L. LBS., INC.			
	0 TO 499	500 TO 1,999	2,000 TO 5,999	6,000 TO 19,999	20,000 TO 31,999	T.L.MIN.WGT.32,000 LBS.	0 TO 499	500 TO 1,499	1,500 TO 4,499	4,500 TO 14,999	15,000 TO 23,999	T.L.MIN.WGT.24,000 LBS.	0 TO 499	500 TO 999	1,000 TO 2,999	3,000 TO 9,999	10,000 TO 15,999	T.L.MIN.WGT.16,000 LBS.	0 TO 499	500 TO 1,499	1,500 TO 4,999	5,000 TO 7,999	T.L.MIN.WGT.8,000 LBS.	0 TO 499	500 TO 2,939	3,000 TO 4,799	T.L.MIN.WGT.4,800 LBS.
	*A	B	C	D	E	F	*A	B	C	D	E	F	*A	B	C	D	E	F	*B	C	D	E	F	*B	C	D	E
#102	138	134	106	76	44	30	167	160	130	98	56	39	201	193	157	120	81	55	241	218	165	88	412	334	221	138
0102	149	142	109	80	45	31	178	171	137	103	41	213	206	165	134	85	57	291	258	225	153	91	442	325	238	144
103	162	156	113	84	47	32	196	187	144	108	59	42	237	228	171	139	89	59	318	269	235	157	96	506	398	254	154
104	172	166	123	87	51	33	203	197	153	111	61	44	250	240	184	145	93	63	338	285	248	164	99	535	411	256	158
105	179	172	127	90	52	34	213	206	159	114	62	46	262	252	191	153	95	68	354	297	255	170	103	558	425	268	164
106	181	175	128	95	52	34	219	210	160	123	62	46	268	258	197	159	97	69	365	307	268	175	109	575	439	280	170
107	185	179	130	98	53	35	222	212	162	127	64	47	271	262	201	165	99	70	374	315	282	181	111	588	448	286	174
108	190	182	134	103	54	37	230	222	165	137	70	48	281	269	208	172	103	72	384	326	296	186	115	605	441	295	181
109	192	187	137	107	56	39	231	223	170	136	73	51	285	275	215	181	107	73	391	335	306	191	117	621	489	304	190
110	197	188	140	109	58	39	235	227	172	140	74	52	292	281	220	188	108	77	405	342	318	197	121	638	503	314	196
111	201	193	145	111	59	41	240	231	181	142	76	53	297	286	224	191	111	80	416	356	326	202	125	657	520	703	
112	203	197	149	112	60																					210	

SUPPLEMENT NO. 99 TO TARIFF NO. 3-K
CANCEL ON PAGE 260 OF TARIFF, PAGE 4 OF SUP. NO. 75 AND PAGE 9 OF SUP. NO. 79 AND ADD IN LIEU THEREOF THE FOLLOWING:
SECTION 3 - TABLE OF CLASS RATES (SD 116)
RATES IN CENTS PER ONE HUNDRED POUNDS
FOR MINIMUM CHARGES, SEE EXPLANATION OF RATE REFERENCE NUMBERS AS SHOWN IN SECTION 9 OF EXCEPTIONS TARIFF (SEE ITEM NO. 5)

New England Motor Rate Bureau class rate tariff excerpt showing truck load minimums, less truck load weight breaks, and other data.

tions were as accurate as they should be, there would be no need for exceptions. The fact is, however, that exceptions to the ratings and rules of classifications for many years have served a useful purpose in that they give carriers more flexibility in dealing with specific competitive situations. Thus, if motor carrier competition develops on a given commodity in a certain territory, the railroads may meet this competition with an exception rating without disturbing the level of rates on that commodity in the rest of the country. Or, if one commodity which for classification purposes is grouped with a number of others, such as in an "N.O.I.B.N." item, starts to move in a far larger volume than the other commodities in that group, there may be justification for reducing its rating by means of exceptions without making a similar reduction of the other commodities in the group.

One of the objectives of the Docket 28310 Uniform Classification investigation was to eliminate exceptions to the greatest extent possible. As a result, LCL exceptions have disappeared and considerable headway has been made in clearing tariffs of those carload exceptions to the old Consolidated Classification which remained in effect. But the task has been complicated by the large number of heavy moving commodities involved and the fact that over many years the resulting rate levels had become deeply imbedded in the freight rate structure and marketing practices of the industries producing those commodities. In some cases it has been possible *to convert them into commodity rate scales,* while in others they have been cancelled, only to reappear as exceptions to the Uniform Classification.

Exceptions also are used to provide *incentive* ratings to encourage heavier loading of equipment. If, for example, the classification gives a stated commodity a Class 40 rating at a minimum weight of 30,000 pounds, the exceptions may publish a lower rating of Class 30 at a higher minimum weight of 50,000 pounds.

Exception ratings and minimum weights take precedence over and *must be used instead of those appearing in the classifications.* If it is intended to give the shipper the benefit of the lower charges accruing from the use of either, it is customary to bring the classification rating forward into the tariff naming the exception rating together with an explanatory note providing for alternation. Since exceptions are used in connection with class rate scales, the rates are expressed in cents per 100 pounds.

■ *Commodity Rates.* Designed to meet specific conditions in a somewhat less general manner than exception ratings, commodity rates are published in a wide variety of forms.

There are *general* commodity rates which are published to apply on a single commodity or group of commodities from or to all points in a designated territory. Some of the older general commodity rate scales never have borne any relationship to the class rate scales and are set up between groups of origins and destinations to preserve traditional competitive relationships between manufacturing and marketing territories. Others at one time were based on the class rates then in effect, but subsequent changes in the class rate structure have obscured this relationship. Still others use the Docket 28300 groupings as their basis or are graduated according to mileage. Among these are commodity column rates, some of them applying on a single minimum carload weight, others on an incentive basis with different numbered columns for each of two or more graduated minimum carload weights and still others naming one column of rates for a given minimum carload weight and another column of lower rates to apply on all weight in excess of that minimum which is loaded in the same car. Because incentive rates are intended to encourage maximum utilization of railroad equipment, it usually is provided that Rule 24 of the classification will not apply in connection with them.

By far the most varied of commodity rates are the thousands of specific point-to-point rates that have been established to take care of individual movements. Justified by many different competitive situations, they are not likely to follow any set pattern, but the well informed industrial traffic man will find it advisable to make a study of the history of those rates which affect his commodities.

For some years, carload and truckload rates have been

published on *freight-all-kinds,* on which the same rate applies on any article in the shipment regardless of classification. These rates usually are restricted only against application on bulk freight, certain light and bulky articles, live stock and a few other items, but may be subject to provisions limiting any one article to from 25% to 60% of the total weight of the shipment or may apply only when a certain number of different articles are included in the shipment. Some of these rates carry provisions permitting the application of class, exception or specific commodity rates when those rates on a portion of the shipment are lower than the freight-all-kinds rate, but may require that the freight-all-kinds rate be used on a stated minimum portion of the shipment. Freight-all-kinds rates are of greatest benefit to freight forwarders and industrial shippers of large quantities of variety merchandise.

Commodity rates usually are expressed in cents per 100 pounds, but there are some commodities, such as brick and coal, with rates per net ton and an occasional rate per gross ton. Certain lumber rates are expressed in cents per 1000 board feet, pulpwood in cents per cord and bulk liquids via motor carrier frequently are rated per gallon. Charges stated in dollars and cents per car formerly were confined to switching and other short-haul movements. The introduction of trailer-on-flat-car service changed that, however, for since 1958 literally thousands of per-car or per-trailer rates have been published to apply on Plan II½, Plan III, and Plan IV piggyback traffic (see Chapter 6).

On the rise in recent years has been the publication of special commodity rates on multiple car shipments, "jumbo" cars, and so on where incentives are involved. Reduced multiple-car rates are conditioned upon the tender of two or more carloads at one time at one point by one shipper for movement over one route to one consignee at one destination. Variations on multiple car rates include unit train rates on which full trainloads of sixty cars or more may move, articulated car rates, and others. Quite often they apply to bulky commodities such as coal, grain, ore, and automobiles. "Jumbo" car rates have been made

applicable to movements via large tank cars having capacities
of roughly 18,000 to 40,000 gallons, large hopper cars, and so
on.

Unless the tariff naming a commodity rate specifically provides alternation, the commodity rate on a given commodity
from a given origin to a given destination must be used instead
of the class or exception rate on that commodity from and to
those points, even though the class or exception rate might produce lower charges.

The railroads of Canada have made use of a system of
commodity "agreed rates" whereby shippers of a substantial
quantity of a certain material who would agree that a major
percentage of that tonnage would move by rail were accorded
rates somewhat below those normally applicable. For a number
of reasons this type of rate is not in general use in the United
States, and only a few intrastate applications exist.

Today there are three major regional groups among railroads, the *Eastern Railroads*, the *Southern Freight Association*
and the *Western Traffic Association*. Within each of these
groups are several tariff publishing agencies, as follows:

Eastern Railroads
   Trunk Line—Central Territory Tariff Bureau
Southern Freight Association
   Southern Freight Tariff Bureau
   Southern Ports Foreign Freight Committee
Western Traffic Association
   Western Trunk Line Committee
   Southwestern Freight Bureau
   Texas-Louisiana Freight Bureau
   Transcontinental Freight Bureau
   Colorado-Utah-Wyoming Committee
   Pacific Southcoast Freight Bureau
   North Pacific Coast Freight Bureau

In addition, Illinois Freight Association and a committee
of east-west Virginia lines each publish tariffs separate from the
three major groups.

Even though the publication of class rates by agencies had greatly reduced the number of class rate tariffs, there were more than 100 of them in effect prior to the publication of the ICC Docket 28300 rates. As a result of the manner in which the ICC Docket 28300, 30416 and 30660 scales were put into tariff form, the entire country's interstate rail class rate structure is contained in 17 issues, a list of which follows:

Tariff No.	Issued by
W—1000	Western Trunk Line Committee
W/S—1001	" " " "
I—1002	Illinois Freight Association
I/S—1003	" " "
SW—1004	Southwestern Freight Bureau
SW/E—1005	" " "
SW/W—1006	" " "
SW/S—1007	" " "
E/S—1008	Trunk Line Central Territory Tariff Bureau
E—1009	Trunk Line Central Territory Tariff Bureau
E/W—1010	Trunk Line Central Territory Tariff Bureau
S—1011	Southern Freight Tariff Bureau
E/SW—1013	Trunk Line Territory Tariff Bureau
1014	Transcontinental Freight Bureau
1015	" " "
1016	North Pacific Coast Freight Bureau jointly with Pacific Southcoast Freight Bureau
SW/E—1040	Southwestern Freight Bureau

The letter prefixes 1000 to 1011, 1013 and 1040 give a clue to the territorial application of each. Tariff 1014 applies between Intermountain Territory and the Pacific Coast States; Tariff 1015 applies between points east of the Rockies and points in the Rocky Mountain states and west thereof; Tariff 1016 applies between points in the Pacific Coast states. Tariffs 1013 and 1040 apply via rail-water routes through Atlantic and Gulf ports.

Tariffs 1000 to 1011 inclusive are governed by tariffs of exception ratings and commodity rate scales issued by the same agencies and bearing corresponding numbers in the 2000 series. Thus, Tariff W-1000 is governed by Tariff W-2000, Tariff W/S-1001 by Tariff W/S-2001 and so on. Tariffs 1013 and 1040 each contain any exceptions to the classification which apply in connection with the rates published therein. Tariffs 1014, 1015 and 1016 are subject to no exception ratings at all, but do contain exceptions to the rules of the classification. Some agencies publish both interterritorial and intraterritorial commodity rates for their member lines, while others leave the intraterritorial and local rates for the individual railroads to publish. *The trend, however, is toward the agency issue,* especially where duplicating rates are published by several railroads between the same points. Except for the class rates mentioned previously, there is no hard and fast rule that will enable a person to tell whether to look in an agency issue or an individual tariff for a given rate.

Motor carriers likewise have created tariff publishing agencies within their various regional associations. But whereas the railroad groups mentioned above act in behalf of all railroads in the respective territories, the same cannot be said of the motor carrier groups. Consequently, there are many overlapping motor carrier bureaus and some carriers represented by no bureau at all. The principal motor carrier groups are:

> New England Motor Rate Brueau
> Middle Atlantic Conference
> Southern Motor Carriers Rate Conference
> Motor Carriers Tariff Association
> Eastern Central Motor Carriers Association
> Central States Motor Freight Bureau
> Central and Southern Motor Freight Tariff Association
> Middlewest Motor Freight Bureau
> Southwestern Motor Freight Bureau
> Rocky Mountain Motor Tariff Bureau
> Interstate Freight Carriers Conference
> Pacific Inland Tariff Bureau

■ *Accessorial Charges.* Grouped under this heading are the

charges made by carriers for a wide variety of services and privileges made available in connection with the transportation of goods. They include charges for switching, loading, unloading, weighing, pickup, delivery and transit privileges such as stopoff for completion of loading or unloading, storage, inspection, grading, repackaging, milling and fabrication. Also included would be charges for demurrage and vehicle detention, as well as allowances paid to shippers and consignees for services performed by them, such as pickup and delivery and the furnishing of shipper owned or leased railroad cars or highway equipment.

■ *Freight Forwarder rates*, both class and commodity, were originally patterned after those published by the railroads and they were governed by the rail classification. Today, the prime regulated competitors of the forwarders are the motor common carriers. Consequently, forwarder tariffs are predominantly governed by motor classifications, and forwarders endeavor to maintain rate levels that do not exceed those of motor carriers.

The basic concept of freight forwarding is to assemble and consolidate "less-load" individual shipments into carload or truckload consignments, which are forwarded from forwarder origin terminals to forwarder destination terminals, where breakbulk and distribution are performed. In essence, separate and distinct parts are combined into a whole and then reduced again to separate and distinct parts. Since the forwarder pays his underlying rail or motor carrier the charges applicable to carload or truckload consignments on the terminal movement, he is able to publish rates of his own to the public on any volume of traffic less than those quantities. Forwarder class and commodity tariffs, as a consequence, name rates on both "less volume" and "volume" shipments. While the vast bulk of forwarder shipments weigh less than 1,000 pounds, a heavy concentration of forwarder tonnage and revenue is to be found in the higher weight ranges.

An enduring, but fallacious, simplification of the forwarder concept is that the forwarder pays carload rates, collects less-than-carload rates, and the difference is his profit. Actually, as previously described, this holds true only on the consolidated terminal-to-terminal portion of forwarder service. It does not take into consideration the cost of assembly, terminal handling, distribution, billing, tracing, claims administration, solicitation, and items of overhead expense. It is therefore necessary to compare the forwarder's total charge to his customer with his total cost of handling the shipment if one is to perceive a meaningful picture, and it is on this basis that forwarder rates are made and maintained, subject to the dictates of competitive necessity.

Forwarder class rates on "less volume" lots between terminal cities are generally competitive with motor carrier rates down to Class 50, but between other points they may be competitive at higher levels to compensate for the higher cost of assembly or distribution or both. Volume class rates usually are maintained to Class 35, regardless of location of origin and destination. As previously mentioned, forwarder rates are not subject to the long- and short-haul provisions of Section 4 of Part I of the Interstate Commerce Act. This feature is often overlooked.

A unique innovation, which has proved of unusual value to LTL shippers and receivers, was the introduction by Acme Fast Freight of the aggregate rate concept to forwarder rate making. Acme's first aggregate tariff became effective on June 8, 1975. The principle of offering reduced rates in return for pick-up savings resulting from multiple tenders of LTL shipments has since been adopted by other forwarders.

■ *Assembly and Distribution rates* are published by many motor carriers for use in connection with shipments originating at or destined to points beyond the terminal areas of freight forwarders or freight consolidators. They appear as both class and commodity rates and usually are 10% or more lower than the ordinary rates applicable between the same points, on the theory that multiple shipments delivered to or picked up at a consolidation point are less costly for the motor carrier to handle. The rules of "'A & D tariffs" usually require that shipments be reforwarded within five working days via common carrier service and that records substantiating compliance with the rule be made available to the assembling or distributing carrier upon demand. These rates are of particular use to the industrial shipper when he maintains a regular consolidation operation either with his own facilities or through a professional consolidator.

■ *Air freight rates* are regulated by the Civil Aeronautics Board rather than the Interstate Commerce Commission. Their structures are somewhat less complicated than those of the rails and the trucks although complications, as is to be expected, are mounting and more of them are in the offing.

Most domestic rates and conditions for air carriage are found in the tariffs published by the Airlines Tariff Publishing Company, Inc., Dulles International Airport, P.O. Box 17415, Washington, D.C. 20041 as agent for the carriers. These are, for the most part, in loose leaf, ring binder compilations. A few tariffs are issued by the airlines and others.

Summaries follow:

Tariff CR 1 contains the rules which govern the rate tariffs and the conditions which attend shipping by air. It limits carrier liability to the higher of 50 cents per pound or $50 per shipment unless a higher value is declared and paid for at rates varying from 10 to 15 cents for each $100 of additional valuation.

Tariff LR 1 is the general and specific commodity tariff which contains local, airport-to-airport rates. Rates generally are expressed in dollars per 100 pounds for minimum weights at various levels, standard categories being 100, 1000, 2000, 3000, 5000 and 10,000 pounds. Commodities are shown in broad groups not necessarily confined to related articles. Rates for the most part apply between large cities. They apply on everything except live animals and certain bulky and valuable articles for which premium rates are given and are expressed in percentages of the normal rates. Trends, under this tariff, are toward more specific commodity descriptions. This is a combination of, and supercedes, two former tariffs, #2 (CAB 8) and #SC 3 (Cab 158).

Tariff JR 13 publishes joint haul rates and complements the single line tariff (#LR 1) immediately above.

Tariff 3 C specifies charges for surface transportation between airports and the cities they serve. There is one set of charges for regular pick up and delivery and another for special trips.

Tariff CT 7 is the container tariff on which developments have been significant. It applies to general and specific commodities and provides discounts on existing rates for those pounds in containers which exceed specified amounts. Large industries, in particular, are among its users and container tonnage has been steadily increasing.

Tariff Circular 6 D is an important one for the air shipper. Articles which are not accepted for air shipment are listed there, as well as those which may travel in limited quantities or special packing. It is being amended as to format.

Other tariffs include those involving commuter lines and so on.

There is further, as an information source, a substantial amount of rate and related data available in brochures and the like published by the air lines. For a shipper investigating, commencing to use, or not substantially involved in air freight these can be helpful and may be sufficient. American Airlines, for instance, has several publications in which examples, rate tables, and the like appear.

An example from one of the publications just referred to shows details of how lower costs (air versus surface) may prevail via that carrier on shipments of just under 500 pounds, door to door, between Dallas and Boston, Buffalo and Los Angeles, and other named cities. Conditions for realizing those costs are spelled out and include the use of a readily available, top loading, light weight container (or its equivalent) not exceeding 42"x29"x25½", shipment tenders between 4 a.m. and 4 p.m., and so on.

As to air freight generally, CAB procedures are often quite

drawn out and complicated. Tariff changes at times arrive at shippers' offices after the effective date and, where important enough, watching services to minimize problems in this regard are advisable. A broad transportation field with many possibilities exists in air freight, however, and the airlines have come up with interesting innovations in freight handling, data processing, freight charges, expeditious movements, and so on. More of this is needed and shippers generally should be accorded, and should take, more important roles as participants in rate making processes and in the development of air carrier services.

In addition to the direct air freight services provided for by the airlines, air freight forwarders are active and available on a nationwide basis as well as an international basis. They are particularly effective in providing economical and efficient services to shippers of smaller quantities. They publish their own tariffs (based on the same underlying principles as surface freight forwarders) and generally provide a top flight control of these shipments on a door to door basis as well as service which has received careful planning.

How Rates Are Published

Even more wasteful, confusing and repetitious than each carrier publishing its own classification was the former practice of individual publication of each carrier's rate tariffs. After Interstate Commerce Commission regulation became effective, competing carriers adhered to the same scales of rates between given points. One of the *main* purposes of regulation was to end the discriminatory rate wars that had characterized the early days of the transportation industry.

Early in the twentieth century the railroads banded together into regional groups, which served as clearing houses for mutual problems, and agents were appointed within these groups to publish tariffs for their members. Thus, instead of one carrier publishing a local class rate tariff from the New York area to Chicago and others publishing joint tariffs with their various

connections from and to the same points, each became a party
to an agency tariff which published a single scale of class rates
that applied via all these routes. This resulted in a tremendous
reduction in the number of tariffs and, while many tariffs still
are issued by individual carriers, for the most part they cover
local provisions or rates within a restricted territory.

There are other interstate groups (generally smaller) as
well as those which publish intrastate rates in a number of
states. Additionally, there are groups representing carriers offering specialized services, a list of which includes the following:

Household Goods Carriers Bureau
Western States Movers Conference
Oil Field Haulers Association
Eastern Tank Carriers Conference
National Automobile Transporters Association
Steel Carriers Tariff Association

How Rates Are Established

*One of the most challenging aspects of traffic work is keep-
ing currently informed on the kaleidoscopic changes that occur
in freight rates.* Every week thousands of changes are proposed; thousands of these proposals are disposed of and thousands of tariff supplements are issued reflecting the decisions of
dozens of rate committees throughout the country. The traffic
man who fails to keep posted is likely to be confronted with
some unpleasant and difficult situations.

These constant changes in freight rates are brought about
in a variety of different ways. In a great number of cases, they
are the outcome of negotiations between shippers and carriers.
In many others, they are proposed by the carriers themselves to
meet the competition of other means of transportation or, as in
the case of general rate increases, to improve their revenues. In
still others, they result from orders of the Interstate Commerce
Commission growing out of investigations such as Dockets
28300, 28310, 30416, 30660 and the various minimum rate orders affecting truck rates.

No one needs to sit by idly and complain that he cannot do anything about his rate situation, for all sorts of remedies are available to him. To be sure, his views will not prevail in every case, but if he has a good understanding of how these things take place he can avoid many situations that might otherwise be extremely troublesome.

Addition of section 5a to the Interstate Commerce Act in 1948, as a result of the Reed-Bulwinkle Bill, exempted common carriers from the operation of the anti-trust laws in connection with agreements developed between themselves and their various regional groups whereby procedures are established for the joint consideration, initiation and establishment of charges for the services they perform. Such agreements must outline all procedures to be followed and must receive the approval of the Interstate Commerce Commission. Basically, all procedures consist of consideration of tariff changes by a *standing rate committee* maintained as a part of the association's staff and, if necessary, reconsideration by an *appeals committee* composed of freight traffic officers of member carriers. All agreements of this nature must guarantee to member carriers the right of independent action.

Generally speaking, proposals for tariff changes may be initiated by shippers, carriers or by the bureau itself on behalf of its members. The dockets giving a brief description of each proposal scheduled for consideration by the standing rate committee are published, usually weekly, and circulated among member carriers and such shippers as may request them. In addition, the rate committees of the railroads and some motor and water carriers advertise their dockets in the weekly TRAFFIC BULLETIN, while a few motor carrier dockets are listed in *Transport Topics*, the weekly newspaper published by the American Trucking Associations (see Chapter 14). The New England Motor Rate Bureau, Middle Atlantic Conference, Southern Motor Carriers Rate Conference, Motor Carriers Traffic Association, Central States Motor Freight Bureau, Middlewest Motor Freight Bureau, Rocky Mountain Motor Tariff Bureau and Pacific Inland Tariff Bureau supply their dockets to shippers gratis or at nominal charges. A tabulation indicating disposition of proposals previously docketed usually is published with each docket.

Thus the traffic man may obtain advance information on proposed tariff changes. If he notes a proposal that will affect his company's operations, he may support or oppose it, as circumstances dictate, either by letter or by asking for public hearing on the matter. The importance of keeping posted in this manner cannot be overemphasized, for decisive action in advance of the actual publication of a tariff change often will forestall the difficulty of obtaining adjustments later.

The report of the standing rate committee will be final unless it is protested within a stated period. However, if it is protested, either by a member carrier or a shipper, it will be scheduled for hearing before the appeals committee, which is known by names such as Freight Traffic Managers Committee, General Rate Committee or Central Committee, and protestants may state their cases either by letter or in person. If the standing rate committee's report is upheld, this usually closes the matter, but if an individual carrier feels very strongly that a proposed provision should or should not be published, he may take independent action and either arrange for publication for his own account or withdraw from participation in the provision, as the case may be. When independent publication of a rate is made by a motor carrier in this manner, it frequently results in a protest and request for suspension being lodged with the ICC by the bureau or others on the premise that the independent action taken constitutes destructive competitive practices or should be cancelled for other reasons. If the tariff provision is suspended, the carrrier then has the burden of justifying the assailed tariff provision.

If publication takes place as a result of standing rate committee or appeals committee action, the law requires that it be made effective on thirty days' notice to the Commission and the public. At this point, *anyone* whose interests are thought to be affected by the published provision may file a protest and *request for suspension* with the Commission's Board of Suspen-

sion, provided it is done at least twelve days before the scheduled effective date and is supported by *good evidence* that the
provision will be unreasonable, prejudicial, preferential or
otherwise in violation of the law. Whether or not the Board decides to suspend, its action may be appealed to the appropriate
division of the Commission. Because of the short time that
usually remains between the Board's announcement of its decision and the effective date, it is of utmost importance that
quick action, when indicated, be taken. Some companies maintain representation in Washington to help in this regard. Suspension, when granted, is for a period of seven months, unless
the case can be disposed of sooner by the Commission or the
publisher of the provision receives the Commission's special
permission to withdraw and cancel the suspended provision. If
the case cannnot be disposed of within the period of suspension,
the rate is allowed to go into effect unless both protestant and
respondent agree to continue the period of suspension until the
Commission's decision is announced. When a provision goes
into effect at the end of the suspension period before the Commission's decision is ready, the investigation of the matter continues and the respondent may be required to cancel the provision at a later date.

Occasionally, the provisions of section 6 of the Act calling
for thirty days' notice of a freight rate adjustment are waived
and the Commission grants what is known as *Sixth Section Permission* to publish on a shorter period of notice. This can be as
little as one day's notice, but it is generally for ten days or
some similar period. Justification for such action must be
strong; the proposed provision must be non-controversial,
must be the result of an order of the Commission or the courts,
or must be to correct a tariff error. In some cases, short-notice
permission will be granted where there has been undue delay
in publishing a duly recommended provision or when the person affected would be severely damaged by waiting the full
thirty days.

From the foregoing, it will be seen that the machinery for
publishing new or changed tariff provisions, though slow and

apparently cumbersome, is designed for the full protection of anyone whose interests are affected. Naturally, only a bare outline of the procedures can be presented here. For those interested in greater detail, a book entitled "Practice and Procedure Before Rate-Making Associations," by G. E. Lowe, the Traffic Service Corporation, Washington, D.C. 20005, offers excellent coverage of this subject and includes both rail and major motor carrier ratemaking bodies.

Rate Adjustments

The skilled traffic manager can exert considerable influence over his company's transportation costs by keeping under constant observation the freight rates applicable to the company's principal raw materials, supplies and products and actively seeking adjustments in those rates when good cause shows itself. A carrier hardly can be expected to reduce its revenues without being asked, and even when it is asked, the request should be reasonable, logical and lawful. But when it is confronted with a carefully worked out proposal for a rate adjustment, any carrier that has a proper customer-relations policy will cooperate to the utmost in seeing that the proposal receives full and fair consideration.

The tremendous variety of our commerce makes it impossible to discuss the standards of rate evaluation and adjustment in any but the most general terms. There are a few points, however, that should be investigated before *any* adjustment is requested of a carrier. The more important of these are:

■ *Lawlessness:* Departures from the "long haul-short haul" requirements of section 4 of the Act, unless maintained under specific relief from the ICC, are prime justification for adjustment in rail rates. The ICC also has ruled that rail or truck commodity rates that exceed class rates on the same article are *prima facie* unreasonable.

■ *History:* It is well to know the history of the rate to be adjusted, whether it was established as the result of an ICC order, and whether that order prescribed it as a *minimun* or *maximum* reasonable rate. It is extremely difficult to obtain a downward revision of a prescribed minimum rate, for formal proceedings must be instituted, asking the Commission to modify its previous order, and supported by the strongest possible justification.

■ *Volume:* The volume and regularity of movement of the traffic involved will have considerable influence upon any adjustment.

■ *Value of Service:* Stated otherwise as "what the traffic will bear," this means that a high priced, high profit item, which may require special equipment or other extraordinary services, must be expected to cost more from a transportation standpoint.

■ *Cost of Service:* No carrier should be expected to publish rates which are below its *out-of-pocket* costs and, except in unusual circumstances, rates should equal or exceed its *fully distributed* costs, which include *all* the factors of doing business. The ICC, through its Bureau of Accounts, publishes several tabulations of such costs and a study of these statements can do much to keep requests for rate adjustments within reason. Also considered under this heading is the commodity's history of susceptibility to damage and pilferage. Likewise, if the movement will help provide maximum utilization of carriers' equipment, through heavier loading or preventing emply return movements of cars or trucks, this may be expected to weigh heavily in favor of the adjustment.

■ *Rate Levels from Other Producing Points:* If, for example, other producing points have commodity rates on a given article equivalent to Class 30, a shipper of the same article with a Class 40 rating has an excellent argument for similar commodity rates.

■ *Market Competition:* Within reason, the effect of a rate upon a producer's ability to compete in a given market may be considered.

■ *Rates on Similar Articles:* Articles of similar nature, use and value often will provide the key to the reasonableness of a rate proposal. Thus, rates on similar articles fabricated from non-ferrous metals, unless extraordinary value is present, should be comparable, whether made from aluminum, brass, bronze, copper, or cupro-nickel. On the other hand, it is extremely unlikely that the rates can be as low as those applicable on the same articles made from steel, although the steel article's producer would have good cause for an adjustment if his rates exceeded those on the non-ferrous articles.

■ *Rates via Other Forms of Transportation:* Although carriers often are aware of their competition and alert to opportunities to meet it whenever they can, it still is good procedure to cite the rates applicable via competitors' services. If common carriers are asked to meet private motor carrier competition, the private carriage costs should be documented carefully and completely.

Although the procedures of all carrier associations provide that proposals may be docketed at the request of the public, the amount of technical information necessary before a rail proposal may be placed upon the public docket makes it desirable that the matter *be handled through an interested railroad* such as the one serving the plant at point of origin or destination.

Motor carrier rate adjustments can be processed by one or more of the carriers, or the shipper can file the proposal direct with the bureau. Most motor carrier bureaus provide standard forms for the presentation of proposals. A common shipper practice is to review the facts with one of its important carriers and cooperate and work fully with the carrier in the handling of the matter to a conclusion. In these cases it can be most helpful to a shipper if carrier representatives who are knowledgeable and experienced can be dealt with. If it is felt unwise for any number of reasons to select a certain carrier or carriers for help, a shipper may proceed on his own with full propriety.

In all cases, the data submitted in support of the proposal should be complete and factual. They should be specific as to the rates sought, for to ask for reduced rates without saying what they should be implies strongly that the proponent lacks sufficient knowledge to judge the propriety of the existing basis.

I.C.C. PROCEEDINGS

If the procedure previously described in this chapter fails to bring about a proper adjustment and a case may be made for unreasonableness, unjust discrimination, undue preference or any other violation of the Act, formal proceedings may be initiated before the Commission, asking for a *cease and desist order* and prescription of rates for the future. If shipments already have moved on assailed rail or water rates, an award for excess charges paid may be asked.

■ *Reparation:* Proceedings along these lines before the I.C.C. are often called reparations cases. The dictionary defines *reparation* as "the act of making amends; atonement; indemnity; also that which is done by way of amends or satisfaction." It thus implies that the petitioner for reparations has been damaged.

Detailed proof of actual damage is required when unjust discrimination under section 2 of the Act or undue preference under section 3 are alleged. Reparations often are awarded, however, as penalties against carriers for unreasonableness under section 1, departures from the long-and-short-haul and aggregate-of-intermediates provisions of section 4, and faulty tariff interpretations under section 6. Generally the fact that petitioner has borne the charges is sufficient proof of damage in these last named instances.

The Commission's power to award reparation is confined to shipments moving under Part I of the Act via all-rail or rail-water routes, with a two year statute of limitations, and Part III, all-water routes, with a three year statute of limitations. The Act provides that the statute runs from the date cause of action accrues and that is defined as the date the shipment is delivered, *not* the date freight charges are paid, if later. However, if charges are collected within 90 days of the end of the limitation period, the limitation period will be extended to include 90 days from the date such charges are collected.

The successful prosecution of a formal reparation case is a difficult and highly technical procedure, best handled by one who has had considerable experience in the work and who has had ample opportunity to observe the methods of others. While a good rate man will unquestionably discover many potential reparation situations, final evaluation of the matter, its development and preparation of the case in accordance with the Commission's General Rules of Practice should be left to the able professional traffic manager, or to an attorney or an I.C.C. practitioner, either or both of whom specializes in such work. In proceedings before the Commission, the quality of the evidence must be such as to establish a clear showing of unlawfulness.

Not all reparation cases need to involve formal proceedings. Even though the carrier agrees with the shipper that a legal published rate is unreasonable or otherwise contrary to the provisions of the Act, the carrier is required by law to charge, and the shipper to pay, the rate. The carrier may petition the Commission for authority to refund and, if a clear showing of unlawfulness has been made and the Commission is satisfied that discrimination will not result, the Commission may issue what is known as *Special Docket Authority* approving the payment of reparation.

Under Part II, the motor carrier part, and Part IV, the freight forwarder part of the Act, the Commission is without power to award reparation. Reversing previous rulings that a shipper had the right to have the reasonableness of past motor carrier rates determined by the ICC, the U.S. Supreme Court in the T.I.M.E. decision on May 18, 1959, declared that Congress had not intended that Part II of the Act preserve the common-law right to damages by which shippers could file a complaint in a court of competent jurisdiction and ask the ICC to determine the reasonableness of the rate in question. This leaves the shipper without the power to recover from motor carriers because of rates unreasonable in the past or to assert "unreasonableness" as a defense in a motor carrier suit to recover published tariff rates. Legislation has been introduced on several occasions in Congress to remedy the situation, but to date, opposition has been such that it has not been passed. In cases where the carrier is in agreement with the shipper as to the unlawfulness of the rate, the carrier may apply to the Commission for authority to refund and permission may be granted under the same conditions as govern Special Docket Authorities, although the procedure is not formalized as in the case of Special Docket Applications.

The foregoing, of course, applies only in the case of interstate shipments. Laws applicable to regulatory bodies in individual states should be checked to determine power to award reparations in cases involving unreasonable charges.

Utilizing Freight Rate Information

If rates are regulated by the ICC and carriers are obligated by law to charge the correct rate, what can the shipper or receiver of freight do about it? Why not obtain any needed rate information from the carriers? How can an industrial traffic man know more about a carrier's rates than the carrier itself? Why go to the trouble and expense of maintaining a tariff file and a staff of rate men?

The answers to these questions lie in the fact that carrier's tariffs, due to the large number of commodities, origins and destinations involved, are very complicated. The multiplicity of rules and regulations governing them, stated as they are in more or less general terms, are open to a variety of interpretations when applied to specific situations. And whereas carriers must deal with *all* the commodities they handle for *all* their customers between *all* the points they serve, an industrial traffic department can *specialize* in the relatively limited number of one company's commodities and locations. Consequently, and this is said without intent to reflect adversely upon the sincere efforts of carriers to be helpful to their customers, the industrial traffic department, properly staffed and equipped, is in a far better position to provide accurate information based on *uniformity of interpretation* and *consistency of policy.*

Furthermore, *it must be remembered that a carrier cannot be held accountable for a mistaken rate quotation or rule interpretation!* Many a company has lost a sale or made a profitless one due to a carrier's misquotation, but in seeking redress has been told by the ICC and the courts that it is given the means (through public posting of tariffs) of ascertaining the carrier's rates beyond question and it is charged with the responsibility of doing so. Delegated to the traffic department, this responsibility can be controlled and made effective. Like ignorance of the law, ignorance of freight rates excuses no man.

■ *Checking Rates:* Acclaim undoubtedly would be earned by those participating in the preparation of this text if they could set down within the confines of this chapter a comprehensive set of instructions for checking freight rates. But alas, no such magic formula is available, nor will it be in the foreseeable future. Much has been said about tariff simplification and, indeed, considerable was accomplished by the railroads' Tariff Research Group and a cooperating committee of the National Industrial Traffic League. Similar activities are continuing and this also is true of the motor carriers and the attention they are devoting to truck tariffs. The sum of this activity in many ways means simply the achievement of a certain uniformity in the meaning of symbols and reference marks, in the language of rules, and in the arrangement of the tariffs. Data processing is being applied to tariffs and has a good future. Much more is to be done there. Currrently, however, the business of checking rates is just as complex as it ever was, and about the most that can be attempted here is a rough outline of the steps customarily taken.

Assuming that the bill of lading description has been determined and it is a rail rate that is to be checked, the first step is to refer to the classification for the class ratings and carload minimum weight. One of the class rate tariffs mentioned earlier is then consulted, according to the territorial location of origin and destination, and the rate bases for both points obtained from the National Rate Basis Tariff. The rate basis number at the junction of the headline columns then is noted and the table of class rates at the back of the tariff referred to for the scale of class rates appearing opposite that rate basis number. The figures in the columns corresponding to the ratings previously determined are the rates per 100 pounds.

Is *that* all? Well maybe, but let's not be too sure. To begin with, the tariff was issued in 1952 and several dozen supplements have been issued, the *latest* of which lists *those* which are currently in effect. So it is necessary to examine each one for a change in rate basis number or in the table of class rates.

Unless there is a possibility that transcontinental LCL commodity rates will be lower *and the class rate tariff contains a rule permitting their use as maximum*, it is reasonably certain that the corrrect rate has been found.

On the other hand, if a carload rate is being checked, many more steps remain. The appropriate exceptions tariff should be consulted for the existence of exception or commodity column ratings. Whether or not any are found, it still will be necessary to look for specific commodity rates from the considered origin to the considered destination; from the considered origin to a point on the same route beyond the considered destination; from a point on the same route beyond the considered origin to the considered destination or a point on the same route beyond it; *for the lowest of them will apply if the tariff publishing them carries the standard intermediate origin and destination rules to comply with the long-and-short-haul provision of Section 4 of the Act.*

But wait; that's not all! The class rate tariff contains a rule which states, also in compliance with Section 4, that if the *aggregate of separately established intermediate rates* via any route over which the class rates apply produces lower charges than the through class rate, the lower charges so obtained will apply via all routes. Thus, if the class rate from Philadelphia to Denver is 255 cents per 100 pounds and there is a rate from Philadelphia to Chicago of 108 cents per 100 pounds and a rate from Chicago to Denver of 130 cents per 100 pounds, the two may be combined to produce a through rate of 238 cents per 100 pounds. Bear in mind, however, *that an intrastate rate may not be combined with an interstate rate, nor may an LCL rate be combined with a carload rate under this rule.* Otherwise, the possibilities under the intermediate origin and destination rules and the aggregate of intermediates rule, or a combination of the two, are limited only by the number of commodity rates published on a given commodity and the imagination of the rate man.

Checking motor carrier rates involves much the same procedure up to a point, but rules providing intermediate application are somewhat more limited in scope and there are no aggregate of intermediate clauses. On the other hand, overlapping motor carrier bureaus often make it necessary to check several tariffs to obtain the lowest rates and individual carriers' exceptions to the application of rates in a single tariff may provide different levels of rates within that tariff. Then, of course, there are the tariffs of individual carriers, which may contain everything from a few scattered local commodity rates published as a result of independent action to a full scale of local and joint class rates, exception ratings and commodity rates. Sometimes it is possible to defeat a through rate by combining the rates of two carriers, one or both of which are not parties to the through rate. All of this requires considerable research and, above all, a very extensive file of tariffs.

Freight forwarder rates present few of the problems of their rail and motor carrier counterparts. There are the class and commodity tariffs of the *Freight Forwarders Tariff Bureau,* to which most of the major forwarders are parties and those same forwarders publish their own tariffs, but there is little or no overlapping. Forwarder rates are not subject to long-and-short-haul nor aggregate of intermediates provisions, but there are differing patterns of rates as between individual forwarders. Whereas Forwarder "A" may be rail or truck competitive from Boston to Kansas City as low as Class 70, Forwarder "B" may be competitive only down to Class 85; yet their positions may be reversed from Boston to Minneapolis.

Of course, as a rate man gains experience, he will be able to modify, and even eliminate, some of the steps described above. But before he acquires that facility, he will have had to repeat those steps many, many times, often fruitlessly and with a sense of frustration. The genuine rate man is never satisfied, though, until he has exhausted *every* possibility.

■ *Auditing Freight Bills:* One of the best means of training a traffic man is to assign him to the audit of freight bills, for from those bills he is in an excellent position to obtain a detailed picture of his company's raw materials and supplies and their sources; its products and markets; its routing policies and practices; and the transportation services available to its various locations. A good rate man can repay his salary many times over, not only by the overcharges he detects, but by the economies he can effect by policing the entire shipping job.

Further, an *alert auditor will observe opportunities to order and ship in more economical quantities; note suppliers' and shipping departments' deviations from proper bill of lading descriptions and prescribed routes; uncover possibilities for consolidations and stopoff arrangements which can reduce transportation charges; and report rates which appear to be out of line!*

Although carriers are required to collect their freight charges before relinquishing shipments at destination, any reputable concern may be accorded *credit arrangements* upon request. By rail or water, from 48 to 120 hours credit will be given, depending upon the location of the consignee and whether shipment is a carload or LCL quantity. Motor carriers, freight forwarders, airlines and express companies may at their discretion extend seven days' credit. Balance-due bills of all carriers must be paid within 30 days. All credit periods are computed from the first 12 o'clock midnight following delivery of the freight or following presentation of the freight bill if it is presented subsequent to the delivery of the freight. If freight bills are mailed, the postmark indicates the date of presentation. In most cases, Saturdays, Sundays and legal holidays are excluded when computing credit periods. Failure to pay bills within the credit period is an offense punishable by fine and can subject the carrier to prosecution for unjust discrimination if he neglects to remind his customers of their obligations and cut off the credit of delinquents. Shippers, also, have obligations in these connections and may be subjected to penalties where violations occur.

■ *Incorrect freight bills may be corrected by a shipper.* If they can be audited and the remainder of their processing completed so that payment may be made within the credit period, considerable expense for filing of claims, processing of balance due bills, and adjustments of records and accounts may be avoided by making the corrections. In such cases, corrections are to be supported by statements of tariff authority or other reasons for the change and such information is sent to the carriers with remittances. If prepayment audits are not possible, the bills may be audited after payment and claims for overcharges thereafter presented to carriers.

Many shippers follow a practice of submitting freight bills to one or more of a large number of reliable freight audit bureaus for reaudit. These firms may not have the specialized knowledge of a concern's materials that its own auditors have, but their familiarity with tariffs plus their experience with other commodities often enables them to detect overcharges that otherwise might go unnoticed. These audit bureaus provide checks on the performance of a shipper's auditing procedures and have other functions. They also will perform the complete audit for concerns that do not do their own work. Their fees vary but may be up to 50% of the amount recovered.

Important to bear in mind in filing claims for overcharges is the *statute of limitations.* On interstate shipments, the statute is three years. This means that carriers may collect their charges and those who pay freight charges may file claims for overcharge within three years of the date shipment is delivered. Intrastate shipments are governed by the laws of the individual states, which provide limitations varying from two to ten years.

■ *Rate Quotations:* One of the most valuable services of

the traffic department is the quotation of freight rates to other departments of the company. These quotations help the purchasing department in the selection of sources of supply and in making comparisons of laid down costs between F O B origin and F O B destination quotations. They can be used by the sales department in arranging distribution methods to the best advantage, in developing profitable marketing areas, in establishing prices to meet competition, and in determining amounts to be allowed on invoices covering goods sold on delivered prices. Manufacturing can use them, too, in arranging for raw materials. Additionally, freight rates play an important role in the selection of new plant locations.

Because their accuracy may have great influence on the profit of a transaction, rate quotations should be in the hands of the most seasoned rate men, preferably those who have had considerable audit experience. An extensive tariff file is essential to a good quotation job.

■ *Consolidations:* Whether it be combining two LCL or LTL shipments into a stopoff carload or truckload or gathering a large number of individual small lots into scheduled pool cars, the success of the operation will hinge to a great degree on the accuracy of the rate information used. Not only must this information be readily available and up-to-date, but it must be under constant review by experienced rate men who can deal knowledgeably with the *effect* of every change in rates.

F O B Terms

(See Chapter 17 for discussion of export and import terms.)

There is a definite interrelation between freight rates and F O B terms, for the F O B terms indicate the purchaser's interest in transportation charges. Conversely, the transportation charges may have considerable influence upon the choice of F O B terms.

"F O B" is an abbreviation for "Free on Board" and implies loading on a conveyance. Several important questions may be answered by the manner in which the F O B terms are stated:

1. Who pays the freight?
2. Where is delivery to be made?
3. Where and when is title and control of the merchandise to be transferred?
4. Where is the point of shipment?
5. How is the laid down cost to be determined?
6. When is payment due?
7. Who pays for packaging?
8. Who is to select and make any necessary special arrangements with carrier?
9. Who absorbs cost of loading into carrier's equipment?
10. Who is to bear the risk of transportation?

As in any legally binding document, ambiguity in a contract of sale will be construed by the courts against the framer. But even if the matter never gets into the courts, improperly stated F O B terms will lead to misunderstandings and ill will between seller and purchaser and should be avoided. It is hoped that the discussion which follows may be instrumental in heading off at least a few of the causes of misunderstanding.

Ordinarily, purchasing F O B destination would appeal to a buyer as relieving him of many bothersome details; but in an operation of any size this simply cannot be done any more than it is possible to buy everything F O B origin. Trade practices, the provisions of the Robinson-Patman Act, and the regulations of the Federal Trade Commission produce a wide variety of F O B terms, many of which cannot be altered at the desire of a single customer, no matter how important that customer may be. Some companies buy F O B origin whenever possible because they wish to control the transportation. This may be important to them. *On the other hand, if an examination of the price indicates that the seller for competitive reasons or otherwise is not including the full amount of transportation, purchases of material F O B destination, absent other considerations, are best.*

In buying F O B origin, title and control of the goods pass to the buyer and invoice becomes payable when the carrier signs for them at that point. It follows that the buyer assumes risks of transportation, is entitled to route the shipment, and also must undertake the responsibility for getting the goods to destination and for filing claims for loss or damage *regardless of who bears the freight charges.* Unless qualified, F O B origin terms place the responsibility for freight charges on the buyer, but the terms may be worded in such a way as to provide for absorption of freight charges, or a portion of them, through allowance or prepayment.

"Freight allowed" and "Freight prepaid" have different meanings and should not be confused. "Freight allowed" means that shipments will move freight collect and, unless qualified, that an amount equivalent to the charges buyer pays to the carrier will be deducted from the total cost of the goods when paying seller's invoice. By this device, seller may quote delivered prices without tying up capital funds in prepaid freight. "Freight prepaid" means that seller will pay transportation charges to the carrier and that buyer will remit the full amount of the invoice without deduction for freight. In either case, if seller is unwilling to absorb charges for premium transportation, the clause may be worded to provide this protection.

Origin F O B points should be designated by naming the city and the use of wording such as "F O B Shipping Point" or "F O B Factory" should be avoided. If the seller has more than one F O B point, the F O B clause should state whether the seller's or the buyer's option governs the selection of the shipping point. If it is the seller's option and material is not sold on a delivered price, provision should be made for the equalization of transportation charges with the seller's shipping point producing the lowest transportation charges to buyer's destination.

When goods are bought F O B destination, the seller retains title and control of them and the invoice covering them does not become payable until they are delivered and the contract of carriage has been completed. The seller selects the carrier and is responsible for the risks of transportation including the filing of claims for loss or damage. Unless the F O B clause states otherwise, he assumes transportation charges either by prepayment or allowance. The buyer may not assign, divert or reconsign the shipment. When the contract of sale contemplates delivery of the material in seller's trucks, or in the trucks of a carrier operating under contract to the seller, such arrangements should be F O B destination, even if a charge is made for the delivery service, for obviously the buyer cannot assume title or control of the goods nor the risks of transportation if the seller has not relinquished them.

The following list includes some of the basic clauses most frequently used in connection with price quotations and contracts of sale. A brief interpretation accompanies each.

"*F O B (City and State at point of shipment).*" This means that material will be placed on the cars or trucks of the carrier indicated in buyer's routing, at seller's expense, and that all transportation charges thereafter will be borne by buyer. Any local trucking charges at point of shipment will be absorbed by seller.

"*F O B (Seller's plant, factory, mill, warehouse or other designated facility, City and State at point of shipment).*" This means that material will be placed on the cars or trucks of the carrier indicated in buyer's routing, at seller's expense, if it can be done at seller's facility indicated. If it is necessary to use local cartage to get the material to the carrier, or if the carrier indicated by buyer makes a charge for picking up at seller's facility, this expense, as well as subsequent transportation charges, will be borne by buyer.

These clauses may be modified to provide for delivered prices through allowance or prepayment of transportation charges by addition of one of the following auxiliary clauses:

"Transportation charges to destination allowed. (Or "prepaid", as the intent may be.)

"On individual shipments of (weight, invoice value of pieces) transportation charges to destination allowed." (Or "prepaid", as the intent may be.)

These mean that the seller will allow (or prepay and absorb) transportation charges via any route of movement and should be used only when this is mutually understood. If protection against charges for premium transportation is desired, one of the following may be used:

"Lowest published common carrier (rail, truck, freight forwarder or water) transportation charges to destination allowed."

"Lowest published common carrier (rail, truck, freight forwarder or water) transportation charges to destination prepaid. When buyer's routing results in higher charges, buyer will be invoiced, and pay, for the excess."

Both of these clauses may be further limited by prefacing them with "On individual shipments of (weight, invoice value or pieces)."

To provide for equalization of transportation charges with seller's other shipping points or competitive shipping points, the following may be added to the basic F O B origin clauses:

". . . . freight charges to be equalized with those applicable from seller's shipping point producing lowest transportation cost to buyer's destination."

". . . . freight charges to be equalized with (city and state)."

If more than one competitive point is involved, "whichever produces the lowest transportation cost to buyer's destination" should be added.

"F O B Destination" or "F O B (City and State of destination)." This means that the seller will undertake to deliver the shipment to the city specified and will absorb the regular transportation charges incident thereto. In the absence of specific provision to the contrary, unloading at destination, as well as any local trucking charges in the city of destination, is to be arranged and paid for by buyer unless carrier's tariff provides that either or both of these services are included in the transportation charge.

"F O B (Street number address, city and state)" or "F O B (buyer's plant, warehouse or similar designation, city and state)." This means that all transportation charges, including those for local delivery to designated address or location, will be absorbed by seller. Arrangements for and cost

or unloading are for buyer's account unless carrier's tariff or F O B clause provides otherwise.

All of the above clauses may be modified to express the intent behind the transaction. The important thing to remember is that *intent must be stated* and stated clearly enough to remove any reasonable doubt.

Recent Developments

Important changes in freight rate basics are made in a new law, the Railroad Revitalization and Regulatory Act of 1976 (45 USC 801), which is sometimes called the 4-R Act and which has as a basic purpose enabling the rails to better compete. One of its principal effects is to permit the rail carriers to change (up or down) their rates more freely and with less government regulation than in the past. New criteria are established under which, very generally speaking, a railroad can, on its own, increase rates as it wishes as long as it does not have "market dominance" and can decrease them to such point as it desires as long as they contribute to its "going concern value". Where rates equal or exceed variable costs for the service it is presumed they contribute to the carrier's going concern value. The criteria that rate changes be "just and reasonable" under the former law are amended or, you might say, made less general by the foregoing. The powers of the I. C. C. to suspend rate changes, along with being limited by the new criteria, are curtailed in other ways, a technical curtailment being that the Commission can no longer suspend on its own motion. Further, the new law establishes substantially more stringent requirements for requests for suspension; a protestant virtually must prove his case in the initial pleading. Much more than rate making and matters related to that subject are covered in this legislation, which is quite extensive. Abandonments, entry requirements, and a number of other aspects of possible specific importance to traffic organizations are affected. It also covers very substantial monetary funding benefits for track betterments, Con Rail, Amtrak, etc. Legislation having somewhat common deregulatory aspects is planned for the motor carriers and for the air lines.

6

FREIGHT ROUTING

EVERYTHING THAT IS PRODUCED, MANUFACTURED OR SOLD MUST be transported at least once to reach its end use or market. Whether it be across town or across the country, decisions as to *how it shall move* are necessary and those decisions properly are the responsibility of the traffic manager. In the business world of today, no firm can compete successfully if its production lines are shut down by a lack of raw materials or if its finished products are not available when and where needed. Its ability to operate profitably will be impaired if it is obliged to tie up capital funds in abnormally large inventories to offset the uncertainties of poorly chosen transportation services. Careful control of the routing of all shipments is an absolute necessity if service requirements are to be satisfied at the lowest possible cost. To a great extent, the traffic manager's value to his company will depend upon the success with which he administers the routing job.

For just as there are differences between the various *types* of services available, so are there vast differences between *individual carriers* in each type of service. Nor is the freight rate the sole element which governs the selection of a routing; there are times when costs will be disregarded and many other considerations will be weighed before an intelligent choice is made. And it is important that *almost every firm develop a basic routing policy,* understood by suppliers, customers and carriers, as well as other interested company departments.

This requires precise knowledge of shipping and receiving facilities at the respective ends of the haul, the operating rights and schedules of the carriers involved and, if a single carrier cannot transport the shipment all the way to its destination, what combinations of carriers will work together to perform an effective through service. It demands a good knowledge of the transportation geography of the country, the location of carriers' terminals and facilities for the interchange of freight, and of the availability of information concerning the location of a shipment while it is in transit. With some commodities the routing man will need to inform himself as to the carriers best able to supply special equipment in which to move the goods. *It will be up to him to utilize to the fullest the inherent advantages of each type of transportation available to him.* To give him this background, he must have an adequate file of tariffs and know how to use them. He can get much help from various trade publications, carrier schedules, maps and routing guides, but one of the greatest aids to education in this field is the *firsthand observation of carrier facilities and equipment.*

It should be remembered that the risks attending the transportation of goods are assumed by the person in whom title vests and that person's failure to protect himself against those risks does not transfer the responsibility to any other party to the transaction. No prudent person would entrust to a stranger the transfer of cash from one place to another; yet shipments valued at millions of dollars find their way into the hands of carriers completely unknown to the owners of the merchandise merely because those owners have failed to face up to their responsibilities and exercise control of the routing. Failure to route shipments makes it practically impossible to expedite them or to intercept them for diversion or reconsignment. There is no way of estimating the cost of delays, losses, damage and excess freight charges that may result, but there can be no doubt that it is far greater than necessary; *greater, of course, than the cost of providing effective control!*

Rail

The right of the owner of a shipment to prescribe the rail route over which it is to travel is set out in Section 15(8) of the Interstate Commerce Act. It is a right which must be exercised with care, however, for the fact that two railroads connect with each other does not always indicate that they participate in through routes with each other; nor does the fact that two railroads serve the same city always mean that they can interchange freight at that point. And it does not always follow that, because a given railroad serves both origin and destination, rates will apply *via* and good service will be provided *by* that railroad.

Specific routing is published in connection with most rates, either in the rate tariff itself or in a routing tariff referred to by the rate tariff. Some specific commodity rates may apply only via one route, while there may be hundreds of routes via which rates apply between other points. It is extremely important to understand this link between the rate and the route, for inattention can be costly. If the shipper specifies a route over which the through rate does not apply, a combination of two or more rates applying between points along the route of movement will be assessed, and it would be a rare case, indeed, if this combination did not exceed the through rate.

In checking out the routes applicable in connection with a given rate, frequently it will be found that both direct and circuitous routes are named. This is where a set of railroad maps, such as provided in the *Official Guide of the Railways,* or as available from Rand McNally, is a valuable adjunct to the routing job. Of course, circuitous routes often are useful, even if very fast service is not obtainable, for sometimes they provide desirable stopoff privileges. Circuitous routes may also be helpful in tonnage distributions, inventory adjustment problems at origin or destination, mileage equalizations when and if required, and so on.

Circuitous routes are numerous. The Baltimore & Ohio Railroad serves both Chicago and Indianapolis. Routing a shipment straight B & O all the way involves it moving into Ohio and then back for a total distance twice that of direct connections. The B & O—Chesapeake & Ohio affiliation has helped, or will help, in this regard, as a glance at the maps of both carriers will show. The Penn Central route between St. Louis and Louisville is longer than others because it goes north through Indianapolis. The situation on circuitous routes bears watching, not only as to the service angle, but as to freight rates. The carriers "flag out" or do not participate in many rates involving circuitous routes because they are not remunerative.

Some of the larger railroad systems publish internal (or local) routing guides which indicate the junctions via which shipments are handled between points served by their lines. These guides are useful in determining whether one point is intermediate to another for stopoff purposes or for the application of rates under the intermediate origin or destination rules.

The routes published in rate and routing tariffs specify the junction points between the railroads named in each route and sometimes these junction points differ for carload and LCL shipments. They may be shown on the bill of lading, but care is required in their selection. Frequently, two or more junction points appear in routes involving the same two railroads and, if the shipper selects one at which little freight is interchanged, it may result in delay to his shipment.

Problems may arise, however, when they are not specified. A carrier generally takes the "long" haul where it can; that is, once it receives a car it moves it the maximum distance it can on its own line. This means ordinarily that it gets the largest share of the revenue on the car. This "long" haul route may not be the best for the shipper. By inserting junctions, faster and better routes may result. In other cases the specifying of junctions can keep cars out of conjested gateways. The Peoria gateway, as an example, has had important use at times in keeping cars out of Chicago.

In still other cases where the originating and delivering carriers are different railroads, the specification of junctions can be used to assure "line" hauls (with their attendant better remuneration) for each of them. Some shippers feel that this is simply good business and that better service results. The foregoing features are by no means complete and the situations of a number of companies may be such that junctions in bills of lading can be by-passed. Where indicated, however, the running of a "tight ship" by a transportation manager can well include providing means to make sure the best junctions are selected and are included in the bills-of-lading routings.

It is the practice of some shippers to show both the rate and the route on the bill of lading. Ordinarily, this alone will have no effect on the assessment of freight charges, for the railroad is obliged by law to charge the legal published rate applicable via the route of movement. However, if the shipper shows a rate lower than that applicable via the route specified, which rate does apply via another route, *the railroad agent must so inform the shipper and ask for instructions as to which route to use.* If he fails to do so ands signs the bill of lading without thus eliminating its conflicting provisions, charges must be assessed at the rate shown on the bill of lading. The practice of showing both rate and route on the bill of lading can be of great assistance to the railroad agent in expediting the preparation of his billing. It should be avoided, however, if carelessness or inaccuracy cannot be overcome to the point where they result in situations which might exert a strain on the relations between shipper and agent.

Less-than-carload: Once an important factor in railroad freight revenues, LCL service was the first to feel the effect of motor carrier competition. For many years, the railroads attempted to head off the loss of this business by reducing rates and overhauling their LCL handling facilities. Some of these measures enjoyed varying degrees of success for a time but none stemmed the loss of the tonnage. The result has been that most parts of the country are without LCL service. At some stations which continue to offer LCL service, the volume handled frequently is insufficient to enable the railroad to maintain its own pickup and delivery service, thus necessitating that shippers and consignees make their own arrangements for getting shipments to and from the freight stations. An allowance usually is paid under such circumstances, but it seldom covers the shipper's or consignee's trucking cost. Such service as remains should be considered only when some special reason exists for using it. Most railroads continue to have applicable tariff provisions to move LCL shipments weighing 6,000 pounds or more when loaded into a car by the shipper, unloaded by the consignee and require no intermediate handling by the railroad. These generally are not used by shippers. The rails themselves incline to look upon this type of shipment as being wasteful of car carrying capacity and may be reluctant to supply equipment, especially in times of car shortage.

Before attempting to make shipment via railroad LCL service, the Official List of Open and Prepay Stations should be consulted to make certain that both origin and destination stations have facilities for the handling of LCL freight. At the same time, if the route contains three or more railroads, it will be necessary to establish that the intermediate lines have no restrictions against the acceptance of this type of shipment.

Carload: The routing of carload freight offers the traffic man many challenging opportunities to demonstrate his effectiveness in controlling his company's transportation costs, for carload shipping provides many advantages not found in other forms of transportation. The smallest box car in common use has about 50% greater cubic capacity and from double to triple the weight carrying ability of the average highway trailer. Recent years have seen the development of still larger equipment in the form of box, hopper, gondola, tank and other special purpose cars with capacities of 100 tons and more. Carloads by rail therefore are the ideal medium for the movement of large masses of goods and this superior carrying capacity frequently enables the shipper to benefit from incentive rates considerably below the lowest offered by motor carriers. Many box cars carry special blocking, bulkheading and other damage prevention devices and some are equipped with extra-wide doors for ease in loading and unloading with mechanized equipment. Additionally, special equipment is being provided,

New auto rack cars, used to haul new automobiles from factory to dealer, are taking on a clean modern look. Attractive white reinforced plastic side panels on these 61-foot, three-level cars serve to reduce damage to automobiles from flying stones, wind-carried grit and other abrasives.

an example being illustrated above. While motor carrier detention charges usually begin within two or three hours of the arrival of the vehicle for loading or unloading, the rail shipper or consignee has 48 hours free time after the 7 A.M. following placement of the car in which complete loading or unloading.

Equally important, however, is a thorough understanding of the disadvantages inherent in rail carload shipping as well as how, even when the carload rate is lower, higher charges may result. Rail shipments usually take longer in transit than do those moving by motor carrier, *and this is particularly noticeable in the shorter hauls.* Rail carloads must be loaded by the shipper and unloaded by the consignee, but the great majority of truckload rates, including some that are the same as or lower than rail, include loading and unloading by the driver of the vehicle. Rail shipping of carloads is confined, in a great measure, to those firms having private sidings, but the flexibility of the motor carrier is such as to permit placement of loads at any point accessible to a passable highway. Carload minimum weights frequently are higher than tuckload minima. There are occasions when the rigid packing requirements of the rail classification make advisable the use of a motor carrier with more liberal provisions. Credit arrangements for the payment of motor carrier freight bills (7 days) are slightly more favorable than rail (120 hours-five working days-maximum).

Because carload shipments involve considerable weight, the saving of pennies in the freight rate often will aggregate very respectable sums. For possible attention in this connection are the various lower rated, or *differential* services that may be available. These will include the all-rail routes through Canada from New England to points in a territory which extends from roughly along a line drawn from Cleveland, Ohio and south on the one hand to the Rockies; on the other, freight routings via water-rail and rail-water-rail between North Atlantic Seaboard points and the southwest may be considered but availability of service is limited. Water-truck combinations are prevalent in several areas. In routings for the growing Alaska trade various combinations should be considered. Quite importantly, routings should be so arranged as to permit the use of rates applicable under the provisions of intermediate clauses.

Some shippers and receivers of freight find important the carload stopoff provisions published by the railroads. Those provisions frequently enable them to obtain the benefit of carload rates on shipments which otherwise would have to move LCL or LTL at the much higher rates applicable to those services. There are a great many variations in stopoff privileges. In general, shipments may be stopped in transit, usually not exceeding three times, for completion of loading or for partial unloading, but not both at the same point. Charges for the shipment are computed on the total weight of the freight loaded in the car at the highest rate or rates applicable from origin or any point at which the car was stopped for completion of loading to the final destination or any point at which the car was stopped for partial unloading. An additional charge of up to

$45, according to territory, is made for each stop exclusive of point of origin or final destination. Ordinarily, the stopoff rules restrict the stopoff points to those which are directly intermediate on the route of movement. Individual railroads, however, publish exceptions to this requirement to meet a variety of competitive situations and by imaginative use of these exceptions a shipper may make up stopoff cars which, from looking at a map, would appear out of the question.

The stopping of a car in transit for completion of loading or for partial unloading at times delays the shipment particularly as to the consignee at the last stop. In most cases this feature is simply an element that is to be taken into account in routing decisions. The carriers have employed various means to help in this regard but have subsequently discontinued them.

One means of help that is continued in a limited way by the western carriers is known as "transloading." It applies to cars to be stopped for partial unloading. Where applicable, a car or cars, loaded with freight for two or more destinations, may be shipped to a point where the railroad offers the transloading service, and the railroad will reload the material for

A new "Big Boy" box car is shown with its little brother, standard size, at right. These cars are longer than a bowling alley and are designed to carry light, bulky loads. As illustrated, they can accommodate a tobacco loading of 124 hogsheads versus 36 for the normal or standard size car.

each destination into a separate car, forwarding the cars to the various destinations just as though they were carloads. Care must be exercised to see that the through rates from origin to each of the destinations apply via routes operating through the transload point. Additionally there are other rules applicable to specific situations connected with transloading which are to be found in the stopoff tariffs of the railroads. Currently the charges applicable are the same as would apply if the shipment were physically stopped in transit for partial unloading. A special additional charge is under consideration.

One of the most important considerations of carload routing is to make certain that delivery can be made at stopoff points and final destination without additional switching. charges. Usually, if the railroad on which the shipper's or consignee's siding is located does not receive a line haul on the car, *it makes a separate charge for handling between the siding and the point of connection with the line-haul railroad.* In order to compete for the business, the line-haul railroad frequently states in its switching tariffs that it will absorb the switching charges of connections and pays the charges of the switching road out of its line-haul revenue. But there is a growing tendency to break away from these traditional reciprocal arrangements, so switching tariffs of both origin and destination carriers should be given careful scrutiny before this type of routing is attempted. When loading or unloading takes place on a public team track, the railroad owning the team track *always* should receive a line haul, for most railroads do not publish switching charges between their team tracks and connecting railroads and when they do these charges are not absorbed by line-haul railroads.

The manner in which a routing is shown on the bill of lading is quite important and may have considerable effect on the service received and on the application of rates. For example, on a carload shipment from Houston, Texas, on the Southern Pacific (SP) to a company in Omaha. Nebraska, whose private siding is served by the Burlington Northern, the following route might be used: SP-MP-BN. This route indicates that each of the three railroads will receive a line haul on the car and, even though the Missouri Pacific serves Omaha, it would be required to turn it over to the BN at some junction short of destination. On the other hand, if the shipper wanted the Missouri Pacific to receive the haul all the way to Omaha and the BN to receive only switching revenue, the route would be written on the bill of lading thus: SP-MP for BN delivery; or, on the routing line SP-MP and on the line headed "Delivering Carrier" BN. Before routing the car to give the Missouri Pacific the long haul, it would be necessary first, to determine that the MP and the BN could interchange cars at Omaha, and second, that the MP would absorb the switching charge of the BN. If this is not done, the shipper runs the risk of incurring excess transportation charges. Junctions could, of course, be specified. See page 79.

Transportation costs on carload shipments of perishables can be influenced considerably by the routing used. The skillful routing man will be sufficiently conversant with types of equipment and with schedules to, if possible and where necessary, avoid re-icing in transit. As to equipment, mechanical refrigerator cars (requiring no icing) are generally of the 50-foot variety, carry rates lower than the 34- to 36-foot types which require icing, and should be used when possible. As to the smaller cars requiring icing, he will choose a route that provides re-icing at the proper time, yet not too often. An extra re-icing often can spell the difference between profit and loss on a carload of produce which may be traded on a narrow profit margin. The National Perishable Freight Committee publishes a list of icing stations and charges for the services rendered at them.

Piggyback: No discussion of rail routing would be complete without an explanation of this hybrid of the transportation family which is known by a variety of names, including *Piggyback, Tofcee, Trailer-on-Flat-Car* and *Flexi-Van*. This consists of loading a highway trailer with goods and moving it over the highways to specially constructed railroad facilities. Here either the entire trailer or just its body is transferred to a railroad flat car built for the purpose and the car forwarded in a train operating on a *fast* schedule to the point having unloading facilities nearest the destination of the trailer. It is then unloaded from the flat car and completes its journey over highways (see page 134).

The basic idea of piggyback is not new, having been used in one form or another for many years. In 1885, the Long Island Railroad placed into operation a so-called "pickaback" plan whereby farmers' wagons loaded with produce were transported, four to a flat car, from outlying points on the island to Brooklyn, whence they were ferried to Manhattan. It was not until the late 1950s, however, that development of the idea by the railroads and acceptance by the shipping public combined to make headline news of the subject. Since that time there has been a steady increase each year in the points at which this service is available and in the number of trailers handled. By early 1971, the railroads were reporting more than 30,000 cars per week loaded with one or more trailers or demountable bodies and, while this represents only about 5 per cent of the railroads' total weekly carloadings, it is desirable and profitable traffic. It appears to offer excellent prospects for growth, judging from the sales effort devoted to it by most railroads, for they feel that at last they have a service with which they can meet the flexibility of motor carrier operation and successfully compete for the business of the smaller concerns and those which do not have railroad sidings. Shippers, on the other hand, find that piggyback provides fast, dependable schedules at charges which appear to be susceptible to far better control than those of motor carriers because labor costs are held to a minimum. Piggyback service is offered under six basic plans, each briefly described as follows:

Plan I—Offered to *motor carriers only* at flat charges agreed upon between railroad and truck line, this substitutes flat car service for over-the-road operations for all or part of the intercity haul. Shippers pay the regular motor carrier rates and may prohibit the use of substituted service but may not order it used. However, they are not likely to know whether or not a given motor carrier uses it.

Plan II—Wherein the railroads pick up freight at shippers' platforms and deliver it to consignees' receiving docks in *railroad owned or leased trailers*. Rates for this service usually are the same as, or slightly lower than, motor carrier rates between the same points and in some cases apply on LTL as well as trailerload traffic. Use of this type of service is elective with the shipper.

Plan II½—Similar to Plan II, except that service is offered *ramp-to-ramp only*, shipper and consignee making their own arrangements for motive power to effect pickup and delivery of loaded and empty trailers from and to railroad piggyback yard. Rates are substantially lower than those applicable via motor carrier.

Plan III—Under which *trailers owned or leased by shippers are* transported on flat cars furnished by the railroads and the railroads perform no terminal service except loading and unloading trailers onto and from flat cars. Rates usually are stated in dollars and cents per flat car up to a stated maximum basic weight of trailer contents with any weight in excess of that at a rate per 100 pounds. They contemplate the loading of two highway trailers or demountable trailer bodies per flat car. Rates are somewhat lower than Plan II½ charges. In some territories, Plans II½ and III rates are published to apply on single trailers at 60% of the two-trailer rates, one-half of the two-trailer maximum basic weight and the same rate per 100 pounds for any weight in excess of the maximum.

As regards commodities certain rate structures are restricted to apply on shipments of those specifically named; others are not limited and are on a freight-all-kinds basis. While the trend is away from restricting the quantity of any one commodity which may be loaded to 60% or some other figure, some tariffs continue to provide such restrictions. Where provided the stated percentage may apply to the total weight or maximum basic weight, which ever is greater.

This illustrates a typical piggyback load except, on an experimental basis, the trailers here are lifted on the car and are placed back-to-back to eliminate possibilities of vandalism and pilferage by making it virtually impossible to open the trailer doors.

Plan IV—Which differs from Plan III in that *the flat car also must be owned or leased by the shipper* and there are no single trailer rates.

Plan V—Resembles Plan II but rates are published jointly with motor common carriers which transport the trailer from origins and to destinations beyond the cities of the railroads' piggyback yards at either or both ends of the rail haul. This service is available on both LTL and truckload shipments.

The use of Plans II and V involves practically the same procedure as regular motor carrier shipments, although there may be some difference in the rules governing. Plan II class rates are subject to the rail classification with ratings which are competitive with motor carrier class rates. Plan V class rates may be subject to either the rail or motor carrier classification, depending upon whether the rates are published by the railroads or the motor carriers.

Plans II½, III and IV present additional problems in that they require that the shipper make arrangements for motive power to get the trailer to and from the railroad piggyback yards at both ends of the haul. Usually there are rail truck subsidiaries or motor carriers in all cities from and to which these rates are applicable which will perform the necessary services, either on a single trailer basis or, in the case of repetitive shipments, on contract. Arrangements must be made in advance, however, and it cannot be assumed that every consignee has such arrangements in force.

Plans III and IV also require that the trailers be owned or leased by the shipper. No difficulty is encountered if there is a two-way movement that will keep trailers under load in both directions, but since the return of empty trailers by piggyback usually costs the same as the loaded movement, any reduction in transportation costs realized on the outbound loaded movement probably will be more than offset by the expense of returning empty trailers. This problem may be solved by trip-leasing trailers from any of a number of firms, which permit the piggyback shipper to be relieved of responsibility for the trailer once it is returned empty to the piggyback yard at destination.

Plan IV, with its requirement that the shipper also own or lease the flat car, likewise requires a two-way loaded movement and thus does not lend itself to general use. It finds its greatest use among freight forwarders and shippers' associations. Territorially, some western carriers provide flat car lease charges for one-way moves and thus help, as to them, in establishing broader general uses of the Plan.

The trend away from weight restrictions on single commodities of freight-all-kinds shipments under Plans II½ and III is making it less difficult for one-product manufacturers to obtain the low rates available through these plans. Many manufacturers in this category have done well in surmounting the hurdle (generally, that no more than 60 per cent of an FAK shipment may consist of one commodity) through their shippers' associations. (See Chapter 9.) These groups, among various functions, arrange the mating of members' shipments to overcome the weight limitations. In most cases they were set up by, and are operated under the guidance of, experienced traffic men. Results have been worthwhile and decisions concerning routings can well involve their use as well as direct use of the plans were single commodity restrictions no longer exist.

Motor Common Carrier

The role of the motor carrier in the development of our country's transportation system has been tremendous. The speed and flexibility offered by highway transportation not only have revolutionized marketing and distribution practices, but have helped take manufacturing plants out of congested city areas and relocate them in the park-like suburban settings that are becoming more and more familiar the country over. The share of intercity tonnage hauled by trucks has been increasing year by year and no one appears to be willing to hazard a guess as to when this trend will level off.

Because of the fact that the average tractor-trailer unit does not have the carrying capacity, either in cubage or tonnage, of the average box car, and because each power unit usually pulls but one trailer as compared to the 100 or more freight cars that may make up a train, motor carrier charges at times are somewhat higher than those applicable via rail. But the speed of the highway carrier and its ability to place a load of goods at almost any point accessible to a passable road often overcome differences in rates which favor railroads. And the lower truckload minimum weights often enable the shipper of smaller quantities to take advantage of volume rates. To illustrate, Iron or Steel Hardware is rated Class 45, carload and truckload, in the rail and motor classification respectively. From Cleveland, Ohio, to Oklahoma City, Okla., the rail rate is $3.14 per 100 pounds, carload minimum weight 30,000 pounds. The truck rate is $3.13 per 100 pounds and, although the truck classification shows the volume minimum weight as 30,000 pounds, there is an exception that reduces the minimum in this case to 24,000 pounds. Thus a shipper with but 25,000 pounds could ship it by truck for $782.50 as compared to the $942.00 it would cost at the rail carload rate and minimum weight.

Most motor carrier rates include loading and unloading by the driver from or to a point adjacent to the tailgate of the vehicle and deliveries inside buildings may be arranged at reasonable additional charges published in carriers' tariffs. Because truck shipments are not likely to receive the impacts in transit to which rail cars are subjected, it is often possible to eliminate the elaborate blocking and bracing necessary in ordinary box cars and the resulting saving in labor and material can be considerable. Ordinarily, motor carrier shipments do not require

On certain highways, motor carriers have found it possible to reduce costs by operating two trailers in tandem behind a single tractor.

the expediting so often necessary to insure prompt delivery of those that travel by rail.

Considerations quite different from those governing rail routing apply in connection with selecting a motor carrier route. Motor common carriers operate on *certificates of public convenience and necessity* granted by the Interstate Commerce Commission which limit the commodities they may handle, describe the area they may serve and, in the case of regular route carriers, define the highway routes they may use. Some carriers may serve all intermediate points along their routes, while others are limited to named intermediate points or none at all. There are certificates permitting service to named points not directly on the described routes, called *off-route points*, and some allow transportation for compensation in one direction only. Every motor common carrier makes public its operating rights, usually in a directory issued by one or more of the rate conferences of which it is a member and referred to by the rate tariffs to which it is a party. In this manner, the public is charged with the knowledge of carriers' operating rights. Under Section 222 (c) of the Act, shippers are made liable, equally with carriers, for any wilful violation of the law; hence it is important that the shipper inform himself either by reference to a directory or by obtaining a written statement from the carrier of the extent to which the carrier may legally serve him and thus avoid any appearance of asking the carrier to depart from the terms of his certificate.

Wherever possible, it is advisable to choose a carrier that offers a single line service from origin to destination, particularly on shorter hauls. Needless interchange only serves to slow up a shipment and may operate to increase freight charges, for there are some class rate scales which are higher for joint hauls than for single-line hauls between the same points, especially below Class 50. When it is absolutely necessary to route over two or more carriers, reference should be made to the specific routing published in connection with the rates, either in the same tariff or in routing tariffs referred to by the rate tariff. Unless these routes are used, combination rates over the point of interchange will apply or the initial carrier may find it impossible to turn the freight over to the second carrier specified. Trailer interchange between carriers is becoming more widespread, but is by no means universal; therefore, it will pay to ascertain whether the routing chosen for truckload shipments provides for through movement in the same trailer, thus saving time and minimizing the opportunities for loss and damage.

Of course, it should be remembered that, unlike Part I, Part II of the Interstate Commerce Act does not confer upon shippers the right to route shipments when two or more motor carriers are required to move them to destination. However, most reliable motor carriers will respect shippers' wishes in this regard wherever possible in the interest of good customer relations, although they will not divide the haul with another carrier when they can reach the destination direct. The Commission has ruled that when the initial carrier selects another carrier or carriers to handle a shipment beyond its line, *it must protect the application of the lowest through charges and to do otherwise is an unreasonable practice in violation of the Act.*

In selecting a motor carrier routing, thought should be given to whether a carrier providing specialized services might be desirable. For example, there are operators specializing in heavy hauling and the transportation of outsize articles such as poles, timbers and pipe. They furnish equipment especially designed for such work, sometimes equipped with winches and cranes for loading and unloading.

Another specialized group consists of tank carriers who will undertake to move almost any liquid and even some free-flowing dry commodities. In addition to speed and flexibility, an advantage of using this type of carrier instead of shipping tank cars by rail is that in most cases the carrier furnishes the tank trailer, whereas railroads do not hold themselves out to furnish tank cars.

Still another group of specialized operators is the automobile transporters. Nearly everyone is aware of the huge, clattering rigs that take new automobiles from factories to dealers' salesrooms, but few realize that, in addition to these initial movements, many automobile transporters have rights for secondary movements, too. They offer two services: *truckaway,* in which two to six vehicles are loaded on a specially equipped trailer; and *driveaway,* in which the transporter merely furnishes a driver and, if two vehicles are handled in tandem, towing equipment. Thus, portions of vehicle fleets or the personal automobiles of transferred employees may be moved from one place to another at a fraction of the cost by rail. Transporters' rates are published to apply on automobiles, trucks, tractors, trailers, chassis, cabs, bodies and parts thereof.

In the selection of any motor carrier, it is important to ascertain the amount of cargo insurance it carries. The Interstate Commerce Act and many state acts provide that certificates may not be issued to a motor carrier or remain in force unless the carrier complies with such rules as may be prescribed for insurance. However, the minimum cargo insurance has been set at extremely low figures and while the larger motor carriers have substantial coverage, some of the smaller lines cannot afford the premiums on policies of this size. If the value of the cargo offered exceeds the amount of insurance carried by the motor carrier, the carrier should be informed so that he may arrange for additional coverage, both for his protection and the shipper's. *The amount of insurance carried in no way limits the carrier's liability for loss or damage, for it is 100 percent liable for the value of the goods, subject only to the exceptions set out in the bill of lading contract.*

Household Goods Carriers

Of all the specialized services available to shippers, none merits more thoughful consideration than those of the common carrier van lines and household goods movers. These carriers have developed into a fine art the transportation of those commodities they are certificated to handle and the alert traffic manager will acquaint himself with the ways they can serve his company. For example, he should be aware of the advantages of having the traffic department make all necessary arrangements for the handling of household goods for employees who are transferred from one location to another.

The average employee has no means of judging the reliability or studying the rates of available carriers. At a time when his mind is occupied with many other particulars, he may be persuaded to order unnecessary and costly special services and without knowledge of the carrier's operations he may suffer delays in the picking up or delivery of his effects. He may experience difficulty in obtaining satisfactory settlement for goods damaged in transit.

In the hands of the traffic department, such moves may be confined to routing via well known van lines of national reputation. Shipments may be timed and coordinated to avoid such extras as warehouse storage or paying for expedited service on smaller lots. If shipments are made in the name of the company, they may be released to the cents per pound valuation which produces lowest rates and any excess may be covered by the company's transportation insurance policy. The responsibility for the handling of claims for loss or damage is assumed by the company, thus assuring proper preparation and prosecution.

A standard set of instructions should be developed and a copy attached to every order for service forwarded to the van line or moving company. Such instructions could well be set up along the following lines:

SHIPPING VIA VAN

1. Prepare and pack goods for shipment.
2. Ship prepaid on Uniform Household Goods Bill of Ladding.
3. Show shipper and consignee as "(name of company) account (name of employee)."
4. Release shipments to value producing lowest rates.
5. Do not furnish separate transit insurance.
6. Have bill of lading signed by the employee or a representative of (name of company).

SHIPPING VIA OTHER SERVICES

1. If you are instructed to forward any part of employee's belongings via other services, charges are to be prepaid and shipments are to be released to the lowest value provided in governing tariffs.
2. Obtain notation of damage and inspection report on any goods arriving at destination in damaged condition.

SERVICING APPLIANCES

(Under this heading list any instructions for the servicing or packing of appliances such as refrigerators, freezers, washing machines, television sets and antenna as may be appropriate.)

GOODS TO STORAGE

(If goods are to be stored temporarily, the mover should be instructed to inform the company of the name of the storage company selected unless the right of selection is reserved to the company. This heading also should contain instructions as to insurance while in storage, delivery from storage and billing of charges for storage services.)

GOODS TO RESIDENCE

(When shipment moves to employee's residence, mover should have instructions as to services desired at that point, such as unpacking of goods, setting up furniture, removal of packing materials and installation of appliances.)

DISPOSITION OF DOCUMENTS

(There should follow instructions as to where to send invoice for services, bill of lading, delivery receipt, freight bill, scale ticket and inspection report.)

The employee likewise should be furnished with information as to what the van line has been instructed to do for him. He also should be instructed to verify number of shipping containers packed by the van line; to avoid entrusting to the van line any jewelry, valuable papers or perishables; to report shortages or damage; and to refrain from ordering the mover to do anything which would alter the instructions given by the company.

Both sets of instructions should be modified and adapted to the policies of individual firms. *The important feature of traffic department control and household goods transfers is that both employee and van line are fully aware of what is to be done.* The development of this control can do much to keep transfer costs at a minimum.

Although these carriers customarily are thought of as being in the business of moving uncrated personal effects and contents of homes, *they are not confined strictly to household goods,* but may be used for many other articles, including office furniture, office machines, delicate instruments and advertising displays. Their rates are published to apply on:

(1) Personal effects and property used or to be used in a dwelling when a part of the equipment or supply of such dwelling;

(2) Furniture, fixtures, equipment and the property of stores, offices, museums, institutions, hospitals or other establishments when a part of the stock, equipment or supply of such stores, museums, institutions, hospitals or other establishments;

(3) Articles, including objects of art, displays and exhibits, which because of their unusual nature or value require specialized handling and equipment usually employed in moving household goods.

Household goods carriers' rates run much higher than those of general commodity carriers, but since this type of service obviates expensive packaging and provides for inside pickup and delivery, their use often can be justified if the commodity to be shipped falls within the standard household goods description quoted above.

Freight Forwarder

Although freight forwarders are regulated under Part IV of Interstate Commerce Act, they are not carriers in the same sense as the other transportation services discussed in this book. They consolidate smaller shipments into more economical shipping quantities and, as discussed in Chapter 5, they derive their profits from the spread between the rates charged the shipper and the total cost of operation, including charges paid to the underlying carriers, which may be railroads, motor carriers, other carriers, or combinations thereof.

As pointed out in Chapter 5, their rates are not always competitive with those of other services, but they do offer definite advantages. One is speed; shipments travel from origin to destination almost as fast as carloads do. Another is free pickup and delivery at the premises of shipper and consignee. Still another is assumption by the forwarder of full responsibility for the shipment from shipper's to consignee's places of business. A firm may welcome the opportunity to give all its shipments to a forwarder in one pickup each day instead of attempting to distribute them among several motor, rail, air, or water carriers.

In cities where forwarders maintain terminals, pickups usually are made in their own trucks or in those of an affiliated company or a local carrier operating under contract. At more distant points they designate motor common carriers as their agents and may have arrangements with several such carriers serving a single city. When shipments are tendered to motor carriers for delivery to forwarders, the forwarder should be shown on the bill of lading as the receiving carrier and the motor carrier should sign it as agent for the forwarder.

There are many freight forwarders operating in the United States, some of them on a nationwide basis, others on a more limited scale and still others specializing in the handling of a single commodity or group of commodities, such as paper. Among the nationwide forwarders are ABC-Trans National Transport, Acme Fast Freight, Inc., Republic Freight Systems and Universal Carloading and Distributing Company. Those with somewhat restricted coverage will include Clipper Exxpress, Merchant Shippers, Western Carloading Co. and others. In order to provide a more frequent service at lower cost than each could furnish singly, two or more forwarders will sometimes pool their available freight (joint load) for movement between terminals. Section 404(d) of the Act permits this and the practice is particularly advantageous at smaller terminal cities.

The introduction of Plans II½, III, and IV piggyback service by the railroads was widely acclaimed by the freight forwarders as a boon to their operations and they utilize these services extensively. The resulting economy and flexibility has enabled them to considerably extend their publication of volume rates, including a large number of such rates with minimum weights comparable to those applicable by truck.

Freight forwarders should not be confused with non-profit shippers' associations which, although they operate on freight forwarder principles, are not subject to regulation under the Interstate Commerce Act. These are discussed earlier in this chapter and in Chapter 9.

Parcel Post

Parcel post was originally designed primarily for small packages, but sizes and weights thereon have increased to a fair extent in recent years. Federal laws and regulations establish parcel post as fourth-class mailing matter. First-class is regular sealed mail and postal cards. Second-class is newspapers and periodicals. Third-class is unsealed envelopes containing announcements, advertising matter, books, catalogs and circulars, merchandise, seeds, plants, and so on, weighing less than 16 ounces. Complete information on parcel post regulations is outlined in the *United States Postal Manual* (see Chapter 14).

The weight and size of parcels which will be accepted for mailing depends upon the class of post office from which the parcel is mailed. Parcels mailed at a first-class office for delivery at another first-class post office are subject to the following:

Limit of weight—40 pounds
Limit of size—84 inches length and girth combined.

Parcels mailed at or addressed for delivery to other than first-class post offices and rural routes are subject to the following:

Limit of weight—70 pounds
Limit of size—100 inches length and girth combined

Post office service includes free delivery, but shippers must take packages to the post office at their expense. There is no limit on the amount of parcel post that can be shipped to any one consignee on the same day. COD shipments may be made in specified amounts at fairly low costs. Special handling service is available for fees ranging from 50¢ to $1.00 per parcel. This provides preferential handling to the extent practical in dispatch and transportation, but does not provide special delivery. Special delivery in limited territories related to the destination post office may be arranged for fees ranging from $1.25 to $2.15. Parcel post shipments are rated *per parcel;* there are no *lot shipment* provisions. United Parcel Service charges are competitive with charges for uninsured parcel post. Distinctions between regular mail and air mail are no longer particularly applicable domestically but continue overseas. Much domestic mail now moves via air.

Insurance is provided by the Post Office Department upon payment of additional fees based on the following scale:

Maximum Liability	Fee
$15.00	40¢
Over $15.00 not over $50.00	60¢
Over 50.00 not over 100.00	80¢
Over 100.00 not over 150.00	$1.00
Over 150.00 not over 200.00	$1.20

The maximum insurance obtainable from the Post Office Department is $200 per package. Commercial insurance for amounts in excess of $200 per parcel post package is not always practical because of reporting requirements for each shipment or the fixing of values as a basis for premium payments. Some shippers of high-value commodities ship via other modes and obtain protection from them as such or in combination with a blanket commercial insurance policy.

Generally speaking, parcel-post charges are among the lowest applicable via the various services. Parcel-post charges are set up on a zone basis, the zones being delineated on charts and further identified by, and related to, the first three digits on applicable postal zip codes. Zones established for postal rates and the approximate distances are as follows:

Local

Zones 1 and 2	Up to 150 miles
Zone 3	Over 150 miles, not over 300
Zone 4	Over 300 miles, not over 600
Zone 5	Over 600 miles, not over 1,000
Zone 6	Over 1,000 miles, not over 1,400
Zone 7	Over 1,400 miles, not over 1,800
Zone 8	Over 1,800 miles

Information on checking parcel post rates involves basically the use of the official zone chart from the office of mailing to the office of address. (The Official Parcel Post Key for the origin city was formerly used for this purpose.) Official zone charts may be obtained free by request to the postmaster at the office of mailing. Data there are to be related to zip codes to determine zones; zones in turn are to be related to tables of parcel post rates by zones; and the final charges are calculated by multiplying the rates with the pounds involved.

A loose-leaf United States Postal Manual is available which contains extensive information on parcel post and mail regulations. It goes into the subject from many different angles, some of them quite removed from average industrial traffic requirements. Pamphlets are issued from time to time, one being "Domestic Postage Rates & Fee" Notice 59 (July 1976) and another "International Postage Rates & Fees" Publication 51 (July 1972). Depending on involvements, these time-saving pamphlets as updated may be sufficient. Further the postal people have a position that, under the law, only they can carry the mail or its equivalent. Industry activities at times becomes involved with this and possibilities of difficulties in this regard should be borne in mind.

With mailing costs increasing and the new postal legislation (see subsequent paragraphs) many traffic people may find themselves in the positions of being able to assume more helpful roles to their companies in the mailing of circulars, advertising, price information, and other items as well as letters and parcel post. The pamphlets just mentioned, as well as the Manual proper, can be worth while in this regard. Appropriate uses of second and third class privileges as well as of the numerous exceptions and special provisions and services that are applicable may result in valuable savings.

Industry postal relations will undoubtedly be affected in many ways by the "landmark" legislation covering parcel post and mailings generally which went into effect July 1, 1971. It is far reaching and created a United States Postal Service (USPS) with broad powers over rates, services, facilities, and operations of the nation's mail. USPS superseded the Post Office Department.

Important industry help went into the legislation. A prime purpose for which it was passed by Congress and signed by the President was to set up postal operations in ways more closely comparable to those of business. Key features of the law include provisions for a gradual decline in postal subsidies with all such subsidies to end after twelve years. At that time the Service would be expected to be self-sustaining. An independent five-member rate-setting board and a nine-member Board of Governors were specified to help in attaining those goals.

The new organization has been active; more liberal parcel sizes and weights have been established; rates have been adjusted; pick-up schedules and mail classifications have been stream-lined and improved. Political and other problems have arisen, however; the financial look-ahead is clouded; competition has increased. Much more needs doing by the Service.

Water

This chapter will discuss only domestic water services, as international trade routes are covered in Chapter 16, which deals with export and import shipments.

Water routes provided the backbone of intercity transportation in the United States long before the advent of the railroads, and all the principal centers of trade were situated on navigable waterways. But as the railroads and other forms of transportation came into being, the broad importance of the water carriers dwindled until today they are relatively few in number and conduct their operations in a considerably different manner than in the past. Most water service is slower, less frequent and less flexible than that provided by competitors and water carriers generally attract tonnage by publishing rates lower than those prevailing via overland services.

At one time, practically all the ports along the Atlantic, Gulf and Pacific Coasts and the Great Lakes were served by domestic boat lines offering a variety of services. They were "break bulk" carriers, however, and handling and stowing individual packages of freight became so costly that today only limited intercoastal service remains. On the Great Lakes, services are confined almost entirely to bulk commodities such as coal, ore, petroleum and grain.

A lively segment of domestic water trade exists in what is basically container transportation or transportation into which the containers of other forms of transport are melded. Included in this category are rail cars for which service is available so that they may be moved by vessel between the Puget Sound area and Alaska as well as to and from British Columbia Canadian points. Seatrain service between the East and Southwest of this type, which came to involve substantial tonnage and which was started in the late 20's, has been discontinued.

Moving from rails to trucks, adaptations of motor carrier operations to vessel movements are extensive. This is sometimes called fishyback service and is closely akin to piggyback but uses truck trailers on ships instead of flat cars. The service was

Modern water-truck freight operation. Loaded truck being transferred to vessel by land based crane.

originally offered in two forms: "Lift-on, lift-off," which involves movement via vessel of trailer bodies, minus wheels and undercarriages, and the transportation of entire trailers on vessels adapted to roll-on, roll-off operations.

Of the two, the vessel movement of simply the trailer bodies enjoys by far the greater acceptance. Roll-on, roll-off service is available to and from Puerto Rico. Aside from this trade, offerings elsewhere are practically non-existent.

Sea-Land Service, Inc. has operations of the combined vessel-trailer body type between eastern points via the ports of New York and Baltimore on the one hand and southern, southwestern and Pacific Coast points via the ports of Jacksonville, Miami, Long Beach, Oakland and Portland on the other. Sea-Land and several other lines provide this type of service also between Pacific Coast ports and Alaska. Additionally it is available between various mainland United States ports and Hawaii, Puerto Rico and the Virgin Islands. Matson, Seatrain and other companies are also among those importantly involved.

Like rail piggyback, this type of operation provides an economical service between shippers' and consignees' places of business in the same vehicle without rehandling of the contents and with a much smoother ride for the greater part of the journey. It thus minimizes packing expense, pilferage exposure, and loss and damage to the goods while in transit. Claims incident thereto (less than ½ of 1%) are among the lowest in the transportation industry.

The use of "pure" containers on ships is also increasing. These take different forms and may be of wood, metal, plastic, or other materials. They are large and generally arrive at or leave the vessel via rail or truck. A great deal of what is said about similar movements of truck trailers is also applicable to them. Freight routings in which they may be utilized also merit consideration.

Not to be overlooked among the available water services are the barge lines that operate among navigable rivers, canals and intracoastal waterways. They and the bulk carriers on the Great Lakes account for the greatest share of water-borne tonnage. There are a few barge lines that have joint routes with rail and truck connections, but in the main their business consists of port-to-port operations. Modern barges are huge affairs, capable of loading some 1,500 tons of freight and volume is a very important consideration in the use of this type of service. The most attractive barge rates are named in connection with minimum weights of from 300 to 1,000 tons.

Domestic water carriers, subject to certain exemptions as to bulk haulers and others, are regulated by the Interstate Commerce Commission as set forth in Part III of the Interstate Commerce Act. Joint services of water carriers with rail and truck lines are subject to the conditions of the Uniform Straight Bill of Lading as prescribed by the rail and truck classifications (See Chapter 4 and Appendix 1). Bill of lading provisions limit carrier liability for the water leg of the move except when tariffs are applicable which provide liability exists. When indicated, insurance should be obtained for this feature.

Ocean-going carriers such as the intercoastal operators are subject to FMC jurisdiction. Thus port-to-port rates do not include marine insurance, for shipments are subject to the conditions of the ocean bill of lading as reproduced in Appendix 2. Separate insurance against the perils of the sea, etc., must be arranged and its cost taken into account in deciding on the use of these services.

Still other cost factors must be considered in connection with these port-to-port rates. Port tolls, wharfage and lighterage, as well as unloading and loading of cars and trucks are to be added (except in those comparatively rare cases where a vessel is able to tie up to the private dock bulkhead of shipper or consignee to receive or discharge cargo). Rates for tollage, accessorial services, etc., are published in tariff form by the owners of the facilities, such as port authorities, ship terminals and railroads. Only railroad charges are under the jurisdiction of the Interstate Commerce Commission.

Air

Air cargo services occupy an important place in modern transportation thinking. Cargo space is available on most passenger planes and more than 600 cities are served by several thousand daily scheduled flights. There are also many all-cargo flights operated by the major airlines as well as by airlines solely in the freight carrying business. Additionally, charter services are available and are offered to those whose situations are such they can use them.

Freight routings via air are common and represent a normal ways of doing business with shippers of fresh flowers, electronic equipment, machine parts, perishable luxury foods, automobile parts, periodicals, clothing, film, aircraft parts, phonograph records, and other articles the successful marketing and distribution of which depend on the shortest possible transit interval. As an example, many items in the fresh fish category enjoy practically nationwide distribution, thanks to air transportation, whereas in the past their markets were confined to narrow geographical areas. The use of the airlines for emergency shipments has been going on since they began, and it continues. Routings of that nature include medicines, insecticides for control where stepped up infestations have occurred, and so on. Transit times, emergencies, and the like are, of course, important at times but economies and related considerations are coming more and more to where it is simply good busines to ship by air. The list of commodities being transported is expanding.

A development receiving considerable attention as portending important air freight use is that large body, 747, jet freighters having 212,000 pound pay load and 24,000 cubic foot volume capacities are in domestic service for American Airlines. Pan American and some of the other foreign service lines also have them. Important advantages include that the main cargo doors on these planes are 10' high $\times$ 11'2" wide and accommodate larger dimension loads than were previously practical.

More economical, improved, and larger containers are being utilized. Sizes 8' $\times$ 8' $\times$ 10' (15,000 pound capacity) are coming more into the picture. At hand, also, are those having the same width and height but 20' lengths (25,000 pound capacity) which also interline with other air carriers and have surface and sea intermodal use capabilities. The latter having the 20' lengths are for the large body, 747s. Further, more containers are being used which have pluses in the material handling and protection fields. They are filled at plant site (say, at the end of a production line) and move from there (intact and under lock and key when indicated) through to the consignee's facilities with no further shipper handling.

There have been innovations, also, in the kinds of services made available. Air Parcel Post continues much as it has in the past; packages weighting over 70 pounds and exceeding 100 inches in overall dimensions are not accepted. With air freight, however, most carriers have developed various types of handling to be accorded their tonnage. This is true of the international carriers as well as domestic. Certain types are dealt with on bases calculated to be faster and more convenient than others and charges are made for this. For a shipper faced with effective freight routing such considerations can be important.

Typical of these are arrangements made by one of the domestic air lines involving essentially three categories: express freight, regular freight, and packages. All may move airport-to-

Jet Freighter. Large body, 747, with cargo loading and handling system.

airport or door-to-door. Additionally in various instances they may move beyond the originating carrier's certificated areas via other connecting carriers. This can be into Canada, Puerto Rico, and so on. Most carriers have available what amounts to these three types of service and generally each will be called by some unique, "catchy" name.

Principal differences between express and regular freight schedules are that the former move on a reserved or designated flight which can be specified by the shipper and presumably represents the best available in the way of service and other features that he needs. A surcharge of 30% is made for this. The surcharge is refunded if the shipment does not so move. Regular freight moves in the first flight with space available to the consignee city. Other differences include a requirement that express shipments must be delivered at least 90 minutes before flight time to the originating carrier versus minimum times of from one to three hours for regular shipments.

In the package category parcels up to 50 pounds in weight having total dimensions up to 90″ (with no one dimension being greater than 48″) are accepted. They are to be tendered at the passenger desk at least 30 minutes before the scheduled departure of the specified flight. Costs are $24 to $60 depending on distance and shipments move on the flight specified or a 50% refund is made. At destination the parcels are available within 30 minutes of arrival time.

Non-scheduled contract and charter services are available at most larger points for use in connection with special airlift requirements. These operators have somewhat more flexibility than the scheduled airlines in that they can go anywhere within the area specified in their permits at any time and are not necessarily held to service between specified fixed termini.

Air Freight Forwarders—Operating much in the same manner as the forwarders using surface transportation, the freight forwarders by air specialize in shipments (generally small) which they consolidate into larger ones. Many forwarder rates are the same as or lower than those applicable via regular Airfreight. Their unique position in the air freight picture is outlined in further detail in the previous chapter.

United Parcel Service

A traffic manager's problem on altogether too many occasions may be the small shipment weighing less than 100 pounds. At one time, low charges gave him the choice of Parcel Post, Express, rail or motor truck, but delivery and other problems on Parcel Post packages, changes in express service, the virtual elimination of railroad LCL facilities and the sharp increases in motor carrier minimum charges have operated to make an orphan of the small shipment.

A welcome relief from small-shipment worries has emerged in United Parcel Service which is available on a nationwide basis. Originally conceived as a delivery service for retail stores, this company now operates a common carrier service covering the 48 contiguous states, the island of Oahu in Hawaii where 82 percent of that state's population resides, and the Anchorage area in Alaska, with about 42 percent of the Alaskan population. Interstate service is provided within this territory and intrastate operations are conducted in practically all of the states served. Requests for additional intrastate operating rights are pending.

UPS also offers an air delivery service in 28 states in the East and 5 in the West. It is designated as its "Blue Label Air" service and includes the use of containers in jet freighters. The company's service to Hawaii and Alaska is part of the Blue Label Air operation. Air service is available to all addresses in the 28 Eastern states on a second-day basis, and between these 28 states and the five western states of Nevada, Arizona, California, Oregon and Washington. Rates for Blue Label are substantially lower than charges made by air express companies. Further territorial expansions are indicated and up-to-date information should be obtained when indicated.

UPS will serve any shipper upon payment of a small weekly service charge which entitles the shipper to an automatic daily call by a pickup driver, whether or not there are packages waiting for him. Additionally packages may be brought to UPS offices for handling. There are some 1,000 of these customer counters which operate at every UPS facility. Occasional pickups may be arranged also. An additional fee is charged for this. No package may weigh more than 50 pounds nor measure more than 108 inches in length and girth combined. Inside delivery will be made without additional charge and if delivery cannot be made on the first call, up to two additional attempts will be made. Undeliverable packages are returned to the shipper without charge. Rates are generally competitive with those of uninsured parcel post. They include protection against loss and damage up to $100.00 per package, with additional coverage available at a reasonable charge. UPS billing and other documentation permit the prompt furnishing of information regarding the delivery of any shipment.

Pipe Line

Considerable inter city tonnage is transported by pipe line. Some pipe line companies are common carriers and some are privately owned. Their principal business is in petroleum products but other liquids and even some dry commodities may be handled by them. Rates on petroleum products generally are published per barrel, subject to various substantial minimum tenders ranging from 5,000 to 25,000 barrels. Some pipe line companies maintain "tank farms" for storage at terminals for the accommodation of their shippers and receivers, and some are regulated under Part I of the Act.

Pipeline use in almost every instance involves having large volumes of material available for movement. The number of them and the areas they serve are limited. Also, dealings in this field are technical, specialized, and heavily weighted toward engineering. The fact that pipelines may be used in freight routings, given the right circumstances, is, of course, to be borne in mind. On the other hand, and while they represent an interesting mode of transport, only in comparatively rare and under very special instances may routings via pipelines be practical.

Basic Routing Policy

All of the Class I railroads, many of the smaller ones, a large number of motor carriers, airlines, water carriers and practically all the freight forwarders maintain extensive sales departments, not only in cities along their lines but at off-line points also. Their purpose is to maintain good will among the shippers presently using their services and, perhaps more important, to develop additional business from those and other shippers. They have an uncanny faculty for discovering potential movements of freight, sometimes before the shipper is aware that it exists. Because of the large number of carriers serving even the smaller industrial areas and competing for almost every shipment, it is manifestly impossible for any concern to satisfy all of them. *Yet to maintain a certain amount of flexibility in his shipping arrangement, to have adequate service available in emergencies, and to insure sympathetic consideration of his rate problems, the shipper usually will find it advisable to distribute his business in accordance with a carefully worked out formula and to deal straightforwardly with those whose services cannot be utilized to advantage.*

As a general but by no means inflexible rule, it is good policy to route carload shipments so that the railroad on whose siding the shipper is located receives its longest possible haul. See also information in the previous chapter in this regard. Exception may have to be made when speed is necessary and that railroad cannot provide competitive transit intervals; also in cases where delivery requirements of a consignee demand that the railroad serving it, or the team track on which it takes delivery, be accorded a line haul. Considerably more freedom in the choice of railroads is available when shippers or consignees are located on more than one railroad or on belt railroads which connect with more than one of the railroads serving their respective cities.

In selecting *motor carrier routes,* those carriers maintaining terminals in or nearest the shipper's town are likely to be entitled to preference. They are most easily reached by telephone for pickups and forwarding information and they usually can get their vehicles to the shipper's place of business more quickly and without having to travel empty for long distances. Of course, in the larger cities, where there may be dozens of terminals, quite likely it will be necessary by more or less arbitrary means to narrow the choice somewhat.

Customers and suppliers, too, should be made aware of a concern's routing policy; otherwise confusion is likely to result. (See also relations with other company departments, Chapter 14). For example, if facilities for handling either rail or truck shipments are limited and the facts are made known to suppliers, there will be a much greater disposition on their part to cooperate, even on material bought FOB destination, than if orders carry flat instructions as to which type of transportation to use. One large steel producer has incorporated in its sales agreements a statement to the effect that its facilities for shipping by truck are limited and that orders bearing motor carrier routing will be accepted subject to possible delay or change in route. This type of frankness will gain far more in good will than it will lose in sales and is likely to be accepted with greater tolerance than will a practice of disregarding customers' routings without explanation. Then too, if certain carriers are known to provide the most reliable service at point of origin, customers buying FOB that point will welcome the benefit of the shipper's experience and usually will arrange their routing accordingly.

Tonnage Distribution: A judicious tonnage distribution policy will insure a fair and equitable division of the total inbound and outbound tonnage among all competing carriers that can be used to advantage. The actual mechanics of setting up such a policy will vary widely according to circumstances, but some companies do so by favoring carriers according to (1), service, (2), cooperation on rate and classification problems, etc., (3) size, and (4) other special considerations. One large company has developed a system that works nicely in its case. The railroads, for example, are divided into regional competition groups, such as C&O-B&O, ConRail, etc., and each road in a group is assigned a predetermined percentage of the total number of carloads handled by that group. The percentages may be altered to conform to changed conditions. They also may be weighted in favor of those roads serving plants or other facilities of the company and the size of the railroad may be taken into account. A report is prepared monthly showing actual percentage received by each carrier and the traffic manager thus is enabled to issue routing instructions adjusting each railroad's share to the predetermined percentage. The same principle may be adapted to motor carrier tonnage.

In the distribution of tonnage, care should be exercised to refrain from distributing it so widely that the carriers favored do not receive enough to enable them to consider the business worthwhile. Obviously, it is wasteful to use a dozen different carriers if each receives but a few hundred pounds per pickup or delivery. Although common carriers theoretically are obligated by the terms of their certificates to handle all shipments within the scope of their authority and published rates, they can hardly be blamed for losing interest in an account which they cannot serve profitably.

The true advantage of effective tonnage control is the "two-way street" results. A traffic manager who knows how much of his tonnage goes to each carrier and can shift it from one carrier to another when circumstances dictate is in a position vastly superior to that of a man who has only sketchy facts and no solid control. His *total tonnage* at all locations can be used to help obtain needed relief at any one of the points under his control. *Customer relations* generally are on a much higher level where the traffic manager is in complete control and operating under a policy which is equitable from the viewpoint of his own company, as well as that of the carriers.

A discussion of tonnage distribution would not be complete without mentioning the current situation regarding reciprocity. Activities of the Department of Justice and the I.C.C. on the subject have increased, the focal point being shippers' sales to carriers of carriers' needs where the shippers also use the carriers for freight movements. Investigations have been made, suits filed, consent agreements entered into, and so on.

Guidelines are not clear or firm on these matters and some industries are more prone to reciprocity entanglements than others. Where possibilities of involvement exist and such has not been done, a traffic department's number one step is to secure guidance from its legal colleagues and possibly from other associates.

Proper and reasonable help from traffic to marketing in this field certainly should not be questioned or felt out of order. As with the I.C.C., where transportation can help it should do so. On the other hand, at times unwarranted interpretations of activities occur. This and other reasons may make it "the thing to do" for the traffic department simply to "open doors" for marketing or, conceivably, maintain a complete hands-off position in reciprocity matters.

7

PACKAGING, LOADING AND
MATERIALS HANDLING

IT IS THE PURPOSE OF THIS CHAPTER TO PROVIDE THE TRAFFIC
manager with a basic outline of packaging, loading and materials handling functions as they affect traffic management.
Hopefully it will lead the serious student to explore the subject
more broadly. Also, this entire handbook is a recommended
study for the packaging engineer whose decisions will then be
based on a better understanding of their effect on traffic managers' operations.

In the opening chapter of this book, it was pointed out
that management of traffic in industry is primarily the complicated problem of securing proper transportation. For example,
it was noted that the traffic manager "must be equipped to
supervise and perform" a number of functions which include
"collaboration with packaging and materials handling engineers." In such collaboration the collective ultimate objective
of the several departments involved must be the over-all effectiveness and economy of the entire program, all in the interest
of maximizing company profits. Broad understanding, appreciation and respect for the problems of all departments involved
is called for. What is wanted eventually is not the lowest freight
rate or the lowest container cost but the lowest over-all cost of
safely distributing the product to ultimate consumers.

The Packaging Problem

The problem that confronts the packaging engineer and his collaborators is a complex one, not solvable through the application of any simple formula. Briefly stated, it is:

"To develop an optimum combination of all the factors concerned with the physical distribution of merchandise from the last manufacturing operation to its ultimate delivery to the consumer."

No attempt will be made to catalog all such factors but certainly high on the list in the sphere of responsibility of the packaging engineer would be the following:

A shipping container that provides low:

(a) Purchase cost.
(b) Packing labor cost.
(c) Sealing or closure cost.
(d) Tare weight.
(e) Cubic displacement.
(f) Rates for chosen means of transportation.
(g) Materials handling cost.
(h) Warehousing cost.
(i) Loss and damage experience.

A shipping container that provides:

(a) Customer conveniences such as reuse possibilities or ease of opening.
(b) Merchandising appeal—miniature billboard or display, etc.
(c) Satisfaction of the personal prejudices that may be encountered in certain areas.
(d) Complete conformance to classification regulations of the carriers.

Obviously no single method of packaging will be likely to offer maximum advantage in all the above areas but they do serve as objectives nevertheless.

One new phase of packaging that is growing in importance is the problem of what size package is most desirable at destination. It is not now considered good policy to pack in units convenient to the factory, but not convenient to the ultimate customer. The factory should not pack in units of fifteen if the customer can better use units of twelve. Similarly, while the factory may be able to handle units weighing 200 lbs., the customer may be much better off with 50-lb. units. Consideration of the customers' needs may help reduce over-all warehouse or handling costs substantially by greatly reducing broken lots at branch warehouses.

It is likewise apparent that traffic management has a distinct interest in many aspects of the final shipping container specification. This specification will affect the final cost of transportation through such factors as weight, size, applicable rates, and loss and damage potential, and others. Only through the understanding collaboration of all parties concerned can the optimum over-all solution to this complex be attained and thereby yield maximum profit to the company.

Too often the packaging problem is over-simplified by management, and a simple but costly result is obtained. Packaging engineers possessing adequate skills have proved their worth and the profession is gaining increased stature at a rapid rate. Universities are including the subject more and more in their curricula and are giving it greater stress and attention. Many short courses and seminars are finding students eager for up-to-date knowledge in the field. Most engineers now actively engaged in packaging have moved into it with backgrounds of education in the older orthodox branches of engineering or with industrial experience only. Their packing know-how has been largely gained by years of experience, which is an all-important requirement because of the great diversity of problems and the many methods of solution. Not only must the packaging engineer know containers, he must also have a rather broad comprehension and knowledge of industry, efficient manufacturing procedures, distribution, and product characteristics.

A great deal of assistance in training personnel and in designing and applying containers is available from container suppliers. Many "box" companies maintain staffs of expert designers broadly familiar with packaging problems. The larger companies usually provide laboratory test facilities and engineers for the evaluation and performance testing of various designs and constructions. Many such laboratories are certified by the National Safe Transit Committee (NST) and can test and certify the adequacy of containers in conformance to the NST standards covered in detail later in this chapter.

Organization of Packaging Function

As is true of the traffic function (See Chapter 14), there is no universal or generally accepted pattern of organization for the packaging function. There are many points of similarity in the two fields such as the need for centralized control, the desirability of having available extensive files of reference material, scarcity of specialists, etc. While this similarity exists between the two functions, the uniquely specialized nature of both is usually recognized by the use of separate staffs. Despite overlapping areas of interest in regulations and objectives, the best over-all job will be accomplished when there is complete understanding, mutual assistance, and collaboration between the Traffic and Packaging groups.

Loss and Damage Claims

Since loss and damage experience often strongly influences both packaging and loading decisions, we will discuss them briefly.

Loss and damage claims paid by the carriers run into millions of dollars (see below.) The trend of claims continues to show a disturbing growth. Frequently in the past the blame for loss and damage has been directed almost solely toward packaging, with the contention that it must be improved. While some claims undoubtedly have been caused by improper or inadequate packaging, extensive investigations conducted jointly by the carriers and the fibre box industry proved that many other causes are of far greater importance. Since the traffic manager is usually charged with the responsi-

Loss and Damage Claim Payments—Certain Carriers		
Year	Rail (1)	Motor Carrier (2)
1970	$228,316,389	$42,277,664
1969	210,100,163	39,850,012
1968	181,995,567	32,357,146

(1) Source: Association of American Railroads (AAR).
(1) Source: American Trucking Association (ATA). Selected items from 57 reporting carriers.

bility for handling and collecting claims, it is important that he be able to recognize the real facts. He should be in a position to promote whatever corrective action is proper rather than being stampeded into the belief that this or that specific cause is the sole culprit. Money spent on excessive packaging will be wasted if, for example, a poorly designed conveyor system is causing damage to the product in the movement to the shipping department.

Claims shown in the tabulation on page 166 tell only part of the story. To these must be added losses sustained by other motor lines and other types of carriers. Facts regarding these untabulated losses are not adequately compiled. Some idea of the enormity of the over-all loss, however, is given from simply the above figures and the millions of dollars spelled out in them. Additionally, these represent sharp increases; claims paid on rail shipments alone were $89 million in 1950 and $120 million in 1960.

Dramatic as these figures are, they probably do not begin to cover the actual losses. The cost to American shippers and carriers may well be in the billion dollars per year area. Careful studies indicate that the total costs of claims average about five times the actual claim dollars paid out by the carriers. Since those claims for all methods of transport can conservatively be estimated to have been at least 10% over the total for railroads and trucks combined, there is a base figure of $250,000,000 which multiplied by five yields a one and a quarter billion total. Adding to the conservatism of the figure with which we start, Chapter 8 points out that the preparation of papers for loss and damage claims is a tedious, expensive procedure, resulting in many companies placing limits under which they will not file claims. Some companies place these limits at figures well above $25 per shipment. Such practice emphasizes the high cost of servicing claims and also means our indicated total is probably well below actual.

The billion-and-a-quarter figure is an attempt to consider the effect of all aspects of the cost, and not just claims paid out. It is based on a report prepared for the National Safe Transit

Committee. The investigation indicated that actual paid-out claims had to be multiplied by five to cover the attendant cost of clerical help, investigation of facts, loss of profits, etc., not recompensed. While it would be impossible to certify such figure, when one considers the many intangible but nevertheless costly results of lost or damaged shipments, it is believed such a figure is entirely justified and reflects the true importance of taking all necessary steps to avoid loss and damage in shipment.

What Is Packaging?

Packaging of the products of industry may be broadly defined as:

"The preparation of merchandise for shipment and marketing involving the provision of necessary and appropriate protective enclosures or bindings to shield it against damage or loss from anticipated handling, storage, and transportation hazards, and to facilitate rapid and economic handling during storage, shipment, and delivery to ultimate consumers."

In industry the terms packing and packaging are used interchangeably to cover the same areas. For simplicity, we have used the term packaging only herein to cover all phases of this topic. It is well to keep in mind, however, that the armed services distinguish between the two terms as follows:

Packing—Application or use of exterior shipping container and assembling of packaged items, or items not requiring packaging, therein, together with necessary blocking, bracing or cushioning, weatherproofing, exterior strapping and marking of shipping container.

Packaging—The use of protective wrappings, cushioning, interior containers and complete identification marking, up to but not including the exterior shipping container.

Packaging in its broadest concept performs many functions. Even a simple listing of major ones is impressive.

1. Protects against rough handling and resulting shocks.
2. Protects against dirt, dust, moisture and other contamination.

3. Prevents pilferage or tampering.
4. Safeguards hazardous materials.
5. Simplifies and makes more efficient piling, warehousing and inventory control through standard shipping units.
6. Defines unit of sale.
7. Provides product identity and definition of quality, quantity, size, etc.
8. Aids merchandising in various ways, particularly by means of the "miniature billboards" attractively printed shipping containers provide.
9. Builds customer good will through convenient reuse features of containers.

It is quite apparent that packaging plays a very important multiple role in the safe, efficient movement of goods from source to ultimate user. It is, therefore, a subject of vital concern to those engaged in industrial traffic management.

The availability of modern, low-cost, high-performance shipping containers has done much to make most of our mass production industries possible. Without such means of assuring the safe delivery of merchandise in good order, we would be severely limited to commodities grown or manufactured in our own immediate communities. Volume of production at any single plant would be restricted to the volume that could be delivered and sold in the immediate vicinity.

Container Regulations

To successfully handle his job, the packaging engineer must be thoroughly familiar with all rules and regulations affecting the design and specification details of shipping containers and methods of closure and reinforcement approved. Since the traffic manager is also vitally concerned with all rules and regulations affecting the shipment of merchandise by various carriers, and is expected to be an expert in the interpretation of these rules, this is an area of strong mutual interest and one providing an opportunity for very effective collaboration. Some of the more common of the many types of shipping containers and container materials available have been mentioned through the text. The traffic manager would be well advised to become familiar with these, at least to the extent of readily recognizing the different types and appreciating properties and differences. This is an area in which the packaging engineer can be of assistance both as an instructor and through reference to suitable literature.

Good sources of general information regarding specific types of materials and containers are the publications put out by industry groups or companies. An excellent example of this is the Fibre Box Handbook compiled by the Fibre Box Association, 224 South Michigan Avenue, Chicago, Illinois 60604, which is available from its members. This publication includes definitions of terms, industry practices, illustrations, and pertinent information regarding a great many standard styles of containers and reproductions of the carrier rules specifically applicable to the construction and use of corrugated fibreboard containers.

The Association also publishes a manual, "Certifications and Other Markings for Fibreboard Boxes," which covers rail, motor, air, express, parcel post, and federal shipments. Such certifications are discussed later in this chapter and are important. Rail, common carrier motor, and REA classifications require that these certifications and markings be of the form, size, type, and wording shown therein and provide that failure to comply with requirements may subject the user to penalties of substantial percentages of the freight charges. A further publication is the Association's "Showcase 70's" outlining packaging innovations, new box types, and so on, which are developing in the field.

Estimates have been made that over 95% of packaged freight moves in corrugated fiberboard containers. It is in order, therefore, to refer to the corrugated container and rules governing its use as examples to pinpoint the discussions that follow.

The assumption is frequently encountered that the provisions included in carrier regulations constitute an all inclusive and safe guide to use in judging the adequacy of a given shipping container. This is not correct. Rule 41 of the Uniform Freight Classification is an important example of the inadequacy of rules alone.

Rule 41 specifically covers the construction and usage of corrugated and solid fibre shipping containers. A rule, such as Rule 41, intended for broad, general application, must be essentially a minimum rule, and Rule 41 is often spoken of in those terms. A more precise definition of what is meant in such a statement has been given by a spokesman for the container industry as follows:

"A minimum Rule 41 is a fibre box specification which in all weight brackets provides, in the bare box, a degree of protection adequate to assure safe delivery of that broad group of easily handled products which makes up the largest part of the volume of merchandise moving in fibre boxes, during transportation cycles involving normal hazards."

Shipped articles vary widely in their characteristics, all the way from coal, sand, and other bulk raw materials requiring no packing whatsoever, to examples of delicate electric gear requiring maximum protection against every known hazard. The hazards to which packed products may be exposed also vary widely both in nature and degree. The definition of a minimum Rule 41 given above, however, attempts to qualify all of these variables so that an adequate concept of the limitations of the minimum rule may be obtained. With these limitations in mind, one can proceed with the development of proper specifications to do a job.

It is extremely important that the packaging engineer and others in the organization who may influence his judgment recognize that in applying a minimum rule of this character, adjustments to fit each case must always be given consideration. For example, it may become necessary to provide increased container values for easily damaged contents or to overcome unusually severe hazards. This may have to be done either by providing greater performance values in the box itself or through the provision of special inner packing. Likewise, if we have a rule that is not completely wide open as to its minimum requirements, it can become necessary for the ruling agency to make exceptions, permitting the shipper of merchandise requiring little or no protection to use a lower-strength container in keeping with the needs of that merchandise.

It is completely incorrect to conclude: "Rule 41 says I can ship 65 pounds gross weight in a box whose dimensions add up to 75 inches, made of board testing not less than 200 pounds per square inch bursting test; therefore, such a pack is suitable for my product, regardless of what it is!"

Such fallacious thinking is often met and management pressure will be encountered to implement such conclusions. While usually not extended to the complete limits as was done above, it results in a continuing emphasis on reduction of margins between the actual facts and the limits of the rule.

Determination of Packaging Specifications

We have pointed out that container construction and container use must conform to requirements of a number of rules, but we have also shown that adherence to only the obvious letter of the law is of little merit as a criterion of shipping container adequacy. Instead, the packaging must consider many factors and, through the application of certain basic principles of protection, ingenuity of design and analysis of the economic feasibility of alternative approaches, arrive at a practical answer.

Taking Rule 41 at face value, it might appear that the only characteristics of the product the packaging engineer must consider are weight and size. Studying the matter further, one will find that the classification contains certain special provisions for a few specific commodities because of special characteristics they possess. However, nowhere in the classification will one find a list of any of the additional characteristics that must be considered, or what to do about them. Selected commodity characteristics for consideration and action appear in the following list but no claim is made for its being all-inclusive.

SELECTED CHARACTERISTICS INFLUENCING CONTAINER SPECIFICATIONS

Weight
Size
Proportion
Design
Shape
Strength
Fragility
Value in dollars
Urgency of need (intrinsic value)
Physical form—liquid, granular, solid, etc.
Susceptibility to contamination
Raw material or finished product

Finish
Set up or knocked down
Unusual hazards, explosives, poisons, etc.
Types of transportation to be used
Trade customs
Manufacturing setup
Storage and distribution setup. Storage life.
Sales practices
Appearance and other merchandising features
Reuse features

The foregoing factors are concerned with the merchandise itself and the conditions or practices surrounding its handling. While those dictate how it should be packed, recognition should also be given to the specific nature of outside factors or hazards that can produce loss or damage. These also dictate the degree of protection to be provided in a package. While hazards vary, both in nature and intensity, they can be broadly classified into seven basic types.

BASIC HAZARD TYPES

1. Piercing blows or pressures.
2. Crushing blows or pressure from heavy loads.
3. Impacts creating shock.
4. Impacts creating rupture or breakage.
5. Contamination.
6. Marking or imprinting through abrasion or pressure.
7. Theft or tampering.

It should be apparent that a single blow or impact may, and usually does, induce several types of hazards that could result in a multiple failure. For example, a container dropped several feet and landing on a corner may ultimately suffer damages described in hazards 2, 3, 4, 5, 6 and 7.

Reversing the above thought, it is well to keep in mind that failure to perform satisfactorily in service is seldom the exclusive result of a single simple hazard. Since many hazards are influenced by poor loading, it is appropriate to discuss this here. Extensive research by the Fibre Box Association in co-operation with the railroad classification committies (Transportation and Packing Survey) some years ago developed certain important and interesting findings which can be of considerable assistance in planning for low-damage performance. These may be summarized as follows:

1. Extensive damage in carload shipments usually results from multiple causes. Cars arriving in good order averaged one-half of a damage cause per car. Cars arriving in poor condition resulting in large claims averaged two damage causes per car or four times as many (See also Loading).

2. Certain damage causes are more serious than others and can be counted on to almost invariably result in damage to the shipment and bring about claims. Broken floor racks in refrigerator cars are an example.

3. Much damage results from careless disregard of obvious details that should be corrected primarily by shippers and carriers such as leaky cars, lack of doorway protection, etc.

4. Nearly every commodity has its critical hazards in combinations peculiar to it. When these hazards are encountered, major damage results. Other hazards will cause relatively minor problems. The peculiar characteristics of a product must be given special attention during package design, car loading, and bracing.

5. Hazards which cause the greatest damage to containers are not necessarily the ones which cause the greatest damage to contents or the largest amount of claims. Frequently, however, there is a close parallel.

The knowledgeable methods engineer learns early in his career to ask himself several all-important questions before he does anything else in making a study of a job: "Is this operation necessary? Can it be eliminated? If not, how can it be improved?"

Likewise, a packaging engineer should ask critically, "Does this part require packaging? If so, what can we do to reduce the need for protection, or to avoid elaborate and expensive container construction, unnecessary weight, etc.?"

To implement this critical approach to the packaging problem, the properly organized company will see to it that its packaging engineering function is so closely correlated with its product design function that this entire packaging question is properly considered and answered while the product is in the design phase. After design is standardized and parts are in production, it is too late for the packaging engineer to make a maximum contribution to cost reduction.

Having crystallized his problem, the packaging engineer has many materials, styles, and designs of containers to choose from. Irrespective of which one he selects, the successful pack, or packs, must provide an adequate degree of protection against physical damage as well as perform the other functions we have noted.

Adequate protection is the result of the proper application of 15 fundamental principles of protection. Every successful low damage container incorporates these principles in its design and construction to the extent demanded by the product characteristics and shipping hazards to be met. Application of these principles, and measurement of the success of their use, is an involved technical subject that space does not permit covering in this text. It is believed, however, that an understanding of their significance can be obtained from a listing of the names of the principles and the result that is accomplished through their proper application. Such an outline follows:

1. Enclosure—The contents have been enclosed by suitable materials and structural design.
2. Compatibility—All packaging materials used are compatible with the contents of the container.
3. Retention—The container incorporates this strength characteristic to the extent needed to prevent loss of contents from any normal cause or their exposure to contamination.
4. Restraint—The container was so designed and built as to eliminate or control all undersired movement.
5. Separation—Adequate dividers, cushions, or other provisions have been made to prevent undesired contact of parts or surfaces.
6. Cushioning—Adequate resiliency or cushion has been provided

in proper parts of the container structure to prevent damaging shocks from reaching the contents.

7. Clearance—Void space or distance has been provided between articles and container walls, etc. to reduce the possibility of damaging contact from any cause.

8. Support—Container and interior packing provides necessary support to resist all stresses and loads that may be imposed as in stacking.

9. Position—The container is arranged and built so that the weakest parts of contents receive the greatest protection.

10. Non-Abrasion—The container incorporates provision to prevent rubbing and marking of critical areas.

11. Distribution—Supporting surfaces contact areas of sufficient size to reduce intensity of pressure to acceptable levels.

12. Suspension—Contents are hung from container in such a way as to prevent abrasion, shocks, and/or contract with critical areas.

13. Exposure—Containers are provided with openings where visual observation of the contents or ventilation is required for maximum safety of contents.

14. Closure—Containers have been adequately closed and sealed, reinforced or otherwise secured against opening.

15. Instruction—Containers include adequate identification, instructions and information regarding contents and their proper storage and handling.

The Real Packaging Equation

The preceding sections have demonstrated there is no simple single mathematical formula for container construction based on weight and size limits only, or for that matter, any other group of variables. Rather, the design must be based on sound fundamentals. On page 177, an attempt has been made to visualize all of this into what might be called the "real packing equation." It is not an exact mathematical formula, for often there can be many usable answers to a given problem. While Rule 41 has been used as this example, any other similar rule or specification could be inserted in its place with equal validity.

The great majority of specific containers used by industry fall in the #3 class of specifications, i.e., they exceed minimum

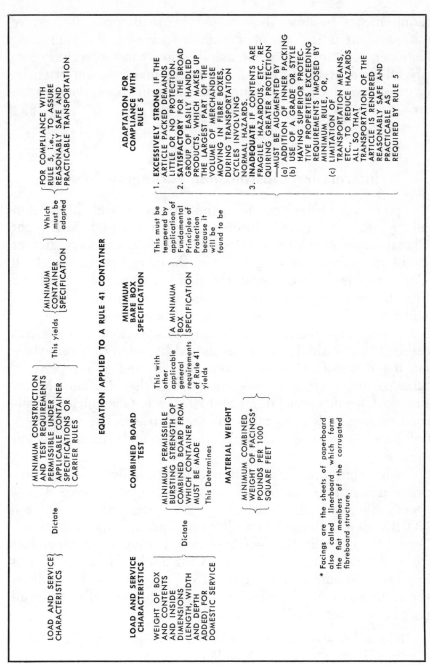

LOAD AND SERVICE CHARACTERISTICS } Dictate { MINIMUM CONSTRUCTION AND TEST REQUIREMENTS PERMISSIBLE UNDER APPLICABLE CONTAINER SPECIFICATIONS OR CARRIER RULES } This yields { MINIMUM CONTAINER SPECIFICATION } Which must be adapted { FOR COMPLIANCE WITH RULE 5, i.e., TO ASSURE REASONABLY SAFE AND PRACTICABLE TRANSPORTATION

EQUATION APPLIED TO A RULE 41 CONTAINER

LOAD AND SERVICE CHARACTERISTICS

WEIGHT OF BOX AND CONTENTS AND INSIDE DIMENSIONS (LENGTH, WIDTH AND DEPTH ADDED) FOR DOMESTIC SERVICE } Dictate {

COMBINED BOARD TEST

{ MINIMUM PERMISSIBLE BURSTING STRENGTH OF COMBINED BOARD FROM WHICH CONTAINER MUST BE MADE } This Determines

MATERIAL WEIGHT

{ MINIMUM COMBINED WEIGHT OF FACINGS* POUNDS PER 1000 SQUARE FEET }

This with other applicable general requirements of Rule 41 yields

MINIMUM BARE BOX SPECIFICATION

{ A MINIMUM BOX SPECIFICATION }

This must be tempered by application of Fundamental Principles of Protection because it will be found to be

ADAPTATION FOR COMPLIANCE WITH RULE 5

1. EXCESSIVELY STRONG IF THE ARTICLE PACKED DEMANDS LITTLE OR NO PROTECTION.
2. SATISFACTORY FOR THE BROAD GROUP OF EASILY HANDLED PRODUCTS, WHICH MAKES UP THE LARGEST PART OF THE VOLUME OF MERCHANDISE MOVING IN FIBRE BOXES, DURING TRANSPORTATION CYCLES INVOLVING NORMAL HAZARDS.
3. INADEQUATE IF CONTENTS ARE FRAGILE, HAZARDOUS, ETC., REQUIRING GREATER PROTECTION —MUST BE AUGMENTED BY
   (a) ADDITION OF INNER PACKING
   (b) USE OF A GRADE OR STYLE HAVING SUPERIOR PROTECTIVE PROPERTIES EXCEEDING REQUIREMENTS IMPOSED BY MINIMUM RULE, OR,
   (c) LIMITATION OF TRANSPORTATION MEANS, ETC., TO REDUCE HAZARDS ALL SO THAT TRANSPORTATION OF THE ARTICLE IS RENDERED REASONABLY SAFE AND PRACTICABLE AS REQUIRED BY RULE 5

* Facings are the sheets of paperboard also called linerboard which form the flat members of the corrugated fibreboard structure.

The Packaging Equation, Basic Equation and Application

requirements because they would be inadequate if it were otherwise. It is the job of a trained specialist, the packaging engineer, to determine what specifications most effectively satisfy all parts of the formula. The traffic manager can often be of great assistance in reaching sound overall conclusions in this area.

Interpreting Classification Packaging Rules

The many rules governing the packaging and shipping of merchandise have been briefly listed in Chapter 3, Freight Classification. It is believed desirable to discuss in some greater detail the several rules governing shipping containers of all kinds. However, because of the dominant use of corrugated fibre boxes in the shipping of packed merchandise, emphasis will be on fibre box construction, use and application. Comment will be limited to the Uniform Classification, which covers railroad rules only. However, it should be noted that very similar, if not identical, constructions are required or accepted by other carriers such as the motor carriers in their National Motor Freight Classification (Items 200-297), etc. Generally the railroad packaging is acceptable to other carriers. The opposite is not always true, so specific regulations should be checked when in doubt.

The Uniform Classification catalogs under some appropriate description practically every article of commerce. If not specifically covered, an article may be acceptable under the NOIBN description (Not Otherwise Indexed By Name—see "Using the Classification"—Chapter 3). Packaging requirements for each article are listed, along with applicable ratings. It is important to note that the type of container used often affects the rating. Because of this fact, it pays to carefully study all possibilities, for example:

> Item 51280—Harness or saddlery NOIBN may be shipped in bags, bales, boxes, crates or Package 903.

The same rating applies to all of the five methods of packing; but

> Item 23340—Chloroform NOIBN: Technical grade provides for several ways of packaging with different ratings and carload minimums applicable as follows:

	Rating LCL	CL Min. Lbs.	Rating CL
In carboys	100	30,000	70
In containers in barrels or boxes	85	36,000	45
In bulk in steel barrels, also CL in tank cars, Rule 35	55	36,000	35

The decision as to whether an article shall be shipped set up (SU) or knocked down (KD) also has an important bearing on ratings, i.e.,

> Item 66810—Tractor seat cabs may be shipped either SU or KD; LCL in boxes or crates, CL loose or in packages. The SU/KD provision, however, has a major effect on ratings and minimums as follows:

	LCL Rating	CL Min. Lbs.	Rating CL
SU	200	10,000R	85
KD	100	24,000R	55

Typical "conditions" covering packaging requirements include the following: In boxes or crates; in bundles; in machine pressed bales; in bags, bales, barrels or boxes or in Package 806; loose or in packages; etc.

A casual review of classification rules or attempt to check the specific needs of a given problem in packaging is difficult for the uninitiated. This is due to the fact that the requirements are scattered in various rules and parts of the classification. Further, the implications of certain words and statements are not entirely clear or perhaps have not been defined. This situation has been improved considerably in the last few years, with respect to Rule 41, by a broad revision of the rule by the Classification Committee. This revision was based on recommendation of the Technical Committee of the Fibre Box Association. The changes were devoted entirely to clarifying the requirements, no change being made in the actual specifications themselves. Included was the addition of many definitions of terms whose specific significance was not clearly apparent in the rules heretofore. Another survey concerned with still further revisions is under way.

Following is a brief review of all of the Uniform Classification rules which deal specifically with packing and shipping container construction:

Rule 2: Provides that when different types of packing affect ratings, the description of packing must be shown on shipping papers. Carriers also have a right to inspect shipments to determine that they are properly described.

Rule 4: Carriers may refuse freight liable to damage equipment or other freight. The packing used may affect a decision in this connection.

Rule 5: Contains important general requirements for the acceptance of freight for transportation by rail. It points out that packing requirements in the classification provide the minimum protection that must be afforded in all cases. However, shipping containers must also be made of materials and construction of such strength as to afford safe handling, reasonable and proper protection of the contents and to protect against damage to other freight or equipment. The carrier may refuse to accept a shipment unless its preparation will render the transportation thereof reasonably safe and practicable. These provisions must be constantly kept in mind because they are an overriding requirement applicable in all cases.

Rule 5 lists and explains the various types of packing which are considered equivalents and the ratings or descriptions that will apply when certain methods not provided for a given article are used. Rule 5 also provides in Section 3, for shipment of fibre boxes in bundles as substitutes for bales or bundles of various kinds and for shipments in drums as substitutes for barrels, and so on. This section should be carefully studied if one is making use of any of these methods.

It is a general principle that if freight is not properly prepared in accordance with the classification requirements, freight charges will be increased 20% on LCL or any quantity and 10% on carload over rates provided for the same articles when shipped in conformity with specific regulations. Section 4a of Rule 5 covers the basis for such charges when various types of containers are used.

Rule 6: Improper or inadequate marking can be a serious cause of loss and even damage in shipment. Rule 6 provides regulations for the marking of freight and particularly requires that packages containing fragile articles or articles in glass or earthenware must be marked "Fragile, Handle With Care," or with similar precautionary marks.

Rule 19: Since advantageously low ratings are applicable to certain items when shipped knocked down as compared with set up, this rule is important. It provides that the bulk of the article must be reduced at least 33% from its normal shipping cubeage when set up for it to be classified as "knocked down."

Rule 21: Provides the definitions of terms "Nested" or "Nested Solid"—Conditions that are often present in the packing of many items such as sets of bowls and other hollow-ware. These again affect ratings.

Rule 22: Wooden articles in the rough, in the white or finished. The condition of certain wooden articles also determines how they may be packed and ratings which apply. The applicable terms are defined in this rule.

Rule 39: Calls attention to the fact that explosives or other dangerous articles will be handled and transported by rail carriers only when all rules and regulations covering containers, etc. as specified by the appropriate tariff have been followed. It provides that when a commodity description in an explosives tariff differs from that in the classification, the former is to be placed in the bill of lading and followed by the latter in parenthesis. These regulations take precedence over any of the rules in the classification. They are quite specific, are rigidly enforced, and are currently receiving extensive attention by the Department of Transportation.

Rule 40: Sets forth specification requirements for a great many miscellaneous types of shipping containers and covers broadly all types except fibreboard boxes dealt with in Rule 41 and fibre barrels, drums, pails and so on, dealt with in Rule 51. Fibreboard boxes with wooden frames are specified in Rule 40, but the fibreboard from which they are made must conform to requirements of Rule 41. Other provisions of general interest include those applicable to single trip containers and their limited re-use, reconditioning of drums, and the like. The principal types of containers covered by Rule 41 in some detail include:

Wood and part wood boxes of various kinds; crates; pails, ferkins, kits and tubs; barrels, casks, drums, hogsheads, kegs, tierces; aluminum barrels, drums, and kits; drums with polyethylene inserts; plastic drums; combined cord fabric and rubber drums and bulk shipping containers; jacketed metal cans; glass and plastic carboys in drums and boxes; fibreboard and veneer drums; paper bags of various kinds; compressed felted pails; and others.

Rule 41: Has been discussed in some detail in the illustrations of the application of packing regulations given heretofore. It provides an elaborate set of requirements to be followed in the construction and use of corrugated and solid fibre boxes. Minimum fibreboard requirements and size and weight limits are specified for a wide range of gross weights as shown on page 183, which is reproduced from Section 3 of Rule 41 as it appears in the Uniform Classification.

These requirements are basic, together with the provision that the corrugating medium must be made of board not less than .009 inch thick, weighing not less than 26 pounds per 1000 sq. ft., and of quality sufficient to produce finished board of adequate rigidity.

When the term fibre or fibreboard is used, it means either corrugated or solid fibre. Corrugated has largely supplanted solid fibre in the market place, however, due to its many advantages.

It is required that fibre box manufacturers certify the materials and construction of boxes manufactured in compliance with Rule 41 and other provisions appearing in the classification. The illustration on page 184 is an excerpt of Rule 41 re this

RULE	SUBJECT	APPLICATION

SECTION 3.-All of the following requirements must also be complied with. Minimum combined weights of facings or component plies must be increased,where necessary,to meet tests specified.

	Corrugated Fibreboard			Solid Fibreboard
	Single Wall	Double Wall	Triple Wall (See Note 5)	

Maximum Weight of Box and Contents (Pounds) (See Note 7)	Maximum Inside Dimensions (Length, Width and Depth (See Note 4) (Inches)	Minimum Combined Weight of Facings (Pounds per 1000 sq.ft.)	Minimum Bursting Test of Combined Board (Pounds per sq.in.) (See Notes 1 and 3)	Minimum Combined Weight of Facings Including Center Facing (Pounds per 1000 sq.ft.)	Minimum Bursting Test of Combined Board (Pounds per sq.in.) (See Notes 1 and 3)	Minimum Combined Weight of Facings Including Center Facing (Pounds per 1000 sq.ft.)	Minimum Puncture Test of Combined Board (Inch oz. per inch of tear) (See Notes 2 and 3)	Minimum Combined Weight of Component Plies (exclusive of adhesives) (Pounds per 1000 sq.ft.)	Minimum Bursting Test of Combined Board (Pounds per sq.in.) (See Notes 1 and 3)

TABLE A.-For all fibreboard boxes other than those described in Section 6,Par.(k).

20	40	52	125	....	....	....	....	114	125
40	60	75	175	....	....	....	....	149	175
65	75	84	200	92	200	....	....	190	200
90	90	138	275	# ① §110 117	275	....	....	237	275
120	100	180	350	# ① §126 153	350	....	....	283	350
140	110	....	....	222	500	....	....	330	500
160	120	....	....	270	600	....	....	360	600
275	120	....	....	....	....	264	1100	....	....

TABLE B.-For double thickness score line boxes,described in Section 6,Par.(k).

| 225 | 60 | 138 | 275 | # ① §110 117 | 275 | .... | .... | 237 | 275 |
| 300 | 60 | 180 | 350 | # ① §126 153 | 350 | .... | .... | 283 | 350 |

① Boxes bearing box maker's certificate indicating applicable minimum combined weight of facings prior to August 28,1969 will be accepted for transportation until January 1,1970.

§ The matter subject to this reference mark is continued in effect under the terms of the order of suspension in I&S Docket No.8495,and,unless it is sooner cancelled,changed or extended,will expire with August 3,1970.

The matter subject to this reference mark is under suspension in I&S Docket No. 8495. Unless sooner cancelled,changed or postponed it will become effective on August 4,1970.

(Rule 41 continued on next page)

For explanation of abbreviations and other reference marks,see last page of this Classification.

Excerpt, Section 3, Rule 41, Uniform Classification. Highlights of Fibre Box Minimum Specifications

RULE	SUBJECT	APPLICATION
41	CORRU-GATED OR SOLID FIBRE-BOARD BOXES	*(see content below)*

CERTIFICATE OF BOX MAKER

SECTION 4.-(a) All fibre boxes that are made to conform to specifications of this rule must bear a legible certificate of a box maker,guaranteeing that boxes do so conform. Certificate must be of following form,size,type and wording,except as otherwise provided in this section

For Singlewall Boxes   For Doublewall Boxes

For Triplewall Boxes   For Solid Fibre Boxes

NOTE 1.-On fibre boxes having length of less than 10 inches or width of less than 9 inches, the above certificates may be reduced in size,but outside diameter must not be less than 2 inches.

NOTE 2.-Fibre boxes made in foreign countries and used for freight imported into the United States and conforming with all provisions of Rule 41 need not have certificate of box maker printed thereon,or the box maker's certificate may be printed in the language of the country in which made,provided shipper certifies on bills of lading that the boxes do so conform.

NOTE 3.-The test stated in this certificate must be the minimum required for the gross weight and dimension limit,except as provided in Note 4 of Section 4,and the combined weight of facings or plies must be the minimum prescribed by Section 3. When the actual test is in excess of the minimum test required,the actual test may be stated below the certificate,but in such case all ratings and rules in this Classification as provided for a box having required minimum test will apply.

(Rule 41 continued on next page)

For explanation of abbreviations and reference marks,see last page of this Classification.

Box Maker Certificate Forms for double thickness boxes and specific package numbers.

RULE	SUBJECT	APPLICATION
41 (Con- tin- ued)	CORRU- GATED OR SOLID FIBRE- BOARD BOXES	(See below)

SECTION 4.-Concluded:
(a)-Concluded:
NOTE 4.-On boxes made to comply with Note 4 of Section 3,which permits increase in size when gross weight is reduced,"size limit" and "gross wt. limit" may be omitted,but certificate must otherwise comply with requirements of Paragraph (a) of Section 4,and below certificate must be printed "Conforms to Rule 41,Section 3,Note 4." On boxes made to comply with Note 6 of Section 3,inner and outer box must bear certificate complying with Section 4 (a) and below the certificate on outer box must be printed "Conforms to Note 6,Section 3,Rule 41."
NOTE 5.-On boxes made to comply with Paragraph (c) (2) of Section 5,certificate must show the actual "size limit" and "gross weight limit" authorized by Paragraph (c) (2) and the certificate must otherwise comply with requirements of this Section,and below certificate must be printed "Conforms to Section 5,Rule 41."
(b) Double thickness score line boxes which conform to requirements of Section 6(k) of this Rule must bear a certificate in the following form,size,type and wording:

BOX CERTIFICATE

THIS DOUBLE THICKNESS SCORE LINE BOX MEETS
ALL OF THE CONSTRUCTION REQUIREMENTS
OF APPLICABLE FREIGHT CLASSIFICATION

BURSTING TEST   GROSS WT LT

LBS PER SQ IN   LBS
(Name of Box Maker Guaranteeing Box.)
(City and State in here.)

(c) Fibreboard boxes,including those referred to as "containers,"not authorized by this rule but which are authorized by package number on page   and succeeding pages of Classification, as amended,for some particular article must bear the appropriate certificate in the following form,size,type and wording:

PACKAGE CERTIFICATE

THIS BOX MEETS ALL CONSTRUCTION REQUIREMENTS
OF APPLICABLE FREIGHT CLASSIFICATION
FOR PACKAGE NO. BURSTING TEST LBS. PER SQ. IN.

000   **000**

(Name of Box Maker Guaranteeing Box)

(City and State in here.)

For triple wall boxes,substitute the words "Puncture Test Units" for "Bursting Test Lbs. Per Sq. In." in the above certificate.
Where numbered packages authorize different tests of fibreboard for bodies and caps,test of the body only need be shown.
On boxes made to comply with Paragraph (d),Section 5,Note 2,certificate must be in rectangular form shown above,enlarged to include certification for Package Nos.1304 and 1305. Such certificate must show bursting test,size limit and weight limits.
(d) When used for LCL shipments,boxes which bear certificate prescribed in Paragraphs (a), (b) or (c) and which boxes do not show description of contents must be marked with an identifying symbol or number and identifying symbol or number must be shown on shipping order and bill of lading.

NOTE 7.-Shipments in fibreboard boxes manufactured on or before October 1,1969,and bearing a form of certificate authorized in Section 4 of Rule 41 as of September 22,1968,will be accepted for transportation if tendered to carriers parties hereto before March 31,1971.

(Rule 41 continued on next page)

For explanation of abbreviations and reference marks,see last page of this Classification.

Excerpt, Rule 41, Uniform Classification. Box Maker Certificate Forms.

box makers certificate or "Class Stamp" as it is frequently called. Shown on page 185 is the special stamp used for specially authorized packages or shipping containers which have been assigned a package number. These box makers certificates are assurance to shippers and carriers alike of the containers' compliance with construction requirements laid down in the classification.

Rule 49: This rule outlines the procedures to be followed when "new" shipping containers or loading or bracing methods are proposed. It is important and, at times, is inadvertently overlooked. It provides the shipper with a means of demonstrating his innovations and outlines the permit, certification, and other detailed requirements incident to these matters.

When the requirements of the rule are met, shipments will not be assessed with increased charges usually applied when containers or loading and bracing methods do not comply with classification regulations. The proposed new procedure or container must be of sufficient merit to warrant the test before a permit will be issued authorizing test shipments.

Frequently laboratory tests are conducted to provide evidence of comparative merit of old and new containers and to demonstrate the suitability of the new for the purpose intended. Since test shipments made under Rule 49 usually involve especially designed containers developed for the packing of specific articles (e.g., a refrigerator), the classification committee often provides for their use after approval by setting up a new "package number" with its complete specification in the section of the classification devoted to "Authorized Packages or Shipping Containers." There are some 160 pages of these, incidentally, at the back of the classification, and they are discussed further at a later point in this Chapter.

Rule 50: Provides for including spare, empty containers which may be needed to recondition carload shipments of commodities packed in such containers.

Rule 51: Gives comprehensive specifications for "Barrels, Drums, Pails, or Greaseproof-Waterproof Tubs." These include details for construction, tests, and so on that are required for dry, solid, semi-solid, and liquids, or articles-in-liquid ship-ments.

The foregoing are the classification rules particularly affect-ing containers used for shipment by rail. There are thirteen of them and they have their counterparts in the classification pub-lications of other transportation carriers. The personnel in the traffic, packaging, loading, and materials handling departments should be intimately acquainted with the contents and proper interpretations of these rules.

Authorized Packages or Shipping Containers

In the final section of the Uniform Classification, under the general subject of Packages and Package Specifications, there appear detailed packing requirements for a large variety of situations. Each individual package carries a number and a complete description or specification for the package is pro-vided. The package numbers and descriptions are arranged in groupings or classes.

It should be noted that many fibreboard containers of special construction are included in the groups listed as Boxes, Cartons, Cases, Packages, Wrapped and Miscellaneous cate-gories as well as in the "F" package category. This last class deals specifically with packages for the shipment of furniture, hence the symbol "F".

Bags	starting with #1	Crates	starting with #530
Bales	” ” #88	Cylinders	” ” #572
Baskets	” ” #165	Drums	” ” #575
Boxes	” ” #170	Loose	” ” #644
Bundles	” ” #280	Packages	” ” #677
Cabinets	” ” #431	Pails	” ” #688
Cans	” ” #447	Rolls	” ” #704
Carriers	” ” #464	Trunks	” ” #715
In Cars	” ” #483	Tubes	” ” #721
Cartons	” ” #492	Wrapped	” ” #742
Cases	” ” #512	Miscellaneous	” ” #783

Package Groups (not shown are F Packages starting with
Package 1F for furniture items)

There are several requirements outlined in the preface to this Package Description Section that are important to know about and understand. Because of their importance it would be better if these were set out either as a separate rule or in some other manner to more adequately call them to everyone's attention. The following should be borne in mind regarding them.

These instructions provide specifically that the special packages, shipping containers, or other authorized forms of shipment set forth under these package description numbers may only be used for articles making specific reference thereto in the individual item specifications in the Classification. Furthermore, the individual packages or containers must comply with the appropriate rule governing the construction of that type container unless exceptions are specifically provided in the individual package description. Where a bursting test is shown for containers made of fibreboard, the fibreboard used must meet the requirements of Sections 2 and 3 of Rule 41. If a special bursting strength is required (one not listed in Section 3 of Rule 41) the fibreboard used must meet the requirements of Sections 2 and 3 for the next lower test shown in the rule and must also meet the minimum bursting test requirement of the individual package description.

Package descriptions were an innovation introduced some years ago and give wide recognition to the fact that special or unique designs of containers, including inner packing, are suitable and acceptable for the packaging of certain articles or types of articles. Since these special packages usually offer superior protection due to inner packing or other unique construction details, and often permit heavier weights, greater dimensions, or other advantages, they are generally used in preference to containers that follow the normal limitations of Rule 41 or other applicable rules. Furthermore, their unique designs usually have been thoroughly tested and approved through extensive laboratory evaluation as a preliminary to test shipping experience under Rule 49. They, therefore, offer a considerable degree of assurance of safe delivery under the prescribed conditions of their use. These packages also reveal engineered concepts of construction found satisfactory by others for the indicated use. While copying someone else's container is not necessarily a recommended practice (unless one knows for sure that his problem really is the same), these basic package descriptions do provide an excellent catalogue of approved construction detail that has proven acceptable to the carriers.

Federal Government and Armed Service Specifications

Space does not permit a detailed discussion of this subject, but the requirements of governmental agency specifications are often so different from usual commercial practice that it is important that the existence of differences be recognized and that some comment be made.

In general, shippers should make no assumptions whatsoever regarding the packaging of merchandise to be delivered against contracts with federal agencies or the Armed Services. A proper approach is to determine from the Government Request for Bid, Contract of Order, how the merchandise for a specific order is to be packed. This information in full should be passed along to packaging engineers, container suppliers, etc., being sure to supply all specification numbers with the proper issue date, or amendment information. Suppliers will then be able to consult the proper specifications and thereby comply with all regular and special requirements that may be imposed. A particularly common mistake is for shippers to ask container suppliers how such and such an article should be packed. The container manufacturer is given no information whatsoever regarding the requirements set forth in the government procurement documents. While the correct answer may be forthcoming, one is always taking a chance that special provisions in the contract are being overlooked when the problem is approached in this manner.

Evaluation of Containers

It is costly and time-consuming to determine whether a given new container is satisfactory by building up shipping experience over an extended period of time. If inadequate, important damage in shipment may result and dealers and customers can be turned against the product and sales lost. Such loss of customer good will and product reputation is more serious than the direct money loss and is extremely hard to live down because the time-consuming, annoying inconvenience is long remembered.

At one time little could be done to plan to control damage situations except to depend upon an occasional test shipment. Such shipments were lacking in real significance, however, since one never knew what, if any, hazards the shipment might have encountered in transit. In the intervening years there has been developed a broad list of sound laboratory testing procedures and equipment. Many of these have been thoroughly studied and standardized by such agencies as The American Society for Testing and Materials (ASTM), 1916 Race St., Philadelphia, Pa. 19103 and The Technical Association of the Pulp and Paper Industry (TAPPI), 360 Lexington Ave., New York, N.Y. 10017.

Laboratories equipped with the necessary testing devices and staffed with trained engineers and technicians competent to use them and to analyze the results are available in several areas. Through appropriate testing programs and analysis of the results, it is possible to measure and evaluate the performance characteristics and relative abilities of both empty and packed shipping containers of all kinds. Such data permit comparison between (a) container types and designs, (b) container materials, (c) modifications of the product itself and (d) container performance and established standards.

The planning, conduct, and analysis of tests of shipping containers is a unique technical area. The test concepts are deceptively simple, but certain factors, such as proper conditioning to standard moisture content, are of major importance in securing accurate results. Superficial unskilled performance of tests can yield gross errors, just as in any other field. It is well, therefore, to be sure that container testing programs are handled by adequately qualified personnel.

National Safe Transit Program

Much work in the application of pre-shipment testing designed to assure successful performance of shipping containers in service, has been done under the program of the National Safe Transit Committee. This program had its beginning in excessive loss and damage being experienced in the shipment of many porcelain enameled products. Determined to do something constructive about it rather than accept threatened rate increases, the Porcelain Enamel Institute inaugurated an activity that led eventually to the National Safe Transit Committee and its program.

After a study of container laboratory testing equipment and techniques in use at that time, the committee adopted three procedures as reflecting the principal hazards encountered in shipment: (1) vibration tests, (2) drop tests, and (3) impact tests. The hazards imposed by these test procedures were correlated with the hazards encountered in shipment as to severity, and standards were established to guide the performance of certification tests by the laboratories using them. The tests themselves are conducted in accordance with standard test procedures established by the American Society for Testing and Materials and the Technical Association of the Pulp and Paper Industry.

Upon verification of the capability of the technical staff and availability of authorized equipment, the National Safe Transit Committee awards certificates to qualified laboratories. These certificates permit them to perform tests and to certify as to the performance of specific items of packed merchandise. This program has been successful, as evidenced by the fact there are some 120 certified laboratories and an even larger number of shippers cooperating in the program.

While a substantial adoption has developed with the appliance manufacturers, Committee procedures have been accepted and used on almost every type of commodity. Additionally the program has been given wide approval by the various transportation agencies. The successful passing of the NST requirements for certification is a major step in assuring shippers that their packaging should have low damage experience in shipping.

The Committee states the philosophy back of its program as follows:

"If you will test your packaged products by these test procedures, and identify them by Safe Transit labels, experience has shown that your damage loss and your packaging cost will be acceptable minimums. It is up to each shipper to decide whether or not he will use these test procedures. The program is entirely voluntary and implies no connection with tariffs, freight rates, claim procedures, or any other existing transit regulations."

It should be noted that the procedures are used to determine the ability of the packaged product to withstand dynamic load conditions encountered in transit and in handling. They do not evaluate the packaged products' protection from other damaging conditions such as cargo security, corrosion, moisture, static compression loading, piercing, contaminating odors, failure to observe proper safety precautions, etc. The packaging engineer should determine whether his product requires special protection and whether additional tests are required to assure safe overall performance against such hazards. He should also determine whether it meets carrier classification requirements in all other respects in addition to subjecting it to the standard NST test program.

At left is illustrated the label which may be attached to packed merchandise that has successfully met the established standards of performance when tested by a certified laboratory. A general review of the Committee's functions is currently under way and a move of its headquarters to Washington, D.C., may occur.

Packaging—Export and Miscellaneous

Our comments on packaging should not be concluded without discussing the important subject of export packaging (also see Chapter 17). Specifications for export packaging are not issued in the same manner as for domestic packaging. As a matter of fact the quality and amount of packaging required on export shipments is left (1) to the packaging influence on the insurance rate (established by the insurance underwriter); (2) to the discretion of the shipper; and (3) to the steamship lines' privilege to refuse freight that, in their opinion, is not well enough packaged to withstand the many potential handlings given foreign shipments.

For particular attention in this regard is the hazard of damage from salt water or moisture. Many shippers line their containers with waterproof paper, polyethylene bags, or other water and moisture barriers to protect against this hazard. So, each shipper must develop a package that will deliver his goods to a foreign customer in good condition.

Commodities shipped domestically in fibreboard containers may require further protection for export shipment. If careful handling and good service is available and well-designed heavy duty containers are being used, they may perform satisfactorily on short shipments to favorable ports. If, however, poor or unknown conditions are to be anticipated, alternative plans should be followed. Typical of these are: Addition of steel strapping, overpacking of domestic fibreboard using "V" board weatherproof fibre boxes, nailed wood or wirebound boxes strapped, packing directly in a suitable special export container including wood or "V" board, and others.

Special grades of fibreboard containers were developed during World War II for export shipment of supplies to the Armed Services. Known as "V" boxes, these containers are made of board combined especially to withstand outdoor storage and exposure to the elements. Lighter grades of the same types are identified as "W" boxes. The complete specifications for "V" and "W" boards and boxes are covered in the following Federal Specifications:

PPP-F-320—Fibreboard; Corrugated and Solid, Sheet Stock (Container grade), and Cut Shapes. (Also covers domestic specifications, essentially same as Rule 41).
PPP-B-636—Box, Fibreboard.

Other related Federal Specifications of interest include:

PPP-B-640—Boxes, Fibreboard, Corrugated, Triple Wall.
PPP-B-1608—Box, Corrugated Fibreboard, Weather-Resistant, Coated

The rail carriers follow performance against their packaging rules through Inspection Bureaus, set up on broad territorial bases, and staffed with personnel trained to investigate, review, and help on shipper packaging, etc. at both shippers' and receivers' plants and en route. One such bureau is the Eastern Weighing and Inspection Bureau, with its headquarters at New York, N.Y. The other three are the Southern Weighing and Inspection Bureau, Atlanta, Georgia; the Western Weighing and Inspection Bureau, Chicago, Illinois; and the Trans-Continental Freight Bureau, San Francisco, California.

Tied in closely with packaging and loading is the use of the impact recorder, a small mechanism that shows the force and direction of each impact and the time the impact occurred. Impact recorders are designed today for use in carrier vehicles, such as freight cars or trailers, and inside the packages themselves. The use of impact recorders inside of packages may well be helpful in making over-all studies to determine at which points packages receive the most strenuous handling. Thus, impact recorders placed inside of containers as merchandise comes off the assembly lines will show the force of impacts during warehouse handling, at both origin and destination, as well as while in transit. Some recorders are designed to show if the position of the container is changed, which might be helpful on "This Side Up" freight. Impact recorders used in carrier vehicles will highlight rough handling of these vehicles en route. The use of such an impact recorder is indicated if, upon delivery, damage is consistently detected and there is a feeling that the packaging and loading are satisfactory but perhaps the handling en route is not satisfactory. There are many different types of impact recorders on the market, designed for various uses.

Other allied features are the cushion underframe box and flat cars and those with loading devices such as movable bulk heads, air bags, and so on. Many cars have both types. They are designed to give "perfect product protection" against impact. The cushion underframe cars are equipped with devices that are combinations of hydraulic units and both fixed and movable friction plates. They are hydraulic impact retarders. Movable bulk heads and air bags help in tightening loads so that shifts in lading do not occur and materials arrive at destination in sound condition. More and more of this equipment is becoming available and arrangements for its use where indicated should be made whenever possible.

Loading

The proper loading of merchandise in trucks, freight cars or other vehicles is closely allied with the packing function. In fact, one may consider that the box car or other carrier being loaded is a master container for all of the smaller packages placed in it. As a master container, it is subject to the same analysis and handling as the packing of individual articles. The 15 Fundamental Principles of Protection outlined earlier in this chapter are likewise applicable. These facts are often overlooked so that it has been found that many of the failures in transit are directly traceable to failure to properly prepare and load shipments.

Loading is the art of placing and bracing freight in cars and trucks to get it to destination safely and to comply with the carriers' regulations. It is an accepted fact that shifting of freight in a car is a major cause of damage in carload shipments. A "Transportation and Packing Survey" sponsored jointly by the railroads and the Fibre Box Association found that most damage was traceable to the following causes—shifting of load due to improper handling of the car in transit, loose loading, and poor arrangement of the load. Together these causes accounted for 62% of the damage found during inspection of 3,440 carloads of merchandise.

When the shipment does not fully occupy the floor area of the car it must be blocked and braced with adequate material properly applied. If this is done and that fact established beyond any reasonable doubt, it can be said that any damage in transit must have resulted from exceptionally rough handling by the carrier. Since the most damaging shocks are lengthwise of the car, the packages or pieces making up the shipment should be placed in the car in an orderly manner using, when necessary, bulkheads, gates or steel bands nailed to the sides and floor of the car.

Under Rule 30 of the Uniform Freight Classification (see Chapter 3), railroads provide dunnage allowances up to 2,000 pounds on bracing used in closed cars and on open cars. This is to encourage shippers to do a good bracing job which so often means the difference between "goods arriving at destination in fine condition" or "goods arriving damaged due to load shifting in the car." The dunnage provision is there to be used and is part of the rails' activities to do their share in damage prevention. While a railroad may be liable for rough handling, it is a two-way street, and a shipper who does not exercise care may find himself in a position of having to stand any damage that may be incurred on a basis of faculty loading.

The AAR publishes a series of pamphlets containing rules concerning the loading of specific kinds of freight in or on cars for rail movement. Its Washington office issues a list of all AAR publications. Costs are nominal and those publications that are applicable to a company's business are worthwhile for reference, review, and study. Transportation departments that are involved should, of course, know and comply with the mandatory rules.

The rules governing open-top cars are mandatory. Loadings in this category involve steel products, including pipe, road and farm machinery, lumber, Department of Defense material, and so on. It is imperative that this kind of tonnage be dealt with so that it does not leave the cars, particularly when they are in transit. Open-top car rules are published by the Mechanical Division (59 East Van Buren Street, Chicago, Ill. 60605) as a book and in sections. Six of the sections concern industry and one the military.

Rules involving closed-top cars are not mandatory except where interchanges between carriers may be involved. The possibility of the loading leaving this type of equipment while in transit is not as great. Types of tonnage in this category are numerous and approximately 40 pamphlets are available. They include furniture, roofing felt, small cylindrical steel containers, and so on. Closed top car rules which are mandatory are in General Rules Circular 42D. Pamphlets are published by the Freight Loading and Container Section of the Freight Claim Division, also of the same Chicago address above.

Carload freight and freight too heavy or bulky for handling by the railroad's station forces or facilities must be loaded into cars by the shipper. Freight loaded by the shipper must be stowed in such a manner as to make transportation reasonably safe and practicable. Temporary blocking, bracing, dunnage or supports, when required to protect and make freight secure for shipment, must be furnished and installed by the shipper and the weight of such blocking, etc., must be noted on the bill of lading, as it is subject to freight charges the same as paid on the articles in the car, less published dunnage allowances.

Freight cars must be sealed when loading is completed, and it is important to keep a record of the car seal numbers placed on each car. A seal should be placed on each door. If the car arrives at destination with seals broken and the consignee has a clear record of this, there is good proof that shortages occurred in transit. Freight car seals will be furnished by the carriers' local agent upon request.

One of the primary considerations in good loading is to plan each carload in advance to be sure that there is at least sufficient weight in the car to meet the carload minimum weight required to apply a carload rate. If the shipper fails to do this, he will be shipping short-weight cars, which means he will be paying for "air". This is costly. For example, if an article is subject to an LCL rate of $1.00 per cwt. and a carload rate of 50¢ per cwt., minimum weight 30,000 pounds, the shipper should see to it that his carload shipment has 30,000 pounds in it. If it has 25,000 pounds he will pay for it "as 30,000 pounds," which means he is paying for 5,000 pounds of air as follows:

25,000 lbs.	@ LCL of $1.00 cwt.—$250.00
25,000 lbs. "as 30,000#"	@ CL of 50¢ cwt.—$150.00
30,000 lbs.	@ CL of 50¢ cwt.—$150.00

Of course, 25,000 pounds for $150.00 is 40% less than it cost LCL; but the cost per 100 lbs. figures out to be 60¢, or 20% more than it would be if another 5,000 pounds were shipped.

To assure application of the lowest charges and to conserve equipment, the smallest car that will accommodate the load should be ordered (see Rule 34, Uniform Freight Classification). Reshipping documents and instructions may be forwarded in cars with the articles covered thereby. The same is true of trucks. Actually, much of what has been said before is applicable to motor carrier shipments and may be followed as to them.

Loading freight shipped via motor vehicles will be performed by employees of the carrier from a place on a platform or dock immediately adjacent and accessible to the tailgate of the vehicle or from sidewalk or doorway when packages can readily be handled by the driver. Necessary assistance must be furnished by the shipper for loading heavy or bulky freight that cannot be handled by the driver of the vehicle. Some variances occur in these practices, but basically they are the controlling features of their loading and unloading operations.

The airlines as well as other carriers are moving ahead fast in developing various types of unit loading and containerization. Much of this is discussed earlier in the text. As a part of using the most economical and practical light weight packaging materials for their loadings via air, shippers will wish to bear in mind and observe the regulations of the surface carriers that will handle them to and from the airports.

The governing rules and regulations for transport of cargo via air are promulgated under the auspices of the Air Transport Association of America for domestic routes within the continental United States. A packaging guide, "Packaging for Profit," is available from them, 1000 Connecticut Ave., Washington, D.C. 20036, on a subscription ($3.00 per year) basis. Parts of the guide are general in scope and include maps showing temperature ranges and humidity by months throughout the country. Special treatment in it is given to automobile parts, cut flowers, live animals, and baby chicks and turkey poults.

Palletizing—Pallets are an important element in the science of materials handling so it is debatable whether palletization should be treated under Loading or Materials Handling. In many ways it belongs to both. A pallet is a platform made in various sizes (according to the job at hand) employing one or two load-bearing surfaces separated by members just wide enough to permit the entry and retraction of a fork lift truck's forks. The pallet is designed to permit the handling and transportation of a vertical load placed over practically the entire area of the surface on which it bears.

The timbers between the two platforms are called stringers or runners and the direction in which they run is always known as the length of the pallet. In quoting pallet sizes, it is proper to quote the length first and the width second.

The pallet permits the tiering or piling of its load, known as a pallet unit load, on top of another resting on the floor, or resting on another load. It is like piling one block on top of another. The program known as palletization transforms a building from a square foot area into a cubic capacity. It utilizes the air space of a structure to the highest possible efficiency.

By far the most popular and widely used pallet is the two-way entry stringer design. Next in popularity is the notched stringer design that allows a four-way entry with fork lift trucks only. The least used is the block design which has a full four-way entry for all types of lift trucks. Four-way entry means that the pallet is so constructed that a fork truck can pick up the pallet from any one of its four sides.

Pallets may be purchased in almost any size, but the most popular size for "shipping" pallets is the 48" x 40", with a maximum pallet weight of 90 pounds. This size pallet is universally interchangeable between most carriers whether land, sea, or air. For instance, these dimensions permit use of the pallet two abreast in the 48" dimension, with ample room for overhang, across railroad freight cars. Since the interiors of motor carriers and van containers are not entirely standardized, it permits either two abreast in the 40" dimension or a pinwheel configuration, loading one pallet in the 40" dimension and its neighbor in the 48" dimension. Here, too, there is maximum flexibility and efficient floor utilization with pallet overhand ranging from 0" to 5" in one or more directions.

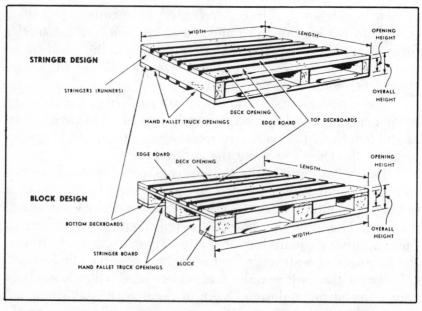

Principal parts and commonly used construction features of the *stringer* "two-way" and *block* "four-way" entrance design pallets.

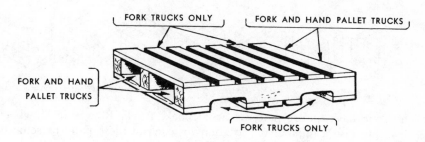

FORK TRUCKS ONLY

FORK AND HAND PALLET TRUCKS

FORK AND HAND
PALLET TRUCKS

FORK TRUCKS ONLY

Courtesy National Wooden Pallet and Container Association.

Notched stringer design allows four-way entry only with fork lift trucks, and two-way entry with hand pallet trucks.

The pallet is designed to permit the handling and transportation of a vertical load placed over practically the entire area of the surface on which it bears. A well built pallet will be designed to support 12,000 pounds static loading. The term "static loading" means the total weight that will rest on the bottom pallet of a pile of two or more pallet loads. In other words, if each pallet load is 2,000 pounds, the 12,000-pound maximum static loading would permit stacking six pallets in one tier, thus placing a 12,000-pound weight on the bottom pallet. A wing-type pallet differs from a flush type in that the runner or stringer is set several inches in from the end board, thereby permitting handling of the pallets by slings, which may be required when loading into ships.

It is important to remember that the bottom deck of a pallet is just as important as the top and is often times subject to more stress in handling and transit. If pallet loads are to be stacked two or more high, it is vital that the bottom deck contain as much surface area as possible to keep it from settling into the package layer directly underneath it.

Think of the right pallet too, in terms of one that will (a) handle as large a load as possible within practical limits, (b) handle materials as few times as possible and (c) utilize mechanical equipment rather than manual labor .

Do not buy pallets on price alone; get the pallet that will

Courtesy National Wooden Pallet and Container Association.

The four basic pallet patterns are: Block, Brick, Row and Pinwheel. There are also a number of variations of each of these patterns some of which leave voids in the center of loads. Block patterns are used for containers or items of equal length and width including cylindrical containers. Block patterns are slightly unstable by nature thus requiring bonding if considerable movement is involved. Brick, Row, and Pinwheel patterns are employed for containers of unequal length or width. All three are customarily arranged in interlocking design which provides a stable load by placing adjoining layers at 90° to each other.

do the job. Also, it should be borne in mind that the kind of wood in a pallet makes a big difference in its longevity.

When pallet loads are placed into a box car the loading time is greatly reduced, because one man with a fork truck can handle a pallet load up to 10,000 pounds in a fraction of the time it would take to handle the same load by individual boxes with a hand truck.

Practically all of the rail tariffs include a provision for free allowances on loaded pallets in carload shipments. This is published as an Exception to Rule 11 of the various tariffs. Many motor carrier tariffs include similar allowances for truckload quantities. These are published as Exceptions to Item 995 in the motor tariffs governed by the National Classification Bureau.

There are three different rules covering rail and motor shipments involving the return of empty, used pallets. One of these is the Free Return Rule, which covers the return without charge of pallets employed in a pool moving in assigned vehicles. Another provides return rates for used pallets substantially below the standard pallet commodity rate.

The third and most recent is known as the "5 for 1 Pallet Rule" and has been adopted by several of the rail freight territories. In essence, this rule allows the free return of 1 car of empty, used pallets for every 5 carloads of palletized freight shipped over the same railroad in the opposite direction. A sample wording of this rule appears in Supplement 54, Trans-Continental Freight Tariff 2-E, Item 468-A and reads:

"Rates contained in this tariff will include the return of pallets, pallet sides, platforms or skids from billed destinations to one origin point via reverse route of that used on one of the cars comprising the inbound movement, subject to the following:

(a) Shipment must be made in one car containing no less than the number of pallets, pallet sides, platforms or skids used in the loading of five carloads of commodities billed at rates provided in this tariff. The bill of lading covering the return movement must show the number of pallets, pallet sides, platforms or skids contained in the car.

(b) No less than five (5) inbound freight bills or copies thereof on which freight charges were computed on a minimum weight or actual weight, whichever is greater, for each car used of not less than 40,000 pounds and dated no earlier than 180 days before the date of the bill of lading covering the return movement. Each freight bill or copy surrendered must show the number of pallets, pallet sides, platforms or skids contained in the inbound car.

(c) Shipments moving under the provisions of this item are subject to Item 833.

(d) No partial unloading in transit privileges on the return movement will be permitted."

Pallet pools can be developed advantageously where two or more companies or plants have a combined two-way pallet need. A pallet pool will operate at maximum efficiency and savings for all concerned if it can be set up with only one type of pallet, i.e., one size, one grade and one design. The pool may be workable with mixed sizes; but standardization is highly desirable.

Some motor carriers do place on their trailers pallets that may be interchanged with an equal number of pallets either at origin or destination. The following pallet interchange rule appears for the account of some 100 motor carriers in Central States Motor Freight Bureau Tariff 500-0 and is a good example of similar rules appearing in other territories:

"This carrier, having equipped certain vehicles with pallets, will furnish such vehicles, when available, upon request. Pallets so constituting part of the standard equipment of the carrier's vehicle, may be removed by consignor, provided such consignor replaces in the vehicle a like number of pallets of identical size and construction, under load; or may be removed by consignee provided such consignee replaces in the vehicle a like number of pallets of identical size and construction, loaded or empty. Pallets so replaced on vehicle will become carrier's property as part of the standard equipment of the vehicle, in lieu of the carrier's pallets exchanged by consignor or consignee."

Naturally, anyone taking advantage of these provisions will have to satisfy the carrier that the pallets to be interchanged are of the proper specifications and in good condition. Some tariffs restrict loading and unloading time to two hours each with charges for detention beyond that period.

Before proceeding to purchase pallets, give all the factors in connection with their use careful study. Look at the kind of movement contemplated, the nature of the material to be palletized and the characteristics of the plant storage areas. Are there fixed or variable paths to travel; what is the distance and frequency of movement; what are the dimensions and density of each commodity? Then note the nature of floors and their capacity weight-wise, per square foot. Floor layouts, aisle space availability, doorways, headroom, supporting columns, elevators, ramps are some of the other factors that may influence a decision on the right size and type pallet.

The importance of selecting the right pallet is further borne out by the general fact that one fork-lift truck will require about 2,000 pallets to keep it busy.

The expendable one-way throw-away pallet made of paper or inexpensive wood is used extensively. It is designed to be used for one warehouse and transportation operation only, and then destroyed. Its cost is about one-third to one-half as much as the reusable, warehouse pallet, its weight much less, and it can be used satisfactorily for loads up to 2,000 pounds per pallet. The saving in labor-handling costs at each end of the movement usually more than absorbs the cost of the pallet. It also eliminates any pallet return transportation expense. There are instances, both domestic and overseas, where some rate concessions are made if cargo is shipped in pallet unit loads.

There are life-time pallets with metal edge clamps, tongue and groove stringers and deckboards. All of the hardware is bolts and teenuts rather than nails.

Pallets have many advantages, such as utilizing air space or the full cubic of a warehouse. The saving in handling goods both by industry and carriers is tremendous. Pallets afford ventilation while goods are stacked in warehouses. They cut down on damage and pilferage.

From the carrier's viewpoint, a properly palletized shipment results in faster vehicle loading and unloading (30-45 minutes) and reduced damage in transit. The key to effective savings is good coordination between shipper and receiver. For instance, the advantages of fast loading and unloading are reduced if a palletized truck must wait in line for hours behind hand unloaded trucks. The solution is bays reserved for palletized freight only. Also, goods must be properly placed on the pallet and securely stowed if damage is to be reduced.

A helpful booklet, *Technical Handbook on Pallets and Palletization*, is available gratis from most established pallet suppliers, or it can be purchased for $1.00 from the National Wooden Pallet and Container Association, 1619 Massachusetts Avenue, N.W., Washington, D.C. 20036.

Other special features of packaging and loading for possible review or attention include the following:

■ *Unit Load*—The term "Unit Load" is used in the strapping industry and does not necessarily imply palletizing. It does describe the bracing of freight in railway cars under the floating load principle. This means fastening two or more packages together by strapping, making them one large unit that is permitted to shift somewhat under impact. This freedom of movement reduces the force of the impact substantially and relies to a great extent on the inertia of the weight concentration of the larger unit. The Unit-Load method of loading cars has been developed to a high degree of efficiency in the handling and loading of such commodities as lumber, steel, paper, bottled goods, furniture, batteries and many others.

■ *Unitization*—This is different than the unit load described above because it applies to any group of packages or pieces fastened together that is shipped as a unit, domestic or overseas. Quite often these are on pallets that are expendable. Such utilization has advantages over containerization since there is no investment in containers, no maintenance and no handling of containers empty or in storage when not in use. An example of an expendable unit-load would be about a ton of bagged material piled crosswise on an expendable pallet. The pile would be topped and sided with heavy fibre board and the whole load steel strapped to the pallet.

■ *Bonded Block*—Another very effective method of loading cars is the "bonded block" method, which is like laying bricks.

■ *Cube Loading*—Identical packages (usually all with the same product) are stacked on pallets or "glued unitized" for handling by grab trucks. These unit loads are stacked so that they can be loaded like blocks or cubes in certain size box cars, filling the cars solidly, with no play or empty space. Thus no bracing or dunnage is required.

■ *Glued Load*—This method requires adhesive with a high shear strength but a low tensile strength. High shear prevents dislodging by lateral force, while low tensile permits easy separation. Glue is applied in two narrow strips 5⁄8″ wide about 2″ in from each side of the box. Thus, during the warehousing and shipping functions, some 20 cartons can be handled as one big carton either by themselves or resting on a pallet.

■ *Bulk Pack*—A development in the packing and loading fields is the Bulk Pack, which is perhaps more of a package than a method of loading. It can be used when the Classification specifies "loose," "in bundles," and where special package descriptions prescribe it. The objective in most instances is to design a large fibreboard box (with whatever interior packaging details are needed) to be substituted for many smaller boxes or cartons.

As an example, a firm manufacturing television speakers has a standard package that meets all carrier requirements and packs four speakers to a carton. For a random lot of 240 speakers, 60 cartons would be needed, equalling 122 cubic feet and weight density of 5 pounds per cubic foot. This would involve light or balloon freight, so that when the speakers are shipped in quantity it would be necessary to pay for air, such as 9,000 lbs. actual weight, shipped "as 14,000 lbs." By packaging the speakers 80 to a bulk pack (45" x 36" x 52" dimensions and 250 lbs. gross weight), it requires only 84 cubic feet for the same 240 speakers and the weight density is increased by 7.2 lbs. per cubic foot. Not only does this reduce the freight charges paid, by shrinking the payment of "air" freight, but it also greatly reduces the "per-speaker" cost of packaging. Another most important advantage is reduction in handling costs in the warehouse and in the factory, since fork lift trucks may be used because of the much larger unit basis than when the same speakers were packaged in 20 separate cartons.

A related development is the use of bulk containers for the shipment and storage of granulated products, such as plastic pellets. While most of these are in the 1,000 to 2,000 lb. range, some have a much higher gross. These bulk containers eliminate the high cost of attending the packing, closure, and handling of many small units. Bulk packs may be mounted on pallets so as to be readily handled by a lift truck. The larger types, however, may be made of rubber or other materials and equipped with lugs for handling by cranes.

Plastic Shrink Wrap Systems. Another interesting development in the package-loading field which is growing in popularity is "plastic shrink wrapping." The system consists of tightly wrapping (or enclosing) with plastic various kinds of shipments to the end that the plastic shrinks, clings, or otherwise closely follows the contour of the lading. A break or tear in the plastic, which ordinarily is readily apparent, indicates possible pilferage or some other occurrence for immediate investigation. At times plastic is used instead of a fibreboard overlap in bulk pack types of shipments.

Containerization

Containers are referred to here as something other than packages, barrels, drums, etc. They are van or shipping containers into which are placed packages, pieces, items, etc. Fibreboard cartons might be on a pallet and the pallet units in turn placed into a container. There are as many ways to use containers as one can imagine. Their use obviously depends on how they affect the total handling and transportation cost of any particular movement. Containers are used to facilitate a through movement, which frequently is from the consignor's door to the consignee's door without any re-handling of the lading. In a sense any over-all protective coverage that facilitates moving goods or units in through transportation at less cost is a container.

In connection with future logistical decision making it can be said that the transport industry has hardly scratched the surface of the ultimate potentials of the container. In warehousing alone the container looms large in future concepts, since there can be no complete mechanization without containers. Cargo security is aided in substantial ways by them. This element, in particular, is assuming increased importance.

Containers of all types have made great progress in recent years. Trailers on flat cars, TOFC service, or piggyback, as forms of containers, have had a meteoric growth. Sea-Land Service, Inc., whose operations are also covered in the previous chapter, has developed in a comparatively short time one of the largest fleets of sea-going vessels which are used for waterborne trailer service. These trailers now include dry cargo, dry bulk, temperature controlled, insulated/ventilated, dry cargo open top, and bulk liquid types of equipment. The territorial extent of their operations is substantial and include domestic and foreign trade.

Large containers (as such and with no prior or subsequent moves on which wheels are attached to them) have developed broad uses and uses that are increasing. The airlines have basically a family of four types for domestic service. The largest of these is of an igloo or hula-hut shape, contoured to fit the interior of the aircraft fuselage and ranges in size from 350 to 625 cubic feet; the smallest is more of a rectangle in shape and has a capacity of 62.5 cubic feet. Not included in these are the belly containers used particularly in the under parts of the aircraft bodies.

Other large containers importantly in this classification are those used in ships, certain rail shipments, and so on. Generally they are used in intermodal trade where two or more types of transport are involved. Common dimensions are 8 feet by 8 feet in height and width, with 20 and 40 feet being their lengths. These quite commonly move within North America to and from the water ports. At least one important company in the business has developed a sophisticated computer system for keeping track of its containers and for its operations generally.

Standardization of containers is important from many angles, perhaps mostly because of the number of different modes of carriers usually involved in one through movement. It is infinitely easier to set up to handle one type of a container than it is to adjust to many different types. The International Organization for Standardization has recommended several types of containers to be used world-wide, and insofar as the U.S.A. is concerned these containers are 8' wide x 8' high with lengths running 10', 20', 30', and 40'. For the most part these containers are metal, though some are made of wood, rubber, or plastics. Some are equipped for reefer and other services and are used domestic as well as overseas.

Standardization needs are reflected from many movements; currently important tonnage is being transported via container truck-rail-truck-water-truck from the midwest to inland Holland, with no handling or rehandling of the lading except the original and terminal loading and unloading.

If containers are to be used, they must contribute to reduce the total cost of the overall distribution, making savings possible for both shipper and the carrier. The principal advantages of containers are as follows:

(1) Reduction in packaging cost.

(2) Reduction in labor cost account less handling.

(3) Reduction in pilferage which is of great importance to both domestic and foreign trade.

(4) Reduction of damage; therefore, fewer claims and lower insurance costs.

(5) From a carrier standpoint, improved equipment utilization; trailers on flat cars are in pay-load use by railroads five times more than are box cars.

(6) Increased efficiency which in many cases will reduce the over-all cost.

There are also reasons why containerization progress has had its difficulties:

(1) Original investment is large because of the high cost of new equipment and facilities.

(2) Maintenance is expensive.

(3) Lack of standardization, including clamps, lifting and other devices.

(4) Lack of coordination between the transportation companies involved sometimes prevents setting up satisfactory interchange arrangements.

Different sizes and types of containers, as well as indications of their various intermodal uses, are shown here. Two "roll-on, roll-off" trailers are included along with 40 and 20 foot "boxes" and even smaller sizes.

(5) Union labor has not always cooperated in working out proposed container services and there have been times when objections have been raised by them.

(6) Even where it is agreed containerization would be good, it has not always been accomplished because no one participant in the movement, either shippers or carriers involved, would provide and maintain it and it could not be worked out where all interests could do it jointly.

A great number of other specialized container applications also exist and they or related ideas behind them are to be kept in mind. One field in which considerable ingenuity has been used is the airline food "portion" business. Outside shipping container involvements there are comparatively remote. The "packages" or trays within them, the transfers to the planes, and the interchange with "finished" trays represent good techniques for adaptation elsewhere when this can be done. National restaurant chains use this plan, too, in their distribution set-up by dropping off freshly loaded container units (some with refrigeration protection) and picking up the used ones. Obviously, good materials handling, along with packaging, are important in many of these situations.

Materials Handling

(See also comments under Loading)

Materials handling is the science of developing most efficient unit loads, improving use of floor and cubic space and professional selection of handling equipment. The development and manufacture of materials handling equipment is a major industry. The wheelbarrow and pry-bar are everyday examples of materials handling equipment, but the range of types with industrial applications is almost endless. These would include: belt, roller and magnetic conveyors; overhead and mobile cranes; fork lift trucks and a variety of mechanized carriers for all types of materials and products; pneumatic loaders and unloaders for bulk granular materials; pallets, skids and dollies; stacking and tiering devices; and so forth.

The materials handling engineer must mechanize a movement-of-goods operation with the objectives of (1) minimizing handling thereby providing increased protection for the material, (2) developing speed in the movement of goods not only by obtaining maximum unit loads per handling but, also, by keeping the equipment working constantly at its maximum potential and (3) obtaining maximum utilization of warehouse space and transportation equipment. Selecting the most suitable materials handling equipment for the job at hand is a primary function. Accomplishments in these areas are sure to result in substantial annual savings.

The first step in improving a handling system is to make a careful survey and cost analysis of the present system. Per unit costs may then be compared, old way vs. new way. It should follow that the unit cost will go down if the quantity handled increases. It has been said that one of the most important prerequisites for the successful materials handling engineer is to have and use a lot of common sense. He must be sort of an efficiency expert, able to study a situation and figure out ways and means to do it better and cheaper. Someone once put it this way, the mostest with the leastest.

First of all, data must be accumulated on each separate move (between successive points of manufacture and storage) about as follows:

(a) Description of material including unit weight, dimensions and over-all volume.

(b) Details of movement: origin, destination, distance, clearances.

(c) Number of employees utilized and time for each employee.

Care must be exercised that any plan developed to save costs does not impair necessary service to factory production and customers and does not involve particular safety hazards to employees.

Selection of the proper materials handling equipment (conveyors, overhead traveling cranes, industrial trucks either hand or power) must not be done hastily. Each type of equipment must be analyzed as to its advantages, limitations, cost and general adaptability. For example, automatic product-lift grab trucks are used to an ever-increasing extent where it is desirable to eliminate the handling and rehandling of pallets and pallet loads. Sometimes it is desirable to start out with a pilot operation on a "trial and error" basis. Frequently the design of a vendor's package must be changed so that incoming materials are received in proper unit packages suitable for power handling. Always remember that one big feature of materials handling is developing unit loads so as to use maximum cubic space; the use of storage to the roof if at all possible can mean good efficiencies. Another phase is loading and unloading shipments to and from carriers' vehicles and equipment mechanically. Constant alertness is needed to assure prompt replacement of obsolete equipment.

Certain features of materials handling are also discussed in Chapter 9. Additionally, The Material Handling Institute, Inc., 1326 Freeport Road, Pittsburgh, Pa. 15238, publishes "An Introduction To Materials Handling" ($2.00 per copy, but single copies will be sent free upon written request) which includes data on recognizing and solving materials handling problems, managing productivity and costs, and appropriately organizing for effective control, presentations to management, and maximum help to other departments. Other publications by them include "Careers With Material Handling Equipment Manufacturers" (single copies free to educators and students, 50¢ each to all others). The institute is a national trade association consisting of over 300 United States manufacturers of material handling equipment, systems, components and normally user specified essential parts. The institute was founded in 1945. A complete list of literature available from it can be obtained by writing for it.

Hazardous Materials

Involvements incident to the transportation of hazardous materials have multiplied in recent years and are treated in a separate chapter which appears later in this text. Included there are the special rules and regulations incident to the packaging and labelling of freight shipments in these categories. The long-time and well-known use of "RED" labels to denote flammables and so on continues. This and other features are discussed more fully in that chapter.

8

FREIGHT CLAIMS

ONE OF THE TRAFFIC MANAGER'S MORE EXACTING DUTIES IS THE recovery of money from carriers for overcharges and for loss of or damage to goods. The success of the claim operation will depend to a considerable degree upon adherence to the procedures outlined in this chapter for each type of claim, as carriers have every right to reject any claim that does not contain full supporting information amply documented.

Freight claims generally divide into two categories: those that involve overcharges on freight bills and those that involve loss and damage to materials shipped. The latter, in turn, divide into ordinary loss and damage situations where the damage is apparent on delivery and those where the damage is concealed and not known until sometime after delivery when, say, a package is opened, a leak becomes apparent, or something else occurs to bring the matter to the consignee's attention. These divisions are hereafter dealt with under general headings. There are certain features of claim work, however, that are applicable to all types of claims or that, perhaps, can best be mentioned at this time and discussions of them follow.

■ *Watch the FOB terms.* Do not spend time and money unnecessarily on claims covering material purchased or sold FOB your plant. Pass your part of the supporting data along to the supplier or customer and let them prepare and prosecute the claims. After all, that is one of the advantages of buying FOB destination, or selling FOB origin. A company selling its goods

FOB its factory is doing so, among other reasons, to relieve it of the responsibility for the cost of, and what occurs in, transit. One company specifies in its general operations manual that overcharge and loss and damage claims shall not be filed by it in these cases and explains that this is more than the views of its transportation people and that it is a company rule with full executive sanction and approval.

■ *Claims Prevention.* Claims prevention is ordinarily associated with such physical matters as better packaging and better handling. It is, of course, important that these have real attention. There are, however, a great number of additional things that can be done, and should be done where practical, to avoid the extra work and expense incident to the filing and processing of claims. These include working with carrier representatives to provide proper freight billings and the checking and correcting to the maximum extent possible of freight bills before they are paid. Available time for paying rail freight bills may be extended to 120 hours when credit is approved under arrangements made since publication of the last edition of this text, and the additional time may well be helpful in reducing claims filed. Other avenues can well include working with marketing and purchasing representatives to approve appropriate FOB terms which reduce claims filed to only those which are necessary. The importance to an industrial company of amounts collected on claims is great, but important also is the realization of those amounts for the company's treasury without time consuming, complicated, and costly claim processing.

■ *Realistic Claim Limits.* Most companies establish freight bill amounts below which bills will not be checked and claim amounts below which claims will not be processed. Some establish one limit for overcharges and another for loss and damage. It is simply good business that this be done, as recoveries that cost more than the checking and processing are obviously not worth while. The limits which are set are generally reviewed at least once a year and in many cases they are spot checked on fairly constant, informal bases by those auditing the bills. The amounts specified as limits vary from company to company. It is not unusual for one division within a company to have one set of amounts and another division a different set. A company's general thinking on matters of this kind is particularly important, along with cost considerations, in establishing limits, and these, plus dealings to be accorded repetitive shipments, spot checks, and other special features, are to be taken into account. Ideally the final judgment on what is specified should be made by the traffic manager in consultation with his treasury colleagues and any others in interest. Simply as information and without suggesting the figures as guides, with one fairly large company a $200 limit for checking bills and a $25 limit for filing claims are currently applicable. Higher and lower limits are used by others, and the specific figures mentioned could well be higher with many companies, particularly in view of cost increases that have occurred.

■ *Rail Claims—Joint Hauls.* Overcharge and loss and damage claims which involve hauls by two or more railroads may be collected from any one of the participating carriers as all have equal responsibility under the law. See Overcharge Mandatory Rule 2, Section A, of Railroad Accounting Rules issued by the AAR Accounting Division and other authorities. This aspect of claims procedures can be helpful and important at times. When one of the participating carriers and the shipper have offices in the same city, claims processing can be handled more conveniently. Also, when one of the carriers goes into reorganization, claims may be collected from the others or, to put the matter another way, when the carrier collecting the freight charges is in bankruptcy the claim may be collected from the carrier at the other end if solvent.

■ *Audit Firms.* Freight bill audit firms have become pretty much a way of life in freight claim work. They operate basically on an understanding that, for a percentage of the recoveries, they will undertake to review a company's freight bills and process to a conclusion any items they find on which overcharges have been made by the carriers. Loss and damage claims are also processed by them under similar arrangements.

Percentage figures are negotiated and are generally in the 30 to
50 per cent area, although they may be higher or lower. Important considerations in setting them are whether the freight bills
have, or have not, been audited previously, whether the bills
involve large freight payments, i.e., $250 versus $1,000, and so
on. Many of these firms provide expert and worth-while services and are used as a means of handling part (or all) of a
company's freight claim work. While at first glance a shipper
may feel it has everything to gain and nothing to lose in these
matters, certain sensitive features can be involved. There may
be times when, for reasons of its own, a traffic department does
not want certain claims filed or processed. Also, the freight bills
which leave the office contain customers' names and other confidential information. These aspects can be of enough importance to some companies to cause them to by-pass the use of an
audit firm. On the other hand, the employment agreement can
provide for the discontinuance without liability of activities on
certain claims at traffic's discretion, and care in the selection of
a reputable audit firm can minimize possible problems incident
to the confidential nature of the data involved. The operators of
many of these firms are men of integrity and reliable. Dealings
with them should be followed periodically to the end that they
are profitable and worthwhile for both parties.

■   *Offsets Not Allowed.* It is illegal to deduct the amounts of
overcharge or loss and damage claims from freight charges on
shipments subject to I. C. C. jurisdiction and within most
states. Such action denies the carrier the right of investigating
the claim to determine its merits. The Supreme Court of the
United States has rendered several decisions on this specific
point. It has held that carriers may not accept service, advertising, property, or releases of claims against them in payment
of transportation. They are required to collect the established
rates and charges on each and every shipment from all alike in
cash or its equivalent regardless of any litigation, claim, debt or
situation on any other shipment or shipments. Possible exceptions exist in a very few states and in other special situations
where litigation on the subject has been minimal.

■ *Ship Cheapest Way.* For a number of reasons some companies may buy materials FOB their destination and specify in the contract of purchase that the materials shall be shipped the cheapest way or via some other means in which the contract provides that the seller shall use the lowest freight rate. In these cases the freight bill becomes part of the final cost and the determination of whether the lowest rate was in fact used by the seller on the shipment to the purchaser becomes an activity of the traffic department of the purchaser. Where the lowest rates are not used, charge backs to the seller or some other method of recoupment is to be employed. The liability to pay the recoupment is, of course, the responsibility of the seller. This, too, can work both ways, i.e., a company may both buy and sell on this basis. It represents a feature to be borne in mind in freight claim work where the practice is applicable. Purchasing and Marketing, in particular, may need help in this regard and care should be taken that this feature is given proper attention.

■ *Undercharges.* On occasion freight bills are paid by shippers which contain charges lower than those legally applicable. Thereafter, through a re-check or otherwise, this becomes known to the carrier and the carrier advises the consignor or consignee of the undercharge and sends him a balance-due bill to bring total charges to the proper amount. Such a balance-due bill represents an obligation that must be paid under the law if the carrier is correct in its position. This is true irrespective of any difficulties or losses that may result to the party liable. As examples, shipper customer accounts may be settled and have to be reopened, or a profit and loss statement may have been issued and have to be adjusted. The signing of Section 7 of the bill of lading (see page 73) operates to prevent shipper liability in these cases and is used to do this. In still other cases undercharges are moot problems for various reasons, and the possibility of difficulties is not important. On the other hand, some companies, because of their situations, tell their carriers when undercharges are observed in their review of the freight bills they pay. The carriers, of course, strive to make their bills right in the first place but slips occur and freight payment work involves appropriate attention to undercharge features where they may be involved.

Some overlapping with what has just been said may occur in the general headings of Overcharge Claims, Loss and Damage Claims—General, and the others which follow. This is minor, however, and the discussions under those headings have been framed to give all help possible on the particular problems that are involved with them. Entire books have been written on various segments of those problems and are available when their use for detailed elaboration is needed. One text in particular, "Paying the Freight Bill," by Traunig and Barrett deals importantly with the far too many, duplicate freight bills that are erroneously submitted and paid.

Overcharge Claims

Claims for overcharge are necessary to adjust carriers' charges to the correct amount when it is discovered that excess charges have been paid as a result of:

—Error in rate
—Error in weight
—Error in bill of lading description
—Duplicate payment of same freight bill and errors in extensions and other calculations.

In each case, the claim must be substantiated by definite supporting evidence. If the rate is incorrect, a detailed statement of tariff authority for the alleged correct rate must be set forth in the claim. Incorrect weights usually will be adjusted only when claim is accompanied by a certificate signed by a sworn weighmaster or other conclusive evidence that the claimed weights are correct. Claims involving a change in bill of lading description will be settled more readily if backed by a ruling from a classification committee, a copy of the invoice, descriptive advertising matter, photographs or other tangible evidence as to the exact nature of the article shipped. Where

Standard Form for Presentation of Overcharge Claims

Approved by the Interstate Commerce Commission; Freight Claim Division, American Railway Association;
National Industrial Traffic League, and the National Association of Railway Commissioners.

C/O 317
(Claimant's Number) §

Mr. R.E. Miller, Auditor   177 X St., Dayton, Ohio
(Name of person to whom claim is presented)   (Address of claimant)

Cross Country Carriers   April 7, 1972
(Name of carrier)   (Date)   (Carrier's Number)

PO Box 91, Centerville, Ill.
(Address)

This claim for $ 38.44 is made against the carrier named above by Ohio Department Store
(Amount of claim)   (Name of claimant)
for Overcharge in connection with the following described shipments:

Description of shipment   Glassware

Name and address of consignor (shipper) Eastern Supply Company, Philadelphia, Pa.

Shipped from Philadelphia, Pa., To Dayton, Ohio
(City, town or station)   (City, town or station)
Final Destination Dayton, Ohio, Routed via Cross Country Carriers
(City, town or station)

Bill of Lading issued by Cross Country Carriers Co.; Date of Bill of Lading March 4, 1972

Paid Freight Bill (Pro) Number 38677; Original Car Number and Initial

Name and address of consignee (Whom shipped to) Ohio Department Store, 177 X St., Dayton, Ohio

If shipment reconsigned en route, state particulars:

Nature of Overcharge Classification and rate
(Weight, rate or classification, etc.)

DETAILED STATEMENT OF CLAIM.

NOTE.—If claim covers more than one item taking different rates and classification, attach separate statement showing how overcharge
is determined and insert totals in space below.

	No. of Pkgs.	Articles	Weight	Rate	Charges	Amount of Overcharge
Charges Paid:	25	Boxes Glassware	825	8.33	$68.72	
		Total	825		$68.72	
Should have been:	25	Boxes Glassware, NOI, actual value exceeding 35¢ per lb., but not exceeding $1.50 per lb.	825	3.67	$30.28	
		Total	825		$30.28	

Authority for rate or classification claimed NMFC A-7, Item 88150, Sub. 2; ECMCA Tariff 31-D
(Give, so far as practicable, tariff reference [I. C. C. number, effective date and page or item].)

IN ADDITION TO THE INFORMATION GIVEN ABOVE, THE FOLLOWING DOCUMENTS ARE SUBMITTED IN SUPPORT OF THIS CLAIM.*

(X) 1. Original paid freight ("expense") bill.
(X) 2. Original invoice, or certified copy, when claim is based on weight or valuation, or when shipment has been improperly
         described.
( ) 3. Original Bill of Lading, if not previously surrendered to carrier, when shipment was prepaid, or when claim is based
         on misrouting or valuation.
( ) 4. Weight certificate or certified statement when claim is based on weight.
      5. Other particulars obtainable in proof of Overcharge claimed: †

REMARKS: Invoice calls for 100 dozen Glass Candlesticks @ $4.55, total
$455.00, or approximately 55¢ per pound.

The foregoing statement of facts is hereby certified to as correct:

Ohio Department Store A P Williams
                            (Signature of claimant)   Traffic Manager

§ Claimant should assign to each claim a number, inserting same in the space provided at the upper right hand corner of this form. Reference should be made
thereto in all correspondence pertaining to this claim.
   * Claimant will please place check (x) before such of the documents mentioned as have been attached, and explain under "Remarks" the absence of any of the
documents called for in connection with this claim. When for any reason it is impossible for claimant to produce original bill of lading if required, or paid freight bill,
claimant should indemnify carrier or carriers against duplicate claim supported by original documents.
   † Claims for overcharge on shipments of lumber should also be supported by a statement of the number of feet, dimensions, kind of lumber and length of time
on sticks before being shipped.
   Claims based on rates quoted in letters from traffic officials should be supported by the original or copies of such letters.

Form No. 2 The Traffic Service Corp., Washington, D.C.

Standard form for presentation of overcharge claims, illustrating manner
of preparation.

duplicate payments occur, the claim papers should be supported by each copy of the freight bills which were paid and, if readily available, a copy of each check (front and back) to support each payment. Overcharge claims may be filed by writing letters in which the basis is fully explained, but they receive much better handling when they are presented on a standard form set up along the general lines of the one shown on page 221. In any case, full identification of the shipment is required by citing the carrier's freight bill or waybill number, or both, and the date thereof, and by specifying the points of origin and destination as well as the shipper and the consignee. Failure to supply this information will delay settlement of the claim, for without it a carrier will find it virtually impossible to locate the transaction in its records.

Most carriers require the surrender of the original receipted freight bill with the claim, but when its loss or other use prevents surrender, they will accept in lieu thereof an agreement on the part of the claimant to indemnify the carrier against loss arising from any subsequent presentation of the original bill. This may be accomplished by signing a separate Indemnity Agreement similar to that shown on Page 223, although the agreement may be incorporated in a firm's printed claim presentation form, abbreviated to read as follows:

> This is to indemnify you against any loss that might arise from payment of this claim when filed without the original bill of lading and/or paid freight bill.

Overcharge claims should include a demand for the payment of interest on the amount of the overcharge at a rate of 6 per cent per annum. There is no statutory basis for this demand and, indeed, motor carriers and freight forwarders seldom pay it. However, the Interstate Commerce Commission has held that such payment of interest does not constitute rebating, and thus the ICC strongly implies that demands for interest are not illegal. The Commission also has held that overcharges refunded within 30 days of their collection are considered cash transactions on which no interest is to be paid. A few railroads resist the payment of interest, but usually they pay at the rate of 4 per cent per annum.

As brought out in Chapter 5, the statute of limitations must be observed in filing overcharge claims, for carriers are forbidden by law to entertain claims filed after expiration of the period provided by the applicable statute. Overcharge claims

Indemnity Agreement

Date..

File No..

We, the undersigned, being unable to produce or supply the..

Company or its connections with the $\begin{Bmatrix} \text{Original Paid Freight Bill} \\ \text{Original Bill of Lading} \end{Bmatrix}$ covering the shipment hereinafter described,

do hereby indemnify and save it, and other interested carriers, if any, harmless from and against any damages

in any way whatsoever connected therewith or arising therefrom. The $\begin{Bmatrix} \text{Original Paid Freight Bill} \\ \text{Original Bill of Lading} \end{Bmatrix}$ cannot be

produced for the following reason:..

DESCRIPTION OF SHIPMENT

Articles..

Consignor.. From..

Consignee.. At..

Date............Car No. and Initial............ Via..

Freight Bill Pro. No..................Date............ Carrier
Issuing Railroad..

Bill of Lading No..................Date............ Carrier
Issuing Railroad..

(Signed)..

Indemnity Agreement

should be filed promptly and without delay simply as a matter of good business and, in some ways, simply because the periods within which they must be filed present the usual problems of inter- versus intrastate requirements, the requirements of one type of carrier versus another, and so on. Some traffic personnel use a "rule-of-thumb" two-year minimum period as applicable in almost all cases. In other words, in "eyeballing" their claims they do not concern themselves with whether they will have limitation problems if the filing is within two years subject to a very few special exceptions. The exceptions where shorter periods govern are minor and involve some airlines which require lesser periods, REA specifies six months from date of payment, and so on.

Actually, there are many cases where the limitation period is longer. The Interstate Commerce Act allows a three-year period with respect to all carriers (railroad, interstate motor carriers, domestic water carriers, and freight forwarders) subject to the Commission's jurisdiction. State law periods vary from two to eight years. Illustrative of the diverse state laws are an Oregon law which allows two years on railroad claims and six on those involving motor carriers, and a South Carolina law which allows two years for motor carriers and six for railroads. Whether longer periods are applicable, of course, becomes important when the two-year "rule-of-thumb" period has passed.

Straight overcharges, the result of charging incorrect rates, should not be confused with reparations, awarded as a result of charging rates found to be illegal. The latter are not handled through normal claim channels, but may be paid only as ordered by the ICC. Comments regarding reparations will be found in Chapter 5.

Loss and Damage Claims—General

Final recourse in loss and damage occurring during transportation is with the courts, and not with the Interstate Commerce Commission. The latter has overcharge claim jurisdiction because of its freight rate regulatory powers. Regarding loss and damage, section 1 (a) of the contract terms and conditions of the railroad Uniform Straight Domestic Bill of Lading reads as follows:

"The carrier or party in possession of any of the property herein described shall be liable as at common law for any loss thereof or damage thereto, . . ."

Motor carrier and freight forwarder shipping papers contain similar provisions.

A great deal has been written about the common law liability of the carriers in these instances. It has significance in that some authorities refer to such liability as making the carrier practically an insurer against all losses of whatever kind except those arising from acts of God and those caused by the public enemy. At times these exceptions have been broadened in some instances to include losses due to acts of public authorities and of the shippers as well as those due to the inherent nature of the goods shipped. It is an unusual and extraordinary liability and is based on considerations of public policy which have survived through the years. Such is the legal foundation on which rests a shipper's right to collect for loss and damage to his shipments.

The practical aspects incident to the filing and processing of loss and damage claims often become quite involved and, taken as classes, the unconcealed damaged claims are generally less involved than are those which are concealed. Reasons for this are obvious in that, when a shipment comes in damaged or with items missing and such is perfectly apparent, exceptions are noted on the bill of lading under regularly observed procedures in these matters. Thereafter the case for liability is clear cut in most instances. With all of these procedures, however, the work incident to them can be enormous and, as indicated earlier in the chapter, some companies establish higher minimum claim figures (below which they will not file) for their loss and damage items.

Loss and damage claims must be filed promptly in writing with the carriers (See Appendix 1, Railroad Bill of Lading,

Section 2(b) providing nine months from notification and two years and a day for filing suit) since they become outlawed within a very short time. Further, the longer the delay in filing the claim, the more difficult it becomes to collect, as the information is old, and therefore may not be as convincing as more current facts. Transportation loss and damage claims must be presented to the carriers within the following time limits to prevent their being outlawed:

Rail carriers, Motor carriers, Freight forwarders	Nine months from the date of delivery on damage claims or after reasonable time for delivery has elapsed (generally considered to be 30 days) on non-delivery or loss claims.
Water carriers, Air freight	Time limit varies. To play safe, file as soon as possible after loss or damage is ascertained.

If a claim is not completed in time to be filed within the allowed time, it is permissible to approximate the amount of the loss or damage and file a preliminary claim on an estimated basis, subject to correction. Please see, however, the new I.C.C. rules outlined at the end of this chapter.

As is to be expected, the time within which concealed loss and damage is discovered, and the carrier notified, is sensitive. The carriers feel that the longer the period goes after the delivery to the consignee the greater are the opportunities for the shipment to be damaged through no fault of theirs. Generally speaking, 15 days after delivery has come to be thought of as a reasonable period for discovery and notification. Where this can be shortened it, by all means, should be done in the interests of good (and fair) carrier relations. The 15 days is not a legal requirement in the sense that claims become void if it is not observed. By observing it, however, shipper recoveries for concealed loss and damage are less apt to run into resistance than if longer periods are involved.

The National Industrial Traffic League has been active with the rail carriers and motor vehicle operators in working

Standard Form for Presentation of Loss and Damage Claims

Approved by the Interstate Commerce Commission; Freight Claim Division, American Railway Association;
National Industrial Traffic League, and the National Association of Railway Commissioners.

Mr. J. J. Jones, Claims Agent   Smithville, New Jersey   L-259
(Name of person to whom claim is presented)   (Address of claimant)   (Claimant's Number)§

Cross Country Carriers   July 20, 1972
(Name of carrier)   (Date)

PO Box 91, Centerville, Ill.   (Carrier's Number)
(Address)

This claim for $ 29.07 is made against the carrier named above by ____ Smith Packing Company ____
(Amount of claim)   (Name of claimant)
for Loss and Damage in connection with the following described shipments:
(Loss or damage)
Description of shipment ____ 100 Boxes Tomato Catsup in Glass Bottles ____

Name and address of consignor (shipper) Smith Packing Co., Smithville, N.J.

Shipped from Smithville, N.J. ; To Westville, Ohio
(City, town or station)   (City, town or station)
Final Destination Westville, Ohio ; Routed via S.J. Trucking c/o Cross Country
(City, town or station)
Bill of Lading issued by South Jersey Trucking Co.; Date of Bill of Lading May 11, 1972

Paid Freight Bill (Pro) Number 87210 ; Original Car Number and Initial ____
Name and address of consignee (whom shipped to) Quality Restaurant Supply Co., Westville, Ohio

If shipment reconsigned en route, state particulars: ____

DETAILED STATEMENT SHOWING HOW AMOUNT CLAIMED IS DETERMINED.
(Number and description of articles, nature and extent of loss or damage, invoice price of articles, amount of claim, etc.)

6 Boxes Catsup - Short at destination	@ $3.23	$19.38
3 Boxes Catsup - Damaged	@ $3.23	$ 9.69
	Total Amount Claimed	

IN ADDITION TO THE INFORMATION GIVEN ABOVE, THE FOLLOWING DOCUMENTS ARE SUBMITTED IN SUPPORT OF THIS CLAIM.*

(X) 1. Original bill of lading, if not previously surrendered to carrier.
(X) 2. Original paid freight (expense) bill.
(X) 3. Original invoice or certified copy.
     4. Other particulars obtainable in proof of loss or damage claimed.

Destination freight bill bearing driver's notation of shortage
and damage.

REMARKS: Damaged boxes contained a total of 44 unbroken bottles with
labels stained and unmarketable. These were returned to
delivering carrier for salvage - receipt attached.

The foregoing statement of facts is hereby certified to as correct: SMITH PACKING COMPANY
A. L. Brown Claims Supervisor
(Signature of claimant)

§ Claimant should assign to each claim a number, inserting same in the space provided at the upper right hand corner of this form.
Reference should be made thereto in all correspondence pertaining to this claim.
* Claimants will please place check (x) before such of the documents mentioned as have been attached, and explain under
"Remarks" the absence of any of the documents called for in connection with this claim. When for any reason it is impossible for
claimant to produce original bill of lading, or paid freight bill, claimant should indemnify carrier or carriers against duplicate claim,
supported by original documents.

Form No. 1   The Traffic Service Corp., Washington, D.C.

Standard form for presentation of loss and damage claims, illustrating manner of preparation.

out equitable rules for dealing with various details of loss and damage claims. This has included coverage of the 15-day concealed loss and damage period mentioned in the preceding paragraph, as well as other features. It covers a wide range of both the unconcealed and concealed involvements in the field; the full text which follows represents the rail memorandum. One along similar lines in applicable to the motor carriers. The provisions are considered reasonable in ordinary circumstances although they are not legally binding as would be the case if they were, say, in the form of a law or a contract.

Along with working with the carriers on general principles to be applied in freight claim matters the League has worked with them and others on forms to be used in presenting claims.

REGULATIONS GOVERNING THE INSPECTION OF FREIGHT BEFORE OR AFTER DELIVERY TO CONSIGNEE AND ADJUSTMENT OF CLAIMS FOR LOSS OR DAMAGE THEREON

Loss of or damage to contents of packages not definitely known to exist at time of delivery by carrier to consignee may be due to negligence in packing, handling or unpacking or abstraction from containers and is the subject of frequent claims and controversy. In order to avoid any discrimination and so that practices may be certain and uniform in the treatment of claims of this character, the following rules are prescribed:

RULE 1—When a package bears indication of having been pilfered while in possession of carrier, it shall be carefully weighed by the delivery agent before delivery and such weight endorsed on the freight bill and a joint inventory of contents of package by carrier and consignee shall be made before delivery or immediately upon receipt by consignee, and claim for shortage so discovered shall be promptly adjusted.

RULE 2—Loss or damage discovered after delivery of shipments to consignee shall be reported by the consignee or consignor to agent of carrier immediately upon discovery, and in any event within fifteen days after receipt, and contents and container held for inspection by carrier, with a statement of facts or circumstances evidencing loss prior to delivery by carrier. Inspection by carrier shall be made when practicable, and in any event within forty-eight hours, and shall include examination of package and contents for evidence of abstraction of the missing goods, checking contents with invoice and weighing for comparison with shipping weight; also investigation of cartman's record of handling shipment. Report of inspection shall be made in duplicate on standard form and signed by carrier's agent and consignee, one copy thereof to be retained by consignee and attached to claim for loss, if made. In case no inspection is made by carrier's agent, consignee's inspection shall be accepted as carrier's inspection. If investigation develops that the loss occurred with carriers, the fifteen days' clause shall not be invoked. (Note—See Rule 7.)

RULE 3—Shortage from a package delivered consignee without exception, when based only upon consignee's failure to find the entire invoice quantity in package, or when package remains in possession of consignee more than 15 days before the goods are unpacked and shortage discovered, shall not be regarded as a responsibility of the carrier unless investigation develops that loss occurred with carrier. When package remains in possession of cartman overnight and not in warehouse, carrier shall require proof that loss did not occur with cartman.

The overcharge form (shown on Page 221) is discussed earlier. A form for loss and damage is used extensively; it is along similar lines and has a similar background. It can be made the basic document in these cases whether unconcealed or concealed aspects are involved. While loss and damage claims can be made via letter and the like, they generally require the inclusion of a fair amount of collateral information (inspection reports and so on) and the form mentioned provides a check list for these (see Page 227).

Special aspects of loss and damage claims are endless. A quite technical one is the basis for the liability which exists versus all motor carriers participating in a joint haul. Overly simplified, in Part II of the Interstate Commerce Act (the motor

---

RULE 4—When a package bears evidence of damage while in possession of carrier, a joint examination of contents by carrier and consignee shall be made before delivery or immediately upon receipt by consignee, and claim for damage so discovered shall be promptly adjusted upon its merits.

RULE 5—Damage to contents of package discovered after delivery of shipments to consignee shall be reported to agent of carrier immediately upon discovery, or in any event within fifteen days after receipt, with a statement of facts or circumstances evidencing damage prior to delivery by carrier, unless investigation develops that the damage occurred with carriers, then the fifteen-day clause shall not be invoked. Inspection shall be made by carriers when practicable, and in any event within forty-eight hours after notice. In case no inspection is made by carrier's agent, consignee's inspection shall be accepted as carrier's inspection. Report of inspection shall be made in duplicate on standard form and signed by carrier's agent and consignee, one copy thereof to be retained by consignee and attached to claim for damage, if made. (Note—See Rule 7.)

RULE 6—Shortage or damage discovered by consignee at time of receiving freight in any quantity from car, warehouse or other premises of carrier shall be reported to agent of carrier before removal of entire shipment, in order that the cause and extent of loss or damage may, if possible, be definitely determined and proper record made thereof. Unloading of freight should not be retarded or discontinued awaiting inspection.

RULE 7—Notice of loss or damage may be given carrier's agent by telephone or in person and in either event shall be confirmed by mail. In case of loss or damage as provided for in Rules 2 and 5, and inspection is not made by carrier's representative, details of findings of inspection by consignee shall be furnished carrier's agent immediately upon completion of inspection.

RULE 8—Failure of consignee to comply with the foregoing regulations shall be regarded as indicating complete delivery of freight by carrier in good order.

RULE 9—When packages which indicate loss of or damage to contents are recovered by the carrier, proper record of this exception shall be noted on the waybill and station records and shall be available to consignee.

carrier part) Section 219 provides their liability shall be the same as the rails. In Part I (the rail part), Section 20, Paragraph 11, provides that each participating carrier in a joint haul movement of freight shall be liable. The rail liability thus becomes also that of the motor carriers. Coupled with this, of course, is the liability created by the bill of lading provisions. Additional aspects are included in subsequent paragraphs.

Disposition of damaged material is important. Under the law the claimant is obligated to minimize, to the fullest extent possible, the loss for which the transportation carrier is liable. This does not mean that he is expected to pass up any legitimate loss, but rather that he is to figure the amount of the loss on the lowest reasonable basis.

If damaged material cannot be used and must be returned to origin, or some other location, for repair or salvage, consideration should be given to the cost of the return transportation as compared to the amount to be recovered. If it is returned it should be routed via the same carriers which transported the original shipment. If the cost of transporting it back to origin, or to some other location, exceeds the total value of the material, the carrier should be so advised and should be requested to dispose of it, with written confirmation. If the damaged material is worthless, the carrier should be requested to furnish disposition, with written confirmation. In this connection, a motor carrier freight claim rule provides that:

"Freight damaged in transit may be returned without charge to initial or intermediate points for repairs or credit, provided return movement is made by the same route as when forwarded, reference to original billing to be shown on return billing."

Additionally, some shippers of "name brand" materials prefer that it be not sold as salvage and special handling of this feature may be needed.

Shipper's Load and Count. Certain provisions of the Bill of Lading Act, which has been effective since January 1, 1917, are important to the legal aspects of loss and damage claims.

Two of them pertain particularly to responsibilities when freight is loaded by a carrier (Section 20) and by a shipper (Section 21). Such provisions are of sufficient interest to reproduce in part:

—*Section 20.*—When goods are loaded by a carrier, such carrier shall count the packages of goods, if packaged freight, and ascertain the kind and quantity if bulk freight, and the carrier shall not, in such cases, insert in the bill of lading, "Shipper's weight, load, and count," or other words of like meaning. If a notation of this kind is made, contrary to the provisions of section 20, said words shall be treated as null and void.

—*Section 21.*—When packaged freight or bulk freight is loaded by a shipper and the goods are described in a bill of lading and are said to be of a certain kind or quantity, or in a certain condition, or words of like meaning, and such statements are true, they shall not make the carrier liable, although the goods are not of the kind or quantity, or in the condition in which they were said to be by the consignor. The carrier may also insert in the bill of lading the words "Shipper's weight, load and count," or other words of like meaning, and if such statement be true, the carrier shall not be liable for damages caused by the improper loading, the non-receipt, or the mis-description of the goods described in the bill of lading: provided, where the shipper of bulk freight installs and maintains adequate facilities for weighing freight and the same facilities are available to the carrier, then the carrier, upon written request of such shipper, and when given a reasonable opportunity to do so, shall ascertain the kind and quantity of bulk freight within a reasonable time after such request, and in such cases shall not insert in the bill of lading the words "Shipper's weight," and if such a notation is inserted, it shall be treated as null and void.

Car seals.—One of the finer points concerns loss or damage in carload lots that move under clear seal records on a "shipper's load and count" basis. Here it is extremely difficult to prove carrier's liability. In the case of loss it is well nigh impossible, if the car was loaded and sealed by the shipper and the seals broken and car unloaded by the consignee. It must be shown that the car could have been entered some way other than through the doors, such as a broken floor leaving an opening. If the car was reloaded en route, there was at least an opportunity for loss. In the event of clear seal records on a carload lot, every obtainable shred of evidence will be needed to prove the loss. And even when a carload is rehandled en route, complete evidence, such as certified copies of load sheets (shipping department detailed record usually used to check material into cars), affidavits signed by individuals loading and unloading the cars, and any other "evidence" that can be produced will be required. Shipments sealed in truck trailers or containers are subject to the same considerations as sealed carloads discussed above.

Stop Offs.—The following excerpt from a factory's advice to its distributors is of interest and to the point:

Distributors sometimes experience difficulties on "stop-off" cars for partial unloading. Such cars contain merchandise for two or three distributors. Cars are consigned to the most distant (from the factory) distributor and are specified by the consignor on the bill of lading for a stop-off to partially unload at the first or nearest (to the factory) distributor. Sometimes a third distributor is added to the stop-off arrangement. In no case are there more than two stop-offs in addition to the final stop. In this way each distributor pays only the carload rate plus stop-off charge instead of the higher less-than-carload rate. Usually freight charges on stop-off cars are on a collect basis so they must be prorated to each distributor by the distributor at final destination who pays the total charge predicated on rate to final destination plus a stop-off, not including final destination. If the distributor at final destination is short certain items, it may be due to the first or second distributor inadvertently unloading more than his stipulated quantity. The final distributor should handle such shortages with the first and second distributor before going to the factory. The first and second distributor, on the other hand, should unload his portion with great care to be absolutely sure he takes out only his part of the shipment. And he should see to it that the car is never left unattended while being unloaded. He should also reseal the car just as soon as his part is unloaded, first inspecting the load to be sure it will 'ride' satisfactorily to the next or final destination. The railroad will not consider claims for shortages from stop-off cars unless opportunities for theft, etc., while the car is in possession of the railroad can be established beyond any doubt.

Trailer-On-Flat-Car Claims.—Considerable difficulty frequently is encountered in obtaining satisfactory settlement of claims on piggy-back shipments handled under Plans II½, III, IV and V. The railroads decline claims unless there is conclusive proof that damage occurred while the trailer was in their possession. Even then, they are inclined to resist payment if the trailer itself shows no evidence of physical damage. For this reason, detailed records of the condition of the trailer at each change of custody during its journey are a necessity.

Measure of Damages.—The question is often asked, "What can we include in a claim besides the invoice value of the material lost or damaged?" The answer is: Anything within reason that constitutes a legitimate "damage" to you. Expenses in connection with claims may well be classified as (1) basic or primary loss, damage or expenses (consequential) and (2) incidental expenses. The major losses may be described as the invoice value, transportation (if not in the selling price), interest, and any other direct cost. Incidental expenses which usually are not included in the claim are telephone calls, cost of tracing, cost of inspection to ascertain extent of damage, and other expenses of filing claim which are not considered to be proper elements of damage.

In the case of perishables, it is a well-founded practice to include any market losses at destination due to the carrier failing to make delivery within a transit-interval period previously established or within what is considered to be a reasonable transit interval. The same principle would apply to perishables that have spoiled in transit, due to unreasonable delays.

There are instances where materials needed at destination arrive damaged and so can not be used. Replacing shipments have to go forward via express or air. Although the original shipments had been routed via rail or truck, the claims may include the extra expense to ship the replacing material via express or air, on the premise that such expense constitutes part of the "damage" to the shipper. Whether collection can be effected can be a problem. It is essential, however, to review each claim very carefully to be certain that all loss elements are included. Two basic court cases defining the measure of damages are Chicago, Milwaukee and St. Paul Railway v. McCaull-Dinsmore, 253 U.S. 97, and Illinois Central Railroad Co. v. Crail, 281 U.S. 57.

Impact Recorders.—The use of impact recorders is fairly common on activities to develop the wheres and hows of damage to shipments. They can be helpful in localizing bad spots or difficulties which may be causes of damage, particularly those of a repetitive nature. They provide means for studying the movements of goods from packaging at the factory to the premises of the customer. In using them the full picture can be developed from which localization may best be obtained. The impact recorder aspect of claim prevention is particularly concerned with damage to shipments and utilization of them can well be a part of the activities of a transportation department in its claim prevention work.

Insurance.—Various features of freight claims serve to highlight areas where insurance coverage may be needed. Bills of lading contain provisions to the effect that carriers shall not be liable for articles of extraordinary value unless they are specifically rated and a stipulated value is endorsed thereon. Freight rates are applicable on some commodities where rates are substantially lower for lower released valuations. Parcel Post and United Parcel have various limitations on the top liabilities they assume. Insurance coverage is generally available for all, or part, of the various damage possibilities that are not recoverable from the carriers. A policy commonly obtained is for contingent floater transportation insurance. Under it the insurer takes care of any losses in using released values and so on. Details of what insurance, if any, should be obtained are to be worked out by a traffic manager with his company's insurance department.

Handling Claims.—Some companies are so structured that it is practically a must that the handling of claims be on a decentralized basis; with other organizations centralized bases are naturals. With still others, claims within certain dollar limits are decentralized and those having higher potentials go to their head office transportation groups for handling. Well trained "claims men" become expert in dealing with the various carrier claim agents and do a great deal to assure better "claims paid" records than can ever be accomplished when they are not in such hands. Employees who are tops in this regard will not only see that the claims are presented properly through the accumulation of all required facts, but will deal with the carriers in a more efficient manner because of greater knowledge of pertinent court cases and other supporting data so often needed to produce a convincing case. From a management standpoint these features are to be borne in mind whether the claims operation is centralized, decentralized, or a combination of both. Opportunities for important recoveries generally abound in claims and the assignment of good people to handle them is important.

Unconcealed Loss Or Damage Claims

Unconcealed loss and damage claims are those that develop from loss and damage which is apparent on delivery. It is of utmost importance with these that, as shipments are delivered, the consignee's representative at the unloading operations specify in writing on the carrier's delivery receipt copy of the freight bill the loss or damage to the shipment. Also, this should be signed by that party and delivery time noted. When this is not done, a carrier may contend that a "clear receipt" has been given and use that as a basis for denying liability. The wording of the exception note should be in sufficient detail to apprize those involved of the facts and can well be in the following manner:

> 1 box short
> 1 box torn, contents damaged
> R.C. Smith
> Jankins Mfg. Co.
> Delivered 8-11-72, 2:45 P.M.

When one of several packages of differently described freight checks short, the identity of the short item should be determined and noted on the delivery receipt. Additionally, care should be taken that unloading personnel known and follow these requirements, that new employees are informed of them, and so on.

The next step upon discovering unconcealed loss or damage is to notify the local freight agent of the delivering carrier, and request that a representative of the carrier call to inspect the damage and prepare an inspection report. While technically there should be no need for an inspection report in case of a loss in the number of pieces shown on the billing, inasmuch as the signature for the goods notes shortage exception, this is done in various cases. As indicated above, by no means should any receiving clerk give a carrier a "clear receipt" for a shipment if it is not complete in accordance with the billing. If there is damage noted, the package or carload should be left just as it is until the carrier's representative has made an inspection. This is to give the carrier an opportunity to determine, if possible, the cause of the damage. It is also added proof that the damage did occur while the shipment was in the carrier's possession. No claim can be collected unless it can be proved that there was loss or damage while the shipment was in the possession of the carrier, and exactly what the loss or damage amounted to in dollars and cents.

The common practice for establishing the value of articles lost or damaged beyond repair is to submit a certified copy of the invoice. This means a copy of the original billing to the customer, which an official of the company signs as a "certification" that it is a true copy of the original invoice. The value for claim purposes is, then, the price at which the seller invoices the material to the customer, plus, of course, the amount of the transportation if not included in the sale price.

If a claim is to cover repair costs, care must be exercised to keep detailed cost figures covering such items as labor (indicate number of hours of labor and rate per hour including loading and any other cost factor) and material. These costs should be itemized on a sheet, to be certified by a responsible plant official.

Carriers at times accept "standard" repair costs for a particular article or part when such costs are shown to be based on reasonable factors and can be proved fair and equitable. If the article must be sent to an outside concern for repair, the transportation may be included and the outside concern should, of course, be required to furnish itemized costs, a certified statement of which should be submitted with claim papers to the carrier.

If a replacement shipment is necessary, and a price change occurs between the date of the original shipment and the replacing shipment, the value for claim purposes should be the established selling price of the replacing shipment plus the amount of the transportation if not included in the sales price.

There is always a question as to the proper value to be used for material not sold, but being shipped between two locations of the same company for another stage of manufacture or for storage. If such material is lost or totally damaged and it can be replaced on the open market, the market price, as invoiced by the supplier, should be used for claim purposes. If it is of your own company manufacture, the amount of loss for claim purposes should be the cost of remanufacture, which would consist of all customary pricing factors with the exception of the profit factor. Since invoices are not usually issued on company shipments, some companies place the following clause on the standard claim form in lieu of a copy of the invoice:

> "We hereby certify that this shipment moved between two of our company locations or from factory to distributing point and that the amount of the claim does not exceed our loss, and does not include any prospective profits, brokerage, overhead expense, percent above invoice or other similar items."

Loss and damage by delay applies to losses or damage sustained (1) because of a decline in the destination market price of the commodity during the period of delay, and (2) by physical damage or deterioration of the commodity caused by the delay. Delay claims must be carefully considered and presented, inasmuch as payment is not usually made without a most exhaustive investigation by the carrier. Under the terms and conditions of the bill of lading the carrier does not guarantee to transport the shipment by any particular train to arrive at its destination at any particular time. Carriers are expected to transport shipments within a reasonable time, and the determination whether the carrier is guilty of negligence, and therefore liable for payment of a claim, can be made by comparing the transit time of the shipment in question with the average transit time provided normally between the origin and destination points. The railroad company's schedules furnish good evidence, but they are not necessarily conclusive. Carriers are not permitted to make agreements to deliver shipments on a certain date, as to do so for a few consignees would set up a discriminatory situation among shippers. In the case of N.Y., P. & N.R.R. Co. vs. Peninsula Produce Exchange of Maryland, 240 U.S. 34, the United States Supreme Court, in giving recognition to loss due to failure to move goods at a reasonable transit interval, stated that there can be no better standard for determining what constitutes a reasonable transit interval than by comparison of the ordinary transit interval with the actual transit interval for the particular shipment. This, of course, was on the basis that there were no acceptable facts that explained and excused the longer transit interval that resulted in the loss. Carriers are not to blame for failures due to acts of God, etc., as defined in the terms and conditions of the bill of lading.

If after a claim for loss has been filed with the carrier, the material is received, the claim should be withdrawn at once.

In the case of loss of coal in transit, it is not customary to present a claim to the carrier unless one or more of the following defects in equipment or load are developed:

> Wreck
> Transfer of load in transit
> Defective hopper cars
> Marked depression in the load

The basis for such claims is the difference between the origin and destination net scale weight and this is generally done without taking into consideration tolerance for moisture, evaporation or scale variation.

To sum up, unconcealed loss or damage claims should be supported by the following papers:

1. Standard form for presentation of loss and damage.
2. Proof of value, in duplicate (certified copy of invoice).
3. Statement of claim (itemized list of all factors making up a total amount of claim).
4. Transportation company's inspection report, if prepared.
5. Paid freight bill or express receipt, as case may be.
6. Original bill of lading.
7. Copies of correspondence with carrier concerning disposition of any damaged material.

Refusing Shipments. A consignee at times will contemplate refusing to accept a freight shipment. This can be for a number of reasons; one that is quite often the cause is the damaged condition in which the goods are tendered for delivery to him by the carrier. Refusing to accept a freight shipment may cause unexpected difficulties. If it is refused because it is damaged, it should be done only with the consent of the carrier, thereby establishing a presumption of carrier liability in connection with the forth-coming claim. If it is refused because the material does not meet purchasing specification, or because of an alleged damage by the carrier (but carrier's Inspection Report does not confirm carrier liability), there should be an understanding with the shipper so that the goods may be returned to the shipper. If terms of purchase are F.O.B. shipper's factory, and the shipper refuses to permit return to him for one reason or another, the consignee's refusal leaves the carrier no recourse but to place the shipment in storage. When the storage charges become substantial and the carrier cannot obtain disposition from either the consignor or the consignee, the goods will be sold at public auction to recover the amount of the transportation and storage charges. In other words, after the shipment is refused, and after expiration of free time, the carrier becomes a bailee or warehouseman, rather than a common carrier. The carrier has a lien upon the goods in its possession until the properly assessed charges are paid. The first action taken by the carrier when a shipment is refused is to forward immediate notification to the shipper. It is only after the shipper declines to accept any responsibility that the goods are placed into storage, and later sold for charges.

Concealed Loss Or Damage Claims

The best way of describing this type of claim is to compare it to the shiny red apple with a rotten core. You may well give the carrier a clear receipt for it, because from all outward appearances there is no loss or damage. However, later, when you open the container, you find a shortage or damage. Right then is the time to discontinue unpacking and leave the package right where it is until you have notified the local agent of the delivering carrier and he has sent a representative to inspect the shipment and prepare an inspection report, a copy of which should be given to you.

Concealed loss and damage claims usually are difficult to collect because real hurdles are encountered in accumulating sufficient evidence that the loss or damage was caused while the goods were in the possession of the carrier and were due to his acts. The difficulty is in definitely locating the responsibility with the carrier, and the carriers point out that, after all, they do not have a monopoly on damaging material or on employing "light fingered" employees. Concurrent with notifying the carrier as outlined above it is also important that the consignee move promptly and carefully to obtain all possible information to support his rights in the matter.

The information to be obtained in this regard varies and depends particularly on the circumstances that prevail. In some cases the data can include the care exercised in packing and unpacking; the experience of the people doing the packing and unpacking and how they have operated through the years; the care exercised with the lading after it was delivered to be sure it was safe; the security proceedures that were applied; and so on. The make-ups of the shipper and consignee statements (hereafter detailed) can suggest other features. The cold, hard facts are that affirmative action should be taken and this should include bonafide assurances to the carrier (and the courts if necessary) that the consignee's operations are so set up that the loss and damage could not have occurred with him. With this, the consignee should be fair with the carrier and recognize his position as well as his problems and any existing facts on his side.

It is a common practice for manufacturers and others to ship large quantities of goods to key points for warehousing and later distribution to surrounding areas. Ordinarily, the original container is not opened and the contents are not examined before their reshipment to final destination. When this practice is followed, it is impossible to determine after delivery to final destination whether loss or damage of a concealed nature occurred before or after reshipping. Further, the merchandise usually traveled many miles before warehousing, while the delivering carrier probably transported it only a short distance. Again, the goods were handled into and out of storage by the warehouseman, and it may be necessary to prove that damage could not have occurred while the goods were in the possession of the warehouseman.

If a claim is filed with the carrier hauling from the warehouse to the final consignee, it may be turned down or settlement offered on a 50-50 or some other basis, because there is not positive proof that the damage did occur while the shipment was in possession of the delivering carrier. Such claims are handled on their individual merits. If, upon delivery, the carton was bent, torn or scratched, or if it rattled when handled, there would be evidence that should result in the delivering carrier paying in full. It is obvious that warehouses cannot open every box or carton they receive and check for concealed damage or loss. Claims on beyond shipments, then, when for concealed loss or damage, must be handled on their merits, with the eventual decision going to that side that can best "prove the point" because of superior facts. In any event, it is proper for the consignee to file a concealed loss or damage claim against the delivering carrier for the full amount of the loss or damage.

The problems of determining where the concealed loss and damage occurred are such that various carrier rules prevail, and have prevailed for some time, concerning prorating between haulers the settlement payments to shippers. Where prorations prevail they may be on percentages of mileage or revenue bases. Details, when needed, can generally be obtained from the freight claim rule books of the carrier associations. Further and insofar as circumstances permit, carriers. will cooperate and assist claimants in collecting balances on such claims from the carrier or carriers rendering the prior transportation. Consignees can usually expedite such settlements by securing the original shipper's and warehouse's cooperation in supplying necessary billing references so that the shipment can be identified in handling with the carrier rendering the prior transportation.

Concealed loss or damage claims should be supported by the following papers:

—Standard form for presentation of loss and damage claims (see page 227).
—Proof of value, in duplicate (certified copy of the invoice).
—Statement of claim (itemized list of all factors making up the total amount of the claim).
—Transportation company's inspection report.
—Paid freight bill, or express receipt as case may be.
—Original bill of lading.
—Shipper's statement in duplicate, see below.
—Consignee's statement in duplicate, see below.
—Copies of correspondence with carrier concerning disposition of any damaged material.

The shipper's statement referred to above should identify the shipment by name of shipper, point of origin, consignee, destination, date of shipment, number of packages and commodity. It then should set forth the following information:

—When and where were the goods packed?

—Were all the articles for which claim is made packed in containers and in good order?

—If property shipped did not fill container to capacity, what material occupied remaining space?

—How was package protected against abstraction of or damage to contents? (Strapped, sealed or otherwise)

—When (date and hour) was shipment delivered to carrier?

—Name of carrier or carriers.

—If not delivered by common carrier, state how delivered.

—What protection was given shipment while in possession of carrier?

In each case, the statement should bear the following certification:

I hereby certify that the foregoing statement of facts is true in every particular.

It should be signed only by a person having first-hand knowledge of the facts, should mention the capacity in which he is employed, the city, state and date.

The consignee's statement should identify the shipment in the same detail as the shipper's statement and provide the following information:

—When (date and hour) was shipment received at consignee's place of business?

—Name of carrier.

—What protection was given shipment while in possession of carrier, to extent known.

—If not received by common carrier, state how received.

—On what date was loss or damage discovered?

—On what date was carrier notified of loss or damage?

—Kind of container.

—How was package protected against abstraction of or damage to contents? (Strapped, sealed or otherwise).

—Was container examined before or after opening?

—If condition of container at time of examination indicated cause of damage, explain fully.

—If condition of interior packing indicated loss or damage, explain fully.

—If property did not fill container to capacity, what material occupied the remaining space?

—What condition of container or contents indicated that loss or damage occurred while in possession of carriers?

The consignee's statement should be certificated and signed in the same manner as the shipper's statement.

Variations on the foregoing may be necessary in the cases of United Parcel, import or coastwise shipments, and others. These, of course, can be taken in a traffic department's stride and handled along the lines of procedures requested by these carriers. The American Trucking Association and the Association of American Railroads have made sincere efforts to place claim procedures, collections, and other aspects on equitable bases and from time to time have issued pamphlets and other publications that can be helpful and of real worth. By writing, these can be obtained.

Within a fairly recent period it has seemed that an increased number of loss and damage claims—unconcealed and concealed—have come to get treatment by carriers which is felt by shippers to be unjustified. This has gotten to the point where special legislation has been advocated that carriers be required to pay attorney fees when suits are filed against them. There appears to be merit to this. With all the controversy, however, fair and forthright treatment by the carrier of the shipper and by the shipper of the carrier basically represents the way to deal with these cases. Law suits are expensive and the selection of responsible carriers by shippers to the end that law suits may be avoided is important.

Another tack at endeavoring to improve matters has been the adoption by the I.C.C. of new rules, effective April 21, 1972*, for handling loss and damage claims. The rules are appli-

* This date has been extended.

cable to all carriers under the Commission's jurisdiction except as to a few minor features applicable to household goods and were issued pursuant to a general investigation (Ex Parte 263 Principles * * For * * Disposition Of Loss And Damage Claims * *) which has been under way for some time. They are available in pamphlet form and will appear in 340 I.C.C. 515.

Highlights of the rules concerned with action by carriers are that they must acknowledge receipt of each claim, investigate it promptly and thoroughly, and "pay, decline, or make a firm compromise settlement offer in writing * * within 120 days * *" after its receipt. When this cannot be done within that period the claimant is to be advised the status and is to be provided similar information every 60 days thereafter until final disposition. Records on salvage activities are also required.

The aspects of the rules which particularly affect claims by shippers deal with the filing of them, the information they must contain, supporting documents that may be necessary, and so on. In certain ways they operate to streamline and tighten up on procedures under which industrial companies have been operating. It is important that they be observed and given precedence where not previously observed or where they are not now being followed.

Pertinent sections follow:

Section 1005.2 Filing of claims.

(a) *Claims in writing required.* A claim for loss or damage to baggage or for loss, damage, injury, or delay to cargo shall not be voluntarily paid by a carrier unless filed in writing, as provided in subparagraph (b) below, with the receiving or delivering carrier, or carrier issuing the bill of lading, receipt, ticket, or baggage check, or carrier on whose line the alleged loss, damage, injury, or delay occurred, within the specified time limits applicable thereto and as otherwise may be required by law, the terms of the bill of lading or other contract of carriage, and all tariff provisions applicable thereto.

(b) *Minimum filing requirements.* A communication in writing from a claimant, filed with a proper carrier within the time limits specified in the bill of lading or contract of carriage or transportation, and (i) containing facts sufficient to identify the baggage or shipment (or shipments) of property involved, (ii) asserting liability for alleged loss, damage, injury, or delay, and (iii) making claim for the payment of a specified or determinable amount of money, shall be considered as sufficient compliance with the provisions for filing claims embraced in the bill of lading or other contract of carriage.

(c) *Documents not constituting claims.* Bad order reports, appraisal reports of damage, notations of shortage or damage, or both, on freight bills, delivery receipts, or other documents, or inspection reports issued by carriers or their inspection agencies, whether the extent of loss or damage is indicated in dollars and cents or otherwise, shall, standing alone, not be considered by carriers as sufficient to comply with the minimum claim filing requirements specified in subparagraph (b) above.

(d) *Claims filed for uncertain amounts.* Whenever a claim is presented against a proper carrier for an uncertain amount, such as "$100 more or less," the carrier against whom such claim is filed shall determine the condition of the baggage or shipment involved at the time of delivery by it, if it was delivered, and shall ascertain as nearly as possible the extent, if any, of the loss or damage for which it may be responsible. It shall not, however, voluntarily pay a claim under such circumstances unless and until a formal claim in writing for a specified or determinable amount of money shall have been filed in accordance with the provisions of subparagraph (b) above.

(e) *Other claims.* If investigation of a claim develops that one or more other carriers has been presented with a similar claim on the same shipment, the carrier investigating such claim shall communicate with each such other carrier and, prior to any agreement entered into between or among them as to the proper disposition of such claim or claims, shall notify all claimants of the receipt of conflicting or overlapping claims and shall require further substantiation, on the part of each claimant of his title to the property involved or his right with respect to such claim.

❊ ❊ ❊ ❊ ❊

Section 1005.4 Investigation of claims.

❊ ❊ ❊ ❊ ❊

(b) *Supporting documents.* When a necessary part of an investigation, each claim shall be supported by the original bill of lading, evidence of the freight charges, if any, and either the original invoice, a photographic copy of the original invoice or an exact copy thereof, or an extract made therefrom, certified by the claimant to be true and correct with respect to the property and value involved in the claim; or certification of prices or values, with trade or other discounts, allowance, or deductions of any nature whatsoever and the terms thereof, or depreciation reflected thereon; *Provided, however,* That where the property involved in a claim has not been invoiced to the consignee shown on the bill of lading or where an invoice does not show price or value, or where the property involved has not been sold, or where the property has been transferred at bookkeeping values only, the carrier shall, before voluntarily paying a claim thereon, require the claimant to establish the destination value in the quantity shipped, transported, or involved and to certify the correctness thereof in writing.

(c) *Verification of loss.* A prerequisite to the voluntary payment by a carrier of a claim for loss of an entire package or an entire shipment shall be the securing by it of a certified statement in writing from the consignee of the shipment involved that the property for which the claim is filed has not been received from any other source.

Among various things, the new rules have considerable promise for simplifying procedures in freight claim matters. They, of course, have yet to stand the test of time and shippers will wish to follow them and do all possible to get the most benefits out of them. The Commission's report, incidentally, also contains recommendations for legislation and cargo insurance as well as other related features.

Santa Fe's 84-car unit train carrying 84,000 tons of coal.

Southern Railway's dropframe rail-highway trailer on the left is used for freight that has high degree of bulk in relation to weight such as furniture. Container on the right is transferred by overhead crane between flatcars and wheeled highway carriages.

A light weight, aluminum-steel gondola car receiving "no hands" rotary dumping.

Delayless container movements. Two types of flexible, mobil units expediting trailer on flat car shipments.

9

DISTRIBUTION & WAREHOUSING

TRADITIONALLY, THE TERM "DISTRIBUTION" HAS BEEN USED TO describe channels of distribution—i.e., whether the product was sold direct to customers, through dealers, or through jobbers or distributors. This chapter, however, will deal with the actual process of distribution: the physical movement of goods through physical systems consisting of transportation facilities, loading and unloading and storage systems, private and public warehouses. It will also deal with the techniques of planning and control applied in order to maximize the efficiency of distribution systems while assuring that they are operated at the lowest total cost consistent with management's standards of customer service.

Distribution

The National Council of Physical Distribution Management defines "physical distribution" as

". . . the term employed in manufacturing and commerce to describe the broad range of activities concerned with efficient movement of finished products from the end of the production line to the consumer, and in some cases includes the movement of raw materials from the source of supply to the beginning of the production line. These activities include freight transportation, warehousing, material handling, protective packaging, inventory control, plant and warehousing site selection, order processing, market forecasting and customer service."

Some schools of thought will argue that this definition is too narrow, others will argue that it is too broad. Rather than get hung up in a sematic trap, we would like to use this definition as a point of departure for our thoughts in this chapter.

■ *Warehousing*—Although warehousing is usually thought of in terms of protection and storage of goods, there are five different types of warehouses whose functions should be clearly distinguished. They are:

—The security warehouse. The primary function of this type is to protect valuable items: documents, pictures, household goods and the like. Such warehouses are fundamentally repositories; they are used particularly by some industrial companies because they are generally more economical and secure for static storage of vital records than on-premise facilities.

—The raw materials warehouse. The function of these warehouses is to permit a company to purchase its raw materials in economical quantities and store them at plants to insure that there will be no production down-time due to nonavailability of materials. This type of warehouse also permits "holding" of raw materials which must be bought seasonally, i.e., crops.

—The production warehouse. Like the raw materials warehouse, the primary function of the production warehouse is the holding of materials to permit production economies, in this case finished goods. In most cases, it is more economical to schedule long runs on a production line well in advance of anticipated sales than it would be to schedule shorter runs at more frequent intervals, and the production warehouse serves to hold and protect these goods until the time they are needed for movement into regular marketing and distribution channels.

—The plant warehouse. The plant warehouse combines the functions of the first three, and a few instances, such as when direct shipment to the customer is the rule, the distribution warehouse.

—The distribution warehouse. The distribution warehouse

serves primarily to facilitate marketing. It does this in several ways. First, it serves as a break-bulk point, permitting the large-lot inbound shipments at low carload or truckload rates over the long haul from the plant to warehouse, with the higher LCL or LTL rates minimized for the relatively short haul from the warehouse to the ultimate consumers. The distribution warehouse also serves as a "mixing point" for different product lines which may originate at a company's different plants; it permits a single shipment of different items to a customer, rather than a number of shipments from different points at relatively higher cost. Traditionally, an important function of the distribution warehouse has been to assure product availability and provide a competitive edge in offering customer service.

Some aspects of warehousing are at times overemphasized. The old adage, "You can't do business from an empty wagon" has been displaced to some degree by modern, high-speed transportation which permits practically the same level of customer service and product availability as a regional or local warehouse, and whose higher cost is often justified by the savings in inventory and warehouse operating and ownership costs it permits. Of course, warehouses also permit many other market-related activities such as (a) finishing of products to special customer orders, (b) cutting steel or printing paper to meet a buyer's special size requirements, (c) assembly of office furniture to incorporate customer specified components, etc., (d) packaging of bulk materials in bags, bottles or drums, (e) operation of showrooms to display company products, (f) furnishing of office space to regional sales forces, and (g) special equipment for handling and protection of high-value, perishable or exotic products.

While many warehouses combine several of these functions, they are generally at some distance from the plant and it is simply not practical that all of them be consolidated.

More will be said in this chapter about the differences between private (company-owned) warehouses and public warehouses; actually, the disadvantage or advantage of either type is a matter primarily of economics and not of the functions outlined above. In most cases, these functions can be performed equally well by either private or public warehouses; the individual company's specific requirements will determine which is best.

Our primary emphasis in this chapter will be on the distribution warehouse; the location and nature of the first four types of warehouse will generally be determined by a company's production requirements, whereas the distribution warehouse offers a wide range of locational choices—and opportunities for excellent work in selecting one. The traffic manager who is responsible for or participates in distribution warehouse activities should familiarize himself with the broad marketing concepts that may be involved as well as the marketing policies of his own company.

■ *General Distribution Problems*—It has been said that 59¢ of the consumer's dollar goes to distribution and 41¢ to manufacturing. That does not mean 59¢ to transportation alone, since distribution covers packaging, handling, sales, retailing, warehousing, and transportation. However, there is no question that the cost for transportation alone is a very substantial figure indeed. More than ever before, management is aware that once their product is manufactured and packaged, there is still the costly function of getting it to market. And they know that not one penny of this expense improves the product; indeed, conversely, rough handling in transit may cause damaged or soiled packages, or even damaged goods.

Emphasis in this book is placed on those expenses that increase the cost of the product rather than the value of the product. These expenses cover the physical movement of goods once manufactured. Thus the traffic man should work closely with materials handling, packaging and warehousing and they in turn, as an interwoven group, cooperate with sales and other company departments interested.

Customer satisfaction is acquired by delivering a product in perfect condition at the time it is needed and service to customers becomes more critical each year probably because "exploding population" means "expanding markets." In the move to maximize profits, lower distribution costs does mean higher profits or an ability to do business at all. At least one third of our citizens live in our 15 largest cities. The concentration of people in cities does indicate that major distribution centers should be located in or adjacent to them.

Because of less handling and some benefits of dual-administration, it figures that the main or primary warehouse should be located as close as possible to the plant. In other words, the completed product would go perhaps by conveyor belt direct from factory to a plant warehouse.

While warehousing of one sort or another has always been required, the approach to warehousing has to be, "is it really necessary to warehouse?" and if so how can it be done with a minimum of physical handling of the merchandise, a minimum of people involved in that handling and, of course, a minimum cost.

Firms generally use both company owned and public warehouses at one time or another. Often goods are stockpiled in public warehouses until product demand requires setting up a company-operated warehouse. Out of this evolves an assembly operation or full-scale manufacturing plant. This cycle sometimes takes a few years—sometimes decades!

The fact that use of warehouses enables companies to take advantage of volume transportation rates for long-haul shipments has long been at the heart of the warehousing operation, but current thinking places it on the same level with inventory costs and competitive advantage.

There are savings if the product can go direct from the manufacturer to the consumer or retailer. The air lines are strong advocates of direct shipping via air freight or express because of speed and the possibility of less expensive packing requirements. But motor carriers, freight forwarders and other forms of transport may perform just as satisfactorily on any given situation. What is needed is a total marketing concept by the company as a whole, not individual units. A distribution audit could be undertaken on a company-wide basis. Direct shipping may be indicated from studies of the real cost of maintaining inventories, giving due consideration to the obsolescence feature, interest, taxes, insurance, transportation into and out of warehouses and the cost of purchasing, maintaining and leasing the warehouse itself. The whole area of inventory control is admittedly complex.

Almost everything that happens to a product after it comes off the production line is part of the cost of selling. Where competing products are basically the same in cost and quality— as in the case of many raw materials and certain consumer items—customer service becomes an important competitive selling tool. Customer service has been defined by one authority as "Having the right product at the right place at the right time, in the right condition . . . at the right price." This suggests all kinds of possibilities: frequent customer deliveries from nearby warehouses, convenience packaging, special protective packaging and protective transportation equipment, unitized shipments, and assistance to customers in solving loading, unloading and storage problems!

These are all well and good, of course, and it is often necessary to offer these and other services to customers simply because the competition is doing so. However, these activities can add so much to the cost of selling as to have a serious effect on profits; so, savings must be found elsewhere in the "distribution system" in order to offset these added costs.

■ *The Inventory Problem*—A major area where such savings may often be effected is that of inventories. The traditional pattern of customer service has been to have many well-stocked warehouses located in principal market areas. To do this a tremendous investment has been necessary, both in inventories and in the warehouses to hold them in anticipation of customer demand. In addition, inaccurate "guesstimates" of customer demand have not infrequently resulted in a high rate of product obsolescence—goods left over at the end of the sales year which have had to be scrapped or sold at greatly reduced prices. This is particularly true when periodic model changes are involved.

With the cost of carrying inventories reckoned as high as 30 cents on the dollar annually by some companies, there has been tremendous pressure by management to reduce inventories whenever possible. This means that the traffic manager may be caught in a type of "squeeze play"—if he uses the lowest-cost forms of transportation plus warehousing to save money in transportation and distribution, then larger inventories and greater periods of time are involved which run inventory costs up. If he uses premium transportation to reduce storage needs and time periods, then his transportation costs are bound to shoot up. Management does not always understand this conflict between inventory and transportation costs; the traffic manager should endeavor to find opportunities to explain it in his management communications.

What can the traffic manager himself do to resolve this conflict between inventories and transportation costs?

In many companies inventory policies are formulated independently of transportation policies, and the traffic manager has to work with this in mind; even though he, personally, doesn't get the blame when inventory costs rise as transportation costs go down, the company's profits can be seriously affected.

Where the traffic manager participates in decisions on the location and number of distribution warehouses—and he almost always has to get involved in one way or another—he can use his specialized knowledge to help remedy this situation. He should always bear in mind that the basic function of warehousing is the same as transportation. It might be good for him to think of warehousing, as some traffic managers do, in this way: "Warehousing = transportation at zero miles per hour." This says that warehousing will achieve the same end as transportation, except that the emphasis on speed has been removed, or, putting it another way it means simply that if there are some instances where transportation can be substituted for warehousing at less total cost, and without sacrificing customer service, then it is perfectly logical to do so. Generally speaking, when we buy either transportation or warehousing, we are buying time; it is good business to pay the lowest total cost.

But there are other ways of buying time, too, and these should be considered as part of the total picture. Paperwork is a good example. If order-processing takes anywhere from three to five days, as it often does, this means that cutting two days out of this operation would give the traffic manager two days more to get his product to customers. This in turn could mean that customers might be served from more distant points, which in turn might permit full or partial discontinuance of some warehouses. Or it could mean using a slower, lower-cost form of transportation and still giving customers the same delivery they were accustomed to. One company took this approach and reduced inventory of one item alone from $5 million to $2 million, at the same time closing a number of its branch warehouses. If order time could be reduced by 24 hours, the company reasoned, customers could be served from warehouses 24 hours more distant and the problem of maintaining complete stocks at numerous locations would be simplified.

Order-picking and assembling for shipping, and packing and loading, may be other time-consuming activities where a speedup would enable the traffic manager to use slower transportation or even to serve his customers from more distant points. If a unit load system, for instance, permits loading a trailer in a half hour as opposed to three hours piece-by-piece, then a total of five hours is saved—two and a half hours on each end of the trip. If you multiply this by the number of handlings an individual shipment may have to go through— sometimes twelve or more—you can see the tremendous potential for savings.

■ The Automated Warehouse—Some companies have found it feasible to invest in highly automated warehouses, with order-picking and assembling, inventory control, and shipping document preparation all controlled by computers. In a typical operation, punch cards will be produced as a byproduct of the order-writing operation; these will be fed to the computer, which will group all orders by destinations, prepare appropriate shipping documents and inventory records, and activate the

Courtesy of The Alvey-Ferguson Company, Cincinnati, Ohio

One section of an automated warehouse of the Colgate-Palmolive Company, Kansas City, Mo. This is an over-all view of discharge end of live storage rack, a portion of order-picking system. Cartons have been automatically discharged from selected lanes and are enroute over collecting belts for delivery onto accumulating lines.

material handling system so that orders are delivered at the appropriate shipping docks in proper sequence for loading and unloading at destinations. In one such operation, the different orders scheduled for one trailer are all color-coded and delivered to the shipping dock in such a sequence that as the driver makes each stop the appropriate order will be immediately in position for unloading and unmistakably color-coded for that destination.

The two previous illustrations provide ideas of automatic warehouses. Whether operated by computer, by tape, by card or by push button, the object of such warehouses is to exploit the full potential of mechanical systems through the use of automatic controls. Heavy moving items can almost always be automated economically; slow movers, split cartons, etc. are not usually automated due to excessive cost. Some electronic controlled warehouses are not conducive to large solid one-item pallet loads. Where automated, they would be covered by another type of automation such as by conveyor belts and by special lift trucks. Automatic systems are simple or very complex, dependent on the problem to be solved. Efficient use of space is No. 1 problem! The heart of any modern warehouse system is live storage!

Remember, the responsibility of planning an automated warehouse should never be attempted without the guidance of a good engineer and possibly a consulting firm that specializes in the field.

A great deal of the advantage of automated warehousing is lost if transportation scheduling is not coordinated. If shipments stay on the dock without trailers to load them into, or in cars on sidings, the time "bought" by the automated warehouse at a rather high price is quickly lost. For this reason, it is always a good idea to proceed slowly before recommending automated warehousing or sophisticated, high-speed handling equipment. It may work fine, but if other parts of the distribution system can not be geared to take advantage of its benefits the greater part of the investment may be wasted.

■ The Physical Distribution Management Concept.—In re-

Courtesy Johnson & Johnson

An automated warehouse.

cent years we have heard a good deal about the "new management art and science of Physical Distribution Management," and there has been discussion as to the part of the traffic manager should play in this function.

Our ability to mass produce goods has far surpassed our ability to get them to the market place. Today, almost any product you can think of spends more time in the distribution system than it does on the production line. Over half the selling price of many consumer goods goes to cover costs incurred after the production process ceases.

The reason for this can be traced, in part, to management's attitude toward the movement of goods. At one time, this movement was considered to be a secondary, but unavoidable, expense in the overall marketing plan. During the first half of this century, management concentrated on the efficiency of the production line. The emphasis was on production, and cost-cutting research was primarily confined to the manufacturing processes.

During the 1950's, many companies realized that they had just about cut their manufacturing costs to the bone. So they turned their cost-cutting efforts to the traditional functions in the company that are involved in getting the goods to the customer. In terms of cost, the traffic department is one of the largest of these functions. As they learned more about the here-and-there expenses incurred for packaging and moving their products, they became quite concerned about the total cost of distribution. Top management started looking for ways to apply the cost-cutting principles of mass-production to the complex problems of mass-distribution.

This look at distribution from the top down—instead of from the inside out—has been called many things: physical distribution, business logistics, materials management, distribution engineering, and logistics management. "Physical distribution" has emerged as the term most generally used to describe this total cost concept of distribution.

Physical distribution is not really a new art or science . . . nor is it as complicated as many of its advocates make it out to be. It is little more than an attempt to coordinate and control all of the elements that contribute to the cost of getting goods to the market. It recognizes the need for greater cooperation between the many traditional functions within a company that are involved in moving goods.

Depending upon what's moving and where it's moving, these functions include such things as (1) traffic and transportation; (2) materials handling; (3) packaging; (4) warehousing; (5) order processing and related distribution center operations; (6) purchasing, production and sales services (insofar as individuals in these latter three functions get involved in the expediting or routing of goods). To a limited extent, it also includes inventory control, unit load planning, site selecting and sales forecasting (although each of these is more of an extension of a traditional company function than it is a true function in itself).

The physical distribution concept is a practical one. It works for small companies as well as for large ones. The key to making it work is coordination—a continuing exchange of information—between the people in the company who manage the traditional functions involved in distribution. This is not the same as saying that to benefit from physical distribution, a company must centralize the control for all of these functions under one man with some type of distribution title. Some companies have found that formalized, centralized distribution departments work best. Others, some good sized companies, have found the opposite to be true. They have found ways to coordinate the functions without consolidating the authority.

The traffic manager should bear in mind that as a part of the development of physical distribution the advent of the computer has made it possible to measure more accurately than ever before the "tradeoff" of costs between transportation and the other activities we have mentioned. And he should be equipped to use the systems approach, not only in terms of transportation but also in terms of all the other activities that relate to it. He should be prepared to recommend spending more on transportation in cases where he knows it will reduce total cost and improve customer service. He should not hesitate to recommend unit loads and improved packaging where they will produce the same results. He will necessarily be occupied a great deal of the time with rate matters, claims and the like, but he should never let these activities become ends in themselves or obscure the fact that his primary transportation responsibility is part of a total system where it may on occasion be outweighed in importance by other elements such as the cost of inventory.

What the traffic manager should realize is that whether or not his company gives organization-chart recognition to the physical distribution concept, it always has a physical distribution system. This is just as true of the company that ships a single bulk product in carload lots as it is of the manufacturer of consumer goods who serves thousands of retail outlets nationally. In the first case, transportation may be the dominant element, whereas in the second inventories, packaging and warehousing will be important elements, but the fact remains that both involve distribution systems and both will benefit from the systems approach—whether it involves unit trains, special hopper cars and bulk terminalling at key points, or computerized order-processing, automated warehousing and premium transportation.

A good example of just what can happen in a combination physical distribution/electronic data processing national distribution arrangement is demonstrated by considering a multiproduct corporation with 40 plants throughout the U.S. Each of these plants ships all of the items it makes to each of 14 distribution warehouses scientifically located close to the corporation's major markets. All customers in each distribution region will be served only from the particular warehouse located in that region. These customers will be supplied by regular shipments, daily if desired, of every item sold by the corporation in mixed shipments from the regional distribution warehouse.

Such a complex is controlled by EDP through only one U.S. service center. Sales offices throughout the country put their area orders on tape which is sent to the service center by teletype. The service center puts the orders on punched cards which are fed into the computers and this is when the magic really starts. Not only do the computers prepare the data for issuing bills-of-lading and loading and routing orders; but they also check the accounts receivable register and determine the customer's credit status and credit limits. The computers also prepare data for issuance of invoices and issue daily stock-status reports used for inventory control.

Salesmen in the field send their orders to the service center by air mail or teletype, as the case may be. After processing for credit check and other functions, orders with full instructions for handling go by teletype to one of the 14 distributing warehouses. There the message is further processed emerging as a loading order, memorandum bill of lading, etc. all set up for the next day's shipping. Next, confirmation of shipment goes back to the service center where stock status inventory control reports are compiled daily for each warehouse. Each regional manager also receives a daily "delivery analysis" report for his area.

The advance scheduling of the use of order handling and carrier equipment removes the necessity of "flooring" goods, one of the costliest routines of most current warehouse and shipping activities. While this is going on the computer will have recorded the reduction in the inventory, made up the shipping papers and notified the customer or consignee that the shipment is moving forward providing necessary details. Operations along these lines have been established. Where indicated, their potentials for economies should be used.

As regards inventories, control charts will not result in perfect conditions at all times. There are sure to be peaks (like just before Christmas) when it may be necessary to use another warehouse temporarily. In these matters, a feature to be remembered is that care should be exercised to see to it that old stock is shipped first and that plans are made which will include this feature.

The traffic manager who trains himself to think in terms of the total system and keeps up on developments in disciplines that relate to his own should not have too much to worry about from the physical distribution concept. In many ways, he is the logical candidate for the top job by virtue of his training and the scope of the job he is doing. If he can demonstrate managerial ability and broad knowledge of fields related to his own within the framework of company obectives, he is well on the way.

While a great deal of physical distribution management appears to have to do with mathematical techniques and computer applications, the traffic manager should bear in mind that the purpose of these is essentially to aid decision-making. The notion that computers can replace managers still persists in some quarters, when the truth is that computers help managers function at the top of their skills. They eliminate the need for routine, repetitive decision-making and paperwork and enable managers to devote more time to major decisions and questions of policy, long-range planning and the like. Naturally, it is in the traffic manager's best interests for him to know something of what computers can do—and what they can't—and to understand how computer programs are written. The general subject of computers is discussed in Chapter 15, and trade journals are devoting considerable space to specific applications. It would be impossible, in this book, to go into all the ramifications of physical distribution management. Many of them are so specialized as to apply only to a relatively small group of companies. But the individual traffic manager has a wide range of literature to choose from, and he is limited only by his own ambition. In this respect, he has a distinct advantage over the traffic manager of even a few years ago, who often found that there was no truly helpful literature on the subect and few courses or seminars.

Company-Operated Vs. Public Warehouses

Large concerns, shipping all over the country, may find it more economical to establish branch houses that they own or lease and operate themselves. The general approach would be to ship into these branch houses or warehouses in carload lots and redistribute to each local area in smaller lots, or, to gather and store an entire product line from different manufacturing locations and reship in mixed loads. The branch house acts as a service unit, as well as a warehousing and shipping unit, keeping in close touch with the customers, handling billing and many "field" services.

A smaller company can accomplish the same results by using public warehousemen. The procedure is to rent warehouse and office space and use the services of a public warehouse for loading, unloading, etc. (see The Public Warehouse in this Chapter). Deciding upon the wisdom of a local warehouse distribution system involves the consideration of many aspects of marketing and transportation. Is the objective primarily getting products into the hands of customers at the least possible cost, or is it to provide better customer servicing at the lowest cost? In the latter case, increased distribution expense may well mean increased sales and profits, and thus will be more economical in the long run. So-called spot stocks are considered good insurance against delays, fires, strikes, storms, etc. The answer to the question of which is the better plan rests mostly with distribution policy as established by the management of each company.

Beware the built-in trap of warehousing, the tendency to think of the warehouse as a permanent fixture. This is to lose sight of its purpose in a distribution system. If for any combination of reasons the warehouse no longer efficiently meshes in the system, it should be wiped out, despite what may be a considerable investment. The right location can become the wrong location because of changing service requirements, transportation requirements, and the rate structures as well as changing customer demands on the company.

Strictly subordinate advantages of using a company warehouse include free advertising—a modern warehouse displaying the company name enhances prestige—and a site for sales offices or display rooms.

If local company owned or leased branch houses is the answer, the next question is, where to locate them? Although transportation will be a primary factor, other factors may be just as determining. For example, we refer to taxes, local labor costs, etc., that affect handling, servicing, billing, packaging, warehousing, value and availability of property and other considerations. A transportation study should be made of the relative advantages of several carefully selected potential locations. This cannot be accomplished by merely checking the carload freight rates to potential warehouse points, and the freight rates beyond. To be of any value, the study must be made on a "weighted average" basis. This will mean taking into consideration the volume of tonnage to and from each destination and origin. A point that is shipping or receiving three times as much tonnage as another must be considered accordingly.

Having given due consideration to the comparative transportation costs from factory or source to each branch house point to be studied, the next step would be to determine or estimate the tonnage to each town in each potenial branch house area. From this data a transportation cost study can be readily made. A comparison of the total transportation in and out costs for each point under consideration would give at least the answer on the comparative transportation costs.

If the weight cannot be estimated specifically for each municipality in the area assigned to each potential branch house, the total estimated figure for each area should be proportioned to each town, based on population. Assuming, of course, that retail sales will be in proportion to the population, it is possible to arrive at a realistic picture of which potential point is the proper one for location of a branch house or warehouse, insofar as the transportation factor is concerned.

Sometimes the distribution problems confronted are relatively simple and capable of solution by using a little high school algebra and plain good sense. Admittedly, some of the material on this subject places exaggerated emphasis on higher mathematics. In other words, the selection of the secondary or regional warehouse locations might be accomplished by a simple mathematical formula which would be developed to show the very best combination of (1) transportation, (2) inventory investment and (3) cost of warehouse operation. Such a formula would not decide on the market areas; but it would decide what is the best location from one of several that might be under consideration.

The overall study to be made will undoubtedly cover a wide field other than the traffic flow. These facts should be generally available:

—Approximate cubic or square foot requirements.

—Floor loads the warehouse must support (cubic density of the product it must house).

—What type of materials handling equipment will be used?

—Is there adequate aisle space for materials handling equipment?

> Do not make the mistake of specifying that all warehouse aisles be, say, 12 ft. wide if the need for the 12 ft. width is restricted to a small percentage of the total material or products to be warehoused.

Courtesy Interlake Steel Corporation

The above illustrates how more storage space can be obtained by the use of racks with good clearance and visibility. It is ideally adapted to inventory control and order picking systems.

Concentrate the heavy items that might require a 6,000 lb. capacity fork lift truck into one section of the warehouse with 12 ft. wide aisles and then set up the balance of the warehouse with 7 ft. or even 10 ft. aisles to accommodate 4,000 lb. capacity fork lift trucks of the narrow aisle type. If this is feasible and can be accomplished, it is obvious that the storage area will be increased with resultant economies.

—Highway and rail shipping and receiving facilities.
—Will customer pick up material or will it be delivered by common carrier or local delivery service?
—What special provisions for small package shipments?
—Sprinklers, humidifiers, heat and cold controls.
—Office and record space.
—Mail and parcel post service.

In some cases it can be worthwhile to make an effort to locate the warehouse in an area having similar distribution warehouses. This community of interest generally brings in more transportation services because a carrier coming into the area can pick up additional freight from other shippers in the vicinity.

Availability of good labor is important. Proper and adequate housing, transportation, restaurant, and other facilities close at hand will attract employees.

There is the question of whether to purchase property and build a warehouse, buy a warehouse already built or lease suitable property. Leasing is considered in lieu of building or buying and not in lieu of employing the services of a public warehouse. Low cost leasing is not always available except on a long-term basis of anywhere from 10 to 25 years. The possible advantage of leasing instead of owning are listed as follows:

(1) Conserves working capital; expenses can be current expenditures, not capital investment.

(2) Provides long-range opportunity for flexibility of location.

(3) May provide a more desirable location than that available for purchase.

(4) Facilitates a move when a presently desirable site deteriorates.

(5) Provides temporary facilities when eventual consolidation of plants is contemplated.

(6) Reduces insurance problems.

(7) Can possibly be advantageous from a tax standpoint.

Some companies expanding rapidly but not wanting to use the services of a public warehouse, find leasing the answer to their needs for desirable locations to service their customers. They say that leasing avoids heavy investments in warehouse facilities before the company is completely sure of its future business. Of course, rental is usually more expensive per square foot than ownership but not necessarily if a company is not too sure of its future requirements. Many concerns use a combination of owning and leasing. This policy permits buying only when permanent need is well determined. Another reason for leasing would be a decision that more earnings can be realized by investing available cash in manufacturing facilities rather than in warehouse buildings. It would seem to be true, however, that the cost of money on a lease basis is higher than the cost of bank loans. It all depends on the cash position of each company and how they figure the best potential, owning vs. leasing.

Another important question is the amount of inventory that should be carried in the branch house or warehouse. This again depends largely on company policy, as established by top management. Low inventories will mean low warehousing costs. But the risk with low inventories can be overcome only by fast, controlled transportation. Frequent, fast shipments may mean employing higher-priced transportation services. Too low an inventory may not take care of those emergency periods when the main plants are closed down. Although this seems to be the day of low inventories, it must be recognized that there is a danger point below which there may be no economy in the long run. This is a matter for each company to decide on the basis of requirements and peculiarities of the individual business.

The Public Warehouse

There are certain differences between a public warehouse and a place of storage. In certain instances those who would distribute through a branch-house plan will find the use of public warehouses less costly than operating their own buildings with their own forces. Through appropriate public warehouse arrangements operational burdens can be taken off the manufacturer thereby leaving him free to devote full time to production and sales.

Public warehouses provide a ready means for the manufacturer to keep his product moving away from the factory and to spread it over a wide territory near his customers. This is a definite competitive advantage in that greater flexibility is obtained. Local merchants sometimes use public warehouses to enable them to purchase goods in larger quantities, securing quantity discounts, or to buy when market prices are most favorable. Seasonal foodstuffs can be canned and warehoused for future markets. The public warehouse can be the reservoir between production and consumption. The principal services of the public warehouse are:

—Storage (custodianship).
—Handling, in and out of warehouse.
—Loading and unloading freight cars and trucks.
—Complete clerical and accounting services involved in distribution of customers' products.
—Accessorial services.

In connection with clerical services, public warehouses also become involved in data communication in the distribution processes of their customers. While warehouses ordinarily keep proper, routine records, present-day inventory controls sometimes require daily reporting of inventories by wire and other similar services. These can be provided by them.

There are many accessorial services; these will vary somewhat between warehouses. The following is a list of the most common of them:

—Leasing space to customers for specialized operations not

readily handled under ordinary warehouse procedure. Office and display space, telephone listing, phone and special clerical services and warehouse labor services are available.

—In-transit storage pending further manufacture, distribution, or sale of goods.

—Provision of controlled temperature and humidity storage.

—Handling and distribution of pool cars and consolidated shipments.

—Operating U.S. Treasury bonded warehouses for storage of imported goods under government supervision, pending the payment of customs duties or legal entry of foreign goods into the United States.

—Operating Internal Revenue bonded warehouses under government supervision for storage of liquor, cigarettes, or other goods manufactured in bond, pending payment of excise taxes and legal release for sale.

—Operating warehouse facilities under the U.S. Warehouse Act for storage of cotton, wool, tobacco, and certain other agricultural commodities.

—Operating warehouse and fumigation facilities under federal quarantine acts for foreign cotton, broomcorn, hides and skins, and other products requiring segregation prior to fumigation or sterilization.

—Furnishing or arranging for transportation by surface, water or air media.

—Loaning, or arranging loans, against merchandise in storage.

—Operating bottling, repacking, and labeling services.

—Operating warehouse facilities for the storage, servicing and distribution of machinery, steel and items requiring special handling equipment and techniques.

—Accepting buk cargo for special storage and rendering a bagging or packaging service prior to order deliveries.

—Operating 'field warehouses.' It is not always economical or practical to move a manufacturer's product to a public warehouse building. The producer may not wish to label or package his output until he knows where or to whom it is to be shipped and what the buyer's wishes may be as to labeling or packaging for shipment. The product may be in bulk, such as ores or pig metals. The manufacturer, however, may have a large amount of capital tied up in these goods and may desire a bank to loan him money, with the goods as collateral, so that he may produce more goods. The bank must have collateral to place in its loan portfolio, and suggests warehouse receipts. The public merchandise warehouseman will, for a suitable fee, appoint a custodian, obtain (through lease or otherwise) appropriate premises, and issue warehouse receipts for the property, keeping it under his supervision and allowing delivery of any or all of it only when it is released by the bank.

Public warehousemen feel that a larger segment of industry will wish to avail itself of the advantages of the public warehouse as more knowledge of the possibilities is distributed. Here are quoted suggestions from a practicing warehouseman as to the possible advantages of using public warehouses:

—"Availability of service. Public merchandise warehouses are

Combination clamp-fork lift truck handling a 300-lb. roll with its clamp attachment.

located in every distribution center. Use of such warehouses allows wider distribution of stocks nearer the markets than would be the case if storers' branch warehouses were used.

—"An actual cash saving will usually accrue. Payment is made only for actual services rendered. No capital investment is required. Fixed rentals and payrolls are eliminated.

—"Flexibility of service. Peaks and valleys of stocks create no problem. The warehouseman handles the large seasonal volume or the minimum off-season stocks at the same "per unit" rates and in the same prompt and efficient manner.

—"Costs of storage are known in advance on a unit basis, allowing intelligent inclusion of such costs in sales prices.

—"Safekeeping of merchandise. Responsible management and trained personnel provide for care of goods often not obtainable elsewhere.

—"Warehouse receipts issued by the public merchandise warehouseman are often acceptable collateral for banking accommodation, reducing the amount of cash capital necessary.

—"The storer is relieved of labor worries. The warehouseman must contract with his own labor.

—"Reduced insurance costs. Warehouses are generally of substantial construction, protected by automatic sprinklers or automatic fire-alarm systems.

—"Accessible to rail, highway, or deep water. Public merchandise warehouses usually are served by railroad sidings, accessible to main highways, and, if in river, lake or ocean ports, often have docks allowing direct handling from boat to warehouse, or vice versa.

—"Equipment for handling any size or weight of packages. Storer could seldom afford the expensive handling equipment with which most public merchandise warehousemen operate.

—"Accessorial services are available to storer. Experienced weighers, samplers, and coopers, as well as labor accustomed to repackaging or bagging merchandise, are usually on the warehouse payroll.

—"The warehouseman will furnish services required in connection with inventory control and transportation into or out of the warehouse along lines similar to those a manufacturer's branch warehouse would perform. Some of these services are reshipping, remarking, furnishing bills of lading, advancing inbound transportation charges, prepaying outbound transportation charges, collecting sight drafts, and prorating inbound freight charges among consignees. The warehouseman may furnish office space for the district salesman, as well as stenographic or clerical service as he may require it. The warehouseman may be furnished by the storer with approved credit lists and be authorized to deliver merchandise to the customers appearing on such lists.

—"Storage in transit is possible at a great many public warehouses, allowing appreciable savings in freight charges on goods reforwarded."

A number of public warehousing companies have adopted a "distribution center" concept for their own operations and, in addition to using highly sophisticated order-picking and handling equipment, also have data processing systems for order processing, inventory control and even customer billing on behalf of their clients. In some cases these warehouses perform such finishing operations as unit packaging of bulk materials, labeling, pricing, etc., and furnish display and office space for their clients. The agreement with the warehouse can be arranged so that the customer pays only for the services needed —and the charges are handled as current expense.

Special laws concerning the receipts issued by warehousemen and the warehousing incident to them have been in effect in many states for many years. These laws some time ago came to be known as Uniform Warehouse Receipts Acts. In more recent years such acts have been consolidated into, and made a part of, the Uniform Commercial Code. The latter is a group of laws concerned with commercial transactions which have uniform provisions. They, generally on the uniform basis, are on the statute books of, and are applicable in, each of the states.

Warehouse receipts may be negotiable or non-negotiable, the latter generally being the more used form. The negotiable receipts have certain attributes similar to negotiable instruments generally. A non-negotiable receipt is an acknowledgment by a warehouseman that the goods specified were delivered to it by the consignor and are held by it subject to release on written order from him. Legal specifications under the Uniform Commercial Code (Sec. 7-104) for the two kinds of receipts are: "A warehouse receipt * * * is negotiable * * * if by its terms the goods are to be delivered to bearer or to the order of a named person; * * *. Any other document is non-negotiable."

Important reasons for these special laws have been that warehouse receipts have been used extensively in obtaining loans. Such use is continuing except that more care is being exercised in this and related types of financing in recent years. In limited instances, but instances involving substantial sums of money, situations have arisen where goods were not as represented in the receipts.

Credit, loan, and other financing activities for an industrial company are responsibilities of its treasury officials and it is remote that its transportation people should become directly involved in borrowings or other similar activities on warehouse receipts. Indirect involvements may occur, however, and these aspects are reviewed here because of this. The data may be of assistance to Traffic in working with Treasury and in trying to be as helpful as possible to them in these matters.

Field warehousing is another type of public warehousing for proper utilization in appropriate cases. Consider a manufacturer who wants to develop a countrywide dealer set-up for a new line of products. It is necessary to deliver a stock to each distributor, complete as to sizes, colors and styles. To keep costs at a minimum, the stocks should be forwarded in carload or truckload lots. If the distributor has no space to store so much stock, he can put it into a public warehouse. An alternate might be appropriate, available space near his place of business. This is where field warehousing comes into the picture.

A field warehouseman may be engaged to open a branch public warehouse near the premises of the distributor, taking custody of the goods and issuing a public warehouse receipt therefor. This receipt would be issued to the manufacturer who would thereby retain title of the goods. As the distributor was able to sell the goods, they would be released to him on the order of the manufacturer and would be paid for as released. In this way and assuming arms length dealings have been conducted and there are no complications, the manufacturer would retain title to the goods through the warehouse receipt.

There is another plan that is more commonly used. A public warehouse can be established at the location of the merchandise. The warehouse receipt is issued to the distributor's bank instead of to the manufacturer and the distributor's bank uses it as collateral for a loan to the distributor which enables him to pay the manufacturer for the goods without any delay.

In either of the above cases, the manufacturer or the distributor's bank has a title that has been established with the holder of the warehouse receipt. The extent to which such a title may be satisfactory to the manufacturing industrial company is a feature for handling by legal counsel for that company. Some companies avoid financing in these matters when the "warehouse" is on the distributor's premises; others do not take exceptions to this feature.

Field warehousing has been applied to various commodities. These have included coal, lumber, and other items. Fairly recent problems incident to these matters, however, have brought on more care in the lending of funds incident to them. Also, even though warehousing may be a transportation function, the financial aspects of these involvements are basically Treasury responsibilities where industrial companies are concerned.

By way of warehousing in general, a warehouseman does not assume full and complete responsibility for goods while they are in his warehouse. His responsibility is for the care that the law requires him to exercise. This, in most cases, is care of a high degree and care similar to that of any other bailee. A warehouseman's rates ordinarily do not include insurance and, where indicated, an industrial company should be sure that goods are fully insured before placing them in a warehouse.

Suggestions On Shipping From Factory to Warehouse

How should an industry ship from its various factory locations to branch houses or warehouses? The primary factor to bear in mind when considering the problem is that every individual handling of freight is an additional risk of loss or damage, and a possible increase in cost. Each handling is a hazard, not only from the standpoint of possible damage to the freight and abuse to the packages, but also each handling costs more money. Consolidation of many small shipments into carloads or truckloads or pooling for carload or truckload shipment presents the greatest savings possibility. Unit loading (see Chapter 7) may be done in quantities acceptable to most customers and this would eliminate substantial handling to and from warehouses. The trend is to package materials in units that can be handled from the factory to the ultimate destination without repackaging at wholesale or branch locations. This trend calls for planning so as to include in a package the number of units best suited to the field stockroom. If these units are palletized (on expendable pallets, if possible, so that no return is necessary), handling costs are tremendously reduced within the warehouse as well as to and from transportation carriers' cars and trucks, not to mention economies at destination and delivery to the eventual consignee.

A regular, heavy movement between a factory and a warehouse presents no transportation problem, since there is enough tonnage to make fairly frequent carload or truckload shipments.

However, if shipments are from two or more factories or supply points, the situation is difficult and requires special traffic department handling. A few suggestions as to this problem are reviewed in the following paragraphs.

Stop-off in transit varies on different carriers but, in general, provides the privilege of stopping off in transit to complete loading or to partially unload, as the case may be. A charge is made for each railroad stop-off. There is great variation in motor carrier stop-off charges, though generally slightly lower than via railroad. In all cases the rate to or from the highest rated point applies on the entire lot. Many cases exist where the intermediate point is not necessarily the lowest rated due to circuitous routing. If a rail carload is shipped from Philadelphia to Kansas City with a stop-off to complete loading at Harrisburg, Pennsylvania, the rate from Philadelphia to Kansas City will apply to the total weight loaded at Philedelphia and Harrisburg. In like manner, a rail carload from Philadelphia to Houston, Texas, with a stop-off to partially unload at Dallas, Texas, is subject to the carload rate to Houston on the total weight for Houston and Dallas. On the other hand, Houston may have a commodity rate established under Fourth Section Authority and not applicable at Dallas; therefore a higher class rate to Dallas would apply. The same principle applies in connection with truckload shipments, the only difference being in the stop-off charge as explained above.

Railroad storage-in-transit privileges may be used economically. The railroad tariffs provide that, under certain conditions, freight may be unloaded and stored in transit. This costs extra for the storage, but the through carload rate from origin to eventual destination is protected.

One form of storage-in-transit called warehouse-in-transit was developed by a large company with the railroads and resulted in saving considerable transportation expense. Fortunately for this plan sales were made to wholesalers (distributors), so orders were usually in large lots. Even then, however, the wholesalers were unable to order carload quantities of every item. To meet this contingency the plan conceived a series of transit warehouses to which each factory or mill would ship in carload lots. The railroads, as a part of the activity, published arrangements whereby outbound carloads from each transit warehouse might be made up of articles which originated in carload lots at two or more mills or factories. Charges are computed on the basis of the through carload rates on each commodity from the respective origins to final destination, from which is deducted the amount paid from origin to the transit point and a charge for the transit privilege added. The freight bills covering the inbound movements are recorded with the railroad agents at the transit point. The outbound shipments are matched against these transit credits. The outbound route must be part of the tariff through route in connection with the published through rate providing the special stop-off provisions. While each wholesaler continues to order in carload lots, he is privileged to order a mixed carload of any item on the company's list, making his own decision as to what quantity of each item he requires. This is a great help to both the distributor and the manufacturer in that it permits the distributor to maintain lower inventories, allows use of the most economical form of transportation and, through more frequent shipments, assures fresher stocks for his customer.

■ *Consolidating.* When a consistent movement between the same points or areas develops that demands shipments of frequent small lots, the situation should be reviewed most carefully to determine how long a period these shipments would have to be held to permit forwarding in carload, truckload or piggy-back lots. This presents a real challenge to the alert traffic executive. However, if the proposition is presented intelligently, and if the possibility of an impressive annual savings in transportation costs can be shown, the pooling arrangement should be inaugurated on a trial basis.

Once in operation it will probably continue, provided that all details are carefully policed and a continuous, worthwhile saving can be effected. The main difficulty is to convince management, unfamiliar with such transportation technicalities, to permit the initial consolidation. This would require a plan to hold sufficient tonnage the number of days necessary to accumulate a volume shipment, a few days, a week or whatever it is. Such a program invariably creates an improved over-all service inasmuch as the controlled volume shipment is faster than when shipped LTL or LCL.

■ A *freight consolidator* receives many small shipments, from any source (but under the control of or for the account of one industrial company), and combines them into one carload or truckload, acting as an independent contractor serving the controlling industrial company. The charge made for this service depends on the requirements of each particular set-up.

A company shipping many small lots to destinations beyond Chicago, and locally in Chicago, could employ a freight distributor at Chicago to whom they would ship at carload, piggyback or truckload rates a car or truck made up of these small lots, all marked for their respective final destinations.

The freight distributor would receive the car or truck at his railroad siding or platform, unload it, and ship the small lots on separate bills of lading. The local Chicago shipments would be turned over to a local drayman, selected by the company employing the freight distributor.

Some freight forwarder subsidiaries act as consolidators. Consolidator's fees vary according to competition, volume potential, the accessorial services required, i.e., marking, preparation of bills of lading, advancement of freight charges, etc.

Freight consolidating has many possibilities. One example would be a company that receives many small shipments at a west coast destination. If these shipments originated east of Chicago, Illinois, Kansas City, Missouri, or other related gateway points, they could be shipped to a freight consolidator in the most advantageous city from a rate and service viewpoint, and the consolidator would load them into a car or truck and ship them as a carload or truckload to the west coast destination, thereby creating savings in transportation costs. This practice adopts the principles of the freight forwarding business (see Chapter 6) to private usage and enables the shipper or consignee to retain whatever reduction in costs accrues. Careful scheduling and expediting of shipments can lay them down at destination at predetermined times. The destination receives a manifest in advance of shipment by airmail, teletype or data communications medium and knows exactly what is in each load. When it is necessary to expedite only one load is involved instead of many small shipments. There is but one delivery instead of many spread out over several days. It is best to confine this activity to situations where there is a steady, heavy flow of tonnage from a somewhat restricted area, for if a regular schedule is not maintained, service will suffer. Further, if small shipments must travel too far to the consolidation point, the profit from the operation will be diminished. In many areas motor carriers' tariffs have very low Assembly and Distribution rates expressly published for small shipment consolidation.

■ *Shippers' consolidating associations.* Private concerns can consolidate for themselves through the simple procedure of shipping their freight under one or more pooling arrangements. Small concerns that do not have sufficient freight of their own to work out pool cars frequently work on an association basis with other companies and accomplish somewhat the same results by reducing members' transportation costs. For example, there are literally scores of shippers' associations in this country which have been organized for the purpose of reducing their transportation costs and obtaining improved service. Then, there are companies selling FOB their factory, which send scheduled pool cars to various destinations for the benefit of their customers.

Shippers' forwarding associations have been increasing ever since 1942 when the Interstate Commerce Act was amended to provide that "a group or association of shippers may consolidate or distribute freight for themselves or its members on a non-profit basis for the purpose of securing the benefits of carload, truckload or other volume rates." The consolidating activities of such organizations are exempt from the Interstate Commerce Act and not subject to regulation. If a common carrier freight forwarder can consolidate and make a profit, then shipper associations can do the same thing, dividing the savings among members in the form of dividends or direct reductions in the distribution of freight charges paid to carriers. At least they can if they have sufficient volume to load cars or trucks up to the full minimum weight at frequent intervals. Of course, they must be operated in a service where the rate spread is great enough to allow for local truck pick up and delivery, loading and unloading cars and trucks, lease of necessary platform and office space and a manager and clerical help. The longer the haul the greater the rate spread and thus, the greater the savings in transportation cost. Another advantage to members is that there is no minimum charge. Some shipper associations insure against losses not covered in the carriers' contract (bill of lading) such as Acts of God, riots, etc. (see Appendix 1).

Although members share shippers' association benefits, if any, they likewise must share any losses. Such an operation should not be attempted, therefore, unless (1) an adequate flow of tonnage is assured (2) experienced supervision can be provided and (3) there is sufficient participation and familiarity with the operation to assure performance strictly within the law (failure to do so can subject the shipper to undesirable penalties)!

One last thought on "shipping from factory to warehouse" is that a well-run warehouse should be so planned that it can accept immediate delivery of all inbound and outbound carload and truckload shipments, and thus eliminate demurrage charges which can be extremely costly if equipment is not loaded or unloaded promptly. More and more, carrier tariffs are increasing and establishing higher detention charges.

Suggestions as to How to Ship from a Warehouse to Final Destination

This class of shipment would ordinarily be almost entirely in the less-than-truckload field. Some shipments might go to truckload weights, and precautions should be set up so as to take advantage of the lower truckload rates wherever possible. The main objective is to distribute products from the warehouse as economically as possible, commensurate with the requirements of the customer. To accomplish this, the local branch-house shipping department or public warehouse must be well-organized with proper rate information so as to differentiate readily between parcel post, air, express, freight forwarder, truck and rail rates, as well as intelligent use of private motor carriage (see Chapters 6 and 11), where indicated. A general traffic department can, and should, furnish such information to each of its company's branch shipping units.

Plant Location

The discussion in this section embraces more than warehouse locations and includes manufacturing facilities as well as others. Transportation considerations to and from all plants have much in common whether those plants manufacture products, warehouse them, combine these functions, or are otherwise involved. Plant installations, particularly new ones, are important focal points for profit possibilities, and high priorities are to be assigned to the attention given them. Generally compromises must be made in these matters and, as new plants go in, all possible should be done that these compromises are kept to a bare minimum.

Traffic men understand that there is a great deal more to selection of a plant location than transportation. While the traffic manager may be called upon to advise particularly as regards transportation in the selection of a site, work on such matters offers him a unique opportunity to participate in top management activities. He must familiarize himself with the over-all considerations so as to visualize better how the transportation functions fit in with the needs and economies for the plant under consideration.

There are no simple rules to assure a successful plant location. Each "location" must of necessity be a custom job. There are, however, a few basic considerations that, though we are generalizing, may be summarized as follows:

—To the extent reasonably possible, areas of responsibility for work to be done should be agreed upon and spelled out in fair detail. Confusion and misunderstanding are avoided by doing this. As mentioned above, what is being discussed here is a plant location, not a distribution center. Naturally its products will have to move to customers, but such movement is simply an element for proper evaluation in arriving at a correct decision concerning the plant itself.

—Manpower or a satisfactory labor market is imperative. Electronic and highly technical plants should generally be located in a community where high level personnel and research facilities are available.

—Raw materials should be close by if at all possible, not only for cheaper transportation but also for fast delivery, eliminating large inventories at the plant. The ratio of raw material transportation costs to finished product transportation costs may be a controlling factor.

—Markets must be mentioned as important. A plant site near the consumption area, all other factors being equal, will save distribution costs and assist in faster customer deliveries.

Note: Raw materials may end up being a high percentage of the finished product, weightwise. If this is so, and the freight charges are appreciably less on the raw materials than the finished product—then, there may be real economy in setting the plant close to the finished product market rather than the source of the principal raw materials.

—Transportation facilities are much more important than ever before, not only because transportation costs have greatly increased but also on account of customers' insistence on low inventories. That means fast and flexible transportation. Plant locations should be near good highways, truck terminals, mainline railroads where a good railroad siding and service will be provided as well as water transportation where it may be needed. A study of both inward and outward transportation costs on locations under consideration is a must contribution by the traffic man. Commitments from carriers prior to site selection must be finalized. In addition, he should review the physical lay-out of the plant to be sure of a sufficient number and right type of truck bays or delivery platforms, as well as suitable railroad siding facilities and sufficiently large and properly equipped shipping and receiving areas. Close cooperation with the company's engineering, purchasing and legal departments is required.

"Get all of the transportation you can" is a particularly

good guide for industrial transportation managers involved in plant site selections. This, of course, is to be tempered so that it is "within reason" and "practical." Plants often exceed expectations, however, and as they are established it is simply the thing to do to look ahead on the basis that every possible transportation need will be met not only on adequate but on excellent, superior, and economical bases.

More specifically, where one location has two or three railroads as against another with only one railroad, this can be an important plus for the first site. Where water transportation may be needed, though remote, proper weight should be given a site with water versus one without. Motor carrier availability of the kind needed should be checked and evaluated. Air, parcel post, freight forwarder, Greyhound, United Parcel, and possibly other transportation services may also be in line for checking and evaluation. Such checking of all of these services should include the costs of them.

Some features of a new plant's subsequent transportation picture are closely tied to its establishment. Tonnage assignments to carriers to and from the plant can be important pluses and minuses. New or lost tonnage may result from it. In the interest of fairness, many traffic managers are particularly careful to deal with this feature where minuses are involved to the end that, as best possible, undue hardships are not created for carriers through loss of business. This is particularly true in the cases of carriers with solid records of providing the shipper with excellent, economical service. Where operating rights for motor carriers must be obtained, the I.C.C. at one time felt the carriers should be "permitted to follow the shipper" and granted new rights. The Commission is not doing this particularly any more. It follows that the shipper is pretty much on his own to do the best he can on tonnage assignments in these instances and will want to conduct himself accordingly.

Also, when operating rights are required for motor carrier service, some shippers include as many carriers as possible. They feel that with wide carrier availability they are better off if, later on, some carrier with rights should endeavor to hamper needed expansion. Other shippers are particularly careful to include, as an incident to operating rights requests, provisions for a contract carrier operation or operations. Along with these features and more, the company's freight rate structure and the freight-rate structures of its competitors should be analyzed and proper arrangemens made with the involved carriers for rate publications on correct bases.

—Most railroads have industrial development or engineering departments that can be helpful, not only in finding locations, but also in advising as to the physical lay-out of the plant and in connection with its transportation requirements. Traffic managers should see to it that contact is made with the proper departments of the railroads that might be involved.

—There are, of course, numerous other considerations that may be important depending on the type of plant to be built. These include price of land, taxes to be paid, proper supplies of water, coal, and so on, sewage disposal facilities, opportunity to expand, school system (sub-standard schools are to be avoided usually), the tone of the community, living conditions, electric and gas utilities, possible ecological problems, a prominent location from an advertising viewpoint, such as on an interstate highway, etc. etc.

Two other important steps of an operating nature are considered "musts" by many industrial transportation managers involved with new plants for their companies. First they personally "get on the ground" at the plant site just as quickly as possible and go over the transportation available, possible transportation alternatives, the terrain, the neighborhood, and the multitude of other physical features with which they will be concerned as an incident to making the plant a successful and profitable operation. Ahead of time, they familiarize themselves with the profit studies, background papers, and so on which are available and on which they have not worked or that are new to them. "On the ground" attention affords one of the best opportunities to deal with the many features that may be important to the plant. Perhaps another site with better transportation facilities should be selected. Perhaps completely different switching service needs to be arranged. Possibilities are many and varied and arrangements for them should be made prior to actual site selection to the fullest extent possible.

The second operational "must" for the transportation manager is to make sure, through appropriate call-ups when necessary, that features needing attention are properly dealt with on time and to a conclusion. This is so basic that no mention of it ordinarily is in order. Getting a new plant and getting it on stream involves so many non-routine activities, however, that this feature is one to be accentuated in these situations. Along wih these follow-up arrangements and related activities, full descriptions and explanations of what are developed from the "on the ground" work are, of course, to be passed on to staff members and others in interest.

Purchased Material Inbound to Plants

Economical distribution also applies for plant inbound shipments of raw materials and supplies. Substantial money can be lost through failure to order or schedule for shipment in quantities that protect the lowest freight charges when such charges are the responsibility of the purchaser.

For example, carload shipments of materials are subject to carload freight rates at specified minimum weights. These carload minimum weights vary from 10,000 to over 100,000 pounds. Most commodities take a carload minimum weight of 30,000 to 40,000 pounds, depending, of course, on the commodity. Thus, if 36,000 pounds of a certain commodity are ordered when the carload minimum weight is 40,000 pounds, it will be necessary to ship "as 40,000 pounds" to obtain the lowest overall charges which would be at the carload rate, thus paying for 4,000 pounds of "air." In other words, ordering an additional 4,000 pounds would mean that the freight cost would be less per commodity unit as the full 40,000 pounds minimum weight would be achieved.

This is even more strongly illustrated in weights from 18,000 to 25,000 pounds, where the carload minimum weight might be 30,000 pounds, but the truckload minimum weight is 20,000 pounds or 23,000 pounds. In such instances—assuming, of course, that the TL rate is not too much higher than the rail CL rate—it would be more economical to route as a truckload rather than as a carload unless, of course, additional material can be ordered to provide the full carload quantity. Motor carriers sometimes publish reduced rates on lots weighing as little as 1,000 pounds. This is an important subject and since there are many variances in the minimum weights for all commodities ordered, it is essential that purchasing department buyers check with traffic department personnel and determine economical quantities on those commodities that are shipped in sufficient quantity to enable motor carrier volume, truckload or rail carload handling. Do not overlook the fact that the heavier the shipment the faster the service, as carriers do not transfer heavier shipments en route as often as they do small shipments. Small shipments moving by truck or rail are subject to minimum charges per shipment. Because of the high cost of making individual deliveries, these minimum charges have risen to the point where the charge for a 50-pound shipment may be as great as that for a shipment of 200 or more pounds.

A more detailed treatment of the aspects of warehousing appears in "Modern Warehouse Management" by Creed H. Jenkins, published by McGraw-Hill, 330 W. 42nd St., New York, N. Y. 10036. As national manager of warehouse operations for one of the leading aluminum and chemical companies, the author brings practical experience and know-how to the text. It is quite comprehensive, particularly as to company-operated warehouses, and contains substantial detail on warehouse equipment, cost control, space utilization, and so on.

Another helpful tract is "100 Ways to Improve Warehouse Operations" by Warren Blanding and Howard E. Way, Jr. (Marketing Publications, Inc., National Press Building, Washington, D.C. 20004).

10

CONTRACT MOTOR CARRIAGE

CONTRACT CARRIAGE HAS EXCELLENT POTENTIALS FOR SHIPPERS in the way of service benefits, rate economies, and freedom to operate with few restrictions in several areas. Overly simplified and as the name implies, this form of operation involves a shipper entering into an agreement under which a motor carrier hauls his tonnage for specified rates. Properly handled it can come close to providing a company with transportation similar in many ways to that which can be made available through the use of its own trucks. Industrial concerns on the alert to obtain maximum help from the inherent advantages of various transportation modes give contract carriage worthwhile positions in their transportation programs when it is possible and practical to do so.

The discussions that follow are along three basic lines: (1) The features of a general nature which are applicable to this type of hauling; (2) the use of contract carriers where operating permits are not necessary, and (3) the use of them where the law requires that operating rights be held, rate schedules be filed, and so on. The operation of vehicles that are privately owned by industrial companies is discussed in the next chapter, as are leases of vehicles by such companies. The features dealing with contract carrier regulation are written with the Interstate Commerce Commission particularly in mind.

Many states regulate contract carriers along the same lines as the I.C.C. and much of what is said is applicable to both interstate and intrastate hauls. Specific state laws, of course, have their particular applicability and should be consulted where indicated.

General

Contract carriers haul for a limited number of companies and are in positions to provide personalized services to them. Their costs can be geared to the particular haulage they perform and their rates can be set on realistic patterns which reflect those costs. It is not uncommon for a contract hauler to work with his shipper or shippers regarding their "look-aheads" as to transportation requirements and to increase or decrease his fleet to meet those requirements. Also, he may go over his books periodically with them to establish that his charges are fair and reasonably profitable. He is in a position to operate free, in many ways, of rate bureau procedural restraints and Reed-Bulwinkle Section 5a involvements, to change equipment and rate schedules quickly when this should be done, and to concentrate on his operations and on doing a good job for his shippers.

To make a contract carrier arrangement worth while there must be enough tonnage available to provide proper truck use. The combined volumes from all of the carrier's shippers can be used to accomplish this. Also, there should be enough tonnage on a year-around basis to provide a nucleus of steady fleet utilization. Back hauls, when they can be arranged, are most helpful. If they cannot be arranged with the materials a company makes, its purchasing people may be able to help, and in some cases, to do so, it may be necessary for them to change purchase terms.

Some think of contract carriers as only those having highly specialized lines of activity, such as heavy machinery haulers combined with rigging operations. While many are specialized, the facts are that contract carriers can haul anything in the way of materials and provide any delivery service that any motor fleet operator can haul and provide, whether he be a common carrier or a private truck operator. Where volumes, distribution patterns, and other aspects permit, some shippers use all three modes—contract, common, and private—alongside each other in their transport activities from or to their shipping points.

The usual shipper practice with this type of hauler is to enter into a memorandum of agreement or formal contract with him. It is simply good business to do this, as the written word helps avoid misunderstandings; also, such agreements spell out that the carrier is an independent contractor and is not an agent of the shipper. This can be important in damage suits and in business activities where contentions may be made that the carrier is the agent for the shipper and, therefore, the shipper is liable for the carrier's acts.

The two formal contract forms that are hereinafter provided are rather lengthy. This gives rise to the question: When should a contract be issued from the standpoint of volume of work to be done? This will vary with different companies and is entirely up to the company policy. Generally speaking it should not be necessary to prepare a formal contract unless the volume of work to be done throughout a one-year period or on a specific job amounts to over $1,000.

Of course the responsibility for bodily injury, etc., is just as great for injuries or damage caused while hauling 50 pounds as it is while hauling large quantities. It is advisable, therefore, to cover local cartage jobs (or any other small-amount, short-term service) by a purchase order if a contract is not negotiated. This purchase order may be a blanket order for a given period or it may be issued on an individual job basis. It should not be used where contracts must be filed with the I.C.C. It should, however, be personalized to the particular transaction or transactions and should embody the following (or similar) wording, which is, for all practical purposes, a miniature contract:

"In acting under this purchase order you agree that any transportation and any other activities to be performed by you hereunder shall be done for your own account and responsibility and as an independent contractor. You will comply with all Federal, State, County, Municipal and other laws, ordinances and regulations, if any, in the work to be done hereunder, and you shall save us and our customers harmless from all damages of any nature whatsoever that we or they may suffer as a result of your failure so to do. All agents or employees furnished by you for the performance of work hereunder shall, at all times and for all intents and purposes, be your agents or employees and you assume full responsibility for and agree to indemnify and save us and our customers harmless from all liability and expenses, including attorneys' fees, for accidents or injuries occurring to such agents or employees or to other persons or for damage to property due to the acts of such agents or employees so furnished by you. You agree to carry suitable workmen's compensation, public liability and property damage insurance, and you agree, if requested, to assume the defense of suits that may be instituted against us or our customers through your failure to conform to laws as herein provided, or as a result of accidents or injuries to persons or damage to property due to the acts of your agents or employees."

Where the trucking work involves substantial sums of freight payments or is to be done over a lengthy period of time a formal, written agreement is advisable. Assuming that there are no legal requirements that the contract be bi-lateral or the like, an agreement form patterned after the one which follows may be used. It makes no provision for either party to guarantee to do anything tangible for the other party. All it does is provide a full set of responsibilities and basis for compensation if the work is performed.

The form is substantially a standard one and is in many ways the equivalent of a letter of intent. It is designed to cover services in the "unregulated" field and, with a few additions to comply with applicable regulatory laws, it can be used where they apply. See later comments and the later form. To it must be added details as to the parties, the nature of the services to be performed, and the compensation applicable for such services. Italics indicate "fill ins" to be made.

Trucking Contract

Contract made this *eighth* day of *February, 1973*, by and between *The Roseland Trucking Company* of the City of *New York*, State of *New York* (hereinafter called the Contractor), and *ABC Company, Inc.* having an office in City of *New York*, State of *New York* (hereinafter called *ABC*)

ARTICLE A—GENERAL PROVISIONS

1. Service. (a) The Contractor shall furnish sufficient labor, including chauffeurs, drivers, helpers and others, motor vehicles, equipment and tools and other accessories necessary to perform efficiently, expeditiously and with safety the services described in Article B.

(b) Although it is *ABC's* intent to use the services of the Contractor, *ABC* reserves the right, if and when in its opinion conditions warrant, to use other truckmen and in such case no accounting or payment will be due the Contractor.

(c) If at any time during the term of this contract, the Contractor shall not be legally qualified to furnish and perform the transportation service by this contract intended to or from or between any of the points herein specified or within the operation hereof, the said points shall be deemed eliminated herefrom during the time such lack of legal qualification shall continue and this contract shall continue as to all other points and services covered hereby. If at any time during the term of this contract any of the rates and charges herein specified for any transportation service shall not be the lawful rates and charges therefor, the lawful rates and charges shall be deemed substituted herein in place and stead of those herein specified and not then being lawful. Instead of permitting this contract to continue as hereinbefore in this paragraph provided *ABC* in any of the contingencies specified in this paragraph may at its option cancel this contract in whole or in any part or parts and if not cancelled in whole, continue the same as to the other portions thereof.

2. Relationship. Contractor and all of its agents shall, as far as

ABC is concerned, be deemed to be at all times independent contractors, and all chauffeurs, drivers, helpers, and other furnished by the Contractor pursuant to this agreement shall for all purposes be considered as employees of the Contractor.

3. Responsibility. The Contractor shall have the sole and exclusive care, custody and control of all goods, wares, and merchandise from the time they are tendered to the Contractor, its agents or servants, until the same shall be delivered to and accepted by the consignee at the destination designated by *ABC*. The Contractor, except as provided in Section 4 hereof, assumes full responsibility for any and all damage to or loss of any goods, wares, and merchandise entrusted to the Contractor hereunder and agrees to reimburse *ABC* for any damage thereto or loss thereof however occurring during the time that said goods, wares, and merchandise are in the Contractor's custody or possession. It is mutually agreed that the measure of damage to *ABC* in all cases of loss or damage shall be based on the invoice price of such goods, wares, and merchandise (or if there is no invoice price, shall be the value thereof to *ABC*), plus transportation charges.

4. Contingencies. The Contractor, however, shall not be held responsible for loss, damage, or delay caused by acts of God or the public enemy provided that the Contractor shall give *ABC* prompt notice of such loss, damage, or delay and shall take all reasonable and proper steps to abate the same.

5. Indemnity. The Contractor agrees to comply with all local, state and federal laws and regulations with respect to the employees of the Contractor engaged in performing services under this contract and with respect to the Contractor's operations hereunder. The Contractor hereby assumes full responsibility for any accidents or injuries to any person (including but not limited to Contractor's employees) and for any loss, damage or injury to property (including but not limited to Contractor's property, vehicles, etc.) as a result of or in connection with or incidental to the performance by the Contractor of the services to be rendered hereunder. In pursuance of such assumption of

responsibility by the Contractor, the Contractor agrees to carry sufficient public liability, property damage, and workmen's compensation insurance fully to protect against any loss, injury, or damage to any person or persons whatsoever, and if requested, the Contractor shall furnish *ABC* with a copy of such insurance policies or certificates which shall be satisfactory to *ABC* in all respects. The Contractor further agrees to undertake the settlement of all claims and the defense of any actions or suits brought against *ABC* and save *ABC* harmless from any and all damage, loss, expense, court costs, and counsel fees arising on account of the performance of any acts required by the Contractor to be performed in accordance herewith.

6. Construction. The construction and performance of this contract shall be governed by the laws of the State referred to at the beginning of this Contract as the location of *ABC's* office, and this contract shall be binding upon the heirs, executors, administrators, successors, and assigns of the respective parties. Waiver by *ABC* of any default by the Contractor shall not be construed as a general waiver, but as a specific waiver applying only to the default waived, and shall not preclude *ABC* from any rights or remedies in respect of any default theretofore occurring which has not been waived or any default occurring thereafter.

7. Assignment. The contract shall not be assigned by either of the parties without the written consent of the other.

ARTICLE B
SCHEDULE OF SERVICES AND COMPENSATION

1. The term of this contract begins *February 8, 1972,* and this contract shall continue in effect until terminated upon thirty (30) days prior written notice of intention to terminate being mailed by either party to the other. The effective date of termination shall be thirty (30) calendar days after such notice has been mailed.

2. The nature of the work to be performed and rate of compensation are as follows:

[*explanation of work covered by the contract inserted here*]

3. The Contractor shall make pickup and/or delivery in each instance except when otherwise specified, at the customary shipping or receiving section at the respective origins and destinations. Work shall be performed daily, including Sundays and Holidays, if requested, and in accordance with instructions issued by *ABC*.

4. The Contractor shall promptly render invoices for services, which shall be payable within 10 days after receipt or at such other intervals as may be mutually agreed upon in writing by the Contractor and *ABC*.

5. Rates of compensation shall be as follows: (Any hourly rates stated in this agreement shall apply from time of leaving garage until return to garage, with deduction made for lunch period, breakdown or other delay or failure on the part of the Contractor. Furthermore, if Contractor permits vehicles to remain on the premises of *ABC* or close by overnight, running time to and from *ABC's* premises will be allowed only to the extent that the truck is actually run to and from *ABC's* premises.)

[*rates to govern work covered by the contract inserted here*]

ABC Company, Inc.   *The Roseland Trucking Company*

By .... By ....
  General Traffic Manager   President

    Contracts can be quite complicated, unless all concerned cooperate to negotiate simple, clearly understood provisions. The simplest contracts to negotiate are those that show hourly rates only. This does not mean that hourly rates are recommended. In fact, quite the contrary is the case. Hourly rates assure a fixed income to the contractor for all the time his vehicles and men are away from the garage, since hourly rates usually apply from the time the vehicles leave the garage until they return to it, with time out, of course, for lunch period and any breakdown of equipment. Hourly rates are not incentive rates as far as the contractor is concerned. They also put the burden of efficient dispatching upon the company hiring the service, making the hirer responsible, in the final analysis, for profitable operation of the equipment.

Tonnage rates or flat-charge rates, on the other hand, are incentive rates, because the more efficiently the contractor operates, the more profit he gets. The contractor supervises the work which, after all, is his business. The company hiring the equipment merely states what has to be done, since the contract provides fixed charges for whatever services are specified. Rates in this category include those that are so much per load, per hundred pounds, per gallon, or any other unit of measurement that industry practice may find desirable. Flat charge rates may be preferable to cover delivery of items that do not always lend themselves to tonnage rates or to material the weight for which is not readily available and where it is more satisfactory to establish rates at a fixed amount for each item or load delivered. Where indicated, rates of this type might be reduced for each item over a fixed number delivered to the same address.

"Tonnage" rates and other charges can be more realistically related to costs with contract carriers than is generally possible with common carriers. Basically, the calculation of these costs involves the proper allocation of those that are fixed and those that are variable. On occasion, such costs are also characterized as involving time and involving distance. Once a truck is bought, the depreciation starts and goes on at all times; this is a fixed cost to be reckoned with on a time basis. Fuel costs increase with the miles run, are a variable, and these are properly to be dealt with on a distance basis. Other time and distance items are to be included in such detail as may be indicated. Along with the depreciation investment charge, the costs of wages, licenses, taxes, and insurance may be included in the time charges. Along with fuel, fuel taxes and other operating charges, tires, paint, maintenance, and miscellaneous items go in the distance category. Reasonable amounts to cover administration, supervision, general office expenses, and profits are also to be incorporated in one or the other of the categories.

Sometimes they are set up separately as "burden," "loading," "overhead," or whatever term may be appropriate.

For "quick" checks of whether freight rates are reasonable which are involved with carriers, some traffic representatives use as yardsticks returns per mile or per hour to the hauler. Such returns are generally calculated by taking the freight payment per load and dividing it by the miles run or time taken. The miles run are obtainable from road maps (be sure they are up to date) and the time taken from estimates of loading and unloading times and time on the road. Either basis can be the foundation for an informal estimate of whether a *prima facie* case of reasonableness exists. With experience, an analyst comes to know the weight to be given these figures, how returns per mile should be higher on short hauls, and so on. When, based on these checks, further calculations or negotiations are indicated, this should be done.

Another somewhat fundamental and common practice in connection with matters related to freight rate dealings is to use graphs of carrier costs as to particular areas or hauls where such costs can be ascertained and calculated on a reasonably accurate and fair basis. These graphs involve using fixed costs as foundations and relating the variables to the miles run. Hypothetically, this results in a graph picture along the lines shown on page 301. Such a graph is more accurate than bare returns per mile or returns per hour figures, is reasonably simple to prepare, and comes up in Line A with cost related rates that at least are in the ball park for important consideration in contract carrier rate matters.

These guide lines and the suggestions made here by no means tell the fully story of truck costs. Truck utilization to the maximum with fast, simple loadings and unloadings will bring down costs importantly. Leasing of equipment may increase them. Guide lines may be difficult to apply where numerous small shipments, split deliveries, local highway congestion, and other features exist. Many elements operate to vary those lines. Transportation cost accounting has a multitude of facets and

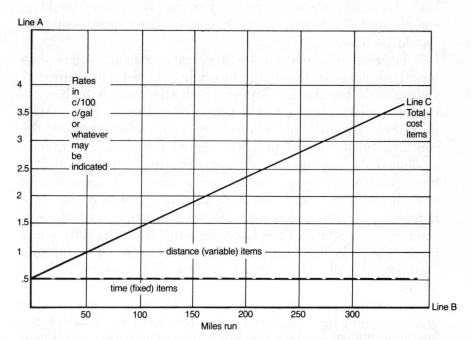

Chart form for relating fixed and variable truck costs to freight rates.

study and attention to them are important. To the exent it can be used appropriately, however, the graph can be a helpful tool because it stems from bed rock fundamentals.

Where "tonnage" rates of the type here discussed are agreed upon their inclusion in the trucking agreement (Article B (5)) could well run that ABC will tender to Contractor truck loads (minimum 30,000 pounds) of leather goods (or whatever may be involved) and Contractor will transport them from and to origins and destinations at freight rates as follows:

Origin	Destination	Rate in cents per 100 pounds
Brown, N. J.	Black, N. J.	25

Mileage scales may be included for use where specific rates are not named, minimum charges may be specified when less truck load shipments are involved, and so on. Generally speaking, complicated wording is not necessary in these agreements and should be avoided.

Turning to hourly rates for contract carriage, where they must be used the rates charged for labor should reflect the prevailing scale for the locality in which the work is to be performed. Scales vary and it is proper that this be done. After the prevailing scale and equipment costs are determined, the contractor's "burden" (including profit) is added. The precise amount that constitutes a reasonable "burden" charge will vary from one contractor to another and in some instances may be as high as 100 per cent, although a figure closer to 50 per cent is realistic in most cases. As a matter of fact, the variations in competitive quotations are likely to result from the differences in the methods used by individual contractors in computing "burden," as all probably are subject to the same scale of wages.

In setting up a scale of hourly charges, the rate for the vehicle should be considered separately from the rate for the chauffeur. The reason for this lies in overtime, for time and one-half or double time should be applied only to the chauffeur's rate and not to that applicable to the vehicle. Where possible, the "burden" item should be computed only on the basic labor rate and not on overtime, on the theory that the contractor's overhead is no greater for overtime than for straight time. Overtime usually is time and one-half for other than regular hours during the week and all day Saturdays; double time for Sundays and holidays. Computed according to the above, assuming that "burden" is 50 per cent and using hypothetical figures, the rates for vehicle and chauffeur at $7.75 per hour, comprising $2.50 for the vehicle and $5.25 for the chauffeur would be as follows:

	Regular time	Time and one-half	Double time
Vehicle	$2.50	$2.50	$2.50
Labor	5.25	7.00	8.75
Total charge	$7.75	$9.50	$11.25

Hourly rates may be subject to minimum compensation for as much as four hours. On the other hand, if there is sufficient prospective use for the vehicle, it is possible to negotiate daily and weekly rates somewhat lower than at the straight hourly basis. For example, the $7.75 per hour charge might be reduced from $62.00 to $55.00 for a full eight-hour day, or from $310.00 to $260.00 for a full 40-hour week, in recognition of the complete utilization of the chauffeur's time thus guaranteed.

The daily basis is computed by reducing the eight-hour charge by approximately 10%, while the weekly rate is $20.00 or $25.00 less than five times the daily rate. In actual practice, other methods may be used to arrive at daily and weekly rates, but many contractors are quite willing to offer such inducements to enable them to stabilize their employee assignments and equipment use.

The principal thought behind any contract basis for trucking operations should be complete coverage and simplicity. The complete coverage eliminates misunderstandings and possible faulty billing while simplicity enables all concerned to understand the application of the charges with their resultant costs in a clearcut fashion.

Contracts should be prepared to fit a particular job to be done. They should be "custom built." The sample contract previously shown in this chapter shows no expiration date but, instead, carries a 30-day cancellation clause. This is done with the idea that either party to the contract is free to renegotiate whenever a change in conditions necessitates a new contract. It also eliminates revision every year if not necessary. Under certain conditions, however, it may be desirable to place the contract on a one-year expiration basis plus a 30-day cancellation clause. This means that once a year both parties get together and decide upon the terms and conditions of a new contract for the ensuing year.

Never hire the contractor to perform services not covered in the contract. This tends to get away from the contract and breaks down the contractual relationship. As conditions and requirements change, the contract should be revised accordingly. Also try to avoid supplementing a contract by a letter. It is always better to reissue the contract in its entirety or revise it by the issuance of a formal supplement, giving all interested parties a copy of the new contract or of the supplement.

Contract Carriage Where No Operating Rights Are Required

The utilization of contract carriers where no operating rights are required is dealt with at times as using them where no regulations are applicable, that is, on a "non-regulated" or "exempt" basis. At other times such employment of them is described as used of them in intraplant and intracity service. These spell out important ways to use them. Special features exist as to these designations, however, and may be important. As examples, intracity moves without permits may properly extend to other nearby municipalities in many instances, and safety regulations may be applicable even though no other regulations are in effect. Further, there are certain commodities that may be transported anywhere without permits. Also, in some states there are no requirements for operating rights as to either commodities or territorial areas on intrastate moves without their borders. Other possible situations that may exist under the regulatory laws may be important to certain shippers and the statutes in this regard should be checked and followed closely.

The Interstate Commerce Act (U.S. Code, Title 49, Part II, Sec. 303(b)(8) provides that no operating permits are required for "* * * transportation * * * wholly within a municipality or between contiguous municipalities or within a zone adjacent to and commercially a part of any such municipality or municipalities * * *." Section 303(b)6 specifies no permit is required for "* * * motor vehicles used in carrying property consisting of ordinary live stock, fish (including shell fish) or agricultural (including horticultural) commodities * * *." The first of these is known as the commercial zone exemption; the second, the agricultural products exemption. It is in these fields, in intraplant trucking, and in the states with no laws imposing regulations that most contract hauling is done without operating rights, that is, on what amounts to a normal, business basis similar in many ways to the manner in which other industrial transactions are handled.

The commercial zones mentioned above are delineated by the I.C.C. as to individual cities and the boundaries of these zones are to be found in the Commission decisions on them. Such delineations are supplemented from time to time, depending on industry growth and other factors, and many industries make special efforts to have their plants included in these extensions. They use the opportunities which arise on occasion to do this and at times take the initiative in extension proceedings. Commercial zones in practically every instance extend beyond the city limits of the municipality involved. The New York City commercial zone is far more extensive than the city boundaries. The same is true of Chicago, St. Louis, New Orleans, and practically all other cities.

The agricultural commodity exemption has been the subject of considerable litigation and the Commission has issued lists of commodities it considers covered and not covered by the wording of the statute. These detailed lists are available in various publications when needed. Permits to haul these products to and from any place in the country are not required.

By way of miscellaneous features, intraplant trucking is, of course, a strictly private affair that does not involve highway use, the public, or have other attributes that impel regulation. Also, laws in a very few states call for regulation of certain aspects of intracity moves on intrastate traffic and should be borne in mind. Additionally, the interstate commerce act (Sec.303,b,9) exempts "* * casual, occasional, or reciprocal transportation * * * by any person not engaged in transportation * * * as a regular occupation or business * * * ." This is little used, however, and is quoted simply as general information.

Most of what is said in the earlier parts of this chapter is applicable to contract carriage where no operating rights are required. Suggestions there are in point here. Arrangements can be set up and carried out with the agreement forms along the lines mentioned very much as would be the case with any other arrangement or contract for materials or service. The dealings to be accorded the hauling can be quite similar.

As regards aspects for particular comment, when it comes to economy, the big potential saving in operating expenses lies in how well the fleet is operated from a functional or dispatching viewpoint. If trucks can be kept busy all day long carrying full loads in both directions and eliminating terminal delays, there is no doubt that the operation is being carried on at its maximum efficiency.

A truck, trailer or tractor sitting idly at a platform is an inefficient unit from a production standpoint. Many companies have found a helpful solution to the idle power unit or tractor problem by inaugurating a shuttle system. By using two or more trailers to each tractor, it is possible to switch the tractor from one trailer to another, the idea being that while the tractor is hauling one trailer, the other or others are being loaded or unloaded, as the case may be. Intraplant and commercial zone trucking lend themselves in particular to such shuttle systems.

If a fleet is hauling too much "air" (is not fully loaded) or is "standing by" for long periods of time, it might be helpful to have each driver prepare a log for a week or so. This log could show all the origins and destinations, percentage of space used gainfully on each trip, and time consumed. An analysis of these logs should permit the working out of a good schedule for each truck, thereby producing an efficient operation.

Other possibilities for increased efficiency include using a good mechanical recorder on each vehicle. A recorder provides accurate data on the actual waiting and running time of the equipment. These are sometimes referred to as tachographs and may have other designations. The particular comments and suggestions made in this and the three preceding paragraphs assume, of course, the existence of relations where both hauler and shipper share in the economies that are effected.

If there are capable haulers available and they are interested, this type of hauling can, of course, be put out on bids in the same fashion as might be done for requirements of other types of service. In actual practice this is not done except on rare occasions, those occasions being generally when a "spot" hauling job is to be done, a new plant comes on stream, or something similar occurs. Even then most companies prefer to deal on negotiated bases with those haulers who have done good jobs for them. Basically, a top-flight contract hauler's work, service, charges, and so on can be such as to meld into and be so tied to his shipper's business that the negotiated route is the one to take and to use as long as each party keeps his relations with the other on excellent bases.

Contract Carriage Where Operating Rights Are Required

The use of contract carriers where operating rights are required is sometimes called intercity use. Utilization of these haulers between cities is, of course, important but at times is on a much broader basis in that operations can extend to counties, be statewide, and so on. There are some 2,000 of these contract operators now hauling interstate traffic, as against some 10,500 common carriers, and the number is steadily growing.

Under the Interstate Commerce Act (U. S. Code, Title 49, Sec. 303,a,15) "contract carrier * * means any person which engages in transportation * * of passengers or property in interstate or foreign commerce, for compensation * * under continuing contracts with one person or a limited number of persons either (a) for the furnishing of transportation services through the assignment of motor vehicles for a continuing period of time to the exclusive use of each person served or (b) for the furnishing of transportation services designed to meet the distinct need of each individual customer." Highlights of other legal regulations are that the shipper-carrier hauling agreement be bilateral, that a schedule reflecting the rates and charges in the contract and the contract itself be filed by the carrier with the Commission, and that an operating permit from the Commission as to commodities and territory be held by the carrier. Applicable also to the carrier are regulations requiring that it be fit and able.

The requirement that the contract be "continuing" and "bilateral" works out in practice that the shipper agrees to tender the carrier a certain amount of traffic during the contract period. This need not be large, an important test being that it should cover a series of shipments during a stated period of time. One calculation used where both parties agree is to make a normal estimate of the tonnage for a year and place a tenth of this figure in an appropriate year's clause in the contract. Unavoidable production changes and other unforeseeable possibilities dictate conservative appropriates to this feature. The requirement that contracts be with "one person or a limited number of persons" is generally dealt with in a broad way by the carrier limiting the number of his contracts to seven at most. The less the number, the better the carrier can tailor his services to "distinct" shipper needs.

Contracts along the lines of the one that follows have been used in these matters for years. The form should be reviewed carefully and amended where indicated to be sure it is in line with shipper-carrier requirements as well as requirements of applicable regulatory bodies. Where Clause 2 and other applicable clauses were appropriately filled in, no exceptions have been taken to them by those bodies. The form is self-explanatory and a separate schedule form for subsequent, formal amendments is also included.

TRUCKING AGREEMENT

THIS AGREEMENT made this .... day of ....
19..........., by and between (..........) whose address is ....
hereinafter called "SHIPPER," and ....

whose address is .... hereinafter

called "CONTRACTOR."

WITNESSETH THAT: The parties hereto hereby mutually agree as follows:

1. CONTRACTOR shall transport by motor truck for SHIPPER, as hereinafter set out, such

quantities of .... as SHIPPER may offer to CONTRACTOR during the term of this Agreement between points specified on schedule No. 1 hereof. As to each shipment made hereunder Shipper shall designate the point of origin and destination thereof, the place within such points where the shipment shall be loaded and unloaded, the time when each such shipment shall be loaded and unloaded, the amount of each such shipment and the particular product or products comprising the same.

2. Each and every shipment hereunder shall be made at the sole option of SHIPPER; provided, however, that SHIPPER shall offer to CONTRACTOR during each contract year of the term

of this contract, for transportation hereunder, not less than... of cargo, said minimum quantity to be reduced proportionately in the event this contract terminates for any reason prior to the end of any contract year. SHIPPER shall not be obligated to offer to CONTRACTOR any products in excess of said minimum quantity, but shall have the right to do so, and CONTRACTOR shall accept and transport as herein provided all quantities offered while this Agreement is in force, provided that CONTRACTOR shall be given at least twenty-four hours' notice of any shipment. All transportation shall be performed with all reasonable dispatch, at CONTRACTOR'S sole risk, cost and expense.

3. Each shipment shall be evidenced by a receipt in form specified by SHIPPER, signed by CONTRACTOR and the consignee showing the kind and quantity of cargo received and delivered by CONTRACTOR at the loading and unloading points respectively. Absence or loss of such receipt form, however, shall not relieve CONTRACTOR from responsibility for the cargo delivered to CONTRACTOR.

4. SHIPPER shall pay CONTRACTOR as full compensation for CONTRACTOR'S compliance with all the terms and conditions of this Agreement, an amount computed in accordance with applicable rate or rates shown on schedule No. 1. Any or all rates specified on said schedule or which may hereafter be agreed upon, whether between the points now listed in said schedule or other points hereinafter agreed upon, may be increased or decreased from time to time by mutual consent of the parties in writing. Such payments shall be made upon the basis of the cargo actually loaded into CONTRACTOR's equipment as shown by SHIPPER'S receipt form for the shipment. For each load of products transported hereunder CONTRACTOR shall furnish SHIPPER with an invoice in duplicate and with the original copy of the receipt described in Section 3 above. SHIPPER shall pay such invoice promptly after presentation but shall not be required to make payments more than once each week.

5. If, from any cause whatsoever, whether within or without CONTRACTOR'S control, a shipment or any part thereof is lost, contaminated, adulterated, discolored, destroyed or damaged in any way, CONTRACTOR shall pay to SHIPPER, within ten (10) days after receipt of invoice from SHIPPER, SHIPPER'S price applicable to the kind and quantity of cargo so lost, contaminated, adulterated, destroyed, or damaged, and, in addition, all taxes, fees and other charges of any kind or nature which SHIPPER may have paid or may be required to pay or collect in respect to or measured by said cargo or the manufacture, storage, distribution, transportation, sale, or any other feature thereof. Upon payment by CONTRACTOR for any contaminated, adulterated, discolored or damaged product or products, title to the same, and the right to possession thereof, shall pass to CONTRACTOR, and he shall immediately remove the same from any prem-

ises of SHIPPER or any consignee at which they may be located. CONTRACTOR shall not resell the same, however, under SHIPPER'S name, trade-marks, or colors.

6. CONTRACTOR shall conduct all operations hereunder in CONTRACTOR'S own name and not in the name of, or as agent for, SHIPPER. In performing all of CONTRACTOR'S obligations hereunder, CONTRACTOR shall act as an independent contractor, and neither CONTRACTOR nor CONTRACTOR'S agents or employees, shall be subject to the control or direction of SHIPPER, except as specifically provided herein.

7. If, under any law or ruling of any government or agency thereof, whether Federal, state or local, SHIPPER, at any time during the term of this Agreement, shall be required to pay rates to CONTRACTOR in excess of any of those fixed pursuant to this Agreement, SHIPPER may terminate this Agreement upon giving written notice to CONTRACTOR of its election so to do.

8. CONTRACTOR, in its operations hereunder, shall comply fully with all applicable laws, rules, orders, and regulations of all governments and agencies thereof, whether Federal, state or local, and shall furnish SHIPPER with satisfactory evidence thereof whenever requested so to do. CONTRACTOR shall report and pay all social security, old age and unemployment taxes, contributions and charges levied on or with respect to CONTRATCTOR'S employees and shall reimburse SHIPPER for and hold SHIPPER harmless from any such taxes, contributions or charges which may be imposed upon, levied against or collected from SHIPPER.

9. All trucks and equipment used in performing CONTRACTOR'S obligations hereunder shall be furnished by CONTRACTOR and maintained by CONTRACTOR in a good, safe and serviceable condition, and shall be suitable for the transportation covered by this Agreement. Trucks and equipment shall comply at all times with applicable standard specifications therefor. No truck or other equipment shall be used by CONTRACTOR except with SHIPPER'S approval of the same, but any such approval shall not relieve CONTRACTOR of any of the obligations imposed upon it under this Agreement.

10. CONTRACTOR agrees to carry the following insurance: (a) Workmen's Compensation Insurance sufficient to comply in full with the laws of the states in which CONTRACTOR operates hereunder; (b) Employers' Liability Insurance in the minimum amount of Twenty-five Thousand/ Twenty-five Thousand Dollars ($25,000/$25,000), covering those employers' risks not provided for in the Workmen's Compensation laws; (c) Public Liability and Property Damage Insurance on all trucks and other equipment used by CONTRACTOR hereunder in an amount not less than $10,000/$20,000 covering bodily injuries (including death) to persons, and in an amount not less than $10,000 covering damage to property. Whenever SHIPPER shall so request, CONTRACTOR shall furnish SHIPPER with certificates properly executed by the insurance carriers evidencing CONTRACTOR'S compliance with CONTRACTOR'S obligations under this Paragraph 10.

11. CONTRACTOR shall indemnify and hold harmless, protect and defend SHIPPER from and against any and all loss, cost, damage, expense, suits, claims, and liability of whatsoever kind or nature which SHIPPER may sustain, suffer, or incur, or which may be instituted or asserted against SHIPPER, resulting from or arising out of any act or omissions during the term of this Agreement of CONTRACTOR, or CONTRACTOR'S servants, agents or employees; provided, however, that SHIPPER shall have the right to participate in the defense of any litigation instituted against it without thereby relieving CONTRACTOR of its obligations under this paragraph.

12. CONTRACTOR shall not assign or subcontract this Agreement, or any of CONTRACTOR'S obligations or rights hereunder, including, without limitation, any money due or to become due to CONTRACTOR hereunder, without the consent in writing of SHIPPER.

13. SHIPPER shall have the right at any time to apply any sum owing by it hereunder to the payment, in whole or in part, of any sum owing by CONTRACTOR to SHIPPER, whether under this Agreement or otherwise, where there are no governmental rulings prohibiting such applica-

tion, and any assignment made of freight earned or to be earned hereunder, even though consented to by SHIPPER, shall be subject to the provisions of this paragraph.

14. New and additional schedule initialed by both parties hereto may be attached to this Agreement at any time by mutual consent of the parties, whereupon such schedules will become a part of this Agreement.

15. If CONTRACTOR fails to perform any obligation imposed upon CONTRACTOR under this Agreement or breaches this Agreement in any respect whatsoever, or if any insolvency, receivership or bankruptcy proceedings, voluntary or involuntary, be instituted against CONTRACTOR at any time, SHIPPER shall have the right, and without prejudice to any other remedy which it may have, to terminate this Agreement by notifying CONTRACTOR in writing of its election so to do.

16. This Agreement shall be and remain in force for a period beginning on the

.... day of ...., 19................ and ending on

the .... of ...., 19................ and from month to month thereafter; provided, however, that the SHIPPER may terminate this Agreement at any time by giving at least thirty days' written notice thereof to CONTRACTOR.

17. This Agreement embodies the entire understanding between the parties with reference to the subject matter hereof and it is agreed that there are no arrangements, agreements or understandings, oral or written, which affect this Agreement in any way.

....
(Shipper)

By ....
Traffic Manager

....
(Contractor)

By ....

SCHEDULE NO. 1 TO TRUCKING AGREEMENT

SECTION	ORIGIN	DESTINATION	RATE IN CENTS PER 100 POUNDS

SCHEDULE NO.   TO TRUCKING AGREEMENT

_____

(Shipper)

_____

(Contractor)

_____

_____

_____

_____

SECTION	ORIGIN	DESTINATION	RATE IN CENTS PER 100 POUNDS

The parties hereto agree that the above Trucking Agreement is hereby amended effective

...., to add the above thereto.

Executed this .... day of ...., 19 ....

....

(Shipper)

By   ....

Traffic Manager

....

Contractor

By   ....

Shippers that have regular contract carriers with operating permits should be careful that the utilization of them is as specified in those permits. Law violations occur when their use is beyond those specifications on commodities and into territories where regulation is applicable. Permit limitations, lack of operating rights, and the ban on hauling for more than a limited number of shippers present real difficulties at times to companies with freight to move who need (or want) contract carriers. On occasion contract haulers with appropriate permits are available. The ATA Contract Carrier Conference, 1616 P St. NW, Washington, D.C. 20036, publishes a directory of those with I.C.C. rights ($7.50). Further, in cases involving armored cars and the like some two to three hundred contracts are permitted.

Generally, however, a shipper with a new origin and no contract carrier with rights or with an origin where more rights are needed faces three motor carrier alternatives: one, setting up or utilizing a private carriage operation; two, using common carriers; and three, having new contract carrier operating rights obtained or existing rights extended. The discussion of private carriage in the next chapter reviews the feature of the first alternative. Common carrier use (negotiated or otherwise) may or may not fulfill requirements. If it does, or can be made to do so, the move to obtain or extend rights may be avoided.

Steps to obtain operating rights for a contract carrier involve the carrier applying for them to the regulatory body involved, the matter being set for a hearing or for attention, and the carrier and the shipper presenting evidence and proving to that body that it is "consistent with the public interest" that the permit be granted. Almost invariably there will be some other carrier or carriers who protest the granting of the rights and who assert they are entitled to make the hauls. Subsequently a decision will be handed down on the granting of the permit.

High-level shipper participation is substantially a must in these matters if they are to be successful. The requirements for the issuance of a permit are not as exacting as those for a common carrier certificate, but the shipper must be prepared to show a need for the carrier's service and how the service must be tailored to the shipper's specific requirements. Rights will not be issued simply because a shipper wishes to increase service availability, simply because rates of other carriers are too high, and so on. A worthwhile article in the December, 1971, issue of the *Transportation and Distribution Management* magazine by H. A. Dubin on the "Role of the Supporting Shipper" in operating rights cases gives further details.

It is advisable at times, also, for the shipper's traffic people to assist in the preparation of papers and in still other stages of these proceedings. No one knows better than they what their companies need, and first-hand attention to many features may save real problems later. Applications should be framed along broad lines as to commodities and territories. As illustrations, in appropriate cases, the right to haul chemicals rather than one chemical product should be sought. Where origin and destination areas are needed they should be delineated and asked for rather than, say, rights between two cities. Requests should be reasonable and represent what is needed to take care of the public served by the shipper in normal as well as unusual and emergency circumstances that have arisen in the past and that may well arise in the future. Other avenues of help can include, when sought, providing the carrier or his counsel with names of attorneys who specialize in these cases. Still others will depend on the particular circumstances and so on.

Various features of the laws pertaining to operating rights and the administration of them seriously need updating and realistic attention in the opinion of responsible traffic executives and, for that matter, of certain of the motor carriers. It is felt these features suppress competition and have other wrongful effects. Rebuttals run that changes may bring on nationalization of transportation and so on. Some carriers have no part in contesting rights requests and spend their time and money on perfecting their own operations. They feel that in this way tonnage assignments result rather than by going to what is set up to be the equivalent of a court of law to try and get them. Legislation is pending to do away with permit requirements for contract carriers and has much in its favor. Such a change in the law would make unnecessary present complicated and expensive proceedings with their nebulous standards and the questionable results that at times come from them.

The data furnished and the suggestions made in the earlier sections of this chapter concerning costs, operating methods, shipper-carrier relations, and the like are also applicable in many ways to contract carriers where operating rights are required. Reference to them should be made when it is appropriate to do so and, along with this, the regulatory structure superimposed thereon should be borne in mind and receive proper attention.

Other regulatory aspects include Commission control of freight rates. Rates of contract carriers in the regulated category may be suspended, investigated, cancelled, and so on, very much as can the rates of the rails and the motor common carriers. The yardsticks of reasonableness as well as others are also similar. When investigations occur, the dealing accorded them can well be along lines usually accorded other investigations of this nature.

As regards contract carrier rights being held by a common carrier hauler it is not customary under existing law for a motor carrier to hold authority to operate as both common and contract carrier. The Commission regards the maintenance by a single carrier of two sets of rates for what may be essentially the same service as an instrument of potential discrimination and therefore not in the public interest. Such dual authority has been granted in a few isolated instances, but only after the Commission has imposed stringent bookkeeping controls and has been satisfied that no violations will result.

An excellent monograph, "The Elements of Contract Carriage", by Blanton Bergen and Colin Barrett ($3.00) has recently been published by The Traffic Service Corp., 815 Washington Bldg., Washington, D.C. 20005. It first appeared as a three issue series in the *Transportation and Distribution Man-*

agement magazine commencing with the December 1971 issue. In the booklet are information at considerable length on utilizing contract carriers, what obligations must be undertaken in the hauling agreements with them, operating rights requirements, and other pertinent and practical information on the subject.

11

PRIVATE MOTOR CARRIAGE

THE MANY INTERESTING FACETS OF A COMPANY OWNING AND operating its own fleet of trucks have attracted a number of them to that activity. Some do it by leasing and lease aspects are included later in this chapter. Some feel the activity is worth while for them and others take views of a contra nature. Representative positions of the latter range from quite firm policies of "leaving the hauling to the haulers" to positions in which private trucking will be considered only when it is clearly developed that regular haulers can not, or will not, provide comparable rates, service, and so on available from the private equipment. The type of business in which a company is involved, i.e. whether seasonal or whatever the case may be, is often important to these positions.

A company owned truck operation is not to be undertaken or dealt with lightly. Such an operation would be much more complicated for a candy company than, say, obtaining and operating another candy manufacturing machine for its production line. In the case of a lumber company the complications would be far greater than buying a car load of lumber and selling it at its facilities. Equipment leasing services at times help in these connections, but complications remain. Also, they have to be paid for directly or indirectly in the long run.

Private truck responsibilities are dealt with organizationally in various ways by industrial companies. Some place them

317

in their transportation departments, some in separate departments, and some elsewhere. To get maximum benefits two important caveats should be observed. The first is that proper staff and help must be provided to run the operation and that it be not relegated to someone already fully occupied with other duties. The second is that the private operation should be carefully coordinated with the company's for-hire motor carrier operations. Every company needs adequate transportation available to it always. A for-hire, private mix can be of help in this regard and, at times, or real importance.

Careful coordination may help also in other ways. Situations in which for hire carriers come to feel the better classes of hauls are going to the private equipment in improper ways may be helped through freight rate adjustment and other work with them by traffic people who are knowledgeable as to what can and can not be done and the ways to accomplish changes. Equipment investments of a top-heavy nature where the money can be used better elsewhere can possibly be reduced. Also, back hauls involving empty movements may be corrected and unused or partially used facilities and equipment may be put to work more efficiently.

One of the country's highly successful companies with a fine record of public responsibility and service follows the practice of not hauling privately if for-hire carriers provide comparable hauling and has announced publicly that this is its position. That company's private truck operations are in a separate department but careful coordination between that department and its transportation people working with for-hire carriers is observed when it is pertinent that this should be done. As distribution patterns are set, or are changed, for-hire and private costs, service, availability, and so on are compared and common or contract carriers are employed when the advantages are in their favor or when all things are equal and a "saw off" prevails as to the types of carriage.

In these matters, of course, the rails and for-hire trucks have various internal considerations to which they must give attention in dealing with private equipment. On many occasions when they consider meeting private truck costs on a particular haul it is their best judgement and conclusion that it is not in their interests to do so. As with an industrial company faced with a possible price cut to meet a particular competitive situation, they may feel that an adjustment will not be isolated, that it will spread, and that over-all revenue considerations are such that they cannot go ahead with it. Many other somewhat related considerations may also be involved.

Most industrial companies are in the private trucking field because of the economies and the service benefits it brings to them. Such operations are relatively free of restraint and regulation and represent ways to get materials hauled that appeal to many. The trucks, by and large, can go anywhere at any time and carry any kind of the company's materials. Proprietary motor carriage is somewhat akin to a person using his own automobile as against using buses, cabs, trains, and airlines. Probably more than half of all U.S. businesses (non-transportation) run their own trucks to haul part or all of their traffic.

Other reasons to go into private trucking may stem from unyieldy regulatory restraints as to for-hire carriage, disenchantment with other modes, a wish for "complete control" as to this segment of a company's business, a need for such trucking to meet competition, and use of drivers as salesmen. These reasons are by no means the only reasons and generally private trucking comes into, and stays in, being because of a number of transportation factors with which a company may be confronted. Once started, a discontinuance may be difficult for various reasons some of which at times may be collateral (job discontinuances, customers wishing continuances of drivers' help, etc.).

The establishment and maintenance of an economic private truck operation is bottomed on having enough steady tonnage to keep a truck or trucks operating fully at over-all costs lower than would be charged by other available transportation services. Materials to be moved should be those of the company as, generally, it will not be able to haul for others. Preferably the hauls should be loaded both ways to avoid unused capacity in empty return movements. Lack of two way loaded tonnage may not be fatal, however, as the real criteria are total costs, private vs for-hire. It is of top importance in almost every case that the available tonnage be year-round and steady enough for full truck operation. Capital commitments and other financial obligations are incurred with trucks. These result in costs that continue whether freight does or does not move. When freight does not move these costs become drags on and red figures to the operation.

It is not practical to attempt to specify any particular minimum volume requirement to keep a truck steadily busy in terms of so many tons per day, week, or other unit of time. Various elements affecting this feature include average shipment sizes, number of units per shipment, service requirements, traffic concentration, what loading and unloading times (as to hours of the day and days per week) will be permitted, and so on. These in turn are to be related to sizes of loads that can be hauled, how much time will be consumed and how many miles will be run per load, and other elements. This matching is necessary to determine whether sufficient volume is available to keep a truck or trucks busy. With many companies the shipment volumes are simply not enough to keep a company truck occupied and operating economically. Appropriate recognition of this at times is simply a fact of life that must be taken in stride to avoid outlays on an uneconomical operation.

On the average and all things being equal, the cost of moving a shipment by private carriage should be less than via for-hire service. Common and contract carriers quite properly have a profit figure built into their rates and a comparable figure need not be a part of private costs. If this is given a hypothetical value of 7%, it does not mean, however, that a 7% return can be expected on a private truck operation. Freight rates vary as to destinations with some having good profits and others representing hauls at losses. Hauling costs as to specific destinations are to be matched, for-hire vs private, when this can be done and it is an important consideration in these matters.

Costs to be used in determining dollars involved in a company truck operation fall into three categories: equipment costs, operating expenses, and overhead. These may be given effect as fixed and variable, time and distance, and so on. They may ultimately be reduced to graph form along the lines of the one mentioned in the Contract Carrier chapter (pg. 301). Possibly they may be lumped into weekly, monthly, or annual totals that are compared with totals constructed from for-hire costs. This latter possibility may be particularly true on peddler, short haul, small shipment, or local operations. A transportation man starting on company hauling should certainly enlist the help of his accounting colleagues in setting up cost figure calculations. Companies differ in their application of accounting practices and cost accounting applicable for one operation may not be the same for another.

Two analysis forms which appeared in the previous edition of this text follow and may be helpful in providing a check on cost items that may be involved in these matters. Some references appear therein to for-hire and lease charges. Where indicated, data in the forms could be broadened to include more details on these two features. Also, those using the forms un-

---

PRIVATE CARRIAGE COST WORKSHEET

Point of Origin	Point of Destination	Mileage (Highway)	Frequency of Movement	Tonnage Per Year	Commodity Description	Density (Loadability)	Common Carrier Costs	
							Rate	Min. Wt.
(1)	(2)	(3)	(4)	(5)	(6)	(7)		

A. Total Miles _____
B. Total Tons _____
C. Empty Miles _____

D. Overflow Tons (Tonnage which cannot be handled by own equipment) ___
E. Equipment Needs _____
F. Driver Requirements _____

Work sheet used in connection with private carriage cost analysis.

PRIVATE CARRIAGE COST ANALYSIS

	Company Owned Equipment	Leased Equipment

I. FIXED COSTS

A. Entire Capital Investment .... $ _____
B. Interest on Investment ....
C. Finance Charges ....
D. License Fees ....
E. Insurance (Property Damage, Public Liability, Buildings, Maintenance, Equipment, etc.) ....
F. Depreciation on Operating Equipment ....
G. Depreciation on Maintenance Equipment and Buildings ..
H. Property Taxes ....
I. Garage Supervision ....
J. Garage Labor (including all insurance, fringe benefits, social security, etc.) ....
K. Garage Maintenance Costs (including building repairs, heat, gas, lights, water, telephone, etc.) ....
L. Costs to replace broken, worn out tools and equipment .
M. Special Equipment Costs (tarpaulins, heaters, refrigerating units, etc.) ....
N. Special Garage Equipment (racks, storage bins, etc.) ..
O. Fleet Supervisor Salary and Expenses ....
P. Administration Expense (includes time management spends on fleet operation problems) ....
Q. Costs for maintenance of records (includes checking, typing, posting and payment of bills, postage, and stationery and supplies, other office work) ....

FIXED TOTAL COSTS $ _____

II. OPERATING COSTS

A. Primary maintenance of equipment (includes washing, polishing, greasing, painting, etc.) .... $ _____
B. Road Service Costs (resulting from breakdowns, wrecks, or other catastrophies) ....
C. Repairs outside company's shop ....
D. Gasoline and oil ....
E. Tires and Tubes (replacement and repairs) ....
F. Replacement parts (Tractor and Trailer) ....
G. Anti-Freeze, Tire Chains, Flares, Lamps and other vehicle accessories ....
H. Cost of equipment retail (when required due to breakdowns or unusual peak load requirements) ......
I. Drivers' Salary (includes all union benefits, insurance, social security, etc.) ....
J. Extra Drivers for vacation periods, sick leaves, etc. ..
K. Toll Road Fees ....

TOTAL OPERATING COSTS $ _____

	Private	Common			
			Miles Operated		
			Cost Per Mile		
			Tons Transported		
Per Mile	_____		Cost per 100 Pounds		
			TOTAL COST	$ _____	
Per 100 Lbs.	_____				

Private carriage cost analysis form.

doubtedly will wish to develop further information on the cases before them. As trucks get older repair costs are relatively higher and they have more down time. Particular cost adjustments as to these may be in order.

After an operation is started ways to be sure it is, and continues to be, economic and also that it is, and continues to be, efficient should be worked out with the accountants. These can relate what is carried (pounds or what ever the case may be) to costs for, say, each month and such costs in turn related to costs by alternative methods. Further, salient operating costs can well be related periodically to miles run or some other standards to permit continuing cost reviews of efficiencies attained. Many feel that the simpler these cost exercises are the better. One company undertakes its private truck investments and keeps track of their operations in the field with four forms. These are called its Truck Justification Record, Rate of Return Worksheet, Truck Performance Report, and Truck Life Record. The basics of what are generally needed in these matters are indicated in the form designations. Where indicated, possible ideas there may be helpful.

Real assistance to a company's owned truck operation can be given by doing the hundred-and-one things possible to promote full and better truck use, to speed up loading and unloading, and to help generally. These often involve working with purchasing and plant staff and others. They are covered in more detail in the Contract Carrier Chapter and elsewhere in this book. Payoffs can be handsome and many. Over and above making the trucking more attractive financially reductions in total inventory and faster and more satisfactory deliveries are but a few of the possible benefits.

The types, makes, mechanical features, sizes and so on of trucks to be acquired and used, as well as the garage and repair facilities to be provided, also need important attention. A unit, depending on the type, will cost between $10,000 and $50,000. Where short haul, local delivery service is involved maneuverability is usually such a controlling factor that smaller sizes of equipment are used. On long hauls the largest carrying capacity possible may be indicated. Truck size, weight, and related laws are to be observed as to these features. Garage and repair facilities need careful selection particularly to the end that down time is kept as near zero as possible and equipment use is kept at its maximum. Engineering problems are common as to these features and company help from its engineers can be beneficial on occasion.

The extent to which private carriers are regulated may at times be particularly important. These regulations are hereafter outlined in the same framework as the earlier outline of this feature for common carriers and for contract carriers. This involves the Interstate Commerce Act and related aspects because they control in many broad ways and because a number of states follow them. Differences that may pertain on certain intrastate hauls are to be dealt with on the basis of the laws of the particular state involved. Compliance with applicable law is close to home with shippers in the use of their own trucks. Obligations to comply are direct rather than possibly indirect as can be the case when for-hire transportation is used.

A "private carrier of property by motor vehicle" is specified by the I. C. Act, U.S. Code 1970, Title 49, Sec. 303(a)(17), to mean "any person not included in the terms 'common carrier by motor vehicle' or 'contract carrier by motor vehicle', who or which transports in interstate or foreign commerce by motor vehicle property of which such person is the owner, lessee, or bailee, when such transportation is for the purpose of sale, lease, rent, or bailment, or in furtherance of any commercial enterprise." Industrial companies, by and large, meet these specifications in the proprietary hauling of their goods to their markets. They operate free of requirements for I.C.C. certificates or permits as to commodities and territories. They are also free of rate and service regulations by the I.C.C. Freedom to move commodities in territories without rate and service regulations is sometimes referred to as being free of I.C.C. "economic" regulation. Congress so recognized shippers' interests in furnishing their own transportation as the Motor Carrier Act was passed. These features are important to private carriers and, to operate as such under the Act, their hauling should conform to its various provisions applicable to them.

While simple proprietary hauling by an industrial company of its own goods to its own markets clearly meets the quoted statutory tests, other situations have arisen which have occasioned court and I.C.C. interpretations that are pertinent. One of prime importance has been the establishment of what is known as the "primary business" rule. Overly simplified it runs to the effect that to be private the haulage must be performed by a company whose primary business is other than transportation. Two commonly referred to "landmark" decisions in this regard are the Woitishek (43 M.C.C. 193) and the Lenoir Chair (51 M.C.C. 65) cases. Both rulings are of the same import.

The Lenoir Chair case involved a furniture manufacturer that sold F.O.B. its factory and transported in its own trucks about one-fifth of its output to its customers. This was done as an incident to supplying their needs and having equipment constantly available. For such transportation the company added separate charges to its invoices comparable to rail or for-hire truck costs. These activities were ruled to not require a change in the furniture company's private carrier status because the primary business of the firm was making furniture and the transportation was subordinate to that activity.

Among other decisions illustrating the application of the primary business test is one by the U.S. Supreme Court in Red Ball Motor Freight vs Shannon 12 L.ed(2) 341. It was there ruled that the purchase of sugar to provide a backhaul in connection with outbound movements of other commodities was within the scope, and in furtherance of, the primary business of a general merchandise enterprise. Important to such decision was the fact that company was in the business of buying and selling many items including sugar.

Other interpretations have caused to be applied on occasion what are sometimes called "control" and "substantial burden" tests. The "control" test runs to the effect that, to be private, the shipper must have the right to control, direct, and dominate the performance of the service and must, in fact, do so. The "substantial burden" test runs that the shipper must bear all, or a preponderance, of the normal risks and burdens associated with the transportation enterprise.

These tests are applied often in leasing cases and it has been held in several of them that the lease arrangements were for-hire rather than private transportation. The H. B. Church case (27 M.C.C. 191) went so far as to establish a presumption that a lease of equipment results in for-hire transportation. It went on to point out, however, that the presumption would yield to a showing by the shipper of meeting the "control" test. In a similar vein Allen vs United States (187 F. Supp. 625) held that in order to constitute private transportation, where equipment is supplied by a lessor, the shipper must have the exclusive right to direct and control the vehicle as well as the driver. In that case an individual experienced in transportation leased trucks to the shipper, supplied drivers, and so on. It was held that the operation as to the shipper was not private.

Other factual situations are numerous. "Buy-and-sell" transactions made simply to have transportation provided are regarded in various quarters as subterfuges and evasions. Normally it is not permissable for one company to cooperate with another and coordinate their private carriage activities through the same fleet of vehicles. This is true even though it permits the use of equipment both ways that normally would return empty, i.e. loads out for one company and loads back for the other. Even when two affiliates of, say, a conglomerate are involved such two-way use of vehicles is normally not permitted.

A further pertinent facet of the economic regulatory picture is the "exemptions" provided in the law under Sec. 303(b)(1) et seq. These apply not only to private carriage but to for-hire carriage as well. They fall into some ten categories. The categories involving "agricultural commodities" and "commercial zone" trucking and perhaps "occasional" hauling may be of particular interest to private carriers as ways to use equipment when needed. The other categories include school buses, taxi cabs, hotel vehicles, trucks of agricultural cooperatives, farm vehicles, and newspaper delivery trucks. Additional information on the "agricultural commodity", "commercial zone", and "occasional" exemptions appears in the previous chapter on Contract Carriage. Please see page 305 in this regard and also the intrastate and state law features mentioned there. They, too, may afford other ways in which to operate with no, or a minimum of, regulations.

Other regulatory aspects can involve drivers' hours, logs, accident reporting, and safety. These were originally I.C.C. responsibilities but are now those of D.O.T. Rules concerning them are obtainable from the latter. Truck license laws and fees, highway use taxes, and the like are to be observed and necessary payments made. Overtime pay standards possibly should be reviewed in that intra versus inter state activities may affect them. Sales taxes may become involved where sales terms are altered and should be checked. In a somewhat related vein a new labor union relation may arise. A new look at a company's insurance may be necessary. Check lists on these can well be prepared and, of course, as an operation gets going the handling of them in many ways becomes routine.

Truck leasing companies occupy an important position in transportation and are enjoying fast growth for several reasons. Not the least of these reasons is that their services permit indistrial shippers (when needed) to employ capital more productively elsewhere than on truck purchases. Other reasons include such protection as they afford against losses due to obsolescence, the assistance they provide in meeting fluctuations in seasonal or cyclical transportation requirements, and the ownership risks born by them. Further, they make trucks available with no initial investment and resulting cash drain and at times help improve company financial ratios by which lenders traditionally measure credit worthiness. When appropriate they provide "full service" leasing which affords a lessee the opportunity to use the more highly specialized maintenance and service facilities, and the trained personnel, of the leasing company.

The other side of the coin on owning versus leasing is particularly the extra costs of the latter. Cases can be made that leasing companies can buy equipment and provide service on less expensive bases than shippers and this may be true in some cases. Such companies quite properly, however, must make profits and these as well as costs must be underwritten and reckoned with even though they may not be too great and not too apparent. Further, not all of the above benefits are attractive in all cases, long term rent obligations may be inadvisable, it may be felt special weight should be given the look ahead on inflation, and benefits where depreciation write-offs help tax-wise may be important. A buy-lease decision needs careful analysis and is to be made within the context of a company's own particular operation.

Other features of the lease picture are that leases are made to large and small companies. They are made on varying payment bases such as so much per mile, per month, or per some other period of time. Some provide payouts are to be made on distance and time combinations. They may include options to purchase the equipment or options to cancel on lease anniversaries or on a certain number of days written notice. Exercise of cancellation options may also be predicated on the payment of certain penalties or on the purchase of the equipment on various bases some of which may be equal to its depreciated value or a figure which may be close to that value. In some areas a typical truck lease is for five or six years but some can run as long as ten years. Short term leases by the month, week, day, or trip are sometimes made available. (See subsequent comment re possible I.C.C. involvements as to trip and other short term leases.) At times comparatively short leases are made to provide industries with "test" periods to determine whether their projections concerning private truck operations are valid.

A large, successful, midwest manufacturing company has a leased fleet of some five dozen large truck-trailer combinations which it uses continuously and extensively to haul a wide variety of products to its markets throughout the country. Some years back it started with leasing a half dozen trucks for some of its hauling and now uses leased equipment for a substantial volume of its tonnage. A leasing company leases the equipment to the manufacturer, maintains it, and services the trucks nation-wide. At least one leasing company concentrates on fleets of more than 100 vehicles and has under lease to one of its clients 3,500-odd autos, vans, and trucks.

Equipment lease forms generally used are of two basic types: those in which simply a truck is provided and those in which the truck plus repair and other service are provided. The first are sometimes known as "finance" or "net" leases and the second as "service" or "full service" leases. The extents of the "service" and "full service" obligations in the latter are, of course, to be spelled out in detail in the lease documents. Agreements to provide drivers are sometimes called leases but whether a shipper can retain a "private" I.C.C. status when someone else (even though he be other than the equipment lessor) provides the drivers is in litigation. At the moment leases of drivers to shippers by other than equipment lessors does not vitiate a "private" status in interstate commerce. In at least one state (Texas) shippers cease to be "private" when drivers are "leased" to them.

Most leasing companies have their own printed forms and a specimen is here shown as an illustration. A representative collection of equipment lease, driver lease, etc. types of forms appears in the text "Model Legal Forms For Shippers" by Stanley Hoffman (1970, 508 pgs.) Traffic Service Corporation, Washington, D.C. 20005. Leasing company forms are to be checked carefully by a shipper's traffic people and its counsel to determine that, among various things, it correctly expresses what is expected of both parties.

The matter of maintaining a "private" status is particularly sensitive to some shippers. In this connection they will wish to check before leasing from a common carrier or an affiliate; these are disproved in some jurisdictions, i.e. New York, but a contra result may be reached by the I.C.C. as to an affiliate.

XYZ
TRUCKING COMPANY

TRUCK LEASE AND SERVICE AGREEMENT

Dated at St. Louis, Mo.

This 15th day of July 1972

THIS AGREEMENT is made between XYZ Trucking Company

whose address is 800 East Farmington Avenue, St. Louis, Ohio 10317
hereinafter called the OWNER, and A.B.C. Company

whose address is 2121 Oxford Street, New York, N. Y. 40004
hereinafter called the LESSEE.

1. PROPERTY COVERED AND TERM:

OWNER does hereby lease to LESSEE and LESSEE hires from OWNER the motor vehicle described in "SCHEDULE A" attached hereto and made a part hereof. This lease shall become effective with respect to each vehicle on the "delivery date" for that specific vehicle as set forth in "Schedule A" and shall continue with respect to each said vehicle until terminated as hereinafter provided.

2.. OWNER AGREES:

A. To provide fuel, oil lubricants, tires, tubes, and all operating supplies and accessories necessary for the proper and efficient operation of the vehicles.

B. To maintain and repair the leased vehicles and furnish in that regard all labor and parts which may be required to keep the vehicles in good operating condtiion. Maintenance to include servicing and washing so that the vehicles shall present a neat appearance.

C. To paint and letter the vehicles according to the LESSEE'S specifications at the time they are put into service.

D. To reimburse LESSEE for the cost of fuel, oil and/or lubricants that LESSEE purchases upon receipt from LESSEE of a receipted bill therefor. However, reimbursement for fuel shall be at LESSEE'S cost or if purchased at a XYZ facility, then at OWNER'S St. Louis, Ohio cost and, in either event, shall not exceed the maximum fuel reimbursement indicated on Schedule A for each vehicle.

E. To release LESSEE from liability for accidental collision damages arising out of each accident to each leased vehicle in excess of the amount specified in "Schedule A," provided such damages are not the result of any violation of the terms of this Agreement.

F. To furnish substitute vehicles, at no extra charge, for any vehicles in "Schedule A" which temporarily may be out of service (ordinary maintenance and servicing time not included), such substitutes to be as nearly as practicable the same size and appearance as the regular vehicle, except that no special painting, lettering, or other alterations need to be made on such substitute vehicles, and they shall be delivered to LESSEE and returned to OWNER at OWNER'S garage. Such substitute vehicles, while in the service of LESSEE, shall be subject to all terms and conditions of this Agreement. Failure of OWNER to furnish a substitute vehicle within a reasonable time shall cause the rental hereunder to abate as to the out of service vehicle until it is returned to service or until a substitute vehicle is furnished; however, the liability of the OWNER in the event of such failure shall be restricted to the abatement of the rental. In the event that the out of service vehicle is specialized and of a type which OWNER would not normally have in its transient rental fleet, the obligation of OWNER to furnish a substitute vehicle shall not be applicable.

G. To procure and maintain in full force and effect public liability and property damage insurance for all vehicles leased hereunder with LESSEE named as an additional assurred in the following limits:

Bodily Injury	$................	per person
Bodily Injury	$................	per accident
Property Damage	$................	per accident

In the event OWNER provides insurance under this Paragraph 2G then LESSEE agrees to indemnify and hold OWNER harmless from and against any claims or causes or cases of action for death or injury to persons or loss or damage to property, in excess of the limits of public liability and property damage insurance provided for herein, arising out of or caused by the ownership, maintenance, use or operation of any vehicle leased hereunder while the same is not in the possession of OWNER, its agent or employees.

H. To release LESSEE from liability for loss or damage to leased vehicles resulting from fire or theft. Conversion of any leased vehicle by an agent or employee of LESSEE shall not be considered theft within the terms of this Agreement.

RTR—2/61—1

Truck lease and service agreement, page 1.

I. To provide the State motor vehicle license for each vehicle for the state in which it is domiciled.

3. LESSEE AGREES:

A. To lease the vehicles described in "Schedule A" and to pay OWNER all rental and other charges provided herein within 7 days of mailing of invoice for the same to LESSEE. Payments shall be mailed to XYZ Trucking Company 800 East Farmington Ave., St. Louis, Ohio.

B. To cause each motor vehicle to be operated only by a safe, careful driver, who shall be a properly licensed chauffeur, at least 21 years of age and who shall be the employee or agent of the LESSEE only, paid by and subject to its exclusive direction and control. Upon receipt of a written complaint from the OWNER specifying any reckless, careless or abusive handling of the vehicle or any other incompetence by or of any driver, LESSEE will immediately remove such individual as a driver of vehicles leased hereunder. In the event that LESSEE shall fail to remove a driver upon receipt of such motive, the LESSEE shall, notwithstanding any other remedy of OWNER or provision of this lease, indemnify and hold OWNER harmless from and against any and all issues or claims resulting from or arising out of any accident or occurence involving OWNER'S vehicle being operated by that driver, including damages to the leased vehicle.

C. To return each vehicle to OWNER'S (St. Louis) garage for a minimum of eight (8) hours in Branch Location each and every week for service, inspection, adjustments, and repairs to eliminate, insofar as possible, interruptions to LESSEE'S use.

D. Not to cause or permit LESSEE'S drivers, employees or agents to make repairs or adjustments to vehicles or to tamper with governors and in all cases of defect or failure to notify OWNER by the speediest means of communication available giving a description of the same and the location of the vehicle and to abide by OWNER'S directions concerning emergency repair service. OWNER will not be responsible for any repair or service to the vehicle while such vehicle is away from OWNER'S garage unless expressly authorized by OWNER and unless LESSEE submits an authentic voucher of the repairs or services including labor and/or materials.

E. To reimburse OWNER in full for damages, including expenses resulting from reckless or abusive handling of the leased vehicles or by operation off a paved road, or overloading beyond the manufacturer's recommended maximum GVW and/or GCW shown in "Schedule A" or for loss of tools, extinguishers and other equipment furnished by OWNER.

F. To procure and maintain in full force and effect (furnishing OWNER with evidence satisfactory to OWNER) standard public liability and property damage insurance for all vehicles leased hereunder written by a company or companies satisfactoy to OWNER and with OWNER named as an additional assured in the following limits:

Bodily Injury $100,000 per person
Bodily Injury $300,000 per accident
Property Damage $ 50,000 per accident

LESSEE further agrees to indemnify and hold OWNER harmless from and against any claims or causes of action for death or injury to persons or loss or damage to property arising out of or causes of action for death or injury to persons or loss or damage to property arising out of or caused by the ownership maintenance, use or operation of any vehicle leased hereunder.

G. To release and hold OWNER harmless for loss or damage to cargo or other property belonging to LESSEE or in its custody or control, and for death or injury to LESSEE, LESSEE'S employees, agents or passengers, or for loss or damage to their property.

H. To notify the OWNER immediately upon the happening of any accident or collision involving a leased vehicle by the speediest means of communication available and to cause the driver to make a detailed report in person at the OWNER'S office as soon as practicable and to promptly render all other assistance to OWNER and/or the insurer hereunder that is requested by either of them in investigation or in defense of all claims and/or suits.

I. That the vehicles will be used and operated only in the normal and ordinary course of LESSEE'S business and upon termination or cancellation of this lease as to each such vehicle, it will be promptly returned to OWNER at its above address unless purchased by LESSEE under the terms of Section 5 hereof or unless the vehicle has been stolen.

J. To pay for any special licenses or any taxes required by the business of the LESSEE and to be responsible for any mileage taxes, ton mileage taxes, highway or bridge tolls which may result from the operation of the leased vehicles and LESSEE shall cause to be kept and make available to OWNER any necessary records relative to the use of the vehicles and pertaining to such taxes.

K. That the vehicles will not be used or operated in violation of any law, rule, regulation, statute or ordinance promulgated by any public body and LESSEE shall indemnify and hold OWNER harmless from and against any and all fines, forfeitures, seizures, confiscations and penalties arising out of any such violation or resulting from the use and operation of the leased vehicles.

4. IT IS MUTUALLY AGREED:

A. That the OWNER shall incur no liability to the LESSEE for failure to supply any vehicle or repair any disabled vehicle or supply a vehicle in substitution of one disabled under the provisions of paragraph 2F hereof if prevented by wars, riots, fires, labor disputes, accidents or other causes beyond its control.

B. Mileage shall be determined from odometer readings. If the odometer fails to function, the mileage for the period in which the failure existed shall be determined from the amount of fuel

Truck lease and service agreement, page 2.

consumed and the miles per gallon record of OWNER averaged for the previous 30 days. Odometer failure shall be promptly reported by LESSEE in writing.

C. The number of pounds specified under manufacturer's recommended maximum GVW and/or GCW on "Schedule A" is the maximum load that may be hauled on each vehicle.

D. Acceptance of a vehicle in service constitutes an acknowledgment that the vehicle complies with LESSEE's specifications; any structural alteration, special equipment, repainting or material alteration in painting, lettering or art work thereafter required by LESSEE shall be made at LESSEE'S expense.

E. This Agreement shall be binding on the parties hereto, their successors, legal representatives and assigns. LESSEE shall promptly notify OWNER in writing prior to all substantial changes in ownership or any material disposition of the assets of LESSEE's business. LESSEE shall not have the right to sublease any of the vehicles leased hereunder, nor to assign this Agreement or any interest therein without the prior writen consent of OWNER.

F. This Agreement contains the entire agreement and understanding between the parties, and its terms shall not be construed as altered by any verbal agreement or informal writing, nor by failure to insist upon performance or' failure to exercise any right or privilege, but alteration or addition shall be accomplished only by written endorsement hereon or amendment hereto, duly executed by both parties.

G. The parties hereto recognize that the rates quoted herein are based upon current fuel prices and that such prices may fluctuate below or above the current price published in the "National Petroleum News" as set forth under the heading Refinery and Terminal Prices, Motor Gasoline and Distillates and Fuels set forth in Schedule A and, in the event of an increase or decrease in such reported price of fuel of each full one ($.01) cent(s) per gallon for the applicable reported city, they agree that the rates shall be increased or decreased as follows:

	Additional Fuel Credit or Charge per Week each vehicle on "Fixed Rental Charge"	Additional Fuel Credit or Charge per Mile each vehicle on "Mileage Charge"
Vehicles with GVW limits up to and including 8,000 lbs.		$.001
Vehicles with GVW limits over 8,000 and up to and including 18,000 lbs.		.002
Vehicles with GVW limits over 18,000 lbs. and up to and including GVW 30,000 lbs. and GCW 60,000 lbs.	not applicable	
Vehicles with .... limits		.003

H. The parties hereto recognize that the rates quoted herein are based on current cost and labor conditions, and that the costs of OWNER'S operation may fluctuate, and agree that for each rise or fall of not applicable index points in the All Items Consumer Price Index for Moderate Income Families in United States Cities (using a 1947-1949 base period), published by the United States Bureau of Labor Statistics, above or below the Index figure applcable for each vehicle leased hereunder as shown on Schedule A, the weekly Fixed Rental Charge and/or the Mileage Rate for such vehicle shall be adjusted upward or downward as follows:

ORIGINAL VALUE OF VEHICLE SHOWN IN SCHEDULE A	ADJUSTMENT IN	
	FIXED RENTAL CHARGE	MILEAGE RATE
Under $3,000.00	$ .50	$.001
$3,000.01 to $4,000.00	.80	.002
$4,000.00 to $5,500.00	.90	.002
$5,500.01 to $7,500.00	1.00	.002
$7,500.01 and over	1.60	.002

Such adjustments shall be effective on the first day of each calendar quarter year and shall be based on the last published Index as of the end of the month next preceding such effective date. The parties further agree that in case there is an increase or decrease of 10% in OWNER'S cost of either tires or labor, they will then negotiate modifications in the rates contained in Schedule A based upon such change in costs.

I. The parties hereto further recognize that the rental charged for lease of the vehicles is exclusive of any sales or use taxes now in force or hereafter imposed and LESSEE agree to pay in addition to the rent specified, the amount of such sales or use taxes and any other new or additional taxes which may be imposed on the use or operation of said motor vehicles or any increase in existing taxes, including license and registration fees.

J. Where tractors leased hereunder will be operated with trailors owned by LESSEE, "Schedule B" shall be executed providing that OWNER shall maintain and service such trailers.

K. The OWNER may finance the property leased hereunder, or any part thereof, and in that connection may, as security give the lender an installment sales instrument or mortgage covering such property or assign rentals due hereunder.

L. That OWNER does not, either by obtaining or by being named as an additional assured under public liability and property damage insurance obtained by LESSEE, incur any liability or responsibility for, or assume any dominion or control over the use and operation of vehicles leased hereunder.

Truck lease and service agreement, page 3.

M. All notices provided for herein shall be in writing and directed to OWNER and LESSEE at their respective addresses as first set forth herein.

5. CANCELLATION AND TERMINATION:

A. Either OWNER or LESSEE (LESSEE not being in default hereunder) may cancel this Agreement on the first and any subsequent anniversary date of its effective date as established by the provisions of Paragraph 1, by giving to the other party sixty (60) days prior written notice of intent to do so. In such event LESSEE shall on the cancellation date promptly purchase for cash all vehicles then being leased under this Agreement as described in "Schedule A," for the sum of the "original value" less the total depreciation which has accrued for each vehicle as set forth in "Schedule A" plus any unexpired licenses and applicable taxes; except, however, that the minimum purchase price at any time shall not be less than fifteen (15%) per cent of the "original value" of each vehicle as set out in "Schedule A."

B. This Agreement may also be cancelled by either party in part by specifying certain vehicles to be eliminated under the same terms and conditions as outlined in Paragraph 5A above.

C. This Agrement shall terminate automatically at the election of OWNER and without notice to LESSEE if LESSEE shall (1) become insolvent, or (2) file a voluntary petition in bankruptcy, or (3) make an assignment for the benefit of creditors, or (4) be adjudicated a bankrupt, or (5) if a receiver be appointed for LESSEE'S business, or (6) make a material liquidation of assets. In the event of any such automatic termination, OWNER may, at its option, demand that LESSEE purchase the vehicles leased hereunder and LESSEE shall promptly purchase them for cash at the purchase price as computed in accordance with the provisions of Paragraph 5A hereof without prejudice to such other remedies as OWNER may have under this agreement or at law.

D. Time is of the essence of this Agreement, and in the event LESSEE breaches or is in default of any of its provisions, OWNER may immediately, without formal notice or demand, take possession of, retain and/or refuse to re-deliver the leased vehicles to LESSEE until such breach or default is cured, without any of such actions being deemed an act of cancellation and without prejudice to other remedies OWNER may have, and LESSEE shall continue to be liable for rent and other charges accruing during the period the leased vehicles are retained by OWNER. If LESSEE's breach or default shall continue for seven (7) days after written notice thereof shall have been mailed to LESSEE, OWNER may at its election, and irrespective of whether OWNER shall have elected to take possession of or retain the leased vehicles as provided above, terminate this Agreement immediately. In the event of such election to terminate, OWNER may, at its option, demand the LESSEE purchase the leased vehicles and LESSEE shall promptly purchase the same for cash at the purchase price as computed in accordance with Paragraph 5A hereof without prejudice to such other remedies as OWNER may have under this Agreement or at law.

E. In the event that OWNER demands that LESSEE purchase the vehicles in accordance with the terms of Paragraph 5A, 5B, 5C, or 5D hereof and LESSEE shall fail to pay the purchase price as herein provided, OWNER may either sell the leased vehicles at public or private sale without notice to LESSEE, whereupon, LESSEE shall be liable to OWNER for the difference between the purchase price as provided in Paragraph 5A and the net amount realized at such sale; or OWNER may pursue such other remedies as it may have under this agreement or at law.

In witness whereof, each of the parties hereto has caused these presents to be duly executed the day and year first above written by a person duly authorized.

XYZ TRUCKING COMPANY

(Owner)

Signed, sealed, and delivered in the presence of:

By _____

_____
As to Owner

Title _____

_____
As to Owner

_____
(Lessee)

By _____

_____
As to Lessee

Title _____

_____
As to Lessee

Truck lease and service agreement, page 4.

TRUCK LEASE AND SERVICE AGREEMENT
SCHEDULE A

Page 1

Add to Agreement:
XXXXXXXXX (Strike One)

Vehicle Number	Date of Delivery	Year	Make	Model and Type	Identification No.	Mfr's Recm. Max. GCW and/or GVW	Lessee's Collision Liability	Original Value	No. of Years	Monthly Depreciation Amount	Fixed Rental Charge Per Wk.	Mileage Rate Per Mile	Max. Mileage Per Wk.	Fuel Reimbursement
......	......	1964	IHC	DCO-405	......	Legal	100%	$13,924		1.5%	$111.50	$.1185		$.26
......	......	1964	Frue-hauf	35' open top tandem trailer	......	Legal	100%	5,774		1.25%	36.00	-0-		......

(a) Current—All Items Consumer Price Index for Moderate Income Families in United States Cities Not applicable.

(b) Current fuel price as published in "National Petroleum News" (Consumer Tank Wagon) for St. Louis (low quotation) is $.145 cents per gallon for Diesel #2, excluding applicable federal, state and local taxes of _____ cents per gallon.

(c) Execution of this Schedule constitutes authorization by LESSEE to OWNER to order and/or purchase the scheduled vehicle for lease to LESSEE.

(d) Mileage Guarantee to reverse side is effective if filled in and initialed.

(e) Required Investment Credit Information on reverse side must be completed and initialed.

This "Schedule A" is hereby made a part of that certain Truck Lease and Service Agreement between the parties dated July 15, 1972,.

XYZ TRUCKING CORPORATION

Signed: _____
             Owner

By _____

Witness _____

1-13 (REV. 2/03)   Dated: _____

Signed: ABC Company
             Lessee

By _____

Witness _____

_____, 19____ .

Truck lease and service agreement, schedule A.

They will wish to check also as to trip or short term leases; bans as to these exist in certain instances where minimum lease lengths are prescribed to avoid subterfuge. They will also wish to check as to "full service" lease provisions when possibilities exist that the "primary business", "control", and "burden" tests heretofore discussed may cause difficulties.

A number of other lease features are to be watched and dealt with which are more along business oriented lines. Bids or the equivalents may well be sought from a number of leasing companies. Clauses dealing with servicing and maintenance should be specific as to what will be done. Provisions specifying that replacement vehicles will be provided when regular equipment is being serviced and for pick-up and delivery service should be clear and unambiguous. Insurance should be obtained and carried by the lessor if lower costs can be obtained in this way. "Present values" of rental payments are to be determined (preferably with the company's treasury people) as a part of calculations of lease costs. "Restricted mileage plans" (under which extra charges are made when miles in excess of certain minima are run) and "uneven depreciation plans" (where charges are based on different depreciation rates for different parts of the trucks, i.e. the chassis and the body) should be checked in particular.

"Balloon" payment provisions at the end of a lease are to be avoided. They are at times included for bidding purposes to minimize rent payments and explanations of them are difficult when they have to be paid. Forfeiture to a leasing company of the residual value of the equipment at the end of the lease is to be avoided as not proper in many cases. Tax considerations i.e. whether rents can be "expensed" and dealings to be accorded investment tax credits, are to be checked with company tax people. The cost, not the value, of the service should be the primary criterion for leasing charges. Such charges should not be based on "what the traffic will bear." Further, particular care should be taken in selecting the lessor. Reliability, maintenance facilities, and personnel are usually to be lived with for years and are of top importance in lease arrangements of this kind.

An excellent pamphlet "The Elements of Private Carriage" (1970, 30 pgs.) on company owned hauling is available from the Traffic Service Corp., Washington, D.C. 20005. It is a reprint from the Transportation and Distribution Management Magazine and includes a worth while supplement on "The Choice of Leasing" by William B. Wagner of the Graduate Business School of the University of Missouri.

In somewhat of a man-bites-dog treatment, to be mentioned also is that situations arise where special trailers or other special equipment are leased by industrial companies to for-hire carriers. Such equipment may be required in a company's business and the practical way to deal with matters is for the company to have the equipment built and to lease it to the hauler so that he may use it in transportation for the company. While this does not happen often, the trade practice in these matters has been to make these leases. As long as they are arms-length, reasonable, and provide for proper charges exceptions have not been taken to them.

A closely related subject to private truck operations can be a company's automobile fleet which may be used by its salesmen and others. Much of what is said before in this chapter is applicable to these cars. Generally, however, an additional option exists through having the employee provide his own transportation and paying a mileage allowance to him for doing so. Dealings accorded company automobile fleets change considerably. A Transportation Department having the responsibility for such a fleet will wish to bear in mind particularly the purchase versus lease considerations here outlined.

Running through this chapter in a myriad of ways is the I.C. Act and what is to be done under it. Observation of its provisions as to both the spirit and the letter of the law in a company's operations are critical and all humanly possible should be done to avoid violations. Penalties for evading regulation may be fines of "not less than $200 nor more than $500 for the first offense and not less than $250 nor more than $2,000 for any subsequent offense" under Sec. 322(a). For failure to make reports a fine may be "not more than $5,000" under (g) of that section. Not to be overlooked also is a careful check by Traffic with its tax colleagues of equipment leases with purchasing provisions. The revenue people rule that conditional sales agreements are created in certain circumstances because of those provisions and upset tax plans concerning "rental" deductions.

Shippers involved in, or contemplating, "leasing" both trucks and drivers will find of interest National Motor Freight Traffic Association vs United States decided recently by the United States Supreme Court (Traffic World, January 15, 1973, pg. 47). It was ruled there that private truck operators may use vehicles and drivers who are supplied by a separate source which is not related to the vehicle leasing agency. Please see in this connection the earlier discussion in this chapter particularly at pages 325 and 326. This decision differs as to the facts from those in the Anderson case cited in that discussion. Both trucks and drivers came from the same source in the Anderson ruling.

12

EXPEDITING AND TRACING

EXPEDITING IS MAKING ARRANGEMENTS FOR THE TRANSPORT OF goods prior to shipment (or ahead of its arrival at junction or transfer points after actual shipment) so as to get them to their destination quicker than they would arrive if moved in a normal manner without assistance. Tracing is following the shipment to get a record of its movement. Both are services normally rendered every day by every traffic department. Expediting and tracing services constitute a traffic department's "firing line." Under normal daily routine, and particularly after a shipment has gone forward, it is more or less true that these services do not produce any particular monetary transportation savings; but there are many important, if less tangible, benefits to be derived from keeping an assembly line going or satisfying a customer. The section "Premium Transportation" later in the chapter explains that there are monetary savings to be obtained by using lower-rated services with possible occasional expediting to assure meeting necessary delivery deadlines rather than utilize higher rated services that presumably would provide an earlier delivery.

Any traffic department can make a fine reputation for itself throughout the whole company simply by rendering effective expediting and tracing service. A traffic man gets real satisfaction out of calling the interested factory (or other) department to report that the desired shipment is on its way to the unloading platform "right now"; perhaps just in time to prevent an emergency situation. A traffic department is a service organization, so the more it accomplishes to facilitate the work of other departments, the more valuable it becomes to its company.

Expediting and tracing usually are delegated exclusively to one or two employees in the traffic department. Many companies will assign younger men to the service jobs. But do not be misled into assuming that an inexperienced individual can step into an expediting assignment and handle it satisfactorily without first gaining some experience. No one can expedite without an understanding of how the various carriers handle their freight.

Some companies handle their expediting and tracing on decentralized or partially decentralized bases. Quite often they will leave to plant transportation personnel these arrangements subject to calling on head office traffic for help in particular cases when indicated. Such practice, when practical, is advantageous in that it may save time in moving to correct delays, possible extra work in the relaying of information to and from the central transportation department, and so on.

With whatever particular practice is used, however, it is essential to know the freight-handling procedure in railroad, truck and air freight houses, to have a clear-cut picture of freight classification yards, local switching arrangements, the physical handling of pickup and delivery services, merchandise cars, piggy-back cars, diversion, reconsignment, and all the many physical and office practices that tie in with the actual job of moving freight. An employee who has had good experience on the expediting and tracing job has obtained a broad and helpful background as to the handling of freight by an industrial company's carriers.

Why not just call up the carrier and tell them you desire your shipment delivered immediately? Actually, this approach would be very inefficient, if not impossible, because all major carriers handle many shipments each day; they cannot reasonably be asked to spend time looking up details on any one particular shipment. If you want results, therefore, you must get the details yourself and then pass them along to the proper individual to get action. Best results will be obtained by educating company departments requesting service to obtain certain pertinent shipping details before calling the traffic department.

Generally the item for best use in having before you shipping details is a copy of the bill of lading, express receipt, air waybill, or other comparable document. Photocopies are easily made, are generally available, and give most of the details applicable to the shipment to receive attention. The car number or numbers on car load shipments can be quite important and at times may be all that are needed to start immediate action to develop where the car is and what can be done about it. Several railroads (the Southern Pacific and others) have data systems that provide information on short order concerning the location of a car when the car number is provided to them.

Where, say, a bill of lading or comparable document is not available (or is in preparation), basic information needed by the different carriers may be tabulated as follows:

Date of shipment.

Consignee and shipping plant location.

Consist of shipment (i.e. 30,000 pounds Aluminum Pipe Fittings).

Car number (truck number or what is pertinent).

Complete Routing (including junctions when specified).

Consignor and delivery location.

To the above are to be added any special data that may be pertinent, i.e., on occasion air way bill and other way bill numbers are important. Conversely, at times only parts of the information shown in the tabulation may be needed. Pluses and minuses as to the tabulation depend to a considerable extent on individual carrier needs and are to be dealt with accordingly.

The best possible background for developing effective expediting and tracing ability is an understanding of how freight is handled by the various carriers. To that end, the following résumé of freight-handling practices is offered together with comments on how to expedite urgent shipments:

Carload

Carload shipments are loaded by the consignor at his private siding or at a public team track. Under certain conditions a carload of freight may be delivered by truck to a railroad freight station platform where it is loaded into a car by the railroad. After loading is completed the car is sealed and a bill of lading to cover is delivered to the office of the local railroad freight agent. The car is then ready to be "pulled" by the carrier.

Switch locomotives perform local switching service which is usually set up at a regular time or regular times each day. The switch locomotive takes the car to the local classification yard where it is placed on a track with other cars going in the same direction and therefore can be forwarded on the same train.

A classification yard consists of a great many tracks, each representing a different scheduled train. The yard is frequently provided with a hump which is a raised track at one end of the yard. Cars are pushed over the hump one at a time, rolling by gravity to the particular track where their train is being made up. The down side is sometimes equipped with mechanical retarders that slow the car up so it will attach itself to the other cars on the track without too heavy an impact.

Recent years have seen the development of electronic classification yards at key points on some of the larger railroad systems. Designed to be operated economically and with maximum automation, they are equipped with closed-circuit television scanners which "read" the "numbers" on freight cars and transmit these numbers to the central control booth and computerized car reporting systems which receive and transmit data on the makeup of trains. These yards are helping to speed up the movement of cars, but there are older yards in which at each hump there is a yard office with windows facing the track. A car recorder sits at a desk facing the track and lists each car number and train to which it is assigned for reference purposes. Where yards have no hump, each car must be moved to its proper location by a switch engine.

The train has a symbol reference, a number or name identifying it as a regularly scheduled freight train. When the train is made up it moves out on a somewhat flexible schedule and proceeds to the next destination classification point where it is broken up and each car put through the classification processes again or switched to a local yard for eventual spotting at the consignee's siding or at a local public team track, as the case may be. A yardmaster is in charge of each yard. A run of a locomotive moving cars is referred to as a "drill."

Ordinarily the prime steps in expediting and tracing are taken with the origin carrier's traffic or sales people at its local office or with its local agent. There is no hard and fast rule as to this, however, and on occasion expediting may involve a call right to the yardmaster's office to assure forwarding on the first available symbol train. Tracing may be handled also by getting records of movements from the car service or car record office which is maintained by every railroad on a system-wide basis. In more and more instances information is made available by means of electronic data processing.

Sometimes a special switch for your car can be arranged with the interested yardmaster. Most symbol trains between large cities go all the way through without any reclassification en route. Most delay is experienced in the local yards. If a car goes "bad order" en route it is taken out of the through train and sent to the closest "rip track" for light repairs. Cars in need of general repair are usually unloaded and sent to the car shops. If this happens, your job as expediter is to point out the need for quick repairs or transfer to another car, obtain the new car number and arrange inclusion in the next through train.

Truckload

Once a truckload of material has been loaded into the trailer or straight truck, as the case may be, it rarely will be transferred to other equipment en route. Most truckloads are handled in tractor-trailer units. Sometimes tractors will be changed at division points, but the trailer load goes right from the consignor to the consignee. Even when it is a two-line haul, the original trailer will probably go through to destination, as many motor carriers interchange trailers. If a trailer goes "bad order," the load will be changed to another trailer, if one is available. Otherwise, the movement is delayed until the trailer is repaired. Most established trucking companies maintain repair and reporting stations for service en route, thereby practically eliminating costly delays in transit.

A good way to expedite a truckload is to get the trailer and tractor number, driver's name and scheduled arrival time at destination. This information should be wired or telephoned to the consignee. In emergency instances it might be well to have the trucking company instruct the driver to telephone the consignee or consignor, as desired, if any unexpected delay is encountered in transit. With such information, steps can be taken with the local representatives or agent of the trucking company to correct the difficulty and rush delivery.

As regards contacts some motor carriers use their sales departments to expedite and trace. Others use their operating departments. Still others have organized customer service departments to handle these problems. First moves to expedite and trace by an industrial company are ordinarily to one or the other of these departments of the carrier picking up the shipment and participating in the first line haul of the movement. At times, when local drayage moves are involved, it is best to go to the line haul carrier. Information obtained from the latter is more complete and its position of being able to help is better.

One more precaution. In expediting a truckload be sure, by checks with the originating truck terminal, that the load is actually on its way. It's disturbing to find out the next morning that your trailer load is still in town due to lack of a driver, mechanical trouble, or some other reason.

Piggyback

One of the benefits to be derived from the use of piggyback services is that generally less expediting and tracing are required. For the most part, these shipments travel in trains which are operating on precise, fast, through schedules. The matters of chief concern to the expediter are getting the trailer to the piggyback yard in time for loading into a scheduled train, making certain that motive power is available for immediate removal from the railroad premises at the end of the rail journey, and prompt unloading at destination. On those occasions where it is necessary to expedite or trace, the procedure will depend to a great extent upon the piggyback plan usd.

Illustrative of the particular situations involved are that neither shipper nor consignee is likely to know if his trailerload travels under Plan I, since use of this plan is the motor carrier's prerogative. Such shipments would be expedited or traced under truckload procedures. Under Plan II, the trailer is in the hands of the railroad from shipper's loading dock to destination; hence the procedure for carloads would be used.

Under Plans II½, III and IV, hauling the trailer from shipper's loading platform to the railroad loading ramp and from the railroad ramp at destination to the consignee's dock is subject to arrangements made by the shipper or consignee, or both, and therefore under their control at all times. Once loaded on a flat car and the number of that car ascertained, the regular procedure for carloads would be followed as to the rail portion of the journey. Plan V involves the use of motor common carrier at either or both ends of the trip and requires the use of both truckload and carload procedures for the respective portions of the haul.

The foregoing illustrations are to be dealt with as representative of the highlights of these matters and guides on which moves to trace and expedite are undertaken. Practically, added complications arise in various cases. At times local cartage companies will be used whose records and handling of the trailers are on the informal side. In some instances a railroad's records will stop as a trailer leaves an unloading ramp. Along with the car number of the flat car used and other information on the shipment, the identification number of the trailer involved can be important. It, too, is to be provided as a part of a shipper's activities when indicated.

Less Than Truckload

The same general procedure outlined for truckloads may be used for less-than-truckload shipments. Less than truckloads may be transferred en route so it is important to have the carrier's waybill number and the location where the load will be transferred. Then the agent at the transfer point should be contacted to protect a quick forwarding on the first available outbound trailer load. Sometimes trucking companies drop lots off en route at locations where they do not maintain a terminal or agent. Be sure they load such a lot near the tailgate; otherwise it cannot be dropped off as desired. If for any reason a lot is to be delivered last, it should be loaded in the nose of the trailer so it would not have to be rehandled with consequent delay.

It may occur to the reader that these are actions that the trucking company would take anyway, so why bother about them. The answer is that when dealing with "expediting" problems, do not leave anything to chance. Check to be sure and thus prevent a delay that, otherwise, could occur.

The greatest potential delay to less-than-truckload shipments is at motor carrier terminals. A shipment may be picked up promptly but not forwarded the same night. It may get to the destination terminal in good time but delivery delayed as much as several days due to failure to unload the trailer or to congestion preventing delivery. Therefore it is necessary to know where the shipment is at all times so that intelligent action can be taken to obtain delivery when needed. Generally speaking, the motor carriers provide good service. Many operate with fairly small terminals making it impossible to accumulate much freight on their platforms. They have to keep it moving. Delays can occur if trailer loads are left standing in the yard instead of being backed up to the platform and unloaded.

Less Than Carload

Less-than-carload freight is either handled into cars at a freight station or at a private siding or team track. At the latter, it will move to the local freight station for rehandling and forwarding or it may be carded direct to another station in another city. When carded direct it is sometimes known as an overhead merchandise or package car.

A so-called peddler car is one in which less-than-carload shipments are loaded for a great many small towns along one railroad. It is stopped at each station while the trainmen and local agent unload the freight for the particular station. This is slow service. In recent years, because of the abandonment of small stations and the removal of agents from others, many railroads have done away with peddler cars. Some have substituted their own trucking system which operates on highways parallel to the right of way of the railroad and handles the freight to and from the small towns with much more dispatch than was possible when using peddler cars.

As has been previously noted (Chapter 6), many railroads have discontinued the handling of less-than-carload freight. Most of the LCL services remaining are not profitable to the carriers and transit times and so on that are available to shippers from them are generally on the slow side and at times are erratic. Expediting and tracing are not in general procedural patterns in which they can be accomplished easily.

Less-than-carload shipments are assigned waybill numbers by the carriers and it is usually important that a shipper or receiver have this waybill number when trying to locate, trace or expedite a shipment. It is assigned by the local freight agent of the originating carrier at the shipping or origin point and all available details of the shipment should be provided to such agent to obtain the waybill number. This local agent is also generally a good starting point when expediting or tracing the shipment. Suggestions relative to such activities for car loads may also be applicable in these matters.

Freight Forwarder

Freight forwarders act the same as shippers, routing their freight in consolidated carloads, piggyback trailers or truckloads via carriers of their selection. It is general procedure that the freight forwarders do their own expediting and tracing although, on occasion, an interested shipper or receiver may find it to his advantage to aid in this work.

Usually the practice is to telephone the forwarder's reference number to the forwarder with a request that expediting or tracing service be rendered, advising the shipper or consignee as to expected and actual arrival times, and so on. The forwarders assign their own reference number in these matters which is known as "bill-of-lading load reference." They also assign a pro or freight bill number to each freight bill. The tonnages they assign and the day-in, day-out routines they establish are such that they are in good positions for tracing and expediting. The occasions when they need help from industrial transportation departments do not occur often. When they do, special reasons and special situations exist which need particular attention.

As a somewhat related feature, forwarders generally employ a manifold (or equivalent) system of billing, whereby the freight bill, the arrival notice, and the delivery receipt are made up in one billing operation. The forwarding office mails this billing immediately to the receiving office at destination, which places the destination agent in the position of knowing the contents prior to arrival. Sometimes the billing is sent along with the shipment if the shipment is in a through trailer.

Air Freight

Air freight service is provided to industrial companies by airline companies much as the rails and motor carriers provide service. The freight may be handled along with passengers on regular scheduled flights or it may be loaded into exclusive freight planes that are not operated on as strict a schedule basis as passenger planes. Freight is sent to (or taken from) the airline at the airport or is transported to or from the airport in pickup and delivery service made available by the air carrier. The airline handles the freight through to destination or turns it over to a connecting airline for delivery.

Tracing and expediting air freight are to be fitted into this pattern. The chief air freight agent of the carrier at the airport of origin is the prime contact on these matters, and he should be given full information on the shipment. Air waybills and flight numbers are often important in these instances. They should be provided, or enough information furnished so that they can be ascertained. Such agent forwards the air bill and flight numbers to the downline stations to locate the shipment after verifying that it has left his station as it should have done.

Tight air schedules, plane availability, and so on afford a considerable area for an industry to help itself in expediting shipments in these cases. It should give the airlines as much advance notice as possible and be sure that space is available. It should be careful to have the shipment at the airport in time to be loaded into the particular plane upon which space has been arranged. In cases involving unusually large or heavy pieces of equipment the airline should have data ahead of time and with appropriate leeway so that special arrangements may be set up, if required. Further, consignees should be given the flight number, the name of the airline over which the shipment is moving, etc., so that airport delivery can be effected as soon as the plane lands and unloads.

Freight moves out on the first flight with space available to the consignee city from the terminal of the originating carrier in normal practice. Delivery is usually accomplished within 24 to 48 hours depending on the prevailing pattern of service. These features and the foregoing paragraphs represent what might be termed the general situation concerning regular air freight.

Over and above regular air freight and the typical dealings to be accorded its expediting and tracing, other types of movements via air have come into the transportation picture which in many ways are traced and expedited (or substantially so) by the organization providing the service. Illustrative of these types of movements are those where specific delivery dates are spelled out, shipments are tracked through to destination, and concurrent with the delivery immediate confirmation is given the shipper.

As is to be expected there are many variations on the foregoing and much depends on the service used and what a shipper is in a position to pay for it. The ultimate are the courier services where vital envelopes, packages, parts, and products are personally taken from one origin to destination by a carrier representative who telephones the consignor as the delivery is accomplished by him (along with obtaining for it a signed receipt and so on). Some services do not go quite this far in providing couriers and, instead, use couriers to and from the airports at the origin and destination cities with parcels moving first class (direct and with no consolidations) via airline airport to airport. Costs vary substantially, important factors being type of service provided, distances, package weights, and whether day or night. One service (courier all the way) currently quotes $40.00 to $70.00 depending on package weights for day time deliveries, Washington, D.C. to New York, with the figures being lower for overnight handling.

Movements in general are, of course, other than those just described and air transport abounds in various types of these in which more than usual expediting and tracing considerations are parts of what is done. One carrier, in particular, specializes in packets and small shipments (ie. more than half of them are under 70 pounds). It has its own fleet of planes, uses a mid-west city as its hub for consolidating and scheduling inbound and outbound shipments, is effective and economical, and provides various tracing and expediting services.

A successful forwarder has an arrangement whereby its shippers may ascertain the location and status of their shipments via phone direct from its data banks simply by dialing two sets of numbers: that of the data center and that of the shipment. Touch tone telephones are used for this and the reports are from the computers and reflect the records which are being tracked by them on the shipment.

The same organization also makes available a service which can help importantly where, say, a purchase is made by a company in New York to be shipped from a plant in Chicago to a location in San Francisco. When the purchase is made in New York the forwarder concurrently arranges through its Chicago people with the Chicago plant to expedite the shipment and, as it leaves, to trace it through to San Francisco. Progress reports on the order, expected delivery dates, and notifications on delays are provided to New York under this service when indicated.

Water Carriers

Expediting and tracing water shipments is fairly simple in approach. Once a shipment is loaded into the vessel there is nothing more that can be done until the vessel arrives at its destination port. Therefore all efforts should be extended to getting it to the forwarding pier in time to be loaded into the ship and then seeing to it that it actually goes aboard. Many a shipment has been left on the dock "shut out" by the steamship line because there is more freight on hand than can be loaded. At destination the job is to get it discharged and placed in an accessible spot for local pickup or loaded into a car, truck or other ship, as the case may be, for a beyond movement.

Each steamship company prepares a ship's manifest upon which is listed all the shipments loaded into any particular vessel. Thus there is always available immediate information as to whether the shipment in question is aboard a designated ship.

Parcel Post and Mail

There is no satisfactory way to trace and expedite parcel post and mail since, once a package or a letter is deposited with the post office, the sender loses control or contact until delivery is made at destination. Some help can be given by using air mail services, special delivery stamps, providing for "special handling," and posting at the right time and place. If a letter or package is undelivered after a reasonable time has elapsed, there is little that can be done (unless it has been registered or insured). Vocal and persistent complaint to postal officials, however, may result in an improvement in service, if not recovery of the individual item.

General — All Services

It is important to keep a good record of persons contacted and date, time, etc., of contact along with the information received when expediting or tracing. This can be done best by using a regular expediting and tracing form (see next illustration). One important action in providing expediting service should take place even before the shipment is forwarded, and that is to find out exactly when the shipment is needed at destination. This should be the final on-the-job "must" date. The traffic department because of its knowledge of the various carriers' transit intervals is able to specify a route that will provide the desired time of delivery at the lowest possible cost. A substantial amount of money can be saved by adhering to this principle.

In dealing with the carriers' representatives, make it a point to develop a pleasing telephone personality. Expedite only those shipments that really are urgently needed. Try to work it out so that the same employee with each carrier handles all of your expediting and tracing work. This employee will become familiar with the character of your business and with the personnel assigned to service functions and they will therefore obtain over-all better results than otherwise. All carriers desire to give their customers good service and are willing to go out of their way to render special handling on urgently-needed shipments; but they have no patience whatsoever with the shippers or receivers who cry "wolf" on almost every shipment. Shippers and receivers should give carriers the same courtesies they expect and look for from the carriers; they should ask for expedited service only on shipments which must be rushed. And importantly, they should give the carrier complete and accurate shipping data.

EXPEDITING — TRACING			TRAFFIC DIVISION	
CONSIGNEE			DESTINATION	
CONSIGNOR			ORIGIN	
NO. OF PIECES	MATERIAL		WEIGHT	
w/s NO.	DATE	CAR NO.	CARDED	
ROUTE				
REQUESTED BY	DEPT.		PHONE	DATE
RECORD				

Expediting and tracing form.

Expediting can be done easily or it can be done strenuously. Actually there are degrees of expediting. A good expediter will know when to go all out and when to handle on a modified basis. The difference lies in how you approach the carrier and how much you yourself will do to assure quick delivery.

Sometimes you need only to "watch" the shipment; other times you must do an all-out job. This might be explained by using the three words: needed — urgent — emergency. If you are a traffic man, do not be too hard on other organizations if they fail to give you all the data you feel they should furnish to you. After all, the traffic department is a service organization and that means do the best you can with what you have. If you do not have all the information you need, go out and get it. By performing in this manner, the traffic department is serving its company to its fullest extent.

Perhaps the simplest and most important function in good expediting is to be sure that the shipments get started right. This means correct billing and marking. Inadequate information on the bill of lading as regards consignee's name, address, route, etc., may cause serious delays. If the shipment is a carload, be sure the bill of lading reaches the local agent in time to permit billing and forwarding on the earliest available train. And in other than carload shipments, check the local shipping platform to be certain that the shipment is not left on the platform but does leave via the right carrier, at the right time, and is loaded in the right manner. This is good "claim prevention" as well as good expediting.

Expediting is sometimes complicated by strikes, embargoes, or other service stoppages. The challenge, of course, is to find a way to move the freight despite such difficulties. In such instances good friends among the carriers pay off in real dividends. They will suggest ways and means. Their help, plus your knowledge and determination, usually will produce results!

Diversion and reconsignment warrants consideration. If you divert a carload shipment you change its destination while it is en route. The consignee remains the same. If you reconsign a shipment you change the name of the consignee and if necessary, the destination while it is en route. While the terms "diversion" and "reconsignment" are not actually synonymous, the same rules govern both and usually are published in the same carrier tariffs.

Generally diversion and reconsignment can be accomplished only if instructions are issued in time to make the changes before the car gets out of route. If the car is already delivered to the original bill of lading destination you cannot reconsign it. Your only recourse then is to reship it on a new bill of lading. Also if you order a diversion from New York to Philadelphia on a car coming from Chicago and the last point at which diversion is possible is Harrisburg, you must see that the carrier issues instruction to Harrisburg before the car leaves there. If you do not, then you are too late to effect either diversion or reconsignment. The charge for either diversion or reconsignment is not great but it varies and is dependent on tariff provisions. Diversion or reconsignment may be undertaken only at the request of the owner of the goods; thus, if you buy FOB Destination, the seller must be asked to make the desired change.

Diversion and reconsignment are indispensable to concerns selling lumber, perishable goods, etc., since cars en route are reconsigned to the most advantageous market as a regular practice.

Diversion and reconsignment privileges are not available on less-than-carload shipments. When the destination of an LCL shipment is changed while en route the shipment will be subject to combination rates in effect via the point where the change is made.

Diversion and reconsignment are not normally practiced to any particular extent by the motor carriers, airlines, freight forwarders or water carriers.

Tracing is relatively simple as compared to expediting, since you are ordinarily following a shipment rather than getting out ahead of it. The main purpose is to locate an undelivered, overdue shipment. If it cannot be found and a reasonable time for delivery has elapsed, instructions should be issued to file claim and duplicate the shipment, if desired. Watch the FOB terms so that claim is not filed if the material is purchased or sold on an FOB your factory basis. If it is, refer to the vendor or customer for handling with the carrier to the end that matters are kept in regular channels and are handled in accordance with the understanding of the parties.

Expediting an urgent shipment is a problem for both the consignor and the consignee as well as the carrier. The consignor should see that the shipment is on its way properly and obtain full forwarding information from the carrier. Then he should wire or phone that information to the consignee along with full routing and the date the shipment is due at destination. The consignee can then contact the delivering carrier and make arrangemens for the shipment to be "pulled in" fast and can also arrange for delivery immediately upon its arrival at the delivering carrier's terminal. This practice also has the added advantage of keeping the consignee or customer informed as to the whereabouts of his shipment. This is an important prerequisite to successful expediting. Here again, FOB terms enter into the consideration. The seller of a shipment sold FOB origin should not be required to expedite or trace a shipment beyond furnishing the buyer with initial forwarding information. On the other hand, good customer relations may well cause the seller to follow an FOB destination shipment all the way to his customer's receiving platform.

Expediting and tracing are made necessary at times because shipping documents are lost or something happens whereby a tie-in between the papers and the shipment disappears. These kinds of shipments are often referred to as "no-bills" (the shipment turns up with no waybill to tell the carrier to whom it belongs or should be sent). There are variations on this, of course, but, generally speaking, situations along these lines become over and short freight to the carrier, and tracing and expediting involve going into its records and what lading it may have on hand in that connection.

Over or short freight is defined as freight with or without marks (including articles in excess of quantity on waybill) which is found in possession of a carrier at any point without a regular revenue waybill. This freight is assigned a "free-astray (F/A) waybill" showing all available details of the shipment, so it can move to a proper destination. The freight charges are controlled by the original revenue waybill, so no charges are assessed on over or short freight, thus resulting in the term, free-astray. If such freight cannot be identified it is put into storage, there to await identification through being claimed or by some other means. In any event, it will not be delivered to the indicated owner without first receiving from him some satisfactory "proof of ownership," as well as a statement from the recipient that credit will be extended to the carrier on any future or previous claim for a shipment with which the material can be identified.

Premium Transportation

This chapter deals primarily with the technique of expediting and tracing, but the transportation cost factor is closely allied to this technique. In other words, if only high-priced services are used, expediting may be easier or may not be necessary. Such use may well be tempered, however, through initiative and know-how so that lower-priced services are used when coupled with expediting techniques used sparingly and in appropriate cases only.

So-called premium transportation cost is defined as the expense for service that is costlier than other cheaper and normally available service. Industrial organizations can keep premium transportation cost at a minimum by:

1. Scheduling shipments to be released for forwarding in the most economical quantities and with sufficient time in transit to permit routing via the lowest-rated services;
2. Contacting traffic personnel prior to actual shipment for the best emergency routing, if normal routing is not considered to be satisfactory.

An example of the first would be raw material shipped via truck in LTL and TL quantities to keep an assembly line going, even though shipping in carloads via rail is cheaper. Once started, the movement continues at the higher transportation costs because the factory just cannot give up the extra days necessary to accumulate enough material for carload shipment. This type of scheduling can run into thousands of excess transportation dollars every year. A great deal of thought should be directed to planning ahead when scheduling raw materials and finished products so that the burden of miscellaneous production failures does not fall on the time left for transporting from supplier to factory, or, factory to customer.

The idea is to specify high-rated routes only when absolutely necessary. A certain corporation made a comprehensive study to determine how much it paid out annually for premium transportation. The resulting sum was given wide publicity through the company to impress all concerned with the real facts as to the excess amount spent annually to move freight at a stepped-up pace. The management of this firm determined that about two-thirds of the extra expense was legitimate. In other words, this company—like most big companies—needed air service, express service, etc., on occasion, to take care of genuine emergency situations. But the company management concluded that at least a third of the premium expense could have been eliminated by handling urgent lots more intelligently. Too often, shipments arrive at a receiving department via premium service only to wait days or weeks before being used in the factory. In other instances, shipments routed via premium service with what were expected to be shorter transit intervals could just as well have been routed at a saving via a regular service with comparable or better transit time.

The same corporation under discussion used a bar chart showing the various factors which added up to its total expense for premium transportation as a part of explaining matters to interested staff. The chart placed the spotlight on the causes of such premium or excess expenses through highlighting nine particular areas in which they were found to exist in its operations. These areas were personalized to its business and, somewhat oddly, showed that parcel post was apparently being overlooked as a way to effect an important percentage (close to 30%) of available savings.

In this connection, it is important to bear in mind that simply because a small shipment moves by air freight or express, it does not necessarily involve premium transportation. With the widespread sharp increases in small shipment charges the air cargo and express charges actually may be lower.

13

DETENTION CHARGES, DEMURRAGE, SIDING AND WEIGHT AGREEMENTS

RAILROADS AND MOTOR CARRIERS INCLUDE IN THEIR COST OF DOING business a factor to cover the expense of furnishing rolling stock in which freight is to be moved over their lines. When this equipment is held by shippers or consignees beyond a time considered reasonable for its loading or unloading, however, the carriers' tariffs provide for the assessment of penalty charges. These indirect costs of transportation, unless carefully controlled, not only will add to the cost of doing business, but are likely to have damaging effects on a company's relations with carriers, for a carrier's ability to operate profitably is dependent to an important degree upon maximum use of equipment.

Today there are substantially fewer freight cars in service than there were in previous years. The freight cars of today, though, differ considerably from those in use in the past; they are larger, they employ damage-control devices, they are built for the specialized handling of certain commodities and they are designed to be operated at much higher speeds than ever before. All of this has been of great benefit to shippers and has enabled the railroads to regain or retain much traffic which otherwise might have been diverted to other modes of transport. At the same time, however, it has brought about a tremendous increase in the railroads' equipment investment and they feel justified in expecting that this expensive rolling stock work harder at producing revenue. It is for this reason that demurrage charges were increased sharply on April 1, 1971, and are likely to undergo further upward revision if detention conditions do not improve.

Demurrage

The word demurrage is a term that has been in use since early in the seventeenth century. Originally, it meant the detention of a vessel beyond its specified time of sailing and the payment made for such detention. With the coming of the railroads its meaning was extended to include freight cars. Demurrage charges are published in one master tariff applicable for the account of all United States railroads. This tariff is published by B. B. Maurer, Agent, 22 West Madison Street, Chicago, Illinois 60602 and is known as "Car Demurrage Rules and Charges—Storage Rules and Charges," Tariff 4 series.

The principal reason for demurrage charges is to prevent the use of freight cars as warehouse space and to discourage "dog-in-the-manger" attitudes on the part of shippers in times of car scarcity. A secondary purpose is to compensate in whole or in part for the per diem charge payable to the railroad owning the car when that car is in the possession of a railroad other than the owner. If the car is not earning revenue, this charge is an out-of-pocket loss to the railroad on whose line the car is detained.

There are two plans for the settlement of demurrage charges. One is straight demurrage; the other is under an average demurrage agreement, which will be discussed later in this chapter. Demurrage rules and charges and related matters are receiving active attention by the I.C.C. and others. Particular care should be taken to update the information here provided where indicated.

Under straight demurrage, a shipper or consignee is allowed 48 hours, or two free days, to load or unload a car. This free time begins at the first 7:00 a.m. after placement of a car on a public delivery track and after notice is sent or given to consignee or party entitled to receive it. In the case of cars to be delivered to industrial connections or private sidings, free time begins at the first 7:00 a.m. after actual or constructive placement.

Actual placement is made when a car is switched to a position accessible for loading or unloading or at a point previously designated by the consignor or consignee. If any cause attributable to consignor or consignee prevents such positioning and the railroad leaves the car elsewhere on a track serving the consignor or consignee (other than a public delivery track), it shall be considered constructively placed, without notice.

Along with free time, during which straight demurrage charges are not payable, certain exclusions from demurrage calculations are provided for Saturdays, Sundays, and holidays. These exclusions, generally speaking, are applicable only within the first week after a car arrives at destination. Also, when they fall after a car has "gone on demurrage" for two days, charges are made for these days as if they are weekdays in the calculations. Additionally, one "$10.00 day" is all that can be excluded.

Overly simplified, exclusions for Saturdays, Sundays, and holidays are made when they fall immediately after, during, or before a free-time period. They are also excluded when they commence with the second day of the "$10.00 per day-4 day" level. Holidays are limited by the tariff to New Year's Day, Washington's Birthday, Memorial Day, Independence Day, Labor Day, Thanksgiving Day and Christmas Day, or the Monday immediately following if one of these holidays occurs on Sunday.

Current straight demurrage charge schedules that take effect subject to free time and exclusion calculations follow:

First 4 days	$10.00 per day
Next 2 days	$20.00 per day
Thereafter	$30.00 per day

Relating these to free time and exclusions and assuming only Saturdays and Sundays are involved, a car placed after 7 a.m.

on Friday goes on the $10.00 level the following Wednesday. A car arriving after 7 a.m. Tuesday has free days of Wednesday and Thursday, incurs a $10.00 charge for Friday, has exempt days for Saturday and Sunday, and resumes the schedule with a $10.00 charge on Monday.

The illustration on page 370, which is included in the discussion on average demurrage agreements, depicts in more detail the workings of straight demurrage calculations.

Demurrage also is assessed on cars held for orders, bills of lading, payment of freight charges, reconsignment, diversion, reshipment, inspection or forwarding instructions. In some of these cases, free time is limited to 24 hours; in others, there is no free time. Charges for demurrage apply per day or any fraction thereof and is not prorated.

Demurrage is not charged on privately owned cars (cars of other than railroad ownership) held on private tracks when the car and the track belong to the same firm. This will include cars leased to the owner of the track when the cars carry a placard or are stenciled to so indicate.

There are several situations in which relief from demurrage charges may be obtained. They include:

- Weather interference, whereby a car may not be loaded or unloaded safely or without damage to the lading;

- When the lading is frozen or congealed, necessitating thawing before it can be removed from the car;

- The presence of floods, earthquakes, hurricanes or tornadoes, including damage to loading or unloading facilities by these natural disasters;

- Bunching, the result of cars shipped from the same origin via the same route on different days being offered for delivery at one time in a quantity exceeding the capacity of unloading facilities;

- Delayed or improper notice by the railroad of the arrival of cars;

- Error on the part of any railroad party to the bill of lading contract which prevents proper tender or delivery, such as making actual placement of constructively placed cars out of arrival sequence in the absence of specific instructions from the consignee—known as "run around";

- Strike interference, when a labor disturbance at shipper's or consignee's premises prevents loading or unloading cars.

In such cases, regular demurrage charges must be paid in full and recovery of excess obtained through filing claims against the railroad within various time limits prescribed in the demurrage tariff. In the case of strike claims, a special charge is applicable of $4.00 per car per day without free time allowance. This amount is being contested before the I.C.C. in proceedings in which the rails contend that the $4.00 figure should be $5.00.

Storage Charges

Demurrage charges should not be confused with railroad storage charges which are of various types. One type involves carload shipments of hazardous materials which are held on a carrier's tracks. This happens at times, an example being a plant where all internal tracks are full because of an influx of business. In addition to being subject to demurrage rules and charges the hazardous shipments are also subject to charges for storage on the railroad's tracks. These charges are prescribed by tariff and vary from roughly $8.00 to $20.00 per day, depending on the rate territory and type of material.

Other examples include LCL lots shipped to consignees at points where there is no free store-door delivery or there is a clause in the body of the bill of lading "Do not make store-door delivery." Upon arrival of the freight the local railroad agent mails an arrival notice to the consignee which states that if the shipment is not called for within the allowed free time, it will be subject to penalty storage charges. If the shipment is not picked up within the free time period, the carrier will consider the shipment as being in storage or, at carrier's option, will place it in a public warehouse. It will be released to the consignee only upon payment of the freight charges, if collect, plus storage charges.

The railroads are not in the warehouse business and these charges are assessed more as penalties than anything else, the theory being that delay in removal of goods increases the railroads' liability for damage or pilferage. Charges are specified in the storage section of the demurrage and storage tariff and the storage principle is set forth in Section 4(a) of the Contract Terms and Conditions of the carrier's bill of lading. (See chart on page 365)

Motor Carrier Detention Charges

Motor carrier detention charges fall generally into two categories: Those where drivers are involved, and those where they are not. Salary payments go on whether a driver is idle and waiting for a load at a shipper's plant or is on the road. That feature is a critical element in determining, not only what the level of the charges should be, but also what, if anything, can be done from an operational point of view to avoid costs of a non-productive nature.

The various rate bureaus have various ways of handling detention charges and the amounts specified and other features vary. By and large, however, motor carrier free time arrangements follow a pattern where one set of detention charges is made in cases of regular operations where drivers are with the equipment and another set where trailers have been spotted at loading or unloading docks in charge of the industries using them and without any employee of the motor carrier being with the trailers. The spotting of trailers can afford benefits to both carriers and shippers and is done subject to availability of equipment and when it is possible to spot them reasonably because of the flexibility inherent in truck operations.

For regular pickup and delivery operations motor carrier free time is ordinarily related to the weight of the goods to be

TABLE OF STORAGE RATES AND CHARGES

Applying in Western, Eastern and Southern Territories described in Notes 25, 24, 15 and 16 of Tariff of Increased Rates and Charges X-267-B. All rates and charges in this chart include increases through Ex Parte 267-B.

Note: Compute any fractional part of 100 lbs. as 100 lbs. and any fractional part of a day as a day.

	TERRITORY			
	WESTERN	EASTERN	SOUTHERN	
	TABLE 12 (12%)	TABLE 14 (14%)	TABLE 6 (6%)	TABLE 12 (12%)
Other than L.C.L. Traffic				
Rule 5, Sec. C:				
Equipment on its own wheels as freight at tariff rates. After 48 hours free time the storage charge per unit per day while held on tracks of the railroad is	$ 4.00	$ 4.07	$ 3.78	$ 4.00
Rule 6, Sec. A, Par. 2:				
Class "A"—More dangerous explosives. After 24 hours free time the storage charge per car per day while held on railroad premises is	*19.89	*20.25	*18.83	*19.89
Rule 6, Sec. B:				
Class "B" and "C"—Less dangerous and relatively safe explosives and Rule 6, Sec. C, Dangerous articles, other than explosives. After free time the storage charge per car per day while on railroad premises is (*) This charge is in addition to demurrage.	* 7.97	* 8.12	* 7.55	* 7.97
On L.C.L. Traffic				
Rule 5, Sec. A:				
After free time the charge per day per 100 lbs. for the first 5 days is	.07	.07	.06¾	.07
Subject to a minimum charge of	1.02	1.04	.96	1.02
Shipment held beyond 5 days the charge per day per 100 lbs. is	.12	.13	.12	.12
Subject to a minimum charge of	1.98	2.02	1.88	1.98
Rule 6, Sec. 3, Par. 1:				
Class "A" explosives—After 24 hours free time the charge per day per 100 lbs. is	1.14	1.16	1.08	1.14
Subject to a minimum charge of	1.98	2.02	1.88	1.98
Rule 6, Sec. B, Par. 1 and Rule 6, Sec. C, Par. 1:				
Class "B" explosives and other dangerous articles. After free time the charge per day per 100 lbs. is	.47	.48	.45	.47
Subject to a minimum charge of	1.02	1.04	.96	1.02
Rule 6, Sec. B, Par. 2:				
Class "C" explosives. After the free time the charge per day per 100 lbs. is	.32	.33	.31	.32
Subject to a minimum charge of	1.02	1.04	.96	1.02

Effective Date April 12, 1971

Chart of Railroad Storage Rates and Charges.

loaded or unloaded, and charges for detention beyond free time are measured in minutes. An example, not necessarily typical, of motor carrier detention rules and charges is provided by Item 50 of Tariff 10 Series, issued by the Middle Atlantic Conference. Sections 3 and 4 of the tariff pertaining to free time and charges are shown below.

Detention rules and charges applicable to trailers spotted at shippers' or consignees' docks appear in Item 80 of the tariff

SEC. 3   Free Time:

Free time shall be as follows:

COLUMN A		COLUMN B	
Actual weight in pounds per vehicle	Free Time in minutes	Actual weight in pounds per vehicle stop	Free Time in minutes per vehicle stop
Less than 24,000	240	Less than 10,000	90
24,000 and less than 36,000	300	10,000 and less than 20,000....	180
		20,000 and less than 24,000....	240
		24,000 and less than 36,000....	300
36,000 or more	360	36,000 or more	360

COLUMN A—Applies to vehicle containing truckload shipments requiring only one vehicle, or to fully loaded vehicles containing truckload shipments requiring more than one vehicle, except as provided in Column B.

COLUMN B—Applies to last vehicle used in transporting overflow truckload shipments requiring two or more vehicles, or to vehicles containing truckload shipments stopped for completion of loading or partial unloading.

SEC. 4   Charges:

When the delay per vehicle beyond free time is:	The charge per vehicle will be:
1 hour or less	$ 10.00
Over 1 hour but not over 75 minutes	12.50
Over 75 minutes but not over 90 minutes	15.00
Over 90 minutes but not over 105 minutes	17.50
Over 105 minutes but not over 120 minutes	20.00
Over 120 minutes but not over 135 minutes	22.50
Over 135 minutes but not over 150 minutes	25.00
Over 150 minutes but not over 165 minutes	27.50
Over 165 minutes but not over 180 minutes	30.00
Over 180 minutes	$30.00 plus $2.50 for each 15 minutes or fraction thereof over 180 minutes.

Motor Carrier Detention Charges. Excerpts Middle Atlantic Tariff No. 10V.

mentioned in the preceding paragraph. Sections 2, 3, and 7 provide free time shall be the eight hours commencing with the 7 A.M. on the day after the trailer is spotted, that Sundays and legal holidays (national, state, and local) shall be excluded, and that a special charge per day shall be made in cases of strikes. Under Section 4, where loading is involved, the charge is $16.38 per 24 hours or fraction thereof after free time; where unloading is involved, charges after free time commence with $19.32 per 24 hours for the first three 24 hour periods and range upwards (25.77 for the fourth 24 hours and $38.65 for the fifth and succeeding 24 hour periods). While far from being on all fours some aspects of these provisions are common to those applicable to the rails.

Motor carriers, as with other carriers, dislike to be placed in a position where it is necessary to charge for detention, feeling that it is far more remunerative to have equipment moving under load and their employees performing the primary duties for which they are paid. They direct considerable effort toward preventive measures and their customers will see the carriers' service vastly improved if they, too, exercise every possible control over the situation.

Average Demurrage Agreement

As a means of minimizing railroad demurrage charges any concern having a steady volume of carload shipments, inbound or outbound, should consider the advantages of an average demurrage agreement. Such an agreement sets up an incentive to the shipper or receiver to load or unload cars quickly, because by doing so some of the demurrage expense can be eliminated. Important railroads also have important reasons to have cars unloaded quickly and all encouragement reasonably possible should be given them in this regard.

An agreement of this type is entered into by the industrial concern and the railroad serving its private siding, industry track or even a specific public delivery track. The salient features of an average demurrage agreement follow:

One credit is allowed for each car released within the first twenty-four hours of free time. Only one credit may accrue per car. One debit per car per day is assessed for each car held after the expiration of 48 hours. Maximum is four debits per car. (Hypothetically, the first level of four days at $10.00 per car per day is "used up".) After four debits have accrued on any one car the regular demurrage charges of $20.00 per car per day for the next two days and $30.00 per car per day for all subsequent days are assessed and may not be offset by credits.

At the end of each calendar month the total number of credits is deducted from the total number of debits and $10.00 per debit is charged for the remainder. Any excess credits remaining are cancelled and may not be used to offset debits in another month.

Credits on cars for loading cannot be used to offset debits on cars for unloading or vice versa. Also, separate average demurrage agreements must be entered into with each railroad serving a given industry at any one station. No agreement may embrace more than one station nor more than one industry. If the industry has two or more plant locations at one station, ordinarily all such locations will be covered by a single agreement with each railroad. The railroad will make individual agreements if desired, but the benefit to be derived is not readily apparent.

The maintenance of current records showing date and time of receipt and release of all cars is necessary when operating under an average demurrage agreement. Car records should be kept on a form designed to include all desired information, but especially the following:

Car Initial Number	Placement Time Date	Date Released	Credits	Debits (Max. 4)	$20 Days	$30 Days	Non-offset Days

Provision may be made on this form for space for summary purposes and, preferably, separate forms should be used to list inbound and outbound cars as the credits on one cannot be used to offset debits on the other. These records have been computerized by some carriers and industries and, in some cases, shipper-carrier computer facilities are being used jointly. Much more can be done in this connection.

The chart on page 370 graphically illustrates the computations to be made under average demurrage agreements as well as for straight demurrage. It provides an elaboration on, and simplification of, the subject which, at best, is complicated and involves substantial detail. Average demurrage statements, particularly for large plants, can be quite lengthy and need close attention.

While, by and large, average demurrage agreements represent good deals for industries and their carriers there may be changes in distribution patterns or other matters which make it best that an agreement be terminated. Some companies maintain periodic call-ups on these agreements because of this. Quite often it is possible for an experienced demurrage man to look at (i.e. "eye-ball") a statement and decide whether a more detailed study should be made. The practice of having this done may well be worth while for some companies.

Those who prepare demurrage records must have a clear understanding of the application of the demurrage tariff; otherwise it will be impossible to audit bills received from the railroad. Also, such records should be subjected to constant analysis as an important factor in any program of demurrage control.

Demurrage control is, to oversimplify, loading and unloading cars within the free time or offset period so there will be no demurrage bill to pay at the end of any calendar month. This cannot be done unless considerable planning goes into the ordering of empty cars for loading and the scheduling of inbound shipments in a manner that will prevent the arrival of too many cars at the same time. Plans must take into account the car capacity of the sidetrack, the frequency of available switching service and the time or times of day at which the switching can be performed. This may be difficult in a busy plant where there is substantial and urgent need for materials or where shipping facilities, on the one hand, and receiving, on the other, have important and vital requirements presenting real difficulties of solution. Coordination of all these factors is

This Chart is Based on Tariff Rules in Effect at Time of Issuance

DEMURRAGE CHART—STRAIGHT AND AVERAGE AGREEMENT BASES

All Days in Computing Free Time and Demurrage Charges Start 7:00 A.M.

	Type of Plan	Monday	Tuesday	Wednesday	Thursday	Friday	Saturday	Sunday	Monday	Tuesday	Holiday	Thursday	Friday	Saturday	Sunday	Monday	Tuesday
Cars	Straight	Placed After 7:00a.m.	FREE	FREE	$10	$10	$10	$10	$20	$20	$30	$30	$30	$30	$30	$30	$30
	Average	FREE	FREE	FREE	Debit	Debit	Debit	Debit	Debit	Debit	Debit	Debit	Debit	Debit	Debit	Debit	Debit
Cars	Straight		Placed After 7:00a.m.	FREE	FREE	10	Excl	Excl	10	10	10	20	20	30	30	30	30
	Average		FREE	FREE	FREE	Debit	Excl	Excl	Debit	Debit	Debit	Debit	Debit	Debit	Debit	Debit	Debit
Cars	Straight			Placed After 7:00a.m.	FREE	FREE	Excl	Excl	10	10	10	10	20	20	30	30	30
	Average			FREE	FREE	FREE	Excl	Excl	Debit	Debit	Debit	Debit	Debit	Debit	Debit	Debit	Debit
Cars	Straight				Placed After 7:00a.m.	FREE	Excl	Excl	FREE	10	Excl	10	10	10	20	20	30
	Average				FREE	FREE	Excl	Excl	FREE	Debit	Excl	Debit	Debit	Debit	Debit	Debit	Debit
Cars	Straight					Placed After 7:00a.m.	Excl	Excl	FREE	FREE	Excl	10	10	10	10	20	20
	Average					FREE	Excl	Excl	FREE	FREE	Excl	Debit	Debit	Debit	Debit	Debit	Debit
Cars	Straight						Placed After 7:00a.m.	Excl	FREE	FREE	Excl	10	10	10	10	20	20
	Average						Placed After 7:00a.m.	Excl	FREE	FREE	Excl	Debit	Debit	Debit	Debit	Debit	Debit
Cars	Straight							Placed After 7:00a.m.	FREE	FREE	Excl	10	10	10	10	20	20
	Average							Placed After 7:00a.m.	FREE	FREE	Excl	Debit	Debit	Debit	Debit	Debit	Debit
Cars	Straight								Placed After 7:00a.m.	FREE	Excl	FREE	10	Excl	Excl	10	10
	Average								Placed After 7:00a.m.	FREE	Excl	FREE	Debit	Excl	Excl	Debit	Debit

1. Under the Average Demurrage Agreement, debit days are $10.00 days.—These can be offset by credits earned on other cars on a one-for-one basis. A credit is earned whenever a car is loaded or unloaded prior to the beginning of the second free day. Credits earned on inbound cars cannot be used to offset debits accruing on outbound cars and vice versa. Intraplant cars must be further separated. The $20.00 and $30.00 days are arbitrary days and these cannot be offset by credits.

2. Demurrage charges accrue for all Saturdays, Sundays and holidays following the second $10.00 or debit day. (See Section 3 for exceptions.)

3. A private car on a private track, when the ownership of the car and the track is the same, is exempt from demurrage. These cars cannot earn credits.

4. Section 3 outlines rules and charges applicable when specifically referred to in the various incentive freight rate tariffs. These items generally restrict the free time to 24 hours and prohibit inclusion of detention in an average demurrage agreement. This chart is not a tariff and the information contained herein is subject to change without notice by tariff revisions or issuance of Interstate Commerce Commission Service Orders and is applicable only within the United States. The tariff should be consulted at all times.

Demurrage Chart. Straight and Average Agreement Computations essential, however, and the traffic manager in cooperation with the plant manager can demonstrate his worth by setting up an arrangement that will be workable by all and still minimize demurrage costs.

High bills for demurrage month after month may indicate that unloading facilities are inadequate for the volume of business being done, in which case enlargement or rearrangement of these facilities may be justified economically. For example, if the length of the building permits, a two-car siding might be enlarged to accommodate four cars; or possibly space would permit the extension of the loading platform along an existing siding. Very often the advice and counsel of the traffic manager to plant construction engineers in the initial planning of a plant's shipping and receiving arrangements will be instrumental in avoiding costly remodeling of these facilities after the plant is in operation.

Excessive demurrage charges also may arise from the lack or inadequacy of materials handling equipment (see Chapter 7). Fork lift trucks, portable conveyor systems and palletizing, among other things, are reducing the reliance upon manual labor, thereby permitting the loading and unloading of cars in but a fraction of the time formerly necessary. This is particularly true in the case of small-package freight. Savings in demurrage charges may contribute heavily to the justification of improved materials handling techniques. The payment of demurrage charges represents a non-productive and unnecessary expense and indicates particular help is needed in over-all plant management.

Side Track Agreement

Railroads actively compete with one another in attracting new industries to the land situated in proximity to their rights of way. They have found that this is an excellent means of obtaining a long haul and maximum revenue on the carload business generated by these industries in addition to making productive use of otherwise undeveloped areas.

An industrial siding is the access by which a railroad is enabled to deliver cars to the premises of an industry on its line. It is connected by a switch to the main track of the railroad and the railroad ordinarily furnishes the motive power for the placement or removal of cars. Sidings vary in size, from those accommodating but a single car to elaborate multi-track layouts with a capacity of several hundred cars. Railroad line-haul rates include one placement on a private siding at origin and destination, but if the arrangement of the siding is such as to put it in the "complicated" category, the railroad is required to make an additional charge for switching.

Except at those plants where switching is performed by the industry's own motive power, the industry and the railroad enter into an agreement covering the construction of and operations over the side track. A so-called industrial side track agreement of this type follows a fairly standard pattern. It describes the location and layout of the track and any trestle, or other structure over which the track is to be built. The industry is called upon to provide, without cost to the railroad, all necessary right-of-way beyond that of the railroad. The agreement confers upon the railroad the right to enter upon the property for the purpose of constructing, maintaining and operating the side track and of removing, upon termination of the agreement, any materials belonging to the railroad. It describes how the materials are to be furnished and generally includes a blue print of the side track to be constructed.

The agreement also establishes how the cost of construction is to be borne. Usually, the railroad assumes the cost of construction from the switch to the clearance point (where the track leading from the switch clears the main track) and the industry pays the rest. Under certain circumstances, however, the railroad may agree to refund part or all of the industry's outlays at rates ranging from $5.00 to $50.00 per car, dependent upon road-haul revenue yielded, for every loaded car originated or terminated (not stopped in transit) on the siding. Cost of maintenance, including removal of snow and ice, is absorbed by the industry, although upon request of the industry, the railroad will furnish the materials and labor and bill the industry for the work. The railroad's right to use the side track for general railroad purposes is established, provided it does not interfere with the use of the track for the industry's traffic, as is the right of the parties to join the track with any other track. Structural clearances in accordance with AAR rules are prescribed which generally mean buildings or objects over the side track less than 21 feet above the top of the rail or alongside the track less than 6 feet from the nearest rail (more on curves) are prohibited.

A typical liability clause in side track agreements is of sufficient importance to reproduce in full:

> It is understood that the operations of the Railroad Company involve some risk of fire, and the Industry assumes all responsibility for and agrees to indemnify the Railroad Company against loss or damage to property of the Industry or to property upon its premises, regardless of negligence of the Railroad Company, its officers or employees, arising from fire caused by or as a result of the operations of the Railroad Company on said sidetrack, except to the premises of the Railroad Company and to rolling stock belonging to the Railroad Company or to others, and to shipments in the course of transportation.
>
> The Industry also agrees to indemnify and hold harmless the Railroad Company from loss, damage or injury resulting from any act or omission of the Industry, its employees or agents, to the person or property of either of the parties hereto and their employees and to the person or property of any other person or corporation, while on or about said sidetrack unless caused by the sole negligence of the Railroad Company; and if any claim or liability, other than from fire or from the existence of the aforesaid close clearances, shall arise from the joint or concurring negligence of both parties hereto, it shall be borne by them equally.

From this it will be seen that the railroad assumes a minimum of liability for occurrences resulting from its operations on the siding and requires the shipper to hold it harmless as to various features on which liabilities can be substantial. The I. C. C. feels its jurisdiction does not include contractual provisions of this sort (61 ICC 120, 25 ICC 352, and 36 ICC 255) and shipper groups have worked with the rails on them. Further attention may well be given them as time progresses.

Many industrial concerns obtain insurance coverage as to these features. In some cases special policy provisions are necessary, and this should be checked where indicated. Additionally, some companies are careful to keep appropriate staff mindful of the liabilities created in these documents as an incident to their safety work and related activities.

Some very large industrial plants have their own trackage on which the placement of cars is performed by their own motive power. In such cases, delivery of cars by and to the railroad takes place on a railroad-owned interchange track. Since the railroad and the industry operate exclusively on their own trackage, no side track agreement is necessary. Industries operating their own trackage may be able to negotiate an agreement with the railroad whereby the railroad will grant an allowance for being relieved of the obligation to perform the switching. This is possible only in situations where it is clear that the switching performed does not fall within the "complicated" category involving extra charges.

Because the practice involves considerable potential for discrimination, the railroads are under some pressure and orders from the Interstate Commerce Commission to refrain from making allowances to industry for performing plant car placing and shifting. While the Commission's attitude is not entirely clear at this time, it is a fact that the railroads cannot undertake to make full reimbursement of an industry's cost of performing this service. Allowances, if any, will be nominal.

Often, the question of responsibility for material in cars standing on private sidings arises. Generally, it is held that the railroad's liability terminates with the placement of the car on inbound shipments. Outbound, the railroad's liability commences when its agent signs the bill of lading, whether or not the car has been removed from the siding, as the bill of lading then becomes an enforceable contract. Unusual circumstances, however, may produce exceptions to this rule.

The carriers, along with making industrial side track agreements, lease sections of their tracks to industries from time to time, generally on a so-much-per-foot basis. This may be done for a number of reasons: To get cars out of a chock-a-block plant, to bring supplies closer for quicker delivery to consuming points, and so on. Strictly from a demurrage point of view, these carry certain pluses quite properly for companies owning or leasing their rail equipment. Such owning or leasing, coupled with the track lease, gives the equipment on the leased track the status of private cars on private tracks for which there are no demurrage charges. Distribution expenses incident to the use of these leases (no matter whose cars are involved) warrants close and complete checking, however, as such expenses can be quite dear when all cost elements are considered.

Weight Agreements

Before discussing weight agreements, it seems to be appropriate to provide some background on the general subject of freight weights. The great majority of freight rates are published to apply on units of weight, *i.e.*, per 100 pounds, per net ton of 2,000 pounds or per gross ton of 2,240 pounds; therefore accurate weights are essential if the railroads are to meet their statutory obligation to charge no more nor less than the correct amount of the transportation of any shipment. They must satisfy themselves that weights shown on shippers' bills of lading are correct, for the acceptance of shipments under short weights will subject both carrier and shipper to prosecution under the Elkins Act, which forbids concessions and rebates.

In the early days of railroading, every shipment was weighed individually; carloads on a track scale, less-than-carloads on a platform scale at the railroad station. Before long, however, mass production and the standardization of packages made this procedure cumbersome and time-consuming. Individual railroad agents were quick to recognize that the weight of products shipped repetitively by industries served by their stations would not vary significantly. A 100-pound sack of feed always weighed 101 pounds, give or take a few ounces; one case of 24 No. 2 cans of peas scaled the same as any other similar case of the same article. Soon it was found that by eliminating unnecessary weighing it was possible to move the freight

EASTERN WEIGHING AND INSPECTION BUREAU   Form EB-8
OFFICE OF MANAGER

WEIGHT AGREEMENT NO.

Two Pennsylvania Plaza
NEW YORK, N.Y. 10001

Effective Date ....19....

This AGREEMENT, entered into, by and between the Eastern Weighing and Inspection Bureau, for and in behalf of the Carriers for which the Eastern Weighing and Inspection Bureau is duly authorized to execute this Agreement,

and

of _____

(Town)   (State)

WITNESSETH: That, in consideration of the carriers, members of the Eastern Weighing and Inspection Bureau, accepting the weights and descriptions as certified on shipping orders, bills of lading or weight certificates for commodities herein specified as the basis for assessing freight charges, it is hereby agreed:

1. The consignor or consignee, as the case may be, shall report and certify to the carrier correct gross weights and correct descriptions of commodities on shipping orders, bills of lading or weight certificates by placing thereon imprint of certification stamp providing for verification by the carriers, members of the Eastern Weighing and Inspection Bureau. When such weights are obtained on track scales the correct gross, tare and net weights shall be given.

2. When weights of uniform or standard weight articles are based upon averages, the consignor or consignee, as the case may be, shall give prompt notice to the authorized representative of the carrier when any change is made which will affect the weight arrived at by the use of the average, including any change made in package or material used.

3. The consignor or consignee, as the case may be, shall keep in good weighing condition all scales used in determining weights and have track scales tested, maintained and operated in accordance with the Track Scales Specifications and Rules approved by The Association of American Railroads and shall also allow the authorized representative of the carrier to inspect and test them.

4. The consignor or consignee, as the case may be, shall keep his records in such a manner as will permit of correct and complete check, and shall allow the authorized representative of the carrier to inspect the true and original weight sheets, books, invoices and records necessary to verify the weights and descriptions of the commodities certified in the shipping orders, bills of lading or weight certificates.

5. The consignor or consignee, as the case may be, shall promptly pay to the authorized representative of the carrier, bills for all undercharges from original point of shipment to final destination, resulting from certification of incorrect weights or improper descriptions, whether shipment is sold f. o. b. at point of shipment or elsewhere. Overcharges developed from check of consignor's or consignee's records, as the case may be, will be promptly certified by the authorized representative of the carrier in writing for proper adjustment.

6. Shipments made under this agreement will be subject to rates, charges, minimum and estimated weights prescribed by classifications, exceptions thereto, tariffs or rules of the carriers interested.

7. This agreement may be cancelled by ten days' notice in writing to either party; it being understood that the consignor or consignee, as the case may be, shall permit check of business and pay undercharges on all shipments made prior to cancellation.
This agreement applies on

....   **EASTERN WEIGHING AND INSPECTION BUREAU**
CONSIGNOR-CONSIGNEE   By ....
By ....   Manager
Title ....   Per ....

Typical weight agreement form.

out much more rapidly, thereby forestalling many tracing requests and avoiding the mixups that always occur in congested freight houses. Gradually, the idea spread to carloads and thus the "average" weight agreement evolved which is shown on page 376.

Because agreed weights must be acceptable not only to the originating carrier but to every other railroad in the route, the railroads do not deal directly with shippers in the establishment of weight agreements. Instead, this function is delegated to weighing and inspection bureaus set up along territorial lines and acting as agents for all railroads in the respective territories. These bureaus have representatives in all major cities who administer the agreements and, in addition, check on bill of lading descriptions and inspect shipments when called upon by the railroads to do so under section 2 of Rule 2 of the Uniform Classification.

An industry desiring to enter into a weight agreement quite often notifies the local railroad agent, who refers the matter to the nearest office of the appropriate weighing and inspection bureau. A representative then is sent to the industry's shipping department, where he determines the classification descriptions of the products to be covered and the various standard packages of each description. He then makes a random selection of at least 10 of each of these packages, weights them separately and establishes an average weight for each size package of each description. If packages are not uniform and an average weight cannot be determined, the shipper's weights may be used if the accuracy of the scales is certified by the bureau representative. If the shipper uses a track scale, it must be tested, maintained and operated in accordance with the Track Scales Specifications and Rules approved by the Association of American Railroads.

Bills of lading involving shipments which are the subject of weight agreements should be stamped with a rubber stamp as shown on page 378. By signing the bill of lading the shipper is bound by the provisions of the certification. Similar informa-

The description and weight indicated on this
bill of lading are correct.
Subject to verification by the
EASTERN WEIGHING & INSP. BUREAU

According to Agreement.

Weight Agreement Certification Form for Bills of Lading.

tion may be imprinted on the bill of lading forms (instead of
using a stamp) provided it carries appropriate "dagger" (†)
marks specifying "Shipper's imprint in lieu of stamp; not a
part of bill lading approved by the Interstate Commerce Commission". (See explanation Chapter 4).

Shippers using weight agreements must notify the bureau
of any change that affects the average weights, keep records in
such a manner as to permit checks by bureau representatives,
allow inspections of scales and records at any time and
promptly pay bills for any undercharges resulting from the use
of incorrect weights. Naturally, the weight and inspection bureau will enter into agreements only with firms of unquestioned
integrity.

Only those firms which have a large volume of carload
business will be able to justify the expense of installing and
maintaining their own track scales, and then only if the major
part of their business consists of straight carloads of a single
commodity. Bills of lading covering carload shipments weighed
on track scales must show the gross weight of the car and its
contents, the tare weight of the empty car and the difference
between the two, which, less dunnage allowance if any, is the
net weight upon which transportation charges are paid. Each
car has its empty weight stenciled on its sides and this weight
usually is checked at regular intervals, particularly if the car
undergoes any modification or rebuilding. Industries with their
own track scales, however, frequently make a practice of run-

ning their own checks on the weights of empty cars, but railroad rules will not permit changes to be made unless check weights differ by more than 300 pounds from the weight stenciled on the car. Each weighing on a track scale produces a scale ticket which is acceptable under a weight agreement as sufficient evidence of the actual weight of a car or its contents.

Shippers of large numbers of mixed carloads will find it necessary to weight shipments before they are loaded or use average weights under an agreement. Otherwise, they will find it impossible to benefit from the provisions of Rule 10 of the classification, which permits the use of the carload rate on each different article in the carload. If a track scale weight were to be used on a mixed carload, the entire weight would be charged for at the highest carload rate applicable to any article in the carload.

Certain perishable commodities, mainly vegetables, move from packing sheds close to the fields in which they are grown. Operations at these sheds being of a seasonal nature, the sheds are not equipped with scales, and since the carloads must be moved to destination without delay, the railroads do not track-scale them. Instead, freight charges on shipments of these commodities are based on a scale of estimated weights developed for each type of commodity and published in carriers' tariffs.

The use of estimated weights is a common practice on certain movements of petroleum, molasses, and other liquids in tank cars. These weights are often found in the items naming the rates; i.e., gasoline at 6.6 pounds per gallon and so on. Uniform Classification Rules 52 and 53 provide estimated weights of 4.7 and 5.2 pounds per gallon for liquefied patroleum gas and butadiene. Some motor carriers also use them.

Freight bills, incidentally, on tank car traffic of liquids moving at estimated weights are generally and fundamentally based on the tank shell capacity of the car. Subject to various qualifications, U.F.C. Rule 35 provides for this. Car capacities are to be found in the Freight Tariff 300 series issued by R. H. Lindsay, Agent, 516 W. Jackson Blvd., Chicago, Ill. #60606.

The qualifications referred to in the preceding paragraph

include loadings into domes, temperature adjustments, required outages for possible expansion of ladings, and so on. They are quite complicated and numerous. Subject to them, where a shipper has 10,000 gallons of gasoline to move via tank car between points taking a rate of 30 cents per 100 pounds at an estimated weight of 6.6 pounds per gallon the freight charges would be $198.00 (10,000 x 6.6 x 30).

This example assumes the liquid moves in a car having a shell capacity of 10,000 gallons. If the shell capacity were 12,000 gallons and only 10,000 gallons were loaded, the shell capacity would control and the freight bill would be $237.60 (12,000 x 6.6 x 30). In matters of this kind "wind weight" payments (here $39.60) require watching and avoidance. Motor carrier tariffs in related fields should be accorded similar treatment.

Although not directly connected with weight agreements, this appears to be an appropriate point to discuss a feature of car weighing, known as "tolerance," which can have considerable influence on the payment of freight charges and the basis of claims for loss. Under the weighing and reweighing rules of the railroads, where carload freight, the weight of which is not subject to change through its inherent nature, is check-weighed or reweighed enroute or at destination, the weight on which freight charges are based will be changed if the difference exceeds 1 per cent or 500 pounds, whichever is greater. On ashes, cinders, clay, dolomite, ganister, gravel, mill scale, ore, sand, all stone that is not cut, brick, soft drain tile and metal borings, filings or turnings loaded in open cars, the tolerance is 1½ per cent or 500 pounds, whichever is greater. If the difference between the original net weight and the weight obtained by reweighing exceeds the tolerance, the car should be weighed a third time if practicable. Should the third weighing produce a still different weight within the tolerance, no change will be made, but if it exceeds the tolerance, the lower of the second or third weights will be used.

The shipper or consignee also is permitted to support a claim for weight difference, subject to the tolerances mentioned above, by means of shipper's authenticated invoice, by weighing the entire load on a platform scale or, if the load consists of uniform packages, by weighing not less than 10 per cent of the load. Any such weighing is to be performed under the supervision of a representative of the railroad. On these tolerance situations the matter of who stands the weighing charges also may become involved and should be borne in mind.

Whenever possible, consignees should check the weights of all inbound shipments. This is good business because it frequently results in the discovery of figure transpositions in billing (e.g., a weight of 5,870 pounds is transposed to 8,570 pounds), it may correct weights which have been estimated inaccurately, and it may even pinpoint evidence of leakage or pilferage of the contents of packages. Correction of weights on freight bills or claims may meet with some resistance on the part of carriers, but the reputation of a firm and the proven accuracy of its scales usually will be the deciding factor. A weight agreement in such cases will at least offer testimony as to the reliability of the scales. As a matter of fact, more and more of these agreements are being entered into for inbound shipments, particularly where iron and steel are involved. The scale inspections, auditing of books, and so on that go with them are regarded favorably by many of those who are involved.

Thus far, the subject of weights has dealt with railroad shipments, but it should be pointed out that the practice of accepting shippers' weights also is followed by motor carriers, water carriers, freight forwarders and airlines. For these carriers to weight each of the millions of shipments they handle would bog down even the most efficient freight terminal and cause no end of delay to the shipments. The motor carriers have their own weighing and inspection bureaus whose representatives conduct continuous sampling checks at carriers' terminals and report inaccurate weighing practices and deviations from correct bill of lading descriptions and packaging provisions. Independently, any carrier may weigh shipments, inspect the contents of packages and test shipping containers at any time. Matters generally work out that there is little risk involved in the acceptance of shippers' weights as a basis for the assessment of freight charges.

14

THE TRAFFIC DEPARTMENT:
ORGANIZING, OPERATING AND EQUIPPING IT;
ITS COMPANY RELATIONS AND PUBLIC RELATIONS

FOR YEARS THE TRAFFIC MAN'S HORIZON HAS BEEN STEADILY broadening. In the early 1900's it was restricted to transportation from a freight station in one town to a freight station in another town. Then it was from the shipper's store-door to the consignee's store-door. Today it is from the end of the assembly line in a factory to a location inside the premises of the final consignee or the retail consumer, thus embracing many phases of the entire transportation and distribution complex.

The traffic man knows that each handling of material costs money and does not contribute any value to the product itself. It is quite obvious that good business practices demand the absolute minimum number of handlings between the time the product leaves the factory and the time it is turned over to the ultimate consignee. This is an important consideration in developing sound and economical operations. The traffic man has always been accustomed to supervising inbound traffic as well as outbound. This has given him diversification. He knows the meaning of FOB terms; he understands transportation, the movement of goods, the practices of other companies similarly situated, costs, loading, packaging, pooling, warehousing, and practically every activity making up and affecting the physical movements of his company's products.

Steps to take, and features to observe, in organizing, operating, and equipping a traffic department run quite a gamut of
considerations. New companies starting operations (and with
no previous transportation experience) are confronted with one
set of requirements. Small, medium, and large size companies
have others. Companies operating in special fields will have
still further variations; requirements will differ from industry to
industry. With some industries transportation costs and allowances will be as much as twenty-five percent or more of gross.
They may be less with others.

It is interesting that certain companies do not know, or do
not have a reasonable approximation of, what they pay and
allow for transportation. They know total costs of wages, of
taxes, and so on. Somehow transportation, however, has been
lumped with other expenses and has not been isolated to a total
figure. Nothing critical should be said about this position in
many cases because with some it has simply been practical to
treat transportation costs in a category similar to, say, most
electric bills—features about which little can be done. Such a
category should be changed, however, as transportation becomes a real expense factor. Something often can be done
about such cost items, and total cost figures can be helpful in
evaluating what should be done and in doing it.

Five classifications form the nucleus for this discussion of
the traffic function. These involve: 1) organization considerations, 2) operations, 3) equipment needs, 4) company relations,
and 5) public relations. They are dealt with on flexible lines
and they follow in the order named. A particular effort is made
to be of help to companies contemplating, or in the process of
starting, a traffic operation. Special discussions of aspects they
may find worth while (eg. rating and routing guides) are
included.

Traffic Organization

Industrial traffic titles and organization set-ups are anything but uniform. The top traffic executive may be designated as general traffic manager, traffic manager, traffic supervisor, manager of transportation, physical distribution manager, traffic director, vice-president in charge of traffic, traffic agent, transportation coordinator, transport control manager, traffic representative, general manager of distribution division, transportation manager, director of physical distribution, etc. He may have no particular title or a title in no way descriptive of transportation. Organization-wise, vis-a-vis the company generally, the traffic department may be a far-ranging, large group with its head having status as a vice president and director. The department may be part of a large transportation and supply group. It may be teamed with purchasing, a distinct distribution group, or other company functions. It may be a one-man activity with that individual also having other duties. The Official Directory of Commercial Traffic Executives, mentioned later, lists these by companies. A top-flight, highly successful chemical company (not particularly given to titles as is, say, the banking business) operates with simply a "Traffic Department," designates the department's head as "Director of Traffic" and accords him a vice-presidential-plus status in its affairs. That department does a particularly outstanding job for its company.

It is a significant achievement to become an expert in traffic matters even though the activity carries a "specialist" classification. Our book deals to a large degree with the principles of being that "specialist"! It also endeavors to point the way to the broader opportunities that exist and are available in the over-all field of company operations. The traditional concept of the transportation department as specialists in freight rates, routing, service, complex transportation laws, etc., has undergone a change. In more and more companies today the traffic man is respected as a full-fledged operating executive, at times on the Vice-President level. Sharp increases in freight transportation costs and the realization that the transportation-distribution complex is a major cost element in almost every industry have had a great deal to do with this change. Beyond that is the realization that transportation is tied in closely with important phases of company profits.

In analyzing this change, there are listed below important operating functions of any business that are dealt with as flexible in that they may be directly under the traffic manager's supervision or may report to some other administrative branch. If it is the latter, the traffic manager has no specific jurisdiction but functions more in an advisory capacity re:

Packaging	Inventory contol
Materials handling	Private carriage
Warehousing	Plant locations
Over-all distribution policy	Export/import traffic

Electronic Data Processing

To the extent that traffic management has assumed administration of the above functions, or has acted to influence their control in a much closer relationship, old concepts and traditions have given way to far-reaching and important "new looks."

The new approach takes nothing away from the proven importance of the traditional traffic functions. Somewhere there must be top level organizational responsibility to centralize and co-ordinate all the varied transportation and related functions of an industrial organization. Where the traffic manager has the capabilities, the training, and the confidence of his management, certainly he has a fine background to carry out successfully and aggressively broader responsibilities.

Companies starting in business and small companies generally do not employ a trained traffic man. The work is done by (1) a shipping clerk, (2) the office manager or similar executive, and (3) outside sources, such as independent traffic consultants, professional traffic bureaus, shippers' associations and chambers of commerce. These outside agencies maintain professional traffic staffs which perform almost all standard traffic management functions for their members or clients. There are over 300 such associations and consultant services in the U.S. The traffic manager of the association or consultant firm is in effect the traffic manager for each of the firms served, and in some cases actually carries a title (with company letter-head) identifying him as such. Some independent traffic management firms represent the shipping interests of as many as 100 or more smaller firms, a situation not unlike that of the corporate traffic manager who controls the transportation activities of as many as 300 or 400 company plants.

Many smaller companies handle routing and carrier selection in accordance with specific instructions furnished them by traffic departments of larger companies to whom they sell. The use of automation for purchase order-writing by such companies has been a factor influencing this, and purchase orders often include pre-programmed shipping instructions. One general traffic department of a major retail chain furnishes such shipping instructions to several thousand of its vendors and has a rule that it will not accept merchandise shipped otherwise.

In a similar vein, these smaller companies will usually permit their inbound shipments to be routed by larger companies from whom they buy because the larger companies employ special skills not available in the smaller companies and do make every effort to give their customers the lowest possible delivered costs.

As traffic expenditures and needs reach a point with a company where the transportation function should be assumed wholly or in part by a company employee, it is preferable that an experienced man be hired for the job. If this is not in order, the individual assuming the responsibility should, if at all possible, take a traffic course or courses at one of the several good traffic schools. Generally the sessions are after work or at night, and the teachers are experienced traffic men having responsible, full-time, day employment in transportation. They do good jobs with their students and provide instruction of a practical nature which is related to day-to-day, often-encountered problems. Tuition is not particularly expensive and in many cases is underwritten directly or indirectly by the employer. Where a traffic school is not practical, a good correspondence course can be of real help.

Moves to be undertaken in the way of obtaining special tariffs, books, and the like can include the acquisition of fairly detailed road and rail maps and subscriptions to one or more pertinent routing guides, motor carrier directories, etc. together with the Official Guide of the Railways. The motor carrier and rail classifications also can well be obtained along with truck, rail, and other tariffs pertinent to the company's operations. Arrangements should be made to receive appropriate trade publications including *Traffic World* and *Transportation & Distribution Management*. See later tabulations for more information on these. Memberships, and participation, in The National Industrial Traffic League, the company's trade association (if it has one and it has a traffic group), and the traffic club of the city of the company's location should be considered. Attendance at pertinent seminars (such as those pertaining to private trucking, computers, and so on) held from time to time at various universities and elsewhere can well be arranged.

The routing guides and motor carrier directories mentioned in the preceding paragraph can be particularly helpful to shippers not experienced extensively in transportation who use less-truckload, truckload, express, parcel post, United Parcel and similar services. These are compilations from official publications in which information is condensed and simplified so that it is readily available and more easily understood. This type of reference work has been around for some time, is used extensively by many shippers small and large, and there are various good ones. Typical of the field are the "guides" published by G. R. Leonard & Co. which are in three basic categories. One includes available service, rate information, and other extensive and detailed data on express, parcel post, and United Parcel shipments; the second contains motor carrier rates to the entire country, and the third contains motor carrier routings to all states. Arrangements can be made for personalizing appropriate shipper information to particular features (i.e., more specific origins when indicated), and so on. Reissues and loose-leaf arrangements are provided to keep information up to date. The services are leased, rather than sold, and costs vary. The most expensive (made up for particular shippers) is $100 per year. Albrechts, an affiliate, specializes in data of a related nature for the West. Similar reference works that may be found helpful include The Shippers Guide, American Motor Carrier Directory, and others.

Office procedures and the like can take their cues from practices in existence and available. By all means make sure good equipment (calculators and the like) are at hand. A possible worth-while step, if it is not already being done, is to arrange for the checking of additions, multiplications, and the like on freight bills over certain amounts. Errors are common here, and recoveries may well make this the thing to do. The checking of rates actually used in the bills by the carriers with the tariffs and other activities requiring more specialization, of course, should also go forward. A filing system can be important. If it can be melded into an existing system, fine; if not, help can be obtained from business books on filing from local libraries. Filing may be by commodity, territory, mode of carriage, or in other ways or combinations of them. Preferably the system should have a basic foundation such as that provided by a Dewey Decimal type of filing. In most cases the papers should be filed by subject chronologically and held in place by punched holes and fasteners; special files for tariffs are on the market and available. Good arrangements for call-ups should be made; they are sure to be needed. A program for destroying old and unneeded files should also be established and followed.

Starting, expanding, or contracting traffic functions are similar in many ways to doing the same thing for a legal, tax, or other like activity. The legal work of some companies is handled by house attorneys as to certain of the work plus a law firm or firms acting as general counsel or on special matters. Similar dealings may be in order for industrial companies starting in traffic or with operations at points where they are working into more coverage of the field. This can be done by using transportation advisory firms and the like which have been previously discussed in this chapter. What might be termed a "full responsibility" traffic department, however, can contribute greatly to the success of an industrial concern, and work to see that this function is so handled properly, aggressively, and adequately can be very much in order.

The features just mentioned as having possible particular application to smaller companies and companies neophyte to transportation are also involved with medium-sized companies and larger companies in many ways. The involvements of the latter are on much broader bases, include more carriers and types of carriage, and are concerned with greater freight bills and opportunities to effect greater benefits for their companies. The traffic departments of all have much in common, however, and what follows in this chapter as well as what appears elsewhere in this text can find application in many instances, irrespective of the size of the industrial organization.

Important fundamentals applicable to all—large and small —are that traffic-wise a company must be kept competitive with others in the same business and that freight cost adjustments which are in order can be of relatively sizeable amounts. With many corporations very substantial sales increases (if they can be accomplished) are necessary to "flow down" to profits amounts which are comparable to those that may "flow down" from freight economies. Other fundamentals are that traffic, to the best of its ability, should reflect the management philosophies and over-all directions undertaken by its company and should work whole-heartedly to follow and support them. Often this is not easy, because they change and at times could be more clear and more consistent. The importance of such support, however, is obvious.

Industry does not allocate responsibilities to its traffic organizations on a uniform basis. Some traffic departments have as their responsibilities the obvious traffic functions of auditing freight bills, routing, claims, expediting, tracing and handling rate and classification problems. Other traffic departments have further responsibilities including, in addition to the above, transportation contracts, distribution arrangements, warehousing, receiving and shipping departments, packaging, materials handling, local or intercity company-owned truck operations, moving employees' household goods, passenger bookings, rental of drive-yourself passenger cars and trucks, and export and import freight as well as domestic freight.

In giving consideration to the presentation of industrial traffic organizations by diagrams, no attempt appears advisable to list in detail all the functions of each individual employee. This will vary greatly between industries and should be developed by each company according to its needs. Since traffic organizations must be established to meet the needs of each company's type of operation, standard organization charts for uniform use are not practical. Certain generalities, however, can be made as to broad features and other aspects.

Organization charts are helpful in enabling someone to understand how a department works and the functions of its various sections. Many knowledgeable executives, however, use these sparingly for even those purposes. Time taken to maintain them may possibly be spent more profitably elsewhere, often the ramifications of particular job situations are of such delicacy that charting presents problems, and so on. At one time charts (and organizations) were set up so that the manager had a dozen or so sections or staff members reporting directly to him. More modern management approaches run to the effect that an "ideal" organization should have two "breakouts" per function or individual. The next chart illustrates this, but modifications of the concept are necessary for practical reasons in many cases. As an example, if the "break-outs" from the General Traffic Manager shown there should be territorial (i.e., East, Mid Continent, and West), they should be so specified. Also, under more modern practices "Clerk" designations in job titles are declining. "Analysts," "Supervisors" and the like are more favored as being more expressive of duties undertaken.

Job assignments can be on territorial, on functional, or on other bases as well as combinations. They should be sufficiently spelled out so that there is a delineation of responsibilities and staff know what is expected of them. Flexibility should be preserved as much as possible, however, so that when someone sees something that needs doing he is not stopped or discour-

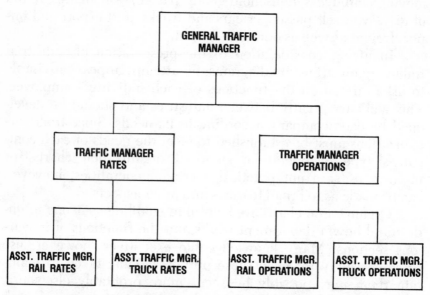

Illustrative Traffic Department Organization Chart

aged from taking steps leading to correct the situation; built into highly structured operations are many restraints to be avoided. "Field Representative" sections (or the like) may be newcomers to some traffic organizations, particularly where decentralization is a fact of life in company operations. Fairly strong adherence to "line" and "staff" organization principles occurs in various cases, one in particular being a quite successful company.

Salaries, benefits, and related aspects of traffic operations (like many other features) are tied to a company's general personnel policies, its profit picture, how much of its gross is paid out for transportation and other items many of which are of a non-transportation nature. As a part of management, traffic leadership should help in the general framework of these when it can. Practically, involvements are so extensive that such help is generally limited. Personnel practices of others similarly situated are to be kept in mind in this framework as well as intra department personnel dealings. Working within reasonable frameworks, traffic management can do a great deal for their companies by taking particular care to reward those who get results, by recognizing increased competence and value through experience and maturity of judgement, and by careful attention to the other elements that are involved in salary administration. Companies with fair and proper salary programs are the most effective and profitable in most cases. As a related item job promotions also should receive particular care with promotion from within the department or the company being so strongly a part that deviations are made only in exceptional cases. The top executive of one of the country's great companies recently pointed out that industry is expected "to pay fair wages and salaries and treat employees well, providing equal promotion and employment opportunities for everybody".

The following functions can well be treated as traditional responsibilities of the general traffic manager of a smaller company:

1. Developing transportation policies and interpreting such policies throughout all company departments.
2. Standardizing traffic procedures at all company locations on a uniform basis.
3. Filing all complaints with government regulatory bodies.
4. Approving all rate and classification proposals and handling them to a conclusion before carrier committees and regulatory bodies.
5. Reviewing and approving all trucking and transportation contracts.
6. Cooperating with sales, purchasing, manufacturing and other company departments on warehousing, storing, packaging, materials handling, private carriage, routing and distribution problems, plant location studies, inventory control, export/import and electronic data processing distribution studies.
7. Conducting continuous studies on all freight movements. Included in this is the development of oppor-

tunities to consolidate small lots into pool cars, pool
trucks or piggy-back direct to final destination or to
strategic points from which they are reshipped to eventual or final destination.

8. Establishing a company-wide tonnage distribution policy for observance in routing freight via all types of
carriers.

As companies expand and traffic men are given additional responsibilities, functions listed above may be broadened and increased. Those listed in Item 6 where traffic is shown as cooperating may well be changed to show traffic as having the
direct administrative responsibility.

The status of transportation in a company's general organization chart is important. The higher it is, the greater is the department's prestige, as a general rule. At times such prestige
may be influential in getting things done with carriers and others. Additionally, other benefits flow from such recognition, including encouragement to help more and further in improving
the company's over-all fortunes, more satisfaction along self-
fulfillment lines on the part of staff that their work is recognized as of real value, and so on. Obviously there are practical
limits to how high this status can be and other features of an
inter-company nature can be as important—often more so. Included in these can be worthwhile pay scales and benefits, opportunities for substantial accomplishments, freedom to do
quickly and simply what should be done, and actual and demonstrated encouragement and appreciation from the rest of the
company (including top management) together with fine and
responsive help from them when needed.

Traffic should be placed high enough in the organization
to assure it the authority and prestige necessary to accomplish
the best results. Further and of equal importance, its situation
should be such that top management encourages and supports
its traffic executive so that he is assured of consistent company-wide cooperation. With these features much more than a
position on an organization chart is involved. The actual deliv-

ery to company operations of *bona fide,* worthwhile benefits is basic. The accomplishment of these and the explanation of them in simple, non-technical terms to those affected helps importantly. "Sales" efforts along these lines, appropriately handled, mean a great deal on many fronts including, when indicated, consideration for assignment to traffic of a higher organization chart stature.

The industrial executive to whom the top traffic man reports (at times called traffic's executive contact) will probably not be too familiar with the complexities of traffic management. Probably too, he will have substantial calls on his time from other company functions. Depending to a great extent on the individual, all reasonably possible should be done as a general rule to see that he has over-all understanding of the functions of the department, its strengths and weaknesses, and its short and long term plans. The going over with him of current items from time to time is also in order. Efforts in these regards may meet with varying reactions. Many in higher management echelons feel that managers should "manage" their departments pretty much on their own and, if that is his position, it should be respected. If some other tack is indicated, it should be undertaken. Relations with its contact are important and traffic should extend itself to the end that he is cordial, helpful, cooperative, and enthusiastically interested in what Traffic does for the company and its advancement. Others in high echelons may be similarly positioned for particular and somewhat similar attention.

The technicalities incident to transportation are such that the going over of current matters in these cases with its executive contact can well be as an attorney or tax specialist would do them. They should be advisable only when more-than-ordinary traffic problems are involved. Presentations should be short, to the point, and in layman's language. Preferably the decision you believe should be made should be presented with the reasons. If he knows of and expresses other considerations that make other moves applicable, they can well modify those you propose. In carrying them out (particularly if they involve

unpleasant features) the best possible should be done to "keep
the boss off the spot" by explaining the facts behind the action
undertaken rather than by expressing the responsibility for the
action as his. Also, if anything extraordinary involving the department commences to loom on the horizon, it is preferable
that this be passed to him right away. Higher echelon colleagues are more effective when they are not "put on the spot"
and are not subjected to "surprises" from "outside" sources.

Important also to traffic's relations with this individual (as
well as other high echelon levels) is that information may be
provided there which will enable it to better assist other members of the company family. Also, guidance may be provided to
enable it to better complement in its operations those of the
company generally. In any number of companies "feedbacks"
to traffic of impending company actions and developments
known at those levels are made to work for the company's benefit. Any number of examples could be cited. One actually occurring recently involved a midwestern manufacturing company that was able to retain a valuable account through a rate
adjustment "triggered" by cooperation of the sort here mentioned.

Traffic Operations

Management principles applicable practically anywhere
are applicable in transportation, and those that have worked
successfully in other connections can well be guides to traffic
effectiveness. John D. Rockefeller's concern with the acquisition of "brains" (rather than properties) and Henri Deterding's
with "simplification" and "getting the best out of people" as incidents to putting together the fine organizations of Standard
Oil and Royal Dutch Shell find particular applications here.
Along with these go the constant looking out for his "money
makers" by Scotsman Alexander Fraser, one of the many excellent Shell Oil presidents who contributed so greatly to its success. Colonel Earl H. (Red) Blaik's winning West Point football
teams were brought to stardom on the precept that true success

takes more than luck or natural gifts and that "you have to pay the price." On a more at-the-moment basis are the thoughts of Avis-fame-and-writer-extraordinary Robert Townsend that business should be "fun" and that the nods for needed executives should go to "anybody who will work full time" and "who doesn't think he's a genius at anything." Reverting to a more serious vein and paramount of all of these, of course, is the always to be remembered, do-unto-others admonition of the Golden Rule.

Management and management leadership techniques are influenced in many ways by those of the company. Due regard is to be given these, and, along with them, such guidance as can be gleaned elsewhere. The American Management Association, 135 W. 50th St., New York, N.Y. 10020, (212) 586-6100, is active in this field and has various texts and publications that may be helpful. Many company personnel departments receive these and are possible sources for information from them. A basic management type which has had consideration in varying forms (but which is being stressed somewhat in various places) is that of "team management." In a recent Association text, "Effective Management Leadership" (1972) by James J. Cribben ($9.75) this was characterized as at once the most difficult, the most effective, and the most rewarding of leadership styles. Under it the executive (i.e., the Traffic Manager) is concerned for both high production and the needs of his people. The building blocks, however, are not individuals but horizontally and vertically integrated work teams. The leader seeks to involve his subordinates in the work through consultation, participation, and joint problem solving. Tensions are openly admitted and dealt with. Attempts are made to make the work more meaningful rather than hard or easy. While a full application of this philosophy to a number of traffic functions could well be going too far, it presents avenues for possibly doing better jobs in various areas and could be worthwhile on that basis.

High on the list for a Traffic Department's attention is the matter of cooperating with other departments and functions

and securing their cooperation in the solution of traffic problems. Sincere work is necessary to be sure a two-way communication in these cases is wide open and moving freely rather
than becoming atrophied. Staff members become occupied with
close-at-hand items, distances intervene, and one thing and another happens if this is overlooked. Across the desk visits with
Accounting, Sales, Manufacturing, and others with appropriate
information exchanges are often of value. Their problems are
Traffic's when Traffic is also involved, and all encouragement
possible should be given them to have Traffic help when it can.
This goes also for the field. When possible, trips can be made
to do double duty. As one becomes necessary, an expansion to
include local marketing offices, plants, and other installations
can well be arranged. Visits there to get up-to-date on what is
going on and so on are in order. In all these contact activities
appropriate traffic staff should do the same thing; also, care
should be taken that the head man of the other function knows
what is going on. The first step on any plant visit can well be a
call on the plant manager or, if he is away, to his office. Further, the idea of letting the other fellow first do the talking is
good in these cases; best results can often be obtained by lis-
tening rather than engaging in a conversation in which traffic
problems overshadow the others. Traffic's time can well come
later.

Another feature on the list for Traffic attention is the delineation of plans for the future. No matter how hard a company tries some of its operations can be improved upon, and
some of the conditions with which it will be faced in the future
need attention ahead of time. Corporate practices today run
more to spelling out goals regarding these than in the past. The
degree to which they are spelled out varies. Such planning includes time tables within which goals are to be reached as well
as the means to be used to meet them. Prospective manpower
requirements are a part of the latter. A wide range of features
may be involved or they may be comparatively simple. Traffic's
look ahead and time tables should be thought out and spelled
out carefully to the end that all operations needing attention

and contingencies that may reasonably be anticipated are recognized and dealt with appropriately. Company budgeting activities into which more traffic functions are being drawn are also to be handled along related lines. Care should be taken that time spent in planning, budgeting, and the like is reasonable and that flexibility is not curtailed because of them.

Changes right and left have been occurring in the personnel picture for traffic. Wider responsibilities, stepped-up activities, and increased complexities in recent years have made this field more critical in many ways. The need for particular knowledge and abilities that formerly existed is still there, but new techniques of automation and containerization, additional regulations, minority groups, wage-hour considerations and other developments have made added skills necessary. Data processing, engineering, and legal talents have been among those added to traffic staffs in increasing numbers. Coming on stronger also has been a general corporate feeling that management in all brackets (lower to upper) should become more attuned to the fact that more and more work must be done by others. Leadership has been expected to concentrate more on educating, motivating, overseeing, and determining that jobs are well done by those to whom work assignments are made. The development of a strong and effective traffic department in these ways has always been important and, if such is possible, it is more so today.

At least two fairly universal truths are applicable to traffic staff, as they are to many other lines of work. First, special capabilities are needed to become a good transportation man, and, second, time is needed to become one. These special capabilities can include a "flair" for detail, being a "digger," and knowing geography. Other faculties can include being tenacious, not easily discouraged, patient, and a "self starter". Many others could well be specified. As regards time needed to become a good traffic man, the range can be from two to ten years, the lesser for narrower responsibilities and the higher for the more important ones. This time span is to be hedged with how capable the individual is, how much exposure he receives, how successfully he handles his assignments, and so on. Employment activities and plans can well include the two features of getting the best employees and the length of time it takes to train them.

Traffic leadership seeking men "to deliver the goods" in their departments go to a number of places. At one time many industrial traffic organizations were staffed significantly with former carrier employees. Carrier ranks are still good nominees in this regard, but ideal traffic employees may also be sought now from other company departments, recruiting at universities (transportation majors and business, law, and engineering graduates are examples), trade associations, other industrial companies, and so on. Some, in particular, are sought from a company's field offices as field experience can be particularly valuable in a head office. Further, educational specifications, i.e., university attendance and degree requirements, are generally kept flexible, particularly if the individual involved obviously has a "will to learn" along with his work and a drive to progress by getting results for the department. Referrals from others, applicants coming in "cold", and others are also nominees, of course, for consideration in work to obtain good employees.

There is no "pat" way to tell whether a prospective employee will or will not be outstanding, or, for that matter, whether once hired he will handle superlatively increased responsibilities as they are assigned to him. Tests of a psychological nature are used by some to help in this regard. Others have tried them and discontinued them. One company in the latter category felt that its managers were using them too much as "crutches" and giving them undue weight in hiring, promoting, rewarding, and discharging. Traffic personnel work with many companies can well be features for the manager's personal participation to the fullest extent possible. This is particularly true when top staff, and staff to which he will look for top personnel performance, are involved.

Undoubtedly many have particular guides which they use in their employment practices. Sometimes these give correct indications of desirable employees and sometimes not. They are, however, often helpful. One experienced in hiring female staff makes it a point (all other things being equal) to hire applicants neatly dressed, well turned out, and obviously careful of their appearance. The reasoning is that those who take care of their appearance well also take good care of the work they do. Others interviewing applicants for jobs review carefully their school records, employment histories, and so on for clues as to whether attributes felt desirable have been demonstrated. Weight is given to the subjects they have taken and the grades they have made. Whether they are in the upper third or better of their class is often given special weight; some companies look for even higher scholastic record percentages. Whether an applicant is, or has been, active in "outside" matters (public speaking, school newspaper work, and the like) are also considered. Good writing ability is important and is a feature for checking. Some interviewers give applicants problems on which to write memos and review and evaluate the memos in this connection. The way prospective traffic employees express themselves verbally, the confidence they display (and inspire), their business acumen, and many other features are also considered and evaluated carefully.

Special and particular skills for good traffic men can be nurtured in many ways by on-the-job training. Steps in this regard often involve responsibility assignments, exposures, and rotations (when indicated) that are determined from a department's functions and needs. Care should be taken that plans made in this regard are followed and not permitted to go fallow because of press of day-to-day activities. In many cases (particularly where younger staff are involved) this training can well be supplemented by traffic and related school work. Top competence should be attained as quickly as possible and school help can be beneficial to such a time table. In such school work, all courses reasonably possible can well be undertaken, including those on I.C.C. law and the like. Also, admission to practice before the I.C.C. can well be sought and accomplished. While a "shingle" to practice may not be needed, the exams given and other aspects require research and attention that can pay off importantly in knowing what to do and in getting good jobs done. Employment arrangements with younger traffic staff in some companies include features regarding school attendance by them.

Other educational activities can well include attaining membership in the American Society of Traffic and Transportation, participation in the functions of the Delta Nu Alpha educational fraternity, and attendance at available university and college courses, seminars, and the like. Some find participation in educational activities other than transportation helpful, such as those of a general business nature and public speaking. The Society is quite outstanding in its contributions. It stresses professional recognition, competence, and conduct for transportation and for physical distribution and provides educational, testing, and related facilities to assist regarding them. Extensive studies in transportation and general business and the passing of comprehensive examinations are necessary to become a "certified member." The requirements necessary to obtain such a certificate make it a meaningful mark of competence and professionalism. An AST&T certificate is to transportation quite a bit what a Certified Public Accountant status is to accounting; it, too, carries with it important pay-offs in knowing what to do and getting good jobs done.

A not uncommon feature of traffic operations is the matter of dealing with "decentralization." With some companies decentralized bases for operating are normal and traffic functions are melded into them effectively, economically, and profitably. Transportation features are decentralized in areas where it is simply smart business that they be that way and are centralized in other areas where it, again, is the wise thing to do regarding them. These dual dealings occur with other functions also (such as legal and tax), and special handling also is required as to them, as it is in traffic. Such special handling in traffic may involve certain features with one mode and other features with others; as an example, more decentralization may be in order with trucks than with rails. Further, considerable variances in these special handlings will occur from company to company.

Decentralization takes place because of such factors as availability of raw materials, concentration of management responsibilities, shifting of market areas, and more economical transportation costs. These and other factors at times cause steps to be taken of a "going overboard" nature that later receive further attention. New lines drawn after such attention on occasion include reverting to more "centralization." Some industries seem to shift through the years from centralization to decentralization, then back to centralization, and so on. Traffic's handling of these involves in most cases keeping as flexible as possible and, as changes arise, being the best architects possible to so organize as to insure for its company the quite substantial benefits that it can provide and make available.

A strong central traffic department has many points in its favor. Able rate men are scarce and their talents can best be used for the company as a whole. The development and maintenance of good tariff files are difficult, costly, and time consuming; good tariff information is best used on a company wide basis. Experts in specialized traffic functions can perform professional jobs for all plants and divisions of a company better and more economically when working together from a central point. It is too expensive and the volume of work does not justify the hiring of comparable talents on individual plant bases. By having those talents in one place and channeling their activities properly, each decentralized unit will receive the full benefit of the best talent that is available.

Centralized traffic organizations do not take any needed prerogatives away from the decentralized units. Quite the contrary is the case. For example, a centralized tonnage distribution policy directing the distribution of over-all tonnage among the carriers results in maximum benefits throughout the company. One unit may give an individual carrier little tonnage. But all units together may favor that particular carrier substantially. Therefore, if a service, rate or classification problem develops with the carrier in connection with one decentralized unit, the full weight of the total company tonnage is available to assist in working out the local problem. Further, particularly with large companies "everybody's business can become nobody's business" and central traffic organizations help importantly in preventing funds from going down the drain in this regard.

Traffic help for decentralized units from a central office is made available in practice in various ways, some or all of which may be used. Reduced to bare essentials, these involve providing the field in uncomplicated form the rate figures and information they must have and in working with, and providing expertise to, the field so that activities there are within the framework of the law and result in maximum benefits of a worthwhile nature. Experience has shown that transportation law complications are such that operating within its framework can be considerably more easily and unintentionally overlooked in decentralized operations.

One program that has worked effectively involves head office traffic furnishing to plants and marketing in the field (and keeping up-to-date) what are called "Master Shipping Instruction" forms. These are prepared for destinations where repetitive business is involved. As the name implies, data therein include the consignee's name and location, the freight rates that may be involved from various shipping points, the routings, and so on. Overly simplified, the plants use these for bill of lading and other purposes to send shipments on their way, and the marketing offices use them as shipments are completed to check freight bills and otherwise. When a form is needed for, say, a new customer, it is provided by central traffic. Also, say, when there is an urgent and good reason to deviate from a routing specified, those in the field do so subject to checking back with head office traffic for alternates or other handling if indicated. In many cases alternates have already been provided on the forms and their use is automatic. The centralized traffic group also prepares and sends to appropriate units "Rate Sheets" which (again as the name implies) give freight rate information on products from numerous origins (including those employed by others) to destinations that may be of interest. These are used in freight studies and in other ways.

Other aspects of this program are that freight bills are checked locally in most cases, with those that cannot being sent to head office. Freight claims are handled locally to the maximum extent possible, with head office being called on for help when needed. Periodic reviews are made in which experienced traffic personnel from the central unit spend time (generally a week or so) going over local transportation work with those assigned to it so that all help possible is given to them. Those doing the work in the field may be in what are called "treasury" or "operating" groups as a general rule, although "transportation supervisors" are designated in some instances. Many do other work in addition to traffic. Important efforts are extended to field installations in other ways from central traffic through (to name a few) rate adjustment work of inbound and outbound shipments, maintenance of competitive positions freight-wise, help on improving carrier service and availability, and general checks of demurrage practices, motor carrier operations, and so on, for compliance with applicable transportation regulations. Periodic studies are also made to assure as much as possible that full benefits are being obtained for any changes in distribution patterns and the like. No particular point is made as to the individual to whom field staff reports as far as head office traffic is concerned; the concentration is on getting a good job done. While a functional reporting to traffic may be important in some cases, it has not been noticeably so in actual practice in the case mentioned. Allocations of outlays for head office traffic costs are made, but time spent on them is held to a minimum and details are avoided; generally the freight bill totals are so great and the amounts of the demonstratable results are so sizable that this is indicated as to this feature.

Help and cooperation in these cases is more than a one-way street; it works both ways. Staff in the field in the instance mentioned do a top job helping their head office traffic colleagues. Their interests and capabilities are such that, when indicated, they are promoted into the central organization. By being on the ground they observe and handle promptly many things that staff miles away cannot deal with nearly as effectively. At the plants, field staff may be particularly concerned with outbound shipments, the scheduling of motor trucks, and making sure sufficient trucks are available for loading. Marketing field staff's concerns may involve shipments inbound to customers, starting in motion arrangements for proper freight rates on them, and so on. Transportation work that may reasonably be done in the field is done there.

Another general step for use in getting best traffic results for companies with decentralized operations can be the location of experienced traffic men in places strategic to company activity. Further, the previous steps suggested can well be modified and improved upon to take advantage of existing and different conditions. The discussion of them is of a particularly broad nature and was meant to be essentially a framework of ideas. Abundantly clear, of course, is that an industrial traffic executive faced with a decentralized operation can proceed with only one philosophy which is to see that the general staff office performs so well that the decentralized units simply cannot get along without the guidance and help of the central office. This general approach should, of course, be coupled with well-organized guidance in all traffic functions and steps along the lines previously mentioned.

It is recognized that traffic management faced with decentralized organization embraces a sensitive area of personal contact with men who have the responsibility for the operations at their local plants or distribution points. Included in that responsibility is the matter of making money, and transportation can do a great deal of good in this regard. One approach that has worked well in similar instances has been to make periodic studies of both the inbound and outward freight movements and present the results, when savings are effected, to the local manager in person so that indicated economies are accomplished by authority of knowledge and actual results attained.

Traffic operations discussed previously in this section and others take their cues in many ways from functions reviewed elsewhere at various places throughout this text. Guides mentioned and indicated there should be observed. Staffing should be adequate. The leadership group should be careful not to let itself get bogged down in detail. Trade publication reading (to follow transportation developments) can well be "spread," particularly to younger staff. A "reading" file technique is normal in many cases. Under it extra copies of all correspondence are made and are passed over the desks of management, section heads, and others where indicated. Among various things, this helps keep them in touch with general developments.

Company passenger travel is traffic's responsibility with many companies. Some use travel agencies for this activity with varying results in actual practice. Where traffic has the direct responsibility appropriate staffing, again, should be adequate and care should be taken that leadership time is not so used that it could be more profitably spent elsewhere for the company. Most travel is now by air and the guides mentioned later include time tables for arranging space and fares for checking charges. Air credit cards have potentials for problems and should be dealt with carefully and concisely. For those travelling extensively short-form plane schedules from most important cities are available. These can be particularly helpful in providing leaving and arriving times and in getting places when irregularities in work schedules are normal and travel activities must be kept as flexible as possible.

Equipping the Industrial Traffic Department

The equipment used by traffic departments readily lends itself to classification into two main categories: one dealing with office lay-out and the other concerning reference material.

Office space for transportation is influenced strongly by a company's offices generally, and many of them work out, on reasonably uniform bases, various space and types of space allocations for their various departments and staff, including traffic. There are two somewhat generally recognized concepts of proper office space at this time, one running to the effect that such space should be made up of offices occupied at most by two people and the other that it should be of an "open" type with a minimum of offices, partitions, and the like. Where the matter can be influenced, the former is preferred for traffic. Distractions are avoided, opportunities for concentration on technicalities are better, and so on.

Other features for appropriate attention can be that employees using the phone most of the day should be isolated somewhat from those working with tariffs, since constant phone conversations are annoying and distracting to anyone trying to concentrate. Employees handling passenger reservations should be placed in a location convenient to visitors calling for tickets or information. Supervisors should be in private offices, since they must interview company associates in other departments, representatives of the various carriers, and employees reporting to them. Typists should be isolated as much as possible because typewriters, too, can be disturbing. Auditors should be near the tariff files. Office lay-out naturally depends on the space available and the floor plan.

There follows in the next illustration an office plan that is included particularly because it depicts how staff may well be located depending on their assignments. Where a "maximum-of-two-to-an-office" allocation exists it can well be a guide to office placements and the like.

Lighting should not be overlooked. Employees working with tariffs must have exceptionally good lighting if maximum efficiency and a minimum of eyestrain are to be maintained. The printing in tariffs is often small, resulting in some eyestrain even under the best conditions. Certain non-supervisory employees frequently have callers from outside organizations and should be provided with proper facilities for reception of visitors. A chair alongside their desks is certainly in order and, where indicated and it can be provided, a separate meeting room or rooms for callers should be available. This would apply particularly to passenger reservations, expediting and tracing, the rate quotations, claims representatives, etc.

The passenger group should be well provided with current

timetables and information on the amounts of charges for various fares. The special restrictions that may be applicable as to when certain fares may be used should also be available to

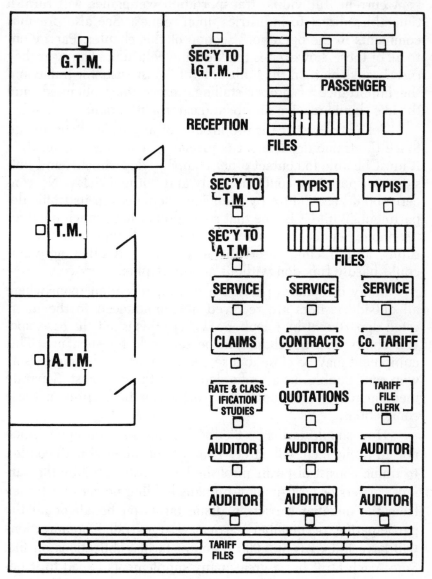

Functional Office Lay-out—Traffic

them. Facilities for checking bills, securing credits, and the like should also be provided where indicated. If possible these functions should be done as bills are received and should be kept current. Individual transportation companies will furnish timetables direct to industries upon request. See also previous comments in the operations section of this chapter. Paramount to all of these, however, is that keeping colleagues happy as they travel ranks high on the multitude of "must" lists for traffic and the importance of proper staffing, reservations obtained, and the like should receive sincere and careful attention.

Telephone service is the lifeline of any traffic department. Since the traffic department is primarily a service organization it must be able to contact other company departments and outside transportation concerns easily and without delay. No concern should economize by reducing telephones in its traffic department. While it is true that some do not have much need for telephone service, it is no less true that all supervisors, expediting and tracing, reservations, claims, and other activities could hardly function without adequate phone service.

Many companies provide a central reception room where all outside visitors are received and announced to the interested department by telephone. Where this is not the case, special chairs or a bench should be set aside for such use. This equipment may be close to a secretary to one of the supervisors who can "double" as a traffic department receptionist. Separate meeting rooms and rooms for callers can be helpful in these connections.

How should tariffs be filed? This is a question upon which not all traffic men will agree. The bulk of inbound mail coming to traffic consist of tariffs published and distributed by the various carriers or tariff-issuing bureaus holding power of attorney from the member carriers to issue tariffs on behalf of all the participating or member carriers. Large traffic organizations will have in excess of 5,000 different tariff publications on file. Since each tariff has a great many supplements issued to it before it is reissued, and since all supplements must be kept on file (even though they are not all effective at any one time) for the auditing of old freight bills or checking freight rates applying at some previous date, there would probably be an average of 10 supplements to each tariff. Even small traffic departments must keep 500 or more active tariffs on file.

There are various kinds of tariff files on the market. Some are of the metal type that come in several sections with small drop-front drawers for filing the tariffs. Each section can be as high as desired, depending on the number of banks of drawers used. Usually they are ordered for a workable height of about six feet. Several tariffs can be kept in each drawer, as it has a holder for identifying name cards. Some files have a shelf between the top two banks of drawers that can be pulled out and used to hold an open tariff while the rate man checks a rate without necessarily having to carry the tariff back to his desk.

It is possible to use regular standard filing cabinets for filing tariffs and special inserts (holders, frames and pockets) are available which makes them reasonably useable. They are not, however, considered as satisfactory as the special tariff filing drawers and cabinets. Some companies, doing a big freight bill audit job, have all their tariffs sitting on open shelves. This may be an inexpensive filing system, but that would be its only advantage. It does not look well and the tariffs get torn, dusty, and unusable.

Tariffs should be filed in accordance with a previously determined plan which is sometimes made available in printed or typed form for the guidance of the rate men and the tariff filing clerks. Individual lines' publications come first in alphabetical order, followed by the agency issues in either alphabetical or geographical sequence. And, of course each group of carriers, such as rail, motor, water and air, is definitely separated from the other groups. Last come special issues, such as the REA Express, Open and Prepay Station List, Uniform Freight Classification, contracts, company or plant tariffs issued by the traffic department for use of the shipping, sales and purchasing departments, etc. Naturally, export and import tariffs would be filed in a separate section, by geographical areas.

A list of the thousands of carrier tariffs currently effective would be very extensive. Each industrial concern must determine what tariff publications are required for the particular commodities, services and territories within or between which that concern is operating regularly. The carriers will supply any tariffs requested, either free or for a nominal expense, unless a request is made for an old issue, the supply of which has been exhausted. Building a tariff file is not an easy task and does take time. A competent traffic man, however, will be able to develop a satisfactory tariff file for the average company within a few months. Since all tariffs are supplemented and reissued from time to time, and new publications are needed as conditions change, any tariff file, large or small, requires constant attention in order to keep it currently useful. Supplements and reissues will arrive daily and should be sorted according to application and filed the same day they are received. This responsibility usually is given to a young clerk who thus has an opportunity to learn something about tariffs.

There are quite a few publications that do not fall into the tariff classification but should be obtained by the traffic man because they qualify as being basic tools or as a source of needed current general information. In the listings that follow, because of certain differences of opinion and in deference to the various publishers, no attempt has been made to judge the relative merits of the publications or to provide any detailed explanation of the subject matter covered. Traffic men will, in most cases, know the coverage. This list is offered primarily as a ready reference to the publications available and as a possible reminder to those who may have overlooked certain publications that, being so reminded, they can take steps to obtain. It is improbable that any traffic department would need all of the publications listed. Just which ones are needed depends, of course, on the scope of each organization's responsibilities. It would seem, however, that most traffic departments would require a substantial percentage of the following publications:

BASIC DATA ESSENTIAL TO TRAFFIC FUNCTIONS

Publication	Address	Subscription Price
Association of American Railroads' Closed Car Loading Rules	Secretary, Freight Loss and Damage Prevention Section, Assoc. of Amer. RRs., 59 E. Van Buren St., Chicago, Ill. 60605	There are some 21 pamphlets, each dealing with a single commodity. Pamphlets cost between 5¢ and 25¢ each
Association of American Railroads' Open Top Equipment Loading Rules	Secretary, Mechanical Division, Assoc. of Amer. RRs., 59 E. Van Buren St., Chicago, Ill. 60605	Seven sections cover loading of various commodities and cost from $1.00 to $3.25 each
Bullinger's Postal and Shippers Guide (issued annually)	Bullinger's Guides, Inc. 63 Woodland Ave., Westwood, N.J. 07675	$30.00 per annual rental copy
National Classification Board Docket (Proposals for changes in rules, descriptions, ratings and minimum weights) issued five times per year	National Classification Board, 1616 P Street, N.W., Washington, D.C. 20036	Published periodically in the Traffic Bulletin
National Motor Freight Classification No. A-12 or reissues (reissued occasionally, and supplemented regularly)	American Trucking Associations, Inc. 1616 P Street, N.W. Washington, D.C. 20036	$9.00 for each issue and supplements
Official Guide of the Railways (issued monthly)	424 West 33rd St., New York, N.Y. 10001	$48.00 per annum
Official Intermodal Equipment Register	424 West 33rd St., New York, N.Y. 10001	(issued quarterly) $15.00 per annum
Official List of Open and Pre-Pay Stations (reissued annually on November 1st)	A. P. Leland, Tariff Publishing Officer, Station List Publishing Co., 827 Syndicate Trust Bldg., 915 Olive St. St. Louis, Mo. 63101	$26.00 per annum (includes November 1 reissue and supplements on first and fifteenth of each month)
Official Railway Equipment Register	424 West 33rd St., New York, N.Y. 10001	(issued quarterly) $30.00 per annum
Pocket List of Railroad Officials, The (issued quarterly)	424 West 33rd St., New York, N.Y. 10001	$12.00 per annum
Postal Services Manual Chapters 1-6	United States Government Printing Office. Washington, D.C. 20402	$14.50 per copy

Publication	Address	Subscription Price
Uniform Classification Docket (proposals for changes in rules, descriptions, ratings and minimum weights)	Uniform Classification Committee 202 Chicago Union Station, Chicago, Ill. 60606	Published weekly in the Traffic Bulletin
Uniform Freight Classification (reissued occasionally and supplemented regularly)	Uniform Classification Committee 202 Chicago Union Station Chicago, Ill. 60606	$9.00 for each issue and supplements

BASIC DATA REQUIRED FOR MANY TRAFFIC FUNCTIONS

Aviation Law Reports (loose leaf—kept currently up to date)	Commerce Clearing House, 4025 W. Peterson Ave., Chicago, Ill. 60646	$315.00 per annum
Automobile Facts and Figures and Motors Truck Facts (issued annually— mid-April)	Automobile Manufacturers Association, 320 New Center Bldg., Detroit, Mich. 48202	Single copies free-on-request
Branham Automobiles Reference Book	Branham Publishing Company, 1422 Beckwith St., Los Angeles, Calif. 90049	$3.75 per annum
Daily Traffic World	The Traffic Service Corp. 815 Washington Building, Washington, D.C. 20005	$340 per annum
Decisions and Reports of the Interstate Commerce Commission	Superintendent of Documents, Government Printing Office, Washington, D.C. 20402	Vary from $4.00 to $6.00 per copy
Digest of Automobile Laws Throughout the United States	Branham Publishing Company, 1422 Beckwith St., Los Angeles, Calif. 90049	$4.50 per copy
Directory of Common Motor Carrier Agency Tariffs and Directory of Forwarding Company Tariffs (loose leaf—kept currently up-to-date)	Transportation Consulting & Service Corp. 4704 W. Irving Park Rd. Chicago, Ill. 60641	$12.00 and $7.50 respectively
Federal Carriers Reports (loose leaf—kept currently up to date)	Commerce Clearing House, 4025 W. Peterson Ave., Chicago, Ill. 60646	$185.00 per annum
The Light Weight Register (loose leaf—kept currently up to date)	Transportation & Consulting Service Corp., 4704 West Irving Park Road, Chicago, Ill. 60641	$12.00 per annum

Publication	Address	Subscription Price
National Industrial Traffic League Circulars and the weekly newsletter, The Legislator (issued regularly)	Office of the Executive Vice President, National Industrial Traffic League, 712 Pennsylvania Bldg., 425-13th St. N.W. Washington, D.C. 20004	Included in dues
Official Airline Guide No. American Quick Reference; International Quick Reference; Pocket Flight Guide; Travel Planner & Hotel/Motel Guide; and Air Cargo Guide	Reuben H. Donnelley Corp., 2000 Clearwater Bldg., Oak Brook, Ill. 60521	$12.00 to $55.00 per annum, dependent on edition
Official Directory of Industrial & Commercial Traffic Executives, The (issued annually)	The Traffic Service Corp., 815 Washington Building, Washington, D.C. 20005	$25.00 per copy
Railway Line Clearances	424 West 33rd St., New York, N.Y. 10001	(issued annually) $6.50 per copy
Rail Carrier, Motor/Forwarder, Civil Aeronautics Board and Federal Maritime Commission Services and Aviation Court Cases (loose leaf—kept currently up to date)	Hawkins Publishing Co., 933 N. Kenmore St., Arlington, Va. 22201 (703) 525-9090	Prices vary with services and range from $85.00 to $125.00 per year
Rand, McNally Commercial Atlas and Marketing Guide (issued annually)	Rand, McNally & Company, Commercial Atlas Service, P.O. Box 7600, Chicago, Ill. 60641	$75.00 per annum
Russell's Official National Motor Coach Guide (issued monthly)	Russell's Guides, Inc., 817 Second Ave., S.E., Cedar Rapids, Iowa 52403	$22.70 per annum
Shippers Advisory Board, Reports of Quarterly Meetings	Individual Shippers Advisory Boards	Free to members
Shippers Telephone and Correspondence Directory of Chicago (loose leaf—kept currently up to date. Also issued for Minneapolis-St. Paul)	Shippers Directory Company, 10731 South Talman Ave., Chicago, Ill. 60655	$24.00 per annum (lease basis)
State Motor Carrier Guide (loose leaf—kept currently up to date)	Commerce Clearing House, 4025 W. Peterson Avenue, Chicago, Ill. 60646	$210.00 per annum (see Federal Carriers Reports)
Traffic Bulletin (issued weekly)	The Traffic Service Corp., 815 Washington Building, Washington, D.C. 20005	$225.00 per annum

Publication	Address	Subscription Price
What's Happening In Transportation and other bulletins	Transporation Association of America 1101 17th St. N.W., Washington, D.C. 20036	Free to members

RATE OR ROUTING GUIDES

A.T.A. American Motor Carrier Directory (official A.T.A. publication)	Guide Services, Inc., P.O. Box No. 13446, Atlanta, Ga. 30324	$48.00 per annum (2 semi-annual issues) (incl two issues)
Chicago Motor Freight (Incl motor, air, water & frt forwarder routings)	1130 South Canal Chicago, Illinois	$12.00 per annum
Leonard's Guides for Parcel Post, Express, Motor Carrier Rates, and Routing	G. R. Leonard & Co. 2121 Shermer Rd. Northbrook, Ill. 60062	Prices range from $15.00 to $50.00 for regular publications and are higher in special cases
National Highway & Airway Carriers and Routes (issued semi-annually)	National Highway Carriers Directory, Inc., 925 West Jackson Blvd., Chicago, Ill. 60607	$38.00 per year (2 semi-annual issues)
New York Motor Express Guide (issued semi-annually)	1130 South Canal Chicago, Illinois	$12.00 per annum
St. Louis Motor Freight Directory (Incl motor, air, water, frt forwarder)	1130 South Canal Chicago, Illinois	$12.00 per annum (incl two issues)
The Shippers Guide	The Shippers Guide Company, 1130 South Canal Chicago, Illinois	$26.00 per annum

PERIODICALS

Cargo Airlift (issued monthly)	P.O. Box 6710, Chicago, Ill. 60680	Free of charge
Container News (issued monthly)	150 E. 52nd St., New York, N.Y. 10002	Free of charge
Distribution Worldwide (issued monthly)	56th and Chestnut Sts., Philadelphia, Pa. 19139	Free of charge
Distribution|Warehouse Cost Digest	221 National Press Building, Washington, D.C. 20004	$35.00 per annum

Publication	Address	Subscription Price
Federal Register (issued Tuesday thru Saturday)	Superintendent of Documents, Government Printing Office, Washington, D.C. 20402	$25.00 per year
Handling & Shipping (issued monthly)	812 Huron Road, Cleveland, Ohio 44115	Free of charge
I.C.C. Practioners' Journal (issued monthly)	Association of I.C.C. Practitioners, 1112 I.C.C. Building, Washington, D.C. 20025	Free to members; $25.00 per annum to non-members
Railway Age (issued weekly)	30 Church Street, New York, N.Y. 10007	$15.00 per annum
Traffic Management (issued monthly)	201 North Wells St., Chicago, Ill. 60606	Free of charge
Traffic World (issued weekly)	815 Washington Building Washington, D.C. 20005	$68.00 per annum
Transport Topics (issued weekly)	American Trucking Associations, Inc., 1616 P Street, N.W., Washington, D.C. 20036	$15.00 per annum
Transportation & Distribution Management (issued monthly)	815 Washington Building, Washington, D.C. 20005	Free of charge

PACKING & SHIPPING

The Industrial Packaging Digest (issued monthly)	Bonnell Publications, Inc., 437 East 5th Street, Plainfield, N.J. 07060	$7.50 per annum
Material Handling Engineering (issued monthly)	812 Huron Road, Cleveland, Ohio 44115	Free of charge
Modern Materials Handling (issued monthly) ·	221 Columbus Ave., Boston, Mass. 02116	$8.00 per annum
National Defense Transportation Journal (issued bi-monthly)	National Defense Transportation Journal, 1612 K Street, N.W., Washington, D.C.	Free to members
Private Carrier, The (issued semi-monthly)	The Private Carrier Conference, American Trucking Associations, Inc., 1616 P Street, N.W., Washington, D.C. 20036	Free to Conference members
Transportation Journal (issued quarterly)	American Society of Traffic and Transportation, Inc. 22 West Madison St., Chicago, Ill. 60602	Free to members

Publication	Address	Subscription Price
EXPORT AND IMPORT INFORMATION		
American Import & Export Bulletin (includes list of licensed foreign freight forwarders and customs house brokers) (issued monthly)	107 So. Tyson Ave., Floral Park, N.Y. 11001	$7.00 per annum (domestic) $8.00 (foreign)
Brandon's Shipper & Forwarder (issued weekly)	Brandon Publications, Suite 1927, One World Trade Center, New York, N.Y. 10048 (212) 423-0750	$7.50 per year (domestic) $13.50 (abroad)
Custom House Guide (issued annually)	Custom House Guide, 107 South Tyson Ave. Floral Park, N.Y. 11001	$43.00 per copy (plus postage and binder)
Export Shipping Manual (loose leaf, weekly supplements)	1231 25th St., N.W., Washington, D.C. 20037	$78.00 per annum
Maritime Reporter & Engineering News (issued bi-monthly)	107 East 31st Street, New York, N.Y. 10016 cost from $1 to $3.25 each	controlled circulation to qualified recipients
Export Document and Shipment Preparation by Durward L. Brooks	The Traffic Service Corporation Washington Building Washington, D.C. 20005	
Exporter's Encyclopedia	Dun & Bradstreet Publications Corp. 466 Lexington Ave. New York, N.Y. 10017	issued annually
MISCELLANEOUS TEXTS AND PUBLICATIONS		
Transportation Law by John Guandolo	William C. Brown Company Dubuque, Iowa	839 pgs. 1969
Law of Freight Loss and Damage Claims (Miller's) by Richard R. Sigmon	William C. Brown Company Dubuque, Iowa	427 pgs. 3rd Ed., 1970
Practice and Procedure Before Rate-making Associations by G. E. Lowe	The Traffic Service Corporation Washington Building Washington, D.C. 20005	62 pgs., 3rd Ed., 1967,
Traffic World's Question & Answers Book	The Traffic Service Corporation Washington Building Washington, D.C. 20005	issued periodically
Model Legal Forms for Shippers by Stanley Hoffman	The Traffic Service Corporation Washington Building Washington, D.C. 20005	508 pgs., 1970

Unquestionably, there are many worthwhile publications that have not been listed, but any oversight is unintentional. Every effort was made to include all of the publications that might be helpful in daily traffic functions. In many instances, subscription prices are lower for a subscription of two years or more than for a single year. Foreign subscriptions are usually available, but at an increased subscription price, upon request to the publishers. The authors have made a detailed check in an effort to obtain correct data, but changes occur frequently so everything shown is subject to change.

To be mentioned also is that some "doubling-up" occurs in that some publications are named in both the text and the foregoing list. Brevity considerations, more than others, are the reasons various publications are not shown twice. Further, most publications are advertised extensively and information on them in most cases is readily available from advertising sources. There are all kinds of traffic publications and the simple fact that they are published does not mean that they are to be acceped without further thought and attention. A recent Harvard Business Review traffic article is illustrative. Any number of questions could be properly raised concerning the validity of various statements in it.

Traffic Department Relations With Other Departments

In many ways a traffic department is a service organization rendering some kind of transportation service to every other department in the company. The traffic department has a primary interest in maintaining the best relations with all other departments. This basic fact sometimes should be accentuated more by traffic executives who become occupied otherwise in their desire to maintain good public relations with the carriers. While it is true that a traffic manager must discharge his responsibility of seeing to it that public relations with all carriers are of the best, it is one of his high priority responsibilities that relations with other departments within his company should be promoted with painstaking care.

The best way to accomplish this is to perform all functions with utmost efficiency. Many times the personnel in the other departments do not clearly understand what the traffic department does or just how it can help them. If this is the case, some salesmanship is indicated. This can be done by several methods. One is by personal contact which, when handled diplomatically, pays rich dividends. Another is by issuing memos from time to time on progress being made in rate adjustment matters and the like in which the addressee is particularly interested and which can mean a great deal to him. The basic proposition that people like to have attention paid to them finds good application in these instances.

As regards periodic, comprehensive reports to management and the like this has at times in the past been quite the thing to do with some companies. It is not so much so now in many cases for several reasons one of them being the time and attention needed to compile them. With top management leaning more to accentuating with transportation managers that they should "manage" their own departments reports of this type have come to be more matters of what traffic has to have to keep performance at top levels and to detect any slippage in any of the things it does, so that corrective steps can be taken immediately. A secondary reason for the reports is, of course, that selected data may be taken from the reports and passed to others in interest. This reason is clearly secondary, however, and for obvious reasons the reports should be streamlined, informal, bare bones affairs that can be compiled preferably from data already handy and with a minimum of effort. When any feature ceases to be needed or where spot checks can take care of the need for that feature, an appropriate deletion should be made.

A report form follows that includes a number of items common to traffic operations. With it is an explanation of the treatment given those items. Data there can well be used as guides where top management wants such information in periodic bulletin form. The information can also be used in determining possible "internal" management needs in the way of statistics and the like for traffic.

This bulletin is designed to enable an industrial traffic department to report practically all of its activities to management. Those activities that are reported by "number of units" require no explanations, since they are easily understood. Those activities that are reported in dollars saved or recovered may not be so easily understood. In "Special other-than-standard routing arrangements" is reflected the savings that result from the alert use of lower-rated or special services (private carriage is an example) that are not used for the greater volume of traffic. These savings can be accumulated by freight bill auditors without too much added effort. Estimating may be used at times, under proper supervisory control. Next, most concerns have regular scheduled pooling arrangements, and it is proper to show the money saved for each shipment. Non-scheduled pooling for a stop-off is another activity that should be included, and a separate heading is shown to cover it. "Arranging for expedited service in lieu of specified costlier service" means that a shipment has been requested to go forward by, say, REA Express, but an alert traffic man will suggest an alternate type of service, motor carrier for instance, providing the desired delivery date. If the suggestion is accepted, there is a saving to the company, and it should be reported. "Transportation overcharges recovered" needs no explanation, except to explain that "Charges billed to distributors or vendors" covers those cases where a distributor or vendor does not use good shipping practices, such as failing to follow lower-rated routing instructions, so a "bill-back" is initiated to cover the amount lost. "Miscellaneous" covers a variety of activities that may be important. This is why all money shown in this column should be explained in a separate sheet headed "Remarks." If a rate is reduced, or a classification rating is adjusted downward, it is proper to show a saving for such activity. It is not feasible to do this on a continuing basis, but it does seem reasonable to estimate the annual savings resulting therefrom, and to show this

Traffic Division: Hqtrs.; Location: Baltimore; For Month of: October **MONTHLY DOMESTIC TRAFFIC BULLETIN**	Month Issued: October NUMBER OF UNITS
EXPEDITERS	891
TRACERS	320

PASSENGER TRANSPORTATION
   Reservations secured
   Reservations cancelled
   Refunds procured
   Air travel cards issued
   Air travel charges audited
	
	103
	10
	8
	3
	86

HOUSEHOLD GOOD SHIPMENTS HANDLED	15
RATE QUOTATIONS	563
TRANSPORTATION CO. TARIFFS AND SUPS. — Received	121

TRANSPORTATION BILLS AUDITED
   Express
   Freight
   Local Trucking
	
	503
	2010
	600

ADJUSTMENT OF TRANSPORTATION CHARGES
   Bills reduced before payment
   Charges billed to suppliers
   Overcharge claims originated
	
	180
	18
	82

LOSS AND DAMAGE CLAIMS	53
ROUTES ISSUED	601
TRANSPORTATION COST REDUCTION	Amount

Special other-than-standard routing arrangements
     Panama Canal (incl. rail & water)
     Other water lines (incl. rail & water)
	
	$ 1,003.00
	4,020.60

Use of company private carriage operations (owned or leased)	$ 2,800.00
Arranging for inclusion of shipments in Scheduled Pool Cars or Trucks (including T.O.F.C. movements, Piggyback Plans II, III, IV or V and use of Shippers' Assocations)	$ 4,010.00
Arranging for Consolidation or Stopping in Transit to partially unload or to complete loading	$ 3,100.00
Arranging for Expedited Service in lieu of specified costlier service (reducing use of Premium Transportation)	$10,600.00

TRANSPORTATION OVERCHARGES RECOVERED
   Freight Charges Reduced before Payment
   Overcharge Claims Collected
   Charges Billed Back to Distributors or Vendors
	
	$12,500.00
	6,025.00
	916.00

LOSS AND DAMAGE CLAIMS — COLLECTED Provide separate sheet with details of any claims outstanding six months or more	$ 1,682.00
MISCELLANEOUS. Detail to be included on separate sheet under "Remarks"	$20,016.00
GRAND TOTAL	**$66,672.60**

TOTAL OPEN UNPAID CLAIMS		DEMURRAGE CHARGES PAID		
Number	Amount	Inbound Cars	Outbound Cars	Total Demurrage
15	$4,000.10	$604.00	$38.00	$642.00

Specimen Industrial Traffic Bulletin—Report Form

annual figure under "Miscellaneous." Thus, the saving is taken only once but for a one-year period. Many other activities such as a contract negotiation for local hauling (where reduced costs result), a plan to reduce demurrage costs, etc., may be shown under "Miscellaneous," either as a lump sum saved by a specific action, or as a sum representing an estimated annual saving. The item for demurrage paid is to acquaint supervision with the amounts so expended. This is particularly helpful on reports received from outlying plant locations.

The traffic department deals with all company organizations on many common functions such as passenger accommodations, movement of employees' household goods, and any and all transportation or allied problems resulting from exporting or importing activities. Additional or more selective traffic activities with other departments are summarized briefly as follows:

■Engineering—Transportation studies on new plant, branch house and warehouse locations.
Advising on siding and other agreements with carriers.
Collaborating with packaging engineer.
Advising on purchase of materials handling and transportation equipment.

■Sales and Distribution—Furnishing rate information and making studies in connection with improved distribution systems.
Quoting freight rates and publishing same where needed.
Providing expediting and tracing service.
Developing pool car possibilities.
Routing via cheapest method.
Assisting customers on claims and other problems.
Arranging warehousing.
Obtaining rate and classification adjustments.
Collaborating on inventory control.
Setting up a private carriage operation.
Supervising weight agreements.

■ Manufacturing—Suggesting improved methods of moving materials intra-plant (between buildings).

Suggesting improved methods of shipping materials inter-city (between plant locations).

Advising as to private carriage operations' ability to haul raw materials.

Advising on package specifications, including unit or pallet loading and/or storage possibilities.

Advising on materials-handling equipment.

Obtaining adequate car and truck supply.

Hiring outside trucks and chauffeurs when required during peak periods.

Expediting and tracing raw materials to keep production lines operating continuously.

■ Shipping—Reissuing information in carriers' tariffs in a simple plant guide to shipping clerks.

Providing classification descriptions for use in preparing bills of lading.

Establishing best bill-of-lading form.

Advising on use of pallets, unit loads or containers.

Obtaining adequate car and truck supply.

Supervising consolidation and pooling of shipments for direct routing or stop-off in transit movement.

Set up procedures for economical use of piggy-back services.

■ Receiving—Handling loss and damage claims.

Routing inbound shipments so as to prevent congestion at receiving platforms.

Expediting and tracing urgently needed materials.

Supervising average demurrage agreement operations.

Inspecting inbound shipments subject to damage due to faulty packing or loading.

Auditing freight bills.

■ Insurance—discussing and advising on all insurance pertaining to any form of transportation.

■ Purchasing—Routing inbound shipments by furnishing routes to be placed on each purchase order.

Advising on quantities to buy and how they should be packaged to protect lowest freight charge.

Quoting competitive freight rates.

Reviewing purchase terms affecting transportation.

Assisting in preparation of contracts.

Arranging transit privileges.

Expediting and tracing urgently needed materials.

Arrange billbacks to suppliers when failure to use good shipping procedure is detected.

■ Accounting—Auditing freight bills.

Auditing transportation charges on invoices.

Collecting transportation overcharge claims.

Cooperation on data processing programs.

Advising on general transportation problems.

Setting up credit arrangements with carriers.

Arranging re-audit (secondary) of freight bills by an outside audit bureau.

■ Legal—Preparing contracts for transportation of materials or rental of transportation equipment.

Advising on transportation legislation as to effect on company operations.

Cooperating in legal cases regarding claims or other transportation matters.

Preparing transportation data for rate cases.

Seeing, in conjunction with legal, that transportation laws and regulations are observed in all fields of company activities.

In connection with the listing under Manufacturing, it is of ever-increasing importance that traffic, the packaging engineer and the materials handling engineer form a sort of triumvirate that works closely on all shipping matters. This group, in turn, should cooperate with sales and other departments in a joint effort to reduce transportation, warehousing and distribution costs through coordination in package, container and materials handling equipment design, etc.

As regards distribution, warehousing deserves careful consideration under any traffic organization discussion because it is part and parcel of the physical movement of goods from factory to customer. Sometimes it involves transportation privileges such as "storage-in-transit" or "processing-in-transit"; but usually it is a pause in the through movement and must be arranged for as economically as possible—and, that surely does bring the traffic executive in close contact with over-all distribution planning. Thus it is that many companies do place the warehousing function, both private and public, directly under the general traffic manager.

The relations of traffic with legal are unique in many companies. Traffic's particular expertise carries with it a knowledge of what may be involved when proper freight billings and payments are necessary, when and how operating rights are to be observed, when and how strict demurrage provisions are to be complied with, and so on. These, and other, quite technical aspects of operating within the framework of applicable transportation laws have placed transportation in a position with legal where each does a great deal of good for the other. The possibility of fines, special damage recoveries, adverse publicity, and other unsatisfactory consequences of what may be an unintentional non-compliance with some transportation law requirement are matters of important concern in a company's operations. Both legal and traffic (legal primarily and traffic secondarily) are looked upon to see that operations are so conducted that difficulties along these lines are not encountered. Where it is indicated that relations of this type in a particular company can be brought closer together, traffic can well move to see that this is done.

Traffic Department Public Relations

In his various activities the traffic manager must depend not only on top relations with other company departments but also on good relations with the carriers and the industrial traffic managers in other companies, particularly those in a similar type of business. So often one hears an experienced traffic man say that the more he learns about traffic the more he realizes how comparatively little he knows. Perhaps it is true that on some things it is not so much knowing it all yourself as it is knowing where to go to get help.

Public relations as covered in this book refer to the industrial traffic man's activities outside of his immediate company. Such relations may well start with the carriers with whom most of the company's business is done. By a judicious tonnage distribution policy and friendly relations a company maintains worthwhile relations between it and all carriers. The purpose of this is to enable its staff to request and get the finest cooperation from the carriers at all times.

Association with other industrial traffic men would seem to be of at least equal importance for most traffic managers. The Rubber Manufacturers Association, the Manufacturing Chemists Association, and the American Petroleum Institute traffic committees are but three examples of many instances where companies of an industry help each other. Industry traffic committees are effective in working with the carriers to solve general service and other problems for their particular fields of operations. Through combined efforts they do for all companies similarly situated what one company (because of wide ramifications) would find extremely difficult, if not impossible, to do on its own.

There are also industrial traffic groups that embrace all types of industries and work with the carriers on over-all transportation problems, both on a local and national level. Chambers of Commerce and local and regional manufacturers associations often maintain traffic men who are also practitioners and offer counsel and functional help to members. Some groups also include carriers. Information in more detail on some of these follows.

The National Industrial Traffic League is the only national organization whose membership is composed exclusively of industrial traffic executives. The League was organized in 1907 and has about 1,800 members representing every line of industry throughout the country. It meets annually and more often when necessary. Most of its work is done in committees that are appointed to cover all phases of transportation of interest to industries on a national basis. The committee chairmen report to the membership at the annual meetings.

The League supports a full-time executive vice president and staff as well as a general counsel. It appears before the Interstate Commerce Commission and other bodies through its general counsel and committee chairmen. Worthwhile circulars and publications are sent to all members informing them on current transportation happenings. Dues depend upon the size of a company, with maximum at a very reasonable figure. It is most helpful and does a great deal of good for transportation.

The National Freight Traffic Association is a fine transportation organization composed of both industrial traffic and carrier executives. Its object is to bring together traffic men who are closely involved in business dealings with the freight traffic departments of transportation companies for the consideration and discussion of their common problems and to encourage a better acquaintance among them which will be helpful in the performance of their duties in representing their companies in the traffic field. It generally meets twice a year at various locations throughout the country. It has a limited membership, so there is always a waiting list of applicants.

The Transportation Association of America is an excellent organization made up of providers and users of, and investors in, transportation. Much of its work is aimed at composing differences between the various segments of transportation to the end that fair and reasonable dealings are accorded them, the basics of private enterprise are preserved, and differences are settled by those directly involved. Work is often done through panels, i.e., rail, air, user, etc. The user panel is made up of top industrial traffic men from all parts of the country, meets regularly, and has a good record of accomplishment. TAA's particular talents are also employed importantly in special situations. Hazardous materials regulations and particular help to certain features of data processing are among the fields in which this has been done.

The Transportation Data Coordinating Committee (1101 17th St. N.W., Washington, D.C. 20036) has as its important responsibility the coordination of transportation data processing activities between industrial companies, carriers, financial institutions, the federal government, and others. It provides means whereby common codes and common computer procedures are established and made available to the end that maximum data processing benefits result for transportation. Work is done by full-time staff and task forces. Knowledgeable industrial traffic men with special data-processing training are members of those task forces and contribute importantly there. Periodic meetings and seminars are held which are open to those in interest. Important support by shippers who are presently involved with computers or who expect to become involved with them is for many reasons appropriate for the committee.

The National Committee on International Trade Documentation (Suite 1406, 30 E. 42nd St., New York, N.Y. 10017) has as its special field the simplification of documents used in foreign trade. Industry, carriers, banks, insurance companies, the federal government, and others are involved in the activity; cooperating groups with similar aims have been established in foreign countries. Progress has been steady with what amounts to about everything specifically accomplished being worthwhile and representing economies over dues costs and the like. A recent publication, "Paper Work or Profits?", ($10.00) on international documentation catalogues and analyzes practices and procedures in this regard and recommends corrective steps regarding them. Support for this activity by industrial companies in world trade is strongly indicated.

The Association of Interstate Commerce Practitioners is a group of attorneys and practitioners who hold certificates permitting them to practice before the Interstate Commerce Commission. Its mission is to maintain high standards of technical procedure and ethics among those who practice or are interested in its field of administrative law. It publishes an informative monthly journal (see listing this chapter) and traffic men admitted to practice should consider membership as a part of their activities. As regards the I.C.C. itself, full time employees may represent their companies before the Commission without being admitted to practice and a certificate of admission is not normally required because of this. Certificates are excellent to have, however. There are two classes of I.C.C. practitioners— lawyer and non-lawyer. Admissions of lawyers to practice are not as complicated as is the case with non-lawyers. The latter must meet certain educational requirements, undertake certain studies, and pass certain tests. Details are available from the Commission. See also earlier comments in this chapter concerning the value to a traffic department of staff with I.C.C. admissions behind them.

Shippers advisory boards, which are sectional and are sponsored and supported by the Association of American Railroads, may also be considered for memberhip by industrial traffic men. They have both industrial and railroad members and are set up by sections such as the Atlantic States Shippers Advisory Board, the Ohio Valley Shippers Advisory Board, etc. They deal primarily with car supply, car conservation, service, etc. and represent a cooperative way for railroads and shippers to solve mutual problems.

Delta Nu Alpha is a fraternity of men who are interested in advancing their usefulness in their chosen field of work by obtaining the benefits of education and technical training and by helping others to obtain these benefits. It is a professional fraternity of those of similar interests and aspirations in the transportation field.

Traffic Clubs offer an excellent medium for contact with other traffic workers. Almost every city of any size has a local traffic club with a membership representing all forms of transportation as well as industrial traffic personnel. There are traffic clubs for women as well as for men. Most traffic clubs are members of the Associated Traffic Clubs of America which functions along lines similar to the local clubs, but on a broader scale. Along with operating as social organizations, local traffic clubs contribute substantially to the welfare of the traffic profession by sponsoring forums, traffic courses in schools, speakers on transportation subjects and the like. They also help and advise members in employment activities, sponsor public speaking courses for members, and so on. A traffic man may well join his local traffic club and support it for a number of reasons. In some ways such action is a bet on himself that he is right in selecting the traffic profession for his life's work.

The American Society of Traffic and Transportation Inc. is discussed earlier in this chapter in connection with staff development. Benefits that may be realized from the Society are, of course, much broader than as indicated in that discussion. Membership, working in, and supporting the organization can well be an important phase of a practical traffic man's personal and public relations responsibilities of uplifting the general professional status of transportation and physical distribution. The Society's aims are high and its work contributes importantly toward making more marked the services of the key transportation group to American industry. Consideration of what a traffic department's leadership can do to participate and help in AST&T affairs merits careful thought, attention, and follow through by that leadership.

The National Council of Physical Distribution Management, also referred to earlier (page 251), has developed considerable popularity in recent years. Generally speaking its undertakings are in areas closely related to traditional transportation functions. Inventory control and warehousing are examples. Participation in its activities can well be of value.

Various other fine transportation groups also have possibilities for consideration for membership and information on them may be found in trade periodicals and elsewhere.

15

DATA PROCESSING IN TRANSPORTATION

THERE HAS BEEN A SUBSTANTIAL STEP-UP IN THE USE OF DATA
processing techniques in transportation in recent years. Some
companies have accentuated it more than others, as have certain
industries. While a considerable amount of the accentuation and
utilization has gone on in the traffic departments of the larger
companies, small to medium sized companies are in the field in
increasing numbers and in increasing ways.

Substantial variances exist in how the techniques are used
and the stresses given them as to functions. These features have
wide ranges. Some companies use them in making sure shipments and the equipment in which those shipments are made
are moving properly and on schedule; others use them in getting maximum efficiency from the equipment available to them;
still others use those techniques in handling rail car, truck, and
other transport equipment supplies, e.g., cars on hand and cars
that can be expected to be on hand for loading each day for,
say, the next week. Data processing is also used in freight bill
payments, in arranging the most economical distribution of
products that are sold and shipped from the origins that have
those products, and in periodic reviews of shipping and distribution patterns and the movements actually made to the end
that nothing is overlooked in the way of possible rate adjustments or other matters needing attention. More particulars on
these appear later in this chapter.

These functional uses by no means tell the full story. There are various other computer applications such as systems used in establishing and operating warehouses and in selecting sites for them. Another is the scheduling of truck fleets so that the best use possible is made of the equipment. The big advantage of effective data processing is that, through it, Traffic is placed in a position, in fact, to administer what it should be administering and to manage what it should be managing. Where no data processing information is available, the alternates are not good. They are myriads of pieces of paper, mostly bills of lading and freight bills. These have to be dealt with individually or through statements that have been tediously hand posted or otherwise prepared with difficulty and that altogether too often contain information that is too little and, actually, too late.

The additions, subtractions, and other calculations that can be made by the computer systems, their "memories" and abilities to "recall" items, the ways they can highlight and "throw out" any "exceptions" when irregularities occur or when mistakes are made, and their flexibility of tying in plants and offices miles apart and in doing work at practically the same time for two or more departments of a company are among the many other valuable features of data processing. The utilization of all features is, of course, to be dealt with on pretty much a company-by-company basis, and the same is true of all or part of the functions previously discussed. Car locations, as an example, will be worthwhile for some and not for others. Important to the subject is that industrial traffic departments know in general the "state of the art" and do for their principals what is best for them.

Companies using, or about to use, data processing in transportation generally do so through their own data processing departments or through service firms having various clients for whom various data activities are performed on a for-hire basis. People in this line, whether within a company or outside of it, have a language of their own and work in a highly specialized field. It is simply on the "must" list that traffic recognize this and look to them for proper help, guidance, and cooperation. Many traffic departments assign broadly experienced, innovative representatives from their staffs to work with the data processing people on these matters. It is interesting that this generally seems better in actual practice than, say, placing a computer man in traffic. Also used are task forces and the like. Particularly on start-ups, a full measure of patience, know-how, and ingenuity is required.

With some companies the formalities to be undertaken with management by traffic in embarking on, maintaining, and enlarging its data processing functions represent following through on general encouragements to move forward on realistic innovations. In those instances traffic has its ground rules of moving when it is profitable that it do so, keeping compatible with the computer group, and so on. Other companies require "justifications" generally of a formal nature. Details required and weight to be given such somewhat intangible features as how soon information is made available will depend to a considerable extent on the company. While some companies may be so far along that it is not indicated as to them, consideration may well be given in many cases to tempering transportation-computer "justifications" (when required) with elements found in research and development (R & D) justifications. Full benefits in these matters often are not readily apparent until actual operations are off and running. In any number of instances the benefits have been much greater than anticipated. Further, these benefits have not been limited to transportation. Supplies, marketing, manufacturing, and other functions have been helped by what traffic does in this regard. In one instance transportation became a particularly valuable ally of the computer group because of the broad spectrum of these benefits to other departments.

Another worthwhile aspect of a good transportation-computer alliance can be the use of data processing equipment when spare time becomes available. Ideal computer operations are round-the-clock and round-the-week. Machine costs run into a great deal of money and those working with the computers quite properly wish to keep them fully occupied. In any number of cases the computer people of a company, in co-operation with traffic, have been able to program and "run" various transportation functions, principally because machine time became available. On occasion this has been done on what might be called test-run bases and on others that were worked out to be permanent arrangements. The test runs are, of course, made permanent, in due course, as their worth is established. Imbalances between machine time available and machine time needs create opportunities on which can well be kept in mind in these matters.

Transportation was not a function to receive early data processing attention with many industrial companies. Payrolls and accounts receivable were among the first with most of them. While these earlier steps were going on in industry the carriers, particularly the rails and trucks, were doing the same thing. A great deal of statistical reporting to the I.C.C., various state commissions, and others is necessary by the carriers, and these statistical requirements were a particularly logical field to which the carriers could turn for further data processing applications.

Reporting on uniform bases by the carriers of the statistics required of them was important and this, in turn, led to the establishment of uniform "codes" or numbers being assigned to certain features. In the case of commodities the applicable uniform code came to be known as the Standard Transportation Commodity Code (STCC). STCC numbers for particular commodities have been previously pointed out in this text in connection with the Uniform Freight Classification. The following excerpt from the Classification is shown at top of page 437 so the reference will be handy and the source for STCC numbers readily established.

Illustrative of what happens would be when, say, a shipment of oakum (third line down on the left) is made by, say, a railroad. It is fed into the data processing facility as 22 941 67. All other oakum shipments are fed in similarly. They are totaled, say, at the end of a given period. The result comes out with 22 941 67 as the control number for the product. That

UNIFORM FREIGHT CLASSIFICATION 10

INDEX TO ARTICLES

STCC No.	Article	Item	STCC No.	Article	Item
39 621 46	Oak leaves,natural,preserved. . . .	32180	34 435 20	Oil and air-separating tanks, pipe line.	88770
08 619 61	Oak seed,jerusalem (worm seed), not ground nor powdered.	85370	34 435 42	Oil and gas-separating tanks, automatic steel.	89170
22 941 67	Oakum	71130	28 996 10	Oil blacks,compressed,electro- statically separated,	
24 994 25	Oars,boat	11780		filtered or granulated,dry	
20 421 40	*Oat and corn chops mixture (chop) .	37230		not activated,not dyes nor	
20 421 63	" *cereal offal feed,not for human consumption	37230		dyestuffs	11160
35 516 22	" clippers,cereal milling 59660, 59760, 159810		28 996 13	" blacks,noibn,dry,not activated, not dyes nor dyestuffs. . . .	11170
20 418 34	" clippings.	47190	26 499 30	" board,paper.	75550
20 421 59	" *feed,flaked,not for human consumption	37230	35 999 48	" burner air register parts, iors.	64960
20 416 10	" *flour.	47010	35 999 47	" burner air registers,iors. . .	64960
20 418 30	" hulls.		28 612 40	" burner oils	
20 418 43	" *groats,feed.		20 939 44	" rape seed	72480
	" meal		20 942 47	" *sea animal.	72480
	steel,or tin plate,single, wall,side seams not closed, nstd 29855, 29880		20 939 44	" *sesame.	72480
			20 923 35	" *soybean	72480
			20 939 44	" *sunflower seed.	72480
29 919 67	Oil,rubber extender	77333			
29 919 67	Oil,rubber processing	77333			
29 912 37	Oil additives,lubricating	δ			

For explanation of reference marks,see top of page 17; for abbreviations,see last page of this Classification

Commodity Code Numbers (STCC) As Used In
Uniform Freight Classification.

number (the STCC number), in turn, is converted back to oakum, and the oakum, along with the total of its shipments, go into the statistics reported. With the other railroads using the STCC number of 22 941 67 for oakum shipments, the necessary uniformity becomes "automatic." Further, similar STCC numbers are used by other carriers along similar lines and for similar purposes. This example, incidentally, is quite elementary, and much more sophisticated uses are made of the STCC in the transportation field and elsewhere.

Another code of particular importance is the Standard Point Location Code (SPLC). As its name implies, it delineates origins, destinations, and other location points. It came (with important motor carrier sponsorship) about the same time as the STCC and employs six digits. The initial number represents a region, the first two a state, and so on. It is widely used by shippers, motor carriers, railroads, and others; it is quite precise, and it is employed in the computer systems of some industries for other-than-transportation purposes, such as state tax computations. Still other codes came into the transportation picture.

These included carrier name codes, carrier equipment codes, patron (i.e. user) codes, vehicle identification codes, and so on. Varying degrees of use and recognition have been accorded these.

Concurrent with early carrier-oriented code developments, many shippers were pretty much going their own way on what might be termed their individual code activities. Quite often only individual plants were involved. These had limited product lists, limited territorial involvements, and so on. Many codes or their equivalents, you might say, were made up by the companies themselves. As data processing horizons expanded, the need became more apparent (as it is today) for broad codes fully compatible between shippers, carriers, banks, governments, and others. Important work on codes was done for the shippers by the National Industrial Traffic League (NITL), and it continues to do such work. The field is so broad and the money involved (millions of dollars) is so great, however, that additional help is needed. This, quite briefly, is one of the reasons for the establishment of the Transportation Data Coordinating Committee (TDCC) which is referred to earlier herein in the Traffic Department chapter. More information on its work (as well as additional code specifics and compatibility activities) appears in its seminar minutes and other publications. Traffic's computer colleagues should be fully informed on the work of TDCC and NITL on these matters. They can be of immense help in effecting savings, advantages, and other benefits as to them.

Proper, efficient, and economical exchange of data is, of course, the aim of compatible codes and the like. Appropriate systems designs are also pertinent to good data exchange. Further, a lot of tariff simplification is needed, because computer systems choke on exceptions and, in somewhat the same vein, international trade aspects require attention. These are to be borne in mind, particularly long term, in work on these matters. In the meantime, STCC, SPLC, and other transportation oriented codes, on the one hand, and codes used by industry, on the other, are being reconciled and made compatible for reasonably common use in many cases by what are called "modifiers" or "bridges". These represent extra steps to be avoided when possible. A tip-top, close-at-hand, common example of what can be done when numbers, machines, and the rest mesh are the checks a person signs on his bank account. The magnetic ink code numbers at the bottom on the left and the amount of the check at bottom right tell the story regarding them. Based on these, the checks are paid, negotiated, processed throughout the country (and some foreign countries) by all the banks, and finally (with correct calculations, print-outs on bank statement forms, etc.) returned duly cancelled to the party originating them.

There are three basic ways of accomplishing the work discussed in this chapter: manually, by punch cards, and by electronic data processing. Operation techniques as to the first two are generally known. When it comes to the third, traffic (in conjunction with its computer colleagues) can well find value in participation, if possible, in what is done by TDCC and NITL. If participation is not possible, information on TDCC activities is available as previously discussed. NITL issues bulletins from time to time and its annual membership circulars contain excellent activity reports by its Data and Computer Systems Committee. The intricacies of computer systems are, of course, for the computer people. Traffic's particular role is to help in pointing out areas for attention and in doing traffic-wise what should be done with data processing developments. Further, when indicated for any general or special research reasons, there are various brochures, magazines, and texts available. Of the latter, two recent are "Funk & Wagnall's Dictionary of Data Processing Terms" edited by Harold A. Rogers (1970) 151 pgs. $7.95 and "Managing The EDP Function" by Ditri, Shaw, and Atkins, McGraw Hill Book Co., (1971) 228 pgs., $14.75.

Activities by industry in transportation data processing along more specific lines have been channeled principally into two fields. One is concerned essentially with operating functions such as rail service, establishing proper distribution patterns, equipment availability, and getting maximum efficiencies from owned and assigned rail car fleets. The second is concerned essentially with treasury functions, such as auditing freight bills, paying them, and the like. No hard line is drawn between operating and treasury functions, and quite often benefits flow to both activities. As to some of these, joint use by industry and carriers of computer systems is made and there is more and more of such use.

A particular joint use situation exists at a paper mill in Mississippi served by the Illinois Central Railroad. Each uses, as appropriate, the other's computer system. Inbound pulp wood supplies via rail are important, and look-aheads as to loads scheduled, arrival dates, and so on are made available to the plant and are used for production planning and other purposes. Bills of lading, waybills, and freight bills as separate pieces of paper are not used. Freight payments are calculated by the computers and remittances are made simply. Outbound movements are kept track of (expedited when necessary, etc.) in part by the carrier's computer system and in part by the system of the shipper. The operation is considered in the "pilot plant" category by the carrier. Various features of the arrangement there are used elsewhere.

Another helpful and considerably used data application is in the Computerized Car Location Message System, sometimes called the "CLM" system. As the name implies, the system involves the acceptance of car location information from the railroads and the mechanized manipulation of such data to conform with the needs of individual shippers. The details of doing this take different forms and the system is used differently by different companies. Ideally it can involve the two computer systems of a plant and its railroad being so hooked up that information on the location of the outbound and inbound shipments and empty cars returning is as available to the plant as to the railroad for expediting, equipment control, production planning, or any other of the many important aspects concerned with rail service and equipment matters. Modifications of these ideal techniques are necessary in various instances for a number of reasons and at times the information cannot be provided or accepted on data processing bases. In actual practice, however, the system finds worth-while use in many cases. Additionally, some plants help their carriers in arranging motive power and so on through facilities that are part of the system.

To the quite substantial group of industries having private car and assigned car fleets, print-outs and other information provided by data processing have created further opportunities to operate those fleets better and more economically. Under old procedures operating information was assembled and prepared manually; data processing brought into being possibilities to change this. Some companies make information from their Car Location System (previous paragraph) part of their car fleet administration system, and this can be helpful. By and large, however, car fleet administration information comes from the data system of the company involved. This information is generally in the form of a weekly or bi-monthly "tab run" (print-out) which shows by origin, by cars, and by shipment transit times and other facts on the private and assigned car fleet on a truly up-to-date basis. Traffic, in turn, takes this information and uses it as a necessary basis to obtain, or arrange to obtain, improved turn-around times for the equipment, more prompt loading and unloading, and so on, where indicated. The plants and others also often help in these cases.

Other operating activities in which data processing techniques have been applied are in the establishment of economical distribution patterns and in determining for a particular destination or destinations the best shipping origin where two or more origins could be used. "Tools" used in this connection are designated variously by various companies but they pretty much boil down to freight rate banks in computer systems from which are taken, automatically, appropriate freight rates. These in turn, are applied to values for the material at the various origins; the rates are added to the values by the computer system; and a "package" comes out showing what are substantially laid down costs as to a territory, destinations, or what ever the case may be from the various origins.

This freight rate bank information is also at times used in

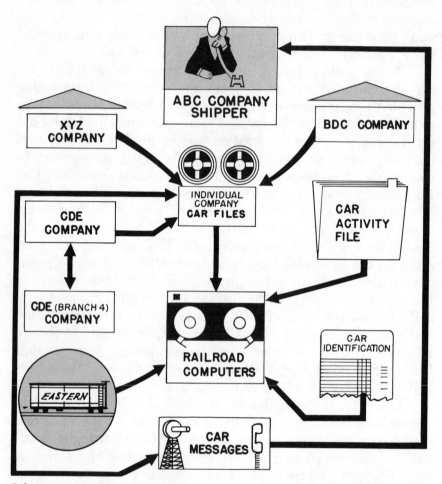

Schematic Diagram—Use of Rail Computer Systems—Car Location Message Purposes and Related Data.

Explanatory note: The above diagram and the diagram on the following page have as their purposes the graphic illustration of certain of the ways in which shipper-carrier joint use of data processing facilities is dealt with and accomplished. They show information flows, facilities used, and other features, including areas where shipper, carrier, government, and other interests may be involved. The diagram above, in particular, shows possibilities for information flows from participating shippers and then back to them.

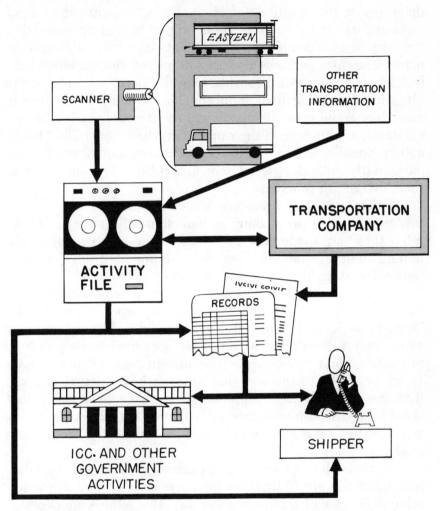

Schematic Diagram—Use of Computer Systems For Other Data Purposes As Well As Car Location Matters.

Explanatory note: The "scanner" feature shown above is concerned with the special multicolored stripes on box cars and the like. Each car has its own stripe. As the car passes certain locations the stripe is electronically scanned or "read" and the information thus obtained is passed to the transportation company's computer operation for retrieval and use when indicated as to that particular car and its contents if it is moving under load.

determining the positions of competitors, i.e., providing their rates and related data from their origins to a given marketing territory or to a destination or destinations where sales may be made. The information is also used in pricing calculations where freight absorptions and the like may be necessary. This quite often involves more than simply making a freight rate quickly available. Some computer systems take the rate, make the calculations, and include in their operation the actual billing transaction. Such "extensive" utilization occurs in a number of cases, particularly in industries where absorptions are ingrained in their marketing practices.

Other activities involving somewhat normal use of data processing occur in making actual shipment reviews. Quite often these are made on "spot check" bases. This involves obtaining periodic "tab runs" showing shipments from (or to) a particular shipping point for, say, the previous thirty days. These are "arranged" in the print-out by product, by destination, or whatever may best suit traffic's purposes, and can be "sorted out" so that shipments are arranged in descending order as to their volumes and so on. This "sort out" is done to help in putting "first things first." The information, in turn, is analyzed by traffic to the end that any particular action is taken that may be indicated. Shipments may have been made that should be discontinued; rate adjustments may be in order; or any number of improvements may be suggested from these analyses.

Various data processing applications particular to international trade are utilized by the carriers and those in carrier-related fields which are considerably along the same lines as those used by companies with private and assigned car fleets. The containers, the language problems, and the intermodal and other aspects for many reasons require special handling, however, and bring on systems that at times may have special benefits to shippers. A large international container company has its communications-computer systems so arranged that automatic translations of commodity descriptions from French to English (and vice versa) are provided in its shipping papers. Particular codes and other techniques are involved in doing this. Further, the great majority of those using the container company's services do not require negotiable bills of lading. In lieu of non-negotiable bills of lading a simple data receipt has been substituted. The information on the receipt (not the receipt itself) is sent by the company's communication system to the port of discharge. Upon proper identification the shipment is delivered there on arrival on the basis of this communication. Among various benefits, potential problems incident to delayed transmissions of bills of lading as pieces of paper are avoided in these cases. Of possible help, also, can be "Computers Sail into Maritime Paperwork," by John H. Robinson (*Transportation and Distribution Management* magazine, June 1972, pg. 32) dealing with freight forwarder-customs broker computer systems applications and the assistance available to shippers from them.

Freight bills, their payment, and their auditing have received considerable attention in data processing and related circles in recent years. A great amount of time, paper work, error correction, and other unsatisfactory features are involved with normal freight bill procedures and the field has been a wide one for appropriate corrective measures. The computer service firms mentioned earlier in this chapter have been active on freight bill matters and, through the use of their computer systems and otherwise, have come up with various applications for small, medium, and large-sized industrial companies that have been found to be worthwhile.

The banks have been continuing with their streamlining activities of debiting and crediting special accounts for freight bills submitted under their bank freight payment plans. They feel that in this they are far ahead of the "checkless society" envisioned for the future. The various transport clearing organizations have been continuing also with their related collecting and remitting operations. Increases have occurred in the use of both these groups and massive work is required of them in many instances; some 22,000 freight bills per day are processed by one upper midwest transport clearing house. The principal thrust of most bank and clearing house plans is to simplify payments. Improper ratings, duplicate payments, and like features are not dealt with by them extensively as a general rule.

In an effort to further streamline matters some industrial companies have set up special, internal procedures for paying for the freight to the carrier within legal time limits after they tender the bill of lading with the material for movement. This is done selectively as to certain kinds of freight and, quite overly simplified, is accomplished by the preparation of what amounts to a check or draft (through carbon paper, data processing, or otherwise) when the bill of lading is prepared. Applicable freight rates from the tariffs are applied to the weights, and calculations of total freight due are computed as the freight carrier would compute them in a regular billing operation. Payments are checked by the carrier, any indicated adjustments are made, and computer systems are variously used in this activity. More accurate freight payments and fewer duplicate payments are among the benefits. It is felt advantages outweigh for the shipper the freight calculating work that he does.

A still more modern method of dealing with freight bills involves the use of a transportation data processing service company for a fee to audit and pay an industrial company's bills. Under such an arrangement a shipper sends its bills of lading to the service company and the carriers also send to the service company their freight bills for the shipments covered by the bills of lading. As the freight bills are received they are audited by the service company, using its data processing system, the bills of lading, and freight rates drawn from its computer freight rate data base. Where the audit results are satisfactory the bills are paid within legal time limits by the service company and it, in turn, is reimbursed by the industry. Where the auditing indicates exceptions should be taken, these are handled appropriately. These companies also furnish statistical reports adjusted to their client's needs from the transactions processed. This activity has many advantages over conventional freight bill handling. It was originally conceived for small to medium sized companies, but large companies also use the service.

Freight bill payment procedures in a broad context, along with activities incident to the related subject of freight rate quotations and the like, are covered in more detail in "Freight Rate Retrieval and Freight Bill Payment," by Herbert S. Rush (The Traffic Service Corporation, 815 Washington Building, Washington, D. C. 20005, 88 pgs., 1969). Reviewed there are ways of using all three systems which are commonly employed: manual, punch card, and electronic data processing. See also, as regards freight bills generally, previous discussions in the Freight Rate and Freight Claims chapters of this text.

A great deal more could be discussed about data processing in transportation. Other particular applications that are working in worthwhile ways include ordering and shipping functions, inventory controls, and so on. Where important to a company, and where a company's data systems will permit, all that is reasonably possible should be done by traffic to secure for its activities the benefits which are practical and possible from automation. Steps in this regard can be many. An interesting article on the moves made in this regard by one of the important divisions of a large chemical company is "Automated Rating at Clairol," by Alfred S. Daviau, in the *Traffic World* issue of December 31, 1971, page 38. Opportunities in the field are many and important to keeping traffic's head above water as to paper work and hand detail that can well be accomplished more economically and efficiently.

Some caveats and suggestions that have been made in these matters include:

—Do not allow transportation information systems to be just information systems. Do something traffic-wise through transportation staff and in other ways about the information provided.

—Get a better understanding of what is shipped and how it is shipped, and take steps to see that the most economical way is used consistent with the level of service required.

—Educate staff and guide the staff capabilities so as to accomplish what should be done where necessary.

—Design systems that are relatively simple and do not make them too complex in the beginning.

—Use a building block approach and, where indicated later, put simple systems together to make them more effective. If a system can not be developed and made operative within a year, do not start it. Redesign the system and commence again.

—Use standard codes when such codes are in existence and are capable of doing the job.

—Concentrate on the problems that affect your company's business in developing a system that satisfies its needs at a cost it can afford within a time period it can endure.

Many of these features are more responsibilities of computer staff (or computer service companies) than they are of traffic. They are of importance to all, however, in meeting needs for good, practical transportation data processing systems.

16

UNITED STATES GOVERNMENT TRAFFIC

THE UNITED STATES GOVERNMENT IS THE LARGEST USER OF transportation services in the world. Furthermore, it ships every conceivable commercial commodity and uses every known form of transportation with consistent regularity. In addition to commercial items, it ships multitudinous types of arms, ammunition and military impedimenta in great volume. Such broad coverage results in a shipping pattern that not only embraces all normal commercial shipping procedures; but, in many cases, seeks to move commodities where no like commercial traffic exists. A high percentage of government domestic traffic moves at rates permitted by section 22 of the Interstate Commerce Act.

Excerpts from section 22 (in Part 1 of the Interstate Commerce Act) of interest follow:

"(1) That nothing in this part shall prevent the carriage, storage or handling of property free or at reduced rates for the United States, state or municipal governments or for charitable purposes. . . .

"(2) All quotations or tenders of rates, fares or charges under paragraph (1) of this section for the transportation, storage or handling of property or the transportation of persons free or at reduced rates for the United States government, or any agency or department thereof, including quotations or tenders for retroactive application whether negotiated or re-negotiated after the services have been performed, shall be in writing or confirmed in writing. . . . Submittal of such quotations or tenders to the Commission shall be made concurrently with submittal to the United States government, or any agency or department thereof, for whose account the quotations or tenders are offered or for whom the proposed services are to be rendered. Such quotations shall be preserved by the Commission for public inspection. The provisions of this paragraph requiring submissions to the Commission shall not apply to any quotation or tender which, as indicated by the United States government or any agency or department thereof, to any carriers, involves information the disclosure of which would endanger the national security."

Because of the volume of government shipping, government traffic has a direct effect on the operation of most types of carriers. Every traffic manager should understand the manner in which government shipping is handled, even though he himself may not be directly involved in shipping government freight.

General

Government traffic management operates under a general policy of distributing cargo equitably between all competing carriers offering equivalent services and rates. In this connection, equitable distribution does not necessarily mean equal distribution; considerations such as the applicable freight rate and the frequency and quality of service offered by each carrier may mean that competing carriers receive varying percentages of the total movement of government freight. The policy of using commercial carriage whenever satisfactory is based on the sound theory that a healthy commercial transportation system is needed both for peacetime economic reasons and for availability in time of war.

Government procurement officers, in common with commercial purchasing men, must consider transportation costs in buying materials. For purchases of any size, it is general policy to request bids both FOB point of production and delivered at the required point of use or storage. One of the first areas of government traffic management, therefore, is to analyze procurement bids together with freight rates available to the government to determine how material should be procured. When it is determined that vendor shipment to destination is cheaper than purchasing FOB plant and letting the government arrange transportation, the purchase is so made, and shipment to the destination point where the government takes delivery will be made as a normal commercial movement. If, on the other hand, procurement FOB origin is advantageous, title is taken at the vendor's plant, and the shipment to the point of use or storage becomes a government shipment, subject to normal government procedures and traffic management.

While state and local governments do purchase transportation services, the federal government is the major shipper by a tremendous margin; therefore the discussion herein will relate to federal government shipments only. There are basically two principal government traffic management authorities; the Department of Defense and the General Services Administration. The function of the Department of Defense is obvious; the General Services Administration provides traffic management for all civilian departments of the government. In addition, the General Accounting Office establishes basic shipping, accounting or clerical procedures for both military and civilian departments, and the Department of Justice represents the entire government in transportation court cases.

The General Services Administration controls shipments through regional offices, and acts for any civilian department requiring transportation services. A certain amount of traffic management authority is delegated to the various government departments, particularly to the Department of Agriculture and State Department for foreign aid shipments. However, for most domestic commercial shipping, the General Services Administration actually routes government shipments (other than military) and issues the required documentation.

The transportation organization in the Department of Defense is understandably complex, since the military are by far the largest shippers of general commodities within the government. Over-all transportation management policy is vested in the Office of the Assistant Secretary of Defense (Installations and Logistics).

The Military Airlift Command (MAC), under the Secretary of the Air Force, is responsible for overseas air cargo and air personnel movements; the Military Sealift Command (MSC), under the Secretary of the Navy, for ocean cargo and personnel movements (other than inland U.S. waterways), and the Military Traffic Management and Terminal Service (MTMTS), under the Secretary of the Army, for the procurement and use of all modes of transportation in the continental United States. This agency manages surface transportation of military cargo and personnel within such area, as well as all military ocean terminals therein with the exception of those used by the Navy in support of fleet activities.

On the subject of government transportation organization, it should be pointed out that the trend is to move away from local traffic management and move toward centralized management on a regional or area basis. This trend is modified to an extent by permitting local government installations to make small or repetitive shipments without reference to the centralized traffic management authority.

Peacetime economy in the use of transportation facilities by the military is important; but more important is whether the system can take on larger and more important responsibilities during an emergency or in case of war. Each military service has peculiar problems of its own and there is no easy answer or quick solution to provide a single system that could be used by all services. In the long run, the military exists for defense of the country. Each service has a job to do and must be capable of rapid expansion, as the net result of any good military transportation system has but one basic objective — to put men and material where needed and do so as rapidly as possible.

Military leaders are now and long have been fully aware of the importance of traffic management as an important segment of military logistics. Advanced transportation study is provided by the Army at the Transportation School at Fort Eustis, Virginia, by the Navy at the U.S. Naval School of Freight Transportation, Naval Supply Center, Oakland, California, and by the Air Force at the Sheppard Technical Training Center, Sheppard Air Force Base, Texas. In addition, all services use various civilian college programs to train transportation specialists.

Domestic Traffic

Domestic government shipments are controlled primarily by the Military Traffic Management and Terminal Service for military departments and the General Services Administration for civilian departments. These agencies prescribe the routing and select the carriers to be used. The MTMTS or GSA select the type of transportation and the carrier giving due consideration to cost, operational factors such as availability of rail sidings, and time-in-transit required for needed delivery at destination. The Military Traffic Management and Terminal Service came about in 1965 as a result of the need to organize military transportation on the basis of greater efficiency and economy. It represents the consolidation of (1) the Defense Traffic Management Service, (2) the Army Terminal Commands (Army/Navy "common user" ocean terminals), (3) the Air Traffic Coordinating offices of the Army, Navy and Air Force and (4) other miscellaneous traffic management functions for military cargo. MTMTS reports to the Department of Defense through the Secretary of the Army and acts as the single *manager* for military traffic in the U.S.A. and all common user terminals for both cargo and passengers. MTMTS was created to provide responsive and economic logistical support to the Joint Chiefs of Staff, the military services and other specified commands.

MTMTS has two area commands through which it controls all domestic land and air transportation for military shipments. It decides whether shipments go via air, water, rail, motor carrier, freight forwarder; it determines port of exit on shipments destined overseas; it reviews all shipment releases for consolidation possibilities and has jurisdiction over all points of origin on all types of cargo regardless of what military agency originates the shipment; it operates military owned rolling stock registered for interchange service.

To sum up, the MTMTS embraces the following responsibilities for movements of military shipments within the U.S.A.:

a. Air shipments from the U.S.A. point of origin to the U.S.A. air terminal from which is moves overseas; except where LOGAIR or QUICKTRANS have jurisdiction. Logair and Quicktrans are airlift services arranged by MAC through contracts with commercial airlines to provide regularly scheduled cargo service between specific points and military bases.

b. All other-than-air shipments from the U.S.A. point of origin to and through the U.S.A. ocean or port terminal from which it will be exported by ocean services.

c. Department of Defense household goods movements and storage.

d. All "common user" military ocean terminals except those used exclusively to support the fleet.

e. Development of plans for the use and control of domestic land transportation resources which would be available to the Department of Defense during emergencies.

As previously stated, domestic transportation is arranged almost entirely with commercial carriers; general policy being that government owned and operated equipment will not be used in the United States in competition with commercial carriers. To illustrate, the Military Airlift Command operates no scheduled domestic air services for either passengers or cargo, but does charter planes from the commercial companies to provide a regular air cargo service between key military supply points. Other domestic military air passenger movements are performed largely by the regular air carriers.

Military trucks and buses do not provide point-to-point services in the United States in competition with commercial services, although charter bus and air services rather than common carrier services may be used to accomplish specific large passenger movements.

Packaging requirements on government orders should not be considered as being the same as for commercial orders. Look at each order carefully to determine if specific packing requirements are provided (see comments Chapter 7).

Overseas Traffic

The Military Sealift Command and the General Services Administration are the primary traffic managers for ocean transportation services. In ocean shipping as with domestic, government policy is to foster a strong merchant marine by using American-flag berth line carriers as the primary source of service. However, in the case of MSC, a nucleus of government owned and operated ships is maintained, so that MSC is both a purchaser of commercial services and a carrier for government passengers and freight. The MSC fleet is maintained primarily to insure that the ships involved will be available on short notice to supplement Navy fleet ships in any emergency. The Navy ships in general are used to complement, rather than compete directly with, commercial carrier service. The size of the fleet, however, is determined by emergency plan requirements, and some services that could be obtained commercially are provided by them. Nevertheless an important part of the military dry cargo has moved in commercial ships, and the 25% that moves in the MSC fleet consists for the most part of cargoes such as Arctic and Antarctic supply movements and other lifts, such as ammunition, which do not fit in with commercial trade route patterns. Troop lift is provided primarily by government (MSC) troop ships, since no commercial passenger ships are currently available for high volume, austere, low cost passenger carriage. Originally, the MSC operated a considerable fleet of passenger vessels (transports); but this fleet has been greatly reduced as use of air service has increased.

Both military and civilian government general-cargo-type freight movements are obtained primarily from scheduled American flag berth line ships operating on commercial trade routes. Such ships normally carry both government and commercial freight on the same voyage.

After the various military services (called Shipper Services) place their requirements on MSC, the local MSC offices book the cargoes with the commercial operator, using an allocation system based on the number of sailings each steamship line makes over its various trade routes.

This berth cargo is distributed as equitably as possible among the American lines, with consideration being given to consolidation of cargoes, where possible, to achieve the lowest possible freight rate.

Bulk lifts of government full-cargo lots such as grain or coal are arranged through normal charter procedures. MSC arranges charters for occasional unusual "general cargo" that cannot be lifted by the MSC nucleus fleet or by available American-flag sailings. To move petroleum products, MSC employs both long-term charters and voyage charters so as to obtain the needed type and number of tankers.

Air Traffic

The Military Airlift Command maintains a sizeable aircraft fleet, which is required to provide airlift of cargoes and troops in the event of military emergency situations. This fleet is used almost entirely for movement of personnel and material between the United States and the far-flung complex of worldwide military bases and for movements between overseas bases. In recent years there has been an increased emphasis on the use of chartered commercial aircraft to provide some of the required airlift on the regular routes flown by MAC. In addition to MAC, which handles military cargo only, some government shipments to overseas destinations are made with regularly scheduled commercial air lines. Quicktrans and Logair are services set up by MAC through contracts with commercial air lines in the U.S.A. to provide regularly scheduled cargo flights between specific points and bases.

Documentation

Shipments of government property in domestic and overseas movements via common carriers are almost always documented on government bills of lading (see next page). Since government regulations do not permit prepayment of freight charges, the total amount due is collected by the carrier from the government after delivery is completed. The government, then, normally has title to the goods at the point of shipment. Shippers of goods sold to a government agency on an FOB origin point basis who substitute their own commercial bill of lading for the government bill of lading (GBL) furnished by the government will be billed by the carrier as the government will not pay the freight charges unless the shipment moves under a GBL. If this happens, it is advisable to endeavor to substitute a GBL for the commercial form as quickly as possible. On the other hand, a consignee of a GBL shipment will be relieved of paying the freight charges by executing the "certificate of receipt of goods" on the GBL and turning it over to the carrier.

Regulations concerning the use of government bills of lading are issued to all government departments by the General Accounting Office in their Policy and Procedures Manual for the Guidance of Federal Agencies, Title 5, Transportation. Instructions to carriers and non-government shippers or consignees are contained on the reverse side of each original GBL. Information to be shown on government bills of lading is identical to that required for commercial bills, insofar as description of articles in accordance with the governing freight classification or tariff and the identification of shipper and consignee are concerned. Certain additional government internal accounting data and shipment control data may also appear on GBLs but is not of direct concern to non-government personnel.

It should be emphasized that the GBL is not used to ship

Standard Form No. 1103
5 GAO 3000
1103-105-67

U.S. GOVERNMENT BILL OF LADING
ORIGINAL

C- 1234567

B/L NO.

TRANSPORTATION COMPANY

TENDERED TO——➤   CHESAPEAKE & OHIO

STOP   THIS CAR OR TRUCK AT

TRAFFIC CONTROL NO.   C-1234567

3C2904953A1GA

FOR
CAR INITIALS AND NO.

CNW 107972

KIND

IMPORTANT
Regulations permit this original bill of lading to be surrendered to the initial carrier or sent immediately to the consignee. The shipping agency will furnish specific instructions with respect thereto.

| CAR-TRUCK LGTH., FT., INS.† | | MARKED CAPACITY † | | DATE FURNISHED † | DATE B/L ISSUED |
| ORDERED | FURNISHED | ORDERED | FURNISHED | | |

†FURNISH THIS INFORMATION IN CASE OF CARLOAD OR TRUCKLOAD SHIPMENTS ONLY.

IF EXTRA SERVICES ARE ORDERED SEE
ADMINISTRATIVE DIRECTIONS NO. 2 ON REVERSE

TRUCK NO.

RECEIVED BY THE TRANSPORTATION COMPANY NAMED ABOVE, SUBJECT TO CONDITIONS NAMED ON THE REVERSE HEREOF, THE PROPERTY HEREINAFTER DESCRIBED, IN APPARENT GOOD ORDER AND CONDITION (CONTENTS AND VALUE UNKNOWN), TO BE FORWARDED TO DESTINATION BY THE SAID COMPANY AND CONNECTING LINES, THERE TO BE DELIVERED IN LIKE GOOD ORDER AND CONDITION TO SAID CONSIGNEE.

FROM

(SHIPPING POINT) ——➤   ANY TOWN, MICHIGAN

FULL NAME OF SHIPPER

SANDY SALT CO.

CONSIGNEE (NAME AND MAILING ADDRESS)

TRANSPORTATION OFFICER
BROOKLYN ARMY TERMINAL

MARKS

DESTINATION

NEW HARBOR, NEW YORK LTGE DELY

VIA (ROUTE SHIPMENT ONLY WHEN SOME SUBSTANTIAL INTEREST OF THE GOVERNMENT IS SERVED THEREBY)

CO-PC-LTGE

CHARGES TO BE BILLED TO (DEPARTMENT OR ESTABLISHMENT, BUREAU OR SERVICE AND LOCATION)
FINANCE CENTER, TDIV
U.S. ARMY
INDIANAPOLIS 49, INDIANA

SEAL NOS.

B-261985-86
SHIPPER

APPLIED BY

FOR CARRIER'S USE ONLY

WAYBILL NO.   FREIGHT BILL NO.

APPROPRIATION CHARGEABLE

97X4961.5103-70 22.1 S11-027

CONTRACTORS WILL RETURN UNUSED OR CANCELED BILLS OF LADING TO GOVERNMENT OFFICE FROM WHICH RECEIVED.

PACKAGES		DESCRIPTION OF ARTICLES	NUMBERS ON PACKAGES	WEIGHTS*	FOR USE OF DESTINATION CARRIER ONLY		
NO.	KIND	(USE CARRIERS' CLASSIFICATION OR TARIFF DESCRIPTION IF POSSIBLE, OTHERWISE A CLEAR NONTECHNICAL DESCRIPTION)			CLASS	RATE	CHARGES
							DOLLARS	CENTS
1282	12/5 PKGS	SALT, TABLE, BAGS ITEM NO. 1	CUBE	78843#			
		TOTAL CUBE		1153.8			

EQUAL EMPLOYMENT OPPORTUNITY
Condition 9 hereof is revised as follows: The Contract clauses in Sec. 301 of Executive Order 10925 (26 F. R. 1977) are incorporated herein, but carriers are exempted from paragraphs 3-7 thereof unless otherwise specifically ordered (26 F. R. 6586, Sec. 60-1.3 (b) (4).

NO DUNNAGE OR OTHER MATERIAL USED
1% EMPTY BAGS INCLUDED
SLW&C

IF THIS SHIPMENT FULLY LOADS THE CAR OR TRUCK USED, CHECK ☐ YES

TARIFF OR SPECIAL RATE AUTHORITIES (C/L - T/L OR VOL. ONLY)

CTR 490-B

CARRIER FURNISHED ☐ PICK UP— ☐ TRAP CAR—
SERVICE AT ORIGIN. INITIALS OF SHIPPER'S AGENT HJN

NAME OF TRANSPORTATION

COMPANY——➤   CHESAPEAKE & OHIO

DATE OF RECEIPT OF SHIPMENT

SIGNATURE OF AGENT

INITIAL CARRIER'S AGENT, BY SIGNATURE BELOW, CERTIFIES HE RECEIVED THE ORIGINAL BILL OF LADING.
☐ YES (INDICATE BY CHECK)

PER

CERTIFICATE OF ISSUING OFFICER

I CERTIFY THAT THIS SHIPMENT IS MADE PURSUANT TO THE TERMS OF CONTRACT OR PURCHASE ORDER NO. CHI-29051-65 DATED

OR OTHER AUTHORITY FOR SHIPMENT, F.O.B. POINT NAMED IN CONTRACT
ANY TOWN, MICHIGAN

ISSUING OFFICE   BROOKLYN ARMY TERMINAL

SIGNATURE OF ISSUING OFFICER

DATE   TITLE   TA FOR TO

WILLIAM NONAME

CONSIGNEE'S CERTIFICATE OF DELIVERY—CONSIGNEE MUST NOT PAY ANY CHARGES ON THIS SHIPMENT

I CERTIFY THAT I HAVE THIS DAY ———— RECEIVED FROM ———— AT ————
(DATE OF DELIVERY)   (NAME OF TRANSPORTATION COMPANY)   (ACTUAL POINT OF DELIVERY)

THE PROPERTY DESCRIBED IN THIS BILL OF LADING IN APPARENT GOOD ORDER AND CONDITION, EXCEPT AS NOTED ON REVERSE HEREOF,   CARRIER FURNISHED ☐ DELIVERY— ☐ TRAP CAR—
SERVICE AT DESTINATION.

———— POUNDS* ————
(GROSS WEIGHT IN BOTH WORDS AND FIGURES)   (SIGNATURE OF CONSIGNEE OR AUTHORIZED AGENT)
*SHOW ALSO CUBIC MEASUREMENTS FOR SHIPMENTS VIA AIR, TRUCK OR WATER CARRIER, IN CASES WHERE REQUIRED.

United States Government Bill of Lading

or pay freight under special government contracts, but is used for shipment by all modes of transportation world wide, where the payment of freight is based on the rates, terms and conditions of published commercial tariffs or specifically negotiated "section 22" rates.

Government shipments made under special contracts or charter arrangements, and shipments moving via government owned trucks, aircraft or ships, are documented on special forms developed for the purpose, rather than on GBL's. Payment to contract carriers for such shipments is made in accordance with the terms of the contract or charter party, and the form used to document the freight may or may not be the basis for payment to the carrier. As an example, the Military Sealift Command has shipping agreements, container agreements, and some shipping contracts with American-flag ocean carriers for the movement of Department of Defense cargo. Each line handling cargo under these arrangements receives a copy of the military manifest listing all cargo on a particular ship. MSC then provides a detailed shipping order for each ship sailing. In these instances no specific bill of lading of any type is issued. Charges are billed by each line against the shipping order copy.

Within the Department of Defense a large number of forms used to document freight moving at other than railroad, motor carrier and freight forwarder rate committee and steamship conference tariff terms were developed over the years. Because many of these forms contained essentially the same information, the Department of Defense established a program to standardize shipping documents to the maximum extent possible with the objective of simplifying military shipping procedures and achieving uniform documentation. This project was titled MILSTAMP, which stands for "Military Standard Transportation and Movement Procedures". MILSTAMP prescribes standard forms to be used by all services in making shipments not documented by government bills of lading and is of particular interest because it is designed primarily as a system in which shipping documents will be prepared and transmitted by electronic data processing equipment. Thus, MILSTAMP documents generally use codes to describe commodities, list origin and destination points and other required data. Shipping documents produced from data processing punch cards or tapes are transmitted over cable or radio circuits (where available) to the designated consignee, who reproduces the required manifests or shipping forms from tapes or cards locally. Complementing MILSTAMP is MILSTRIP which stands for "Military Standard Requisition and Issue Procedure". MILSTRIP is a "supply issue" documentation procedure intended to accelerate the supply distribution process. In combination, MILSTAMP and MILSTRIP are designed to speed the delivery of material to military units and to improve logistic efficiency while permitting a degree of inventory reduction.

The following initials and explanations cover those most frequently used in connection with government traffic:

DSA — Defense Supply Agency

GAO — General Accounting Office

GSA — General Services Administration

LRU — Less Release Units (Refers to LCL or LTL lots)

MAC — Military Airlift Command

METS — Mechanized Export Traffic System

MILSTAMP — Military Standard Transportation and Movement Procedures

MILSTRIP — Military Standard Requisition and Issue Procedure

MOT — Military Ocean Terminal

MSC — Military Sealift Command

MTMTS — Military Traffic Management and Terminal Service

NSC — Navy Supply Center

USNS — United States Naval Ship

17

INTERNATIONAL SHIPMENTS

THE FUTURE WELFARE OF THE UNITED STATES, BOTH ECONOMICALLY
and politically, depends more and more on its international relationships. Isolationism is almost a forgotten word. Because international trade is essential, the scope of industrial traffic management now more than ever embraces exports, imports and
other foreign transportation as well as domestic traffic.

There are many detailed technical procedures connected
with the transportation of materials between different countries
as well as the sale and purchase of those materials. The right
form of transportation (giving due consideration to cost, service and handling) must be determined. Preparation of bills of
lading, dock receipts, export declarations, consular invoices and
other documentation, is most important. The need for export
and import licenses must be checked. Packing suitable for
proper handling must be provided. There is the matter of terms
of sale and whether payments will be on open account, by letter of credit or some other means. In the important export field
a basic consideration, of course, is whether the exporter is prepared to price his goods so they can be landed at a foreign destination at an over-all price equivalent to or lower than that of
a foreign competitor and what his transportation people can do
to help in this regard. This chapter is intended to provide a
broad outline of the pertinent facts involved.

General features for recognition and for due attention include the matter of industrial corporate set-ups, which vary considerably in the international field. Some companies operate as simply and on as near a one-corporation basis as possible with their own transportation departments having the responsibility for both domestic and foreign trade. Other companies have separate corporations organized specifically for their foreign activities, with close ties to the parent company but at the same time with their own traffic departments. Still others have corporate affiliates duly organized in other countries, with autonomy in varying degrees as to their various activities, including traffic. These varying corporate set-ups in almost every instance have as backgrounds government relations, applicable taxes, and other considerations not necessarily related to transportation. Traffic people that are involved should do all possible to keep abreast of these considerations and to arrange their operations to help and complement them. When organization changes are indicated to do a better transportation job they should, of course, work to those ends.

Another feature for general consideration by traffic departments involved in these matters is the extent to which brokers are employed. These have their special fields of activity and their operations are essentially in three categories: First, independent ocean freight forwarders; second, customs representatives; and third, freight, chartering, and ship brokers. They provide helpful, specialized, and technical talents and have important stature with many companies, including some with large international operations. The costs of utilizing their services are generally not great, and more details concerning them are in the section on broker activities in this chapter. Those in the first category differ from the forwarding companies that are in the business of consolidating and forwarding shipments. All three categories, when indicated, can be important adjuncts to the proper movement of goods in foreign commerce.

A further feature for general recognition is that Canada and Mexico may represent situations for special attention as to many companies using border-crossing transportation. Industries located there may be the only companies with which a

U.S. based company does any export-import business. Other situations will vary and, at what might possibly be termed the other end of the spectrum, are Canadian and Mexican based companies whose major sources of business are from the U.S. Much of what is said later is also applicable in these cases and should receive attention on that basis. Relations basically, however, are relatively uncomplicated; most of the actual movements are across the borders via rail or truck; customs requirements are ordinarily reasonably well understood, and so on. The traffic manager of a large, extensive Canadian company maintains master shipping instruction forms giving complete information, including customs data and so on, for shipments. These forms are kept up to date and are provided to origins, destinations, and others in interest when indicated. This system is of real help in avoiding trouble, delays, and other problems on shipments. Incidentally, on inbound rail movements from the U.S. to Canada this company's traffic department handles customs and related matters direct and essentially with the destination carrier in Canada. On truck shipments, Canadian customs brokers at border points are used (with full powers of attorney and so on). In the case of Mexico, many U.S.-based companies make it a point to maintain broker connections at border crossings, for customs and other reasons, to assist on inbound and outbound movements. Also, problems incident to language differences are helped considerably by doing this.

Exports, that is, sales abroad, are currently in the limelight. They are of tremendous importance; it is right that they should be; and much of what is said later in this chapter deals with them. On the other hand it should not be overlooked that, as applied to the responsibilities of industrial traffic departments, international trade may have three functional divisions: Exports, imports, and commerce between foreign countries. Quite a bit depends on how a department is organized as to the importance of these break-outs to them. Where they are important, care is taken to give all three proper attention at all times. As an example, a movement of steel pipe from a U.S. to a Spanish port which is the responsibility of the traffic department of a U.S.-based steel manufacturer may well represent to that department important items of "export" work as it leaves and "import" as it arrives. This may be particularly true where, say, the destination is a warehouse or other facility of the shipping company.

Not only do responsibilities for arrangements for transportation on foreign trade vary with corporate systems, with different countries, and so on, they also vary within organizations as to what is expected of their transportation departments. With some, responsibilities are limited and may involve only selecting the most advantageous method of transportation and arranging for appropriate bills of lading. These responsibilities generally, however, are much broader in extent and may include some or all of freight rate negotiations, customs clearances, the procurement of proper cargo and other insurance, preparation of foreign trade documents, setting up financial arrangements with banks or others for appropriate payments, and on-the-ground arrangements abroad for loading, unloading, and storage facilities, as well as others. In some cases these responsibilities are shared, i.e., financing arrangements may be made by both treasury and traffic people.

With all of the complications that are seemingly inescapable in global matters, foreign traffic people have a great many things going for them. Important help to them and their carriers comes from government sources, federal, state, and local. The Maritime Commission, Department of Commerce, various state and local activities, the port authorities, and others are aiding in a number of ways the improvement of international trade. Of real importance, also, are the far reaching developments on sea, air, and land in new ships, new containerization, new aircraft, new equipment, new documentation, and other innovations. These have operated pretty much to bring a new ball game to this field in recent years and there are more improvements yet to come.

A discussion of items concerned with the dealings that might be accorded day to day operations of an international traffic department as well as new developments at hand and coming could be tackled in a number of ways. To some, certain features would be more important and, to others, the accentuation could well be elsewhere. A somewhat broad-based way to approach those items, however, would be by the specifics that follow. The discussion of them is as much along the indicated chronological lines as possible: (1) Conventional cargo movements, (2) utilization of up-dated shipping modes; (3) bills of lading and inland practices and costs; (4) ocean freight rates; (5) customs duties and procedures; (6) financing payments; (7) insurance and claims; (8) packaging; (9) the 1970 Merchant Marine Act and other laws; (10) employment of independent ocean freight forwarders, customs representatives, and freight, chartering, and ship brokers, and (11) airlines, parcel post, and non-vessel operating common carriers by water.

Conventional Cargo Movements

Despite the changes that are in the offing and the mounting enthusiasm for those changes, conventional cargo movements via water for export and import will undoubtedly be an important part of international transportation for some time. It has been such a predominant factor and has been so important for so long that switches to other modes will be far from automatic when, and if, they occur. Various shippers have given serious attention and study to new services offered and have concluded that it is best for them that their tonnage should continue to move via conventional vessels.

Reduced to simple terms, a conventional cargo shipment involves timely delivery of cargo to shipside, loading of the cargo aboard the vessel, transportation of the cargo from origin to destination by that vessel, and unloading it from the vessel at destination. What is tantamount to a break in the bulk of the cargo occurs as it is loaded and as it is unloaded and, because of this, a conventional cargo movement is often referred to as via a "break bulk" carrier. The before and after features of these movements as well as the water movements themselves represent elements to some shippers which, taken as a whole, are so handled that economically and service-wise the use of break-bulk carriers is in order and is to be continued.

Available service from conventional cargo carriers falls into two broad fields: Liner service and tramp service. Liner service is sometimes called berth service. Definitions of the two services follow:

■ *Liner service*—Liner service is performed by vessels operating as common carriers. They serve particular trade routes and carry chiefly a wide variety of packaged goods for many shippers. They adhere to known, regular schedules in spite of fluctuations in cargo offerings much the same as a bus or street car line runs its set route on schedule regardless of the number of passengers. A substantial majority of the liner companies are members of steamship conferences which have to do with ocean freight rates, the use of certain ships, and so on. These are discussed later in this chapter.

■ *Tramp service*—Tramp service is performed by vessels operating not as common carriers but as contract carriers. They serve no fixed route, adhere to no regular schedule and often carry homogeneous cargo from one loading port to one or a few discharge ports for a single shipper who charters the entire vessel for that purpose. Unlike the regular route scheduled service given by streetcars or bus lines, tramp vessel service is more like that given by taxicabs. There are no tramp operators in steamship conferences.

It is good practice to have a shipment at destination on just as firm a schedule as possible and just as quickly as possible. This pleases the customer and may reduce handling. Use of the larger, well-established liner steamship companies generally assures benefiting not only from the best in scheduled sailing frequency but also from the shortest transit interval to the foreign port. Tonnage assignments with these features in mind are, of course, quite important at times.

Those industries using conventional cargo carriers also give consideration to the use of vessels that are units of the U.S. merchant marine. The term "U.S. merchant marine" is a phrase used to designate ocean-going, privately owned, freight and passenger ships (generally over 1,000 gross tons), documented under the American flag. To qualify as an American-flag ship and therefore as a unit in the American merchant marine, a ship must be built in the United States to specifications of the American Bureau of Shipping, be registered with the United States Customs, be owned and operated by American citizens with an American crew, and be governed by safety regulations of the United States. Many of these vessels are subsidized and more details on the subsidy features are given in that part of this chapter concerned with government and regulatory activities.

There are two kinds of berth, or scheduled, operators—the subsidized and the non-subsidized. The latter, while frequently publishing schedules, are free to switch to other more remunerative routes or endeavors if they so desire. In other words, the non-subsidized lines are free to engage in tramp operations on occasion. The subsidized operator, as a part of its subsidy, agrees with the U.S. government to provide a minimum and maximum number of regular sailings on one or more of a total of some two-dozen-plus, specified, essential trade routes. These agreements give the government such control that a steamship operator of freighters may not deviate from specified trade routes unless special permission is obtained in each instance from the Maritime Administration. As this book goes to press, there are 12 subsidized lines in the United States viz.:

American Export Isbrandtsen Lines, Inc.
American Mail Line, Ltd.
American President Lines, Ltd.
Delta Steamship Lines, Inc.
Farrell Lines, Inc.
Lykes Bros. Steamship Co. Inc.
Moore-McCormack Lines, Inc.
Pacific Far East Line, Inc.
Prudential Grace Lines, Inc.
States Steamship Company

The Oceanic Steamship Company

United States Lines Company

All these lines provide regular liner service in connection with their established trade routes with modern ships. Service reasons are important in using this type of carrier.

Various cargo preference laws (and related resolutions, policies, and rulings) are also observed, and should be observed, in tonnage assignments to American flag operators. Foreign aid, loans to foreign governments for capital improvement projects, the military, and others are particularly involved in these preferences. Such laws have been a great boon to the American-flag operators, both liner and tramp. Rates have been fixed at levels to enable the tramp operator to take full cargoes of certain kinds of commodities outward and to return home without cargo when this has been necessary and no practical alternative was available. It has been stated that were it not for the cargo preference laws, the U.S. tramp fleet as it is now constituted could not exist. U.S. government-sponsored cargoes comprise very substantial percentages of the cargo carried by the tramp fleet.

The country-wide shippers' organization, The National Industrial Traffic League, has and has had for a number of years a standing resolution on its records outlining a clear policy of supporting an adequate American Merchant Marine and of urging American importers and exporters to utilize American-flag shipping for their ocean transportation. League policy further urges that its members endeavor to sell their products on a delivered basis, such as CIF or C & F, and to purchase products on an FOB or FAS basis in order that they retain the routing control of ocean transportation and thus support the American Merchant Marine to the maximum extent possible. (Details on "CIF" and the other terms appear later).

Cargo vessels of certain special types that are conventional as well as unconventional could well be discussed in this or the following section. The most important of these are the bulk carriers. Petroleum, grain, ores, and other materials are hauled by them with a new entry in the field being liquefied natural gas. Volumes transported are substantial. In 1970 these aggregated 415 million tons, or more than 85% of the U.S. import-export tonnage movement. Some vessels may be, and are, used interchangeably in grain, oil, and other services. Benefits under the 1970 Merchant Marine Act, discussed later, are applicable to them, and new ships planned for construction include certain OBO's for ore/bulk/oil service. Bulk cargo fleet developments are as dramatic, progressive, and on the high technology side as those for other vessels. The use of these ships is such that often particular, special attention is given them by industry through separate marine departments.

Utilization of Up-Dated Shipping Modes

The conventional "breakbulk" method of shipping, described in the previous section, has dominated the ocean shipping scene for hundreds of years. Many trades are still predominantly breakbulk routes and breakbulk ships continue operations in most trading areas.

The last decade, however, witnessed essential changes in shipping methods which provide a new range of shipping options for ocean transportation. Indeed this climate of change is continuing into the 1970s. In this section, we briefly review some of these new services from which a merchant firm can select the shipping option most advantageous to his own needs. Actually, a single shipper may advantageously use more than one mode on different trade routes or even on the same trade route. At the very least, the variety of these new options places a burden on the industrial traffic department to keep abreast of the rapid changes and refinements, and to weigh the various modes so as to select the most advantageous to his needs of the moment.

■ *Containerization*—By almost any standard of measurement, the wide-spread use of containers throughout many world trade routes was the most dramatic change in international shipping during the 1960s. This shipping mode shows continued growth and is projected by most analysts to continue expansion for years to come. It is already the dominant shipping method on some trade routes, such as, for example, U.S. North Atlantic and Europe. Containerization is essentially the consolidating of multiple shipper packages into standardized and specially constructed shipping units, which are basically like truck-trailers without wheels. Although there were experiments in ocean containerization prior to the 1960's, the wide-spread use of this shipping mode began within the last 10 years. There continues to be international efforts towards standardizing container units used in world trade. Physically, the field is dominated by units 20 and 40 feet in length and 8 feet wide. Most such containers are either 8 or 8'6" high. Certain steamship operators do provide their own containers in different lengths of 24, 27 and 35 feet. In addition to the standard containers, some operators make available specialty containers, which include such features as open tops, bulk liquid tanks, refrigeration and there are even half height containers measuring 40 feet long by 4 feet high. There is continuing investigation which may ultimately lead to other specialty types.

Concurrent with the large scale introduction of containers and specially adapted container carrying ships was the systems concept, usually described as intermodalism. In its most basic sense, this concept encourages the loading of cargo into the container at the originating manufacturing or processing plant, thence proceeding undisturbed until unstuffing at final destination. The effort is to provide a system where the standard container units move with physical, regulatory and economic efficiency by the various connecting modes of transportation. This could involve rail, truck or perhaps barge movement of the container to a coastal port where it is retained until it is loaded aboard ship. The procedure is reversed at the destination port with the container ultimately arriving for unstuffing at the consignee's facilities.

The degree of available container service does vary significantly from trade to trade. Service between some areas, such as the United States and Europe, certain ports of the Far East and, to a degree, the Mediterranean have experienced rapid growth of containerization whereas other trade routes have moved more slowly in implementing this concept. Traffic rules vary significantly from trade to trade and often times between operators in the same trade. Generally speaking, ocean carriers offer tariff provisions which cover containers owned or rented by the carrier and with the tariff rules based on classifications of pier to pier, house to house, pier to house or house to pier rates and terms. Each classification often includes minimum revenue requirements per container and frequently includes a demurrage scale of charges after a designated free time period for containers which move to an originating plant or similar location for loading by the shipper. Similar provisions for demurrage cover delivery and unstuffing locations.

In arranging container transportation the desires of the consignee as well as possible physical limitations of his unstuffing capabilities must be determined in advance if delays and extraordinary expenses are to be avoided. Various plans by railroads including COFC and TOFC as well as over the road restrictions must be explored so as to avoid possible penalties. In over the road movements there are significant variances from state to state and from region to region in this country, and limitations exist overseas as well. The field of containerization is a constantly changing one and regulations which are applicable today may well be modified within a short period of time, both here and abroad. In addition to the basic determination of whether or not containerization is best option, modern traffic executives are faced with determining precisely what size and type of container is most advantageous as well as familiarizing themselves with possible variances between operators on such matters as costs, container rules and physical characteristics of the containers themselves.

Although containerization is now in wide-spread use, the industrial traffic manager must continue to be aware of potential difficulties which can cause unexpected delay or expense. Typical examples include varying Customs' requirements where the question of acceptance of shippers' seals and the seals of customs authorities in other countries need to be determined. Documentation still remains time consuming in many trades and, with the rapid speed increases of many new container ships, this feature of document transmission deserves close attention to avoid delivery delays at destination. The question of packaging individual pieces within a container requires examination by shippers as the needs of such packaging may vary significantly from requirements on breakbulk ships. The shipper must balance the obvious desire to minimize packaging costs with the need for cargo to arrive at destination in undamaged condition. The loading of cargo into containers at plants and other interior locations has created a whole new set of potential problems. People unfamiliar with the rigors of ocean transportation sometimes tend to load cargo into containers in the same way that they load domestic boxcars and trucks, often with expensive results at overseas destination. Ocean carriers wish to avoid damage in transit and most such companies will provide guidance on such matters as packing and shipper planning of stowage in containers.

This brief review is far from all inclusive but is intended to provide insight into a whole new set of potential problem areas which must be considered in order to maximize the use of containerization with satisfactory results. The containerization field is rapidly growing and is undergoing constant change. It warrants close attention by general cargo shippers and industrial traffic management.

Substantial, additional specifics on this subject and its various intermodal aspects (water, rail, highway, and air) are in "Container Services of the Atlantic" (2nd ed., 1970, 396 pgs.) by John R. Immer, published by Work Saving International, 1638 19th St. NW, Washington, D.C. 20009.

■ *Barge-Carrying Ships*—A shipping mode which made its operational debut as recently as 1969 is constituted by the barge carriers. While there was just one operator in 1969, rapid growth of this shipping method in the 1970s seems likely as there are well over 20 of these ships already operating or under contract for construction. The fleet of supporting barges in the

U.S.-foreign trade already numbers over 1,000, with additional ones under construction.

In simplified terms, these systems are based upon the concept of moving specially designed barges or lighters to cargo loading and discharging locations rather than a complete large ocean going freighter. These barges will be collected at designated areas for subsequent loading aboard large ocean going ships for the deep sea passage.

To date, two distinct such systems are in operation. The LASH (lighter aboard ship) type predominates in numbers and already offers service from the Atlantic, Gulf and Pacific coasts on various trades. One operator has introduced its own barge carrying concept, named SEABEE (sea barge). These systems are all still so new that there continues to be variation between the different operators as to service.

LASH-España, of Prudential Grace Lines

Lykes SEABEE maiden voyage.

The SEABEE system combines breakbulk shipping and containers.

SEABEE vessel with hatch covers in place. Sixteen 40 foot containers may be loaded over each loaded barge.

All the LASH barges have standardized exterior dimensions with their overall length being 61'6" with width of 31'2". They each contain a space capacity of approximately 19,900 cubic feet and a maximum weight capacity of approximately 370 long tons. There is some variance between operators as to interior characteristics and hatch covers types. The SEABEE standard barges have exterior dimensions of 97.5 feet long and 35 feet wide. Interior (bale) cubic capacity is 39,100 cubic feet and maximum weight load capacity, 833 long tons. Above is shown a new SEABEE vessel now in service. To be noted in particular are its size and the various facilities it provides.

To date, LASH ships in operation are either full barge types where approximately 80 barges are carried for full load

SEABEE vessel discharging barges at Bremerhaven

or a combination of barge and cellular containerization. In this latter type, a portion of the ship is devoted to cellular container stowage to supplement 40/50 barges which provide breakbulk space. The SEABEE ships are all identical and carry a maximum 38 standard barges, with containerization being provided by 20, 30 and 40 foot containers inside of barges as well as on container beams on top of barges and, possibly in the future, on a portion of the upper deck.

Proponents of these systems advocate that barge-carriers represent a shipping system which combines modern container service with an up-dated breakbulk capability. Regardless of the mechanical means used, virtually every barge ship operator includes a provision for container carriage. The barges represent mobile breakbulk cargo holds which can be distributed to various ports and in some cases inland loading locations for loading or discharge of breakbulk shipments. Such operations also permit a reduced number of ports of call for the large ocean going barge carriers and provide opportunities for faster voyages and more accurate long range scheduling.

There are significant variances in existing tariffs for these services. Some operators provide barge ship service primarily from coastal port to coastal port, whereas others, with access to interior waterways, include tariff provisions for loading cargo to barges at interior river ports. Some tariffs provide single commodity rates in the following four categories: coastal port to coastal port, inland point to coastal port, inland point to inland point and coastal port to inland point. Some operators also advocate tariff incentive reductions when full or multiple barge load size shipments are made. Because this method of operation remains very new, it may be expected that there will be continued differences. These differences should lessen as operators and industrial traffic managers have opportunities to work out shipping programs which can use their full potentials. Ultimately there should be a wide variety of breakbulk and container form shipping possibilities, loading and unloading locations, and other innovations.

As in the case of pure containerization, barge ships present a whole new set of potential problem areas which suggest intensive investigations by traffic departments. Where transportation is negotiated in barge load lots slight modification of package size or pallet loads might provide a significant increase in the tonnage shipped in a single barge. There are presently considerable differences in interior cargo hold characteristics within individual barges. Some provide more locations to secure cargo than others. The size of hatch openings vary which can be a factor in long length cargo. Sizes range from roughly 44 to 84 feet. Under hatch heights also vary. Customs' regulations and cargo clearances must be factors, also, for attention. There have been existing cases where overall through transportation economies are achieved by negotiating free in, or free out, or FIO terms. Special dock discharge or loading within a specific port might represent a savings feature. These barge ship operators usually issue bill of lading coverage from point cargo is loaded to a barge to the point it is discharged from the barge.

In summary, barge-ships are increasing in number and are simultaneously presenting a whole new set of shipping possibilities at the same time that pure containerization is expanding. The opportunity of designing a specific traffic program which could include packaging options and transportation programmed to production and sales as well as inland loading and discharging presents the traffic department with a greater number of variables than ever before. This field is one which requires continuous up-date to determine the full potential of economies and benefits.

■ *Other Shipping Methods*—In addition to full breakbulk ships, container ships, and the barge carriers there are other shipping methods that are perhaps not as wide-spread but are none the less important in certain trades. The roll on/roll off concept has shown growth in recent years. This is especially true in relatively short voyage trades such as to and from the Caribbean area and mainland United States. Limited service between the U.S. and Europe is also available, however, and service from the west coast to the Orient is planned. RO-RO ships range from relatively small vessels to very large ships providing up to over 150,000 square feet on which to park wheeled vehicles. This type service is based on ships providing flat decks with connecting ramps so that wheeled vehicles and trucks can be delivered directly on board and conversely connecting cabs or the vehicles themselves driven off the ship at destination ports. Special facilities such as refrigeration connections are generally provided and these services run on a regular schedule between specific ports.

Another method of transporting general cargo which has shown recent growth are the tug-barge systems which are distinct from the barge carrying ship approach. Tug-barge systems provide large ocean going enclosed barges which, after leaving harbor waters, are towed on a hauser by sea-going tugs. Some of these huge barges stress palletization of cargo and provide regularly scheduled service on relatively short hauls. At present, there is no such scheduled service on the long trans-Atlantic or trans-Pacific trades and the United States mainland. They are currently going principally to off shore states such as Hawaii and Alaska as well as to Puerto Rico and the surrounding areas. There are movements across the ocean by sea-going tugs where specialty units such as oil rigs are transported, but these are individually negotiated and do not offer a regular liner type service. The tug-barge concept is undergoing a continuing investigation by both industry and government and some proponents believe that such new systems may provide transocean service in the future.

A large percentage of available service from virtually every United States' coast involves ship operations combining the various shipping modes. For example, there are an increasing number of former breakbulk ships that are being lengthened by the addition of a center section devoted to containerization, thereby providing the shipper with both breakbulk space and container space on the same sailing. Roll on/roll off capability has been combined with containerization so that wheeled vehicles as well as regular containers can be shipped. This is not yet wide-spread but is available to a limited degree. We have already mentioned how the barge carriers combine container carriage with breakbulk capability. This is done in a large measure through the use of mobile cargo holds within the barges.

The availability of these many types of service varies significantly from trade to trade and they are not all available from every United States' coast or in every foreign trade area. Each of them, however, points up and suggests the wide and growing range of shipping options as well as the constantly changing nature of ocean transportation resulting from continuing innovations in this field. Never before have traffic executives had as many different means for moving goods to foreign destinations by water. This variety of service demands constant attention and investigation for the purpose of selecting the best transportation means that are available, or can be made available, to or from each area. Specifics as to costs, service, savings, availability, and so on for individual movements must of necessity be worked out between transportation people and the shipping company. Opportunities for worthwhile results are excellent.

Bills of Lading and Inland Practices and Costs

Bills of lading used in foreign commerce have as their basic document the ocean bill of lading form, the provisions of which appear in detail in Appendix 2. Complementary to the ocean form are the "through export" forms, which have considerable in their favor but have limited territorial and carrier use, and the domestic forms, which are commonly used in the movement of goods between inland points and the ports. These have variances and related forms in the same categories (dock receipts and so on); all have particular uses.

Closely related to the bill of lading subject are the important practices, freight rate structures, port charges, and other aspects of the inland costs. These are particularly involved in exports, but several features are also of concern to import activities. They are reviewed later in this section. Rates, costs, and the like which stem from the ocean transportation proper and the conference methods of establishing those charges are reviewed in this chapter, in the next section.

■ *Ocean Bills of Lading*—Ocean bills of lading have considerable in common with their domestic counterparts. A notable exception is that in the ocean form the carrier's liability to a shipper for any loss and damage to his shipment is not as extensive. Ways in which these liabilities differ and the reasons for the differences are discussed in more detail later in the section in this chapter on Insurance and Claims. Under applicable law, however, both the ocean and the domestic forms are the contracts between carriers and shippers and the provisions therein are binding as to them. The ocean form, like the domestic form, is to be read and used with this in mind.

The typical provisions of the ocean form outlined in Appendix 2 become bills of lading proper, as shown in the following illustration, when they are processed by the carrier. "Short" form ocean bills of lading along lines similar to the "short" forms used in domestic trade are common, and the illustration used is a "short" form. All clauses and conditions of the carrier's regular ocean form are deemed a part of the short form contract and it is so stated therein. All steamship companies

Form No. 1190	Lykes Continent & United Kingdom Bill of Lading	Lykes Lines

SHIPPER	DOCUMENT NO.
ABC PAPER SALES INTERNATIONAL, CORP. 1 CANAL BLVD NEW ORLEANS, LA.	EXPORT REFERENCES — EXPORT DEC. NO.

CONSIGNED TO ORDER OF	FORWARDING AGENT — REFERENCES — FMC NO.
JJJ PAPER SALES LTD. ROTTERDAM	BOSWELL FORWARDING CO. 3-3567
	POINT AND COUNTRY OF ORIGIN

ADDRESS ARRIVAL NOTICE TO	DOMESTIC ROUTING — DELIVERING CARRIER — CAR NUMBER-REFERENCE
SAME	THE SCOPE OF THE VOYAGE IS BETWEEN U. S. GULF PORTS AND UNITED KINGDOM AND NORTH EUROPE PORTS INCLUDING SCANDINAVIAN AND BALTIC PORTS, AND VICE-VERSA, IN ANY ORDER, AND WITH LIBERTY DESCRIBED IN CLAUSE 3 HEREOF. THE CARRIER IN ADDITION HAVING THE LIBERTY OF LOADING AND DISCHARGING AT ANY PORT OR PORTS IN OR OUT OF GEOGRAPHICAL OR CUSTOMARY OR ADVERTISED ROUTE. BACKWARD OR FORWARD OR ANY COMBINATION THEREOF. A.B.C. TRUCKING CO. TO HENRY CLAY AVE WHARF
	ON BOARD (Without liability to Carrier, see Clause 17 hereof)

BARGE	SHIP	VOY.	PORT OF LOADING	BARGE LIFT-ON POINT (where Barge placed aboard Ship)	BARGE LIFT-OFF POINT (where Barge removed from Ship)
	DOCTOR LYKES		NEW ORLEANS	NEW ORLEANS	ROTTERDAM

PORT OF DISCHARGE	FOR TRANSSHIPMENT TO (See Clause 12 hereof)	ONWARD INLAND ROUTING
ROTTERDAM		

		PARTICULARS FURNISHED BY SHIPPER		
MARKS AND NUMBERS	NO. OF PKGS.	DESCRIPTION OF PACKAGES AND GOODS	GROSS WEIGHT	MEASUREMENT
JJJ PSLTD NO 1/5000 MADE IN USA	5000 BALES	**ON BOARD** OCT 10 1972 LYKES BROS. STEAMSHIP CO., INC. WOODPULP UNDER DECK STOWAGE REQUIRED	2,800,321#	

Ocean Bill Of Lading Form. Basic information and ways in which it should be treated appear on face. Spacing and location of data are in accordance with international approved format. Provisions on reverse side (not shown) are standard plus additional clauses to cover where up-dated shipping methods are used.

today use practically the same ocean bill of lading, and such documents may be either a straight (non-negotiable) or an order (negotiable) form.

A bill of lading set should contain five or more copies (sometimes up to 25 or more copies) to satisfy all the various interests desiring a copy. The first three copies are such that generally any one of the three may be used to claim freight at destination. An advantage of the "short" form is the ability to

---

ORIGINAL

FREIGHT PREPAID

"UNITED STATES LAW PROHIBITS DISPOSITION OF THESE COMMODITIES TO THE SOVIET BLOC, COMMUNIST CHINA, NORTH KOREA, MACAO, HONG KONG, SOUTHERN RHODESIA OR COMMUNIST CONTROLLED AREAS OF VIET NAM AND CUBA UNLESS OTHERWISE AUTHORIZED BY THE UNITED STATES."

ISSUED UNDER AGREEMENT WITH THE LIVERPOOL BILL OF LADING CONFERENCE COMMITTEE WITH RESPECT TO SHIPMENT OF COTTON.

RECEIVED from the shipper herein named, the goods or packages said to contain goods, in apparent good order and condition, except as otherwise noted herein, and except where the goods or packages have been loaded in a container or SEABEE BARGE by shipper, in which case condition, nature and description are unknown, to be transported, subject to all the terms of this Bill of Lading, to the port of discharge, and there to be delivered or transshipped as provided herein. With regard to the Particulars Furnished by Shipper above, the Carrier is not concluded as to the correctness of such particulars.

In any situation whatsover, including, but not limited to, the goods being shut out, Carrier has the right, in its sole discretion, to carry the goods in any SEABEE or non-SEABEE SHIP, or in any SEABEE BARGE, always subject to this Bill of Lading, irrespective of any specific ship or barge named herein as carrying vessel. **THE TERMS AND CONDITIONS OF THIS BILL OF LADING ARE CONTINUED ON THE REVERSE HEREOF.**

IN ACCEPTING THIS BILL OF LADING, any local customs or privileges to the contrary notwithstanding, the shipper, consignee and owner of the goods agree to be bound by all of its stipulations, exceptions, and conditions, whether written, printed or stamped on the front or back hereof, as fully as if they were all signed by said shipper, consignee and owner of the goods.

FREIGHT AND CHARGES

CUBIC	POUNDS	RATE AND TERMS	FREIGHT CHARGES	
			$	
FREIGHT PREPAID — TO COLLECT			TOTAL	$

IN WITNESS WHEREOF, there have been executed __3__ Bills of Lading exclusive of non-negotiable copies, all of the same tenor and date, one of which being accomplished, the others to stand void.

Dated at New Orleans   Oct   10   1972
                            MONTH DAY YEAR

LYKES BROS. STEAMSHIP CO., INC.

BY _____

CONTRACT NO.	B/L NUMBER
	7

prepare the bill of lading in master setups along with dock receipts, the shipper's export declaration, and other documents.

Master standard formats for documents in foreign trade have had varying uses in recent years and have been helpful in simplifying and keeping correct the preparation of the paperwork involved. They have been helpful, also, in the standardization of forms and, along with other factors, in the elimination of some of them. Additional use of formats is planned. Ideally, the format starts with the duplicator master and includes the shipper's export declaration, drawback application, ocean bill of lading, delivery instructions, dock receipt, certificate of origin, and insurance certificate, as well as other specialized documents that can be integrated into the package such as invoices, delivery orders, forwarder's waybills, arrival notices, acknowledgments, advance shipping notice, etc. The single typing and checking operation reduces the chance of error and, of course, as many copies as are needed can be made.

Carriers' liability for loss, damage, and other related features of the transportation they undertake is heavily influenced by legislation as well as by the clauses in their bills of lading. As mentioned in the section on Insurance and Claims, the Harter and the Carriage-of-Goods-by-Sea Acts are the two important statutes in this regard. The summaries of these laws which appear there should be referred to in this connection. Also, not to be overlooked are such clauses as number 17 in the ocean bill of lading form, purporting to limit liability to $500 per package unless a higher value is declared, and so on. Most companies insure their shipments and feel it is good business to do so. A pertinent reason for doing this is the general situation concerning ocean carrier liability.

Steamship companies do not surrender executed export ocean bills of lading to shippers or their agents until all freight charges due the steamship company have been paid, unless special credit arrangements (due bill privileges) have been established.

Due bill privileges are extended to shippers with satisfactory credit ratings. The shipper or his agent (freight forwarder) signs a statement guaranteeing payment of the freight charges within a specified time (usually from five to seven days) and as a result receives signed bills of lading from the carrier. In many cases the shipper requires the negotiated bill of lading to obtain payment from the bank for the goods and prepaid transportation. Thus the due bill privilege enables the shipper to get his money before paying the carrier. Proposals within steamship conferences to curtail or eliminate due bill privileges have been considered from time to time.

In connection with inbound shipments it is customary to surrender the bill of lading and remit all freight charges due prior to taking delivery of the shipment at the steamship pier. In some cases receivers can obtain a Bank Guarantee in lieu of a negotiable bill of lading from their bank whereby the bank guarantees ownership of the goods to the steamship company which then releases the freight when freight charges have been paid. Importers should "follow-up" with their bank and cancel the guarantee once the bill of lading has been delivered and freight paid; otherwise the bank has it standing as a "debit" against the importer.

Ocean bills of lading are customarily issued as either "received for shipment" or "on board." The "received for shipment" bill of lading, which is used most frequently, means the freight has been received by the steamship company and is under its custody on the dock. It does not guarantee, of course, that the freight will be loaded on any particular steamer. The "on board" bill of lading is not signed and surrendered until the merchandise is loaded on board the steamer. Steamship companies with the cargo on the dock may receipt bills of lading with an on board certificate in advance of actually loading to the ship—but without a certification date. The date is added later, when the freight is in the ship. It is important, therefore, to request an on-board bill of lading with a date certification.

A so-called frustrated bill of lading covers a shipment that cannot go through to its indicated destination because of various changed conditions making delivery or acceptance virtually impossible (strikes, riots, war, disaster, etc.) so shipment is diverted for delivery to another port at which point the steamship company considers it has fulfilled its obligation.

Letters of indemnity are used when a shipper, because of terms in the letter of credit or for other reasons, requires a clean bill of lading (no exceptions such as mars and scratches, dented drums, etc). In appropriate cases a clean bill of lading will be issued in return for a signed letter of indemnity guaranteeing to protect the carrier against claim liability on whatever exceptions are noted by the carrier at the time the cargo is delivered to his care. A specimen letter utilized in these connections follows as the next illustration. The propriety of these indemnity letters has been questioned, but their use is widespread and at this point it would seem that they are fairly entrenched in foreign trade activities.

```
Lykes Bros. Steamship Co., Inc.                          New Orleans, Louisiana
Commerce Building
New Orleans 12, Louisiana
                                                           July 15, 1972
                                      S.S.          GEORGE MC CALL

In consideration of your omitting the clause(s), I.E.: Bale #2 torn and mended Bales #3
                                       and 10 - wire straps broken

From Bill of Lading No. 7

Covering shipment of    10 bales Cotton Piece Goods

Marked:    FF - Manila - #1/10

Shipped by:    Franklin Fabrics Company, Inc.

Loaded on board the S.S.    GEORGE MC CALL

Port of Discharge from the Ship:    Manila, P.I.

Consigned to:    Order

and thereby handing us clean documents, we and/or principals and/or others concerned, hereby
undertake and agree to hold the Line, Master, Owners and Agents perfectly harmless and fully
indemnified against all consequences, loss, damage and expense due to the aforementioned
clauses being omitted from bill of lading, and further, if any claims are presented, we will
adjust them directly with claimants relieving you entirely and in case of any payment made,
or expense incurred by you, we will reimburse you in full. Further, the consignees are
being advised fully as to the terms of this agreement.

                                     Franklin Fabrics Company, Inc.
                                              (Shipper)


                          Per:
                                   James Franklin, Jr.
```

Letter of Indemnity

■ *The Through Export Bill of Lading*—The uniform through export or overland bill of lading (either "straight" or "order") is a combination of the domestic rail and the ocean bills of lading. It was designed as a convenience to inland shippers. It is not the general practice to use through export bills of lading on LCL shipments.

The through export bill of lading (hereinafter referred to as the "through bill of lading") covers the shipment from point of inland origin to the foreign destination port. It contains all the rules and regulations of the domestic bill of lading and the ocean bill of lading. It contains full details as to the name of the steamship line beyond the port of exit, package numbers and markings, destination port, etc. The shipper pays the railroad both the rail and ocean charges and subsequently the railroad pays the ocean freight charges to the steamship line.

Under the through bill of lading the shipper does not receive a separate ocean bill of lading since both the domestic and ocean contracts are included in the one through bill of lading. The through bill of lading is not issued for all foreign shipments. Applicable tariff circular provisions restrict the application of the through bill of lading to only those countries designated in the circular. Neither is the through bill of lading applicable to destinations beyond the foreign port. In other words it can be used only to cover transportation from a United States inland shipping point to any foreign port in a country listed in the tariff circular as one of the countries to which through bills of lading are applicable. Further, the use of these bills of lading is restricted as to U.S. inland origins. Generally speaking they are used in the West, that is, from the States of North and South Dakota, Nebraska, Colorado, New Mexico and states west thereof; and from points in Canada east of the Saskatchewan-Manitoba boundary line.

The through bill of lading is not executed at the inland origin point until the local railroad foreign freight agent has received all necessary documents such as a consular invoice, export license, import license, shipper's export declaration, steamship permit or booking number, etc. Since the shipper works with the railroad's foreign freight agent in accumulating these documents, the use of the through bill of lading may help to eliminate the necessity of employing the services of others to assist with the shipments. Thus, use of the through bill of lading may result in reducing the over-all cost of exporting.

Another advantage of through export bills of lading is not having to pay handling, wharfage, and other port accessorial charges. These are subject to absorptions (all or in part) by the rail and steamship carriers and depend on current tariff provisions. Also, certain selected commodities moving under through bill of lading are subject to published reduced rates which are the result of collaboration by both the rail and steamship carriers.

The through bill of lading is not used universally because some shippers, receivers and banks object to it since, under it, there is no guarantee that a shipment will "clear" on a certain steamer. The shipper has a tendency to relax once the through bill of lading is signed by the railroad, whereas when separate domestic and ocean bills of lading are employed, the shipper or his agent must follow through and procure the ocean bill of lading thus exerting more pressure to get the shipment abroad the first available steamer.

Foreign importers may insist on an on-board ocean bill of lading which is absolute evidence that the shipment is en route on a specified steamer. It is for this reason that a bank may refuse to make payment under a letter of credit when through bills of lading are used. This is because the letter of credit may specify that ocean bills of lading must be dated and signed prior to the expiration date on the letter of credit. Thus the date on the through bill of lading is of no value since it is the date from the inland shipping point, not from the port of exit. Also, it is sometimes impossible to use the through bill of lading because the ocean rate must be known before ocean freight charges can be prepaid, and when the rate is optional, weight or measurement, it is not always possible to determine the measurement accurately. This is because in most instances the steamship company insists on measuring the cargo when received at its dock.

If, after a through rail bill of lading has been signed, it develops that a letter of credit or other requirements would be better served if the through lading were not used, there is no difficulty in having it exchanged for a local rail lading and an ocean bill of lading (certified on board, if needed).

The through bill of lading's greatest application is via Western rail carriers through Pacific ports where it started and where some inland rail export rates (lower than the domestic rates) will not apply unless a through bill of lading is used. Many rail shipments via Pacific ports to Hawaii and other Far East points are on through bills of lading. Freight forwarders and household goods carriers, in particular, find it useful.

The document simplification aspects of through bills of lading are truly worthwhile, and further developments along those lines are certainly in order. At this time, however, practically all motor common carrier moves between inland points and ports are on domestic bills of lading and the same is true of rail shipments, except in the West. Domestic bills of lading are discussed in Chapter 4, and the data there are applicable in general to those documents.

■ *Inland Practices and Costs*—As heretofore indicated, the discussion in this subsection is intended to be along broad lines. Such discussion includes industry practices, rates, routings, port charges, and the many other features of these inland moves which may be directly and indirectly involved in costs to a shipper in foreign trade.

A worthwhile savings area in this connection can be that certain freight rates on export shipments are lower than for the same material moving domestically. The practice to publish rail rates that are lower on export or import shipments than on domestic shipments is general throughout all territories. These rates are subject to I.C.C. jurisdiction and are to be found in appropriate carrier tariff publications.

Routing export freight to a port involves several factors if it is to be done successfully. Although it is risky to release ship-

ments for the rail move until the freight has been booked or
accepted for shipment by the steamship company, some inland
shippers will do so anyway in order to have their freight somewhere near the port when the requested steamer space is secured. This is a gamble that is made on the shipper's confidence
in being able to secure the space. Steamer space is booked by
either the shipper or its forwarder. This is accomplished by
negotiating a steamship freight booking contract, which shows
a contract number and is a confirmation of the booking of the
specified cargo on a named ship at a departure time to a particular destination. It may show the freight rate or merely state
"at a rate applicable at time of shipment". The "contract" is
issued upon the express condition that all clauses and conditions
of the carrier's ocean bill of lading are deemed to be part of the
"contract." If a freight booking contract is not issued by the
steamship company involved, then it is well to confirm the
booking by letter.

Routing items for special consideration are the selection of
a carrier or carriers participating in tariffs naming the lowest
inland rate when all other factors are equal. For consideration
also is the selection of the fastest service since it is best to be
sure the freight is at the port in time to make the desired
steamship sailing date. Where rail rates are involved, even
though the rates of competing railroads may include delivery
to the vessel's loading terminal, it is well to route into the port
via the railroad serving the pier where the steamer is loading.
Where terminals are served by a belt railway any carrier may
be properly specified in almost all cases.

Ownership and operation of port facilities may be important on occasion. At one time many of the piers at the major
ports were owned and operated by the railroads. In recent
years railroad operations of piers has decreased. Piers and the
like have come to be owned more by port authorities, municipalities, and other government agencies. Such facilities may
also be operated by them or may be leased for operation and
use to terminal operators or steamship companies. Rail service
via belt railways exists in some cases. If these features come to

be important to an industrial company they should, of course, be checked out on an individual basis.

The final selection and designation of a port of export or import, the steamship company, and the inland hauler for a particular movement should be made on the basis of both service and total cost. This involves much more than selecting a port because it is the nearest in distance to the inland shipping or destination point, and more than selecting a port where the ocean freight plus the inland freight are lowest. Distance and freight charge elements are important and are to be reckoned with in these matters.

Along with these, however, port facilities for handling cargo, frequency of sailings, speed in deliveries, and other features may be involved and should be weighed into port selections and inland carrier-steamer tonnage assignments. Interest costs and costs of inventory may well be important also to these calculations. Total costs, giving effect to all elements, are to be sought and made the basic for the steps taken.

Each company will have its own set of facts that are controlling in these matters. An example would be a Chicago-based exporter having sales in South Africa with lower inland rates from his plant to New Orleans than to any of the Atlantic ports. Assuming the ocean rates from New Orleans to be the same as from Atlantic ports to South Africa and assuming all other features (frequency of sailings and so on) ex New Orleans to be on a par with Atlantic ports, the selection should, of course, be New Orleans. On the other hand, a paucity of sailings with indirect, slow service ex New Orleans to the destination port versus an excellent picture as to these from another port could well swing the selection to the latter.

Of importance also at times to inland costs and to competitive conditions are port "differentials" which result in more favorable rate structures for certain ports and certain areas. Such differentials might result in, say, certain freight rates from and to port B being 3 cents per hundred pounds over port A, port C being 3 cents over port B, and so on. Mixed blessings are not uncommon in rate structures of this kind. In the past they have been somewhat arbitrary, quite rigid and not easily changed. Freight absorptions may be necessary to get business when the differentials are against an industrial company. When they are favorable they are, of course, to be used and, if possible, their use should be extended.

Most steamship companies issue a delivery or shipping permit before freight can be delivered to the dock. This is to provide the steamship company with advance information necessary to formulate a plan for loading the ship and to protect against more freight being delivered than can be stowed into the ship or held conveniently on the pier. The shipping permit usually is not requested from the steamship line until the freight actually arrives at destination. The shipper or its freight forwarder domiciled at the port of exit arranges for this permit.

Inland carriers' "shipside rates," which were quite prevalent at one time, have been discontinued at eastern, south Atlantic, and Gulf ports. Under these rates the inland carriers, generally speaking, would absorb the cost of placing the cargo at, or removing it from, the vessel's terminal facilities.

When delivering freight to the dock the shipper presents the delivery order plus a dock receipt. The dock receipt is a steamship company form, copies of which are made available to shippers (or their agents) so they can be prepared in advance (usually in master format—see bill of lading comments) thus avoiding delay at the piers. The dock receipt controls the ownership of the goods until the ocean bill of lading is issued. All pertinent shipping information must be included in the dock receipt, which is prepared in at least quadruplicate so that the shipper, the freight forwarder, the dock forces, and the steamship company's office can each have a copy.

After the cargo is delivered to the steamship pier, the steamship company computes the ocean freight charges and inserts the detailed freight charges on the ocean bill of lading, which usually has been delivered to the steamship company in the interim by the shipper or his agent along with all other required documents. Practically all export shipments are sent prepaid as a general practice. The steamship company will not release a signed ocean bill of lading until total charges have been paid or credit has been arranged.

Shipments from inland points transported to the port of exit should preferably be consigned to the ocean carrier in care of the consignor or its forwarder handling clearances, etc. The consignor's agent will arrange for delivery to the proper pier for loading to a specified steamer.

Carload shipments may at times be routed with the specification "Free Lighterage For Export," to certain ports. This means that on other than short hauls the railroad rate will include unloading the freight from the car into a lighter or barge and towing the barge alongside the steamer from which the freight will be loaded directly to the steamer with ship's tackle or transferred to the pier for subsequent loading to the ship.

LCL or LTL shipments can be routed via motor carrier, freight forwarder, possibly rail, and other means, depending on the circumstances. If an LCL shipment is to be handled at the port by a domestic freight forwarder that also renders a foreign freight forwarder service and has service from the inland point to the port, the shipment should be routed via that forwarder. At some ports motor carrier, freight forwarder, and related rates are sometimes subject to additive charges when shipments move to piers.

■ *Imports*—Thus far the discussion under inland costs has referred importantly to outbound or export shipments. The comments made also apply in general to inbound or import shipments.

Carriers hauling freight from piers frequently are "bonded carriers." They have given a bond to the U.S. Treasury Department which permits them to transport import freight prior to the time it has been released by customs. The freight is "in bond," which means that it is still in the possession of the U.S.; the carrier will not deliver it to the inland receiver except upon an "order" or "release" issue by the collector of customs. This is done as a convenience to importers and to avoid congestion at seaports; it is only possible when the shipment is destined to a city where there is a customs office. Thus the shipment is "in bond" to whatever destination the local customs office releases it. Carriers transporting goods "in bond" to "interior ports of entry" are required to prepare a simplified form of entry referred to as an "I.T." (immediate transportation entry). This form permits immediate transportation of the shipment to the "interior port of entry."

Bonded warehouses are those which give bonds to the U.S. Treasury Department so that they can receive and hold import materials before they are finally released by customs. The privilege of warehousing goods for later payment of duties is obtained by executing an "entry for warehouse" form which is a simple document designed to remove the goods from the pier as quickly as possible.

A particular type of installation for landing, storing, and possibly reshipping goods with a minimum of customs control and without a customs bond are the foreign trade zones. These are essentially duty-free resting places from which imported material may be exported without going through customs. It is possible to mix U.S. with foreign goods in these zones and ship them on duty free. When foreign trade zones are available they are at or near other port facilities.

Costs in foreign trade are influenced at times by the "free" time allowances made at the ports. These are the periods during which cargo may occupy public wharves, warehouses, transit sheds, and other facilities without being subject to storage or demurrage charges. Such allowances permit time for accumulating cargo for outward vessels and for removing inward cargo preparatory to forwarding it to ultimate destination. Practices in this connection vary and are subject to change. Specific information on free time allowed on export and import cargo as well as wharfage, tollage, demurrage, and other charges in effect at the various U.S. ports may be found in the respective port and other appropriate tariffs. Illustrative of other tariffs that may be involved are the steamship tariffs which contain free time data on imports to New York.

Further highlights of the free time situation are that the rails generally provide five days' free time (Saturdays, Sundays and holidays excluded) on carload shipments at Atlantic, Gulf, Pacific and Great Lakes ports from the time of arrival at the port until unloaded at shipside or pier. After the free time freight may be held in cars at carrier's option. If it is not so held and the freight is not unloaded within the free time, the rail carriers start collecting demurrage charges for detention of the freight cars.

Port authority practices vary as to free time, a general feature being that more extended periods are often provided for exports than for imports. Special provisions on time allocations are made at times for relief and aid cargo, cargoes stored on open piers, and so on. Belt railways at some ports such as New Orleans may provide still further time periods. These ordinarily are not great, but on occasion they may be extended by average demurrage agreements. Motor carriers do not provide much if any free time. The barge lines, though having limited involvements, generally make free time provisions.

Steamship lines use either public or privately owned piers as terminals. In some locations they arrange for space either on a long-term lease or "preferentially" (they can have the use of the space as long as their cargo activity justifies such use). In either case they recognize the port rules and practices as to free time allowed cargo delivered to the pier before storage charges are assessed.

Ocean Freight Rates

Ocean freight rates, rules and regulations are published by the individual steamship lines and by freight conferences. Applicable laws require that they be made available to the public and this is done in tariff form, as is the case with rail and motor carriers on domestic traffic. Published ocean rates are filed with, and subject to the jurisdiction of, the Federal Maritime Commission (FMC). Important volumes of cargo movements are transported under the individual lines' tariffs. Rate structures are world-wide in character and often include contract and non-contract rates. These last named rates are on the unique side and are discussed in more detail later in this section.

The conference method of operating has been in existence many years and the conferences proper are voluntary associations of competing liner companies, usually flying the flags of many nations. Most of the steamship lines regularly serving United States foreign trade routes are members of those conferences that cover their trade routes. There are numerous conferences and they are located at various places throughout the world. Each conference is composed of member lines much as are the domestic freight rate bureaus with their rail and motor carrier members.

In various ways the conferences operate more informally and less rigidly than domestic bureaus. Meeting calls are not particularly formal and meetings are held more often as a general rule. Member lines are free to elect to withdraw from participation. The conferences operate under anti-trust exemptions along lines similar to those accorded the rail and truck lines domestically. The agreements under which they take collective action are subject to FMC approval.

The FMC publishes a list annually of conferences operating with its approval. This includes names, trade areas, member lines, and so on. Selected examples of the information which is shown follow:

FAR EAST CONFERENCE

Raymond J. Flynn, Chairman
11 Broadway, Room 760
New York, New York 10004

Trade From U.S. Atlantic and Gulf Ports

To   Japan, Okinawa, Korea, Taiwan, Siberia, Manchuria, China, Hong Kong, Vietnam, Philippines, Cambodia and Loas.

Dual rate contract in effect

Members
A. P. Moller Maersk
American Export Isbrandtsen Lines, Inc.
American President Lines, Ltd.
Barber Line A/S
Japan Line, Ltd.
Kawasaki Kisen Kaisha, Ltd.
Lykes Bros. Steamship Co., Inc.
Maritime Company of the Philippines
Nippon Yusen Kaisha
States Marine Lines
The Merchantile Marine, Ltd.
United States Lines
Yamashita Shinnihon Line

ATLANTIC & GULF/WEST COAST OF
SOUTH AMERICA CONFERENCE

C. D. Marshall, Chairman
11 Broadway
New York, New York 10004
    Direct or Transshipment

Trade From U.S. Atlantic and Gulf Ports

    To   West Coast of South America

Dual rate contract in effect

Members
    Chilean Line
    Colombiana International De Vapores
        Limitaoa
    Grancolumbiana Line
    Gulf and South American Steamship Co.,
        Inc.
    Hapag-Lloyd Magellan Service
    Peruvian State Line
    Prudential-Grace Lines, Inc.

PACIFIC WESTBOUND CONFERENCE

W. C. Galloway, Chairman
635 Sacramento Street
San Francisco, California 94111

Trade From U.S. Pacific Coast Ports excluding
    Alaska and Hawaii

    To   Far East Ports

Dual rate contract in effect

Members
    American Mail Line, Ltd.
    American President Lines, Ltd.
    Barber Line A/S
    Japan Line, Ltd.
    Kawasaki Kisen Kaisha, Ltd.

Knutsen Line—Joint Service
Maritime Company of the Philippines
Mexico Line
Mitsui O.S.K. Lines, Ltd
Moller-Maersk Line—J/S
Nippon Yusen Kaisha
Pacific Far East Line, Inc.
Scindia Steam Navigation Co. Ltd.
Sealand Service Inc.
Shipping Corporation of India
Showa Shipping Ltd.
States Marine Lines
States Steamship Company
United Philippine Lines
United States Lines, Inc.
Waterman Steamship Corp.
Weyerhauser Line
Yamashita Shinnihon Line

GULF/MEDITERRANEAN PORTS
CONFERENCE

John T. Crook, Chairman
Suite 927 Whitney Building
New Orleans, Louisiana 70130
    CABLE CONFERENCE
Except sulphur, grain and phosphate rock
in bulk

Trade From U.S. South Atlantic and Gulf Ports

    To   Mediterranean Ports including Mo-
       rocco

Dual rate contract in effect

Members
    Compania Maritima Del Nervion
    Concordia Line—Joint Service
    Deep Sea Shipping Company
    Dampskibs A/S Torm A/S
    Hellenic Lines, Ltd.
    Lykes Bros. Steamship Co., Inc.
    Nordana Line/Det Forende/
    States Marine Lines
    Trans-Mex Line
    Zim Israel Navigation Co., Ltd.

The conferences, in turn, may belong to associations with related interests; for example, the Atlantic & Gulf/West Coast of South America Conference (above) is a member of the Associated Latin America Freight Conferences (same address). Copies of the FMC publication "Approved Conference, Rate, and

Interconference Agreements of Steamship Lines in the Foreign Commerce of the United States," may be obtained from the U.S. Government Printing Office, Washington, D.C. 20402 (2-yr. subscr. $4.50)

Sources for ocean freight rates, rules, and regulations are: (1) The conferences, (2) the steamship companies, and (3) the tariff files of the FMC in Washington. As a practical matter, an industrial company having important foreign trade interests will wish this information direct from the publisher and will arrange to receive tariffs as issued. Subscription costs for these from the conferences are not substantial and will range roughly from $50 to $100 per year. Rate changes and other changes are forwarded to subscribers as they occur, and information concerning changes is thus kept current. Arrangements for individual lines' tariffs are made direct with the carriers involved. Watching services (generally in Washington, D.C.) for rates filed with the FMC are available. Illustrative of tariff publications and information shown therein are the title and rate pages (Far East Conference Tariff 25 and page 237, 17th revised) which follow. Their formats, the information shown, and other data have much in common with domestic rail and truck tariffs.

Class rates, as distinguished from commodity rates, have some stature in ocean freight rate structures in that some rates are published on class bases. The tonnage moving under them, however, is not as great in volume as that moving under commodity rates. Ocean carriers generally think in terms of commodity rates in arranging price schedules for their services. To an even greater degree than with some domestic rail rates, distance is not too controlling as a factor in many port-to-port freight charges. The value of the commodity, or the price at which it will be offered on the international market, generally receives important attention in the rate making processes. Many rates are published with expiration dates.

Steamship lines and conferences must file their tariffs with the FMC immediately on change. Increases in contract rates must be on file at least 60 to 90 days and increases in non-contract rates at least 30 days. Decreases become effective simply

2ND REVISED TITLE PAGE	
CANCELS: 1ST REV. TITLE PAGE	
EFFECTIVE: January 12, 1972	

Far East Conference

Freight Tariff No. 25   **F.M.C. No. 5**

(CANCELS FREIGHT TARIFF NO. 24 AND CORRECTIONS THERETO)

Correction No.	Cancels Corr. No.
2656	**2550**

NAMING CONTRACT AND NON-CONTRACT COMMODITY RATES

FROM: UNITED STATES ATLANTIC and GULF PORTS.

TO: JAPAN, OKINAWA, KOREA, TAIWAN (Formosa), HONG KONG, PHILIPPINE ISLANDS, VIET NAM, CAMBODIA, LAOS, and MAINLAND CHINA.

VIA: DIRECT CALL OR TRANSHIPMENT.

FOR RATES TO THE FOLLOWING GROUP PORTS REFER TO THE COMMODITY RATE PAGES PUBLISHED HEREIN

Group 1 Ports: NAGOYA, YOKOHAMA, KOBE, OSAKA, MANILA and HONG KONG

Group 2 Ports: CEBU and ILOILO

Group 3 Ports: TAKAO (Kaohsiung) and KEELUNG (Chilung)

Group 4 Port : SAIGON

REFER TO PAGES NOS. 1 and 2 HEREIN FOR THE NAMES OF THE PARTICIPATING CARRIERS.

FOR RATES TO OUTPORTS AND THEIR APPLICATION REFER TO THE OUTPORT SECTION OF THIS TARIFF.

RATES PUBLISHED HEREIN ARE SUBJECT TO THE RULES AND REGULATIONS OF THIS TARIFF UNLESS OTHERWISE INDICATED IN THE INDIVIDUAL COMMODITY ITEM.

Issued: January 15, 1969   Effective: January 15, 1969

GERALD J. FLYNN, Chairman

11 Broadway

New York, N.Y. 10004

I: New Matter effective January 12, 1972.

Illustration: Typical Conference Ocean Freight Title Page Showing Trade Areas, Commodity Rates Involved, and Other Information.

			ORIG./REV.	PAGE
			17th Revised	237
			CANCELS	PAGE
			16th Revised	237

Far East Conference

Tariff No. 25   **F. M. C. No. 5**

From: UNITED STATES ATLANTIC and GULF PORTS.
To: JAPAN, OKINAWA, KOREA, TAIWAN, HONG KONG, PHILIPPINE ISLANDS, VIET NAM, CAMBODIA, LAOS and MAINLAND CHINA

EFFECTIVE DATE
June 1, 1972

CORRECTION NO   3086
CANCELS CORR. NO.   2845

EXCEPT AS OTHERWISE PROVIDED HEREIN, RATES APPLY PER TON OF 2000 LBS., OR 40 CUBIC FEET, WHICHEVER PRODUCES THE GREATER REVENUE.

"C" denotes "CONTRACT" rates.   "NC" denotes "NON-CONTRACT" rates.

Commodity Code	Commodity	Rate Basis	Group Ports 1 — Nagoya Yokohama Kobe Osaka Manila Hong Kong	2 — Cebu Iloilo	3 — Takao Keelung	4 — Saigon	Item No.
			$	$	$	$	
	Iron and Steel Articles Plain or Galvanized (Not including Stainless Steel) Viz: (cont'd)						
	Bale Tires, Wire	C 2240 A:	54.00	57.50	61.00	56.00	
	Billets	NC lbs.	62.10	66.10	70.15	64.40	1353
	Blooms	or 40					
	Bolt Stock, Steel	cu.ft.					
	Bolts, Mine, Roof						
	Bolts, Railway						
	Bolts, N.O.S.		Apply the following rates as special rates on				
	Clevices		STEEL BILLETS TO PHILIPPINE SAFE PORTS;				
	Conduit Fittings, (not Cast Iron)		HONG KONG (Rule 1(f)(7) not applicable):				
	Cuttings, N.O.S.		Rate declared Open subject to tariff rules				
	Cuttings, Plate		and regulations and also subject to minimum				
	Cuttings, Sheet		quantity of 1000 revenue tons per vessel per				
	Expansion Shells	()	port of loading and port of discharge.				
	Forgings, not machined		Effective through September 30, 1972.				
	Forgings, not machined beyond deburring, with or without lifting lugs.		PIPE FITTINGS, NOT CAST IRON - TO TAKAO: Effective through September 30, 1972, the				
	Hoop Steel	A:	following rates will apply:				
	Hoops		C - $58.75 - NC - $67.55 per 2240 lbs. or				
	Ingots	A:	40 cu.ft., Berth Terms, or at Ship's Option.				
	Nails, Common Wire		C - $52.50 - NC - $60.35 per 2240 lbs. or				
	Nails, Leadhead		40 cu.ft., Free In Stowed - 50% discount in				
	Nuts		Heavy Lift Charges.				
	Piling, N.O.S.						
	Pipe Fittings, not Cast Iron						
	Rivets						
	Screw Stock						
	Screws						
	Screws, Brassplated, Bronze plated, Cadmium plated or Copper plated						
	Shafting, not forged						
	Shafting, not machined						
	Sheet Bar						
	Skelp						
	Slabs						
	Spikes, Boat						
	Spikes, N.O.S.						
	Spikes, Railway						
	Strips, N.O.S.						
	Strips, Copper Coated, N.O.S.						
	Studs						
	Thread Protectors, Pipe						
	Tire Bead Wire		(Continued on next Page)				

A: Advance in rates effective June 1, 1972.
() Expiration date extended from May 31, 1972.

Illustration: Ocean Freight Tariff Page Naming Rates and Other Information on Specific Commodities.

on filing, as a general rule. There is no minimum-period requirement on decreases. Some tariffs have firm cargo booking provisions which may operate to somewhat extend the above periods applicable to increases.

Ocean rates which become "open" rates and the incidents to declaring rates "open" may be important to shippers in conference procedures. Where a member line adjusts a rate on a certain commodity to meet competition and the other lines are unwilling to go along with such action, the activity usually involves a declaration that the rate is "open" as to the conference. This sets up the rate, generally speaking, as free of the conference tariff rules and provisions. Whether this is completely free or only partially so depends on the particular situation. Certain features, such as surcharges, may continue to be applicable, and these should be watched.

Another particular feature for possible attention with "open" rates is that when they are involved there is no assurance that a rate quoted by a steamship line today will be good tomorrow. It may stay the same or go up or down. Changes may occur quickly, and shippers should check currently and carefully with carriers regarding applicable rates when such rates become especially important to them. Rates may be "nailed down," so that they cannot be changed, by (1) firm bookings at the specified rate for a given shipping period to which both carrier and shipper agree or (2) a "refusal" in which the steamship company agrees with the shipper to protect the rate for a specified time, generally 24 hours or at most a few days. During that time the shipper may accept or decline to use the rate.

Both the weight and the measurement of cargo receive particular attention in the assessment of ocean freight charges. At times, rates will be on a weight basis (W) and at times on a measurement basis (M). Quite often they alternate (W/M). This alternation is generally accomplished by tariff provisions along lines similar to those shown at the top of the tariff page previously illustrated, which run to the effect that rates "apply per ton of 2,000 pounds or 40 cubic feet, whichever produces the greater revenue." Space considerations are particularly critical in vessel operations and alternation provisions in many ways are necessary and fair in these rate structures.

Rates published on weight bases generally are on tons of 2,000 pounds. Long or gross tons of 2,240 pounds and kilo or metric tons of 2,204.6 pounds are specified at times. Also specified at limited times are rates in cents per 100 pounds. Additionally rates are assessed occasionally on a "per 1,000 board feet" basis (lumber as an example) or on a specified percentage of the value of the shipment.

Rates bases on measurements require calculation by, or for, the steamship companies after cargo is delivered to the dock and before it is loaded into the ship, as a general rule. This activity is often called "putting the stick to it". Basically the cubage determination of a package is made by measuring the length, width, and height in inches, multiplying the three, and dividing the answer by 1728 (the number of cubic inches in one cubic foot). Some tariff rules provide for dropping fractions of less than one half inch and for using one half inch and more as a full inch in measurement calculations. When such rules do not exist, fractions are generally increased to full inches to avoid controversies.

Normally each shipment is measured in accordance with the rules and regulations of the governing conference or other applicable authority. Highlights of these rules involve requirements for using the greatest, or extreme, outside measurement of the largest dimension. Measurements on wooden barrels, casks, and kegs are to be taken on the square of the greatest bilge. In measuring rolls and cylindrical packages, the measurements are taken on the square of the mean diameter.

Freight charges are generally computed on the gross weight or on the overall measurements of the individual pieces (whichever produces the greatest revenue) when tariff provisions specify that the rates are on a weight-measurement, ship's option basis. Weight-measurement agreements on regularly moving commodities in standard packages along lines similar to those used domestically may be arranged between conferences and shippers in appropriate cases. Several conferences use inspection bureaus to perform, or assist in, measurement functions. At times all of this work for a conference will be done by one bureau. Some ready reference figures in connection with freight calculations are available in commercial publications. For example, cubic measurement tables are published under the names "The Expeditious Measurer", the "Ready Calculator", the "Unz Cubic Contents Tables" and "Tweed's Accurate Cubic Table". Certain conferences standardize on one "table".

The usual procedure for shippers and receivers seeking an adjustment in a freight rate or rule is to direct a letter to the chairman of the steamship conference having jurisdiction. This is the preferred method rather than make a request through one steamship member of the conference. Some call in person on the chairman, a conference committee, or appear before the entire conference membership for a personal discussion of all phases of the application. In the case of homeward conferences (domiciled abroad) shippers may go direct by letter or handle with a member carrier which will present the proposal to the conference along with its recommendations. Letters should state all possible data such as complete description of the commodity, origins, destinations, value per pound, weight per cubic foot, damage factor, volume expected to move, F.A.S. selling price and freight rate from foreign country if request is to meet foreign competition, how packed including package dimensions, comparative rates on similar commodities in the same or other trades, and anything else that will assist the conference in making its decision. Most conferences use traffic analysis forms for this purpose along the lines of the one shown on Page 502. Some firms send a copy of their conference transmittal letter to all conference member steamship lines with whom they route or might route shipments. Adjustments to be made direct with the steamship companies are, of course, to be handled with their representatives.

As mentioned earlier in this section a particularly important facet of ocean freight rates to industrial traffic managers at times are "contract" and "non-contract" rates. Overly simpli-

BM 2-63 J. B.

ASSOCIATED LATIN AMERICAN FREIGHT CONFERENCES TRAFFIC ANALYSIS FORM

1. Name of article and its trade name, if any: Clay Tile

2. Description of article: Clay Tile including ceramic, wall and floor and quarry floor tile

3. What it is used for: Decorative floor and wall covering

4. State if hazardous or inflammable: Neither

5. State what label is required for ocean shipment: None

6. State if liquid, paste, flake, powdered, granulated or solid: Solid

7. State how packed (box, barrel, bale, carton, crate, etc.): Crates

8. Package Dimensions: Length 17"   Width 10"   Height 4½"   Cu. ft. per package: 0.5

9. Package gross weight is 40   lbs.   24   Cu. ft. per 2,000 lbs.:

10. From U. S. port of: New Orleans   To foreign port of: Rio Haina, Dominican Republic

11. Present rate: $79. per 2,000 lbs.   Rate proposed by applicant: $50. per 2,000 lbs.

12. Place where material is made or produced: Various points in U. S.

13. How article is described for railroad movement: Clay Tile

14. How described in Shipper's Export Declaration: Clay Tile

15. Schedule B Commodity No.: D662.4610

16. Tonnage of present movement to foreign port named in Item 10: Nil

17. Extra tonnage expected to move at proposed rate: 240 tons per annum

18. State if movement is continuous, seasonal or sporadic: Continuous

19. F.A.S. value per pound or package (state which): $6.00 per package

20. Name of competitive or substitute article: Tile from other countries

21. F.A.S. value per pound of competitive article: Unknown - C.I.F. about $350. per ton
    (If this information is not obtainable, but the delivered competitive price is
    the basis of this application, it must be indicated at least approximately)

22. Reason for proposed change:
    Shipments to other areas, competing with other supplying countries, are on the
    increase. Therefore, feel if comparable freight obtainable here, business
    would increase.

23. Application submitted by: Slippery Floor Co., Inc.

                        Per: George Mudd, T. M.

Date: Address: 678 Oak Street, Catalpa, Alaska

Note.-Applicant to keep one completed copy of this form. The remainder to be mailed to
      C. D. Marshall, Conference Chairman, Room 2100, 11 Broadway, New York 4. N. Y.

Steamship Conference Traffic Analysis Form

fied, these dual rates are provided by most conferences and, under the system they represent, a shipper is granted rates which are approximately 15% lower if he will route all of his freight and the freight of his affiliates in a given trade via conference member lines. Formal, written contracts are required from shippers in these connections and it is basically from this feature that the designations of "contract" and "non-contract" have come to be used. Contracts are available to all shippers, large, or small, and signers obtain the lower rates regardless of the volume of their shipments. The system is ingrained in the rate structures and has been so for many years.

While each conference has its own forms, and these should be referred to for details, the contracts have many points in common. All are subject to FMC jurisdiction as well as to federal legislation. Particularly important parts of this legislation were passed after a U.S. Supreme Court decision (May 19, 1958) adverse to the system. This legislation is incorporated into the "Shipping Act of 1916" (as amended), Section 14b being especially pertinent. Various features of these laws and the rules promulgated by the FMC as an incident to its work are discussed later. As with the contract forms proper, these laws and rules are to be referred to for more details where indicated for in-depth consideration of a shipper's rights and liabilities in these cases.

Features that often cause particular problems with these contracts are those involving requirements that concern the routing of all freight and those involving the extent to which company affiliates are bound. Complications incident to international trading, particular trade practices in certain foreign countries, and other practical considerations operate to produce situations that are far from clear cut in the "all-freight" routing function. Company affiliations vary, have differing lines of corporate authority, and conduct their traffic work in so many different ways that just what are affiliates for "contract" rate purposes may be difficult of determination.

Basic statutory controls as to these features are that the shipper's obligation to route "covers only those goods" for which he has "the legal right at the time of shipment to select the carrier." Further, he may not divest himself (or permit himself to be divested) of the "legal right to select the carrier" before the time of shipment "with the intent to avoid his obligation under the contract." The FMC and the conferences endeavor to interpret these realistically; important considerations are the routing features of the arrangements between the seller and the buyer, when title passes, the kind of title involved (i.e. whether title is retained simply for security purposes), who is shown as shipper on the transportation documents, the extent of the shipper's participation in the making of the transportation arrangements, and so on.

In these matters a shipper is not obligated to refuse a sale simply because a customer insists on making his own transporation arrangements and, when they are so made, they may be followed without a contract violation. The FMC has taken a firm position to this effect, and clauses so providing are to be found in the various contracts. Terms of sale may be important in determining when title passes and an obligation to route occurs, but such terms are often so loosely used that they are simply a factor for consideration. As an example, FOB can be "free on board" a vessel or dock any place, and further specifics would be needed to make the term truly controlling and binding. A conference may, at its option, provide in its agreement that where a shipper participates in the transportation arrangements or where his name appears as shipper on the bill of lading or export declaration there is a presumption (which is rebuttable) that he had the right to route. Proof in "prima facie" matters of this kind at times presents problems.

As regards affiliates, where a contract signer regularly exercises direction and working control in relation to shipping matters of a parent, subsidiary, or associated company, all of the shipments of such companies are also to be routed via the vessels of the conference with which the contract is made. An "affiliates clause" along these lines appears in the agreements of the various conferences and normally the parent and other companies involved are specifically named in the appendix.

Where a company is one of a family of companies these clauses usually require particular consideration, attention, and study, as non-compliance can be costly.

Highlights of other features generally applicable to these contracts are that when reduced rates are negotiated by anyone after a contract is signed such reduced rates apply also for the account of the contract signer. Conferences have the right to inspect those parts of a shipper's files that may pertain to a claimed breach of contract. Usually disputes are settled by arbitration. Resort to the FMC is available to a shipper when he believes he has had improper or arbitrary treatment at the hands of the conference.

Excluded from the provisions of these agreements are dry cargo loaded in bulk without mark or count and liquid bulk chemical and petroleum shipments. Also excluded are shipments in vessels owned by a shipper or fully chartered by him for six months or more, provided such vessels are used only for the carriage of the shipper's owned goods. "Open" commodities, previously discussed, are excluded as long as they remain "open" as to the conference procedures.

Where suitable vessel space cannot be provided, a shipper is relieved of his obligations to patronize conference vessels, provided he has given the conference ten days' written notice and an opportunity to meet his needs during that time. Contracts may be cancelled by shippers on 90 days' notice and on even shorter periods when increases in rates have been promulgated. Where a contract is breached by a shipper, the measure of damages is the amount of the contract rate less loading and unloading costs. In other words, such damages represent the the freight charges actually lost by the conference, less out-of-pocket expense that a carrier would have incurred. Generally, the burden of proof in establishing a breach is in the conference.

The general approach is that shippers who sign conference contracts do so in good faith in order to avail themselves of the lower contract rates. In many instances the legal interpretation problems presented here do not develop. If they do, it is a matter for the shipper and conference chairman to settle and this should be done before a violation occurs. Conference chairman are focal points for shippers who are, or may be, confronted with dual rate problems.

Counsel for certain shipper interests has stated that there is nothing in the law or the shippers' contracts to prevent foreign buyers, acting independently, from varying their purchase terms so that some shipments will move on non-conference vessels and some will be controlled by the seller and entitled to contract rates. Buyers generally seek the most satisfactory terms, and shippers frequently must sell on the conditions the buyer stipulates. Carriers and conferences, however, do check out alleged failures to live up to the terms of dual-rate contracts and prosecute to the fullest extent possible.

Conferences can, and do, exist without a dual rate system. There are not many of these, however, and the lines find it helpful, because of rate stability and economics, to handle these systems, as well as rate and tariff matters generally, with both the shipping public and the government through a central office. In the instances in which the lines publish their own tariffs there are usually particular reasons for them to do so.

Customs Duties and Procedures

Customs duties and procedures are another way of saying "government levies and regulations." Foreign shipments are subject to various governmental duties regulations, restrictions, etc., at both the forwarding and receiving ends. Usually, when customs are mentioned, the first thing that comes to mind is imports. They involve duty payments and this is quite proper. On the other hand, much the same payments must be made and procedures undertaken on exports (at the countries of importations) and, for that matter, on commerce between non-U.S. ports. Customs requirements along broad lines related to those of the United States exist throughout the world and should be dealt with accordingly.

An increasing influence in the amounts of duty to be paid

in this country and abroad as to some goods are the "anti-dumping" laws. They exist in a number of places, and tougher enforcement policies regarding them have recently been given higher priority here. Overly simplified, the U.S. version provides that imports cannot be sold by a foreign marketer at less than their fair value. A test in this regard is whether sales in the U.S. are made at prices lower than in the home market. Where less than fair value sales occur, the Treasury makes a finding to that effect, passes the finding to the Tariff Commission, and the latter adjusts duty charges upward or makes such other changes therein as may be appropriate. In some companies the traffic departments have the responsibilities of handling these cases in addition to dealing with the aspects that are concerned with the amounts of duty payable.

The discussion which follows involves, in the order named, highlights on customs duties and procedures as to imports, exports, and other foreign trade. As more specific data in these fields come to be required various publications are available with more details. These include the Custom House Guide, the Exporters' Encyclopedia, and others. Contained therein are many of the specifics that are so often needed in these matters. Such publications can be most helpful and additional information on them appears in appropriate context later. Also, many of the documents and forms referred to in this text may, hopefully, soon be in limbo, eliminated, or otherwise dealt with so that a much simpler, more streamlined documentation situation exists. The National Committee on International Trade Documentation is doing a great deal in this regard of an important nature.

■ *Imports*—American importers are subject to customs regulations at the port of entry. The United States Customs is a branch of the Treasury Department. The country is divided into customers collection districts. There is a collector of customs and a customhouse at all major ports. The U.S. Customs assumes ownership of all materials arriving from a foreign port and maintains its ownership until all duties have been paid and other requirements met. When the importer has complied with all regulations he presents the necessary documents to the Customs office and the "entry" is made. The "entry" is a term used to designate the act of complying with the law and obtaining release of the material.

The usual procedure is to submit to the Collector of Customs a form of entry showing a complete description of the goods, particulars of the shipment and duty rates. This form is called a "duty paid" or "consumption entry" form.

Duty is assessed in accordance with laws passed by Congress which list dutiable goods and the amount of duty for each item. Duty is assessed on the basis of "ad valorem," "specific," or a combination of the two. Ad valorem means according to total value while specific is per unit as "10¢ per bushel." Ocean insurance and freight charges are exempt, so duty is assessable only on the consular invoice value at foreign port of exportation.

From the laws passed by Congress is evolved what is called the United States Customs Tariff. It is intricate and importers should give their foreign exporters explicit instructions so that details as to commodity names, descriptions, and so on, are spelled out clearly. All packages should be marked with the country of origin as "product of ...." and should also be numbered in sequence with identifying symbols.

Schedules of amounts to be paid in duties for the importation of various commodities appear in the publication, "Tariff Schedules of the U.S.," 1971 Edition, U.S. Tariff Commission, Washington, D.C. 20436 and in the Customs House Guide. Each has certain advantages, i.e., the Guide's commodity list is on more of an alphatbetical basis, and a number of companies use both. Usual procedures involve the "entry" being passed to the customs appraiser for checking and the ultimate assessment of duties by the Collector. If problems develop, such as a need for more information, this is provided by the importer. Most of the time, satisfactory assessments are made at this level. When this is not the case, however, appeals may be taken to the Customs Court and matters may be adjudicated there. The usual practice is to employ attorneys as an incident to these appeals. Some companies hire them on annual retainers and, in addition, pay them percentages of recoveries effected, which range from 15 to 50%, depending on work involved, the size of the case, and so on.

All shipments must be cleared through customs even though they consist of duty-free commodities. The practice is for the local agent of an inbound vessel to present a copy of the ship's manifest to the collector of the port who issues a permit authorizing the docking of the vessel and the landing of the cargo. Entry must be made for payment of duty or an "in bond" application submitted within 48 hours after the entry of the vessel. Failure to comply with the 48-hour time limit will result in the goods being sent to a bonded warehouse under a phase of the law called "General Order".

It is expensive when goods are sent to a "General Order" warehouse since the importer must pay transportation to the warehouse, handling charges in and out and at least one month's warehouse charges. If the required documents are not available when the goods are unloaded from the ship, a bond can be executed for later surrender of the documents. Bonds must be executed for the amount of the value plus duty on consumption entries and double the duty on warehouse entries. As a general rule, importers make a practice of filing a "general bond" which obligates them to conform to the import laws. This is sometimes referred to as a "general term bond" and is renewed yearly.

The law states that the ocean bill of lading and the invoice must be attached to the entry. If no bill of lading is available the freight will be delivered under a bond, provided the bond is for an amount twice the value of the shipment. If the invoice is not available, it may be substituted for by a pro-forma invoice which is used when papers are late. The bond, of course, must accompany the pro-forma invoice. This invoice represents the importer's best effort to reproduce the provisions of the true invoice.

The United States customs requires a special customs invoice on ad valorem shipments but a visa is not necessary.

These invoices are not needed unless the shipment is valued in excess of $500.00. Because of this requirement it is important that American importers be certain that sales agreements, letters of credit, etc., stipulate that a customs invoice must be issued. These invoices must include all particulars concerning each shipment in addition to the purchase price in the currency purchased, persons from and to whom sold, time and place of sale and other pertinent details.

If a shipment is to be placed in a bonded warehouse and that fact is known at time of shipment from the foreign country, the ocean bill of lading should state, "In bond to John Doe Warehouse Co., New York, N.Y." If the goods are to move to a bonded warehouse in a location other than the port of entry, an "I.T." entry (immediate transportation entry) can be obtained. This is a simplified form that will permit immediate movement. The government does not assess any duty on merchandise shipped to a bonded warehouse. The duty is assessed only when the goods are removed from the control of the government and from the bonded warehouse.

Goods placed in a bonded warehouse may be removed for export from the United States without paying duty. This is done by executing a "withdrawal for export" form. Duty is not assessed on goods inspected and rejected since they are returned to the foreign shipper. Neither is duty assessed against American goods being returned to the United States because of rejection by the foreign buyer or for any other reason.

A drawback is an application to the customs office for a refund on duty paid on materials used to manufacture a product that is exported. The government permits a duty refund on all imported raw materials that are shipped out of the country as part of a finished product. The necessary forms call for full particulars as to date and details of the importation, where the exported product was manufactured, and certifications, etc. as to the manufacturing process. The duty refund is 99 per cent of the duty paid on the imported raw materials.

Customs appraisers attached to the customs office are responsible for inspecting merchandise to determine the quantity and value for customs purposes. They must prepare a report to the Collector of Customs, who determines the amount of duty based on the appraiser's report, customs invoice, and other documents furnished. They do not always perform a complete inspection of those materials not subject to duty and, on those commodities subject to duty, they may not inspect every piece. It is advisable, however, that a proper inspection be accomplished before the goods are removed from the dock or appraisers' stores on behalf of the cargo owner. Loss or damage to the goods may have occurred and, if so, prompt action to recover should be taken.

Reference texts for duty charges by commodities, tariff decisions, and the myriad of other things that go into customs work include the 2,000-page Custom House Guide and its supplement, the American Import Export Bulletin. These are published annually and monthly, respectively, by Budd Publications, Inc., 107 S. Tyson Ave., Floral Park, N.Y. 11001, (212-347-8724). Details in these publications are voluminous and they can well be valuable tools to an industrial traffic department where their use is indicated. Additional publications are available from federal, state, and other governments, chambers of commerce, port authorities and other sources.

■ *Exports*—The exporter must obtain an export license, where applicable, (application forms are obtainable from the Bureau of International Commerce, Department of Commerce, and contain both general and specific instructions) to forward his shipment out of the country and an import license, where applicable, to ship it into the destination country. If he can obtain one and not the other, he just cannot export the material. This type of government license is usually based on political and economic considerations. A certain country may decide that too much money is being spent outside the country so the government passes a law banning all imports, except certain staple commodities, and then only if a license to import is obtained for each order placed. The United States may decide that certain countries should not receive any of a selected list of items

on the theory that they may be diverted to uses that would result in action unfriendly to the United States. Also, certain
commodities in short supply in the United States may have to
be controlled for emergency stockpiling. Thus the exporter and
importer may be confronted with problems over and above
those presented by customs regulations requiring such routine
documents as shipper's export declaration, consular invoice,
certificate of origin, consumption entry, et cetera.

The Bureau of International Commerce of the Department
of Commerce issues export licenses in accordance with the government's current policy on export control. Foreign traders may
find themselves out of certain markets if their product does not
fit in with the policy of a recovery program or an emergency
situation of one type or another. The Bureau may desire to
hold prices down on controlled commodities so that foreign
countries may obtain more goods with money loaned to them
by the United States. In such a situation the government would
issue export licenses to those exporters with the lowest prices.
Or, if the foreign country was in dire straits, a steel exporter
proposing to sell steel to be used to manufacture shoe polish
boxes would be turned down in favor of a steel exporter selling
steel for repairing a railroad bridge. This would be issuing export licenses under an "end use" policy.

Shipper's Export Declarations must be prepared for shipments that go beyond the borders of the United States and
their preparation is part of the "custom's clearance" procedure.
The declaration form (next illustrated) shows information involved as well as other data. It, too, may be designed for use
with a master duplicator arrangement, discussed earlier in the
section on ocean bills of lading. The government uses the "export dec" in the compilation of various statistics on foreign
trade. It also assures that the identity of cargo is checked by a
U.S. customs inspector prior to loading on board the export
vessel.

The Declaration must be prepared in full. It must specify
the number and kind of packages, description of commodities,
export license number and expiration date, if any, and other

Shippers Export Declaration

data as set forth in the instructions on the reverse side of the form.

The use of proper commodity descriptions is important with these papers. Such descriptions should conform to those on any export license that may be involved. They also should conform to those specified in the U.S. Commerce Department "Schedule B" commodity list and should include the commodity code number for that commodity specified there. These are seven-digit numbers and are used in the Department's data processing activities for the statistics mentioned previously. Schedules may be obtained from most Commerce Department offices. Additionally, the descriptions should be closely related to, but not necessarily exactly the same, as the description on the ocean bill of lading. Further refinements may be necessary with hazardous materials, where import requirements may make certain phraseology advisable, and so on.

The declaration must be signed by an officer of the exporting company, although power of attorney may be issued by an officer to permit signing by another employee or a foreign freight forwarder. The form is usually prepared in quadruplicate, with the original and one copy retained by the custom house; the third copy, duly numbered, is delivered to the steamship company at the time of delivery; and the fourth copy, bearing the custom house number, is retained on file by the freight forwarder or the shipper. The steamship company is required to attach a copy of each declaration to its ship's manifest which is filed with and validated by the Collector of Customs, before sailing clearance papers can be issued.

Shipper's export declaration forms are used as export control documents as well as for statistics. This control is evidenced by the issuance of a license, which is the equivalent of a permit. Government licensing of the export may be by a formal document or by endorsement on the export declaration. Such a license is required on many shipments to foreign countries.

The exporter also must obtain a visaed consular invoice (see next illustration) as a prerequisite for shipping materials to many countries. Most foreign countries have appointed consuls in the United States. There is a consul for most countries in all major ports and even in some interior cities. These consuls represent their respective countries in various capacities, subject to the general supervision of the ambassador to the United States from each particular country.

The exporter or his forwarding agent prepares the consular invoice on forms designed for that purpose and then submits them to the consul for certification. Consular invoices must be prepared on special forms purchased from the various consuls. The purpose is to provide the foreign country with a "certification" as to the character of the goods which it can use with confidence in assessing import duties. Sometimes the invoice is prepared in the language of the country to which the shipment

FA Form Nos. 48/49
July 1, 1957 (Consolidated)
(Submit in quintuplicate)

FOREIGN SERVICE OF THE PHILIPPINES

CONSULATE GENERAL OF THE PHILIPPINES
New York

For sale only by the
Consulate General of the Philippines
New York, N. Y.

G 28976

ORIGINAL

CONSULAR INVOICE OF MERCHANDISE

Purchased ☐   Not Purchased ☐

New York, N. Y.
Place

, 19
Date

Invoice of ...... Cotton Piece Goods
general description of merchandise

Supplied by ...... Franklin Fabrics ...... of ...... New York, N. Y.
manufacturer/seller/consignor .... address

To ...... Philippine Merchandise Co. ...... of ...... Manila, P. I.
purchaser/consignee .... address

To be shipped per ...... S.S. "GEORGE MC CALL" ...... on or about ......
carrier .... date of departure

Place of exportation ...... New York ...... Port of entry ...... Manila

Terms (whether FOB, CIF, FAS, etc.) of selling price ...... CIF Manila ...... ; of export value $30,000.00

MARKS AND NUMBERS	TYPE AND NO. OF PACKAGES	QUANTITY AND DESCRIPTION OF GOODS	SELLING PRICE (1) TO PURCHASER Unit	SELLING PRICE (1) TO PURCHASER Total	CURRENT EXPORT (2) VALUE Unit	CURRENT EXPORT (2) VALUE Total
◇FF◇ #1-10	10 bales	Cotton Piece Goods (10,000 yards) As per Attached Commercial Invoices	US $ 3.00 p. yd.	US $ 30,000.00		
(3)						
		TOTAL		$30,000.00		

CHARGES INCLUDED IN OR EXCLUDED FROM THE ABOVE EXPORT VALUES: [Whenever an imported article is subject to an ad valorem rate of duty, the duty shall be assessed upon the market value or price at which, at the time of exportation, the same, like or similar article is freely offered for sale in the principal markets of the exporting country for exportation to the Philippines, in the usual wholesale quantities and in the ordinary course of trade (excluding internal excise taxes to be remitted or rebated), plus ordinary expenses prior and incidental to the lading of such article on board the vessel or aircraft at the port of export (including taxes or duties, if any) and freight paid as well as insurance premium paid covering the transportation of such article to the port of entry in the Philippines.]

NATURE OF CHARGES	(2) AMOUNT Included	(2) AMOUNT Excluded
1. Value of materials for packing for export purposes	$ 5.00	
2. Labor in packing the goods into packages for export purposes	50.00	
3. Inland freight and other charges to the dock area, airport or post office including inland insurance	89.00	
4. Cartage to rail, docks, airport or post office	none	
5. Pier and handling charges	2.00	
6. Internal taxes to be remitted or rebated	none	
7. Commission	none	
8. Export duties and taxes	none	
9. Ocean freight	250.00	
10. Marine insurance premium	330.00	
TOTAL		

(1) In currency of corresponding commercial invoice.

(2) In currency of exporting country. The export values are as indicated in the supplier's latest effective export price list published on ...... ; otherwise, indicate here the reference ......

(3) If this space is not sufficient, use as many pages with the same headings as may be necessary, number the pages and securely attach them to this sheet.

Consular Invoice

is being forwarded. Occasionally, it must be accompanied by a Certificate of Origin indorsed by the consul with prior certification or by an accredited Chamber of Commerce or Trade Bureau.

Be sure the consular invoice is prepared correctly, since it is the prime document in connection with customs entry at the port of destination. The consul may be delegated to check the price in case of a "non-dumping" policy in the foreign country. It is quite customary for a consul to charge a fee for visaing a consular invoice; and foreign freight forwarders assess a special fee for each consular invoice prepared by them.

Customs duties and the customs tariffs which levy those duties vary considerably from country to country as to amounts charged, designations of articles on which duties are to be paid, and so on. Varying economic conditions, regulatory philosophies, and other factors are reflected there. Some moves to standardize these have been made but they have not been particularly fruitful. Specific references to the texts proper for commodity names, amounts, and other information are advisable when justified. Discussions of further details on the situations in Canada and Mexico follow and illustrate further these facets of duty charges and the tariff "price lists" establishing them.

Shipments from the United States to Canada are subject to customs regulations and charges similar in many ways to shipments to other countries. Waybills properly filled out must accompany all shipments. They are required to be typed or written in ink or indelible pencil in a clear and legible manner, and to give the full name and address of the consignee, the marks and numbers on the packages, and adequate descriptions of them.

Canadian customs invoices which are properly certified are required and at least four copies are to be prepared (two for customs entries, the third for statistical purposes, and the fourth for the importer). These are combination forms that include the invoice proper, the exporter's declaration, and a certificate of origin. Regular commercial invoices may be used on shipments valued at less than $100. There are various customs invoice forms. Two in particular are important: Form M A for goods sold prior to shipment and N A for goods shipped without sale.

Canada's customs tariff is based generally on its own unique customs nomenclature and not on any of the other "standard" tariff systems such as the Brussels Tariff Nomenclature or the Standard International Tariff Classification system. It has three columns with the rates of duty for each property item dependent on the country of origin. One column shows "preferential" rates (ie. those for the United Kingdom), the second shows rates for "most favored nations" (ie. the United States), and the third covers "general" situation rates (ie. where no treaty or similar document exists).

As regards Mexico, a large number of products are subject to import control. Import licenses by that country for these goods are required before firm orders are placed. "Open end" import licenses may be granted as to some materials which permit limited importation for six months to a year. Invoices must contain certain specified information, ie. the complete name and address of the consignee, the sea or border point of entry, and so on. They must be legalized and visaed by Mexican authorities and should be in Spanish. Some importers prepare invoices with the Spanish text below the English and this has been acceptable to the Mexican customs people.

Mexico's current customs tariff has a revised nomenclature to conform to the Brussels Tariff Nomenclature system. The rate structure is composed of a specific duty, based on weight or quantity, plus an ad valorem duty. As with other countries, certain products enter duty free. Regulations applicable to shipments via border points are similar in many ways to those via the ports.

Consular and other forms required in exports (and imports, for that matter) can be of real importance. At times they are prescribed by the countries involved and can be obtained only from the representatives of those countries. Many can be obtained from good stationery stores. Unz & Co., 24 Beaver

St., N.Y., N.Y. 10004 (212-944-2075) publishes a great number of them. A free, illustrated catalogue and price list are available from them and will be sent upon request.

Of the reference texts particularly applicable to exports the Exporters' Encyclopedia published by Dun & Bradstreet Publications Corp., 466 Lexington Ave., New York, N.Y. 10017, among various things, explains in substantial detail what is involved in shipments to each of the countries of the world. This is done by country, with appropriate maps showing ports involved, ship and other transportation service available, licenses and documents needed, customs requirements, and so on. The volume covers many facets of foreign trade and can be a worth while tool for an involved transportation department. As with texts on imports, additional data concerning exports are available from government, consular, chamber of commerce, and other sources.

■ *Commerce Between Foreign Ports*—U.S. based traffic departments are being called on more and more to arrange transportation of cargo between foreign countries. This may be from Mexico to Holland, Liberia to France, Canada to Japan, or, for that matter, practically anywhere. The almost endless possibilities in this regard present real challenges to dealing effectively with the customs and related requirements that may be involved. This largely stems from the fact that each country's particular set of requirements requires "digging," research, and effort to determine them and to relate them to the particular problems at hand.

Much of what is said earlier in this chapter is also applicable in a broad way to these movements. The country of export, as a usual proposition, will have its equivalents of export declarations, licenses, and so on and the country of import will have its requirements which may involve payments of duty, customs clearances, and other procedures. The details on these should be determined and appropriate dealings should be accorded the requirements that are developed.

Steps to determine details vary; the consular offices of the particular countries involved are generally good sources for information. Others can be the particular carriers providing transportation to and from those countries, financial institutions involved there, insurance underwriters, chambers of commerce, and so on. Assistance may be obtained also from the two reference texts specifically mentioned previously. The 1972 Exporters' Encyclopedia previously mentioned in this chapter can be particularly helpful on country-by-country requirements for these movements. A plus, of course, for the digging out of these details is that other valuable information as to sales possibilities and so on may also be obtained in the process.

Financing Payments

Transportation departments engaged in international operations become involved to quite an extent as a general rule in the financial arrangements whereby their companies are paid for the merchandise they sell or the remittances they make for goods sold to them. These arrangements have been intimately tied through the centuries to the transportation used and they represent courses of dealing that are in important trade practice channels for the financial institutions, carriers, and others involved with them. Over and above the precedents that exist, there are other reasons for these involvements. After all, possible complications incident to paying a bill to, or getting it paid by, someone half-way around the world can be much greater than someone half-way around the block. The carriers, banks, and others with representatives on the ground are in particularly good positions to help when assistance is needed.

Many fundamentals of domestic finance are also involved in foreign finance matters. Drafts, credit insurance, and open accounts (at times) as well as other similar arrangements are used in both these areas. In international trade, however, more government underwritings, guarantees, and so on are utilized and it is important to bear in mind differing monetary systems and related problems. Possible fluctuations is exchange rates of dollars for francs, marks, and other currencies are among these as are the possibilities of having to deal with a "blocked" currency which makes a remittance problematical. Also more banking services are used in foreign trade and many banks have special foreign departments. Delineations between commercial risks and political risks are made in the credit insurance which is written and the coverage may include one or the other or both.

Foreign financing carries with it added paper work and it cannot be emphasized too strongly that absolute accuracy in preparing and executing documents is essential! Errors or discrepancies can be costly and, if serious enough, may result in prolonged delays in receiving payment or in the loss of payment entirely. Along with accuracy, extra care should be taken so that the information on the various forms is properly reconciled. Variations in such information can bring just as unsatisfactory results as those produced by errors. Finance, shipping, billing, and other papers go out as "packages" in many cases and the need for all of them to "tell the same story" is important. Illustrative of practices needing attention in this regard is the experience of one of the leading foreign trade banks which reported discrepancies in more than 30% of the documents involved with letters of credit.

With particular reference to U.S.-based companies exporting to other countries, they will, of course, wish to satisfy themselves with a buyer's ability to pay, a step that may be accomplished most readily through checking with major banks engaged in international finance and through commercial credit agencies. In addition to these familiar steps, however, an exporter must apply his credit principles and knowledge to his buyer's country. Exchange regulations, both domestic and foreign, must be examined and the political and economic climate of the importing nation carefully appraised, both as to present and probable future conditions. The U.S. government, for example, requires export licenses on some products, and in many foreign countries exchange payments are controlled through the issuance of import licenses. It is up to both exporter and importer to make certain that such requirements have been met, or will be met, prior to the consummation of the transaction under consideration. The information necessary to carry out the requirements of and make the judgments needed in this step may be gathered from such sources as the U.S. Department of Commerce or commercial banks engaged in international trade, most of which publish reports containing this type of information.

Normal terms of sale are: F.O.B. (free on board), F.A.S.- (free along side), C & F (cost and freight), and C.I.F. (cost, insurance, freight). It is important in using these terms to clearly understand that they may refer to the inland carrier or the vessel at the port of ocean shipment to another point of departure or to a named point in the country of importation.

To put the matter another way, in arranging an export-import contract for goods on an F.O.B. price basis the what and where elements of the "free on board" feature should be agreed upon and clearly specified in the contract. Typically, this might be F.O.B. vessel at a named port of shipment. It could, however, be at any other mutually-agreed-upon place or on any other basis. Contract terms F.O.B. vessel at, say, San Francisco, California, would mean the seller would provide the goods and deliver them at his expense upon the overseas vessel provided for, or by, the buyer at the named port of shipment. An F.A.S. basis would carry similar obligations except, instead of delivering on the vessel, the seller would be obliged to deliver the goods at San Francisco alongside of the vessel within reach of its loading tackle.

C.&F. and C.I.F. terms should be dealt with similarly although, generally, a specific, unambiguous destination is all that is necessary to be agreed upon and provided for in the contract. Where more than such a destination is involved, however, data thereon should be included. A seller's agreement to furnish goods C. & F. San Francisco would mean the seller's price would include the goods and providing transportation at his expense to the named port of destination. C.I.F. terms involve the same obligations plus the seller providing at his cost marine insurance.

Additional costs and responsibilities are inherent to the F.O.B. and other terms just discussed as well as to still further terms used by exporters and importers. More details may be found in "Revised American Foreign Trade Definitions—1941" promulgated by a joint committee representing the National Foreign Trade Council, Inc., the National Council of American Importers, Inc. and the Chamber of Commerce of the U.S. These definitions supercede an earlier issue published in 1919 and have important recognition in trade circles. "Incoterms— 1953" promulgated by the International Chamber of Commerce is along similar lines and has also been published to provide a set of international rules for the interpretation of the chief terms used in foreign trade contracts. "Uniform Customs and Practice for Documentary Credits" approved by the nineteenth Congress of the International Chamber of Commerce at Mexico City in 1963 is also important in this field, particularly as to financing. Some differences exist in the three texts and, where indicated, reconciliations or other features regarding them can be dealt with by appropriate agreement provisions. See later comments regarding where these are available. Highlights of them appear in the Exporters Encyclopedia previously mentioned.

An exporter or importer should, for his protection, be sure that his contract clearly defines the scope of coverage meant when quoting any abbreviated or similar trade term or provision. The decision as to which terms of sale to apply is often as important as determining the method of payment. This has merit in the face of the fact that, in foreign trade, the method of payment is an important factor in meeting competition. Requirements that competitive methods of payments be maintained are especially true of capital goods which lend themselves to extended payment terms.

Payments for, and the financing of, foreign shipments particularly for export are often dealt with in two broad categories: first, short term and, second, medium-long term. Short term generally contemplates payment within one year and medium-long term one to five years (longer in some cases). Usual methods of payment are: (1) Cash upon receipt of the order, (2) open account, (3) a draft or drafts, (4) letters of credit, or (5) extended terms. Consignment, i.e., "floor plan" financing, and other methods are also used.

In each case, the documentation required will be determined by the terms of sale, the means of shipment, the manner of payment, and the regulations of both the U.S. government and the government of the importing country. For consumer goods, the most popular methods are payment by draft or drafts against presentation of documents or payment under a letter of credit. In the case of the exportation of such capital goods as heavy machinery, the granting of extended terms is in demand as a means of settlement.

Referring to the first of the usual payment methods, cash upon receipt of order involves payment in advance of shipment. Considerable time elapses between the date of payment and the date the goods are delivered as a general rule and this is a disadvantage to many consignees. Further, an importer needing dollars may not have a reserve in the U.S. which he can use or he may have problems buying dollars in his country. Limited use only is made of this method of payment.

Open account terms are used most often in the settlement of shipments between a parent and its foreign subsidiary or to very reliable customers, agents or representatives. Such terms are granted only when complete confidence exists between the buyer and seller. Under them the exporter in a normal case would make shipment, await payment, and bear the brunt of all of the financing. This method, also, is a little used one as an ordinary proposition.

Settlement by draft is the most prevalent way of effecting payments in international trade with a fair second being by letters of credit. This is particularly the case with short term financing. In many transactions both drafts and letters of credit may be used and at times they may be used interchangeably. Drafts are also known as bills of exchange and are documents which are members of the negotiable instruments family. Some drafts are essentially the same as a check that, say, a company would use in paying for domestic merchandise. Others have added features similar to those of promissory notes in that they are to be paid in 30, 60, 90, or 180 days or some other period.

Letters of credit are what their names imply. They essentially are written representations by banks that funds are available and will be paid for goods sent to an importer on presentation of bills of lading and other documents that will permit him to take delivery of those goods. Such letters, generally speaking, mean that both the bank and the importer are liable when the terms of the sale are fulfilled by the exporter. Bank acceptances and acceptance credits are also used in these financings and carry with them what are the quivalents of agreements by banks to pay the exporter promptly for the goods and to allow the importer time (usually a short period) in which to pay for them.

Drafts, letters of credit, bank acceptances, and the like lend themselves readily to bank financing and bank handling. The facilities of many banks are geared to handle these on a day-to-day, routine basis. These banks also are generally closer to, and better equipped to handle, exchange matters, currency availability, and related problems than are most industrial companies. Further, when banks are involved, greater care is exercised that payments are not delayed or other difficulties caused because of possible reflections on the credit standings of the importers and exporters involved. Additionally, under applicable rules in certain important situations, U.S. industries must first go to their banks for financing before going to the federal government. Good banking connections and extensive use of them are important and indispensable to companies in foreign trade.

Three types of drafts are in general use in foreign trade-sight, time, and date. With sight draft, documents-against-payment arrangements, a traditional handling of the matter would be for the exporter to have the draft, bill of lading, and other papers forwarded through his bank to its branch or correspondent at the importer's location. There the importer would pay the draft and take delivery of the documents which would permit him to obtain the merchandise from the carrier. The branch or correspondent in turn would remit to the exporter's bank for credit to the exporter's account.

While such traditional handling survives it is apt to be outdated in various cases in actual practice. Air mail generally brings the draft "package" to the importer quickly and there may be a substantial time lag between its receipt and the arrival of the merchandise. Payment in such cases may be burdensome to the importer. Also, where dollar payments are involved there may be times when they are not available. Further, some countries forbid payment for merchandise before customs are cleared. While this last named possibility is generally dealt with by provisional deposits of local currency and agreements to adjust in the event of changes in exchange rates, potential problems exist in such cases. These features are simply to be borne in mind in sight draft, documents against payment, situations. When advisable, other types of arrangement may be practical.

Time drafts usually stipulate documents against acceptance or documents against payment. The former is the more used of the two. It means the importer gets the shipping and other documents on "accepting" (agreeing to pay) the draft and then has a stipulated time (usually 30 to 120 days) in which to make actual payment. Time drafts, documents against payment, are little used except in certain areas such as the Far East where banks are accustomed to handling them. With this type of draft the importer is given time to pay (usually 30 days and upward) but control of the documents remains with the exporter until payment is made. Under these arrangements the foreign bank has the responsibility of clearing and warehousing the merchandise.

Date drafts are forms of time drafts that have specific maturities. Usually they are framed to mature a certain number of days after their date. They have advantages in extensions of credit in that payments are clearly and unambiguously due on certain dates rather than on dates dependent on "acceptances," the times of which may be subject to variances. An importer may be able to delay his acceptance of a draft until the goods have arrived when ordinary time drafts are used.

Other aspects of the use of drafts are that exporters at times finance them at their banks on what are known as loan or discount bases. The former is more often used and, under it, the drawer receives an immediate credit of the full amount of the draft or an agreed upon percentage of it. If the drawee (i.e., the importer) does not pay the exporter must. Most short term financing of this nature by banks is done "with recourse" and on the basis of the credit standing of the exporter. Some finance houses and a few banks, however, will discount this paper "without recourse" and relieve the exporter of any contingent liability if the importer does not pay. Additional costs are involved in these cases.

While there is a divergence of practice on the subject dependent on the country of destination and competitive conditions, relatively few exporters charge interest on their time drafts. The exceptions generally may be found in the Far East and certain British Commonwealth markets. When time drafts are not used to obtain immediate funds by an exporter they are usually sent abroad by him for collection through his banking connections.

Letters of credit, as before indicated, are written representations by banks that credit has been established to pay for goods. Importers, exporters, their banks, and the corespondents of the latter are among those that become involved with them. Various classifications for these letters exist such as whether the banks are in the country of the importer or the exporter. An import letter is the authorization addressed to the beneficiary in one country by the credit issuing bank in another under which the beneficiary is given the right to draw drafts up to a specified sum and within a definite time. The credit issuing bank undertakes to honor these drafts when presented and is generally in, or near, the country of the importer. An export letter of credit in a broad way is the advice from a bank to the beneficiary that a credit has been opened in his favor by a foreign bank and that he may present his drafts to the notifying bank for negotiation. "Notifying" banks in these cases are generally in, or near, the country of the exporter.

Other classifications involve stipulations concerning conditions that must be met before payments are made. A letter agreeing to honor drafts drawn by the beneficiary only when accompanied by bills of lading and other papers is classed as a documentary letter of credit. When such stipulations are not included, the letter is a "clean" or "open" one. Still other classifications involve whether letters are "revocable" or "irrevocable," that is, whether the issuing bank reserves the right to withdraw from its undertaking or whether it is specified that the bank cannot do this before the termination date. A further classification involves whether a notifying bank (see previous paragraph) in the same country as the exporter will add its unqualified assurance that it will pay if the foreign bank does not. When such assurances are included the export letter of credit becomes a "confirmed" one. When it is not the letter is "unconfirmed".

Open, irrevocable, confirmed export letters of credit are, of course, to be preferred for use by U.S. exporters when this kind of financing is used. These give important protection that bills will be paid with a minimum of possible adverse developments. Financing by letters of credit has become extensive in recent years because of delays in draft payments, dollar shortages, and other reasons. Trade practices have brought on the designation of certain foreign markets as "letter of credit" markets and such letters are used for those areas unless special reaons to the contrary exist.

Bank acceptances and acceptance credits take their names from the acceptance by banks of certain financing aspects and the credits that flow from those acceptances. Their use is not limited to overseas markets, but to U.S. exporters they represent undertakings of a practical nature that may possibly be used at times to obtain funds quickly. They may be utilized under letters of credit or draft arrangements. Under the former the exporter draws a draft against an accepting bank and obtains immediate payment. Concurrently the importer has a time credit to finance for which he may have the facilities of an American bank at his disposal where probably a more favorable rate is obtainable. When used with draft arrangements an exporter delivers the shipping documents together with his draft on the foreign bank to his bank. Concurrently he draws a second draft on the American bank for a similar amount which the bank accepts. He discounts the draft and funds are made available to him.

As regards differing values in currencies, many countries have eased exchange restrictions and their currencies usually are convertible into U.S. dollars. Thus, there are increased occasions for the safe making of sales which call for payments in foreign countries. In such cases, banks may open credits requiring drafts drawn in foreign currencies. When future payments are to be received in a foreign currency, however, the exporter may feel he should protect himself against any fluctuation of that currency. Ordinarily he may do so by selling an amount of foreign currency (usually through his bank) equivalent to the amount which he will eventually receive, at delivery dates coinciding with the maturities of this foreign currency receivables. These so-called "forward" sales are made at predetermined rates and enable the exporter to know in advance the amount of dollars he will receive, thereby eliminating the exchange risk.

U.S. government involvements in foreign financing stem principally from the Export Import Bank (Eximbank). Other such involvements include the Agency for International Development, which administers aid to less developed countries, the Commodity Credit Corporation, which deals with the export of surplus agricultural commodities, the International Bank for Reconstruction and Development, which makes long term development loans, the Inter American Development Bank, which is a joint operation of the American republics except Cuba, and the Department of Defense, which finances or guarantees certain military related U.S. exports.

Exporters with special financing problems which may be concerned with the Agency for International Development and the other groups subsequently named are probably best served by going to them direct or with their banks or finance companies. The lines are not as clearly drawn as to them as are the lines to Eximbank. Approaches to the latter are to be made by an exporter only after a definite determination that his requirements can not be met by his own bank or finance company. Eximbank does not compete with commercial banks and does not finance loans that they will handle. Additionally its operations are conducted so that commercial paper is kept to the best extent possible in private financial markets. When Eximbank takes participation in a transaction, the prerequisites, roughly stated, are that the foreign buyer pay 10 to 20% of the invoices involved and that the exporter retain 15 to 30% of the balance.

Insurance against export credit risks is available to exporters from the U.S. or its territories including Puerto Rico through the Foreign Credit Insurance Association (F.C.I.A.), 250 Broadway, New York, N.Y., 10007. This as an association of some fifty American insurance companies which administers export credit insurance in cooperation with Eximbank. Depending on the policies either or both commercial or political risks are covered, F.C.I.A. assuming the former and Eximbank the latter. Some policies cover short term (up to 180 days) financing and others medium term (181 days to 5 years-longer in some cases). Products that are eligible for the insurance vary, a feature that they have certain ties of U.S. origin being important. Comprehensive policies are also issued. Premium rates on comprehensive short-term policies average 50¢ per $100 of invoice value. Medium term rates are somewhat higher. Recognition of, and assistance to, non-recourse financing is also included in some policies. The Association has branch offices in Chicago, Cleveland, Houston, Los Angeles, and San Francisco.

SF 131B (L) REV. 5-66
PRINTING OF 10-70

COLLECTION INSTRUCTIONS

FROM
J. L. Mercantile Corp.

DATE
June 30,

ADDRESS
1375 Aisle Street, New York, N. Y.   00001

TO: **FIRST NATIONAL CITY BANK**
NEW YORK

THIS BOX FOR BANK USE ONLY
TYPE OF CURRENCY
U.S.

WE HAND YOU OUR DRAFT FOR	☐ PURCHASE OR ADVANCE SUBJECT TO FINAL PAYMENT	☒ PAYMENT TO US AFTER COLLECTION

AMOUNT
$35,000.00

DRAWN ON (DRAWEE)
Ambre Importer

TENOR
Sight

ADDRESS
Rio De Janiero, Brazil

OUR REFERENCE
AOX 2235

THE FOLLOWING DOCUMENTS COVER SHIPMENT OF (MERCHANDISE)   CONSIGNED TO

*UNLESS INDICATED TO THE CONTRARY BELOW:

1. SEND ALL COMMUNICATIONS VIA AIR MAIL.   2. DO NOT INCUR CABLE EXPENSE.   3. DO NOT PROTEST.

DOCUMENTS ▶	DRAFTS		BILLS OF LADING		INSURANCE		CONSULAR INV.		CERTIFICATE OF ORIGIN	INVOICES		MISCELLANEOUS
	ORIG.	DUP.	ORIG.	DUP.	ORIG.	DUP.	ORIG.	DUP.		VISED	PLAIN	
ORIG. ENCL.	X		X		X	X	X				X	Freight Receipt
DUP. TO FOLLOW												

PLEASE FOLLOW INSTRUCTIONS MARKED "X"

	TO BE FILLED IN BY FNCB		PLEASE FOLLOW INSTRUCTIONS MARKED "X"		
	DELIVER DOCUMENTS AGAINST ACCEPTANCE	POSTAGE	X	CABLE PROCEEDS	OUR EXP.	X DRAWEES EXP.
X	DELIVER DOCUMENTS AGAINST PAYMENT	ACCEPT LOCAL CURRENCY DEPOSIT		CABLE ADVICE OF PAYMENT	
X	ALL CHARGES ACCOUNT DRAWEE	COLLECT OUR CHARGE OF $		CABLE ADVICE OF NON-ACCEPTANCE AND REASON	
X	AIR MAIL DOCUMENTS AT OUR EXPENSE	COLLECT OUR POSTAGE OF $	X	CABLE ADVICE OF NON-PAYMENT AND REASON	
	AIR MAIL DOCUMENTS AT DRAWEES EXPENSE	INTEREST IS TO BE COLLECTED		PROTEST FOR NON-PAYMENT	
X	SUBJECT TO CONDITIONS ON REVERSE SIDE			PROTEST FOR NON-ACCEPTANCE	

ALLOW A DISCOUNT OF 2%		COLLECT INTEREST AT THE RATE OF 8% % PER ANNUM
X IF PAID on first presentation		FROM Maturity TO Date Paid

SPECIAL INSTRUCTIONS:

Present documents through your Rio De Janiero Branch

IN CASE OF NEED OR DIFFICULTY COMMUNICATE WITH
Jose Quantero, 116 Ave Santurce, Rio De Janiero, Brazil

X WHOSE INSTRUCTIONS HERETO YOU MAY FOLLOW WHETHER OR NOT IN ACCORD WITH THE INSTRUCTIONS HEREBY GIVEN

WHO WILL ENDEAVOR TO CAUSE THIS BILL TO BE HONORED AS DRAWN

UNLESS YOU ARE HEREINABOVE INSTRUCTED TO THE CONTRARY. PRESENTATION FOR ACCEPTANCE AND/OR PAYMENT OF EACH BILL ON LATIN AMERICA. INDIA. MALAYSIA. SINGAPORE. BRUNEI OR THE PHILIPPINES (IF ANY) MAY BE DEFERRED UNTIL THE ARRIVAL OF THE CARRYING VESSEL.

*WHENEVER YOU MAY HAVE PURCHASED ANY BILL OR MADE AN ADVANCE THEREAGAINST. YOU MAY IN YOUR DISCRETION REQUEST CABLE ADVICE OF NON-ACCEPTANCE AND/OR NON-PAYMENT. NOTWITHSTANDING ANY INSTRUCTIONS CONTAINED HEREIN TO THE CONTRARY. ANY EXPENSE INCURRED BY YOU RELATIVE THERETO SHALL BE FOR OUR ACCOUNT.
YOURS VERY TRULY.
J. L. Mercantile Corp.

TO BE FILLED IN BY BANK

SEND TO	AMOUNT OF BILL	DEDUCTIONS	PROCEEDS	INSTRUCTION LETTER	
				PREPARED BY	CHECKED BY
	SPECIAL PAYMENT INSTRUCTIONS			REMITTANCE LETTER (CHECKED BY)	
	☐ ISSUE CHECK ☐ CREDIT ACCOUNT			OUTSTANDING LIABILITY $	
RATE				APPROVED FOR PURCHASE BY	

Customer's Foreign Collection Letter

The mechanics of moving forward on, and dealing with, collections for goods sold in international trade vary. Some basic document forms which appear on the previous page and hereafter. The first is a customer's foreign collection letter addressed by an exporter to his bank enclosing a draft and other documents mentioned therein and specifying how they should be handled in connection with a shipment. The export-import contract in this instance was on the basis that payment would be made on delivery of the goods and this is reflected in the instruction letter. A letter form along these lines is generally the initial step in collection matters of this nature.

The draft forms which follow call for immediate (sight) payment and for payment in 90 days. They illustrate the use of features of these negotiable instruments as checks and as promissory notes. The obscure phrase, "First of Exchange (second unpaid)", incidentally, has been ingrained in these instruments for years (probably centuries) and at one time had significance when drafts were often lost and copies were provided for contingencies. With modern mail service and so on, however, the phrase is no longer a particularly pertinent one.

Next is a specimen of an irrevocable, confirmed letter of credit. It is not a "clean" or "open" letter, however, in that the presentation of appropriate documents is a prerequisite to pay-

---

$35,000.00   New York   June 30,   19 72

       Sight   DAYS AFTER   OF THIS

FIRST OF EXCHANGE (SECOND UNPAID) PAY TO THE ORDER OF

FIRST NATIONAL CITY BANK

Thirty-five Thousand and 00/100 Dollars

VALUE RECEIVED WHICH CHARGE TO THE ACCOUNT OF

Ambre Importer

Rio De Janiero   J. L. Mercantile Corp.

Brazil

SF 1362 REV. 6-62

Sight Draft

$35,000.00			New York	June 30,	19 72
			CITY	DATE	
	90 days	DAYS AFTER	Sight		OF THIS

FIRST OF EXCHANGE (SECOND UNPAID) PAY TO THE ORDER OF

FIRST NATIONAL CITY BANK

Thirty-five Thousand and 00/100 Dollars

VALUE RECEIVED WHICH CHARGE TO THE ACCOUNT OF

Ambre Importer

Rio De Janiero   J. L. Mercantile Corp.

Brazil

Ninety Day Draft

ment. Parties to transactions of this nature often agree to such prerequisites. The letter in essence says $35,000 has been made available to the exporter and, as shipments are made and documents are provided, funds will be remitted to him up to that amount. Two banks irrevocably stand behind the credit and drafts must be presented by a certain date.

Costs incident to using banking services in these matters are generally fractional when compared to the total amount of the transaction. Letter of credit charges are most often paid by the importer and run very roughly 1/4% of the value of the credit. A confirmation of the letter of credit would be roughly another 1/20% for every three months. Acceptance financing runs approximately an additional 1½ to 3% per annum. These figures may vary considerably in practice and, of course, actual charges should be developed when indicated.

Word use in the financing of payments for goods in foreign trade varies considerably. "Term" or "Time" drafts may become "Sight" drafts to some in certain circumstances. "Letters of Credit" become "Credits", "Commercial Credits," and so on. The basics, however, are as hereinbefore outlined and, where indicated, should be supplemented with other texts and information. Most banks in the field have publications which

FIRST NATIONAL CITY BANK

CABLE ADDRESS "CITIBANK"

111 WALL STREET, NEW YORK, N. Y. 10015

CONFIRMED IRREVOCABLE STRAIGHT CREDIT

DATE June 24, (Current Year)

J & L Mercantile Corp.
1375 Aisle Street
New York, New York 00001

ALL DRAFTS DRAWN MUST BE MARKED
DRAWN AS PER ADVICE CCF 100000

DEAR SIRS:

WE ARE INSTRUCTED BY Banco De Importacion, Rio De Janiero, Brazil

TO ADVISE YOU THAT IT HAS OPENED ITS IRREVOCABLE CREDIT No. 16   IN YOUR FAVOR

FOR ACCOUNT OF Ambre Importer, Rio De Janiero, Brazil

FOR A SUM OR SUMS NOT EXCEEDING A TOTAL OF $35,000.00 (Thirty-five Thousand Dollars)

AVAILABLE BY YOUR DRAFTS AT Sight   ON US TO BE ACCOMPANIED BY

1. Full set on board ocean bills of lading issued to order blank endorsed; notify Ambre Importer evidencing shipment from New York to Brazil dated not later than July 14, (Current Year).

2. Consular invoice

3. Full set negotiable marine insurance certificate including war risks.

4. Commercial invoice in four copies stating it covers grinding equipment and spare parts as per order number XLG dated January 15, (Current Year).

THIS ADVICE IS SUBJECT TO THE UNIFORM CUSTOMS AND PRACTICE FOR DOCUMENTARY CREDITS (1962 REVISION), INTERNATIONAL CHAMBER OF COMMERCE BROCHURE NO. 222.

THE ABOVE-NAMED OPENER OF THE CREDIT ENGAGES WITH YOU THAT EACH DRAFT DRAWN UNDER AND IN COMPLIANCE WITH THE TERMS OF THE CREDIT WILL BE DULY HONORED ON DELIVERY OF DOCUMENTS AS SPECIFIED IF PRESENTED AT THIS OFFICE ON OR BEFORE July 21, (Current Year)

WE CONFIRM THE CREDIT AND THEREBY UNDERTAKE TO HONOR EACH DRAFT DRAWN AND PRESENTED AS ABOVE SPECIFIED.

YOURS VERY TRULY,

COM 511 (L) S PARTS REV. 6-70
PRINTING OF 1-71

AUTHORIZED SIGNATURE

ART 906

Irrevocable Confirmed Letter of Credit

are helpful. Illustrative of these is "Introduction to Commercial Letters of Credit" by Leonard A. Back which was published for distribution recently by the First National City Bank, 399 Park Avenue, New York, N.Y. Included therein are the full texts of "Revised American Foreign Trade Definitions" and "Uniform Customs and Practice for Documentary Credits" which have been previously referred to in this section. Also included are some five pages of explanations of English, Spanish, French, German and other abbreviations commonly used in international trade.

Insurance and Claims

Here are subjects of vital interest and importance to every company operating in international trade. They should be given studious attention at all times. While steamship companies are liable for loss or damage due to their negligence, fault or failure in loading, storage, unloading, carriage, or care of merchandise, they are not liable for losses due to the perils of the seas, acts of God, acts of the public enemy, inherent defects of cargo or packages, or to negligence attributable to the shipper. Also, steamship companies can risk cargo and deviate from their intended voyages in order to save life or property at sea. There are many opportunities for misunderstandings and differences of opinion as to responsibility for loss or damage to foreign shipments, and every person making them must be sure that he has the best possible insurance protection. Concurrent with this, careful selection of carriers is important to the end that responsible, proper, and equitable handling is given any claims that might arise against such carriers.

Insurance and claim matters will doubtless be affected in some ways as the use of newer and more up-to-date international shipping modes progresses. Conceivably certain carrier-shipper liabilities may be altered as on incident to them. Additionally, the work being done on document simplification will help importantly in making less complicated insurance and claims papers, reports, and so on. The information which follows is written with this in mind. Fundamentally, however, much of what is said in this text has its origins in conventional cargo carriage.

■ *Insurance*—In order to obtain the best possible contract with an ocean marine underwriter, it is wise for those in foreign trade to seek the assistance of a reputable and experienced marine insurance broker. The broker, acting as the representative of the assured, will check to see that:

1. the insurance contract is tailor-made to fit the scope and method of operation of the individual trader,
2. the marine rates charged the assured are predicated upon a careful analysis of his own actual shipping experience; i.e., premiums paid for insurance against losses paid by underwriters,
3. the adjustment of claims is expedited; and that detailed information concerning the improving of packaging and conditions in various ports and places in the world that may affect the assured's shipments are made readily available,
4. the declaration to the underwriters of shipments insured under the policy is processed efficiently with a minimum of effort and time on the part of the assured,
5. the underwriter selected is well known not only in the marine insurance field as a whole but also for his knowledge of the particular commodity or commodities that are to be insured.

It is the purpose of this chapter to discuss in a broad way the subject of marine insurance and, under the following subheadings, to present in simple outline a few of the basic considerations involved in arranging ocean cargo insurance coverage.

■ *Insurable Interest*—The basic and fundamental principle behind all insurance is that of insurable interest. The same holds true in marine insurance. In marine insurance a shipper or receiver has an insurable interest in a cargo of goods when he is directly affected materially by the safe arrival or the loss or damage of the goods he has contracted to buy or sell.

In order for the assured to have an insurable interest in the goods, he must determine at what point the title to the property actually passes from the seller to the buyer. Terms of sale directly affect the insurable interest of the owner in the goods. He must know when his interest attaches and when it ceases. In other words, he must determine if the obligation is his to arrange marine and war risk insurance protection under the contracts of sale. Exporters who sell on F.O.B./F.A.S. terms port of shipment in the United States can extend their marine policies to cover such shipments in those instances where the buyer is obligated to furnish ocean marine insurance.

Misunderstandings and confusion as to where the responsibility rests for obtaining insurance may cause double insurance to occur. If, through error, both parties to the contract have placed insurance, the underwriter whose assured has no responsibility for declaring the shipment is usually willing to cancel his insurance, and return any premium charged when full particulars of the sale are disclosed. Double insurance can cause unnecessary trouble to insurers if the buyer and seller of the goods are not careful in their negotiations.

■ *Contingent Interest Insurance*—An American exporter who extends credit to an overseas buyer should make every effort to control the insurance covering the goods until he has been paid regardless of the terms of sale. Quite frequently United States shippers who sell on F.O.B. vessel terms insist on arranging the primary insurance coverage where they have sold to overseas buyers on sight draft, open account or other delayed payment terms. This is not always possible, however, if the country to which the goods are being shipped has insurance regulations which state that imported goods must be insured with local insurance companies. In other instances the foreign buyer may be so insistent upon controlling his own insurance that the exporter goes along with the request rather than jeopardize the sale.

In order to adequately protect his financial interest in the goods the shipper can arrange by endorsement to his open marine policy automatic contingent interest insurance protection. Under the terms set forth in the endorsement, shipments from United States made by the shipper on terms whereby he is not obliged to furnish ocean marine insurance are excluded from his policy. The insurance company agrees however that in respect to shipments reported prior to any known or reported loss or accident and in consideration of the declaration of the value of the shipment and payment of premium for same, they will guarantee to the shipper the prompt collection of losses which otherwise would have come within the terms of the policy. This means that if the goods are lost or damaged and the consignee does not pay the shipper, despite the terms of sale, the shipper is protected by means of his contingent interest insurance. This coverage is non-assignable and is for the benefit of the shipper only. The shipper declares such shipments to underwriters in the normal manner. Special policies or certificates are not required as it is not necessary to pass any insurance documents on to third parties. It is strictly an agreement made between underwriter and assured. The premium charge in most instances for this coverage is approximately 50% of the marine rate.

■ *Methods of Insuring*—Specific insurance (insurance placed for each specific shipment) is usually handled by a "special risks" department of an insurance brokerage firm for those shippers whose volume of business does not require an open policy, or for those firms whose shipments are of such a unique nature as to require placement in particular domestic and foreign markets.

Under an open policy the assured may take out insurance providing continuous coverage for all shipments he may make until cancelled by himself or the underwriter; the assured has automatic protection, subject to limits stated in the policy, from the time the goods leave the original warehouse until delivered to the consignee's warehouse. It is not necessary for the shipper to advise his broker of the export of goods prior to each sailing.

The declaration of shipments insured under an open policy should be made, however, as soon as practicable after the commencement of the transit of the goods. This is usually done by:

1. issuing a certificate when a negotiable document is required by the bank to satisfy a letter of credit; or
2. when a negotiable document is not required, forms supplied by the broker or underwriter are filled out by the assured and sent to the broker for transmission to the underwriter.

Under an open policy when full information is not known about goods in transit, the assured may bind a specific shipment with his underwriter by submitting a provisional declaration. When full particulars are available, the provisional declaration can be made final.

■ *Types of Coverage*—In order to satisfy the terms of a letter of credit or the request of a buyer or seller abroad, an exporter or importer must have more than a passing acquaintance with the various terms and conditions of the insurance coverage he may be called upon to supply.

Coverage given by the free of particular average (F.P.A.) policy is the narrowest in common use. This clause restricts coverage generally to total losses. In addition, it provides that partial losses are recoverable only in the event that the vessel or interest insured has been stranded, sunk, burnt, on fire, or in a collision. There are two forms of F.P.A. coverage, "under deck" and "on deck." The under-deck coverage is customarily written according to English conditions (F.P.A.-E.C.) which are:

> Free of particular average (unless general) or unless the vessel or craft be stranded, sunk, burnt, on fire, or in collision with another vessel.

The on-deck coverage is customarily written according to American conditions (F.P.A.-A.C.) which are:

> Free of particular average (unless general) or unless caused by stranding, sinking, burning, or in collision with another vessel.

In the English form, partial losses resulting from sea perils are recoverable, provided one of the stated accidents has taken place, without requiring that the damage actually be caused by the peril. In the American form, partial losses are not recoverable, unless the damage is caused by the stranding, sinking, burning or collision of the carrying vessel. Under both English and American forms, both general average and salvage charges are recoverable.

With Average (W.A.) coverage is a broadening of the basic F.P.A. form and may be stated as follows:

> Free of average under three (3%) per cent unless general or the vessel and/or the interest hereby insured be stranded, sunk, burnt, on fire, or in collision with any substance (ice included) other than water, each package separately insured or on the whole.

In simpler terms this clause means that if the vessel is stranded, sunk, burnt or in collision, partial loss from these sea perils is paid without regard to amount. However, if the vessel is not stranded, sunk, burnt or in collision and the partial loss is due to another sea peril such as salt water or unusually heavy weather, the loss is paid in full if it amounts to 3% or more. Insured losses not amounting to the 3% are not collectible.

The all risk clause which is widely used and is the most complete of the coverages available reads:

> Against all risks of physical loss or damage from any external cause (excepting risks excluded by the F. C. & S. [Free of Capture & Seizure] and Strikes, Riots and Civil Commotions warranties unless covered elsewhere herein), irrespective of percentage.

■ *Exclusions*—In all the forms of insurance coverage previously mentioned, certain perils are excluded. The risks of war, strikes, riots, and civil commotions are especially excluded, but can be included by special endorsement, or by a separate war policy. Claims for loss of market and for loss, damage or deterioration arising from delay are excluded. These are claims of consequential and indirect nature and not ones of physical loss or damage caused by an external force.

Another exclusion in every policy is that of inherent vice.

Damage that can be foreseen, or is due to the internal structure or nature of the commodity, is known as inherent vice. In other words, the claims that are allowable under the marine contract are in most cases caused by an external force. "Trade" losses such as normal loss of weight of certain types of foodstuffs, chemicals, and organic substances are not recoverable. Allowances for such weight discrepancies are taken into consideration by traders when negotiating for the merchandise.

When determining the type of coverage needed, an exporter or importer should obtain the most complete coverage practical to suit not only his buyer or seller but also the goods he is shipping. He must determine with the help of his broker whether or not F.P.A., W.A., or all risks conditions are warranted, taking into consideration, of course, the cost of the insurance and the susceptibility of the cargo to damage.

■ *Marine Insurance Rates*—Marine insurance rates are based on the premium and loss experience of the individual assured together with the over-all experience of certain types of commodities shipped to and from various places in the world. In determining rates, careful consideration is given to commodity, packaging, destination, ocean carriers and connecting conveyances involved, climatic conditions encountered during the voyage, and whether there is any additional storage and transshipment throughout the venture. An exporter or importer, by cooperating with his broker and underwriter, may often improve his loss experience by careful attention to these various factors and by being acquainted with the reliability of the foreign customers with whom he is dealing.

■ *General average*—(G.A.) is a marine insurance term referring to assessment against all shippers or interests to cover loss sustained when some cargo is jettisoned to save the vessel and the remaining part of the cargo. General average has been authoritatively described as "that which has been destroyed for all shall be replaced by the contributions of all. A general average loss is the result of a sacrifice voluntarily made under fortuitous circumstances of a portion of either ship or cargo or a voluntary expense for the sole purpose of saving the common interest from total destruction."

The expenses, losses, and sacrifices involved in a sea disaster are borne by all those with an interest in the goods on the ship and also the ship itself. The cargo and ship owners must contribute together and recompense those who have suffered loss or damage to their goods.

The method of arriving at the contribution of each is handled by general average adjusters. Some cases are solved and settled quickly, but if there are many interests involved, the process of the general average adjustment is a complicated one and may take months to settle.

In order for there to be a General Average situation, four conditions must be present: first, there must be an immediate impending physical peril, common to vessel and cargo; second, there must be a voluntary sacrifice or extraordinary expenditure to avert the peril; third, there must be a successful result; and fourth, there must be no fault on the part of those claiming contribution.

If the shipper is insured against general average losses his underwriter will usually furnish the guarantee for the general average bonds or security. The deposit receipt for such a bond is a negotiable instrument and should be held in readiness to be presented to the adjusters upon completion of the adjustment for refund if there should be an excess payment over and above the general average contribution.

Suppose, for instance, the outbound *Charles Cushing*, on which due diligence has been exercised to make seaworthy, is in collision in the Gulf of Mexico with another vessel, and as a result the *Charles Cushing* sustains a gash in its port side. The vessel is now unseaworthy and cannot continue its voyage. If the gash is extensive, it could place the *Charles Cushing* in jeopardy of sinking, or at least sustaining more damage. Thus we have the first condition—a physical peril common to vessel and cargo.

At this point a decision must be made. The voyage could be abandoned; and give the shippers back their cargo, and let them find some other means of getting their goods to their respective destinations; or the damage can be repaired and continue the venture. Most steamship companies are not in the habit of abandoning voyages and leaving their customers stranded, so it is elected to make repairs and continue to destination.

However, to do this the *Charles Cushing* must return to New Orleans, a port of refuge, discharge enough cargo to get to and repair the hole in the side, reload the cargo, and resume the voyage. The sacrifices and extraordinary expenditures in satisfaction of the second condition are: delay to the vessel in returning to a port of refuge; docking and wharfage fees; tug hire; pilotage; stevedore charges for discharging and reloading cargo; surveyor's fees for keeping account of the cargo being discharged and reloaded and the damages to cargo sustained thereby; and certain fees and expenses incurred by the general average adjusters.

In the case of the *Charles Cushing* let us suppose the value of the cargo was $100,000, and the value of the vessel was $400,000—a total of $500,000. The sacrifices were $150,000 and represent the amount to be "made good" in General Average.

The ratio of $500,000 to $150,000 is 30 per cent; therefore, the ship contributes 30 per cent of its value of $400,000, or $120,000, while cargo contributes 30 per cent of its value of $100,000, or $30,000, the total contribution being $150,000, the amount to be "made good". Of course, each individual shipper's contribution is 30 per cent of the value of his cargo, so if his cargo was worth $1,000, his proportion is $300.

There is a popular misconception among some shippers that they are required to pay costs of damage to the vessel sustained in the peril, but this is not true. Only sacrifices and extraordinary expenses incurred after the peril or to avoid the peril are charged into general average.

In all general average losses the shipper is called upon to do the following:

1. Post security in order to release cargo at port of destination.
2. Establish documentary evidence of the value of his cargo.
3. Pay the general average contribution when assessed by the adjusters.

If the shipper is insured against general average losses his underwriter will usually furnish the guarantee for the general average security in lieu of the cash deposit which would have to be made if the shipment was not insured. The receipt for such deposit is a negotiable instrument and should be held in readiness to be presented to the adjusters upon completion of the adjustment for refund if there should be an excess payment over and above the general average contribution.

■ *Determining the Correct Insured Value.*—The marine insurance policy is a "valued" policy; that is, when the value of the shipment is declared a certain policy value is agreed upon. In case of total loss, the total amount insured is paid; if a partial loss, a percentage of the total insured value is recoverable, based upon the extent of the damage to the goods.

An importer or exporter wishes to receive in return for damage to his merchandise a sum of money that will represent full indemnification. The various factors that go into making up the insured value include invoice value, freight charges, packing, consular charges, other fees, and insurance premiums. Anticipated profit of the transaction is also taken care of by adding a percentage of advance to the total value of the various factors above. While usually ten percent, an advance may be varied as an assured deems desirable to protect his position. It is most important that a trader in commodities such as sugar, coffee, burlap, rubber, cotton, etc., which are subject to price fluctuations in the open market, make certain that his valuation clauses are so drawn as to give him protection not only for his original costs but also for market changes.

■ *Duty.*—Import duties are collected on goods delivered into a country whether the goods are in a sound or damaged condition upon arrival. On such goods the U.S. Government demands duty to be paid and makes no allowance for depreciation due to damage unless the package containing the goods arrives empty or is so damaged as to be worthless. In such cases refund of duty may be allowed.

It is wise then for an importer to consider insuring duty on goods delivered into the U.S. so that in the event of damage he can recover the same percentage of loss on the duty amount as is recoverable on the insured value of the goods themselves. Because there is no risk on duty until the goods arrive in the U.S., the additional premium charged for insuring duty is approximately ½ of the marine rate applicable to the goods.

■ *Warehouse to Warehouse Clause.*—The Warehouse to Warehouse clause, normally a part of every policy, states when the insuring conditions attach and terminate. Goods insured are covered from the time they leave the warehouse for commencement of transit, during ordinary transit, and until delivered at the final warehouse at destination, or until the expiration of 15 days (30 days if an interior destination), whichever shall first occur. In case of delay beyond the assured's control, the goods are held covered subject to additional premium payments.

■ *Marine Extension Clause.*—This clause is designed to broaden the Warehouse to Warehouse Clause by eliminating the ordinary-course-of-transit-be-maintained provision, extending the 15/30 day time limit at destination limitation, and providing additional protection if goods must be off-loaded short of the original destination. This is considered interruption and suspension of transit beyond the assured's control. Unusual circumstances within his control and beyond the time limits provided in the policy would be:

    (1) Interruption of normal course of transit for repacking and consolidation for export at warehouses or even in the supplier's premises prior to start of transit, or

    (2) Import goods temporarily held in U.S. warehouses

pending sale. In this case an endorsement would be added and could be written to include transit to the final destination designated by the importer.

(3) When goods are sold on sight draft, open account or other delayed payment terms.

Obviously, because of the greater benefits to the assured, premiums for coverage within assured's control are slightly higher than for beyond assured's control.

■ *Streamlining Insurance Reporting Procedures.*—Cutting down on today's high cost of processing paper work can save as much or more money than a reduction in premium costs. Every effort should be made to eliminate unnecessary repetition of detail and the documentation of reports. Shippers should periodically review methods of operations with their insurance brokers to determine the possibilities of cutting down or simplifying methods of insurance reports. Certificate forms tailormade to a particular shipper's operational needs and acceptable to banking facilities throughout the world are available to overseas shippers. In any event shippers should certainly avail themselves of sets of certificates printed with one-time carbons or included in manifolds with other documents such as the invoice or bill of lading.

■ *Worldwide Wrap-up of Cargo Insurance.*—As U.S. industry spreads abroad or consolidates already existing facilities open marine cargo insurance policies arranged here in the United States can be extended to include shipments made by overseas manufacturing facilities and premiums may be paid in the local currency of the country of manufacture, if required. Consolidation of coverage can in many instances result in broader protection under master cargo policies at more competitive rates than before. Leading U.S. marine cargo insurance brokers and underwriters make available, through their U.S. and foreign facilities, service to handle the consolidation of marine insurance for all international shipments.

In actual practice interests and activities of marine insurance brokers and underwriters in international trade extend considerably beyond the policies they write. Some provide claim adjustment service abroad, others are active in packaging, and so on. The "Ports of the World", publication discussed in more detail in the Packaging section which follows also outlines port conditions (by ports) throughout the world and has cargo loss prevention features.

■ *Claims*—As a practical proposition, claims for loss and damage to cargo in foreign trade are insured in many cases. The practice of looking to insurers for reimbursement in these matters is quite prevalent. This is as it should be for many reasons. One in particular is that underwriters work daily with these matters and bring to them a worthwhile expertise and familiarity. Even with insurance, however, there can be problems; without insurance, complications can be staggering. To illustrate, a traffic department of a U.S.-based manufacturer having cargo moved without insurance by an ocean carrier from Europe to Africa could well find the complications simply too great to start legal collection proceedings on a loss or damage claim disputed by the carrier.

Another somewhat special facet of these matters is that often both the cargo owner and the ship operator are insured. The latter commonly has what is known as "P. and I." coverage, that is, property and indemnity insurance. Also, it is not unusual for ship owners having this insurance to be self-insurers up to certain dollar amount limits and to be insured for amounts in excess of those limits. The dual coverages result in a fairly common practice in, say, cargo damage instances for the cargo owner to make a claim against both the ship owner and his (the cargo owner's) insurer for the damage. The ship operator or its insurer may pay. If neither pays, the underwriter for the cargo owner does and then proceeds against the ship operator as subrogee. Alternatively, the cargo owner's insurer may pay in the first place and then proceed against the ship owner. These practices at times are quite helpful in avoiding delays and complications.

As a fundamental proposition, however, ship operators must transport cargo safely for the owners entrusting shipments to them irrespective of what insurance they may have. They are obligated to their shippers much as the rails and truck lines are obligated, except there are important differences in the ground rules and liabilities. As with domestic shipments, the bill of lading provisions are important. Sections 18 and 19 of the Ocean Bill of Lading, Appendix 2, are basic in this regard. They require certain written notice to the carrier at the port of discharge in certain circumstances and within certain time limits. They require also that suit must be brought within one year after date of cargo delivery or date when it should have been delivered. Reference to these provisions should be made for full particulars.

The important laws specifying liabilities in these cases are the Harter Act and the Carriage of Goods By Sea Act (U.S. Code 1970 ed. Title 46 Secs. 190–195 and 1300–1315). These have been in effect for some time and provide that a carrier may not include in the contract of carriage (the bill of lading) any clause, convenant, or agreement that relieves the carrier or the ship from loss or damage arising from negligence, fault, or failure in the duties and obligations as provided in these statutes. In other words, the law does not permit the carrier to soften their provisions by agreement. The Carriage of Goods by Sea Act is the more important of the two. It applies (Sec. 1313) "to all contracts for carriage of goods by sea to and from all ports of the United States in foreign trade."

The provisions of these laws which are concerned with cargo liability may be summarized as follows: A carrier must use due dilligence to make his ship seaworthy, to properly man, equip, and supply it, and to make its parts fit and safe for the carriage of goods. He is required to properly and carefully load, handle, stow, carry, keep, care for, and discharge the goods carried. Additionally he shall issue bills of lading as specified and so on. He is not liable for the unseaworthiness of the vessel unless it is caused by want of diligence on his part, fires unless due to his fault, acts of God, war, or public enemies, omissions of the shipper, latent defects, insufficiency of packing, and others. He is not liable for loss or damage result-

ing from deviations in attempting to save life or property at
sea.

The bill of lading provisions, the statutes summarized, and
the court interpretations of them are the high points of cargo
liability which govern the shipment from tackle-to-tackle, i.e.
from the time the goods are loaded on board until discharged
at destination; and represent the limits of the ship's responsibility. But that is not the end of it as far as the steamship company is concerned. Cargo comes into custody of the carrier
from trucks, railroads, and barges, frequently some time before
the vessel for which it is intended arrives in port. The carrier
then becomes a warehouseman or bailee, a bailee being a person to whom goods are committed in trust and who has temporary possession of them. A bailee also has a responsibility for
them and in several respects this responsibility is greater than
when these same goods are aboard a vessel. In this instance,
the steamship company does not have the protection of the
special laws mentioned because they do not apply ashore before the cargo attaches to the ship's tackle or after leaving the
tackle at port of discharge. The bill of lading terms do not
apply because the bill of lading has not been issued.

Consequently, the carrier usually protects his legal liability
for goods in his custody with insurance sometimes called
"Shore Risk". This covers the liability of the assured for physical loss or damage to cargoes, etc. from any cause whatsoever
(including the risks of strikes, riots and civil commotions) but
excluding war risks, while such properly is in, on or about his
premises at locations named in the policy, subject to stated limits of liability. Generally the cargo owner also has insurance as
to these steps in the movement of his shipment and, when
losses occur, substantially the same routine is followed as that
hereinbefore outlined for other types of claims. Essentially he
will let his underwriter handle the matter. Where the cargo
owner does not have insurance, however, reimbursement
should come direct from the carrier or the latter's underwriter.

■ *Collecting Claims for Losses.*—When an assured suffers a
loss to merchandise insured under a marine policy through one

of the stipulations of the policy, he should make every effort to protect the damaged goods from further harm and arrange for the proper inspection of the goods by qualified surveyors. After notifying the nearest agent of the insurance company of the loss, a written notice of claim upon the goods must be made.

When a foreign customer receives goods in a damaged condition, after their having been insured by the U.S. exporter, he examines the reverse side of the original insurance certificate, or policy, and determines the nearest representative of the insurance company. Through him, the survey report can be drawn up, and other details surrounding the loss can be discussed. Any reasonable charges incurred at this time by the consignee, such as the survey fee, and the repacking and reconditioning expenses are allowable as part of the claim. A U.S. importer of goods from abroad, when discovering damage, will immediately notify his underwriter, who will in turn arrange for the survey. A formal claim upon the carrier must also be initiated.

Upon receipt of the certificate of damage, the assured is in a position to present his claim to the underwriters. The following documents are those that make up a complete claims presentation.

1. The original and duplicate copies of the insurance certificate or policy.
2. A copy of the claim letter upon carrier, and reply, if obtainable.
3. A copy of the bill of lading.
4. A copy of the original invoice.
5. A copy of the packing list and weight certificates.
6. The surveyor's report, or certificate of damage, showing extent of loss.

An experienced insurance broker can be of invaluable assistance to the exporter or importer if, upon receipt of all the documents required, he will draw up the formal claim and present it to the underwriters for payment. Claims are made up in accordance with the valuation clauses of each policy. The loss may be one of a part of the goods which are missing upon arrival at destination, or it may be one in which the goods arrive in a damaged condition at destination. Additionally, marine policies are particularly difficult to understand and trade usage is important to the effect to be given a great deal of their wording. A good broker, working with them every day, can be most helpful in this connection.

Packaging

There are few published rules and regulations concerning packaging in foreign trade. Because of the varying conditions from origin to destination, competition, and for other reasons, international packaging standards have not been spelled out on particularly clear cut bases. Packaging, nevertheless, is an important phase of exporting, importing and transportation between foreign countries. Chapter seven, dealing with domestic packaging, has much in common with this section. Much of the information there is also applicable to this discussion.

The package must be designed to withstand all of the hazards of salt water, stevedore handling, shipment, and warehousing in foreign countries. At the same time, it must be as light as possible to keep freight costs at a minimum; and to keep customs duties at a minimum because some countries levy duties on gross, rather than on net or legal, weight of goods. Even when duties are levied on value, the levy may be on the value of the package as well as on the goods, or even on the total transportation charges paid from the originating port to destination.

Discussion with almost any steamship official as to the many problems of operating foreign service is sure to bring forth, sooner or later, an opinion that some companies with foreign operations do not either package or mark their freight as well as transportation conditions may well require. They will say that too much attention is paid to the "cost-of-packaging" factor and not enough to the "safe-arrival-at-destination" factor. Or, they may say that domestic packaging is used with the entirely erroneous idea that shipments forwarded to foreign countries are not subject to any more hazard than domestic shipments. The fact is that over-all losses due to faulty packaging of goods in foreign trade are in the millions each year.

Even a good loading job into the ship is not the complete answer to satisfactory handling to destination. A freighter has three or more hatches into which freight is loaded. The average dry cargo freighter, depending of course on size, will transport anywhere from 4,000 to 10,000 tons and up of cargo. Packages loaded into a ship may be subject to a strain from outside pressure of as much as 1,000 pounds per square foot. The rolling and pitching of the vessel is bound to cause the strain to shift, thereby resulting in weak packaging giving way, with resulting damage to the merchandise.

The use of containers, cribs, platforms and pallets, even though the pallets are removed once the cargo is in the hold of the ship, greatly improves ship-to-pier and pier-to-ship handling.

For shipping valuable commodities in small packages, which are subject to theft, metal shipping containers that hold a number of small wood or fiberboard packages are used by many steamship companies to permit the handling of numerous small shipments as one unit load.

Even if freight is handled properly, loaded properly and stowed into the ship properly, there is still the sometimes much greater hazard of unloading, handling, and reshipment at foreign ports. Many foreign ports have facilities requiring unloading to open piers or from the ship anchored off shore into lighters or barges, thence to the dock and the beyond carrier (rail, truck, air, barge, cart or even muleback).

Another problem is theft or pilferage. Packaging should be designed to prevent access to contents. The many handlings of some foreign shipments offer opportunities for freight handlers, etc., to break a carton or open a package, remove part of the contents, and efface any evidence of tampering. Steamship companies can refuse to pay claims for concealed loss or damage. It is well to keep in mind that, if at all possible, packaging should be designed so that it cannot be opened readily. There is "pilfer-proof" packaging that is constructed and sealed in such a way that, if it is broken into, it cannot be resealed or repaired. Result: The theft is discovered at the next inspection, and the approximate time and place of the pilferage can be determined.

Weather at destination or enroute is another packaging factor that is given important attention. High humidity, rain when goods are stored on open piers, etc., cause rust, mildew, or fungus growth, and destroy the binding strength of cartons fastened with glue as well as causing other damage. A ship moving through the tropics enroute to destination generates considerable heat in the holds, and this can cause damage due to melting, sweating, etc. The answer is better packaging. Waterproofing can be accomplished (or made better) by using waterproof solid and corrugated cartons, or lining cases with heavy tar paper or other waterproof material; by plastic wrappings; by oiling tools, machinery and similar items; by creating a sealed vacuum; and by depositing in the case a supply of silica gel or some other moisture-absorbing agent, of which there are several on the market today. Inhibitors that will prevent corrosion can be placed in packages.

Good business demands getting the product to destination in perfect condition. Competition for foreign markets quite often mean that the exporter performing the most satisfactory packaging job will obtain the business. Foreign importers are often familiar with the type of packaging required to get goods to their country safely and may specify packing requirements in the sales agreement or as part of the specifications laid down in the letter of credit. Experience plus the advice of the receiver will provide the right answer sooner or later.

Some countries assess a duty on the finished product but not on parts. Therefore, if the item can be shipped as parts with instructions to the receiver as to how to assemble, there may be a saving in duty expenses.

The steamship companies have not issued any standardization regulations on packaging, for several reasons. One reason is the obvious fact that some foreign steamship lines would be reluctant to accept any standards, feeling that it might jeopardize their competitive situation. The Federal Maritime Commission has not mandated packaging standards for the shipment of overseas cargo for similar and other reasons. The Bureau of Foreign and Domestic Commerce of the Department of Commerce has issued some approved packaging methods which are optional with the shipper. Some military packaging standards are excellent, but are often considered to be too rigid and expensive for commercial purposes.

Some steamship conferences publish tariffs that contain packaging provisions, but these are more to determine the applicable rates on a single commodity packed in different types of containers than to set up any particular packaging requirements.

Firms handling measurement cargo (i.e., cargo that is charged for by its total dimensions rather than by its weight) in foreign commerce would do well to study their package design, as it is sometimes possible to change the dimensions only slightly and still materially reduce the cubic content, resulting in a decrease in the ocean freight costs.

Hazardous and dangerous cargo is subject to special packaging, marking and stowage rules and regulations. Agent R. M. Graziano's Water Carrier Tariff No. 24, republishes United States Coast Guard regulations governing the transportation or storage of explosives, combustible liquids, and other dangerous articles or substances on board vessels together with restrictions covering the acceptance and transportation of explosives and other dangerous articles by carriers parties to the tariff. A copy of this publication may be obtained from the Bureau of Explosives, Room 620, American Railroads Building, Washington, D.C. The cost is $18.00 to members of the Bureau or $22.00 to nonmembers. See also comments in the chapter on Hazardous Materials later in the text.

Various other publications dealing with the packaging of international shipments include "Ports of the World" by the Insurance Company of North America, P.O. Box 7728, Philadelphia, Pa. Package requirements and other features involved with preventable loss and damage are included. Cautionary markings in English and their counterparts in French, German, and other languages are also shown. Marking symbols such as a drawing of a hook with an "X" over it meaning "use no hooks," for use where illiteracy may prevail, are also presented. The text is now in its ninth edition and copies are available gratis on request. Insurance underwriters have been taking an increasing interest in good export and import packaging. Their emphasis on improved packaging as it affects insurance rates has been helpful in numerous cases.

Marking is a most important consideration in connection with all overseas shipments. Some countries have customs regulations that specify that marking must be accomplished with a

SHANGHAI
301/400

Example of packing case mark.

stencil and indelible ink. Frequently good paint applied with a brush is satisfactory. It is well to mark at least two sides of a package as it may be in a pile where only one side is showing.

Marking follows a well-defined practice. An example of the usual practice is:

First there is the symbol of the importer. This is followed by the destination port and the consecutive case numbers. The symbol suffices for the name of the consignee. This is done when it is desirable not only to keep the customer's name from becoming known to competitors, or when consigned to a broker for resale, but also to disguise the nature of contents as an antipilferage measure. Then follows a double number system in that the first number is the individual piece number while the second number represents the total number of pieces in the lot.

Thus in the example the piece would be number 301 of a 400-piece lot. The next piece would be marked 302/400, the following 303/400, etc.

In addition, it is often necessary to show on each piece the gross, legal and net weights in pounds or kilograms and the cubic measurement (in feet and/or meters) of the package. Marks should be 2″ or 3″ high and run from 12″ to 15″ across the package. Since foreign longshoremen often cannot read English and since steamship companies stow freight by destination port, it is of the utmost importance to provide clear markings.

The 1970 Merchant Marine Act and Other Laws

The United States, as with other countries, has important responsibilities in dealing with the indispensable role foreign trade plays in economic development. Exports and imports have been steadily rising, the total figure for 1971 being almost $90 billion, composed of $43.6 billion for exports (up 2% from the previous year) and $45.6 billion for imports (up 14% from the previous year).

Prior to the 1950s there was no question but that the United States enjoyed a "favorable balance of trade" as it was a creditor nation with its exports, both agricultural and industrial, exceeding its total imports. However, about 1959 world wide competition of foreign countries, particularly of manufactured products, increased too and along with lowering of tariff restrictions, imports into the U.S. became higher than ever.

A most vital factor affecting U.S. exports is the ever-increasing competition of foreign countries. Domestic U.S. inflation has upped costs to an extent that overseas nations, with a new will-to-do, are under-selling U.S. concerns on many items. In fact, some foreign goods have the ability to compete right in the U.S. The technological revolution that began in the U.S. at the turn of the century has now swept across the world at a vigorous pace which means rough competition for the U.S. everywhere.

We hear a lot about "balance of payments deficit" of the U.S. This deficit is caused primarily by huge expenditures (outgo) of U.S. dollars in other countries for the large programs involving excess agriculturals, loans, military aid, tourism, etc. Persistent payments deficits cause a continued large accumulation of dollar holdings by foreigners. Besides being a claim on United States gold reserves, this surplus tends through the law of supply and demand—and psychologically —to weaken the value of the dollar internationally. United States overseas shipping is one of the largest sources of strength to the country in this regard and is its principal intangible export.

Regulatory philosophy toward "free trade" is modifying. Trade on this basis normally means reducing or eliminating duties so that foreign countries may compete freely with American manufacturers and vice versa. The sponsors of free trade argue that in the long run everyone is better off because the country that can produce a certain item most economically will produce that item to the advantage of all concerned. The foreign country has an opportunity to sell some of its products and will spend some of the profits in the United States for items produced cheaper than in the foreign country. The American consumer, on the other hand, can purchase cheaper and thus has more money wherewith to buy other goods, thereby improving conditions all around. Modifications, thus far, are directed against certain countries and are applied to certain products. Stepped-up anti-dumping activities are also a part of these modification, all of which require watching.

The United States is not a self-sufficient country. A long list of commodities must be imported to keep United States industry operating on a normal basis and its people supplied adequately with necessary goods. Transportation of these items depends almost entirely on ships. To be assured of a continuous flow of all essential commodities, the United States must see to it that its merchant marine is kept strong.

Operating and construction subsidies and other help by the federal government for carriers are, and have been for many years, simply a way of life in international trade. Tangible returns in higher tax collections and in other ways come from these and good cases are made for the help that is given. On the business front more than carrier subsidies exist, however, in that particular, special legislation of a helpful nature as to industrial companies with foreign operations are also on the statute books. Prime reasons for all of these are those hereinbefore outlined as well as other conditions elsewhere, steps taken by other countries, and so on. Coupled with them are our own important international needs, requirements for adequate defense, and other considerations.

The 1970 Merchant Marine Act is one of the most significant U.S. laws in recent years dealing with international shipping and represents a substantial step in opening wider the doors of international trade. Overly simplified it calls for a ten year 300 ship building program and has been the spring board for some in the trade to speak of the 1970's as the "Decade of the Shipper". Financial assistance is provided for the building of more modern ships, larger and more economical ships, ships in bulk cargo trades and others. Industrial traffic managers working with carriers on these matters will wish to familiarize themselves to the extent necessary with the provisions of this Act that may be of value to them. Data thereon are available in various government publications.

The general program that produced these encouraging benefits of particular interest to the carriers also made available tax benefits to industrial companies for participation in foreign trade. Known as the DISC legislation, the law provides that such companies may form Domestic International Sales Corporations as separate marketing subsidiaries to engage in international sales and that 50% of the earnings on such sales may be deferred or otherwise receive special treatment. DISC companies have been formed by a number of industrial concerns. Benefits are worth while in many cases and possibilities are to be investigated in this field where indicated. "Boom in DISCs", an article in Barron's for August 28, 1972, gives more details on these.

The Webb Pomerene law (Export Trade Act of 1918) may also be of importance to industries at times. Immunity from U.S. anti-trust statutes is available under it to them in their export activities. It was passed to enable American producers to meet the competition of foreign combinations. The law is administered by the Federal Trade Commission, and companies using this law generally do so through associations. These associations, one step short of being cartels, are most successful when the member firms export the same or generally the same commodities. Under the association set-up they can cooperate and consolidate on sales, pricing, shipping and distribution. They can quote one set of prices, consolidate shipping control as well as actual shipments, and achieve long term continuity of product and service through joint distribution channels.

Employment of Independent Ocean Freight Forwarders, Customs Representatives, and Freight, Chartering, and Ship Brokers

As mentioned earlier in this chapter, the use of brokers can be of real help in foreign trade. Considerations forming the basis of their employment will vary. Some companies do not use them. Others use them on all of their work. Still others use only certain kinds, i.e., customs brokers. To an industrial company commencing international activities or to one having only a few international shipments, brokers can be particularly helpful because their special lines of work are technical, and mastery of them takes time, money, and attention. To many they represent "built-in" sources for moving ahead in business fields of a non-routine and not-normally-encountered nature.

When brokers are employed, however, it is not enough for exporting and importing concerns to establish arrangements and then feel that every necessary action has been taken. Such concerns should have working understandings of foreign trade sufficient to enable them to deal properly with their agents and to be sure that such agents are taking actions with which they would agree. Additionally shippers should keep actively in touch with the work being performed to the end that all help possible is being given to the broker operation. Details of the various services offered follow.

■ *Independent Ocean Freight Forwarders*—The services of these forwarders and of customs house brokers are the two types most used by most shippers. Both must have licenses, the first from the Maritime Commission and the second from the Treasury Department. Many independent ocean freight forwarders are also customs brokers and hold licenses to act as both. Customs clearances are, of course, concerned with imports and the holding of the two licenses is a "natural" for those involved in that such licenses clear them to represent their principals in both export and import procedures. Along with obtaining a license from the Maritime Commission before commencing operations, ocean freight forwarders must also post performance bonds.

An independent ocean freight forwarder is defined as "a person carrying on the business of forwarding for a consideration who is not a shipper or consignee or a seller or purchaser of shipments to foreign countries, nor has any beneficial interest therein, nor directly or indirectly controls or is controlled by such shipper or consignee or by any person having such a beneficial interest." They occupy unique positions similar, say, to tax experts, and their responsibilities differ from those of domestic and foreign forwarding companies that consolidate and move on freight shipments.

Ocean forwarders are specialists in their field. They book cargo and perform many other functions. They will trace or expedite shipments from inland shipping point to shipside. They will supervise unloading with "domestic" equipment at the port of exit and arrange for inspection, strapping, marking, sorting, re-packing, relabeling, cartage, lighterage and some at times will check merchandise going aboard the steamer. They prepare all documentation such as dock receipts, customs declarations, ocean bills of lading, certificates of origin, consular invoices and arrange for marine insurance with needed certificates. They will distribute documents as required and as directed by their clients.

Forwarders are familiar not only with sailings, rates and services of the various steamship companies, but also with the documentation required before the steamship company can accept the shipment. The forwarder invoices the exporting or importing company, say, $25.00 or more per shipment for services rendered, i.e., documention, expediting and tracing, arranging marine insurance, attending to banking requirements, etc., including advice and guidance in negotiating freight rates and other related matters. Their fees to their shipper clients will vary in proportion to the functions performed.

Interestingly enough, the "forwarder" may also receive a commission or compensation from the steamship company. It is paid to him for bringing the business to the steamship company, and while the usual amount paid to him by the steamship carrier is 1¼% of the total freight paid, some steamship lines on certain high rated commodities in limited trades pay as high as 5 per cent.

Legal sanction for this trade practice provides that steamship common carriers may pay a commission to certified independent foreign freight forwarders when such a forwarder has solicited and secured cargo (actually booked it with the carrier). The law states that the forwarder must sign a certification, usually placed on the forwarder's invoice, which must be in the possession of the steamship company before any compensation can be paid. The certification reads as follows:

"The undersigned hereby certifies that it is operating under license No. .... (or application No. .... and registration No. ....) issued by the Federal Maritime Commission, or its predecessors, and has performed in addition to the solicitation and securing of the cargo for the ship, or the booking of or otherwise arranging for space for such cargo, two or more of the following services (Check services performed):

1. The coordination of the movement of the cargo to ship-side;
2. The preparation and processing of the ocean bill of lading;
3. The preparation and processing of dock receipts or delivery orders;
4. The preparation and processing of consular documents or export declarations;
5. The payment of the ocean freight charges on the cargo."

Commodities not subject to mark and count, (usually bulk cargo subject mostly to "open" rates) are exempt from this certification requirement. While some ocean forwarders work with these bulk commodities, such work generally represents only a small percentage of their business.

The practices under which ocean forwarders receive compensation on the same shipment from two sources—the shipper and the carrier—has been in existence for many years. Information concerning lists of them and their headquarter locations, as well as trade association and other data, appear at the end of the next subsection on customs brokers.

■ *Customs Brokers.*—The principal functions of customs house brokers are concerned with imports. They arrange for the payment of correct duty (which often times is technical and detailed), clearances into and out of bonded warehouses, payment of freight charges due, and so on. They also perform such special functions as securing refunds of excess duties, appeals from appraisement, preparation of withdrawal papers for articles in bonded warehouses, etc. Many importers arrange for shipments to be consigned direct to their customs broker.

The licenses that must be obtained by them from the Treasury Department are issued by ports to both individuals and corporations. To secure a license an individual must pass both a written and oral examination after which he must appear before a Review Board to be sure that he is thoroughly familiar with customs laws and procedures. A fee is required to obtain the license, which is then good until cancelled. Corporations receive licenses too, but only if two or more of their officers have individual licenses and, if these licensees appear before the Review Board, a customs brokerage license will then be issued in the name of the corporation.

Typical of situations where customs brokers can be helpful would be the case of an Ex Dock shipment arriving at a U.S port of entry. The term "Ex Dock" is used fairly regularly in import trade, as are "Ex Quay" and "Ex Pier". Purchases on an Ex Dock basis would be subject to check to be sure a foreign seller to a U.S. buyer was paying all fees that come under this responsibility. A good customs broker would understand this and take what steps might be necessary to protect the importer accordingly. Under Ex Dock the foreign seller must:

(1) Provide and pay for transportation to named port of importation,

(2) Pay export taxes, or other fees or charges, if any, levied because of importation,

(3) Provide and pay for marine insurance,

(4) Provide and pay for war risk or related insurance,

(5) Be responsible for any loss or damage, or both, to cargo until the expiration of the free time allowed on the dock at the named port of importation or the removal of such cargo within that time by the consignee (whichever occurs first).

(6) Pay the cost of certificates of origin, consular invoices, legalization of bill of lading, or any other documents issued in the country of origin, or of shipment, or of both, which the buyer may require for the importation of goods into the country of destination and, where necessary, for their passage in transit through another country.

(7) Pay all costs of landing, including wharfage, landing charges, and taxes, if any;

(8) Pay all costs of customs entry in the country of importation,

(9) Pay customs duties and all taxes applicable to imports, if any, in the county of importation.

The above conditions would be applicable to an import sale of this nature except where the terms of the sales contract or other agreements establish different provisions. The buyer's responsibilities would start when he takes delivery on the dock at the named port of importation within the free time allowed. If delivery is not taken within that time, the cost and risk of goods are his as the free time expires. Parenthetically, the specification of Ex Dock terms on U.S. exports is generally avoided.

All of the various customs procedures must be correctly accomplished to avoid delays and possible extra expense. As a part of this and for various other reasons customs brokers frequently receive a power of attorney from the importer so they can endorse bills of lading and file entries for account of the importer. Also, when a bond is needed two sureties are required. The customs broker can act in the capacity of one surety, which is a great convenience. Additionally, situations may arise where a customs broker may represent both the seller and the buyer in a transaction and this should be borne in mind. Customs brokers fees will vary with the functions required and may run from $25 and more per entry.

A current list of ocean fowarders and customs brokers and their locations is available in the Customs House Guide, issued annually. The list is supplemented monthly in The American Import and Export Bulletin. Their publication address is 107 So. Tyson Ave., Floral Park, N.Y. 11001 (212-347-8724). Many operators in these two groups hold memberships in the National Customs Brokers and Forwarders Association of America, Inc., One World Trade Center, Suite 1109, New York, N.Y. 10048 (212-432-0050).

■ *Freight, Chartering, and Ship Brokers.*—Brokers in the freight, chartering, and ship fields do not, as a general rule, have much to do with what is usually considered general cargo.

Insofar as cargo is concerned their work is more with bulk shipments involving no marks or counts and on certain open rated commodities. Their fields are quite broad and some specialize in particular parts of those fields.

Licenses are not required in operations in this category and, if a broker in these operations should perform the services of a freight forwarder without being certificated as such, he would be liable for prosecution as being in violation of a federal statute. These brokers do not handle documentation work such as preparing bills of lading, passing of "decs" (export declarations), and so on.

Freight brokers do not usually work bulk lots of less than 500 tons. They bring together a shipper of a full cargo or a large parcel of bulk cargo with a tramp or liner steamship operator. They develop or negotiate rates and terms (laydays, demurrage, dispatch, F.I.O., F.I.T., etc.) and then prepare a charter party or a contract of affreightment which the shipper and carrier sign. Brokers also arrange for ship trip or time charters between shipping companies. Further, there are ship brokers who sell ships; they are specialists in ship sales.

There is no generally prescribed commission or brokerage to be paid in these matters. This is a negotiated feature of any "fixture" and goes from 1¼% to 5 per cent, or even higher, dependent on how many interests are represented. Sometimes there are two or more brokers involved each wanting a share of the fee as well as other involvements such as "address" commissions (extra, special payments) and the like.

Many brokers in this field are members of The Association of Ship Brokers & Agents, Inc., 17 Battery Place, New York, N.Y. 10004. 212-422-2786.

Airlines, Parcel Post, and Non-Vessel Operating Common Carriers by Water

The airlines, parcel post, and non-vessel operating common carriers by water have particular positions in foreign trade. Each provides certain unique and special benefits to a shipper and their judicial use can be profitable and helpful in many ways. Further, many changes in their rate structures, shipping schedules, size of shipment availabilities, and other features of their operations are such that a particularly open mind should be kept in industrial traffic circles concerning their use. On any number of kinds of shipments they may well be, or come to be, the best nominees for carriage.

■ *Airlines.*—The use of containers is the current, number-one feature of foreign air shipments as it is with domestic air carriers. The international and domestic air freight pictures have much in common in this connection. Container formats and sizes are comparable, special freight rates are made regarding them, and so on. The earlier discussion in this text on containerized domestic air freight should be referred to for further details. Reference also should be made to other features of that discussion. As to many of those features, comparable situations exist. Internationally, foreign airline companies are added "starters" available to make a company's shipments.

Airplanes of U.S. and foreign registry, destined from the U.S. to foreign countries, operate from and to international airports in the United States and over routes authorized by the Civil Aeronautics Board, in most cases in conjunction with agreements established between the United States and foreign governments. Airfreight within or between foreign nations is generally subject to regulation by those countries. Rates, rules and regulations involving U.S. entries and exits are published in tariffs that must be filed with the C.A.B. and some foreign governments. Major overseas airlines are members of the International Air Transport Association (I.A.T.A.) which publishes rates jointly for its members. Air cargo tariffs include domestic and foreign routing for joint carriage under through rates and air waybills. Rates are usually in cents per pound from base points with arbitraries applying from non-base points. In many cases they apply either on a volume or a weight basis; volume is cargo with overall dimensions exceeding a certain number of cubic inches per pound while weight is less than that number of cubic inches. The greatest rectangular dimensions of each package, or group of packages tied together, are used in determining the cubic measurement of a shipment.

There are specific commodity rates and general cargo rates. Additionally minimum charges often apply per waybill. Each airline publishes and distributes its own memorandum tariff which contains rates and other details on shipping overseas by air cargo services including any special individual line situations.

An International air waybill is commonly used and will be issued as a through waybill from any interior point by the local agent of the airline. It is typed with at least ten copies to satisfy all needs. Memorandum tariffs show a sample waybill with reference numbers explaining spaces in detail. For example, "N.V.D." shown in a waybill means "No Value Declared".

Cargo may be delivered to or received from the airline directly at the local airport. Pickup and delivery trucking services at published rates are available also at principal cities in the United States and Canada. Downtown airline receiving deppots have been established in some cities.

Many airlines provide a reservation service for air freight in the same manner as for passengers; in these cases the shipper may book in advance specifying the schedule and routing he wishes. It is well to be sure in advance that the airline equipment will accommodate the cargo.

The size and weight of air freight shipments are limited only by the dimensions of hatches and compartments, and the floorbearing ratings of the various types of aircraft. Large shipments, including five and ten ton units, are normally handled on the all-cargo planes; smaller shipments may be transported on either all-cargo aircraft or the combination passenger-cargo schedules. Dangerous and certain other commodities are restricted. Carriers can refuse cargo if not properly marked and packed. Packing requirements are generally on the less critical side, but temperature changes plus getting shipments to and from airports must be kept in mind.

The overseas airlines, as with the domestic carriers, promote use of their services with the suggestion that despite lower rates elsewhere there may actually be savings by using air freight because of other factors. For example, they ask shippers to analyze their over-all costs re the following: packaging; insurance; domestic transport; storage enroute; brokerage; embarkation port charges; transportation overseas; discharge port costs; customs duties and onward transportation. The airlines suggest that some of these items are non-existent via air or so much lower, that the over-all costs will favor use of air freight. This may be particularly true in foreign trade on small lots, say those of less than 1,000 pounds.

The airlines go further and claim there are hidden costs via other transportation that do not apply via air freight in the following areas: overseas warehousing, inventory outlays and losses, cost of time in transit, lost sales account distributor/customer dissatisfaction, and claims. More specifics on calculations that may be used in determining a company's costs in these matters appear in "A Formula for Determining Air Feasibility" published in the September 18, 1972 Traffic World. Copies are currently available gratis from E. T. Whalen, Director Cargo Sales, Japan Air Lines, 655 Fifth Avenue, New York, N.Y. 10022.

Customs, licenses (export and import), financial remittances, and related features of international air shipments may be characterized as receiving streamlined attention in some ways. Basic requirements as to these features, however, must be met. Export declarations (and licenses) may be processed at some inland origins as an incident to tendering cargo for shipment and using the waybills as "through" documents.

■ *Parcel Post.*—International parcel post service (surface and air) is available between the United States and most countries as well as between the foreign countries themselves. Current U.S. surface rates to North and Central America and a limited number of near-by countries are $1.20 for two pounds or less and 35¢ for each additional pound or fraction thereof. Shipments to other countries take slightly higher figures. Air rates vary considerably by country and range from about $1.50 to

2.25 for the first 4 oz. plus $0.25 to $1.25 for each additional 4 oz. or fraction thereof. General dimensional limits are: greatest length 3½ feet, greatest length and girth combined 6 feet. As to some countries parcels may be 4 feet long if not more than 16 inches in girth. Maximum permitted weights vary (roughly) from 22 to 44 pounds.

Special delivery and insurance availability vary from nation to nation. Each is obtainable in about half of them. Further, recoverable amounts on insurance (when available) are low. Availabilities of other features are: registration—very limited, COD and certified mail—not available, and special handling—between mailing point and U.S. point of departure only. Letters and the like move on a more expedited basis as "postal union" mail and small packets (1 to 2 pounds depending on the country) may also be sent (regular or air and at a higher cost) under the "postal union" category.

Prohibited articles include, radio-active materials, firearms capable of being concealed on the person, and others. Parcels should be more carefully packed than those for domestic delivery. Certain forms are required where dutiable articles are involved. These include a completed parcel post sticker (Form 2922) and at least one customs declaration (Form 2966). To some countries a dispatch note (Form 2972) is also required. These forms are obtainable at most post offices.

The foregoing highlights are, of course, subject to change and are presented simply as broad guides. Publication 51 (July 1971), "International Postage Rates and Fees," is obtainable gratis at many post offices and gives more details. Publication 42, "International Mail," gives still further details. This last named post office publication is available for review at many post offices. Copies may be purchased from the Government Printing Office, Washington, D.C. 20402. Considerable use is made by companies of the mails in foreign shipments and their help at times to transportation people is worthwhile and important.

■ *Non-Vessel Operators.*—Comparatively new in significance to the ocean trade are the non-vessel operating common carriers (sometimes referred to as NVOCCs or NVOs). In other countries they are nicknamed, and known as, combined transport operators (CTOs). They do not own or operate vessels. They do, however, hold themselves out (as a common carrier would hold itself out) to accept and handle foreign and domestic offhsore shipments for industry. Generally the shipments they handle have intermodal features and involve the use of other kinds of transportation in addition to the use of the vessels of the water carriers. They publish their own tariffs.

The basic concept of their field of operations differs from the activities undertaken by the independent ocean freight forwarders previously discussed. In some ways the NVO concept is more like that of the domestic freight forwarding companies although they are not regulated along the same lines as the latter and there are other points of differentiation. As examples, motor carriers and van line operators, as well as domestic forwarders, issue through bills of lading as NVOs for the transportation of freight to overseas destinations. Problems as to the extent to which NVOs should be regulated, the liabilities they assume under their bills of lading, and so on are receiving attention. Their operations are not substantial at the present time. They do, however, provide benefits to shippers in certain instances and may be helpful to them.

18

THE TRANSPORTATION OF HAZARDOUS MATERIALS

THE SUBJECT OF THIS CHAPTER, NEW FOR THIS TEXT, LOOMS QUITE importantly in transportation affairs. Recent years have seen a substantial increase in the volume of hazardous materials transported via all modes. A wide variety of new chemicals, insecticides, pesticides, gasses, and radioactive products in commercial quantities are being transported long distances, often in railroad cars, motor vehicles, and vessels of greatly expanded size and capacity. A new regulatory agency, the Department of Transportation, has been made responsible for federal regulations applicable to such materials. State, municipal, and other requirements have become more stringent in a number of cases.

This group of products requires particular care in transportation and in the related fields of packaging, shipping, and handling. Regulations involving them are binding on both shippers and carriers; penalties may be as high as $10,000 per violation or 10 years in prison, or both, if death or bodily injury result. External and internal concerns of industry as to these have a wide and complicated range. Fundamentally, the materials should be dealt with so that accidents are reduced or eliminated to the extent reasonably possible. Employees should know, understand, and comply with the regulations. All possible should be done to be sure that the regulations that are promulgated are proper and reasonable. Many aspects of these features are in the domain of traffic, directly or indirectly, at many companies.

The handling of hazardous material shipment problems in an industrial company in almost every case involves a number of departments. These can be functionally and territorially extensive. Nine committees (insurance, legal, and others), as well as representatives throughout the country, worked on the Manufacturing Chemists Association Chem Card Manual, which is discussed in more detail in subsequent pages. Coordination within a single company may well take its cue from the usual handling of problems of this type. Task forces are used by some; others center responsibility in one department (i.e., a safety group) with the understanding that it will effect necessary coordination, and so on. Full and adequate attention in strong and experienced hands are, of course, salient organizational features in these matters. Further, "non-hazardous" materials companies will wish to bear in mind coloading practices in which, say, their materials may be loaded with hazardous materials in the same equipment.

Products classed as hazardous materials for purposes of regulation were originally the explosives. The list has grown through the years. Explosives, flammable liquids and solids, gases, corrosive materials, acids, poisons, oxidizing agents, radioactive materials, and, for air shipments, magnetized materials are now in this group. Where specific commodities become involved reference to the DOT regulations can well be the first step in determining whether they are in a hazardous classification and, when they are, the rules to which they are subject. Carrier tariffs also provide similar information and are reviewed later. While DOT's regulations consist of several sets pertaining to to various modes (rail, highway, air, pipelines, etc.), the most used and comprehensive are those that originally came from the rail, highway, and shipper regulations of the ICC. These are currently published in Title 49, Code of Federal Regulations (CFR), Parts 170 to 179; they generally serve as the model for regulation via other modes. Copies of the Code are obtainable from the Superintendent of Documents, Government Printing Office, Washington, D.C. 20402.

The next illustration is a page from the Code showing how

Chapter I—Hazardous Materials Regulations Board   § 172.5

§ 172.5 List of hazardous materials.

(a) For explanation of signs and abbreviations see § 172.4.

Article	Classed as—	Exemptions and packing (see sec.)	Label required if not exempt	Maximum quantity in 1 outside container by rail express
Acetaldehyde (*ethyl aldehyde*)	F. L.	173.118, 173.119	Red	10 gallons.
Acetone	F. L.	173.118, 173.119	do	Do.
Acetone cyanhydrin	Pois. B	173.345, 173.346	Poison	55 gallons
*Acetone oils	F.L.	173.118, 173.119	Red	10 gallons.
Acetonitrile	F.L.	173.118, 173.119	do	Do.
Acetyl benzoyl peroxide, solid	Not accepted			Not accepted.
Acetyl benzoyl peroxide, solution	Oxy. M	No exemption, 173.222	Yellow	1 quart.
Acetyl chloride	Cor. L	173.244, 173.247	White	1 gallon.
Acetyl peroxide, solid	Not accepted			Not accepted.
Acetyl peroxide, solution	Oxy. M	173.153 (b), 173.222	Yellow	1 quart.
Acetylene	F. G.	173.306, 173.303	Red Gas	300 pounds.
Acid carboys, empty	See § 173.29 (c)			
Acids, liquid, n.o.s.	Cor. L	173.244, 173.245	White	5 pints.
Acid picric. *See* Picric acid.				
*Acid sludge. *See* * Sludge acid.				
Acrolein, inhibited	F. L.	No exemption, 173.122	Red	1 quart.
Acrylonitrile	F. L.	173.118, 173.119	do	10 gallons.
Actuating cartridges, explosive, fire extinguisher or valve.	Expl. C	173.114		150 pounds.
*Adhesives, n.o.s. *See* Cement, liquid, n.o.s.				
*Aeroplane flares. *See* Special fireworks.				
*Aerosol products. *See* Compressed gases, n.o.s.				
Air, compressed	Nonf. G	173.306, 173.302	Green	300 pounds.
Aircraft rocket engines (commercial).	F.S.	No exemption, 173.238	Yellow	550 pounds.
Aircraft rocket engine igniters (commercial).	F.S.	No exemption, 173.238	do	25 pounds.
*Alcohol, n.o.s.	F.L.	173.118, 173.125	Red	10 gallons.
Alcohol, allyl	Pois. B	173.345, 173.346	Poison	55 gallons.
Aldrin	Pois. B	173.364, 173.376	do	200 pounds.
Aldrin mixtures, liquid, with more than 60 percent aldrin.	Pois. B	173.345, 173.361	do	55 gallons.
*Aldrin, cast solid	See §173.376(b)			
Aldrin mixtures, dry, with more than 65 percent aldrin.	Pois. B	173.364, 173.376	Poison	200 pounds.
*Aldrin mixtures, dry, with 65 percent or less aldrin.	See §173.376(b)			
*Aldrin mixtures, liquid, with 60 percent or less aldrin.	See §173.361(b)			
*Alkaline caustic liquids, n. o. s.	Cor. L	173.244, 173.249	White	10 gallons.
Alkaline corrosive battery fluid	Cor. L	173.244, 173.249, 173,257	do	Do.
Alkaline corrosive battery fluid with storage battery.	Cor. L	No exemption, 173.258	do	400 pounds.
Alkaline corrosive liquids, n. o. s.	Cor. L	173.244, 173.249	do	10 gallons.
*Alkyl aluminum halides. *See* Pyroforic liquids, n.o.s.				
Allyl alcohol. *See* Alcohol, allyl.				
Allyl bromide	F. L	173.118, 173.119	Red	Do.
Allyl chlorocarbonate. *See* Allyl chloroformate.				
Allyl chloroformate	Cor. L	No exemption, 173.288	White	5 pints.
Allyl trichlorosilane	Cor. L	No exemption, 173.280	do	10 gallons.
*Aluminum alkyls. *See* Pyroforic liquids, n.o.s.				
Aluminum dross	See §173.173			
*Aluminum liquid (or paint). *See* *Paint, enamel, lacquer, stain, shellac, varnish, etc.				
Aluminum nitrate	Oxy. M	173.153, 173.182	Yellow	100 pounds.
*Amatol. *See* High explosives.				
Ammonia, anhydrous. *See* Anhydrous ammonia.				
Ammonium arsenate, solid	Pois. B	173.364, 173.365	Poison	200 pounds
Ammonium bichromate (ammonium dichromate).	F.S.	173.153, 173.154, 173.235	Yellow	100 pounds
Ammonium nitrate	Oxy. M	173.153, 173.182	do	Do.
Ammonium nitrate fertilizer, containing 90 percent or more ammonium nitrate with no organic coating.	Oxy. M	173.153, 173.182	do	Do.
Ammonium nitrate—carbonate mixtures.	Oxy. M	173.153, 173.182	do	Do.
*Ammonium nitrate mixed fertilizer.	Oxy. M	173.153, 173.182	do	Do.
Ammonium nitrate (organic coating.)	Oxy. M	173.153, 173.182	do	Do.

15

Excerpt—Hazardous Materials Code,
Department of Transportation

specific commodities and articles are listed. Where a company is concerned with, say, a truck shipment of acetone, reference to the chart (second line) shows the commodity as a flammable liquid subject to various packing and other requirements and as "taking" a red label for warning purposes. The abbreviations in the "Classed as—" column for the other products stand for flammable liquids, poisons in various classes, oxidizing materials, corrosive liquids, explosives in various classes, and so on. The "Exemptions and Packing" column refers to other sections of the regulations dealing with particular features; for example the 173.118 figure for acetone refers to a section applicable to packing. The "Label required" column is self explanatory and (in addition to red) covers other products for which Yellow, Green, White, and other colored "warning" labels are required. The last column is in point only in particular situations.

Articles or products not specifically shown in the commodity list but classified as dangerous under the various generic definitions in the regulations (for explosives, flammables, and so on) are to be prepared and offered for shipment in compliance with the regulations for the appropriate hazard classification. Special permits for waivers or exemptions to depart validly from usual regulatory provisions may be obtained when justified and when an adequate and reasonable degree of safety would prevail. The rules (49 CFR 170.13) for obtaining such permits have been considerably formalized with the advent of DOT and, as a general proposition, the time it now takes to secure the issuance of a special permit has been considerably lengthened.

As regards the numerous other facets of the DOT regulations picture, the Code is divided into several parts. Part 172, as is indicated by the page just reproduced, is concerned with the listing of hazardous materials and other features. Part 173 contains regulations applying specifically to shippers and includes definitions of such terms as "flammable," "poisonous," "compressed gas," etc. This Part also prescribes specifications and numbers for packages, information to be shown on shipping documents (the dangerous articles description, the hazardous classification, and the certificate of compliance), and label regulations. Parts 174, 175, and 176 contain regulations for railroads, express, and baggage service. Part 177 contains regulations applying to for-hire and private motor carriers of dangerous articles. Companies operating their own fleets may be particularly concerned with Part 177. Part 178 contains detailed and technical shipping container specifications. Part 179 contains specifications for tank cars. The regulations are quite complicated. When they apply to a company's operations the necessity is very real and important to know and to understand those that are applicable and to see that compliance with them is effective.

The various transport modes have their own hazardous materials tariffs as mentioned earlier. These reflect, in particular, the regulations applicable to the shipments each of them carry. Supplements are issued as changes occur and, where carrier requirements are imposed in addition to those specified by DOT, such requirements are also applicable. In some ways a company having relatively few hazardous movements which are, say, all by rail would consider itself "covered" by using simply the rail tariff. On the other hand publications of this sort are relatively inexpensive and the complications may be so involved and time consuming that many companies feel it best not to limit the information they obtain. Another vote for having both carrier and government publications is the possibility of carrier requirements in addition to those of DOT. See earlier comments in this paragraph. Publishing agents and other data on these issues follow:

Rail Carriers—Bureau of Explosives Tariff No. 23
(R. M. Graziano, Rm. 620, American Railroads Bldg., Washington, D.C., 20036)

Water Carriers—Bureau of Explosives, Tariff No. 24
(This contains Coast Guard regulations and is published by R. M. Graziano, same address as above)

Motor Carrier Explosives and Dangerous Articles—Tariff No. 14
(American Trucking Associations, Inc., 1616 P Street, N.W., Washington, D.C. 20036)

Air Transport Restricted Articles—Tariff No. 6D

(Airline Tariff Publishers, Inc., Dulles International Airport, P.O. Box 17415, Washington, D.C. 20041)

By way of auxiliary information which may be helpful, the Office of Hazardous Materials of DOT (400 Sixth Street, Washington, D. C. 20590) issues periodic news letters summarizing changes. It also issues kits of prescribed placards, brochures illustrating such placards, shipper and carrier "guides," abstracts of hazardous materials definitions, lists of authorized containers, and so on. The Bureau of Explosives publishes a number of informative pamphlets including its No. 6 "General Information Relating to Explosives and other Dangerous Articles," and No. 22, "Handling Collisions and Derailments Involving Explosives, Gasoline, and Other Dangerous Articles." More publications are available at libraries, in trade papers, and elsewhere. Additionally seminars on the subject are conducted by several universities, colleges, and others.

Depending to a large extent on the involvement of a particular company, data on its hazardous products together with the regulations concerning them are quite often made the subject of specific instruction sheets for shipping origins and others by, say, a central traffic or safety group. Where products move by tank car the placards to be applied (and reversed and removed) are specified, requirements concerning loading with outlet caps off and not loading into domes are spelled out, and so on. When products move in drums, the types of drums and the labels, etc., that may be used as well as other features are outlined. The colors of labels and other markings help in identifying products. They have been and are important and information on them should be included. Broadly stated, red labels are used for flammable liquids and gases, yellow for flammable solids and oxidizing materials, and white for acids and other corrosive liquids. A "red label" product to an experienced freight handler at a loading point receives careful, respectful treatment. Such instruction sheets have much in their favor. They permit a "personalization" of needed information as to a company's particular products, save "digging out" time on the regulations by plant personnel, and permit more helpful explanations of pertinent industry activities which often are not particularly available at plant levels. They need to be kept up to date, but up dating is necessary in any event. Once started, the matter of keeping them current is generally not too onerous.

Organization-wise several groups within DOT concern themselves with hazardous materials. At times, to avoid overly complicated explanations, it is simply stated that DOT took over ICC safety functions. These functions, however, involved principally rail, highway, and shipper interests and, as a matter of detail, air and other safety responsibilities in other branches came to be under DOT also. For various reasons (principally legal) responsibilities for safety functions were not all placed in one focal point. In lieu of such a step certain coordinating mechanisms were established. These are the Office of Hazardous Materials and the Hazardous Materials Regulations Board. The former currently reports to the Assistant Secretary for Safety and Consumer Affairs. The Board is made up of various modal representatives and others. The Safety and Consumer Affairs Assistant Secretary is Chairman and the Hazardous Materials Office Director is Secretary. The Hazardous Materials Office and the Hazardous Materials Regulations Board are the groups with which shippers deal in most cases in these matters.

Activities leading to the issuance, amendment, or repeal of hazardous material regulations have as their first steps what are called "rule-making" proceedings before the Hazardous Materials Regulations Board (49 CFR 170.1). These may be instituted by the Board or through petition to the Board by a person in interest; notices of proposed rule making actions are published in the *Federal Register* but these may be dispensed with in appropriate cases. Procedures are considerably different from those formerly effective with the ICC. Oral hearings are seldom allowed and cross-examination of witnesses is not permitted. All proceedings are considered non-adversary and neither an exchange of pleadings or service of any kind is required. Limited provision for reconsideration is made but there is no automatic stay pending such consideration. The decision of the Board need not be based solely on the record of the proceeding.

Various trade associations have been of help in numerous ways in the hazardous materials field to industrial companies. Generally a great deal of the work is done through committees of industry members with association staff coordinating activities and assisting in keeping matters moving. The providing of expert and knowledgeable help and a spread of the work load are among the worthwhile advantages that can be attained from this course of dealing. The Manufacturing Chemists Association (MCA), the American Petroleum Institute (API), The Fertilizer Institute (TFI), all of Washington, D.C., and the Compressed Gas Association (CGA) of New York, are among those that have been particular participants. The Transportation Association of America (TAA), also of Washington, is comparatively new as a special aid to shippers in these matters.

One particular area of trade association help has been in "rule-making" proceedings involving DOT. An undertaking to have a substantive hazardous material regulation issued, amended, or repealed is an involved activity. Where assumed by one company it is particularly expensive, time-consuming, and takes considerable talent. Further, the Board on its own motion commonly undertakes changes in regulations via the "rule-making" route. The various associations, at one time and another, have furnished representation to their members in these matters and have dealt with the "rule-making" proposals as best possible in the circumstances. Varying results have been attained in these cases; some results have been in accordance with the positions taken by the companies involved; others have not been as favorable.

Another area of assistance is the information made available to their members by certain of the associations. The regulations are particularly complicated and many of the associations have bulletin and memoranda procedures which interpret developments. These are issued to the membership to keep them informed of current problems, changes, and other occurrences of special value to the recipients. They are generally framed so that, say, The Fertilizer Institute places particular emphasis on fertilizer transportation matters, and so on. Further, they are generally framed to express what goes on in about as simple and quickly understandable terms as possible. Some companies have these bulletins sent directly to their plants to keep them informed generally and supplement them with company memos when for any reason such action appears advisable.

Two particularly helpful programs, "Chem-Card" and "Chemtrec," have been pioneered by the Manufacturing Chemists Association. Its more than 160 member companies assisted in the preparation of the information involved. Both programs represent worthwhile steps in making promptly available data concerning certain hazardous properties of various chemicals. Actions taken within a comparatively short time after a containment rupture are critical in many cases, and the "Chem-Cards" and the "Chemtrec" help are designed particularly to provide practical information at these times to carrier employees, cargo handlers, police, fire, and other emergency personnel, and to bystanders.

The "Chem-Card" program is a transportation emergency guide consisting of a manual and some 85 cards on various individual chemicals in fairly common use. It was compiled as a reference for the safe handling of each of those chemicals if they should become involved in a transportation emergency. While designed for tank truck carriers, the manual and cards are used by other modes. Each manual includes a general explanation and a set of cards; separate cards, however, are available. Illustrative of these is the copy of the "Chem-Card" on anhydrous ammonia which follows. While the copy shows as black and white, the originals use red backgrounds for the "in case of accident" and "fire" lines. When poisons are involved, red skull and crossbones are added. Where, say, a tank truck driver with a load of the material experiences a highway spill, he has a ready reference on what to do through either the manual and the card or through the separate card on the material. The wording is short, to the point, and non-technical. Considerable use has been made of the program; more than 66,000 copies were printed through mid-1970. Copies are available at $1.00 each from the MCA, 1825 Connecticut Avenue N.W., Washington, D.C. 20009.

"Chemtrec" gets its name from the Chemical Transportation Emergency Center. It is operated by the MCA around the clock every day of the year to provide immediate information about hazards of chemicals involved in transportation accidents anywhere in the continental United States. Firemen, police, carrier personnel and others handling emergencies involving chemicals can get immediate help by dialing a toll-free nationwide number now carried on shipping papers issued by most MCA members: 800-424-9300 (in Washington, D.C. the number is 483-7616). When an emergency call comes in to "Chemtrec," the man on duty immediately responds with information on whether the chemical is hazardous, and what to do in case of spills, leaks, fire, or exposure—enough information for the first steps needed to control the emergency. The communicator also relays details of the accident to the shipper who can provide additional expert help. "Chemtrec's" what-to-do data are stored in tub-type files covering thousands of chemicals—cross-referenced by company and both generic and trade names. These files are being constantly updated as member companies supply hazards information on additional products. "Chemtrec" started in the fall of 1971. More than 800 calls were received during the first four months of its operations. Many were minor and were concerned with small leaks and spills. Some, however, were larger. Illustrative of the latter was a poison leak in the East where immediate features were handled from "Chemtrec" information and where, on a call from "Chemtrec," the shipper sent help and equipment. Between all hands involved, matters were cleaned up in short order.

A great deal of attention is given hazardous materials by the carriers. The Bureau of Explosives, originally established by

MCA CHEM-CARD — Transportation Emergency Guide

CC-44
August 1965

ANHYDROUS AMMONIA

Compressed, liquefied gas; extremely pungent odor

HAZARDS

FIRE *Can catch fire, but requires high ignition temperature.*

EXPOSURE *Vapor extremely irritating. Liquid causes severe burns.*

IN CASE OF ACCIDENT

IF THIS HAPPENS   **DO THIS**

SPILL or LEAK
Keep upwind from small leaks. Evacuate area in case of large leaks or tank rupture. Shut off leak if without risk. Use gas mask around small leaks, and self-contained breathing apparatus around large leaks or spills. If necessary to enter spill area, wear full protective clothing including boots. Water spray is extremely effective in absorbing ammonia gas and should be used around leaks of gas only. **Do not put water on liquid ammonia.**

FIRE
Move tank promptly out of fire zone. If removal is impossible, cool tank with water spray.

EXPOSURE
Remove to fresh air and call a physician at once. If not breathing, apply artificial respiration, oxygen. If breathing is difficult, administer oxygen. In case of contact with liquid, immediately flush skin or eyes with plenty of water for at least 15 minutes; remove contaminated clothing and shoes at once. Keep patient at rest.

Published by the Manufacturing Chemists' Association, Inc. in cooperation with the Compressed Gas Association, Inc. While prepared from sources believed reliable, the Associations make no warranty that the information is, in all cases, correct or sufficient.
© Manufacturing Chemists' Association, Inc., 1825 Connecticut Ave., N.W., Washington, D. C. 20009, 1965.   Printed in USA

the railroads in 1906, has a unique position in the field. The ICC was specifically authorized by law in 1921 to "utilize the services" of the Bureau, and under this authorization it became an important factor in regulatory matters. Its staff, offices, laboratory services, field force, and general, practical know-how came to have the respect not only of the carriers but of the shippers and others. Its assistance to the military has been particularly valuable at various critical times. Also its expertise came to be drawn on by the ICC in the regulation of carriers other than the railroads. While the statutory authority to use Bureau of Explosives services is applicable to DOT, a number of features have intervened and such functions are not being used as in the past. The Bureau, however, continues to provide a number of essential investigatory, technical, and other services and publishes the hazardous materials tariffs named earlier. It also continues with its assistance to shippers and others via publications previously detailed and otherwise.

Activities by individual carriers and their particular groups on hazardous materials vary. Most carriers make instructions on, and the handling of, these materials part of their safety programs. Operating seminars are arranged in some cases in which applicable regulations and what do about them are reviewed and studied. The National Tank Truck carriers have sponsored this type of seminar for a number of years at a large north central university and have publications on the subject. Some of the railroads, along with other things, maintain what is about the equivalent of a Chemtrec operation as to their lines. Illustrative of this is the program of the Southern Railway. Instruction kits are provided for authorized personnel throughout the Southern's system, covering matters generally. The Southern also has a safety team composed of trained and qualified personnel prepared to move on a moment's notice, day or night, with necessary equipment to the scene of an accident. Other dealings also are accorded accident prevention and handling by the Southern, these being the highlights of the positive action taken by that railway system for preventing trouble and increasing its capabilities of handling an emergency when it does occur.

A wide variety of miscellaneous features are also involved in hazardous materials transportation. One in particular is with reference to federal law applicable to vessels in international trade. As to these "goods of an inflammable, explosive, or dangerous" nature may be landed, destroyed, or rendered innocuous without compensation if the master has not consented to move them with knowledge of their nature and character; also, the shipper "shall be liable for all damages and expenses directly or indirectly arising out of" such shipment. Additionally, along with the new chemicals and other general developments previously mentioned, particular changes have occurred in the operations of certain of the modes. The rail transition from a lessening of LCL involvements to a heavier dependence on piggyback is particularly pertinent. Further, most of the modes are becoming increasingly involved in movements of containers in which a variety of shipments are included. New looks at hazardous materials may be involved in these and related cases.

At times state and local laws and regulations have particular effects on hazardous materials transportation. An example is Michigan where certain "extra" requirements have been made applicable to shipments in this category from, within, and to the state. Usually compliance with federal rules carries with it local compliance but this is not always true. As is the case in most transportation matters, local regulations should be checked when indicated.

Also to be borne in mind is that DOT has under consideration various regulation changes. One in particular is in its "Hazard Information System" on which an "Advance Notice of Proposed Rule Making" (Docket HM-103) appeared in the June 27, 1972 *Federal Register*. Features involved include sweeping changes in the identification of the hazards of materials in transportation and the accentuation of a numbering system new to present requirements. Another proposal (*Federal Register*, June 15, 1972) would redefine "flammables" and add "combustibles" as a new class to hazardous materials. These developments are two of many that are pending or that can be expected. Industry has an important stake in the regulations. Work on them in a helpful, thoughtful vein by industrial companies in cooperation with DOT, the carriers, and others is needed to the end that proper, practical, and knowledgeable solutions are found and made effective.

APPENDIX 1

RAILROAD BILL OF LADING

(The same terms, slightly modified, also apply for motor carriers and freight forwarders.)

Contract Terms and Conditions

Sec. 1. (a) The carrier or party in possession of any of the property herein described shall be liable as at common law for any loss thereof or damage thereto, except as hereinafter provided.

(b) No carrier or party in possession of all or any of the property herein described shall be liable for any loss thereof or damage thereto or delay caused by the act of God; the public enemy; the authority of law; or the act or default of the shipper or owner, or for natural shrinkage. The carrier's liability shall be that of warehouseman, only, for loss, damage, or delay caused by fire occurring after the expiration of the free time allowed by tariffs lawfully on file (such free time to be computed as therein provided) after notice of arrival of the property at destination or at the port of export (if intended for export) has been duly sent or given, and after placement of the property for delivery at destination, or tender of delivery of the property to the party entitled to receive it, has been made. Except in case of negligence of the carrier or party in possession (and the burden to prove freedom from such negligence shall be on the carrier or party in possession), the carrier or party in possession shall not be liable for loss, damage, or delay occurring while the property is stopped and held in transit upon the request of the shipper, owner, or party entitled to make such request, or resulting from a defect or vice in the property, or for country damage to cotton, or from riots or strikes.

(c) In case of quarantine the property may be discharged at risk and expense of owners into quarantine depot or elsewhere, as required by quarantine regulations or authorities, or for the carrier's dispatch at nearest available point in carrier's judgment, and in any such case carrier's responsibility shall cease when property is so discharged, or property may be returned by carrier at owner's expense to shipping point, earning freight both ways. Quarantine expenses of whatever nature or kind upon or in respect to property shall be borne by the owners of the property or be in lien thereon. The carrier shall not be liable for loss or damage occasioned by fumigation or disinfection or other acts required or done by quarantine regulations or authorities even though the same may have been done by carrier's officers, agents, or employees, nor for detention, loss, or damage of any kind occasioned by quarantine or the enforcement thereof. No carrier shall be liable, except in case of negligence, for any mistake or inaccuracy in any information furnished by the carrier, its agents, or officers, as to quarantine laws or regulations. The shipper shall hold the carriers harmless from any expense they may incur, or damages they may incur, or damages they may be required to pay, by reason of the introduction of the property covered by this contract into any place against the quarantine laws or regulations in effect at such place.

Sec. 2. (a) No carrier is bound to transport said property by any particular train or vessel, or in time for any particular market or otherwise than with reasonable dispatch. Every carrier shall have the right in case of physical necessity to forward said property by any carrier or route between the point of shipment and the point of destination. In all cases not prohibited by law, where a lower value than actual value has been represented in writing by the shipper or has been agreed upon in writing as the released value of the property as determined by the classification or tariffs upon which the rate is based, such lower value plus freight charges if paid shall be the maximum amount to be recovered, whether or not such loss or damage occurs from negligence.

(b) As a condition precedent to recovery, claims must be filed in writing with the receiving or delivering carrier, or carrier issuing this bill of lading, or carrier on whose line the loss, damage, injury or delay occurred, within nine months after delivery of the property (or, in case of export traffic, within nine months after delivery at port of export) or, in case of failure to make delivery, then within nine months after a reasonable time for delivery has elapsed; and suits shall be instituted against any carrier only within two years and one day from the day when notice in writing is given by the carrier to the claimant that the carrier has disallowed the claim or any part or parts thereof specified in the notice. Where claims are not filed or suits are not instituted thereon in accordance with the foregoing provisions, no carrier hereunder shall be liable, and such claims will not be paid.

(c) Any carrier or party liable on account of loss of or damage to any of said property shall have the full benefit of any insurance that may have been effected upon or on account of said property, so far as this shall not avoid the policies or contracts of insurance: Provided, That the carrier reimburse the claimant for the premium paid thereon.

Sec. 3. Except where such service is required as the result of carrier's negligence, all property shall be subject to necessary cooperage and baling at owner's cost. Each carrier over whose route cotton or cotton linters is to be transported hereunder shall have the privilege, at its own cost and risk, of compressing the same for greater convenience in handling or forwarding, and shall not be held responsible for deviation or unavoidable delays in procuring such compression. Grain in bulk consigned to a point where there is a railroad, public or licensed elevator, may (unless otherwise expressly noted herein, and then if it is not promptly unloaded) be there delivered and placed with other grain of the same kind and grade without respect to ownership (and prompt notice thereof shall be given to the consignor), and if so delivered shall be subject to a lien for elevator charges in addition to all other charges hereunder.

Sec. 4. (a) Property not removed by the party entitled to receive it within the free time allowed by tariffs, lawfully on file (such free time to be computed as therein provided), after notice of the arrival of the property at destination or at the port of export (if intended for export) has been duly sent or given, and after placement of the property for delivery at destination has been made, may be kept in vessel, car, depot, warehouse or place of delivery of the carrier, subject to the tariff charge for storage and to carrier's responsibility as warehouseman, only, or at the option of the carrier, may be removed to and stored in a public or licensed warehouse at the place of delivery or other available place, at the cost of the owner, and there held without liability on the part of the carrier, and subject to a lien for all freight and other lawful charges, including a reasonable charge for storage.

(b) Where nonperishable property which has been transported to destination hereunder is refused by consignee or the party entitled to receive it, or said consignee or party entitled to receive it fails to receive it within 15 days after notice of arrival shall have been duly sent or given, the carrier may sell the same at public auction to the highest bidder, at such place as may be designated by the carrier: Provided, That the carrier shall have first mailed, sent, or given to the consignor notice that the property has been refused or remains unclaimed, as the case may be, and that it will be subject to sale under the terms of the bill of lading if disposition be not arranged for, and shall have published notice containing a description of the property, the name of the party to whom consigned, or, if shipped order notify, the name of the party to be notified, and the time and place of sale, once a week for two successive weeks, in a newspaper of general circulation at the place of sale or nearest place where such newspaper is published: Provided, That 30 days shall have elapsed before publication of notice of sale after said notice that the property was refused or remains unclaimed was mailed, sent, or given.

(c) Where perishable property which has been transported hereunder to destination is refused by consignee or party entitled to receive it, or said consignee or party entitled to receive it shall fail to receive it promptly, the carrier may, in its discretion, to prevent deterioration or further deterioration, sell the same to the best advantage at private or public sale: Provided, That if time serves for notification to the consignor or owner of the refusal of the property or the failure to receive it and request for disposition of the property, such notification shall be given, in such manner as the exercise of due diligence requires, before the property is sold.

(d) Where the procedure provided for in the two paragraphs last preceding is not possible, it is agreed that nothing contained in said paragraphs shall be construed to abridge the right of the carrier at its option to sell the property under such circumstances and in such manner as may be authorized by law.

(e) The proceeds of any sale made under this section shall be applied by the carrier to the payment of freight, demurrage, storage, and any other lawful charges and the expense of notice, advertisement, sale, and other necessary expense and of caring for and maintaining the property, if proper care of the same requires special expense, and should there be a balance it shall be paid to the owner of the property sold hereunder.

(f) Property destined to or taken from a station, wharf, or landing at which there is no regularly appointed freight agent shall be entirely at risk of owner after unloaded from cars or vessels or until loaded into cars or vessels, and, except in case of carrier's negligence, when received from or delivered to such stations, wharves, or landings shall be at owner's risk until the cars are attached to and after they are detached from locomotive or train or until loaded into and after unloaded from vessels.

Sec. 5. No carrier hereunder will carry or be liable in any way for any documents, specie, or for any articles of extraordinary value not specifically rated in the published classifications or tariffs unless a special agreement to do so and a stipulated value of the articles are indorsed hereon.

Sec. 6. Every party, whether principal or agent, shipping explosives or dangerous goods, without previous full written disclosure to the carrier of their nature, shall be liable for and indemnify the carrier against all loss or damage caused by such goods, and such goods may be warehoused at owner's risk and expense or destroyed without compensation.

Sec. 7. The owner or consignee shall pay the freight and average, if any, and all other lawful charges accruing on said property; but, except in those instances where it may lawfully be authorized to do so, no carrier by railroad shall deliver or relinquish possession at destination of the property covered by this bill of lading until all tariff rates and charges thereon have been paid. The consignor shall be liable for the freight and all other lawful charges, except that if the consignor stipulates, by signature, in the space provided for that purpose on the face of this bill of lading that the carrier shall not make delivery without requiring payment of such charges and the carrier, contrary to such stipulation, shall make delivery without requiring such payment, the consignor (except as hereinafter provided) shall not be liable for such charges. Provided, that, where the carrier has been instructed by the shipper or consignor to deliver said property to a consignee other than the shipper or consignor, such consignee shall not be legally liable for transportation charges in respect to the transportation of said property (beyond those billed against him at the time of delivery for which he is otherwise liable) which may be found to be due after the property has been delivered to him, if the consignee (a) is an agent only and has no beneficial title in said property and (b) prior to delivery of said property has notified the delivering carrier in writing of the fact of such agency and absence of beneficial title, and, in the case of a shipment reconsigned or diverted to a point other than that specified in the original bill of lading, has also notified the delivering carrier in writing of the name and address of the beneficial owner of said property; and in such cases the shipper or consignor, or, in the case of a shipment so reconsigned or diverted, the beneficial owner, shall be liable for such additional charges. If the consignee has given to the carrier erroneous information as to who the beneficial owner is, such consignee shall be liable for such additional charges. On shipments reconsigned or diverted by an agent who has furnished the carrier in the reconsignment or diversion order with a notice of agency and the proper name and address of the beneficial owner, and where such shipments are refused or abandoned at ultimate destination, the said beneficial owner shall be liable for all legally applicable charges in connection therewith, If the reconsignor or diverter has given to the carrier erroneous information as to who the beneficial owner is, such reconsignor or diverter shall himself be liable for all such charges.

If a shipper or consignor of a shipment of property (other than a prepaid shipment) is also the consignee named in the bill of lading and, prior to the time of delivery, notifies, in writing, a delivering carrier by railroad (a) to deliver such property at destination to another party, (b) that such party is the beneficial owner of such property, and (c) that delivery is to be made to such party only upon payment of all transportation charges in respect of the transportation of such property, and delivery is made by the carrier to such party without such payment, such shipper or consignor shall not be liable (as shipper, consignor, consignee, or otherwise) for such transportation charges but the party to whom delivery is so made shall in any event be liable for transportation charges billed against the property at the time of such delivery, and also for any additional charges which may be found to be due after delivery of the property, except that if such party prior to such delivery has notified in writing the delivering carrier that he is not the beneficial owner of the property, and has given in writing to such delivering carrier the name and address of such beneficial owner, such party shall not be liable for any additional charges which may be found to be due after delivery of the property; but if the party to whom delivery is made has given to the carrier erroneous information as to the beneficial owner, such party shall nevertheless be liable for such additional charges. If the shipper or consignor has given to the delivering carrier erroneous information as to who the beneficial owner is, such shipper or consignor shall himself be liable for such transportation charges, notwithstanding the foregoing provisions of this paragraph and irrespective of any provisions to the contrary in the bill of lading or in the contract of transportation under which the shipment was made. The term "delivering carrier" means the line-haul carrier making ultimate delivery.

Nothing herein shall limit the right of the carrier to require at time of shipment the prepayment or guarantee of the charges. If upon inspection it is ascertained that the articles shipped are not those described in this bill of lading, the freight charges must be paid upon the articles actually shipped.

Where delivery is made by a common carrier by water the foregoing provisions of this action shall apply, except as may be inconsistent with Part III of the Interstate Commerce Act.

Sec. 8. If this bill of lading is issued on the order of the shipper, or his agent, in exchange or in substitution for another bill of lading, the shipper's signature to the prior bill of lading as to the statement of value or otherwise, or election of common law or bill of lading liability, in or in connection with such prior bill of lading shall be considered a part of this bill of lading as fully as if the same were written or made in or in connection with this bill of lading.

Sec. 9. (a) If all or any part of said property is carried by water over any part of said route, and loss, damage or injury to said property occurs while the same is in the custody of a carrier by water the liability of such carrier shall be determined by the bill of lading of the carrier by water (this bill of lading being such bill of lading if the property is transported by such water carrier thereunder) and by and under the laws and regulations applicable to transportation by water. Such water carriage shall be performed subject to all the terms and provisions of, and all the exemptions from liability contained in the Act of the Congress of the United States, approved on February 13, 1893, and entitled "An act relating to the navigation of vessels, etc.," and of other statutes of the United States according carriers by water the protection of limited liability, as well as the following subdivisions of this section; and to the conditions contained in this bill of lading not inconsistent with this section, when this bill of lading becomes the bill of lading of the carrier by water.

(b) No such carrier by water shall be liable for any loss or damage resulting from any fire happening to or on board the vessel, or from explosion, bursting of boilers or breakage of shafts, unless caused by the design or neglect of such carrier.

(c) If the owner shall have exercised due diligence in making the vessel in all respects seaworthy and properly manned, equipped, and supplied, no such carrier shall be liable for any loss or damage resulting from the perils of the lakes, seas, or other waters, or from latent defects in hull, machinery, or appurtenances whether existing prior to, at the time of, or after sailing, or from collision, stranding, or other accidents of navigation, or from prolongation of the voyage. And, when for any reason it is necessary, any vessel carrying any or all of the property herein described shall be at liberty to call at any port or ports, in or out of the customary route, to tow and be towed, to transfer, trans-ship, or lighter, to load and discharge goods at any time, to assist vessels in distress, to deviate for the purpose of saving life or property, and for docking and repairs. Except in case of negligence such carrier shall not be responsible for any loss or damage to property if it be necessary or is usual to carry the same upon deck.

(d) General Average shall be payable according to the York-Antwerp Rules of 1924, Sections 1 to 15 inclusive, and Sections 17 to 22, inclusive, and as to matters not covered thereby according to the laws and usages of the Port of New York. If the owners shall have exercised due diligence to make the vessel in all respects seaworthy and properly manned, equipped and supplied, it is hereby agreed that in case of danger, damage or disaster resulting from faults or errors in navigation, or in the management of the vessel, or from any latent or other defects in the vessel, her machinery or appurtenances, or from unseaworthiness, whether existing at the time of shipment or at the beginning of the voyage (provided the latent or other defects or the unseaworthiness was not discoverable by the exercise of due diligence), the shippers, consignees and/or owners of the cargo shall nevertheless pay salvage and any special charges incurred in respect of the cargo, and shall contribute with the shipowner in general average to the payment of any sacrifices, losses or expenses of a general average nature that may be made or incurred for the common benefit or to relieve the adventure from any common peril.

(e) If the property is being carried under a tariff which provides that any carrier or carriers party thereto shall be liable for loss from perils of the sea, then as to such carrier or carriers the provisions of this section shall be modified in accordance with the tariff provisions, which shall be regarded as incorporated into the conditions of this bill of lading.

(f) The term "water carriage" in this section shall not be construed as including lighterage in or across rivers, harbors, or lakes, when performed by or on behalf of rail carriers.

Sec. 10. Any alteration, addition, or erasure in this bill of lading which shall be made without the special notation hereon of the agent of the carrier issuing this bill of lading, shall be without effect, and this bill of lading shall be enforceable according to its original tenor.

APPENDIX 2

Ocean Bill of Lading
Contract Terms and Conditions

(These contract terms and conditions are typical; the various steamship lines do not necessarily use identical terms and conditions; some of them use short forms which adopt their long forms by reference, as do the railroads and others.)

Received from the Shipper hereinafter named, the goods or packages said to contain goods hereinafter mentioned, in apparent good order and condition, unless otherwise indicated in this bill of lading, to be transported subject to all terms of this bill of lading with liberty to proceed via any port or ports within the scope of the voyage described herein, to the port of discharge or so near thereunto as the ship can always safely get and leave, always afloat at all stages and conditions of water and weather, and there to be delivered or transshipped on payment of the charges thereon. If the goods in whole or in part are shut out from the ship named herein for any cause, the Carrier shall have liberty to forward them under the terms of this bill of lading on the next available ship of this line or substitute therefor, or at the carrier's option, of any line.

It is agreed that the custody and carriage of the goods are subject to the following terms on the face and back hereof which shall govern the relations, whatsoever they may be, between the shipper, consignee, and the Carrier, Master and ship in every contingency, wheresoever and whensover occurring, and also in the event of deviation, or of unseaworthiness of the ship at the time of loading or inception of the voyage or subsequently, and none of the terms of this bill of lading shall be deemed to have been waived by the Carrier unless by express waiver signed by a duly authorized agent of the Carrier:

1. This bill of lading shall have effect subject to the provisions of the Carriage of Goods by Sea Act of the United States of America, approved April 16, 1936, which shall be deemed to be incorporated herein, and nothing herein contained shall be deemed a surrender by the Carrier of any of its rights or immunities or an increase of any of its responsibilities or liabilities under said Act. The provisions stated in said Act (except as may be otherwise specifically provided herein) shall govern before the goods are loaded on and after they are discharged from the ship and throughout the entire time the goods are in the custody of the Carrier. The Carrier shall not be liable in any capacity whatsoever for any delay, non-delivery or misdelivery, or loss of or damage to the goods occurring while the goods are not in the actual custody of the Carrier. If this bill of lading is issued in a locality where there is in force a Carriage of Goods by Sea Act or Ordinance or Statute of a similar nature to the International Convention for the Unification of Certain Rules Relating to Bills of Lading at Brussels of August 25, 1924, it is subject to the provisions stated in such Act, Ordinance and rules thereto annexed which may be in effect where this bill of lading is issued.

(a) The Carrier shall be entitled to the full benefit of, and right to, all limitations of, or exemptions from, liability authorized by any provisions of Sections 4281 to 4286 of the Revised Statutes of the United States and amendments thereto and of any other provisions of the laws of the United States or of any other country whose laws shall apply. If the ship is not owned by or chartered by demise to the Federal Maritime Commission or the Company designated herein (as may be the case notwithstanding anything that appears to the contrary) this bill of lading shall take effect only as a contract with the owner or demise charterer, as the case may be, as principal, made through the agency of the Federal Maritime Commission or the Company designated herein which acts as agent only and shall be under no personal liability whatsoever in respect thereof. If, however, it shall be adjudged that any other than the owner or demise charterer is carrier and/or bailee of the goods all limitations of and exonerations from liability provided by law or by the terms hereof shall be available to such other.

2. In this bill of lading the word "ship" shall include any substituted vessel, and any craft, lighter or other means of conveyance owned, chartered or operated by the Carrier used in the performance of this contract; the word "Carrier" shall include the ship, her owner, master, operator, demise charterer, and if bound hereby the time charterer, and any substituted carrier, whether the owner, operator, charterer, or master shall be acting as carrier or bailee; the word "shipper" shall include the person named as such in this bill of lading and the person for whose account the goods are shipped; the word "consignee" shall include the holder of the bill of lading, properly endorsed, and the receiver and the owner of the goods; the word "charges" shall include freight and all expenses and money obligations incurred and payable by the goods, shipper, consignee, or any of them.

3. The scope of voyage herein contracted for shall include usual or customary or advertised ports of call whether named in this contract or not, also port in or out of the advertised, geographical, usual or ordinary route or order, even though in proceeding thereto the ship may sail beyond the port of discharge or in a direction contrary thereto or return to the original port, or depart from the direct or customary route, and includes all canals, straits and other waters. The ship may call at any port for the purpose of the current voyage or of a prior or subsequent voyage. The ship may omit calling at any port or ports whether scheduled or not, and may call at the same port more than once; may for matters occuring before loading the goods, known or unknown at the time of such loading and matters occurring after such loading, either with or without the goods or passengers on board, and before or after proceeding toward the port of discharge, adjust compasses, dry dock, with or without cargo aboard go on ways or to repair yards, shift berths, make trial trips or tests, take fuel or stores, remain in port, sail with or without pilots, tow and be towed, and save or attempt to save life or property; and all of the foregoing are included in the contract voyage.

In view of the necessity for the expeditious employment of all the available Merchant Marine, the exercise by the carrier or master or any of the liberties granted herein with respect to loading, departure, scope of voyage, arrival routes, ports of call, stopping, discharge, destination, surrender, delivery, or otherwise, shall be presumed to be for the purposes of conserving and utilizing war time, sea mileage or shipping space, and therefore prima facie reasonable and necessary in the assembling, transportation or distribution of materials essential to the war effort.

4. In any situation whatsoever and wheresoever occurring and whether existing or anticipated before commencement of or during the voyage, which in the judgment of the Carrier or the Master is likely to give rise to risk of capture, seizure, detention, damage, delay or disadvantage to or loss of the ship or any part of her cargo, to make it unsafe, imprudent, or unlawful for any reason to commence or proceed on or continue the voyage or to enter or discharge the goods at the port of discharge, or to give rise to delay or difficulty in arriving, discharging at or leaving the port of discharge or the usual or agreed place of discharge in such port, the Carrier may before loading or before the commencement of the voyage, require the shipper or other person entitled thereto to take delivery of the goods at port of shipment and upon failure to do so, may warehouse the goods at the risk and expense of the goods; or the Carrier or the Master, whether or not proceeding toward or entering or attempting to enter the port of discharge or reaching or attempting to reach the usual place of discharge therein or attempting to discharge the goods there, may discharge the goods into depot, lazaretto, craft, or other place; or the ship may proceed or return, directly or indirectly, to or stop at any port or place whatsoever as the Master or the Carrier may consider safe or advisable under the circumstances, and dischage the goods, or any part thereof, at any such port or place; or the Carrier or the Master may retain the cargo on board until the return trip or until such time as the Carrier or the Master thinks advisable and discharge the goods at any place whatsoever as herein provided; or the Carrier or the Master may discharge and forward the goods by any means, rail, water, land, or air at the risk and expense of the goods. The Carrier or the Master is not required to give notice of discharge of the goods or the forwarding thereof as herein provided. When the goods are discharged from the ship, as herein provided, they shall be at their own risk and expense; such discharge shall constitute complete delivery and performance under this contract and the Carrier shall be freed from any further responsibility. For any services rendered to the goods as hereinabove provided, the Carrier shall be freed from any further responsibility. For any services rendered to the goods as hereinabove provided, the Carrier shall be entitled to a reasonable extra compensation.

5. The Carrier, Master and ship shall have liberty to comply with any orders or directions as to loading, departing, arrival, routes, ports of call, stoppages, discharge, destination, delivery or otherwise howsoever given by the government of any nation or department thereof or any person acting or purporting to act with the authority of such government or of any department thereof, or by any committee or person having, under the terms of the war risk insurance on the ship, the right to give such orders or directions. Delivery or other disposition of the goods in accordance with such orders or directions shall be a fulfillment of the contract voyage. The ship may carry contraband, explosives,

munitions, warlike stores, hazardous cargo, and may sail armed or unarmed and with or without convoy.

In addition to all other liberties herein the Carrier shall have the right to withold delivery of, reship to, deposit or discharge the goods at any place whatsoever, surrender or dispose of the goods in accordance with any direction, condition or agreement imposed upon or exacted from the carrier by any government or department thereof or any person purporting to act with the authority of either of them. In any of the above circumstances the goods shall be solely at their risk and expense and all expenses and charges so incurred shall be payable by the owner or consignee thereof and shall be a lien on the goods.

6. Unless otherwise stated herein, the description of the goods and the particulars of the packages mentioned herein are those furnished in writing by the shipper and the Carrier shall not be concluded as to the correctness of marks, number, quantity, weight, gauge, measurement, contents, nature, quality of value. Single pieces or packages exceeding 4,480 lbs. in weight shall be liable to pay extra charges in accordance with tariff rates in effect at time of shipment for loading, handling, transshipping or discharging and the weight of each such piece or package shall be declared in writing by the shipper on shipment and clearly and durably marked on the outside of the piece or package. The shipper and the goods shall also be liable for, and shall indemnify the Carrier in respect of, any injury, loss or damage arising from shipper's failure to declare and mark the weight of any such piece or package or from inadequate or improper description of the goods or from the incorrect weight of any such piece or package or from inadequate or improper description of the goods or from the incorrect weight of any such piece or package having been declared or marked thereon, or from failure fully to disclose the nature and character of the goods.

7. Goods may be stowed in poop, forecastle, deck house, shelter deck, passenger space or any other covered in space commonly used in the trade and suitable for the carriage of goods, and when so stowed shall be deemed for all purposes to be stowed under deck. In respect of goods carried on deck all risks of loss or damage by perils inherent in such carriage shall be borne by the shipper or the consignee but in all other respects the custody and carriage of such goods shall be governed by the terms of this bill of lading and the provisions stated in said Carriage of Goods by Sea Act notwithstanding Sec. 1 (c) thereof, or the corresponding provision of any Carriage of Goods by Sea Act that may be applicable. Specially heated or specially cooled stowage is not to be furnished unless contracted for at increased freight rate. Goods or articles carried in such compartment are at the sole risk of the owner thereof and subject to all the conditions, exceptions and limitations as to the Carrier's liability and other provisions of this bill of lading; and further the Carrier shall not be liable for any loss or damage occasioned by the temperature, risks or refrigeration, defects or insufficiency in or accidents to or explosion, breakage, derangement of failure of any refrigerator plant or part thereof, or by or in any material or the supply or use thereof used in the process of refrigeration unless

shown to have been caused by negligence of the Carrier from liability for which the Carrier is not by law entitled to exemption.

8. Live animals, birds, reptiles and fish are received and carried at shipper's risk of accident or mortality, and the Carrier shall not be liable for any loss or damage thereto arising or resulting from any matter mentioned in Section 4, Sub-section 2, a to p, inclusive of said Carriage of Goods by Sea Act or similar sections of any Carriage of Goods by Sea Act that may be applicable, or from any other cause whatsoever not due to the fault of the Carrier, any warranty of seaworthiness in the premises being waived by the shipper. Except as provided above such shipments shall be deemed goods, and shall be subject to all terms and provisions in this bill of lading relating to goods.

9. If the ship comes into collision with another ship as a result of the negligence of the other ship and any act, neglect or default of the Master, mariner, pilot or the servants of the Carrier in the navigation or in the management of the ship, the owners of the goods carried hereunder will indemnify the Carrier against all loss or liability to the other or non-carrying ship or her owners in so far as such loss or liability represents loss of, or damage to, or any claim whatsoever of the owners of said goods, paid or payable by the other or non-carrying ship or her owners to the owners of said goods and set-off, recouped or recovered by the other or non-carrying ship or her owners as part of their claim against the carrying ship or Carrier.

The foregoing provision shall also apply where the owners, operators or those in charge of any ship or ships or objects other than, or in addition to, the colliding ships or objects are at fault in respect of a collision or contact.

10. General average shall be adjusted, stated and settled, according to York-Antwerp Rules 1950, except Rule XXII thereof, at such port or place in the United States as may be selected by the carrier, and as to matters not provided for by these Rules, according to the laws and usages at the port of New York. In such adjustment disbursements in foreign currencies shall be exchanged into United States money at the rate prevailing on the dates made and allowances for damage to cargo claimed in foreign currency shall be converted at the rate prevailing on the last day of discharge at the port or place of final discharge of such damaged cargo from the ship. Average agreement or bond and such additional security, as may be required by the Carrier, must be furnished before delivery of the goods. Such cash deposit as the Carrier or his agents may deem sufficient as additional security for the contribution of the goods and for any salvage and special charges thereon, shall, if required, be made by the goods, shippers, consignees or owners of the goods to the Carrier before delivery. Such deposit shall, at the option of the Carrier, be payable in United States money and be remitted to the adjuster. When so remitted the deposit shall be held in a special account at the place of adjustment in the name of the adjuster pending settlement of the general average and refunds or credit balances, if any, shall be paid in United States money.

In the event of accident, danger, damage, or disaster, before or after commencement of the voyage resulting from any cause whatsoever, whether due to negligence or not, for which, or for the consequence of which, the Carrier is not responsible, by statute, contract, or otherwise, the goods, the shipper and the consignee, jointly and severally, shall contribute with the Carrier in general average to the payment of any sacrifices, losses, or expenses of a general average nature that may be made or incurred, and shall pay salvage and special charges incurred in respect of the goods. If a salving ship is owned or operated by the Carrier, salvage shall be paid for as fully and in the same manner as if such salving ship or ships belonged to strangers.

11. Whenever the Carrier or the Master may deem it advisable or in any case where the goods are consigned to a point where the ship does not expect to discharge, the Carrier or Master may, without notice, forward the whole or any part of the goods before or after loading at the original port of shipment, or any other place or places even though outside the scope of the voyage or the route to or beyond the port of discharge or the destination of the goods, by any vessel, vessels or other means of transportation by water or by land or by air or by any such means, whether operated by the Carrier or by others and whether departing or arriving or scheduled to depart or arrive before or after the ship expected to be used for the transportation of the goods. This Carrier, in making arrangements for any transshipping or forwarding vessel or means of transportation not operated by this Carrier shall be considered solely the forwarding agent of the shipper and without any other responsibility whatsoever.

The carriage by any transshiping or forwarding carrier and all transshipment or forwarding shall be subject to all the terms whatsoever in the regular form or bill of lading, freight note, contract or other shipping document used at the time by such carrier, whether issued for the goods or not, and even though such terms may be less favorable to the shipper or consignee than the terms of this bill of lading and may contain more stringent requirements as to notice of claim or commencement of suit and may exempt the on-carrier from liability for negligence. The shipper expressly authorizes the Carrier to arrange with any such transshipping or forwarding carrier that the lowest valuation of the goods or limitation of liability contained in the bill of lading or shipping document of such carrier shall apply even though lower than the valuation or limitation herein, provided that the shipper shall not be compelled to pay a rate higher than that applicable to the valuation contained in such bill of lading. Pending or during transshipment the goods may be stored ashore or afloat at their risk and expense and the Carrier shall not be liable for detention.

12. The port authorities are hereby authorized to grant a general order for discharging immediately upon arrival of the ship and the Carrier without giving notice either of arrival or discharge, may discharge the goods directly they come to hand, at or onto any wharf, craft or place that the Carrier may select, and continuously Sundays and holidays included, at all such hours by day or by night as the Carrier may determine no matter what the state of the weather or custom of the port may be. The Carrier shall not be liable in any respect whatsoever if heat or refrigeration or special cooling facilities shall not be furnished during loading or discharge or any part of the time that the goods

are upon the wharf, craft, or other loading or discharging place. All lighterage and use of craft in discharging shall be at the risk and expense of the goods. Landing and delivery charges and pier dues shall be at the expense of the goods unless included in the freight herein provided for. If the goods are not taken away by the consignee by the expiration of the next working day after the goods are at his disposal, the goods may at Carrier's option and subject to Carrier's lien, be sent to store or warehouse or be permitted to lie where landed, but always at the expense and risk of the goods. The responsibility of the Carrier in any capacity shall altogether cease and the goods shall be considered to be delivered and at their own risk and expense in every respect when taken into the custody of customs or other authorities. The Carrier shall not be required to give any notification of disposition of the goods.

13. The Carrier shall not be liable for failure to deliver in accordance with marks unless such marks shall have been clearly and durably stamped or marked by the shipper before shipment upon the goods or packages, in letters and numbers not less than two inches high, together with name of the port of discharge. Goods that cannot be identified as to marks or numbers, cargo sweepings, liquid residue and any unclaimed goods not otherwise accounted for shall be allocated for completing delivery to the various consignees of goods of like character, in proportion to any apparent shortage, loss of weight or damage. Loss or damage to goods in bulk stowed without separation from other goods in bulk of like quality, shipped by either the same or another shipper, shall be divided in proportion among the several shipments.

14. The goods shall be liable for all expense of mending, cooperage, baling or reconditioning of the goods or packages and gathering of loose contents of packages; also for any payment, expense, fine, dues, duty, tax, impost, loss, damage or detention sustained or incurred by or levied upon the Carrier or the ship in connection with the goods, howsoever caused, including any action or requirement of any government or governmental authority or person purporting to act under the authority thereof, seizure under legal process or attempted seizure, incorrect or insufficient marking, numbering or addressing of packages or description of the contents, failure of the shipper to procure consular, Board of Health or other certificates to accompany the goods or to comply with laws or regulations of any kind imposed with respect to the goods by the authorities at any port or place or any act or omission of the shipper or consignee.

15. Freight shall be payable on actual gross intake weight or measurement or, at Carrier's option, on actual gross discharge weight or measurement. Freight may be calculated on the basis of the particulars of the goods furnished by the shipper herein but the Carrier may at any time open the packages and examine, weight, measure and value the goods. In case shipper's particulars are found to be erroneous and additional freight is payable, the goods shall be liable for any expense incurred for examining, weighing, measuring and valuing the goods. Full freight shall be paid on damaged or unsound goods. Full freight hereunder to port of discharge named herein shall be considered completely earned on shipment whether the freight be stated or intended to be

prepaid or to be collected at destination; and the Carrier shall be entitled to all freight and charges due hereunder, whether actually paid or not, and to receive and retain them irrevocably under all circumstances whatsoever ship and/or cargo lost or not lost or the voyage broken up or abandoned. If there shall be a forced interruption or abandonment of the voyage at the port of shipment or elsewhere any forwarding of the goods or any part thereof shall be at the risk and expense of the goods. All unpaid charges shall be paid in full and without any offset, counterclaim or deduction in the currency of the port of shipment, or, at Carrier's option, in the currency of the port of discharge at the demand rate of New York exchange as quoted on the day of the ship's entry at the Custom House of her port of discharge. The Carrier shall have a lien on the goods, which shall survive delivery, for all charges due hereunder and may enforce this lien by public or private sale and without notice. The shipper and the consignee shall be jointly and severally liable to the Carrier for the payment of all charges and for the performance of the obligation of each of them hereunder.

16. Neither the Carrier nor any corporation owned by, subsidiary to or associated or affiliated with the Carrier shall be liable to answer for or make good any loss or damage to the goods occurring at any time and even though before loading on or after discharge from the ship, by reason or by means of any fire whatsoever, unless such fire shall be caused by its design or neglect.

17. In case of any loss or damage to or in connection with goods exceeding in actual value $500 lawful money of the United States, per package, or, in case of goods not shipped in packages, per customary freight unit, the value of the goods shall be deemed to be $500 per package or per unit, on which basis the freight is adjusted and the Carrier's liability, if any, shall be determined on the basis of a value of $500 per package or per customary freight unit, or pro rata in case of partial loss or damage, unless the nature of the goods and a valuation higher than $500 shall have been declared in writing by the shipper upon delivery to the Carrier and inserted in this bill of lading and extra freight paid if required and in such case if the actual value of the goods per package or per customary freight unit shall exceed such declared value, the value shall nevertheless be deemed to be the declared value and the Carrier's liability, if any, shall not exceed the declared value and any partial loss or damage shall be adjusted pro rata on the basis of such declared value.

Whenever the value of the goods is less than $500 per package or other freight unit, their value in the calculation and adjustment of claim for which the Carrier may be liable shall for the purpose of avoiding uncertainties and difficulties in fixing value be deemed to be the invoice value, plus freight and insurance if paid, irrespective of whether any other value is greater or less.

18. Unless notice of loss or damage and the general nature of such loss or damage be given in writing to the Carrier or his agent at the port of discharge before or at the time of the removal of the goods into the custody of the person entitled to delivery thereof under the contract of carriage, such removal shall be prima facie evidence of the delivery by the Carrier of the goods as

described in the bill of lading. If the loss or damage is not apparent the notice must be given within three days of the delivery. The Carrier shall not be liable upon any claim for loss or damage unless written particulars of such claim shall be received by the Carrier within thirty days after receipt of the notice herein provided for.

19. In any event the Carrier and the ship shall be discharged from all liability in respect of loss or damage unless suit is brought within one year after the delivery of the goods or the date when the goods should have been delivered. Suit shall not be deemed brought until jurisdiction shall have been obtained over the Carrier and/or the ship by service of process or by an agreement to appear.

20. To avoid or alleviate preventions or delays in prosecution or completion of the voyage incident to the existence of hostilities, the Carrier has liberty and is authorized by the shipper and the owner of the goods to agree with the representatives of any government to submit the goods to examination at any place or places whatsoever and to delay delivery of the same until any restriction asserted by any governmental authority shall have been removed. The Carrier may put the goods in store ashore or afloat at the risk and expense of the owner of the same pending examination; and thereupon the Carrier's responsibility shall end. Any damage or deterioration occasioned by such examination or by delay and other risks of whatsoever nature shall be solely for account of the owner of the goods. All expenses incurred by the Carrier in relation to such detention of the goods shall be paid by the shipper or consignee or owner of the goods.

21. This bill of lading shall be construed and the rights of the parties thereunder determined according to the law of the United States.

22. Cargo skids and labor on quay are to be provided by ship's agent for account of consignee at current rates, and any cargo which may be ordered for delivery into fiscal deposits, must be taken by an official cartman appointed by the agent of the ship, at current rates for account and risk of consignee.

23. If any bagged or baled goods are landed slack or torn, receiver and/or consignee shall accept its proportion of the sweepings. Ship not responsible for loss of weight in bags or bales torn, mended or with sample holes.

24. COTTON. Description of the condition of the cotton does not relate to the insufficiency of or torn condition of the covering, nor to any damage resulting therefrom, and Carrier shall not be responsible for damage of such nature.

25. SPECIE. Specie will not be shipped or landed by the Carrier; it must be put on board by the shipper, and will only be delivered on board on presentation of the bills of lading properly endorsed; it may be carried on at consignee's risk if delivery is not taken during the ship's stay in port, and in every case the liability of the Carrier shall cease when the specie leaves the ship's deck.

26. SPECIFIED DOCK DISCHARGE: If the carrier makes a special agree-

ment, whether by stamp hereon or otherwise, to deliver the goods hereby receipted for at a specified dock or wharf at the port of discharge, it is mutually agreed that such agreement shall be construed to mean that the Carrier is to make such delivery only if, in the sole judgment of the Master, the ship can safely under her own power, proceed to, lie at, and return from said dock or wharf, always afloat at any time of tide, and only if such dock or wharf is available to the ship immediately the ship is ready to discharge the goods and, that otherwise, the ship shall discharge the goods in accordance with Clause 12 of this bill of lading, whereupon Carrier's responsibility shall cease.

27. All agreements of freight engagements for the shipment of the goods are superseded by this bill of lading, and all its terms, whether written, typed, stamped, or printed, are accepted and agreed by the shipper to be binding as fully as if signed by the shipper, any local customs or privileges to the contrary notwithstanding. Nothing in this bill of lading shall operate to limit or deprive the Carrier of any statutory protection or exemption from or limitation of liability. If required by the Carrier, one signed bill of lading duly endorsed must be surrendered to the agent of the ship at the port of discharge in exchange for delivery order.

GLOSSARY

Definitions and abbreviations of traffic and transportation terms in general or common use appear in the list which follows. A limited number of data processing items are included.

"A" end of car—The end opposite the end with the hand brakes (which is the "B" end).

A. & D. rates—Rates published to apply on freight moving to assembly (consolidation) points and from distribution points.

A.A.R.—a. Against all risks (insurance clause).
b. Association of American Railroads.

Absorption—One carrier assumes the charges of another, such as switching, without any increase in charges to the shipper.

A/C or acct.—Account.

Accessorial service—A service in addition to the line-haul service, usually at an added cost, such as heating, packing, loading, storage or the like.

Act of God—An act beyond man's control such as lightning, flood, earthquake.

Actual weight (A/W)—Gross shipping weight.

Ad valorem (Ad. Val.)—According to value.

Admiralty (Adm.)—Refers to marine matters such as an Admiralty Court.

Adoption notice—A notice given where one carrier takes over another carrier's operations, or agrees that the other carrier's tariff is also binding on it.

Advanced charge—Transportation charges advanced by one carrier to another to be collected by the latter carrier from the consignor or consignee.

Affidavit—A written statement generally sworn to before a notary public.

Agency tariff—A tariff published by an agent on behalf of several carriers.

Agent (Agt.)—An individual authorized to act on behalf of another person or company.

Aggregate of intermediates—The sum of the intermediate rates. Section 4, Part 1, of the I. C. Act prohibits through rates higher than the sum of the intermediate rates.

Agreed valuation—The value of a shipment agreed upon in order to secure a specific freight rate.

All commodity rate—A freight rate applying, generally with certain restrictions, on any and all commodities.

All rail (A.R.)—Exclusively by railroad.

All water (A.W.)—Exclusively by water.

Alternative rates—More than one rate with privilege to use the one producing the lowest charges.

A.M.M.I.—American Merchant Marine Institute.

A.T.A.—American Trucking Associations.

Analogous articles—Articles with similar characteristics.

Any-quantity (A.Q.)—Usually refers to a rating that applies to an article regardless of weight (i.e., in any quantity).

Arbitrary—A stated amount over a fixed rate to one point to make a rate to another point.

Arrival notice—A notice to the consignee advising that freight has arrived.

Assigned siding—A sidetrack owned by a rail line and assigned to the use of one or more parties for the loading and unloading of cars.

Assignee—One to whom an assignment of rights or property is made.

Assigner—One who makes an assignment.

Astray freight—Freight that becomes separated from the waybill while in transit.

Average demurrage agreement—An agreement to offset car detention debits with credits (see Chapter 13).

Avoirdupois pound—Same as 0.4535924277 kilograms.

"B" end of car—The end on which the hand brake is located. See "A" end of car.

Back haul—Hauling of a shipment back over part of a route already traveled.

Bailment—A delivery of goods by one party to another to be held and dealt with according to the purpose of the delivery and to be returned when that purpose is accomplished.

Barratry—The action of officers or crews of a ship in willfully destroying or injuring it or its cargo.

Basing point—A point, the rates to and from which are used in constructing through rates between other points. Also, a location named in a sales contract on which to make price calculations.

Bbl.—Barrel.

Bdl.—Bundle.

Beam—The greatest width of a ship.

Belt line—A switching railroad operating within a commercial area.

Bilateral—A contract term meaning both parties agree to provide something for the other.

Billed weight—The weight the carrier shows on the waybill and freight bill.

Bill of Lading (B/L)—Either a straight non-negotiable or order negotiable document which is a contract for transportation between the shipper and the carrier (see Chapter 4 and 17).

Bill of sale—A contract for a sale of goods.

Blanket bond—A bond covering a group of persons, articles, or properties.

Blanket rate—A rate applicable to or from a group of points. A special rate applicable to several different articles in a single shipment.

B/L—Bill of lading.

Bls.—Bales.

B/M—Board measure.

B.O.—Bad order.

Bonded warehouse—A warehouse under Treasury Department bond for the observance of revenue laws.

Bond of indemnity—A certificate filed with a carrier relieving it from liability to which it would otherwise be subject.

Booking—Arrangements with a carrier, often a steamship or airline, for the acceptance and carriage of passengers or freight.

Box car—A closed freight car.

Break bulk—To unload and reship the contents of a car.

Brief—A written abstract of testimony, pleadings, and commentaries in a legal proceeding.

Bulk freight—Not in packages or containers; but shipped loose as grain in a box car, coal in a hopper car, or sulphur in the hold of a ship.

Bulkhead—a. A partition separating one part of a ship, freight car, aircraft, or truck from another part.

b. A structure to resist water.

Bunching—The accumulation and tender of railroad cars for loading, generally at an industrial plant, contrary to normal schedules.

Bunker charge. An extra charge sometimes added to steamship freight rates having as a justification higher fuel costs.

Burden of proof—The duty of proving a particular position in a legal proceeding where the failure to perform this duty calls for judgment against the party on whom the duty is imposed. An important aspect of I.C.C. proceedings, the Act provides the carriers have the burden of proof to show that rate, etc. changes are reasonable.

Bx.—Box.

C.A.B.—Civil Aeronautics Board.

C.A.F.—Cost, assurance and freight.

C. & F.—Cost and freight.

C. & S.M.F.T.A.—Central and Southern Motor Freight Traffic Association.

Car pooling—Use of individual carrier equipment through a central agency for the benefit of carriers and shippers.

Car seal—Small metal strip and lead fastener used for locking freight car or truck doors. Seals are numbered for record purposes.

Car float—A barge equipped with tracks on which up to about 12 railroad cars are moved in harbors or inland waterways.

Cargo—Freight loaded into a ship.

Cargo ship tonnage—is either "weight" or "measurement." The weight ton in the United States is 2,000 or 2,240 pounds and in British countries is the English long or gross ton of 2,240 pounds. A "measurement" ton is usually 40 cubic feet.

Carload (CL)—The amount of freight required for the application of a carload rate.

Carload minimum weight—The lowest weight at which a shipment is subject to a carload rate.

Carload rate—A rate applying to a quantity equal to or above the carload minimum weight.

Car mile—Refers to the movement of one freight car one mile. Used to measure costs, revenues or volume.

Carrier—Any individual, company or corporation engaged in transporting goods.

Cartage—Usually refers to intracity hauling on drays or trucks.

C.A.S.L.—Committee of American Steamship Lines.

Cash against documents—Payment for goods upon presentation of documents evidencing shipment.

C.E.—Consumption entry.

Certificate of origin—A certified statement showing where goods originated.

Certificate of public convenience and necessity—Authority granted by a government regulatory body to operate as a common carrier.

Certiorari. A writ used in appellate court procedure under which a court of review brings a case up from a lower court.

C.F. (Cu. Ft.)—Cubic feet.

C.F.A.—Canadian Freight Association.

Chartered ship—A ship under lease by its owners to others.

Charter Party, C/P—Form of contract between merchant and shipowner.

C.I.—Cost and insurance.

C.I.F.—Cost, insurance and freight.

C.I.F. & C.—Cost, insurance, freight and commission.

C.I.F.C.I.—Cost, insurance, freight, collection and interest.

C.I.F.I. & E.—Cost, insurance, freight, interest and exchange.

C.I.F. & E.—Cost, insurance, freight and exchange.

Cir.—Circular.

Circuitous route—Other than direct route.

Claim—A document showing evidence to recover loss by damage or overcharge.

C.L.—Carload.

Class I motor carriers—Those motor carriers with average annual operating revenue of $1,000,000 or over for the three immediately preceding years.

Class II motor carriers—Those motor carriers with average annual operating revenue of $300,000 and over but under $1,000,000 for the three immediately preceding years.

Class III motor carriers—Those motor carriers with average annual operating revenue of less than $300,000 for the three immediately preceding years.

Class I railroads—Those railroads with an annual operating revenue of $5,000,000 or more.

Class II railroads—Those railroads with an annual operating revenue of less than $5,000,000.

Class and commodity tariff—A tariff publication including both class and commodity rates.

Classification—A publication, such as the Uniform Freight Classification (railroad) or the National Motor Freight Classification (motor carrier), which assigns ratings to various articles and provides bill-of-lading descriptions and rules.

Classification rating—The designation provided in a classification by which a class rate is determined.

Classification yard—A railroad yard with many tracks used for assembling freight trains.

Class rate—A rate resulting from the application of a rating named in a classification.

Clean bill of lading—A carrier-receipted bill of lading without any exceptions whatsoever noted such as "shortage," "damage," "shipper's load and count," etc.

Clear record—A record of a shipment indicating no exceptions whatsoever.

Clearance limits—The measurement beyond which cars or loads cannot be handled due to bridges, tunnels, etc.

Cleat—A strip of wood or metal used to afford additional strength, to prevent warping, or to hold in position.

Coastwise—Water transportation along the coast.

C.O.D.—Collect (cash) on delivery.

Code—A set of rules, numbers, etc. that is used to convert data from one representation to another in data processing.

C.O.G.S.A.—Carriage of Goods By Sea Act.

Col.—Column.

Collector of Customs—A U.S. Treasury Department official in charge of a customs zone to collect duties, etc. on import shipments.

Com.—Committee or commission.

Combination rate—A rate made up of two or more factors, separately published.

Commodity—Article shipped.

Commodity clause—I. C. Act Sec. 1(8) which makes it unlawful for a railroad to transport any commodity, other than timber and its products, which it owns or in which it has an interest except those intended for its use as a carrier.

Commodity rate—A rate published to apply to a specific article or articles.

Commodity tariff—A tariff published to show specific rates on specific articles.

Common carrier—A transportation company operating under a Certificate of Convenience and Necessity which holds itself out to provide service to the general public at published rates.

Common law—That part of the law which derives its force and authority from consent, custom, and usage rather than from the statutes.

Common point—A point served by two or more carriers.

Competitive point—A point served by two or more carriers that compete for traffic.

Competitive rate—A rate published by one line to compete with another.

Competitive traffic—Traffic for which two or more lines compete.

Complainant—An individual or company that makes a complaint.

Concealed damage—Damage that is not evident from viewing the unopened package.

Concurrence—A carrier document filed with a regulatory body to show participation in rates published in a tariff by an agent.

Conference rate—Freight rates arrived at by a conference of carriers, generally water carriers.

Consignee—The receiver to whom goods are shipped.

Consignor—The shipper who forwards goods.

Consolidation—The act of assembling LCL or LTL shipments into carloads or truckloads.

Consolidation point—A point where several shipments, usually LCL or LTL, are assembled for reshipment as consolidated shipments.

Consolidator—A person or firm performing a consolidation service for others.

Constructive mileage—An arbitrary mileage specified for a carrier in dividing joint rates, etc. on a mileage pro rata basis.

Constructive placement—Freight cars placed other than at a siding or other location usually designated, because of some interference.

Consul—A government official representing his country in foreign locations.

Consular invoice—A document that lists particulars of a shipment and that must be certified by a country's consul before goods may be exported to that country.

Consulate—The office or premises occupied officially by a consul.

Container car—A specially designed car for transporting portable freight containers.

Contraband—Traffic that is prohibited.

Contract carrier—Usually refers to a for-hire motor carrier, other than a common carrier, hauling under contracts in accordance with a permit issued by a government regulatory body.

Conversion—Appropriation of freight by a carrier.

C/P—a. Custom of the port.
            b. Charter party.

Cr.—Credit.

C.S.M.F.B.—Central States Motor Freight Bureau.

C.S.T.—Central standard time.

C.T.R.—Central Territory Railroads.

Cu.—Cubic.

Custom House—A U.S. Treasury Department office where duties, etc. on foreign shipments are handled.

Customs tariff—A schedule of charges assessed by a government on imported or exported goods.

Cwt.—Hundredweight (U.S.A. is 100 lbs.; United Kingdom 112 lbs.).

D/B/A—Doing business as.

D.F. car—Box cars equipped with special bracing material sometimes called "damage free cars."

Dbk.—Drawback.

Dead space—Space in a car, truck, vessel, etc., that is not utilized.

Deadweight tonnage, D/W—expresses the number of tons of 2,240 pounds that a vessel can transport of cargo, stores, and bunker fuel. It is the difference between the number of tons of water a vessel displaces "light" and the number of tons it displaces when submerged to the "load line".

Deld.—Delivered.

Delivering carrier—The carrier that delivers the shipment to the consignee.

Dely.—Delivery.

Demurrage (Dem.)—A penalty charge against shippers or receivers for delaying carrier equipment beyond allowed free time.

Density—The weight of freight per cubic foot or other unit.

Density of traffic—Amount of traffic over a carrier's route per mile or other unit.

Deposition—Certified, written testimony.

Detention charge (motor carrier)—see demurrage.

Differential (Diff.)—The difference between rates from or to several points. Differential rates are established to one point at fixed amounts over or under a rate to another point or via another route.

Discrimination—Giving some shippers or receivers rates or other privileges not accorded others under practically the same conditions.

Displacement—of a vessel is the weight, in tons of 2,240 pounds, of the vessel and its contents.

Distributor—A person or firm performing a service of distribution on pool cars or consolidated shipments at destination.

Divert—The route of a shipment changed in transit from that shown on the original billing. The word is used interchangably with reconsign.

Division—Carriers' practice of dividing revenue received from through rates where joint hauls are involved. This is usually according to agreed formulae.

Dock—a. The water alongside a pier or wharf.

b. Loading or unloading platform at an industrial location or carrier terminal.

Dockage—Charge for use of a dock.

Dock receipt—A document given to a shipper when goods are delivered to a pier.

D.O.T.—Department of Transportation.

Draft—The number of feet that a ship is beneath the water line.

Draft, bank—an order issued by a seller against a purchaser directing payment of money usually through an intermediary bank. These usually are "negotiable instruments" and are similar in many ways to checks on checking accounts in a bank.

Drawback—Refund of duty paid on imported material subsequently shipped out of the country.

Drayage—Refers to charge made for local hauling by dray or truck.

Drill—Movement of a car into a local switching yard or on a private siding.

Due bill—a. Usually called balance due bill and usually covers additional charges because first bill was issued too low and in error.

      b. A receipt signed for ocean bills of lading delivered with specific credit privileges.

Dunnage (Dge.)—Lumber or other material used to brace material in carriers' equipment.

Duty—The charge assessed by the government on shipments imported or exported.

D.W.—Dead weight.

E.C.M.C.A.—Eastern Central Motor Carriers Association.

E.D.S.T.—Eastern Daylight Saving Time.

Elevating charge (vessel)—A charge for services performed in connection with floating elevators; also charges assessed for the handling of grain through grain elevators.

Elkins Act—An Act of Congress (1903) prohibiting rebates, concessions, misbilling, etc. and providing specific penalties for such violations.

Embargo—Carrier or regulatory-body order to restrict the hauling of freight.

Emergency rate—A rate established to meet some immediate and pressing need, and without due regard to the usual rate factors.

En route—Along the route of movement.

Entry—Customs documents required to "clear" a shipment imported into the country.

Est. Wt.—Estimated weight. A specific weight provided in a carrier tariff for application on a certain commodity regardless of the actual weight.

E.W.I.B.—Eastern Weighing and Inspection Bureau.

Ex. B.L.—Exchange bill of lading.

Ex dock—The freight is away from the dock. This term is used principally in United States import trade. It has various modifications, such as "Ex Quay", "Ex Pier", etc., but it is seldom, if ever, used in American export practice.

Ex parte—From, or in the interest of, one side only.

Exceptions to classification—Ratings or rules that differ from and take precedence over those shown in the normally governing classification.

Excess freight—Freight in excess of that shown on the original carrier billing.

Exchange bill of lading—A bill of lading prepared to be substituted for another bill of lading as a straight bill of lading for an order bill of lading or vice-versa.

Expense bill—The freight bill used to invoice freight charges.

Expiration notice—Issued in connection with tariffs to advise that stated provisions will expire at a certain time.

Export (Expt.)—Shipment of goods to a foreign country.

Export declaration—See Shippers' Export Declaration.

Export license—A government document permitting designated goods to be shipped out of the country.

Ex post facto—After the fact.

F.A.A.—Free of all average.

Fabrication in transit—Material stopped in transit for a manufacturing process, protecting through rate from origin to destination.

False billing—Description of commodities on shipping papers that does not reflect the true contents of a shipment.

F.A.S.—Free alongside ship.

F.B.—Freight bill.

Federal Aviation Act—An Act of Congress (1958) which superseded the Civil Aeronautics Act of 1938 regulating air transportation.

F.D.—Free discharge.

Feeding in transit—The stopping of shipments of livestock, etc. at a point located between points of origin and destination to be fed and watered.

Ferry car—A freight car loaded with several LCL shipments by a shipper to a railroad or by a railroad to a receiver. A trap car.

Finance docket—I.C.C. dockets of matters involving carrier financings, extensions, abandonments, and consolidations.

Fighting ship—term used to define a ship set up by conference lines to combat non-conference competition. This is done by making rates on these ships so low that the competition is forced out of business or influenced to quote rates economically sound. Fighting ships are illegal under the Shipping Act of 1916.

F.I.O.—Free in and out to the ship.

Firkin—A capacity measurement equal to one-fourth of a barrel.

Fishyback—The transportation of highway trailers or demountable trailer bodies aboard ship.

Flag station—Trains stop only upon signal from the station.

Flammable liquids—Liquids that give off vapors which become combustible at a certain temperature. These are sometimes called "Inflammable" but "Flammable" is preferred.

Flat car—A freight car without ends, sides, or top.

Float bridge—A mechanical device that lowers or raises tracks connecting a car float with land railroad tracks.

F.M.C.—Federal Maritime Commission.

Font—A data processing term referring to type size, style, etc.

F.O.B.—Free on board.

F.O.R.—Free on rail.

Foreign car—A car owned by one railroad but on the rails of another railroad.

Formal complaint—A complaint filed with the Interstate Commerce Commission charging violation of federal laws and decided under formal procedure as per the rules of the Commission.

F.O.T.—Free on truck.

Fourth Section application—A carrier application to the Interstate Commerce Commission requesting permission to publish rates not in accordance with the Fourth Section which provides that rates to any destination cannot be higher than to a more distant point over the same route. The issuance of a Fourth Section Order favorable to the carrier by the I.C.C. grants the relief sought.

F.P.A.—Free of particular average.

Free astray (F.A.)—A shipment which is lost and then found is designated to be "astray" and is sent to its proper destination free, i.e., without additional charges.

Free of particular average (F.P.A.)—A marine insurance term meaning that the assurers will not allow payment for partial loss or damage to foreign shipments except in certain circumstances. See the insurance section of the International Shipments Chapter.

Free port—A restricted area at a seaport for the handling of duty exempted import goods. (Foreign Trade Zone).

Free time—The time allowed shippers or receivers to load or unload cars before demurrage, detention or storage charges accrue.

Freight forwarder—An individual or company accepting LCL shipments from shippers and combining them for forwarding in carload lots. A foreign freight forwarder handles customs procedures and documents on export shipments.

Frt.—Freight.

Fwd.—Forward.

Gateway—A freight interchange point between territories.

G.B.L.—Government bill of lading.

General average (G.A.)—A marine insurance term referring to assessment against all interests to cover loss sustained when some cargo is jettisoned to save the vessel and the remaining part of the cargo.

G.F.T.C.—E.R.R.—General Freight Traffic Committee—Eastern Railroads.

Gondola car—A freight car with low sides and ends. Most have no tops but some are equipped with removable or retractable covers.

Grandfather clause—A provision of the law protecting vested interests. Motor carriers operating prior to October 1, 1935 were given protection under the Grandfather Clause of the Motor Carrier Act in that they could continue their operations previous to that date by simply establishing the extent of them.

Gross ton (G.T.)—2,240 pounds.

Gross tonnage—Applies to vessels, not to cargo. It is determined by dividing by 100 the contents, in cubic feet, of the vessel's closed-in spaces. A vessel ton is 100 cubic feet.

Gross weight—The total weight of merchandise and container. Also, the total weight of a freight car and its contents.

Hearing—A time and place designated by the Interstate Commerce Commission or a carrier rate conference to permit presentation of evidence by parties interested in a particular case being considered.

Heater car—An insulated box car equipped with heating apparatus for the protection of perishables.

Heavy lifts—Freight too heavy to be handled by regular equipment (usually refers to ship's tackle).

Hold track—A track where cars are placed pending disposition orders from shippers or receivers.

Home car—A car on the track of its owner.

Hopper car—A car for bulk dry freight which unloads, usually by gravity, through vents in the underside. Some are open; others have tops.

Hump—Used in railroad classification yards; a high track from which uncoupled cars roll by gravity to desired classification tracks.

I.C.C.—Interstate Commerce Commission.

Identity of shipment—Preservation of original character of shipments stopped in transit so that no substitution occurs outbound from the transit point.

I.F.A.—Illinois Freight Association.

Incldg.—Including.

Indemnity bond—An agreement to hold harmless a carrier as regards a liability to which it would otherwise be subject.

Individual tariff—A tariff published by one transportation line to apply to traffic moving locally between points served by the issuing carrier or jointly with a limited number of participating carriers.

Industrial carrier—A short railroad owned and operated by one or more industries for their exclusive purposes or as a common carrier.

GLOSSARY

Inflammable liquids—See Flammable liquids.

Informal complaint—A complaint filed with the Interstate Commerce Commission on an informal basis with the desire to obtain the Commission's decision through correspondence without the recourse to a formal complaint and with general understanding to that end between the complainant and the defendant.

Information retrieval—As used in data processing, the methods and procedures for recovering specific information from stored data.

Initial carrier—The carrier that receives the first line-haul on an outbound shipment from the shipper.

Initials, car—The initials of the car owner before the car number as "SCCX 185".

Ins.—Insurance.

Int.—Interest.

Interchange point—A location where one carrier delivers freight to another carrier.

Interchange track—A specific track location where one carrier delivers freight to another carrier or to an industrial switch.

Intercoastal—Water service between two coasts usually referring to water service between points on the Atlantic and Pacific Coasts.

Interface—A data processing term indicating a shared boundary, e.g., one code will "interface" with another, etc.

Interline waybill—Carriers' waybill when more than one carrier is involved.

Intermediate clause—A clause in tariffs providing for the application of rates from or to points not listed that are the same as those published from or to more distant points via the same route.

Intermediate point—A point located en route between two other points.

Interstate traffic—Generally speaking this is traffic crossing state lines in the course of transportation.

Intervene—To take action and participate in proceedings that have been instituted by others.

In transitu—In transit or in passage.

Intra-plant switching—Moving cars between locations within an industrial plant.

Intrastate traffic—Traffic moving between points within one state and not leaving the state in the course of transportation.

Inv.—Invoice.

Investigation and suspension docket (I & S)—Cases before the Interstate Commerce Commission dealing with applications or orders for suspension of rates or rules.

Issuing carrier—The carrier issuing transportation documents or publishing a tariff.

I.T.—Immediate transportation, refers to an "I.T." Entry (U.S. Customs).

Jct.—Junction.

Jettison—Act of throwing cargo or equipment overboard when a ship is in danger.

Joint agent—An official designated to act for two or more carriers.

Joint boards—These are hearing groups consisting of members from interested states which are generally involved in motor carrier operating rights requests. They are created under the I. C. Act (Motor Carrier Part, Sec. 205).

Joint rate—A rate applying via two or more carriers.

Joint traffic—Freight that moves between stations on two or more carriers.

Judicial notice—Consideration of facts generally known by the court or commission when its attention is directed to them without production of proof that they exist.

Junction point—A track connection between two lines or two branches of the same line.

Kilogram—2.2 lbs.

Knocked down (K.D.)—Articles that are taken apart so as to reduce the cubic foot displacement or to make a better shipping unit.

Knot—The nautical mile (6082.66 feet).

L. & D.—Loss and damage.

Lading—Refers to the freight shipped; the contents of a shipment.

Land grant rate—A special rate applied on government traffic in consideration of a land grant.

Legal weight—A foreign trade term referring to the weight of of the merchandise and its inner or immediate container but not to the outer shipping container.

Less than carload (LCL)—A shipment weighing less than the weight required for the application of a carload rate.

Less than truckload (LTL)—A shipment weighing less than the weight required for the application of a truckload rate.

Letter of credit (L.C.)—A letter of agreement by a bank stating a foreign purchaser has established a line of credit in a sellers' favor and confirming that payment for goods sold will be made upon presentation of certain documents.

Lic.—License.

Lien—A legal claim upon goods for the satisfaction of some debt or duty.

Lighter (Ltr.)—An open or covered barge towed by a tugboat and used mostly in harbors.

Lighterage—Refers to carriage of goods by lighter; also to the charge assessed therefor.

Line-haul—The transportation from one city to another as differentiated from local switching service.

Liter—1.06 liquid quarts.

Local rate—A rate applicable between points served by the same carrier.

Local station—A station served by only one carrier.

Local traffic—Freight transported between points served by the same carrier.

Long-and-short-haul clause—Refers to Fourth Section of the Interstate Commerce Commission which prohibits carriers from charging a higher rate for short haul than for a long haul when en route except by special I.C.C. permission, See Fourth Section Application, supra.

Longshoreman—Individual employed locally in a port to load and unload ships.

Long ton/l.t. or l.tn.—2,240 pounds.

Loose—Without packing.

M.A.C.—Middle Atlantic Conference.

Mandamus—A writ issued by a court requiring that specific things be done.

Manifest—A statement listing the particulars of all shipments loaded in car, ship, truck, etc. Usually refers to ship's manifest.

Marked capacity—The weight limits of cargo loaded into a car as stenciled on the side of the car.

Marriage rule—An arrangement whereby, instead of physically stopping a car for completion of loading, the railroad will place a separate car at the stopoff point to receive the freight.

Master tariff—A tariff filed with the Interstate Commerce Commission applying to a large number of applicable tariffs. Used mostly to publish general rate increases.

Max.—Maximum.

Maximum rate—The highest freight rate permitted by a regulatory body to apply between points.

M.C.T.A.—Motor Carriers Traffic Association.

Measurement cargo—Freight on which transportation charges are calculated on the basis of measurement.

Memorandum bill of lading—Generally the third copy of a bill of lading.

Merchandise car—A car loaded with two or more less-than-carload shipments.

Meter—39.37 inches.

Metric ton—2,204.6 pounds.

Mileage allowance—a. A mileage allowance made by the railroad to private owners of freight cars.

b. Allowance made to employees using own automobiles on company business.

Mileage tariff—A carrier tariff naming rates based on mileage.

Milling in transit—The operation of stopping in transit certain commodities such as grain for milling with through rates applying from origin to destination.

Min.—Minimum.

Minimum carload weight—The lowest weight for which a carload freight rate can be assessed.

Minimum charge—The lowest charge than can be assessed to transport a shipment.

Minimum rate—The lowest freight rate permitted by a regulatory body to apply between points.

Min. Wt.—Minimum weight.

M.I.P.—Marine Insurance Policy.

M.I.T.—Milling in transit.

Mixed carload rate—A rate applicable to a carload shipment composed of two or more different articles.

M.M.F.B.—Middlewest Motor Freight Bureau.

Modified procedure—A shortened and simplified method of handling I.C.C. proceedings under which part of the testimony may be handled in writing by sworn statements.

Motor Carrier Act—An Act of Congress effective October 1, 1935, placing the motor carriers under federal regulation (Part II of the Interstate Commerce Act).

Mullen (or Cady) Test—Mechanical equipment used to test the strength of fiberboard containers.

N.E.M.R.B.—New England Motor Rate Bureau.

Nested—Articles packed so that one rests partially or entirely within another thereby reducing the cubic foot displacement.

N.E.T.R.—New England Territory Railroads.

Net ton (N.T.)—2,000 pounds.

Net tonnage—is a vessel's gross tonnage minus deductions of space occupied by accommodations for crew, by machinery, for navigation, by the engine room and fuel. A vessel's net tonnage expresses the space available for the accommodation of passengers and the stowage of cargo.

Net weight—The weight of merchandise without the shipping container. Also, the weight of the contents of a freight car.

N/M—No mark.

N.M.F.C.—National Motor Freight Classification.

N.O.I.—Not otherwise indexed.

N.O.I.B.N.—Not otherwise indexed by name.

Non-agency Station—A station where there is no representative of the carrier.

N.O.S.—Not otherwise specified.

N.P.C.F.B.—North Pacific Coast Freight Bureau.

O/C—Overcharge.

Open insurance policy—A marine insurance policy that applies on all shipments over a period of time rather than on a single shipment.

Operating ratio—A comparison of a carrier's operating expense with its gross receipts.

Order-notify (O/N)—A bill-of-lading term to provide for surrender of the original bill of lading before freight is surrendered; usually handled through a bank.

O.S.&D.—Over, short and damaged.

Overcharge—A charge on a freight bill based upon an erroneous rate, weight or rating thereby resulting in excessive charges.

Over freight—Freight in possession of a carrier without way-bill or identifying marks.

P/A—(a) Particular average.
　　　(b) Private account.

Package car—A freight car containing two or more less-than-carload shipments that a railroad cards through (dispatches) from origin point to a principal break-bulk point to improve service.

Package freight—Less-than-carload shipments.

Packing list—A statement prepared by the shipper, not necessarily required by carriers, to show merchandise packing particulars. A copy is usually sent to the consignee to assist in checking the shipment when received.

Pallet—A platform (usually two-deck), with or without sides, on which a number of packages or pieces may be loaded to facilitate handling by a lift truck.

Panama Canal Act—A federal law applicable to railroads and their ownership of water carriers with whom they compete.

Paper rate—A published rate that is never assessed because of no freight movement under it.

Participating carrier—A carrier that is a party to a tariff published by an agency or another carrier or which is designated in a route.

P.D.—(a) Property damage (insurance term).
    (b) pd.—paid.
    (c) Post dated.

Per annum (Per An)/(per Ann.)—For one year.

Per diem (P.D.)—For one day; refers to charges made by railroads against other railroads for use of the owner railroad's cars while on other lines.

Perishable freight—Food and other commodities subject to spoliage en route.

Per se—By itself.

P. & I.—Protection and indemnity—an insurance term.

Pickup—The act of calling for freight by truck at the consignor's shipping platform.

Piggyback—The transportation of highway trailers or demountable trailer bodies on specially equipped rail cars.

P.I.T.B.—Pacific Inland Tariff Bureau.

P.L.—Public liability (insurance term).

Port—a. Harbor with piers or docks.
    b. Left side of a ship when facing the bow.
    c. Opening in a ship's side for handling freight.

Port of entry—A port designated by the government as satisfactory for handling import shipments.

Power of attorney—Authority given by the first party to the second party to act for the first party. Used in transportation when carriers give power of attorney to an agent to publish tariffs for account of those carriers.

P.P.—Parcel post.

Prepaid (Ppd.)—Freight charges paid by the consignor.

Prepay station—A non-agency station to which freight charges must be prepaid.

Prima facie—Means on first appearance; used as "prima facie evidence" or "prima facie case" whereby a premise is established as a fact unless challenged and proven by rebuttal.

Private cars—Cars whose ownership is vested in a person or company not engaged primarily in common carrier service.

Private siding—A railroad track serving an industrial plant owned or rented by the plant.

Program—A data processing term meaning a plan for solving a problem or devising a plan for solving a problem.

Pro number—A serial number assigned by a carrier to its freight bill. The term pro comes from the word progressive.

Proportional rate—A rate between two points that applies only when certain requirements are met as to a movement beyond one of the two points.

Proportional tariff—A tariff naming proportional rates.

Proximo—In or of the next month after the present.

P.S.F.B.—Pacific Southcoast Freight Bureau.

P.U.&D.—Pickup and delivery.

R.&L.—Rail and lake.

R.&O.—Rail and ocean.

R.&T.—Rail and truck.

R.&W.—Rail and water.

Rate basis number—The number by which a given scale of class rates is identified.

Rate group—The group in which a given point is located for the determination of rates in a tariff.

R.E.A.—Railway Express Agency (REA Express).

Receivers certificate—An acknowledgement of indebtedness issued by the receiver for a carrier (with court authority) to provide funds for equipment supplies, fuel and the like for the carrier's operations.

Reciprocal switching—An arrangement where two or more railroads serving the same point agree to absorb each other's local switching charges. Example: Where this exists an industry on "A" railroad in a switching district served by "A" and "B" railroads can route its shipments via "B" without paying extra charges for switching by "A".

Reconsignment (R/C)—The act of changing the bill of lading provisions as to consignee or destination while shipment is still in transit. Diversion has substantially the same meaning.

Red label—A label required on shipments of articles of a flammable character.

Reefer—Refrigeration equipment.

Refrigeration car—A car built with icing compartments and ventilators or mechanically operated cooling devices for transporting perishable freight.

Refund—A sum of money returned to the shipper or receiver because of an overcharge collected at the time transportation charges were billed and paid.

Release rate—A rate that applies when the carrier assumes responsibility for a limited, less-than-actual value of the freight.

Reparation—Refund ordered by the Interstate Commerce Commission as award of damages when charges paid are adjudged unlawful.

Retroactive—Applying a tariff, rule, etc., to a date prior to the date of publication of the tariff, rule, etc.

Revenue load—A load of freight in a car, truck, vessel, or plane for which freight charges are assessed.

R.L.&R.—Rail, lake and rail.

R.M.M.T.B.—Rocky Mountain Motor Tariff Bureau.

Route (Rte.)—The manner in which a shipment moves, i.e., the carriers handling it and the points via which they handle it.

R.S.L.—Other articles rated the same or lower. Used in describing mixed packages when only the highest rated article is named.

Salvage—What is saved after damage has been done; the value of the goods after being damaged.

S/D—(a) Sight draft.

(b) Sea damage.

Seal—Small metal strip and lead fastener used for locking freight car or truck doors. Seals are numbered for record purposes.

Semi-trailer—A freight-carrying vehicle without motor power that is attached by means of a "fifth wheel" to a tractor resulting in a tractor-trailer combination.

Set-up (S.U.)—Designates an article that is ready for use; other than knocked down; completely assembled.

S.F.A.—Southern Freight Association.

Ship chandler—An individual or company selling ship's equipment and supplies.

Shipper's export declaration—A form required by the U.S. Treasury on export shipments and listing full particulars of the shipments.

Shipper's load and count—Carload or truckload shipments loaded and sealed by shippers where the contents are not checked or verified by the carriers.

Shipping permit—a. Privilege extended by carriers to shippers to forward specific shipments contrary to existing embargoes.

b. Permit issued by steamship lines to shippers authorizing specific shipments to be accepted at pier receiving locations.

Ship's bells—Time on board ships is designated by bells that run from one to eight bells every half hour each four-hour period. One bell would be 12:30 o'clock, two bells on o'clock, three bells 1:30 and so on up to four o'clock which is eight bells. Four-thirty, then would start all over at one bell.

Shipside—Pier or off-shore side of a vessel docked for loading or unloading.

Ship's manifest—A statement listing the particulars of all shipments loaded to one ship for a specified voyage.

Ship's tackle—All rigging, etc., utilized on a ship to load or unload cargo.

Short ton—2,000 pounds.

Shortage (Shtg.)—That part of a shipment that remains undelivered.

Side-track—A spur track from a regular railroad track usually alongside the regular track. A siding.

Side-track agreement—A contract executed by a railroad and a shipper or receiver to cover mutual responsibilities for the use and operation of a siding serving the shipper or receiver.

Sixth Section relief—I.C.C. permission to make freight rate changes effective on less than the statutory (30 days) notice requirements of the Act.

S.L.&C.—Shipper's load and count.

S.L.&T.—Shipper's load and tally.

Sling—A large net into which freight may be placed and then hoisted into or out of a ship.

S.M.C.R.C.—Southern Motor Carriers Rate Conference.

S.O.—a. Seller's option.
    b. Ship's option.
    c. Shipping order.
    d. Stop off.

S.P.A.—Subject to particular average.

S.P.F.F.C.—Southern Ports Foreign Freight Committee.

Spotting—Refers to placing freight cars or trucks for loading or unloading.

Spur-track—A track extending a fairly short distance from a regular railroad track.

S.S.—a. Shipside.
    b. Steamship.

Standard gauge—The distance between the rails of practically all Northern American railroads, 4 ft. 8½ in.

Starboard—The right side of a ship when facing the bow.

Statutory notice—The length of time required by government regulatory bodies for carriers to give notice of tariff rate and rule changes.

Stds.—Standards.

Steamship freight contract—An agreement between a shipper and steamship line for space and rates in connection with future sailings.

Stevedore—Individual or firm that employs longshoremen.

Stopoff—An arrangement whereby a carload or truckload may be started at one point and stopped at another en route for completion of loading or for a partial unloading.

Storage in transit—A tariff privilege permitting freight to be stopped and stored en route with rate from origin to final destination applying.

Store door delivery—Delivery to consignee's place of business by motor vehicle.

Stowage—A marine term referring to loading freight into ships' holds.

Subrogate—To put in place of another, i.e., when an insurance company pays a claim it is placed in the same position as the payee as regards any rights against others.

Supplement (Sup.)—A tariff publication adding to or changing the subject matter of the original tariff.

Surcharge—An extra or additional charge.

S.W.F.B.—Southwestern Freight Bureau.

Switching (Swg.)—The transfer of cars from one location to another within a local railroad area.

Tacking—Through common carrier motor service achieved by "tacking" one set of operating authority to another, e.g., regular with irregular, "limited commodity" with "open" authority, etc.

Tank car—A car for bulk liquid freight, sometimes divided into two or more compartments.

Tare weight—The weight of packing material or, in carload shipments, the weight of the empty freight car.

Tariff (Trf.)—A publication setting forth the charges, rates and rules of transportation companies.

Tariff circular—An Interstate Commerce Commission publication setting forth carrier tariff publishing rules and regulations.

T.C.F.B.—Trans-Continental Freight Bureau.

Team track—A track established by a railroad for general use of the public in loading and unloading freight cars.

Terminal charge—A charge made for a service performed in a carrier's terminal area.

Terr.—Territory.

Through rate—A rate that applies from origin to destination.

T.O.F.C. (Tofcee)—Trailer-on-flat-car; piggyback.

Tolerance—A weight allowance made to reconcile weight variations of certain commodities.

Ton-mile—Refers to the movement of one ton of freight one mile. Used to measure costs, revenue or volume.

Tonnage—Generally refers to freight handled.

Trace—The act of locating a shipment that has not arrived at destination.

Trackage right—The privilege granted one railroad to operate over the tracks of another railroad.

Tractor—Unit of highway motive power used to pull one or more trailers.

Trailer—The truck unit into which freight is loaded as in tractor-trailer combination.

Tramp steamer—A steamer not operating on regulars runs or schedules.

Transit privilege—The privilege, provided in tariffs, of stopping shipments en route for milling, treating, storage, etc.

Transit rate—A rate applying to traffic stopped en route for milling, treating, storage, etc.

Trans-load—A service whereby a stop-off carload is reloaded at a point en route.

Trans-ship—Usually refers to the physical break-bulk transfer of freight shipments between carriers such as from a rail to a water carrier.

Trap car—A freight car loaded with less-than-carload freight by a shipper generally to one consignee.

Truckload (TL)—A shipment via motor carrier weighing the amount required for the application of a truckload rate.

Truck mile—Refers to the movement of one unit of highway motive power one mile. Used to measure costs, revenue or volume.

Trunk line—A railroad operating trains a substantial distance.

Undercharge—To charge less than the proper amount.

U.F.C.—Uniform Freight Classification.

Unilateral—A legal term used in connection with contracts meaning a contract in which only one party is specifically bound as to tonnage hauled, service furnished, etc.

Unit load—Several packages that are loaded on a pallet in a crate or any other way that enables them to be handled at one time as a unit.

Vessel ton—One hundred cubic feet.

Via—By way of.

Vol.—Volume.

Volume minimum weight—Used in motor carrier tariffs, it is the minimum weight in connection with which any specific volume rate, other than truckload, applies.

Volume rate (V.R.)—Used in motor carrier tariffs to denote any rate applicable in connection with which a volume minimum weight applies.

Warehouse receipt—A negotiable or non-negotiable document given by warehouse companies as a receipt for goods placed in warehouses.

Waybill (W.B.)—A carrier record issued for each shipment showing details. Copies are often sent to all interested agents of the carrier.

Weight agreement—A carrier-shipper agreement under which the carrier accepts the shipper's goods for transportation at certain agreed weights.

Wharfage (Whfge.)—Charge assessed by a pier or dock owner against freight handled over the pier or dock, or against a steamship company using the pier or dock.

W/M—Weight or measurement—basis for assessing freight charges.

W.P.A.—With particular average.

W.T.L.—Western Trunk Line.

Yard—A railroad local classification, storage or switching area.

Zones—(a) Express. Districts established for rate making purposes for express shipments, sometimes known as "blocks."

(b) Parcel Post. Areas used as bases for establishing parcel post rates.

(c) Time. Districts used for time-making purposes, e.g., Eastern, Central, Mountain, and Pacific Time Zones.

INDEX

A

accounting, private carriage, 320-323, 335

Act to Regulate Commerce, 19

adjustments, classification, 44, 46, 47

    rate, 104-107

    rate, steamship, 501, 502

agencies, government traffic, 451, 452

    tariff publishing, 92-94, 97-99

Agency for International Development, 528, 529

aggregate of intermediates, 111, 112

agreement, average demurrage, 367-371

    contract truck 293-298, 308-312

    indemnity, 222, 223

    side track, 371-375

    truck lease, 330-334

    weight, 77, 375-381

agricultural exemption (I.C.C.), 304, 305

air freight, 97-99

air, rates and routing, overseas, 564-567

Air Transport Assn. of America, 199

allowance, mileage, salesmen, 336

American Merchant Marine, 466-469

American Society Traffic & Transportation, 402, 431

American Trucking Associations, Inc., 37, 101, 244

Amtrac, 120

anti trust, relief, foreign trade, 558

Reed Bulwinkle Act, 17, 101, 292

Domestic, Sec. 5a I.C.C. Act, 101 292

Contract Motor Carriers, 292

Webb Pomerene law (Export Trade Act of 1918), 558

antidumping, foreign trade, 30, 506, 507, 556

auditing freight bills and audit firms, 113, 114, 217, 218

Associated Traffic Clubs of America, 430

Association of American Railroads, 196, 197, 244, 377

associations, shippers consolidating, 282, 283

automatic data processing (A.D.P.) —see data processing

B

balance of payments, 555, 556

Bank Guarantee, 483

billing, false, 41

bill of lading, domestic, general, rail, truck, etc. Ch. 4, 65-80, Appendix I, 585-591

bill of lading, ocean, general, 69, 479-487, 509, Appendix 2, 593-602

bill of lading, air, domestic, 70

    international, 566

    government 71, 457-459

master format, 482, 490

memorandum, 66, 71, 72

preparation of, 66-71, 75-80

rates—inserting 74, 79, 80, 125

routes and junctions—specifying, 79, 80, 125, 130, 131

Section 7—signing, 73, 79, 80

shipping order, 66, 71

short form, 67, 78

signature, 73-75

through export, 69, 479, 485-487

   uniform live stock contract, 68, 69

   uniform order, 67, 68, 76

   uniform straight, 67, 68, 76-80

   unit, 67, 72

Bills of Lading Act, 65, 230, 231

Bulletin—Report Form—Traffic Dept., 422

booking, cargo, export, import, 487-493

brokers, chartering, 563, 564

   custom, 561-563

   freight, 558-561

   ship, 563, 564

bulk load, 206, 207

C

Canada, shipments within, to and from, 462, 463, 485, 516, 517

Cargo measurement and inspection bureaus, 501

Carriage-of-Goods-By-Sea Act, 482, 547

carriers, unregulated, 9, 10

cars and light trucks, operating, 336

Certificate of Origin, 516

certificates of public convenience and necessity, 138

charges, accessorial, 83, 94, 95

   detention, 127, 364-367

   storage, 363-367

Civil Aeronautics Act, 18

Civil Aeronautics Board, 11, 17-19, 27, 28

organization charts, 18, 28

claim prevention, 216, 234

Claims, audit firms, 217, 218

   concealed loss or damage 226-230, 240-244

   export, import 534, 435, 546-550

   freight, 215-247

   F.O.B. terms, 215

   I.C.C. rules (new, 1972), 244-247

   joint hauls (rail), 217

   loss and damage, 117, 166-168, 215-218, 220, 224-247, 408

   offset not allowed, 218

   overcharge, 114, 220-224

   realistic claim limits, 216, 217

   ship cheapest way, 219

   unconcealed loss or damage, 235-240

   undercharges, 219

classification by analogy, 42, 44, 54

classification, exceptions to, 35, 36

Classification, Consolidated, 34, 36

Classification, Coordinated, 37, 38, 51-64

Classification, Illinois, 33

Classification, National Motor Freight, 31, 37-41, 46, 51-63

Classification, Official, 33

Classification, Southern, 33, 34

Classification, Uniform, 35, 36, 42-51, 436, 437

Classification, Western, 33, 34

commercial zones (I.C.C.), 23 305

commission, forwarder, broker, 558-564

Commodity Credit Corporation, 528

commodity code, (S.T.C.C.), data processing, 50, 51, 436, 437

common carrier system, 8-10

complaints, formal, 47, 104, 105, 107-109

informal, 108
conferences, steamship, 25-27, 493-506
Congressional committees, transport responsibilities, 16
Conrail, 80, 120
Conrail routings, 78, 80
consolidations, 96, 115, 280-283
consolidators, freight, 281-283

Consular Invoice, 514-518
containers, 208-211, 469-477, 551
    air freight, 208, 209, 565
contract, bilateral, 294, 308-312, 501-506
    bill of lading, 65-80, 225, 234, 364
    steamship booking, 488
    trucking, 291-316
contract form, motor, 293-298, 308-312
contract motor carriage, 291-316
contract system, steamship conference, 493, 501, 503-506
control, demurrage, 369-371
Crail case, 234
credit arrangements, 73, 113, 114, 128, 482, 519-534
credit, letters of, types, 523, 524, 526-528, 531-534
customs brokers, 462, 558, 559, 561-563
customs invoice, 509, 510
customs procedure, export, import, 506-519

D

dangerous articles, see hazardous materials
dangerous cargo, export, see hazardous materials
data processing, 2, 50, 51, 71, 72,
    258-260, 263-265, 386, 433-448
decentralization, industrial traffic functions, 402-406
Delta Nu Alpha, 402, 430
demurrage, 359-363, 367-371
demurrage, hazardous materials storage, 363
Department of Commerce, 464, 512, 513
Department of Transportation, 11-17, 28, 29, 571-579, 582-584
    organization charts, 12-15
descriptions, bill of lading, 31-34, 41-52, 77, 78, 220, 513
detention charges, 127, 364-367, 492, 493
differential services, 128
DISC law benefits, foreign trade, 557
distribution, physical, concept of, 251, 252, 260-265
diversion, 354, 355
dockets, classification, 44, 46, 47
    dockets, ICC 28300, 36, 37, 84, 88, 90, 93, 100
    ICC 28310, 35, 89, 100
    ICC 30416, 36, 37, 84, 88, 100
    ICC 30660, 36, 37, 84, 88, 100
    motor carrier, 101, 102
dock receipt, 490
documentation, export, import, 506-534
    government, overseas, and domestic, 457-460
    insurance, export, import, 534-546, 548-550
drawback, 482, 510
dual-rate system, 26, 501-506
due bill privileges, export, import, 482-483
dunnage, 196
duty, imports, 507-511

duty free trade zones, 492

E

electronic data processing (EDP)
—see data processing
engineer, material handling, 211-213
   packaging, 163, 165, 169-172, 174-178
environment laws (recent) and transportation, 29, 30
equalization, freight, 5, 117, 119
equipment, materials handling, 211
equipment, traffic department, 407-419
expediting, 339-358
   air express, 349, 350
   air freight, 348, 349
   carload, 342, 343
   freight forwarder, 348
   less than carload, 347
   less than truckload, 346
   parcel post and mail, 351, 352
   piggyback, 344-346
   truckload, 343, 344
   water carriers, 350, 351
explosives—see hazardous materials
Export-Import Bank, 528-529

F

Federal Maritime Commission, 11, 17-19, 24-27, 464, 493-499, 503-505, 553, 559
   organization charts, 18, 25,
Federal Trade Commission, 558
Fibre Box Association, 170, 174, 179
financial procedure, export, import, 519-534
fishyback, 151
flammables—see hazardous materials

FOB terms, 4, 5, 114-120, 159, 215, 216, 239, 354-356
FOB/FAS terms, 468, 504, 521, 522, 536
   Ex dock, ex quay, ex pier, 562, 563
Foreign Credit Insurance Association, 529
foreign trade, 463, 464, 555-558
   DISC law benefits, 557
Foreign Trade Definitions, 522
foreign trade zone, 492
form, expediting and tracing, 353
   loss or damage claim, 227, 239, 242
overcharge claim, 221
forwarder, freight, 95, 96, 144, 145, 155, 487, 491
   freight, foreign, 462, 465, 558-561, 563
   shipper association, 282, 283
4 R Act, 120
free time, 127, 360-371
   export, import, 492, 493
free trade, 556
freight bills, audit of, 113, 114, 390, 404, 405, 408
freight, over or short, 356
functions, clerical, 7
   decentralized, 402-406
   managerial, 7
   traffic manager, 386, 393-396

G

general average, 540-543
government traffic, how handled, 449-460
government agencies, organization charts, Executive branch, general transportation, 12, 13
   Department of Transportation, 14, 15

Congressional Committees, 16
General regulatory agencies, 18
Interstate Commerce Commission, 21
Federal Maritime Commission, 25
Civil Aeronautics Board, 28
guides, rate, routing, 388, 389, 416

H

Harter Act, 482, 547
hazardous materials, transportation, general, 11, 59, 149, 214, 513, 514, 553, 571-584, 588, 595, 596
Bureau of Explosives, 553, 575, 580, 582
Chemcards, 572, 579-581
Chemtrec, 579-582
international, 513, 514, 553, 582, 583
Office of Hazardous Materials, DOT, 576
rail storage charges, 363
State and local laws, 583
Uniform Frt. Classification Rule 39, 59

I

impact recorder, 194, 195, 234
imports, routing of, 491-493, 507-511
inspection bureaus, railroad, 194
insurance, cargo, motor carrier, 140
export, import, types of, 536-546
marine, 534-546
transportation, 234
Inter American Development Bank, 529
interest, payment of, 222, 223
intermediate application of rates, 111-113, 128

International Bank for Reconstruction and Development, 528, 529
international shipments, 461-569
Interstate Commerce Act, 18-24, 27, 28, 31, 33, 35, 41, 65, 66, 73, 83, 101-103, 107, 108, 111, 138-140, 144, 152, 157, 222, 234, 229, 230, 304, 305, 307, 314, 324, 326, 336
Part 1, 19, 20, 28, 41, 107, 108, 139, 157, 230
Part II, 19, 37, 41, 108, 109, 139, 229, 230, 304, 307
Part III, 19, 20, 22, 41, 107, 152
Part IV, 19, 22, 41, 108, 144
Section 1, 35, 41, 107
Section 2, 107
Section 3, 107
Section 4, 20, 104, 107, 111
Section 5a, 101, 292
Section 6, 21, 103, 107
Section 13, 35
Section 15, 123
Section 20, 231
Section 21, 231
Section 22, 449, 450, 459
Section 219, 230
Section 222, 138
Section 303, 304, 305, 307, 324
Section 322, 336
Interstate Commerce Commission, 11, 18-23
organization charts, 18-21
inventory control, 7, 256-260, 264, 267, 268, 270
invoice, commercial, export, import, 509, 510, 516, 517

L

laws, motor carrier, 291-294, 304, 305, 307, 324, 326, 336, 337

lease, truck, sample of, 330-334
leasing, agreement, form of 330-334
   private carriage, 327-337
   reasons for, 327-329
   truck, 327-337
Lenoir Chair case, 325
letter of credit, types of, 526-528
letter of indemnity, 484
limitations, statute of, 107, 114, 223, 224
loading, cargo, 195-211
   types of, 203-207

M

Maritime Administration, 12, 24
marking, export, import, 553-555
Master Format, 482, 490
materials handling, 211-213
McCaull-Dinsmore case, 234
measurement, international cargo, 499-501
Merchant Marine Act of 1970, 469, 555-557
Mexico, shipments to and from, 462, 463, 516, 517
Military Sealift Command, 452, 455, 456, 459, 460
minimum weights, carload, 33, 50, 57, 58, 128
   truckload, 50, 64, 128
motor carriage, intercity, 307-316
   intraplant and intracity, 304-307
   safety and related regulations, 327

N

National Classification Board, 41, 47
National Committee on International Trade Documentation, 429, 507
National Freight Traffic Association, 428
National Industrial Traffic League, 110, 226-229, 388, 427, 428, 438, 439, 468
National Motor Freight Traffic Association, Inc., 37
National Safe Transit Committee, 165, 167, 191, 192
National Tank Truck Carriers, 582
non-contract system, steamship conference, 493, 494, 501-506

O

Official Guide of the Railways, 123, 388, 413
Official List of Open and Prepay Stations, 126, 413
Open account, international shipments, 519, 523
organization, traffic department, 383-407

P

packaging, airlines, 198, 199, 565-567
   definition of, 168, 169
   export, import, 193, 194, 550-555
   government specifications, 189
packing, *see packaging*
pallet, 199-206, 278, 551
palletization, 199-206
parcel post, foreign, 567, 568
passenger cars, 336
penalties, criminal, 31, 41, 65, 336, 337, 571
Peninsula Produce Exchange Case, 238
periodicals, export and import, 418
   transportation, 416-418
permit, delivery, 490

permit, ICC, contract carrier, 304, 308, 313-316
physical distribution, concept of, 251, 252, 260-265
piggyback, 91, 131-136, 145, 233
placement, actual, 360, 361
  constructive, 360, 361
plant location, 284-288
policy, routing, 121, 122, 158-161
policy, transportation, national, 19, 20
practitioners, I.C.C., 401, 429
price control laws (recent) and transportation charges, 29
private motor carriage, 317-337
  cost of, 319-324, 327, 328, 335, 336
  definition of, 324
  development of, 320-324
  hazardous material, 575
  hidden costs, 317, 318, 327, 335
  leasing, 317, 327-337
  reasons for, 319, 327, 328
  risks of, 317, 319, 320, 324
publications, traffic or transportation, 413-418
public relations, industrial traffic, 384, 426-431

R

rail demurrage and hazardous materials storage, 363
Railroad Revitalization and Regulating Act (1976), 120
rates, agreed, 92
  air freight, 97-99, 565-567
  assembly and distribution, 96
  class, 32-36, 83-88, 496
  combination, 111, 112, 123
  commodity, 83, 90-92, 496
  defined, 60, 61, 81
  exception, 83, 88-90
  freight-all-kinds, 41, 90, 91

freight forwarder, 95, 96
freight, ocean, 493-506
inland, export, 479, 487-491
marine insurance, 535, 537, 540, 544
ratings, class, 32-41
  defined, 61
  exception, 35, 36, 89
  incentive, 89
receipt, warehouse, 273-277
reconsignment, 354, 355
Reed-Bulwinkle Act, 17, 101, 292
regulations, container, 169-172
  inspection, loss or damage, 228, 229
  motor carrier, contract, 304-316
  private carriarge, 324-327, 335-337
regulatory and other government functions (general), 11-30
relations, traffic, other company departments, 384-386, 419-426
reparation, 107-109, 224
reports, insurance, 545
  traffic department, 3, 420-423
responsibility, traffic manager, 393-396
Robinson-Patman Act, 11C
routing, air freight, 153-155, 564-567
  carload, 126-131
  domestic, water, 149-153
  freight, 121-161
  freight forwarder, 144, 145, 155
  household goods carrier, 140-143
  inland, export, 479, 486, 487-491
  inland, import, 491-493
  less-than-carload, 125, 126
  motor carrier, 136-140
  ocean transportation, 465-479, 556, 557
  parcel post, 145-148, 567, 568
  piggyback, 131-136

pipe line, 157
rail, 123-131
specialized motor carrier, 139, 140
United Parcel Service, 156, 157
water domestic, 149-153
rules, classification, 51-64, 170-172, 176-189, 196
overflow, 79
packaging, 176-189, 196
tariff publishing, 21, 487

S

safety and health laws (recent), transportation applicability, 30
safety regulations, motor carrier, 327, 571, 575, 577, 579, 582
salesmen, cars for, 336
salvage, damaged material, 230
Schedule B Commodity Number, U.S. Commerce Department, 513, 514
service, transportation, 2-6
Sherman Anti-Trust Act, 558
shipment, defined, 54, 75, 76
shippers' associations, 145, 282, 283, 558
shippers' guides, 338, 389, 416
shipper's export declaration, 512-514
shipper's load and count, 77, 79, 230, 231
Shipping Act of 1916, 17, 25-27, 503
shipping, factory to warehouse, 278-283
inbound to plants, 288, 289 ·
warehouse to customer, 283, 284
sidings, rail, 371-375
siding, rail, hazardous materials, 363

Sixth-section relief, short notice publications, 21, 103
Special Docket Authority, 108
standardization, containers, 209
Standard Point Location Code (SPLC), 84, 437
Standard Transportation Commodity Code, (STCC), 43, 51, 436, 437
State regulatory commissions, 23, 28
stopoff privileges, 113, 123, 124, 128-130, 278-280
storage charges, 363-365
storage-in-transit, 279, 280
subsidized lines, U.S. steamship, 466-468, 556, 557
suspension of tariff provisions, 102, 103
suspension of tariff provisions, under 4 R Act, 120
switching, 130, 131
absorption of, 131

T

tank car freight calculations, 379, 380
tariff files, 410-412
testing, containers, 186, 189, 190
theft and pilferage, 207, 240, 551
shrink wrap systems, 207
titles, traffic management, 384, 385
tonnage distribution, 159, 160
tracing, general, 339-358
trade routes, U.S., 466, 467
trade zones (duty free), 492
Traffic Bulletin, 47 101, 415
traffic clubes, 388, 430, 431
traffic data, publications, 413-418
traffic departments (general), 383-431
traffic, government, 449-460

transloading, 129, 130

transportation, premium, 2-4, 339, 356-358

Transport Topics, 101, 417

Transportation Association of America, 428, 578

Transportation Data Coordinating Committee, 429, 438, 439

trucks, light, 321, 323

U

undercharges, carrier freight bills, 219

Uniform Classification Committee, 41-47

Uniform Commercial Code, 275

Uniform Customs and Practices for Documentary Credits, 522

Uniform Warehouse Receipt Act, 275

unit load, 205, 206, 469-479

V

valuation, actual, 39-41
    released, 39, 40, 141, 234
value, declaration of, 69-71, 77
vehicles, motor ownership of, 317, 319

W

warehouse, automated, 258-260
    bonded, 272, 492, 509, 510
    field, 276-278
    public, 271-278
    public vs. private, 253, 255, 265-270
    types of, 251-254
warehouse-in-transit, 278-280
waybill, air, 566, 567
Webb-Pomerene law, 558
weight agreements, 375-381
weights, estimated, 379, 380
    minimum, 33, 50, 57, 58, 64, 128, 179, 197, 198
weight tolerance, 380
Woitishek Case, 325